# ADOLESCENCE

WITHDRAWN

# ADOLESCENCE

## Michael L. Jaffe

Kean College of New Jersey

John Wiley & Sons, Inc.

New York • Chichester • Weinheim • Brisbane • Toronto • Singapore

| Executive Editor | Christopher J. Rogers |
| Aquisitions Editor | Ellen Schatz |
| Marketing Manager | Karen Allman |
| Production Editor | Deborah Herbert |
| Cover and Text Designer | Karin Gerdes Kincheloe |
| Photo Editors | Elaine Paoloni, Mary Ann Price |
| Illustration Editor | Anna Melhorn |
| Cartoon Illustrator | Justin Jaffe |
| Text Illustrator | Wellington Studios |
| Cover Photo | From the Hip Collection |

This book was set in 10/12 Palatino by University Graphics, Inc. and printed and bound by R. R. Donnelley & Sons Company (Crawfordsville). The cover was printed by The Lehigh Press, Inc.

This book is printed on acid-free paper. ∞

The paper in this book was manufactured by a mill whose forest management programs include sustained yield harvesting of its timberlands. Sustained yield harvesting principles ensure that the numbers of trees cut each year does not exceed the amount of new growth.

*Library of Congress Cataloging-in-Publication Data*
Jaffe, Michael L.
     Adolescence / Michael L. Jaffe.
          p. cm.
     Includes bibliographical references and indexes.
     ISBN 0-471-57190-3 (pbk. : alk. paper)
     1. Adolescent psychology. I. Title.
BF724.J33 1998
155.5—dc21

97-24350
CIP

Printed in the United States of America

10 9 8 7 6 5 4 3 2

# PREFACE

**W**hat other life period is shrouded in as much mystery and myth as adolescence? Surely, part of the reason is that our remarkable physical metamorphosis from infertile child to fertile adult occurs during this time. It is not easy for young people and the adults who care about them to make sense of the myriad changes that occur while "coming of age," not only in body, but also in mind, spirit, and behavior.

The popular media often portray adolescents as collections of deficits—lazy, uncooperative, rude, obnoxious, even dangerous. Those willing to look beyond the stereotypical adolescent "attitude problem" are likely to encounter someone searching for his or her place in society and a primeval yearning for independence and self-regulation. The more we learn about adolescents as active participants in their own development, the better able we are to assist them through this bumpiest of life stages.

An excellent way to understand adolescents is to become familiar with the extensive research literature on adolescent development and the ingenious theories that attempt to organize and summarize research findings. Another way is to live or work with adolescents; to get to know them as clever, witty, skeptical young men and women waiting not so patiently for their turn to "be in charge." Part of my interest in this time of life stems from the joy of raising two adolescents, who at this writing are ages 16 and 21. (Truth-in-advertising: My 16-year-old son tells me that I know **nothing** about teenagers—ouch!). My curiosity also reflects two and a half decades of teaching child and adolescent psychology, and my years of work as a family therapist and textbook author (Jaffe, 1997). In these roles and in this book, I try to understand the strong bonds that keep families together and the occasional breakdowns in communication and trust between parent and child.

Writing about adolescents (or members of any group) can be frustrating because at the same time that we emphasize their diversity (no two are alike) we must also view and characterize them as members of groups. Imagine a textbook that consisted of an exhaustive case study of just one unlucky adolescent. And how much of what we would learn about this overly examined individual would apply to other young people? Although social scientists try to understand people both as individuals and as members of groups, when we characterize any group (e.g., 14-year-olds, high school seniors, Native-Americans, virgins, underachievers), we almost certainly are overgeneralizing. When the available research literature allows, I try to shed light on individual, gender, and cultural differences in development as well as the enormous diversity we observe within each gender, cultural group, and even individual.

In addition to surveying and summarizing current research and theory in adolescent development, I have tried to capture in these pages a little of the subjective side of adolescent life—what it feels like to be an adolescent today. If what you read in these pages rings at all true to your own experiences, I will consider my efforts to be successful.

## FEATURES

Study aids in each chapter are included to promote interest, learning, and retention. Chapters begin with preview questions that highlight the main topics or issues of the chapter and with disclosures, quotes from adolescents that get right to the heart of a chapter's contents. Most selections of the text begin with a study question (or chapter heading in the form of a question) that can be answered by reading the section. Thought questions can be found throughout each chapter, helping students integrate what they are learning with what they already know. Most chapters have Spotlights and Boxes featuring supplementary information. Each chapter ends with a numbered summary, a glossary containing definitions of key terms, additional thought questions, and a multiple choice self-test. Answers to the self-test questions are located at the end of the text. The last chapter is followed by an Epilogue that reviews the main themes of this textbook. Students might want to peruse the Epilogue first to behold the adolescent forest before examining the individual trees. An Instructor's Manual, which includes test items, is available.

## OVERVIEW OF CONTENTS

Chapter 1 provides an introduction to the topic of adolescent development. Who are adolescents, why do we study them, how are they perceived by adult society, and how were "youth" viewed and treated by our ancestors? Chapter 2 reviews influential theories that attempt to summarize and make sense of what we think we know about this life period. Understanding adolescence is not a simple task, given the vast number of biological, social, emotional, and cultural factors that affect human development and the ways in which they interact. Chapter 3 addresses physical growth and development. How do adolescents change during puberty and what do these changes mean to them, their family members, and friends?

In Chapter 4, we examine cognitive development. How do adolescents think and reason and what do they think and reason about? Chapter 5 considers moral development in adolescence—coming to understand the difference between right and wrong. In Chapter 6, we turn our attention to adolescent identity, self-concept, and self-esteem. How do adolescents see themselves and what do they think and feel about what they see? Chapter 7 presents adolescents in the context of family life—balancing the desire to stay connected to parents with the need to become "your own person."

Chapter 8 views adolescents in a social context, as friends and acquaintances. How does popular culture influence adolescents and vice versa? In Chapters 9 and 10, we explore many different facets of adolescent sexuality, romance, and intimacy. Topics include sexual orientation, dating, sexual behavior, sex education, and the potential hazards of careless sexual activity.

Chapter 11 addresses the topics of schooling and achievement. How do adolescents manage the most important role that they are assigned during the preadult years, that of student? Chapter 12 considers one of the most intimidating questions facing adolescents—How will I earn a living? Chapter 13 explores the problems of adolescents in crisis. Although most adolescents adjust well to the changes and transitions of the teenage years, a significant number suffer from disorders that require intervention from family members or members of the community. The Epilogue reviews the main themes of this textbook. The Appendix provides a comprehensive account of the methods that researchers use to observe and understand adolescent behavior and development. Instructors can assign reading of the Appendix at the time that they discuss research methodology in class.

I gratefully acknowledge the following colleagues who thoughtfully reviewed the manuscript for this text:

Patrick T. DeBoli, St John's University

Lee B. Ross, Frostburg State University

Nancy E. Meck, The University of Kansas Medical Center

Roslyn Mass, Middlesex County College

Stephen S. Coccia, Orange County Community College

Gene V. Elliott, Rowan College of NJ

Thomas R. Sommerkamp, Central Missouri State University

Thomas S. Parish, Kansas State University

Bernard Rosenthal, Western CT State University

Alan Keniston, University of Wisconsin-Eau Claire

Lori F. W. Wynters, Greenfield Community College

John J. Mirich, Metropolitan State College

Lee K. Hildman, University of Southern Mississippi

Karen L. Salley, Southern Oregon State College

Robert E. Schell, State University of New York-Oswego

John L. McManus, Eastern Michigan University

Jennifer Connolly, York University, Ontario Canada

*Michael L. Jaffe*

When we were looking for a cover for this text, we wanted a photo image that captures the energy and excitement of adolescence. One of our editors brought us the photograph that appears on the cover. This photo is part of the From the Hip Collection. From the Hip is a nonprofit youth program headquartered in Durham, North Carolina. This group asked over 100 young photographers, ''Does the public know who young people are?'' A number of remarkable photos resulted, which are distributed nationally through a professional photo bank. We felt that the question asked of this group of photographers is the same question that the author of this text is trying to help his readers answer: Who are these young people we live and work with? We are pleased that the proceeds from our use of the photo will be used to support an organization that empowers adolescents as they navigate their way through this remarkable life stage.

*Ellen Schatz, Psychology Editor*

# BRIEF CONTENTS

# CONTENTS

# ONE

# INTRODUCTION TO ADOLESCENCE

◆

## Preview Questions

1. How will you benefit from the study of adolescence?
2. Does research support or contradict common stereotypes of adolescents?
3. How might certain characteristics of adolescents, such as their alleged "attitude problem" or their strong orientation to peers, reflect cultural practices that are imposed on them?
4. How can we distinguish between who is an adolescent and who is an adult?
5. How does daily life for today's adolescents differ from daily life in past eras?
6. What are four common concerns of today's adolescents?

◆

## Disclosures

"How do I feel about being 18?" I kind of like it and kind of dislike it. I feel mature at 18 but I always want to be older. That's how most teenagers think. You can't wait until you're 21. For my age, I'm having a good time—hanging out with my friends and going to clubs. I like to be stupid at times and do little kid things. People expect, 'cause you're 18, you're mature now, you have responsibilities. That gets in the way of the child inside of you."

*(18-year-old girl)*

"I like being bigger—I don't get picked on—sometimes it's good, sometimes it's bad. I fit in. I have a lot of friends. I don't like shaving. It's a pain in the butt and cuts your face up. It doesn't bother me at all. It's just one of those things. It's gonna happen sooner or later. It happens to everyone."

*(17-year-old boy, 6 foot 3, 230 pounds, brown hair, brown eyes,*
*"pretty average person," so he says)*

"The first thing they gotta realize, they can't make kids do anything. Actually, if you tell them not to do it, they're going to do it. Kids rebel against things." *(17-year-old girl, quoted by Verhovek, 1995, p. 24)*

# Contents

Paul wanted to go to a party in Summit tonight, but he surprised me when he accepted my 'no.' I said he had a hockey game which wouldn't be over until 10 P.M. and I thought that was too late to go out. I also said I thought he had been out enough this week. For the first time in his teenage years, Paul did not argue with me about this. He came home from his hockey game, called a girl from town, went over to her house, and was home at about midnight.

In the afternoon, before the game, he studied and worked on college boards. When I asked him why he is accepting our concern about all of his extracurricular activities, he said that we were probably right. He couldn't forget that getting into a good college was his first priority this year. This new focus on what he must do in the present to prepare for the future is amazing. As we're learning in class, Piaget claims that this is an element of formal operational thinking. I wonder if it will continue, or if it will be like all the other growth stages—two steps forward and at least one step back. Paul seems torn between the commitment he wants to make and his ability to carry out the steps necessary to realize it.

*(From the journal of the mother of this 17-year-old boy)*

This entry from the journal of a parent enrolled in my adolescent psychology course captures an exciting and unexpected moment in her parenting history. Something seems to have "clicked" in her son's personality. He is taking care of his business, not to avoid an argument with his mother (she assumes), but because he is thinking about his future. In her eyes, he is beginning to take his plans for the future more seriously, acting in ways that might fulfill his personal goals. Paul's actions, to some extent, relieve his mother of that responsibility. Many parents recognize similar moments when something clicks, when children begin to take their lives into their own hands.

Perhaps you, the reader, have recently "come of age" and are embarked on a new and equally challenging period of life: young adulthood. From this more seasoned vantage point, take a moment to look back over the past 10 or so years of your life. What do you remember about your own bodily changes? How did you feel when you first realized that your body was growing and developing? Did your development begin before that of your closest friends, at about the same time, or afterward? Did you feel normal or different from your peers? Were you proud of or embarrassed by what you saw in the mirror?

Can you recall how your relationships changed during early adolescence? Was there better communication with family members or more arguing? Do you remember occasionally feeling moody, alienated, or confused? If so, who did you talk to about these uncomfortable feelings? Did you discuss them with your parents or friends or keep them to yourself?

Do you recall having romantic or sexual feelings that you dared not express to anyone? As a young adolescent, did you have any sense of who you were, of who you wanted to be, or of where you fit in? Finally, was there something like a moment of awakening when you realized that, at least in your own eyes, you weren't exactly a child anymore?

In this text, we raise many questions about those we call adolescents, including the following: How do they see themselves? How do they spend their time? What are their goals and aspirations? What types of life tasks are they working on? What are their major problems and concerns. Perhaps the biggest obstacle we face in answering these questions is the existence of **individual differences** (Scarr, 1992). Adolescents are so different from each other in so many ways—physically, socially, intellectually, emotionally—that almost any generalization we make can be challenged as simplistic or misguided. The very diversity that makes adolescents as a group so interesting to study keeps us on our toes when we are tempted to paint broad strokes when finer points are called for.

One additional word of caution. Life does not begin at adolescence. Some of you have completed developmental courses such as those in child psychology or adult psychology. What you have learned in these courses may help you to understand how adolescence fits into the rest of the life span. There is an old saying: "The child is the father to the man." What we go through in each life period sets the stage for what is to follow. This idea is at the core of developmental psychology.

The main theme of this introductory chapter can be stated in the form of an intriguing question: Does adolescence really exist as a unique stage of the life span? There is overwhelming evidence that teenagers exist (Palladino, 1996), but some theorists claim that the modern *idea* of adolescence arose in the late 19th century as a way of justifying the restrictions and expectations that adults impose on young people today. Are those whom we call adolescents really different from younger children and adults or are they just some strange amalgamation of the two? The quotes that begin this chapter demonstrate that adolescents themselves aren't very clear about their status in society. And if there really is a distinctive stage of life called adolescence, does its form vary from culture to culture and from one era to the next (Riley, 1993)?

In pursuit of answers to these questions, we begin by considering why it might be worth our while to study adolescent development. To gain some historical perspective, we then explore how young people (referred to as **youth** by our ancestors) were viewed and treated in the past. We return to this chapter's main theme by considering whether our current view of adolescence is a modern invention or a discovery of something that has always existed but was never recognized. Midway in this chapter, we address the issue of who is and who is not an adolescent. Finally, we look at how adolescents live today, emphasizing the joys and opportunities of adolescent life and the problems and issues many young people face.

Subsequent chapters of this text will shed light on many other topics—what happens when children's bodies transform into adultlike bodies, how young people grapple with family relationships, and why young people think and act as they do. Along the way, use your recollections of your own adolescent experiences and your current encounters with young people as a way of connecting the material in this text to your understanding of the fascinating period of life you are about to study.

## WHY STUDY ADOLESCENCE?

Adolescents are different from other age groups physically, cognitively, socially, and emotionally (Graber & Brooks-Gunn, 1996; Hoffman, 1996; Scheer, Unger, & Brown, 1996). Like all people, they deserve special appreciation and understanding. Adults who work with or teach adolescents but who remain uninformed about adolescent development increase the risk that their efforts will fail.

I study adolescence partly because the knowledge I gain helps me as a therapist, as an educator, and as a parent. Teachers, coaches, counselors, social workers, people employed in the juvenile justice system, and others who work closely with young people can do a better job when they have good information about the young people they serve. Media portrayals of adolescents generally are of little use. They can mislead us into seeing adolescents stereotypically—

as alienated, obnoxious, spoiled, and lazy (Snyder, 1995). (See Spotlight • Stereotyping Adolescents, pp. 6–10.)

As a family therapist, I find working with adolescents intriguing. My typical adolescent client is not self-referred but is usually brought in by a concerned parent. At the first meeting, many adolescents are guarded and distrustful, probably feeling uncomfortable about having to see a "shrink" (Young, Anderson, & Steinbrecher, 1995). No small number feel misunderstood, blamed, or mistreated by adults (perhaps that's one reason they are in counseling). Many have low self-esteem and feel lonely, depressed, or anxious. Some tell me that their parents or teachers hate them or that adults do not take their concerns seriously.

Realizing that many teenagers are wary of authority figures and assume that therapists are in cahoots with their parents, I try not to come on too strong. Through my work with young people and my study of adolescent psychology, I have learned that it takes time to establish rapport, earn trust, and persuade adolescents to participate in assessment and treatment (Young et al., 1995). Eventually, most let down their guard and discuss the obstacles that they encounter in becoming more independent while trying to stay in touch, emotionally and socially, with their family members and friends.

As a parent, my knowledge of adolescent development helps me maintain a sympathetic stance when my own children test the limits that my wife and I place on their behavior. When my older son came home one day (at age 16) with a pierced ear and an earring, our immediate response was not congratulatory. However, seeing his behavior as a statement about who he felt he was at that moment (and remembering my own shoulder-length hair in the mid-1960s and my parents' less than supportive reaction) helped me to understand and come to terms with his daring deed. *Interest in the adolescent point of view enables parents to stay close to their children even when they are correcting their behavior or disagreeing with their opinions.*

Researchers study adolescence mainly to gain knowledge. They may be interested in why adolescents begin to smoke cigarettes, why so many sexually active adolescents take few if any precautions to avoid unwanted pregnancy, or why some adolescents excel academically while others struggle or drop out of school. Lois Hoffman (1996) suggests that the recent rebirth of interest in adolescent development partly reflects the belief that adolescents are responsible for (or victims of) a disproportionate share of today's social problems. She mentions as examples crime, substance abuse, unwanted pregnancies, eating disorders, and depression. The knowledge we derive from research has practical value in helping us understand and address adolescent problems. It also helps those of us who work with and serve adolescents to get along better with them, devise effective programs to encourage prosocial behavior, and design educational materials that are stimulating and challenging. A discussion of the methods that researchers use to study adolescent development and some very interesting examples of adolescent research (including an explicit account of sexual awakening) can be found in the Appendix.

In this century, adolescence has been described as a transition stage between childhood and adulthood and as a period of preparation and training

**The knowledge that we gain from developmental research often has practical value for those who work or live with young people.**

for adult living (Graber & Brooks-Gunn, 1996). Because it comes between childhood and adulthood, adolescence provides researchers with an excellent vantage point for looking back and looking forward, that is, studying how adolescent development reflects earlier life experiences and foretells adult outcomes. More than childhood, adolescence is the time when adult life paths are set in motion. *Understanding life course trajectories (how we change over time) is the main goal of developmental psychology* (Hoffman, 1996).

Although belief in the importance of early experience led developmental researchers to focus on early childhood for much of this century, knowledge of adolescence and adulthood furthers our understanding of human development and personality. The idea that adolescence is a transition stage (actually, it is a series of transitions) is a useful perspective, but adolescence also is a unique period of life, worthy of study in its own right (Stattin, 1995).

*Thought Question: Adolescents frequently are viewed as having an "attitude problem." How might a better understanding of the heightened pressures of early adolescence help parents and teachers treat young people more sensitively?*

## SPOTLIGHT • Stereotyping Adolescents

*One of the reasons today's adolescents are out of control is that they demand constant stimulation and have never been disciplined to defer satisfaction.*

*(Excerpt from a letter to* The New York Times, *January 27, 1994)*

Are adolescents really "out of control"? Do they really demand constant stimulation? Stereotypical depictions of adolescents are not new. Many are found in English literature from Chaucer to Dickens (Violato & Wiley, 1990). William Shakespeare, for example, in his play *Romeo and Juliet*, depicted youth as passionate, irresponsible, impulsive, and self-destructive. In a national survey of adults released in 1997, two-thirds of the adults applied adjectives such as *rude, wild,* and *irresponsible* when asked to describe teenagers (Applebome, 1997c). Modern dramatic depictions on TV and in movies perpetuate this view.

A **stereotype** is an overgeneralized way of portraying members of a given group (Hilton & von Hippel, 1996; Judd, Park, Ryan, Brauer, & Kraus, 1995). When we stereotype a group (e.g., women drivers), we imply that all members of the group share common characteristics (Krueger, 1996). Stereotypes generally are unflattering, misguided, and resistant to change (Brooks-Gunn & Petersen, 1984). Gender and racial stereotypes sometimes are accepted by members of the targeted group (Alfieri, Ruble, & Higgins, 1996), who, as a result, may "freeze up" in challenging situations where they would otherwise perform well (DeAngelis, 1996a; Steele, 1992). In other words, being stereotyped puts pressure on people to disprove the stereotype.

Albert Bandura (1964) suggested that a self-fulfilling prophecy plays a role in adolescent development. If a society believes that adolescents are obnoxious, rebellious, and out of control, and if this image is reinforced in the media, some young people will identify with these qualities or at least accept them (Snyder, 1995). According to one high school freshman, "Some [stereotypes] are true, some aren't. I can be obnoxious at times, secretive—you want to be to yourself. All teenagers are rebellious because they're all trying new things, experimenting with different things." Although news reports and films paint a not-so-appealing picture of modern teenagers, there is evidence that most adolescents view themselves realistically (Falchikov, 1989).

Do the young people you know conform to the stereotypes of adolescents listed in Table 1-1? The first problem with these characterizations is that they imply that all adolescents are alike. Were you just like your friends during adolescence? Did you and your peers share exactly the same personal qualities? Or were you a group of individuals, diverse in mood, mannerisms, opinions, aspirations, and prejudices? One of the most glaring errors we commit when we broadly characterize members of any group (e.g., "jocks") is to overlook the considerable diversity among group members.

A second problem with overgeneralizations is that stereotypes often contradict each other. Are adolescents idealistic or are they cynical? Are they rebellious or conforming? Most people, regardless of age, display at least some of these qualities some of the time. Human personality is dynamic, not fixed. What we refer to as personality consists of hundreds of different behaviors, moods, ideas, dispositions, and qualities. These are variously elicited by ever-changing life circumstances, as well as by complex historical, motivational, and biological processes. Further, any particular behavior can be characterized in positive or negative terms. Are adolescents secretive or do they value privacy? Are they impressionable or are they open-minded?

The main reason for disputing stereotypes is that they are simply not accurate. They are confirmed neither by research nor by careful everyday observation (Stattin, 1995). For the most part, most adolescents get along well with their parents and teachers and with each other (Laursen & Collins, 1994; Offer & Schonert-Reichl, 1992). Some stereotypes that sound as if

### Table 1-1  Common Stereotypes of Adolescents

What images come to mind when you think of adolescents? Over the years, my students have brainstormed the following characterizations. Adolescents supposedly are awkward, lazy, spoiled, materialistic, disrespectful, confused, promiscuous, moody, arrogant, manipulative, passionate, obnoxious, innocent, opinionated, irresponsible, idealistic, vulnerable, cynical, rebellious, secretive, conforming, antisocial, narrow-minded, and just plain difficult. Do your own encounters with adolescents support or contradict these generalizations?

Informal observation and objective research confirm that stereotypical depictions of adolescents as obnoxious, rebellious, and lazy are not valid.

they apply to adolescents—for example, materialistic—may apply equally well to children and adults.

If stereotypes are not valid ways of perceiving people and groups, why do they persist? The **grain of truth hypothesis** implies that adolescents possess some of these qualities more than do younger or older people. For each of the personal qualities cited in Table 1-1, it would not be hard to find adolescent behaviors that support the stereotype. In their struggle to become "their own persons," many adolescents challenge adult authority and request (or demand) more freedom. Is this being rebellious or independent? Adolescents begin to resent the sometimes intrusive monitoring of their behavior by their parents ("Where are you going?" "Who are you with?") and, like adults, they desire more privacy. Is this being sneaky or mature? Adolescents going through puberty experience fluctuating hormone levels that give rise to emotional arousal. Is this being moody or is it being alive?

Bandura (1964) also noted that the media sensationalize adolescent behavior. "Since the deviant adolescent excites far more interest than the typical high school student, the adolescent is usually portrayed in literature, television, and in the movies as passing through a neurotic or a semi-delinquent phase of development" (p. 227). Additionally, since antisocial behavior receives so much media attention, the public may stereotype all adolescents on the basis of a nonrepresentative sample of poorly behaved youth (Falchikov, 1986). *Thought Question: Why are there so few positive portrayals of adolescents in the media?*

It is important that we view young people accurately and realistically, partly out of fairness and partly because our perceptions of youth guide our parenting behaviors, school practices and curriculum, and social policies. If we perceive teenagers as dangerous and out of control, as the letter to the editor beginning this section suggests, then we feel compelled to limit their freedom and increase our control. If we perceive young people as biologically or emotionally unstable, we are unlikely to offer them opportunities to display responsible and trustworthy behavior. We must resist the temptation to view adolescents stereotypically—as difficult, antisocial, or out of control—and the idea that the status of "adolescent" is in any meaningful way inferior to that of "adult" (Lesko, 1996).

In this spirit, let's end this section with another letter to the editor, one that may be introducing a new adolescent stereotype: scapegoat. "I am a police officer who likes teenagers. Leave them alone: There's always someone who thinks that the kids are to blame for everything! Teenagers are scapegoats for [automobile] insurance companies, which simply want to continue raising our costs." (*The New York Times*, New Jersey Section, March 16, 1997)

## HISTORICAL CONCEPTS OF CHILDHOOD AND ADOLESCENCE

*Study Question: What distinctions did our ancestors make regarding different ages or stages of life?*

Rejecting stereotypical formulations, perhaps we can shed some light on modern adolescents by studying their predecessors. Most of what we know about human history comes from written records. Before literacy became common in this century, relatively little was written about children, families, and everyday life (Cleverley & Phillips, 1986). Documents that exist tend to be vague, inconsistent, or of questionable accuracy. As a result, our understanding of the origin of concepts like *childhood*, *youth*, and *adolescence* is far from complete.

Aries (1962) concluded that until the 17th century, our ancestors recognized only two stages of life: infancy and adulthood. Painters such as Brueghel the Elder depicted children as miniature adults (Cleverley & Phillips, 1986). Aries maintained that "people had no idea of what we call adolescence, and the idea was a long time taking shape" (p. 29). Schlegel and Barry (1991) contend that Aries misapplied to earlier eras the modern usage of the term *adolescence*. "While adolescents as we know them—kept in the natal home under the authority of parents, attending school, and bedeviled by a bewildering array of occupational choices—are a modern phenomenon, adolescence as a social stage with its own activities and behaviors, expectations and rewards, is well recorded in the history and literature of earlier times" (p. 2).

Indeed, there is abundant evidence that our ancestors, although not explicitly acknowledging a period of life dedicated to preparing for adulthood, did recognize many of the qualities that we associate with modern children and

Our ancestors had little basis for distinguishing between children, adolescents, and adults.

adolescents (Elkind, 1988; Pollack, 1983). The idealism (Juliet refers to Romeo's "dear perfection") and cynicism attributed to the romantic lovers in *Romeo and Juliet* are familiar to parents of modern adolescents, although not usually expressed so poetically by today's high school students. Going further back in history, Socrates, the illustrious Greek philosopher, complained that youth annoy and contradict their parents and that they eat too much. Aristotle, Plato's gifted student, also portrayed male youths stereotypically (see Box 1-1).

When asked why they want to become parents, modern adults often respond that they like children. Ancestral parents valued their children partly for their labor and for the security they offered when parents could no longer support or care for themselves. In earlier centuries, children and adolescents may not have been well treated, at least according to modern standards of child care (Aries, 1962; Gies & Gies, 1987).

Premature death due to infectious diseases was common before the invention of immunizations and antibiotics. Parents may have been wary of becoming too attached to offspring who could perish at any time. Large numbers of children and adolescents suffered and died because of parental abuse, neglect, exploitation, and ignorance (Aries, 1962). *Thought Question: Is it fair to use contemporary standards to judge the child-rearing methods and values of our ancestors?*

Nowadays, most parents would not seriously consider (for more than a few hours) placing their teenage children in the service of other families as apprentices or domestics. The practice of **placing out** boys and girls who were between the ages of 12 and 15 years was common in Western Europe and

Box 1-1
Aristotle's
View of Youth:
"They Think
They Know
Everything"

How did Aristotle, the brilliant Greek philosopher, view male youths of his time 24 centuries ago? He characterized them as having strong desires, and "whatever they desire they are prone to do. Of the body desires the one they let govern them most is the sexual; here they lack self-control" (translated by Cooper, 1932, p. 132).

Aristotle viewed young males as passionate, impressionable, quick to anger, shy, impulsive, brave, resentful, trustful, quick to hope, and easily deceived. Aristotle's no-holds-barred characterization echoes some of the modern stereotypes listed in Table 1-1. It also anticipates the idealistic conception of young malehood conveyed by the modern Boy Scout oath: a scout is trustworthy, loyal, helpful, friendly, courteous, kind, obedient, cheerful, thrifty, brave, clean, and reverent.

Aristotle proceeds to tell us that youth "carry everything too far: they love to excess, they hate to excess—and so in all else. They think they know everything" (p. 134). Further, "they are fond of their friends, intimates, and associates—more so than are men in the other two periods of life" (p. 133). Aristotle certainly was on target regarding this last point. Adolescents spend more time with friends than do persons of any other age group.

colonial America. It encouraged children to learn adult roles while remaining semidependent upon adults who were not family members (Modell & Goodman, 1990). There is little reason to believe that these children were well treated by their employers. As we shall see in Chapter 12, teenagers today who work part-time sometimes complain of harsh treatment by insensitive supervisors.

By the 14th century, artists no longer portrayed children as miniature adults. Paintings were more sympathetic and sentimental in their rendering of children as immature and even helpless. During the 16th and 17th centuries, influential philosophers John Locke and Jean Jacques Rousseau suggested that childhood is a distinct and important stage of life. They recognized that children are impressionable and have special needs.

As church teachings became more widespread, parents began to view children as vulnerable and innocent. Philosophers and theologians advocated that, to preserve children's purity, they must be shielded from adult corruption and vice. This relatively enlightened view of childhood was offset by the belief that, to save their immortal souls, children require strict, even brutal discipline (the "Spare the rod, spoil the child" philosophy) (Aries, 1962; Cleverley & Phillips, 1986; Gies & Gies, 1987).

Thus, what we now call childhood gradually became accepted as a formative stage of life, that is, one during which adult character begins to develop (Aries, 1962). Many philosophers advocated that children be educated and trained for a vocation. In the first schools, children of all ages were taught together, but eventually they were segregated by age. Age-related grading was but one of many factors that led to the recognition (or invention) of adolescence as a distinct life stage in the late 19th century (Klein, 1990).

# ADOLESCENCE: INVENTION OR DISCOVERY?

*Study Question: Does adolescence exist as a natural and universal stage of life or is it an invention of modern industrial societies?*

Although Aristotle, Shakespeare, and other perceptive observers realized that youth are different from children but not quite adults, many of our ancestors recognized only two life stages: infancy (from birth to about 7 years) and adulthood. Where were the children and adolescents? Given the relative simplicity of life roles practiced by our ancestors and their considerably shorter life span, finer distinctions between age groups apparently were not needed and thus not recognized (Aries, 1962).

During the 16th and 17th centuries, philosophers and theologians began to recognize childhood as a distinctive life stage, one that intervenes between infancy and maturity. During the late 19th century, psychologists such as G. Stanley Hall (1904) came to view adolescence as a crucial stage of life. Today, developmental psychologists have little difficulty distinguishing among eight or more life stages.

Does human development really occur in leaps and bounds (stages) or is development one continuous albeit bumpy process of change from conception to death? Do terms like *child*, *adolescent*, and *adult* refer to natural life periods or are they merely terms of convenience, rooted in historical and sociocultural forces? For distinctions among natural life stages (such as adolescence and adulthood) to be convincing, we must be able to demonstrate that stages are qualitatively different from each other (different in kind rather than more or less of something), that the stage sequence is fixed and universal, and we should be able to describe what conditions lead to a transition from one stage to the next (Crain, 1992). Most stage theories, for example, those of Erik Erikson and Jean Piaget, so far have succeeded only on the first task.

If adolescence is a natural (universal and timeless) stage of life, we should be able to identify features of this stage that are common to young people in every culture and every era and that are free of social and historical influence. On the other hand, if the term *adolescent* is no more than a convenient designation for middle-class youth in industrial societies, we should discover both historical changes and cultural differences in who is considered an adolescent (Lesko, 1996). It is also possible that both points of view have some validity. Perhaps adolescence is a distinctive and universal period of physical, social, cognitive, and sexual maturation, but its exact form or expression depends on specific conditions existing in a particular time and culture (Lesko, 1996).

According to the **inventionist model** of adolescence, a society perceives and employs its young people according to its current economic and political needs (Enright et al., 1987). An agricultural society sees young people as manual laborers. A country at war views them as courageous warriors and defenders of the homeland. During economic depression, youth may be seen as competitors for scarce jobs and as additional mouths to feed.

According to inventionists, modern competitive, technological society views young people (adolescents) in several ways that satisfy its present needs: (1) as students in preparation for adult roles such as citizen, parent, and employee; (2) as a source of cheap, part-time labor; (3) as performers or athletes who entertain us with their physical stamina and prowess; and, importantly, (4) as consumers whose impulsive spending benefits our national economy (Schlegel & Barry, 1991).

Inventionists maintain that Western society's current interests are served by viewing adolescence as a **moratorium arrangement**, that is, as a period of deferred adult responsibilities and deferred adult privileges. It is secondary schooling, they claim, more than anything else, that propels our current model of adolescence (Lapsley, Enright, & Serlin, 1985).

Fasick (1994) reviews the factors that contribute to the familiar form that adolescence takes in most Western societies. These factors include (1) the stable, small-family system that allows parents to concentrate their economic and emotional resources on a small number of offspring; (2) the movement of young people from the workplace into schools, where they can form close relationships with age-mates; (3) the financial dependence of adolescents on their parents that results from full-time schooling; (4) the commercialization of youth culture in clothing, music, and other media; (5) the diversification of jobs, with young people being trained for eventual full-time employment; and (6) urbanization, which encourages the existence of age-graded secondary schools, recreational activities, and commercial outlets aimed directly at adolescent comsumers. We can add to this list the existence of legal categories such as *juvenile delinquency* and diagnostic categories such as *conduct disorder* that distinguish (on the basis of age) adult offenses from antisocial behaviors committed by young people (Table 1-2).

What adolescents gain from the moratorium arrangement, according to inventionists, is prolonged financial support from their families and the nurturance and security of family life. By attending school, adolescents are shielded from the pressures and competition of the adult work world. They are granted food, shelter, limited household responsibilities, and leisure time to spend with peers, to watch television, listen to music with pounding bass, and sleep for prolonged periods when possible. What adolescents temporarily give up in this arrangement are the adult privileges enjoyed by their counterparts of previous

**Table 1-2  Factors Contributing to the Modern Conception of Adolescence in Western Societies**

Small, stable family system

Urbanization of family life

Child labor laws

Mandatory education leading to daily contact with same-aged peers

Financial dependence on parents

Commercialization of adolescent subculture

Diversification of jobs

Special legal and diagnostic categories

(From Fasick, 1994)

centuries, the very freedom that adolescents long for during their teenage years (Lapsley et al., 1985).

The key point of the inventionist model is that *the moratorium arrangement is designed to serve society's current needs.* If young people happen to benefit from this arrangement, all the better. Some may claim that humanitarian treatment of children, not their "exploitation," should be society's primary goal. But if it were, would the serious problems of so many young people—poverty, drug abuse, violence, unwanted pregnancy—remain so prevalent (Chung & Pardeck, 1997; Hamburg, 1992; Simons, 1993)?

Some inventionists view the moratorium arrangement as "state enforced status deprivation and the prolongation of childhood" (Lapsley & Rice, 1988, p. 211). In other words, adult society deprives adolescents of the adult privileges that young people enjoyed until this century. Instead, they are forced to remain dependent on their parents until their early to mid-20s. Lapsley and Rice suggest that what we refer to as the adolescent attitude problem (i.e., noncompliance, moodiness) is an unconscious reaction to their enforced status as children. According to Lapsley and Rice, adolescence is best defined not by the transition into adult roles but by the *exclusion of adult freedom and privilege.*

*Thought Question: Do child labor laws, compulsory education, and the juvenile justice system (which emphasizes rehabilitation rather than punishment) support or contradict the idea of a moratorium period (deferred freedom, deferred responsibility) during adolescence?*

Why do today's youth tolerate status deprivation? Well, what choice do they have? Years ago, David Bakan (1972) suggested that adolescents believe in the promise "that if a young person does all the things he is 'supposed to do' during his adolescence, he will then realize success, status, income, power, and so forth in his adulthood" (p. 83). This implies that adolescents who do not believe in the promise will reject the trappings of middle-class life. The alienation of large numbers of disadvantaged youth supports this view.

*Thought Question: If there were a national referendum of high school students offering them full adult privileges* and *full adult responsibilities, would it pass?*

## Summary and Analysis

The inventionist model addresses the most basic question that we can raise about adolescence as a life stage: does it exist? Although the existence of this life period in modern society seems obvious, our ancestors did not view the teenage years as we view them today, as a period of dependency and as preparation for adulthood. Since there were relatively few roles for adults to occupy before industrialization, extensive preparation for adult life (and *age consciousness*) was not necessary. Adulthood in a competitive technological world requires extensive training and thus a long period of dependence on caregivers and teachers. This view is supported by the absence of an adolescent (moratorium) stage in many modern nonindustrial cultures.

Inventionists contend that adolescence, as a stage of life, is whatever a given society needs it to be, or it may not be needed at all. Variation in the roles that adolescents adopt in different cultures supports this view (Arnett & Taber, 1994; Riley, 1993). However, some theorists view adolescence as a time of preparation for adulthood during which *social role learning* occurs in all societies, past and present (Schlegel & Barry, 1991). If this is the case, then adolescence has existed all along (in different forms) and we have merely rediscovered qualities of youth that Aristotle and Shakespeare noticed and described centuries ago. Inventionists counter that adolescence as *a period of preparation for adulthood* is not an inevitable stage of human development.

The fact remains that adolescence is not so clearly demarcated in nonindustrial societies. In cultures where adult roles can be learned and practiced during childhood, adolescence, at least as a moratorium stage, is unnecessary. Apparently, adolescence serves as a training period for adulthood only when a training period is needed.

## SPOTLIGHT • G. Stanley Hall

No one person deserves more credit than does Granville Stanley Hall (1844–1924) both for popularizing adolescence as a formative stage in development and for encouraging research on this topic. He has been described as the father, the discoverer, and even the inventor of adolescence. Who was G. Stanley Hall? Well, for starters, Hall was the first person in the United States to earn a Ph.D. in psychology (from Harvard in 1878). He also was a founder and the first president of the American Psychological Association (in 1892).

Although his theorizing about adolescence was speculative and often misguided, his monumental two-volume text *Adolescence: Its Psychology and Its Relations to Physiology, Anthropology, Sociology, Sex, Crime, Religion and Education* (1904) popularized adolescence as an important developmental stage. Hall's writings established adolescence as a legitimate field of scientific study. His text is a compendium of (often questionable) information about physical growth in adolescence, sexual and intellectual development, adolescent adjustment, antisocial behavior, emotions, religion, and love (Table 1-3). Throughout the two massive volumes, Hall was generous in his advice to teachers and parents about the rearing and education of adolescents.

G. Stanley Hall has been described as the father, discoverer, and even inventor of adolescent psychology.

Hall's views reflected the 19th-century perception of adolescence as a period of biologically induced agitation and turmoil. He reasoned that the distinctive behavior patterns that we associate with adolescents are biologically rooted and therefore universal. Adult patience and nurturance, Hall maintained, are necessary for healthy adolescent development. What can parents do but wait patiently for their children's natural impulses and desires to run their course? Hall used the German phrase **Sturm und Drang** ("storm and stress") to characterize what he (and Aristotle) saw as the passionate, moody, rebellious nature of the adolescent personality. His characterizations reinforced the persistent cultural stereotype of turbulent adoles-

**Table 1-3  G. Stanley Hall's *Adolescence***

G. Stanley Hall's two-volume set, published in 1904, included the following chapters:

**Volume I**

*Chapter*

 1  Growth in Height and Weight
 2  Growth of Parts and Organs during Adolescence
 3  Growth of Motor Power and Function
 4  Diseases of Body and Mind
 5  Juvenile Faults, Immoralities, and Crimes
 6  Sexual Development: Its Dangers and Hygiene in Boys
 7  Periodicity
 8  Adolescence in Literature, Biography, and History

**Volume II**

 9  Changes in the Sense and Voice
10  Evolution and the Feelings and Instincts Characteristic of Normal Adolescence
11  Adolescent Love
12  Adolescent Feelings toward Nature and a New Education in Science
13  Savage Public Initiations, Classical Ideals and Customs, and Church Confirmations
14  The Adolescent Psychology of Conversion
15  Social Instincts and Institutions
16  Intellectual Development and Education
17  Adolescent Girls and Their Education
18  Ethnic Psychology and Pedagogy, or Adolescent Races and Their Treatment

cence. Modern research does not support Hall's idea that adolescence is inherently stressful (Compas, 1987a, 1987b). Yet, as we have seen, Hall's stereotypical depiction of adolescent turmoil persists in the media and in many people's minds.

Hall's understanding of development was based on the **recapitulation** principle. The principle states that "every child, from the moment of conception to maturity, recapitulates, very rapidly at first, and then more slowly, every stage of development through which the human race from its lowest animal beginnings has passed" (Hall, 1923, p. 380). In effect, each of us, in our individual development, reproduces the evolution of our species. This strange idea was based on Hall's belief that evolutionarily older parts of the brain mature before more recently evolved brain areas.

Hall hypothesized that infancy reflects the animal stage of our evolutionary development. Children 5 to 7 years of age reveal humanity's cave-dwelling, hunter-gatherer stage. Children 8 to 14 years old, referred to as *youth*, display both sides of human nature—savage impulses as well as susceptibility to learning and discipline. William Golding's novel (also a film) *Lord of the Flies*, dramatizes this idea. How would children turn out if cut off from the restraints of adult supervision and socialization? According to Hall, childhood activities provide opportunities for a healthy release of primal impulses that otherwise would be carried into adulthood.

In Hall's model, children between the ages of 14 and 25 (adolescents) reflect in their behavior the stage of human evolution when our ancient ancestors were undergoing a transition from savagery to civilization. Presumably, this was a turbulent transitional phase. Thus, Hall viewed adolescence as a period of instability. According to Hall, the advent of adulthood symbolizes the beginning of human civilization.

Reflecting these views, Hall encouraged the creation of adult-sponsored youth organizations, such as the YMCA and the Boy Scouts, to provide adolescents with socially acceptable outlets for their instinctual drives. Hall's writings and speeches encouraged parents and teachers to be tolerant of youngsters. Eventually, he asserted, harried parents would see the light at the end of the adolescent tunnel.

### Evaluation of Hall's Model

If adolescence as we know it was discovered (rather than invented), then G. Stanley Hall must be credited as the discoverer. Nevertheless, his description of this life stage was based more on speculation and stereotype than on objective research. Hall's portrayals of adolescent angst were overstated. Rather than creating a convincing body of empirical research (most of his data were collected using questionnaires), Hall formulated an ideology of adolescent development. His presumptions elicited critical reactions from many psychologists and sociologists. Like Sigmund Freud, Hall exaggerated the role of biology (especially pubertal hormones) in adolescent development. He underestimated the importance of family influence. He did acknowledge the role of the peer group, setting the stage for numerous studies of peer relationships and peer influence. Unfortunately, he lumped all adolescents into narrow categories, inadvertently creating unappealing stereotypes.

To his credit, Hall raised important questions. He drew attention to the distinctive needs and problems of adolescents. His basic point remains valid: *adolescence is a unique and important stage of physical, cognitive, emotional, and social change.* Hall's speeches and publications helped launch the Child Study Movement, leading eventually to increased understanding of adolescents (Kett, 1977).

In the early 20th century, his writings had a positive influence on educational and social institutions. After decades of relative neglect, there has recently been a rebirth of interest in adolescent psychology (Hoffman, 1996). Questions and issues concerning adolescent development first raised by G. Stanley Hall are again receiving the rapt attention of developmental researchers (White, 1992).

# DEFINING ADOLESCENCE

*From early adolescence on, I was thought of as a mature young man. I did all my chores, got good grades in school, and never got into any big trouble. Being a good kid and not causing trouble are the two most important measurements of maturity. I lived up to everyone's expectations, and then some. But I think it was my intelligence and the lessons of my upbringing which led to my fulfillment of adult expectations. I was used to working hard and doing a good job. And I had learned that if I did a good job, I would be trusted with a greater share of freedom. That was the way I considered maturity when I was younger, as a social contract. If you do this, you get that.*

*(20-year-old-male, quoted by Garrod, Smulyan, Powers, & Kilkenny, 1992, p. 54).*

This is one person's view of his attainment of maturity. If you act like an adult and people treat you like an adult, then you must be an adult. But what do the terms *adult* and *adolescent* mean? We might think we know one when we see one, but deciding who is and who is not an adolescent is not as simple as it sounds (Arnett & Taber, 1994).

Not too long ago, adulthood was said to begin when one graduated from high school, joined the army, married, or simply left home. Today, about half of all high school graduates attend college, extending their financial dependence on their parents. Following college graduation, many return home in what some call the **return to the nest** phenomenon. In developed countries, about half of all people in their early to mid-20s live with their parents (Chisholm & Bergeret, 1991). Not all of them are employed full time. Are they adolescents or adults? Let's consider several ways of defining adolescence, noting the strengths and limitations of each definition.

## Dictionary Definition

The term *adolescence* literally means "to grow into adulthood," although some dictionaries define the term as "to come of age." (The word *adult* comes from *adultus*, the past participle of *adolescere*, which means "to grow up.") Many dictionaries define adolescence as "the period of life between puberty and maturity." The onset of puberty is a convenient marker for the beginning of adolescence, as we discuss below. However, the definition does not tell us what maturity is (we could look it up) or how we know when someone has achieved it.

To be mature implies that someone is a complete person or "fully cooked," ready to take on adult roles and responsibilities. Being mature implies that someone has the social, cognitive, and emotional resources that we expect to find in an adult. Presumably, these resources include independence, responsibility, good judgment, and coping skills. But how would we measure these qualities to distinguish those who are ready for adulthood from those who need more cooking?

## Puberty as a Marker

Biological definitions of adolescence are appealing because of their relative simplicity. They equate the beginning of adolescence with the onset of puberty (relatively rapid physical growth and sexual maturation). Physical growth and the development of secondary sexual characteristics such as body hair and a deeper voice are universal and relatively easy to observe and measure (Montemayor & Flannery, 1990). Similarly, we could define the end of adolescence as the completion of growth and sexual maturation.

Although adolescents are qualitatively different from younger children in their growth and sexual characteristics, there are problems with defining adolescence in strictly biological terms. One problem is that for different children, puberty can begin at strikingly different ages. Early-maturing girls begin puberty between 8 and 9 years of age, while late-maturing boys do not show pubertal changes until they are about 16 years old. Besides the fact that they are entering puberty, what else do these 8- and 16-year-olds have in common to suggest that they are entering the same stage of life?

Further, there are no obvious biological markers that indicate the end of adolescence. Physical growth eventually ends, but at different ages for different individuals. Although sexual maturation is complete and adult size usually is attained by the late teenage years, these physical changes do not guarantee the emotional, intellectual, and social maturity that we hope to find in young adults.

## Age or Grade Status as Markers

Why not use age, a convenient marker, to indicate the beginning and end of adolescence? For example, we could define adolescence as the second decade of life (Petersen, Silbereisen, & Sörensen, 1996) or equate adolescence with being a teenager, spanning the ages 13 to 19 years. In either case, one might be conferred adult status on one's 20th birthday. This is the case in Japan. On January

Equating the onset of adolescence with puberty is appealing because physical growth and maturation are universal and relatively easy to observe and measure.

15th of each year, 20-year-old Japanese declare their legal (if not their financial) independence from their parents. The event, known as the **coming-of-age day**, is one of Japan's most colorful rituals and ancient traditions. To keep their young people interested, Japanese officials treat the affair as one big national party with prizes, beer, and pop music (Sanger, 1993).

Since they are nearly universal within cultures, school transitions could serve as a convenient way of defining adolescence. After all, we do view adolescence as a time to learn how to be a productive member of society. The predominant characteristic of adolescent life today in developed societies is prolonged school attendance and expectations of achievement and career attainment (Hurrelmann, 1996). We could equate the beginning of adolescence with entry into secondary school and the end of adolescence with graduation from high school or college (Elder, 1975; Hollingshead, 1949). Middle school begins at about the same time that the average child is experiencing puberty. For many, high school or college graduation signals entry into the adult work world.

One problem with defining adolescence in terms of one's age or grade is that, like physical growth and sexual maturation, age and grade are not very good predictors of emotional, cognitive, and social maturity. Nevertheless, society's treatment of its members and granting of privileges are based largely on age, hence the proliferation of fake IDs among high school and college students.

## Rites of Passage

More than half of all societies mark the transition from childhood to adulthood with rituals known as **rites of passage** (Paige, 1983). Their function is to help make clear to young people and others what will be expected of them as they take on adult roles and responsibilities (Alsaker, 1995). Rites of passage occur cross-culturally and have been performed for thousands of years to mark one's entry into the adult community. They include elaborate celebrations such as the coming-of-age day in Japan; traditional food, songs, and clothing; initiation rites including fasting and prayer; formal ceremonies; and other ways of instantly conferring adult status and privileges. Rituals usually include temporarily separating the young person from society, preparation or instruction from an elder, and a welcoming back into society with public acknowledgment of the adolescent's new status (Delaney, 1995).

Delaney describes a rite of passage known as the **vision quest** that is common to many Native American tribes. Fourteen- and 15-year-old boys are brought individually into a sweat lodge where their bodies and spirit are purified by the heat of burning cedar. A medicine man advises each child and assists him with prayers. Subsequently, each boy is brought to an isolated spot where he fasts for 4 days. "There he will pray, contemplate the world of the medicine man, and await a vision which will reveal to him his path in life as a man in native society" (p. 893).

Most Western cultures, including the United States and Canada, lack formal rites of passage. Adult privileges are granted largely on the basis of age. How-

In Japan, an annual rite of passage known as coming-of-age day marks Japanese youths' formal entry into the adult community.

ever, many ethnic, religious, and other subcultural groups in the West arrange ceremonies such as confirmations and bar mitzvahs to symbolize the child-to-adult transition (Sebald, 1992).

*Thought Question: How do rites of passage, such as religious confirmations or vision quests, increase adolescents' commitment to and investment in their community and culture?*

Delaney (1995) suggests that for middle-class families in the United States, high school graduation has become a rite of passage. In industrialized societies, at specified ages, individuals acquire adult rights of passage such as the right to drive an automobile, purchase alcohol, work full time, and marry without parental consent. Although one might become "legal" at age 18, the ages at which society grants adult privileges vary considerably and somewhat arbitrarily. Minors can free themselves from parental authority through marriage, by living apart from parents, and by being self-supporting (Rodman, 1990). In many nonindustrialized countries, milestones in education, work, and family life mark the transition from adolescence to adulthood. Markers of adulthood include acquiring desired skills, finding employment, and living independently of one's parents (Arnett & Taber, 1994).

To impress their peers, some adolescents create rites of passage of their own. They adopt "adult" behaviors such as sexual intimacy, drinking alcohol, and smoking cigarettes. Some who lack the means or opportunity to gain recognition for worthwhile accomplishments seek peer approval by engaging in deviant activities such as stealing cars or even going to jail.

## Social and Emotional Changes

Anthropological and sociological definitions characterize adolescence as a stage of social, cognitive, and emotional learning that intervenes between childhood and adulthood as young people prepare for an active role in the community (Schlegel & Barry, 1991, p. 8). According to this view of adolescence, young people are learning about specific roles that they are expected to take on as adults. However, during this time they remain subordinate to, and dependent on, adults, who must be responsive to their current needs as well as prepare them for the future.

We do observe remarkable social and emotional changes during the early teenage years (Graber & Brooks-Gunn, 1996; Montemayor & Flannery, 1990). Children begin to distance themselves from their parents, embrace their peers (literally and figuratively), and adopt more **gender-typed** behavior (predicted by one's gender). We are also likely to notice a modest increase in moodiness and irritability during early adolescence. Can these changes be used to mark the transition between childhood and adolescence? Or are young adolescents so diverse that looking for predictable patterns of social or emotional change is fruitless?

The word **adult** means one who is mature. As we have seen, the word *mature* means full-grown or complete. Becoming an adult suggests that one has attained some minimal level of physical, social, and emotional growth. We expect young adults to be self-reliant, economically independent, and responsible, to show good judgment, to have direction in their lives, and to partake in close relationships (Erikson, 1963; Zahn-Waxler, 1996). We also expect them to have coping resources that will allow them to handle the stresses and strains of contemporary adult life. Although such qualities are not sufficient in themselves to define adulthood, they are necessary components of any reasonable definition. Even well-adjusted adults, however, are quite diverse regarding their social skills and emotional resources (Arnett & Taber, 1994).

## Cognitive Change and Moral Development

The concept of maturity also implies minimal attainment of intellectual ability and moral development. Piaget (1972) and others have described remarkable advances in intellectual abilities during adolescence. At about age 11 or 12 years, adolescents begin to shift away from the concrete, black-and-white thinking we associate with younger children and increasingly display more flexible reasoning and problem-solving strategies. Compared to the self-concepts of younger children, those of adolescents' are more differentiated, abstract, and integrated (Montemayor & Flannery, 1990). Young adolescents have a deeper understanding and appreciation of human motivation and everyday life events than do younger children. They can solve math problems and understand poems that are incomprehensible to most preadolescents. More skillfully than younger children, adolescents can distinguish between what is real and what is not real, between what is possible and what is not possible.

Adults are even better than adolescents at posing hypotheses and deducing solutions to problems, so improvements in reasoning ability could serve to define the onset of both adolescence and adulthood. However, most adolescents and adults (in Western and non–Western cultures) do not exhibit the advanced reasoning skills that Piaget called *formal operational thinking* (Arnett & Taber, 1994).

The late psychologist Lawrence Kohlberg observed that adolescents display sophisticated moral reasoning skills that distinguish them from younger children. For example, more than younger children, adolescents can take into account situational factors that affect decision making. They are better able to weigh the consequences of their actions. The emergence of moral reasoning during the early teenage years could provide a convenient marker for the beginning of adolescence. Unfortunately, the cognitive abilities described by Piaget and Kohlberg are not always found in adolescents or even in most adults (Blasi & Hoeffel, 1974; Colby & Kohlberg, 1987; Lapsley, 1990).

Although adolescents generally exhibit reasonable impulse control and comply with social conventions most of the time, as a group teenagers display a much higher rate of reckless and deviant behaviors (such as drunk driving and shoplifting) than younger children or adults (Arnett, 1992a, 1992b). Certainly, they face more serious temptations involving sex and drugs. However, as we shall see in Chapter 5, it would be unfair and stereotypical to define adolescence as that life period characterized by weakened impulse control and reckless behavior.

## Life Challenges and Role Transitions

Finally, we can consider defining adolescence in terms of the specific life challenges and role transitions that modern adolescents face: handling family conflict, becoming more self-regulating, exploring a variety of ways of acting and thinking, inhabiting a wider social world, forming close relationships with peers, and eventually separating from one's family and becoming self-sufficient (Havighurst, 1972; Hill, 1993; Holmbeck & Updegrove, 1995).

Entrance into adulthood usually is defined in non-Western societies by a specific social event such as marriage. In the West, however, where independence is highly valued, entry into adulthood is defined individually. Someone may be considered to be an adult if he or she lives separately from parents, is financially independent, and is self-sufficient in other ways. "This means relinquishing the role of dependent child and taking greater responsibility for themselves: washing their own clothes, paying their own bills, and making their own day-to-day life decisions. This increased personal responsibility can take place while still living in the parent's home, but it is usually accompanied and promoted by residential independence" (Arnett & Taber, 1994, p. 532).

## The Subjective Experience of Achieving Adulthood

Is there a particular point when one feels like an adult? Nearly two-thirds of the college students Arnett (1994) interviewed were uncertain about their adult status. Scheer, Unger, and Brown (1996) asked 113 male and female teenagers whether they considered themselves to be adults, and if they didn't, when they would be. Although the group had only a mean age of 16.7 years, most (78.8%) considered themselves to be adults. More than a third equated adulthood with "reaching maturity/taking responsibility for my actions." Other criteria included "making my own decisions" (14.2%), "financial independence/having a job" (12.4%), or some combination of the three (20%). *Thought Question: Some adolescents apparently consider themselves to be adults long before their parents and teachers do. How might this affect adult–adolescent relationships?*

Many adolescents can identify a particular event in their lives that left them with the sense of achieving adulthood. A 17-year-old girl gave the following account to one of my students: "I remember I received a phone call from the police. I thought it was a joke, one of my friends calling me, telling me that I had to go pick up my mother at the police station because she was picked up for drunk driving. I got one of my friends to go with me. I felt like an adult, even though I was 16 years old. For the first time, I was taking control of something, whereas my mom had always had control of me. When I had to pick up my mother at the precinct, that's when I felt that I really grew up." As powerful as such experiences are, their personal nature precludes using them to distinguish between childhood, adolescence, and adulthood. Nevertheless, this adolescent's disclosure reminds us that part of becoming an adult is feeling and believing that one is "grown up."

## A Working Definition of Adolescence

We have discussed several potential markers for the beginning and end of adolescence. It is clear that the transitions from childhood to adolescence and from adolescence to adulthood are characterized by continuity *and* change. Both transitions, consisting of developmental tasks and challenges that are relatively universal, require new modes of adaptation (Graber & Brooks-Gunn, 1996; Holmbeck & Updegrove, 1995). Because there is no single criterion that establishes someone as an adolescent, we hereby invoke two plausible markers: the onset of puberty and the shift from elementary school to middle school. "It is the interplay of pubertal maturation with school transition, and other life changes, which make the transition from childhood to adolescence unique" (Montemayor & Flannery, 1990, p. 295).

When does adolescence end? Because there is no precise biological or social marker for the attainment of maturity, our definition of adulthood includes a combination of personal qualities and role transitions. These include (1) being behaviorally and emotionally self-regulating, (2) being financially independent of one's family, and (3) taking on adult roles, such as homemaker, worker, and spouse. Thus, **adolescence** is the life period that begins with the onset of puberty or the shift to middle school and ends when an individual is economically self-sufficient and has taken on several adult roles. Keep in mind the limitations

**Box 1-2 Three Substages of Adolescence**

Given the length of the adolescent period, it is helpful to divide it into three substages that correspond to three important school transitions. For convenience, *early adolescence* will refer to the middle school years (about 11 to 13 years), *middle adolescence* will refer to the high school years (about 14 to 17 years), and *late adolescence* will refer to the college years (about 18 to the early 20s). Although this division is somewhat arbitrary, it reminds us that not all adolescents are working on the same life tasks and challenges.

of these definitions. Young people's life circumstances are so diverse that we cannot expect everyone to fall neatly into one or the other category.

In Western societies, "adulthood emerges gradually over many years, and there is no specific age or event when emerging adulthood can be deemed definitely to have ended and full adult status definitely achieved" (Arnett & Taber, 1994, p. 534). Adolescents become increasingly adult-like as they become fertile, graduate from school, take on adult roles and responsibilities, leave their parents' home, become economically self-sufficient, and perhaps start a family of their own (Arnett, 1994; Rindfuss, 1991).

Hurrelmann (1996) notes that increasing numbers of adolescents are *not* entering adulthood following the completion of their education. Living at home and underemployed, they are independent of their parents socially, morally, politically, and sexually but not economically. He wonders, is this the beginning of a new stage of development: postadolescence? (See Table 1-4.)

### Table 1-4  Possible Criteria for Distinguishing Between Childhood, Adolescence, and Adulthood

**Dictionary definition:** "to come of age" or "period of life between puberty and maturity"

**Biological definition:** adolescence begins with the onset of puberty and ends with the completion of growth and sexual maturation

**Age or grade status:** one becomes an adult at age 18 or 21 or upon graduating high school or college

**Rites of passage:** celebrations, rituals, and ceremonies that confer adult status and privilege

**Social and emotional change:** self-reliance, responsibility, good problem-solving and coping skills

**Cognitive change:** emergence of formal operational thinking and sophisticated moral reasoning

**Life changes and role transitions:** forming close relationships, separating from one's family, taking on adult roles, self-sufficiency

**Subjective experience:** feeling like an adult

Our working definition of adolescence: Adolescence is the life period that begins with the onset of puberty or the shift to middle school and ends when an individual is economically self-sufficient and has taken on several adult roles.

# ADOLESCENCE IN NORTH AMERICA

*Study Question: How did the rural youth of the past evolve into the modern teenager?*

A variety of political, cultural, and economic changes during the 19th century, to a large extent reflecting urbanization (family relocation from farm to city), industrialization, and compulsory schooling, led to our modern view of adolescence. Before industrialization, most children in North America and Europe lived on farms and labored mightily alongside their parents and siblings. Children served as apprentices, learning agricultural skills that they would need to survive. Unlike children today, daily contact with same-age peers was rare (Gies & Gies, 1987).

In the absence of formal schooling, there were few special markers such as promotion or graduation to indicate transitions to new life stages. The average age of puberty onset was 3 to 4 years later than it is today, with longevity averaging about 40 years. There were few specialized roles to distinguish the teenage years from either childhood or adulthood (Chisholm & Hurrelmann, 1995; Kett, 1977).

Prior to industrialization, there was a labor shortage that was alleviated but not solved by immigration and the exploitative practices of slavery and child labor. Industrialization, greater occupational choice, and the abolition of slavery encouraged many families to leave their farms and to head for the cities.

Machines replaced children as more efficient sources of labor. For the first time, children spent extended periods of time away from their families. A new model of childhood was emerging, one that emphasized the importance of preparing children, mainly through formal education, to live and work in an increasingly competitive industrialized society. For adults, working outside of the home led to the formation of relationships in the workplace with other adults. One of the most important social consequences of industrialization was the separation of the home from the workplace (Chisholm & Hurrelmann, 1995).

The family unit was also changing. Now that fathers worked away from home, mothers accepted greater responsibility for the moral upbringing of their children. "Practices such as sacrificing for one's children and refusing to accept wages from them became one characteristic demarcating the middle from the lower classes of society. The period from 1870 to 1930 (later in European countries) marks the transformation in America from the nineteenth-century's 'useful child' to the twentieth-century's sentimentalized 'priceless child'" (Modell & Goodman, 1990, p. 99).

In the late 19th and early 20th centuries, federal courts prohibited child labor and mandated compulsory public education for all children. Reformers like G. Stanley Hall, fearing the exploitation of abandoned and runaway children in the cities, created the *Child Study Movement*. This crusade was committed to "taking youth off the streets, putting them in schools, stretching out the normal home-leaving age from 14 to 18, and in general, prolonging a developmental period" (Teeter, 1988, p. 15).

Various social institutions, including high schools and scouting organizations, aided parental attempts both to protect children from harm and to build moral character. In industrialized countries, the gradual emergence of universal schooling (for males *and* females) accelerated and institutionalized the process of generational separation (Chisholm & Hurrelmann, 1995). "Within these adult-sanctioned groups, adolescence could be recognized, named, analyzed, and perhaps channeled in desired directions" (Modell & Goodman, 1990, p. 101).

Self-styled experts offered advice about child rearing to parents. Boys should be encouraged to be masculine, strong, and independent. Girls were taught to be feminine, affectionate, and pure. For the first time, books and pamphlets addressing "moral problems" were written specifically to be read by young people. Demos and Demos (1969) cite the following titles: *A Voice to Youth, How to Be a Man, Papers for Thoughtful Girls, The Young Lady's Companion, On the Threshold,* and *Lectures to Young Men.*

G. Stanley Hall and many others portrayed youth as the critical transition period in life. Together with an emerging juvenile justice system, these landmark changes required a precise definition of the boundaries between childhood, adolescence, and adulthood. The institutionalization of adolescence as a distinctive period of life led to a new set of ideas and practices concerning young people's cognitive abilities, emotional nature, privileges and obligations, and expectations about courtship, education, and work (Chisholm & Hurrelmann, 1995).

Hurrelmann (1996) notes that initially adolescence was limited to middle-class children because only middle-class parents could afford to provide an extended period of self-exploration and self-definition for their children in the service of career preparation. Eventually, young people from working-class and rural families and ethnic minority families also entered adolescence. "Postwar teenagers had very different expectations of their rights and responsibilities, expectations that were directly linked to the economic prosperity their families now enjoyed. They were coming of age in a world of expanding opportunities and increased leisure time, and they intended to make the most of their good fortune. The war had taught them the meaning of sacrifice, to be sure, but it had also stirred their appetites for records, clothes, cars—the 'stuff' of teenage life. Thanks to full employment and a buoyant economy, a larger proportion of American families could now afford to support their teenagers in style.... For teenagers, this economic prosperity was quickly translated into personal freedom and enjoyment" (Palladino, 1996, pp. 100–101).

Whereas ethnicity and social background used to dictate people's position in society, today it is economic achievement that mainly determines one's social status and lifestyle. In effect, educational and occupational institutions have largely superseded families regarding children's integration into adult society and roles. In nonindustrial societies, vocational training still usually occurs within the family.

Although this text mainly addresses the nature of adolescence in Western, industrialized societies, especially in North America, we must repeat that some aspects of what we call adolescence are universal across cultures and some are

The biological, emotional, and cognitive transitions of adolescence appear to be universal across cultures, but a young person's experience of adolescence varies according to the individual's unique life circumstances.

culture-specific. There is considerable evidence that the biological, emotional, and cognitive transitions of adolescence are universal (Graber & Brooks-Gunn, 1996). Almost all children experience puberty, emotional development, and intellectual growth. But there is also evidence that even these changes, rooted in our human genetic structure, reflect the influence of different economic, ecological, cultural, and social conditions in each society (Hurrelmann, 1994; Riley, 1993). For example, all children acquire beliefs and values, but the specific beliefs and values that they hold reflect the specific circumstances of their lives and the prevailing beliefs and values of their communities. Even within the United States, we can expect to find that the "experience" of adolescence will vary according to a young person's race, ethnic group, gender, economic class, geographical area, and so on.

Most youth in non-Western societies live in modernizing societies that place them in an "educational system grounded in the humanistic and scientific traditions of the West. For better or for worse, within the last century Western culture has become a global culture, more so than any competing set of knowledge and values" (Schlegel & Barry, 1991, p. 201). Schlegel and Barry note that Third World adolescents are probably learning about the scientific view of the world in a European language such as French or English (probably on the Internet). As a result, some of these young people develop a cross-cultural appreciation of their world; others may experience confusion and loss. "Having inadequately learned their own culture, they fail to become adept in the one they encounter in school. . . . Rock musicians, film stars, and sports heroes are the idols of adolescents worldwide, personifying adolescent fantasies of wealth and freedom" (pp. 201–202). Throughout this text, cross-cultural studies are cited to shed light on the universal and culture-specific nature of the adolescent experience.

## ADOLESCENTS TODAY

As society changes, so does adolescent life, with new sets of challenges and potential problems (Chisholm & Hurrelmann, 1995). Since World War II, when teenagers were first identified as such, prosperity has allowed middle-class adolescents in the United States to exert a significant influence on the national economy through their spending and by influencing their parents' spending. The adolescent consumer market is worth about 89 billion dollars annually, and parents contribute an additional 200 billion dollars for their teenagers' care and treatment (Palladino, 1996). Although prosperity has increased the number of adolescents who live in demographically advantaged households, the proportion of adolescents living in poverty also has increased (Cornwell, Eggebeen, & Meschke, 1996).

The growing number of dual-earner and single-parent families has resulted in less parental supervision of adolescents compared to earlier eras. Family members today each have their own time and activity schedules and spend relatively little time together. Rapid technological change and specialization in careers require that adolescents spend more time in school. Compared to their predecessors, most adolescents today face a less predictable future, especially in the world of employment (Chisholm & Hurrelmann, 1995; Fryer, 1997; Schulenberg & Ebata, 1994).

Because of the relatively early onset of puberty and because increasing numbers of adolescents attend college, the period of life we call adolescence is expanding. Parents worry that their children's physical and sexual development are out of step with their social and emotional maturity. Despite their children's rapid growth, parents know that teenagers are not yet ready to take on adult roles and responsibilities. Children and adolescents are neither expected nor allowed to carry their weight economically. Compared to adolescents in other cultures, relatively few Western adolescents are given positions of responsibility. Unlike youth of the past, who spent their waking hours at their parents' side chopping wood, tending livestock, and harvesting crops, many of today's adolescents, lacking meaningful personal challenges, even balk at making their beds and cleaning their rooms.

To be fair, most young people spend many hours each day in classrooms and try to satisfy their obligations at home. Adults expect adolescents—in school, at home, and with peers—to prepare to meet the problems and challenges that await them as adults. The adolescent years are an exciting time of life for most young people as they gain privileges such as driving a car, voting, and seeing "adult" movies (Siegel & Shaughnessy, 1995). The later teenage years and the early 20s are spent in a state of semi-independence during which young people continue to prepare for their future roles and responsibilities while enjoying a considerable measure of freedom (Schulenberg & Ebata, 1994).

Unlike youth of previous centuries, young people in industrialized societies usually have leisure time to spend with peers or by themselves, perhaps shopping, listening to music, or watching television. Although many have part-time jobs, a career is something most give little serious thought to until well into the high school years. College students have serious misgivings about their economic future. "In an age of automation, plant closings, corporate downsizing, and dual-career families, they are learning the hard way that middle-class comforts are not guaranteed" (Palladino, 1996, p. xix).

Compared to their predecessors in the 1960s, today's students appear to be less interested in social affairs. For example, a 1994 survey of 333,703 students at 670 colleges and universities reported that that year's college freshmen were less interested and involved in politics than any entering class in the previous 29 years. Relatively few freshmen reported keeping up with political affairs (32%) or discussing politics (16%) (Higher Education Research Institute, UCLA, *The New York Times*, January 9, 1995).

Csikszentmihalyi and Larson (1984) used an innovative method to gather self-reports from 75 ethnically diverse Chicago high school students regarding these adolescents' daily thoughts, activities, and feelings. The investigators wanted to know what high school students "go through" during a typical week. Participants in the study carried an electronic pager and a pad of self-report forms. At a random moment within every 2-hour period for a week, the pager beeped or vibrated to signal the adolescent to complete a self-report form.

"Adolescents participating in this research reported doing all the things they normally do, from cutting classes to teasing friends, from shopping for dental floss to watching the Miss America Contest. Because the schedule is systematic, it provides a representative sample of their life, a profile of what each teenager's daily experience is like" (p. 33). A total of 2,700 self-reports was collected for all subjects.

What did the study reveal about these teenagers' lives? They spent most of their time (41%) at home. More time at home was spent in their bedrooms than in any room. They spent 32% of their time in school (mainly in class) and 27% of their time in public, much of it with friends or at work. How did they spend their time? Forty percent was spent in such leisure-time activities as socializing (16%), watching TV (7.2%), reading, playing games, and listening to music. Thirty-one percent of their time was spent in "maintenance" activities such as doing chores, eating, and traveling.

Twenty-nine percent of their time was spent in productive activities, including studying (12.7%), classwork (12%), and doing non-school-related work (4.3%). The investigators noted that the students in this study, compared to students in other industrialized societies such as Japan, spent relatively little time in productive activities such as studying and a lot of time in leisure pursuits and socializing. As a group, students in the United States appear to be less committed to their school work than students in other technologically advanced societies.

About a quarter of the teenagers' day was spent alone, a quarter with classmates, and a quarter with friends; relatively little time (8%) was spent with parents and siblings. Considerably more time was spent with mothers than with fathers. The investigators categorized the social world of teenagers this way: (1) unstructured time spent alone, (2) structured time spent in school and with family members, and (3) "spontaneous time" spent with friends, figuring out what to do next. Boys and girls in this study were surprisingly similar in how they spent their time. There were some age differences. For example, older adolescents spent less time with their families than did younger ones.

The study also revealed variability in the teenagers' moods, but this doesn't mean that they were not happy. "Adolescents whose moods change most, report being as happy and as much in control as their steadier peers, and they appear to be as well adjusted on other measures" (p. 123). Rather, the emotional changes seem to reflect "the conflicting experiences in their lives. At one moment they are sitting in class, expected to learn materials (and earn grades) that will have a crucial bearing on their future life; the next moment the bell rings and they are with friends, impelled by an expectation to have a good time" (pp. 124–125).

Some psychologists, notably David Elkind (1984, 1994b), maintain that adult concerns are being imposed on young people prematurely. In his book *All Grown Up and No Place To Go* (1984), Elkind observed that parents are so preoccupied with their own problems that they cannot provide their children with adequate guidance and emotional support. Even concerned parents sometimes feel powerless regarding the multitude of choices their children face. These include pressure to date, to be sexually active, to experiment with drugs, and generally to adopt adult roles and behaviors before they are ready. *Thought Question: Do young people today have lives that are more pressured or less pressured than those of their counterparts of previous eras?*

## JOYS AND OPPORTUNITIES, PROBLEMS AND HAZARDS OF ADOLESCENCE

Although adulthood is hardly a time of unlimited freedom, it probably looks that way to children. Children need adult permission to do almost anything worth doing. The cognitive advances of adolescence that we will study in Chapter 4 give young people a "fresh perspective" with which to view their first-time experiences in the worlds of relationship, responsibility, and romance. "Adolescence is a time of one's first kiss, first dance, first job, first date, first crush, and first 'love.' Childhood had been a period of 'make believe' with much adult supervision. In adolescence, the teenager is confronted with 'the real thing' for the first time" (Siegel & Shaughnessy, 1995, p. 217).

Many are the joys and opportunities of the adolescent years. The emotional investment that teenagers bring to their daily affairs intensifies each experience, magnifying the peaks and valleys of their social lives. Adult roles and responsibilities are edging closer, but one can always find time to party. Teenagers know that there will be less time for having fun after each successive graduation.

Alas, the adolescent years are not just for "chilling." Most teenagers have serious concerns, such as getting along with family members, earning good grades, being accepted by their peers, and finding a decent job (Adwere-Boamah & Curtis, 1993). In one study of the hassles that adolescents face, girls reported having more problems than boys reported in the areas of social alienation, excessive demands, romantic concerns, loneliness, and unpopularity.

**Table 1-5  Common Concerns of Adolescents**

Getting along with family members

One's appearance

Rejection from peers

Peer pressure

Parental divorce

Academic failure

Getting into college

Preparing for the future

Being a victim of crime

There were no gender differences regarding decisions about schooling and their personal futures (Kohn & Milrose, 1993) (Table 1-5).

Large numbers of today's adolescents have serious life problems, such as suffering through their parents' separation and divorce or living in a society where ethnic or political violence is a common occurrence (Garbarino, 1996; Ladd & Cairns, 1996; Lomsky-Feder, 1996). Adolescents in many cultures feel imperiled by political and economic events that threaten their sense of security (Gottlieb & Bronstein, 1996) and by interpersonal encounters that occasion denigration and embarrassment (Ravo, 1996; Yamamoto et al., 1996). Further, many young people participate in high-risk activities that could jeopardize their health and survival. These activities may involve alcohol and other drugs, weapons, vehicles, unsafe sexual practices, and sexual exploitation (Hamburg, 1992; Simons, 1993; Smith & Rosenthal, 1995).

Tens of thousands of children and adolescents live in poverty and are exposed daily to violence and drugs (Martin & Murray, 1996). So-called street children inhabit large cities throughout the world, "gambling, smoking, sniffing solvents, taking up with locals or tourists for a night of 'big money,' taking on odd jobs to get some money to ease their grumbling stomachs or to take home to starving family members" (le Roux, 1996, p. 965). Slavery and child bondage are widely practiced in Asia and West Africa. Child trafficking for the

**Many adolescents participate in high-risk activities that could jeopardize their health and survival.**

sex industry is increasing worldwide. In Asia there are approximately 1 million child prostitutes, and the number is rising in Africa. Worldwide, 250 million, 5- to 14-year-olds are employed, half of them full time, many in hazardous industries (*The New York Times*, November 12, 1996).

Inner-city youth in the United States have a high probability of exposure to violent crime, as witnesses or as victims (Berman, Kurtines, Silverman, & Serafini, 1996; Warner & Weist, 1996), leaving many expecting their own violent death (Hinton-Nelson, Roberts, & Snyder, 1996). In a poll of 2,000 teenagers released by Louis Harris & Associates in early 1996, one in eight young people reported carrying a weapon for protection. One in nine admitted cutting classes because of a fear of violence.

A 1995 study released by the Carnegie Council on Adolescent Development reported that one out of five adolescents is growing up in poverty. One-third of 13-year-olds in the study acknowledged using illegal drugs. Lacking family or peer encouragement for academic achievement, thousands of teenagers drop out of school each year and face low-paying jobs or chronic unemployment (Patterson, 1997). With little prospect of achieving the American dream, many will be tempted to engage in drug dealing, drug use, gambling, and other self-destructive behaviors (Hamburg, 1992).

Adolescents who are susceptible to deviant peer pressure or who lack adequate parental supervision are at greater risk of displaying antisocial and self-destructive behaviors. Short-term consequences of these self-destructive patterns include social rejection, sexually transmitted diseases, serious accidents, addiction, and unwanted pregnancies. Long-term consequences of self-destructive patterns such as alcohol and drug use and poor nutrition include chronic illnesses, cardiovascular disease, and cancer (Hamburg & Takanishi, 1989).

The main concern of any culture is its survival. A culture can thrive only if it provides its young people with a sense of purpose and activities that they find meaningful (Sebald, 1992). It is remarkable that so many youngsters who encounter obstacles not of their own creation make such a commitment. Yet, there is also widespread distrust and resentment, especially among minority youth whom we might characterize as disadvantaged or underprivileged (Martin & Murray, 1996; Wood & Clay, 1996). We are losing too many promising young people to drugs, violence, disease, and other forms of self-destruction. We must do better.

## SUMMARY

**1.** There are many good reasons for studying adolescence, including that it is a fascinating and challenging time of life. Like younger children, adolescents have distinctive needs and require special understanding. The better we understand adolescents, the more supportive we can be as parents, teachers, coaches, and counselors.

**2.** Adolescents are often portrayed in unflattering terms—for example, as moody, rebellious, and irresponsible. The truth is more complicated and more interesting than these stereotypes suggest. Because adolescents are such a varied group, no simple characterization fits them all. Some stereotypes, such as moody and materialistic, may have a grain of truth, but most adolescents are hard-working, responsible, and well adjusted.

**3.** Our ancestors divided life into two stages: infancy and adulthood. Given their relatively short and simple lives, two stages were sufficient. But over the past several hundred years, childhood and adolescence have come to be recognized as distinct formative periods of life. Current theories identify eight or more different life stages, each with its own unique characteristics and challenges.

**4.** Does adolescence exist as an inevitable and universal life stage or does each society invent its own version? Inventionists maintain the latter position, noting that children in industrial societies require an extended period of preparation for adulthood. Adolescence, they suggest, was invented to serve this function. School attendance in particular requires that teenagers remain dependent upon their parents financially and emotionally for an extended period. Yet even in societies that do not require prolonged dependency on parents, young people still undergo physical, sexual, and cognitive changes that could be used to define a unique stage of development.

**5.** Partly due to G. Stanley Hall's pioneering efforts, adolescence has become a legitimate field of scientific inquiry. Hall depicted adolescence as an important and interesting period of life, but one rooted in "storm and stress." Today we view adolescence as a time of exploration and experimentation, an extended life period during which we are expected to "find ourselves."

**6.** Terms like *child*, *adolescent*, and *adult* are inherently vague. After considering many possible definitions, we define adolescence as the life period that begins with the onset of puberty or entry into middle school and ends when one has taken on adult roles and is relatively self-sufficient.

**7.** Most Western adolescents live at home with their parents, attend school, and spend their leisure time with friends, listening to music, or watching television. Young people worry about school, being accepted by peers, and having to choose a career. For most, adolescence is a time of exploring and occasionally for risk taking. Those who are susceptible to deviant peer pressure or who lack adequate parental supervision are at greatest risk of developing self-destructive behaviors.

# GLOSSARY

**Individual differences** Variations in normal development from one person to another

**Youth** The traditional term for those not yet considered adults

**Stereotype** A set of characteristics assumed to be shared by all members of a designated group (e.g., women drivers)

**Grain of truth hypothesis** The idea that every stereotype has a grain of truth behind it

**Placing out** The practice of parents' placing their teenage children in the service of other families as apprentices or domestics

**Inventionist model** The idea that adolescence as a stage of life was invented to serve the current needs and interests of industrial societies

**Moratorium arrangement** The modern idea that adolescence is a time of deferred adult responsibilities and deferred adult privileges

**Sturm und Drang** The German phrase for "storm and stress," used to imply that adolescence is inherently conflictual

**Recapitulation** G. Stanley Hall's idea that the development of each individual replicates the evolution of our species

**Return to the nest** The modern phenomenon whereby adult children return to live at home, usually after college or divorce

**Qualitative differences** Differences in kind rather than amount

**Quantitative differences** Differences in amount rather than kind

**Coming-of-age day** A national holiday in Japan when 20-year-old Japanese declare their legal independence from their parents

**Rites of passage** Rituals that mark the transition from childhood to adulthood

**Vision quest** Native-American rite of passage for male adolescents

**Gender typing** Process by which individuals learn gender roles

**Adult** According to the text, a time of behavioral and emotional self-regulation, financial independence, and taking on adult roles

**Adolescence** The life period that begins with the onset of puberty and the shift to middle school and ends when an individual is economically self-sufficient and has taken on several adult roles

## THOUGHT QUESTIONS

**1.** List five general qualities that you associate with adolescents. Are they stereotypical or are they valid descriptions of adolescents you know?

**2.** According to your own definitions of these terms, are you an adolescent or an adult? Justify your response.

**3.** Describe any rites of passage you experienced during your adolescence as a member of your community, ethnic group, or religion.

What did the rituals or ceremonies mean to you?

**4.** What aspects of adolescence are universal across cultures? What aspects reflect the economic, educational, and employment opportunities of a particular culture?

**5.** What would you tell your children about your adolescence to help them through this distinctive period of life?

# SELF-TEST

1. Researchers study adolescents mainly
   a. to create meaningful social policies
   b. to provide interventions for clinicians who work with young people
   c. to design interesting and effective educational materials
   d. to gain knowledge

2. Stereotypes usually are
   a. unflattering
   b. misguided
   c. resistant to change
   d. all of the above

3. The historical study of youth suggests that
   a. children generally were well treated by their families
   b. parents valued their children partly for the labor and security children could provide
   c. childhood was recognized as a distinct stage of life as early as the Middle Ages
   d. ancestral parents were as strongly attached to their children as parents are today

4. Adolescence was first recognized as a unique and important stage of life by
   a. Aristotle
   b. Shakespeare
   c. G. Stanley Hall
   d. Erik Erikson

5. Inventionists maintain that a society perceives its young people according to its
   a. current economic and political needs
   b. ethnic and religious traditions
   c. level of industrialization
   d. ethical and moral beliefs

6. The moratorium arrangement of adolescence refers to
   a. mandatory universal schooling
   b. deferred freedom and deferred responsibilities

    c. laws that protect children from exploitation

    d. property rights extended to male and female children

**7.** G. Stanley Hall

    a. popularized adolescence as an important developmental stage

    b. devised the first intelligence test

    c. rejected Darwin's theory of evolution

    d. encouraged parents and teachers to be strict and punitive

**8.** The return to the nest phenomenon refers to

    a. hawks and eagles

    b. late adolescents and young adults

    c. coaches and counselors

    d. developmental researchers

**9.** The coming-of-age day is celebrated by

    a. gays and lesbians

    b. Jews and Catholics

    c. Japanese youth

    d. all of the above

**10.** Rites of passage

    a. are practiced cross-culturally

    b. include elaborate celebrations

    c. indicate the transition from childhood to adulthood

    d. all of the above

**11.** After considering many alternatives, the chapter defines the onset of adolescence in terms of

    a. biological and school transitions

    b. cognitive and intellectual changes

    c. social and emotional changes

    d. rites of passage

**12.** About what percentage of adolescents live in poverty?

    a. 5

    b. 10

    c. 15

    d. 20

# TWO

# THEORETICAL PERSPECTIVES

## Preview Questions

1. Does development occur gradually or in "leaps & bounds"?

2. What is the relationship between theory and research?

3. Does biology or life experience play a greater role in personality development?

4. What is the key assumption or premise of each of the following types of developmental theories?

   a. Biological-ethological
   b. Cognitive-developmental
   c. Psychodynamic

   d. Psychosocial
   e. Phenomenological
   f. Learning

5. In what way do interactional and contextual models offer more plausible explanations of child and adolescent development than simpler direct effects models?

◆

———

# Contents

Micaela is captain of her high school track team. She is a bright, highly motivated, appealing 17-year-old. Somehow, she is able to balance her school work and extracurricular activities with an active social life and a part-time job. She would assure us that it's not easy.

Micaela usually has positive feelings about herself and her parents, but she complains that they place too many restrictions on her. For example, there is some family strain regarding her on-and-off again relationship with a boyfriend. Additionally, her parents are not pleased about how she spends the money she earns at work. They implore her to save some money for college. They are proud of her academic and athletic achievements and try to be supportive, but occasionally family tensions increase to a boiling point and there is heated conflict and angry confrontations.

Over the past few years, Micaela has experienced remarkable physical, emotional, and cognitive changes that would make her almost unrecognizable to a younger version of herself. Although she is not so different from other high school seniors, understanding how Micaela came to be the person she is now is not easy. How has she been affected by her gender, ethnicity, parents, friends, teachers, TV, and popular culture?

Unfortunately, there is no single *theory of development* or personality that can make sense of all of Micaela's changes or accurately predict her future life course. Instead, there are dozens of theoretical perspectives, each of which sheds some light on how adolescents like Micaela are transformed from a child into an adult. Keep in mind that as individuals like Micaela develop (show orderly change over time), so do families, communities, and societies (Lerner, 1986).

In this chapter, we briefly review several developmental theories and models, each of which addresses a fairly narrow domain of development. (The term *model* sometimes is used interchangeably with the term *theory* but more narrowly describes the application of a general theory to a more specific field of interest [Whitley, Jr., 1996]). Having given much thought to the role that conflicting emotions play in personality, Sigmund Freud might have wondered how much of Micaela's bickering with her parents reflects frustration displaced from her relationship with her boyfriend. Jean Piaget's interest in cognitive development might have led him to wonder how Micaela uses her impressive reasoning abilities to promote her point of view during family discussions.

Freud and Piaget are proponents of **stage theories** which view developmental change as occurring in fairly predictable stages or steps. Stage theorists contend that the changes that occur during each life period build on previous changes and set the groundwork for subsequent development. Parents often employ a stage model when trying to understand their children. Micaela's father, for example, views her stubbornness as a stage that she is going through. This helps him cope with what he sees as her unpredictable mood swings and occasional bad attitude. Since it's just a stage, he assures himself, it will pass. Current research in development has been shifting away from stage models toward process models that emphasize interactions between individuals and the varied social contexts in which development occurs (Lerner, 1996; Petersen et al., 1996; Wachs, 1996; Zahn-Waxler, 1996).

Existential and behavioral theorists do not view developmental change as occurring in stages. They claim that adolescence is not qualitatively different (different in kind) from any other period of life. Rather, we change slightly each day (Figure 2-1). Existential theorists view the adolescent as "a whole being who not only exists in the here and now but is inextricably linked to a past childhood leading imperceptibly to a future adulthood" (Hacker, 1994, p. 302). Existential theorists would be interested in Micaela's awareness of her existence as a unique individual, the meaning that she attributes to her everday life experiences, and her willingness to take responsibility for her actions and decisions.

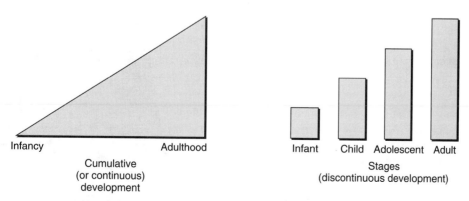

FIGURE 2-1  **Comparing cumulative change models to stage models.**

Behavioral (learning) models like that of B. F. Skinner view developmental change cumulatively. They acknowledge that each day we change a little bit, but they see no dramatic changes or shifts from one period of life to the next. Given the important role in personality development that they attribute to behavioral consequences (rewards and punishments), behaviorists would be interested in how Micaela's parents, teachers, and peers use positive reinforcement (e.g., praise) and punishment (e.g., criticism) to encourage certain behaviors in Micaela and discourage others.

Skinner might have noted that Micaela is more self-disclosing with her peers than with her parents, perhaps because her friends are not as critical and demanding. In other words, her friends (who, unlike her parents, are her equals) reinforce self-disclosures (e.g., about possible sexual encounters with her boyfriend) that Micaela's parents might punish through criticism or disapproval.

Psychosocial theorists, such as Erikson (1963) and Havighurst (1972), would bring our attention to the developmental tasks and challenges that Micaela faces as a middle-class adolescent in a highly competitive technological culture, including coming to terms with her emerging sexuality, becoming more independent, adjusting to new peer group standards and pressures, and especially, formulating an adult self-concept. According to Erikson, Micaela's self-concept must integrate the various roles she has taken on in her community, as well as her personal values, spiritual beliefs, and vocational aspirations.

The interactional-contextual model of development, the last and most comprehensive model that we consider in this chapter, emphasizes the complex relationships between individuals and the various settings that they inhabit (Lerner, 1996). This model reminds us that Micaela's development does not occur in a vacuum. On a typical day, she spends her time in several different places (e.g., home, school, workplace) and with many different groups of people (e.g., parents, teachers, peers). Like all of us, Micaela is influenced by cultural media such as music and TV, members of her community, her socioecomic status, religious instruction, national events, and the sexism and racism that are inherent in most human cultures (Watts, Machabanski, & Karrer, 1993). Her encounters in one particular setting with one group of individuals will influence her behavior and feelings in other settings. For example, she may be inattentive in math class after an argument with her sister.

In subsequent sections of this chapter, we will elaborate on these and other models of developmental change. Note how each model sheds light on certain aspects of Micaela's development. Keep in mind that although most models address a somewhat narrow slice of adolescent development, throughout this text we will try to view the adolescent as a whole, complete, yet developing person.

# DOMAINS OF DEVELOPMENTAL CHANGE

*Study Question: How can we organize the myriad changes of adolescence into a small number of useful categories?*

We can assign each of the features of Micaela's life cited in the previous section to one of three categories of developmental change: physical, cognitive, and psychosocial. The **physical domain of development** includes bodily changes such as growth, sensory and motor development, and sexual maturation. Micaela is larger, stronger, and faster than she was as a younger child. Her well-proportioned body and long legs are physical qualities that help her to compete successfully on the track team.

The **cognitive domain of development** includes mental and intellectual abilities that allow us to make sense out of our everyday experiences. Micaela's ability to think and reason about her life as an adolescent is much more impressive than when she was younger. Micaela can think in complex ways about her relationships and family problems. For example, sometimes she notices inconsistencies, even contradictions in her parents' reasoning. She writes amusing poems and stories with symbolism and abstract ideas and composes fiction that transcends her own life experiences. Cognitive abilities involving memory, learning, thinking, and reasoning emerge and change over the course of the life span, but most dramatically during childhood and adolescence.

The **psychosocial domain of development** includes changes in personality, motivation, emotions, self-concept, and social behavior. This domain is called psychosocial because the changes it addresses involve the interplay of psychological (personal) and social factors. Micaela views herself as a member of and participant in a variety of groups including her family, her ethnic group, her crowd at school, her soccer team, her relationship with her boyfriend, and the school community. She senses that her behavior and emotions are inextricably woven into the fabric of her family life, peer relationships, and community obligations.

Although most physical growth and cognitive development is complete by early adulthood, important psychosocial changes in personality, relationships, and roles continue throughout the adult years. Keep in mind that *changes in one domain of development usually lead to changes in the other domains.* For example, in the next chapter, we will see how the physical changes of puberty affect virtually every other aspect of adolescent development. (Table 2-1). As Micaela's body became more shapely during puberty (physical domain), her identification and appreciation of herself as a female deepened (cognitive domain), and people (especially boys) treated her differently (psychosocial domain). ***Thought***

### Table 2-1  The Three Domains of Developmental Change

**Physical domain:** growth and maturation—heredity, physical growth, sensory and motor development, sexual maturation

**Cognitive domain:** how we know the world—development of perception, memory, learning, thinking, reasoning, problem solving, intelligence

**Psychosocial domain:** changes in personality, emotions, and social behavior

*Question: What changes in the psychosocial domain of development might lead to changes in the physical domain?*

## THEORIES OF DEVELOPMENT

*The major task in any science is the development of theory. A good theory is simply a good explanation of the processes that actually take place in a phenomenon. . . . But to construct theories, one must first know some of the basic facts. . . .*
*(Schmidt, 1992, p. 1177)*

Each year in the United States, about 1 million unmarried teenage girls become pregnant. How can we understand why so many sexually active teenagers avoid taking precautions that would avoid unwanted pregnancy? Don't they understand the relationship between intercourse and pregnancy? Do they really want to become pregnant? Do they just hope and pray that it won't happen to them? Or do they think that getting an abortion is no big deal? Before we can have any hope of solving this serious social problem, we must understand the key factors involved. That is, we need relevant information. One goal of science is to satisfy society's continuing thirst for useful knowledge about human behavior and development.

Because human affairs are complicated and usually difficult to explain, behavioral researchers initially speculate about how life events influence behavior and development. Perhaps some boys don't use condoms during sex because they are too embarrassed to buy them. Maybe some girls are coerced into having sex by boyfriends who threaten to abandon them if they do not submit. Hypotheses like these are predictions (guesses) about how events are related to each other. Research hypotheses usually are based on the (often limited) evidence available, casual observation, or even intuition. **Theories of development** are intended to describe, predict, and explain changes in behavior over the life span, from conception to death (Box 2-1).

Theorists attempt to organize and summarize existing facts "in a reasonable, internally consistent manner. A theory should also make predictions [hypotheses] concerning phenomena not yet investigated and allow clear tests of these predictions. At their best, theories explain phenomena as well as describe and predict them" (Plomin, 1994, p. 159).

As the quote that begins this section implies, all worthwhile theories begin with existing knowledge (Schmidt, 1992). When organized into a body of knowledge, they offer useful perspectives that we might otherwise overlook. Theories are always tentative; we can never know anything with absolute certainty. Are you consciously reading this sentence now or are you dreaming it? How can you tell? The results of any particular study may support or contradict our predictions but cannot establish their truth or falsity. A good example is Charles Darwin's theory of the origin of species. We can never know for sure what happened yesterday, let alone thousands or millions of years ago. However, so much evidence in so many diverse disciplines supports Darwin's theory of evolution that its basic premise (evolution through natural selection) is

A theory is a set of statements about how variables are related. Most developmental theories attempt to describe, predict, and explain specific changes in behavior over some part of the life span. To do so, they must generate testable predictions, that is, ones that can be confirmed or disconfirmed. In other words, the statements that comprise a theory must have been verified by research or are potentially verifiable (Whitley, Jr., 1996). When research results confirm a theory's predictions, our confidence in the theory is strengthened. When research findings contradict a theory's predictions, the theory is modified accordingly or abandoned.

Not all theoretical assumptions are subject to empirical testing. Environmentalists like John Watson assumed that learning plays the major role in human development, whereas ethologists assume that heredity and evolution are the key factors. Most modern theorists assume that almost all developmental change depends upon the interaction between heredity and life experience, but this assumption is almost impossible to prove.

Good theories do not contradict themselves, are in agreement with what is already known about a topic, and are consistent with related theories. They are parsimonious (not unnecessarily complicated), and their terms are clear and well-defined. The best developmental theories serve three purposes: They help us to organize what we believe we know about development, they extend our knowledge, and they guide future research and theorizing (Whitley, Jr., 1996). Since the ultimate goal of a developmental theory is to further our understanding of behavior and personality, we hope that a theory is useful, that is, applicable to what some call the real world.

**Box 2-1**
**Characteristics of Developmental Theories**

accepted as fact by most reasonable people. Only disconfirming evidence or a better theory would lessen our confidence in Darwin's theory. *Thought Question: What role should faith or personal belief play in a behavioral science?*

Darwin's theory of evolution and Sir Isaac Newton's laws of motion are impressive because they are relatively easy to understand, yet they explain so much about the natural world. And they are **testable**, that is, both models generate hypotheses that can be confirmed or disconfirmed through objective observation and measurement. Elaborate theories like Freud's and Erikson's generate hypotheses that are not as easily tested. For example, Freud's postulation of an unconscious "death wish" to explain self-destructive behavior is almost impossible to confirm or refute. In any case, there is no one theory of development that can make sense out of everything that we know about how people change. Instead, we find many theories, most being attempts to explain one particular aspect or domain of development. *Thought Question: Why are successful theories harder to develop in the behavioral sciences than in natural sciences such as physics, chemistry, and biology?*

Developmental theories differ not only in the particular domain of development that they address but also in how they view the nature and causes of development. Some theorists, such as G. Stanley Hall and his student Arnold

Gesell, heavily emphasized the role of biology (nature) in development, especially heredity and maturation. Most biological theories view development as a process in which our biological nature gradually unfolds according to some unique inherited design. It is partly because people prefer conceptually simple answers to questions about behavior that biological models are so popular (Regan, 1996).

To environmentalists like John Locke, John Watson, and B. F. Skinner, development reflects primarily the conditions of rearing (nurture), diverse life situations, and personal encounters that gradually shape our behavior and personality. The role of biological factors and individual differences usually is minimized. Interactional models of development, discussed later in this chapter, acknowledge both biological and environmental influences on development. They attribute developmental change to dynamic interactive processes between individuals and their environments involving inherited dispositions, socialization, family dynamics, cultural practices, and an individual's unique life situation (Plomin, 1994; Zahn-Waxler, 1996).

## EARLY THEORIES OF DEVELOPMENT

### John Locke

John Locke (1632–1704) was a British philosopher and statesman. He advocated a perspective known as **empiricism**. Empiricism is the assumption that all knowledge is derived from experience (especially sensory experience) and mental reflection. In other words, we know the world by observing it through our senses and then by reasoning about what we have observed.

Before Locke's influence was felt, it was widely believed that people were born with innate ideas and morals, presumably instilled by God. Locke challenged this belief. If the mind contains innate ideas, he reasoned, then all people should have the same ideas. Obviously, this is not the case. According to Locke (1690, 1693), at birth a child's mind is a **tabula rasa**—that is, a blank slate devoid of knowledge or ideas. All knowledge, he claimed, comes from our experiences with the world and from our ability to reflect on (reason about) these experiences. However, he acknowledged that children differ intellectually and, therefore, in what they can learn. He also allowed for differences in children's temperaments, suggesting that at birth children's personalities, unlike their minds, are not totally blank (Crain, 1992).

Locke's empiricism, predating by centuries the radical environmentalism of behaviorists like John Watson and B. F. Skinner, emphasized the importance of nurture (rearing and education), practice, imitation, and rewards in children's development. He opposed the use of punishment. Many of Locke's learning principles—repetition, rewards, imitation, minimal use of punishment—have been incorporated into modern learning theory and educational practice. His observation that children's personalities are different from adult personalities provided the groundwork for modern theories of development (Hergenhahn, 1992). Locke certainly would approve of the child-focused nature of modern life and of the use of positive incentives by parents and teachers to

**John Locke (left) and Jean Jacques Rousseau (right) began a nature-nurture debate that continues to this day.**

help today's youth become productive members of society. However, having so valued self-control, Locke might be a little dismayed by the lack of discipline and resolve that he would observe in so many of today's teenagers.

## Jean Jacques Rousseau

Unlike John Locke, the French philosopher Jean Jacques Rousseau (1712–1778) favored nature (biology) in the **nature-nurture controversy**. He emphasized what he called *natural processes* (biological maturation) in development. According to Rousseau, nature allows children to develop different abilities at different stages of growth. Jean Piaget later expanded on this insight—the emergence of new abilities is age-related.

To Rousseau, child rearing and education were either irrelevant or negative forces in development. He had little faith that parents or teachers could allow children the freedom that they needed to become healthy individuals. Better to minimize adult guidance and let the child explore the world through her senses. Let her think for herself (Crain, 1992; Hergenhahn, 1992). Parents tend to raise their firstborns in the spirit of John Locke ("You will sit there and eat those vegetables") and their laterborns according to the gospel of Rousseau ("You're going to marry your tennis coach? What a wonderful idea!").

Rousseau formulated the first stage theory of child development, citing infancy (birth to 2 years), childhood (2–12 years), late childhood (12–15 years) and adolescence (15–20 years). Each stage, he maintained, has distinctive psychological characteristics that should be taken into account when rearing and educating children (Crain, 1992).

What we refer to today as adolescence begins at puberty, a "second birth" for children, marked by increasingly passionate behavior. "A change of temper, frequent outbreaks of anger, a perpetual stirring of the mind, make the child almost ungovernable" (Rousseau, 1762, p. 172). To his credit, Rousseau observed that youth are more sociable and less selfish than younger children and more subject to peer pressure. Sexual feelings, he surmised, lead to an interest in and attraction to the opposite sex and perhaps a readiness for marriage. Rousseau also acknowledged cognitive advances in adolescents that allow them to think like adults about scientific and moral issues. To a surprising extent, Rousseau's 18th-century depiction of adolescents anticipated many modern conceptualizations of this period of life (Crain, 1992). *Thought Question: If we took Rousseau literally and raised children with minimal socialization and education, how do you think they would turn out?*

## MODERN THEORIES OF ADOLESCENT DEVELOPMENT

### Biological and Evolutionary Models

#### Gesell's Maturational Model

**Arnold Gesell overemphasized the role of biology in development and minimized the role of the environment.**

Like Rousseau, Arnold Gesell (1880–1961) viewed development as the gradual unfolding of a child's biological nature (Gesell & Ilg, 1943). Children differ in how quickly they develop—for example, the age at which puberty begins and its duration. However, almost all children show the same *sequence* of developmental changes. Gesell and Rousseau maintained that each of us possesses an innate "timetable" that dictates when new behaviors and abilities will emerge. Both theorists urged parents to be flexible in rearing their children and to avoid pushing a child in one direction or another. Instead, parents should respect the natural, inevitable flow of their children's development. One can only wonder what their reaction would be to the hectic pace and pressures of family life in the late 20th century.

Today we know that development is not static and fixed but rather unfolds over the life span. As we mature, each of us becomes increasingly **differentiated**, that is, more complex and unique, more of an individual. Some developmental changes are essentially continuous, notably aging. Other changes involve transitions from one form to another, such as the pubertal metamorphosis from child to adult body (Graber & Brooks-Gunn, 1996). The extent to which development is **continuous or discontinuous** is still debated by theorists, but as we noted in Chapter 1, we observe both quantitative change (change in amount) and qualitative change (change in kind) during adolescence.

Most current models of development view biological and experiential factors as reciprocal and interactive (Ge et al., 1996; Wachs, 1992, 1996). That is, biological change both influences and is influenced by an individual's psychological, social, and historical development. The question no longer is "Which is more important to development, nature or nurture?'' but rather ''How do biology and life experience interact to produce developmental change?''

### Evolutionary and Ethological Theory

Charles Darwin (1809–1882) did not originate the idea that life on earth evolved from simple to complex organisms over long periods of time. Greek philosophers suggested this possibility over 2,000 years ago. However, Darwin was the first to describe the mechanism, **natural selection**, by which a species' habitat perpetuates certain traits rather than others. The main tenet of natural selection is that traits that promote an organism's survival proliferate through sexual reproduction.

Charles Darwin's theory suggests links between evolution, heredity, and current adolescent behavior.

Genes, the basic units of heredity, give rise to the biological ''packaging'' that we call bodies. Because children inherit their genes from their parents, we are not surprised by the physical resemblance usually seen among family members. Human genes evolved over long periods of time and do not seem to have changed substantially during hundreds of thousands of years. Our physical makeup is not very different from that of our ancient ancestors. On the average, we are larger and healthier than our ancestors and live longer. This is mainly attributable to modern diet, sanitation, and medical technology but could also reflect changes in our genetic makeup (Figure 2-2).

In trying to understand adolescent development, theorists known as **ethologists** invoke evolutionary theory. They look for connections between evolution, heredity, biology, current life circumstances, and adolescent behavior (see Spotlight • Can Evolutionary Theory Help Us Understand Adolescent Behavior?). Puberty and sexual maturity are particularly important concepts in ethological models of adolescent behavior. Ethologists are interested, for example, in how secondary sexual characteristics such as body hair, breasts, and body shape signal fertility to potential mates. Ethologists cite genetic and evolutionary principles when trying to understand parent–adolescent and peer relationships, unwed motherhood, self-concept, sexual orientation, psychological gender differences, antisocial behavior, puberty rites, and parental investment in child rearing (Angier, 1997; Buss, 1995; Elkins, McGue, & Iacono, 1997; Savin-Williams & Weisfeld, 1989). Environmental theorists usually are less than enthusiastic about such conjectures, which are difficult to test empirically.

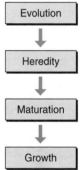

FIGURE 2-2 Relation between evolution, heredity, maturation, and growth.

### SPOTLIGHT • Can Evolutionary Theory Help Us Understand Adolescent Behavior?

Evolutionary models of development propose that any complete picture of adolescent development must take heredity into account. Belsky, Steinberg, and Draper (1991) present a provocative developmental model based on evolutionary principles. They hypothesize that individuals who have endured very stressful childhoods later adjust their mating and parenting behaviors accordingly.

Children whose caregivers are untrustworthy, abusive, or unavailable, Belsky and his colleagues suggest, develop a set of reproductively adaptive characteristics, such as early puberty and precocious sexuality. These characteristics improve reproductive success for children raised under less than optimal conditions. None of these adaptations is presumed to be conscious or intentional. *Critical Thinking Question: Why would early fertility and sexual precociousness be adaptive for teenagers who were raised in troubled families?*

According to Belsky's hypothesis, during adulthood individuals who have had unstable childhoods become involved in unhealthy relationships and show little patience with their own children. Belsky hypothesizes that children who enjoy stable family relationships and nurturant parenting in their early years avoid early sexual encounters and eventually have stable, supportive adult relationships. One corollary of this model is that closeness to parents during childhood delays the onset of puberty, perhaps reflecting evolutionary pressure to inhibit incest (Steinberg, 1988, 1989). The key point of this evolutionary model of socialization is that "early experience 'sets' the reproductive strategy that individuals will follow in later life" (Belsky et al., 1991, p. 647) (Figure 2-3).

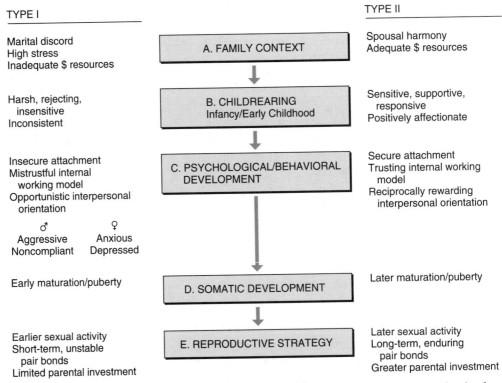

**FIGURE 2-3 Relationship between early stressful experiences and reproductive behavior. (From Belsky et al., 1991, p. 651)**

Belsky's model is controversial (Maccoby, 1991) because it suggests that reproductive and mating strategies during adolescence and adulthood are programmed to some extent by early childhood experiences. (How would Freud feel about this idea?) Belsky's hypothesis has received mixed research support (Graber, Brooks-Gunn, & Warren, 1995). In one longitudinal study of 16-year-old girls (Moffitt, Caspi, Belsky, & Silva, 1992), the effect of family stress on the timing of menarche was not found to be mediated by child behavior problems (contradicting the model). However, family conflict and father absence in childhood did predict earlier onset of menstruation (supporting the model). Another study found that compared to girls from intact families, girls from conflicted and divorced families have earlier onset of menstruation (Wierson, Long, & Forehand, 1993). Can you think of an explanation for this observation that is not stress-related?

## Cognitive Developmental Models

Cognitive models of development, such as that of Jean Piaget (1896–1980), emphasize the critical role that thinking and reasoning play in development. In Chapter 4, we will examine at length Piaget's model of cognitive development as it applies to adolescents. We know that adolescents' reasoning abilities are more advanced than those of younger children but not quite as sophisticated as those of young adults. We teach geometry to high school students, not to elementary school students, yet we do not consider most high school students to be responsible enough to marry or to raise children (although many do).

Despite shortcomings in his model of cognitive development, Jean Piaget has contributed more than anyone else to our understanding of how young people think and reason about the world and about themselves.

Since thinking and reasoning influence our feelings and behaviors, it is important to understand how adolescents think and reason about the world, especially their social environment and their own behavior. The *information-processing* approach attempts to understand adolescent reasoning by determining exactly what is happening when adolescents receive, perceive, and remember information and how they think about and use information. (This and other approaches to intellectual development are described in Chapter 4.) The key point to remember about cognitive models of development is that *how we know the world changes over the course of childhood and adolescence. And how we know the world has an enormous impact on our self-concept, behavior, and emotional life. Critical Thinking Question: What is the relationship between how we know and what we know?*

## Freudian (Psychodynamic) Models

Freudian theory offers a storm and stress view of adolescence, emphasizing the role that family conflict and sexual tension play in motivating adolescent behavior (Elman & Offer, 1993). Sigmund Freud (1856–1939), the founder of psychoanalysis, viewed adolescence as a psychological reaction to puberty. According to Freud, during puberty adolescents experience a variety of powerful impulses, including sexual feelings toward the opposite-gender parent and rivalry with the parent of the same gender. For example, boys feel attracted to their mothers and competitive with their fathers. The increase in tension causes ''both unpleasurable and pleasurable sensations, to which a person must and will adapt in various ways. These adaptations then form the basis of personality development during adolescence'' (Richards & Peterson, 1987, p. 39).

In effect, adolescents must find a middle ground between indulging their impulses and completely denying or suppressing them. Freud (1920) considered the most important task of adolescents to be separating from their parents and establishing a life of their own. Incestual sexual impulses and rivalries hasten this separation. Because sexual desire directed toward family members is socially unacceptable, it ultimately encourages adolescents to seek intimacy from peers (Blos, 1962) (Figure 2-4).

Anna Freud, Sigmund Freud's daughter, elaborated on the role that emotions play in helping adolescents separate from their families. She saw adolescence as a ''normative developmental disturbance'' (A. Freud, 1969) that occurs when adolescents' conflictual feelings compel them to flee from the family environment. Anna Freud viewed family tensions as normal and even desirable because they help adolescents accomplish one of the most difficult tasks they face: separation (A. Freud, 1958). *Critical Thinking Question: What factors other than family tensions motivate adolescents to want to become independent?*

Psychodynamic theories link early childhood experiences, family tensions, and adolescent behavior. One problem with a turbulence model of adolescence is that it perpetuates the stereotype of the troubled teenager. Teenagers who are easygoing and compliant are seen as pathological. Further, if emotional disturbance during adolescence is considered normal, it does not have to be

**Sigmund Freud and his daughter Anna agreed that adolescents' conflictual feelings facilitate the process of separation from their parents.**

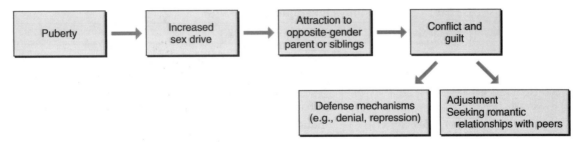

**FIGURE 2-4** Freud's direct-effects model.

taken seriously ("Well, she's depressed again, but she'll grow out of it"). Many young people who are having a hard time do not grow out of their problems and need help (Elman & Offer, 1993).

Research contradicts the stereotype of the adolescent in turmoil. Most adolescents get along fairly well with their parents, teachers, and friends and prefer to avoid conflict when possible (Offer, 1985). Nowadays, most psychodynamic theorists deemphasize the role of sexual tensions in adolescent personality and instead focus on how the ego or self contributes to adolescent functioning (Sandler, 1992).

## Psychosocial Developmental Models

The developmental models described by Gesell, Freud, and the ethologists addressed mainly the physical (biological) domain of development. Psychosocial developmental models, such as those of Erik Erikson and Robert Havighurst, view the sequence and timing of key life events as crucial factors in development. Adjustment depends on successful completion of critical tasks facing an individual at different points in life, including acquiring the cognitive and social skills valued by one's culture and community (Klaczynski, 1990).

Erikson (1963) described eight psychosocial stages of development that encompass the life span (Table 2-2). At each stage of development, individuals face distinctive tasks, conflicts, and challenges. One's readiness to address a particular task reflects mainly biological maturity and motivation to rise to the challenge. We will revisit Erikson's model and its implications for adolescent identity in Chapter 6.

Havighurst (1972) defined a **developmental task** as one "which arises at or about a certain point in the life of the individual, successful achievement of which leads to his happiness and success at later tasks, while failure leads to unhappiness in the individual, disapproval by society, and difficulty with later tasks" (p. 2).

Most developmental tasks, such as becoming more self-sufficient, creating an adult identity, or acquiring values, are not specific to any particular life period. But certain life periods (like adolescence) provide excellent opportunities to work on tasks such as those just mentioned.

Havighurst and Erikson agreed that identity formation is the central task

According to Erik Erikson, at each stage of life individuals face distinctive developmental tasks, conflicts, and challenges.

### Table 2-2 Erikson's Developmental Stages

| Stage | Developmental Task |
| --- | --- |
| Infancy | Trust vs. mistrust—will infant trust or mistrust its caregivers? |
| Toddlerhood | Autonomy vs. shame and doubt—will toddler feel pride or shame in its new abilities? |
| Early childhood | Initiative vs. guilt—will child take initiative or fear failure? |
| Middle childhood | Industry vs. inferiority—will child learn the skills of its culture or feel inferior? |
| Adolescence | Identity vs. identity diffusion—will adolescent create a satisfying adult identity or lack direction? |
| Early adulthood | Intimacy vs. isolation—will young adult form close relationship with another or feel isolated? |
| Middle adulthood | Generativity vs. stagnation—will adult contribute to the next generation or feel interpersonally impoverished? |
| Late adulthood | Integrity vs. despair—will elderly person accept his/her life or feel unfulfilled? |

(From Erikson, 1963)

of adolescence. Havighurst described eight other tasks that most adolescents must address (but probably won't complete) before young adulthood (Table 2-3). Each subtask supports the creation of a personal identity: (1) developing mature relationships with male and female peers, (2) accepting a masculine or feminine sex role, (3) accepting one's body and physical appearance, (4) becoming emotionally independent of parents, (5) preparing for marriage and family life, (6) preparing for economic independence, (7) acquiring values that will guide one's behavior, and (8) exhibiting socially responsible behavior.

Keep in mind that the specific tasks and challenges that one faces vary according to one's gender, culture, ethnic group, and personal circumstances. Specific life tasks could include attaining an impressive SAT score, knowing how to sail, being good with children, or memorizing portions of the Bible.

### Table 2-3 Havighurst's Developmental Tasks of Adolescence

Forming mature relationships with male and female peers

Adopting a masculine or feminine social role

Accepting one's body

Achieving emotional independence of parents and other adults

Preparing for marriage and family life

Preparing for a career and becoming self-supporting

Acquiring values that guide one's behavior

Exhibiting socially responsible behavior

(From Havighurst, 1972)

Some tasks, such as acquiring a set of meaningful values, may be applicable to a wide range of adolescents from dissimilar backgrounds, but adolescents from different social, cultural, or ethnic backgrounds face different tasks at different points in their lives (Klaczynski, 1990).

Awareness of developmental life tasks helps adults to be more supportive of children's development. For example, it is important for parents and teachers to view adolescent questioning of their authority as a normal and healthy desire for autonomy rather than as an "attitude problem" that requires a forceful display of adult power.

## Existential Models

Existential (also known as *humanistic* or *phenomenological*) psychologists seek to understand the meaning of human existence, not from the point of view of an objective observer but from the point of view of the developing person. They ask, "What does it feel like to be an adolescent?" Existential psychologists like Abraham Maslow (1971) and Carl Rogers (1961) view each person as a complete thinking and feeling individual with enormous potential for growth rather than as just a collection of behaviors, stages, or domains of development.

Existential concerns of adolescents include the meaning of life, isolation, love, alienation, mortality, and taking responsibility for the decisions they make (Hacker, 1994). Existential theorists assume that each of us has **free will**, or the ability to make choices that are free of influence. *Critical Thinking Question: Does the premise that each of us is ultimately responsible for his or her own behavior require the assumption of free will?*

Existential psychologists are interested in adolescents' cognitive development, but only to the extent that advanced reasoning abilities help adolescents gain a deeper awareness of their existence in the world (Hacker, 1994). Although mainstream psychologists criticize existential psychology's philosophical base and subjective methodology, existential models often provide plausible and dramatic depictions of adolescent life. There are domains of adolescent experience (e.g., spiritual awakening) that are interesting and important even though they are not very susceptible to direct scientific examination.

Fischer and Alapack (1987) offer an existential analysis of adolescent first love. They use personal accounts provided by students in an adolescent psychology class. These investigators attempted to capture the reported first love experiences using the following qualities: absolutes ("I love everything about you"), uniqueness ("Nobody has ever loved like we love"), perfection ("My one and only true love"), and togetherness ("We did everything together"). Such an analysis allows us to view adolescent first love from the adolescent's point of view rather than from the theorist's. Those who live with or work with adolescents would respond more sympathetically during hard times if the adolescent's point of view were better understood.

*Critical Thinking Question: As a researcher, how much credibility would you give to adolescents' personal accounts of their sexual experiences? What could you do to increase their credibility?*

Existential psychologists are interested in what it feels like to be an adolescent.

## Learning Models

Virtually all behavioral scientists acknowledge the important role that learning and the social environment play in human development, agreeing with John Locke that knowledge and character are strongly rooted in everyday life experience. John Watson (1878–1958) originated the behaviorist school in modern psychology, asserting that the only proper subject matter of psychology is observable behavior. To a behaviorist, in effect, you are what you do.

Ivan Pavlov (1849–1936) and B. F. Skinner (1904–1990) discovered principles of learning that account for the acquisition, persistence, generalization, and suppression of behavior. Although learning models do not address learning in any particular life period, they imply that most adolescent behavior is learned and maintained according to principles of classical conditioning (Pavlov), operant conditioning (Skinner), and observational learning (Albert Bandura).

For the most part, learning models ignore or downplay biological factors such as hormones and reject hypothetical mentalistic concepts such as mind, ego, and self. In explaining behavior, behavioral (learning) models focus on how the environment shapes and maintains behavior rather than on feelings and cognitive abilities, which are less accessible to empirical examination. Skinner (1974) and Bandura (1986) disagreed about the role that cognitions or interpretations play in behavior. Skinner advocated an objective environmental model, whereas Bandura maintains that cognitions usually mediate between the environment and behavior (see Figure 2-5). Both probably are right some of the time.

Bandura and Skinner would agree with most other psychologists, however, that behavior and development are **determined** by environmental events, especially socialization and education. Both theorists rejected the possibility that humans, and therefore adolescents, have free choice. However, both would

**B. F. Skinner (left) and Ivan Pavlov (right) described powerful learning principles that help explain cumulative changes in human behavior and development.**

allow that adolescents partly create the environment that determines their behavior. Bandura (1986) stresses the importance of encouraging **self-efficacy** in young people, the belief that they can solve their problems and cope with their emotions. A Skinnerian view of adolescent behavior emphasizes the importance of behavioral consequences (reinforcers and punishments) in shaping adolescent behavior. Prosocial behavior earns money, grades, recognition, and approval. Punishments such as disapproval, poor grades, and speeding tickets discourage selfish, lazy, and antisocial behavior. Skinner believed that society should provide young people with opportunities to gain meaningful reinforcers for achievement and prosocial behavior. Nonbehaviorists criticize learning models as offering a passive and simplistic view of child and adolescent behavior. Nevertheless, parents and teachers who understand basic principles of learning and motivation are more likely to socialize their children using posi-

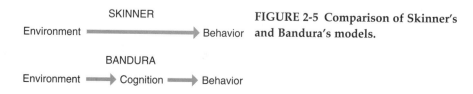

SKINNER

Environment ⟹ Behavior

BANDURA

Environment ⟹ Cognition ⟹ Behavior

**FIGURE 2-5 Comparison of Skinner's and Bandura's models.**

tive rather than coercive strategies. *Critical Thinking Question: What limitations would existential psychologists see in a strictly behavioral view of adolescence? What limitations would behaviorists see in the existential model?*

## Interactional-Contextual Models: The Ecology of Human Life

The earliest developmental models proposed that biological and environmental factors have direct and universal effects on development. For example, as noted earlier, Freud claimed that pubertal hormones exert a direct (unmediated) influence on adolescents' social behavior and adjustment. However, we now know that how puberty affects development depends on specific contextual conditions, including an adolescent's self-esteem, family stability, peer group support, and cultural factors (Lerner, 1992, 1996).

*Interactional-contextual (ecological) models of development* take into account all categories of influence on human behavior—heredity, family history, socioeconomic status, quality of family life, ethnic and cultural background—and analyze how they interact with each other to generate developmental change. The *interactional-contextual* model (Bronfenbrenner, 1979, 1989; Lerner, 1996) proposes that each individual's development is embedded in a complex physical and social network of parents, siblings, peers, neighborhood, school system, community, and culture. Changes in one level of organization (e.g., the family) are dynamically related to developmental changes in other levels (e.g., the peer group). Thus, patterns of development and behavior that are rooted in biology or family life are maintained or changed by encounters beyond the family. This process continues over the life span (Figure 2-6).

**FIGURE 2-6  The four layers of the environment in ecological systems theory. The microsystem refers to relations between the child and the immediate environment, the mesosystem to connections among the child's immediate settings, the exosystem to social settings that affect but do not contain the child, and the macrosystem to values, laws, and customs of the child's culture. (From Berk, 1996)**

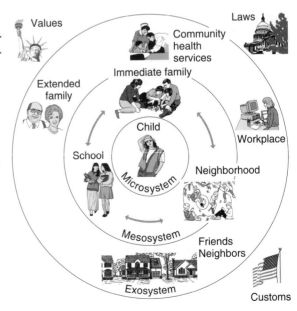

The interactional-contextual perspective describes multiple interacting paths of influence at different "levels" of an individual's environment (Bronfenbrenner, 1979, 1989; Wachs, 1992, 1996). Unfortunately for developmental researchers, there are a large number of factors interacting (influencing each other) at biological, personal, and environmental levels. A given level of organization influences and is influenced by all other levels. It is the pattern of relations among levels at a given point in time that "causes" behavior and development (Lerner, 1992, 1996).

Consider, if you will, two sisters who attend the same high school. The older one excels academically and the younger one struggles to get passing grades. The older sister has a close relationship with her mother, who happens to be unmarried. The younger, less achieving sister is more emotionally distant and has frequent conflicts with her mother and sister. At first glance, it seems odd that sisters would differ so much in their relationships and in their academic achievement. As siblings, they share approximately half their genes, the same home and school, and the same parent. How do we go about understanding, let's say, the divergence in their school performance?

The number of factors affecting the girls' academic achievement is sizable, including their mother's educational background, the level of family functioning, each parent–child relationship, socioeconomic factors, the quality of instruction they receive, the high school environment, peer relationships, and so on. Some of these factors encourage similarities in the girls' development; others generate differences.

The effect that an environmental factor such as parental education has on some aspect of development such as achievement almost always depends on a host of other so-called **mediating variables** (Figure 2-7). Technically speaking,

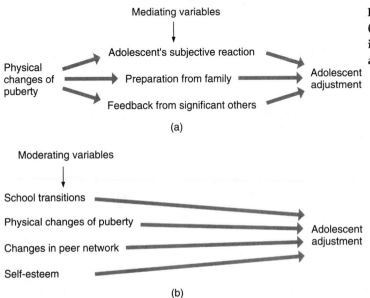

FIGURE 2-7 Comparing mediator (*a*) and moderator (*b*) variables using effect of puberty on adjustment as an example.

mediators are variables through which the **independent variable** affects the **dependent variable**. When asked what effect a particular independent variable has on behavior or development, we can almost always answer, "It depends." "It depends" means that other factors mediate between the environmental variable and the behavior of interest. The effects of parental divorce on a child's adjustment, for example, depend on the child's age, gender, emotional resources, and so on.

**Moderator variables** usually take the form of individual differences and situational factors that interact with an independent variable to produce behavioral and developmental outcomes. For example, an adolescent's self-esteem (the moderator variable) can weaken or strengthen the effect of peer influence (the independent variable) on deviant behavior (the behavioral outcome).

By emphasizing person–context relations, interactional and contextual models offer a more plausible view of development than do the simplistic direct-effects models described earlier in this chapter. The down side of the contextual approach is its potential complexity. To understand your own development and personality, for example, we must take into account your unique biological packaging and dispositions, your family and educational history, your current life circumstances, cognitive abilities, and so on. Much of what we would need to know about you to understand your personality (i.e., why you turned out the way that you did) would not be readily available to researchers or even to you.

### Table 2-4  Developmental Models of Adolescence

**Biological models** emphasize the importance in development of heredity and maturation, especially as manifested during puberty.

**Ethological (evolutionary) models** focus on adaptive behaviors or qualities that we observe in adolescents and their possible origins in the evolution of our species.

**Cognitive models** of adolescent development describe the sophisticated thinking and reasoning abilities that emerge during adolescence and the crucial role that these abilities play in the formation of adolescent self-concept, identity, and relationships.

**Psychodynamic models** describe how sexual and other unconscious impulses lead to family conflict, which in turn motivates adolescents to become more self-sufficient.

**Psychosocial models** of development emphasize the interplay between individual and social factors. They maintain that adolescent development is best understood in terms of specific crises or developmental tasks that adolescents face such as creating an adult identity or acquiring prosocial values.

**Existential models** describe what it feels like to be an adolescent and highlight adolescents' search for meaning in their lives.

**Learning models** emphasize environmental influences, especially observational learning and the effects on adolescent behavior of positive and negative encounters with others.

**Ecological-interactional (contextual) models** take multiple levels of influence into account, ranging from an adolescent's immediate family environment to peer, school, community, and cultural influence.

The interactional-contextual model highlights the important role played by the links that exist between two or more settings that family members inhabit. What happens to the girls at home affects their behavior at school (and vice versa). For example, family arguments make it harder to concentrate in school; schoolwork interferes with getting chores done. Some of Mom's encounters at work (e.g., advice from friends) may affect her parenting behavior at home. Work-related stress reduces her emotional availability to her daughters when they need comfort or reassurance. At the highest level of contextual influence, Western culture provides Mom and the girls with certain beliefs, resources, opportunities, limitations, and hazards that can have a considerable impact on the course of their lives (Table 2-4).

## SUMMARY

**1.** Those who study human development are interested in several types of changes: physical growth, cognitive-intellectual advancement, and changes in emotions, personality, and social behavior. Theories of development, by organizing and summarizing existing knowledge, are intended to describe, predict, and explain changes in behavior, thinking, emotions, and experience.

**2.** There is no single theory of adolescent development. Several types of theories are described in this chapter, most focusing on a particular aspect of development. Biological models emphasize the importance in development of heredity and maturation. Evolutionary models focus on adaptive behaviors or qualities that we observe in adolescents and their possible origins in the evolution of our species.

**3.** Cognitive models of development describe the impressive thinking and reasoning abilities that emerge during childhood and adolescence and the crucial role that they play in almost all aspects of adolescent development. Psychodynamic models describe how sexual and other tensions lead to family conflict, which, in turn, motivates adolescents to become more self-sufficient.

**4.** Psychosocial models of development stress the importance of social factors in development, especially relationships with family members and friends. Erikson and Havighurst suggested that adolescent development is best understood in terms of specific life tasks or challenges that adolescents face, such as creating an adult identity or acquiring prosocial values.

**5.** Existential models attempt to describe what it feels like to be an adolescent. Learning models emphasize cumulative environmental influences, especially the effects on adolescent behavior of positive and negative encounters with other people.

**6.** Most factors that affect development do not operate independently. Rather, individual influences interact with each other to produce outcomes that are often difficult to predict. Hence, ecological-interactional models offer a more plausible view of adolescent development than direct effects models, mainly because they take multiple influences into account. Further, the effects of one variable on development, such as father absence, usually is mediated or moderated by other variables, such as a custodial mother's coping resources.

**7.** Most current models of adolescent development acknowledge the existence of similarities and differences among adolescents. Understanding the origin of individual differences requires consideration of several factors, including gender, family socioeconomic level, ethnic group membership, and differences in cultural norms. Most current models of development also acknowledge mutual (reciprocal) influence between adolescents and the important people in their lives.

# GLOSSARY

**Stage theories** Theories that view development as occurring in discrete steps or stages

**Physical domain of development** Changes in the body, nervous system, sensory capacity, and motor skills

**Cognitive domain of development** Changes in how we know the world

**Psychosocial domain of development** Changes in personality, emotions, and social behavior

**Theories of development** Systematic attempts to describe, predict, and explain changes in growth, maturation, and behavior

**Testability** The ability of a hypothesis or theory to be confirmed or disconfirmed by objective evidence

**Empiricism** The assumption that all knowledge is derived from experience (especially sensory experience) and mental reflection

**Tabula rasa** John Locke's idea that at birth the mind is a "blank slate" upon which experience writes

**Nature–nurture controversy** Disagreement about the relative importance to development of biology and experience

**Differentiation** Over time, individuals become more complex and unique

**Continuity versus discontinuity** Disagreement about whether development occurs cumulatively or in stages

**Natural selection** According to Darwin's theory of evolution, nature (the environment) favors traits that have survival value

**Ethologists** Scientists who study animal behavior and emphasize the importance of evolution and heredity

**Developmental task** A life task or challenge associated with a particular stage of development

**Free will** The assumption that people can make choices that are free of external influence

**Determinism** The assumption made by scientists that all natural events, including human behavior, have natural causes

**Self-efficacy** The belief that one can perform successfully on a task

**Mediating variables** Variables through which an independent variable affects a dependent variable

**Independent variable** A variable that is manipulated in an experiment to determine its effect on other (i.e., dependent) variables; in psychology, any observable variable that influences behavior or development

**Dependent variable** A variable that is measured to determine whether and how it is affected by an independent variable

**Moderator variable** Variables that take the form of individual differences and situational factors that interact with an independent variable to produce behavioral and developmental outcomes

# THOUGHT QUESTIONS

**1.** What is your theory of adolescent moodiness and irritability? What evidence supports it?

**2.** Which one of the various theories of development discussed in this chapter is most useful to you in understanding your own development?

**3.** What is your position on the nature–nurture issue? Do you believe that one of these factors is more basic to personality development than the other?

**4.** Can you identify a significant developmental task or challenge you are now facing? How will mastery of this task prepare you for your future?

**5.** What implications does the free will concept have for a science of behavior?

# SELF-TEST

**1.** Stage theorists propose that development occurs

   **a.** as a continuous process

   **b.** in a step-like progression

   **c.** independently of age

   **d.** unpredictably

**2.** Which one of the following theorists did not propose a stage theory of development?

   **a.** Erikson

   **b.** Piaget

   **c.** Skinner

   **d.** Freud

**3.** In which domain of development does sexual maturation fall?

   **a.** physical

   **b.** cognitive

   **c.** social

   **d.** emotional

**4.** Theories of development attempt to _____ knowledge about development.

   **a.** organize

   **b.** summarize

   **c.** explain

   **d.** all of the above

**5.** Which one of the following theorists offered the least biological model of development?

   **a.** Bandura

   **b.** Freud

   **c.** G. Stanley Hall

   **d.** Gesell

**6.** The assumption that all knowledge comes from experience is called

   **a.** nativism

   **b.** empiricism

   **c.** tabula rasa

   **d.** determinism

7. Evolutionary (ethological) theory emphasizes the role in development played by
   a. reinforcement
   b. observational learning
   c. defense mechanisms
   d. natural selection

8. The role played by sexual feelings in adolescence was emphasized by
   a. Erikson
   b. Rousseau
   c. Freud
   d. Havighurst

9. Erikson and Havighurst agreed that the central task of adolescence is
   a. identity formation
   b. separation from one's parents
   c. self-regulation
   d. accepting one's body

10. Existential concerns of adolescents include
    a. allowance
    b. curfews
    c. peer pressure
    d. the meaning of life

11. Skinner and Pavlov would be most interested in how adolescents
    a. think
    b. learn
    c. feel
    d. interpret their experiences

12. The link between family, peer group, and school setting is emphasized by what theoretical approach?
    a. social learning
    b. cognitive
    c. interactional
    d. existential

# THREE

# PHYSICAL GROWTH AND DEVELOPMENT

## Preview Questions

1. What does it mean to say that physical changes in adolescents' bodies have *social stimulus value*?
2. How do developmental researchers actually measure physical change during puberty?
3. How does *growth spurt* during puberty affect adult expectations?
4. What is the difference between a primary and a secondary sexual characteristic?
5. What is the secular trend?
6. What biological factors trigger the onset of puberty?
7. How do the advantages and disadvantages of early and late maturation vary according to gender?
8. What aspects of bodily change cause self-consciousness in boys and girls?

◆

## Disclosures

Adolescence is when everyone goes through their changes, and girls get their period, boys get crazy, and you start going out with guys and stuff.... I was in fifth grade at school and I went to the bathroom and realized I got "it." I had no clue. I wasn't nervous, but I felt stupid like everyone was looking at me when I went back to class. I now know that they didn't know, but I felt like they did.

*(16-year-old girl)*

My first day of seventh grade I was scared. I thought, "Oh God, I hope I don't mess up, I hope I don't say something or do something that makes me different." But before school even started, this boy comes up to me and says, "Hi, Miss Piggy! Hi, Miss Piggy!" He thought it was okay to pick on me just because of how I look. Then I had to go to school. And nobody even gave me a chance. It was like they were afraid to talk to me because I was fat, like I had a disease.

*(Lisa, eighth grader, interviewed by Orenstein, 1994, p. 100)*

I check my look in the mirror. I wanna change my clothes, my hair, my face.

*Bruce Springsteen, "Dancing in the Dark"*

◆
―――――
**Contents**

What would happen if a child were given an adult body and the opportunity to spend a few weeks in the world of adult work, competition, and romance? In the movie *Big*, Tom Hanks plays a 12-year-old boy (Josh) who magically finds himself in the body of a young adult. The movie's appeal lies partly in Tom Hanks's ability to use his adult body, voice, and mannerisms to convey the childish innocence and vulnerability of Josh's personality. Through luck and creative

**By the end of the movie *Big*, Josh (played by Tom Hanks) realizes that he is not ready to take on adult roles.**

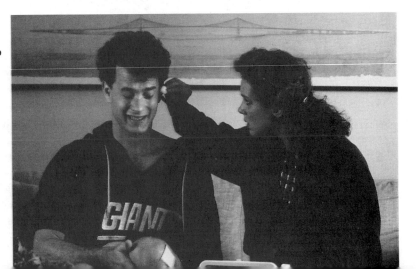

thinking, Josh manages to put on an almost convincing front, but by the end of the film it is clear to Josh and to the film's audience that he is not yet ready to handle the stresses and strains of adult life. He is given back (again magically) both his young adolescent body and the many more years he'll need to prepare for being a grownup.

Early in the movie, Josh awakens and looks in the mirror to see for the first time his physical transformation. The changes that real-life adolescents see in the mirror are much more gradual than Josh's, but the feelings that accompany his startled reaction are not so different. How strange to look in the mirror and see that one's appearance is changing, slowly but inexorably. How odd to become larger and stronger and to feel the first pangs of sexual desire.

As noted previously, the onset of puberty is a reasonable marker for the beginning of adolescence. Puberty appears to be one of the few domains of adolescence that is inevitable and universal. Most of the physical changes that comprise puberty are observable and measurable, lending themselves to scientific examination. As noted in Chapter 1, the main drawback of using a strictly biological definition for the onset of adolescence is the wide variation in age (8 to 16 years) at which puberty can begin.

Changes in hormone levels, bone structure, fat deposits, and sex organs begin almost simultaneously, markedly altering the appearance of **pubescent** girls and boys (those beginning puberty). Adding to adolescent anxiety, there is no way of knowing what one will look like when the process is complete! Changes

**The size and shape of adolescent bodies have social stimulus value—people notice and react to them.**

in appearance have what psychologists call **social stimulus value**—people notice them and react to them. Adolescents who appear to be physically mature have to adjust to the heightened expectations of parents, teachers, and friends. Because physical maturity usually precedes social and emotional maturity, young people may have difficulty meeting this challenge.

Teenagers receive a lot of feedback about their bodies. They realize that their appearance plays an important role in their popularity with peers. Depending on how they evaluate their "look," adolescents may experience excitement, confusion, or dread. Puberty provides one of the most clear-cut examples of how biological change can have important social and psychological consequences (Downs, 1990). Although physical changes are important in their own right, people's reactions to these changes usually have an even greater impact.

Physically attractive adolescents typically gain considerable attention and are perceived positively by peers and adults (Sorell & Nowak, 1981). Taller males enjoy an enviable dating advantage (Hensley, 1994). Changes in appearance and sexuality set the stage for social and emotional adjustments by adolescents and their family members that will continue until young adulthood and beyond (Keelan, Dion, & Dion, 1992; Paikoff & Brooks-Gunn, 1991). Even as adults, many males are preoccupied with their size and height and many females with their weight and breast size (Ayalah & Weinstock, 1979; Rosenbaum, 1979).

The meaning assigned to pubertal change varies from one culture to another and from one community to another. Most societies acknowledge the importance of becoming fertile with rituals, ceremonies, and celebrations (Hurrelmann, 1994; Paige, 1983). Such recognition is less common in Western culture, perhaps reflecting mixed feelings about sexual maturation (Delaney, 1995). Unfortunately, many parents do not provide the emotional support and understanding required by pubescent children for optimal adjustment. Most tell their children little that would help them prepare for or understand their physical metamorphosis (Brooks-Gunn & Reiter, 1990). For example, girls generally are given inadequate information about the onset of menstruation and about the sexualized attention that their developing bodies will attract from boys.

In this chapter, we raise several intriguing questions concerning adolescents' physical development, especially regarding the interrelatedness of bodily change and psychological functioning. How and why does the body change during puberty? What biological factors initiate rapid growth and sexual development? How do children, especially those who are "off time" in their physical development, feel about their growth and sexual maturation? How do powerful pubertal hormones affect children's mood, behavior, and relationships? And how do cultural forces and socialization moderate the expression of biological processes?

These questions are not easily answered. As the interactional-contextual model of development (Chapter 2) makes clear, biological change does not occur in a vacuum. At about the same time that children are maturing physically, they are also experiencing dramatic intellectual and social changes that help transform their self-concepts. The timing of maturation, family reactions to the physical change, stressful life events, and cultural assumptions are examples of contextual variables that moderate the effects of pubertal change on adolescent behavior and adjustment (Brooks-Gunn & Reiter, 1990; Lesko, 1996; Markstrom-Adams, 1992).

## HOW DO PSYCHOLOGISTS STUDY PUBERTY?

The role of puberty in adolescent development received scant attention from researchers prior to the 1980s, perhaps reflecting society's discomfort about sexual and bodily matters (Brooks-Gunn & Reiter, 1990). Many parents, children, and educators still resist requests from researchers who want to interview or examine adolescents regarding their physical changes (Brooks-Gunn, 1990).

A variety of methods are available for assessing pubertal status, including physician ratings, parent ratings, and self-ratings (Graber & Brooks-Gunn, 1995). Although blood, saliva, and urine tests and physical examinations yield precise physiological and physical measurements, parents, adolescents, and school officials find self-report measures less intrusive. Self-ratings provide useful information about adolescents' perceptions of their development and social status (Brooks-Gunn, 1990).

Chronological age is not a very good predictor of a child's physical growth or sexual maturity. Thus, researchers have devised rating scales to measure a child's **pubertal status**, or current level of pubertal development. The pubertal assessment instrument that is most widely used by health professionals is the five-stage Tanner scale, which evaluates primary and secondary sexual characteristics. When given a little instruction about how to identify bodily changes, adolescents provide fairly accurate assessments of their pubertal status. Not surprisingly, adolescents are aware that their bodies are changing (Downs, 1990). Their self-assessments correlate reasonably well with those of their parents and with those of trained health care personnel (Dorn, Nottelmann, Inoff-Germain, Susman, & Chrousos, 1990).

One group of researchers has designed a **Pubertal Development Scale (PDS)**, a short self-report instrument (Petersen, Crockett, Richards, & Boxer, 1988). Adolescents rate their maturational status of five pubertal markers using a 4-point scale. The five markers include (1) development of body hair, (2) the occurrence of the growth spurt, (3) changes in complexion, breast development (girls), and menstruation (girls), (4) voice changes (boys), and (5) facial hair growth (boys). The 4-point scale includes the following choices: has not yet begun, has barely begun, is definitely under way, growth or development is complete.

Another group of investigators (Robertson et al., 1992) administered the PDS to seventh graders in rural Iowa and suburban Chicago. The two groups were matched on gender, age, race, and school grade. In their self-reports, the rural children reported greater pubertal change than did the suburban children on 9 of the 10 markers. As expected, girls in both locations showed earlier changes than boys in growth, body hair, and complexion.

It is possible that rural children have more stressful lives, which, in turn, precipitates early maturation. This interpretation supports the hypothesis of Belsky and his colleagues (described in Chapter 2) that stress during childhood triggers early maturation. *Critical Thinking Question: What other environmental or socioeconomic factors could account for maturational differences between rural and suburban students?*

## WHAT IS PUBERTY?

### Growth

**Puberty** is the period of transition from reproductive immaturity (nonfertility) to reproductive maturity (fertility) (Cameron, 1990). It takes place over an av-

**Identical twins have identical genes and nearly identical maturation.**

erage period of 4 years and varies in duration from 2 to 6 years (Brooks-Gunn, 1987). The internal and external changes of puberty are orchestrated mainly by heredity. Identical twins, having identical genes, display nearly identical patterns of growth and maturation, even compared to fraternal twins, who share only about half of their genes. For example, identical twin girls experience **menarche** (the onset of menstruation) within 3 months of each other on the average, compared to 10 months for fraternal twins (Petri, 1934). The exact timing of pubertal events for specific adolescents reflects a complex combination of biological and psychosocial factors (Graber et al., 1995). Growth and maturation are adversely affected by extreme environmental conditions such as malnutrition, chronic stress, neglect, and abuse (Belsky, 1993; duToit, 1987; Mallik, Ghosh, & Chattopadhyay, 1986).

Rapid skeletal growth, known as the **growth spurt,** begins at about age 9 or 10 for girls and at about age 11 for boys. During the growth spurt, boys and girls grow an average of 10 inches, about 2½ inches a year over a 4-year period. Boys are a few inches taller than girls when the growth spurt begins, so they are taller when it ends. Boys and girls gain an average of 40 pounds during this period. As height and weight increase, there is an accompanying growth spurt in internal organs such as the heart and lungs (Graber & Brooks-Gunn, 1995).

Gradual growth continues during the high school years and is complete at about 17 and 20 years, respectively, for girls and boys. African-American girls develop secondary sexual characteristics at a slightly younger age than white girls and are more physically developed at the same age (Harlan, Harlan, & Grillo, 1980; Udry, Halpern, & Campbell, 1991). Figure 3-1 displays the sequence and duration of key pubertal events for girls and boys. Almost all pubertal growth occurs between 9 and 19 years of age (Richards, Abell, & Petersen, 1993).

Growth in size and muscle mass leads to increased strength and improved motor performance for boys and girls (Graber & Brooks-Gunn, 1995). Boys usually are larger, stronger, and faster than girls after puberty, giving them a competitive advantage athletically. Sports that allow an equal number of males and females on each team (e.g., mixed doubles in tennis) minimize any gender advantage in size, strength, or speed.

## Sexual Maturation

**Sexual maturation** refers mainly to achieving fertility but also refers to other bodily changes that support the reproductive process. Menarche, the first menstrual period, symbolizes the emergence of femininity even though it occurs relatively late during puberty (at about 12.5 years), 2 years after breast budding. Ethologists note that conspicuous changes in the shape of the female body help distinguish females from males and have social stimulus value for most males. Breast development in particular, one of the first indications of puberty in females, "advertises the capacity for reproductive functioning" (Savin-Williams & Weisfeld, 1989, p. 263).

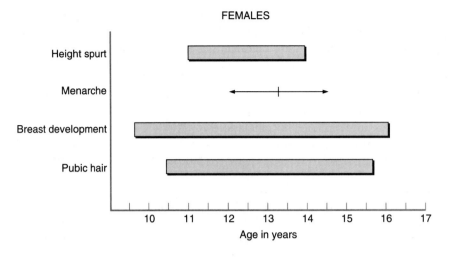

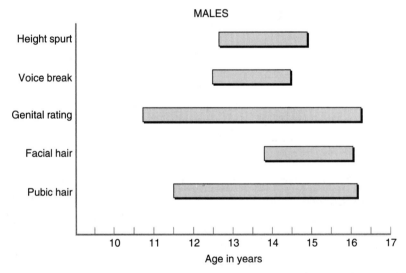

FIGURE 3-1 The developmental course of pubertal events for females (top) and for males (bottom). (From Richards, Abell, & Petersen, 1993)

### Primary Sexual Changes

**Primary sexual changes** include changes in male and female organs that are involved directly in reproduction (Table 3-1). These include the vagina, ovaries, fallopian tubes, and uterus for females and the penis, testes, and seminal vesicles for males. The maturation of the ovaries leads to an irregular ovarian cycle that becomes increasingly regular (monthly) over time. **Ovulation** usually begins several months after menarche. A regular cycle of ovulation emerges months or years after menarche. During the growth spurt, a female's pelvis widens. This allows easier passage of a fetus during birth (Apter & Vihko, 1977;

## Table 3-1 Pubertal Development in North American Boys and Girls

| Girls | Average Age Attained | Age Range | Boys | Average Age Attained | Age Range |
|---|---|---|---|---|---|
| Breasts begin to "bud." | 10 | (8–13) | Testes begin to enlarge. | 11.5 | (9.5–13.5) |
| Height spurt begins. | 10 | (8–13) | Pubic hair appears. | 12 | (10–15) |
| Pubic hair appears. | 10.5 | (8–14) | Penis begins to enlarge. | 12 | (10.5–14.5) |
| Peak of strength spurt. | 11.6 | (9.5–14) | Height spurt begins. | 12.5 | (10.5–16) |
| Peak of height spurt. | 11.7 | (10–13.5) | Spermarche (first ejaculation) occurs. | 13 | (12–16) |
| Menarche (first menstruation) occurs. | 12.5 | (10.5–15.5) | Peak of height spurt. | 14 | (12.5–15.5) |
| Adult stature reached. | 13 | (10–16) | Facial hair begins to grow. | 14 | (12.5–15.5) |
| Breast growth completed. | 14 | (10–16) | Voice begins to deepen. | 14 | (12.5–15.5) |
| Pubic hair growth completed. | 14.5 | (14–15) | Penis growth completed. | 14.5 | (12.5–16) |
| | | | Peak of strength spurt. | 15.3 | (13–17) |
| | | | Adult stature reached. | 15.5 | (13.5–17.5) |
| | | | Pubic hair growth completed. | 15.5 | (14–17) |

*Notes:* These milestones represent overall age trends. Individual differences exist in the precise age at which each milestone is attained.

*Sources:* Malina & Bouchard, 1991; Tanner, 1990.

Apter, Viinikka, & Vihko, 1978; Cameron, 1990; Paikoff & Brooks-Gunn, 1991). For males, increased production of testicular hormones leads first to enlargement of the testes (at about age 11.5 years) and then to pubic hair growth. The production of mature sperm, growth of the penis and scrotum, increased muscle mass, and facial and development of body hair follow (Cameron, 1990). Due to large increases in testosterone production, boys and girls experience a heightened sex drive (Cameron, 1990; Hopwood et al., 1990).

On average, boys become fertile several years before girls, even though puberty begins earlier in girls. **Spermatogenesis,** the production of sperm by the testes, begins as early as age 11 in boys, although ejaculation usually occurs considerably later. Ovulation begins at about age 15 in girls (Stein & Reiser, 1994). *Critical Thinking Question: How can we explain the marked age difference between the onset of male and female fertility? Hint: Why would premature fertility be more costly to females than to males?*

### Secondary Sexual Changes

**Secondary sexual characteristics** include the growth of body hair (including genital, underarm, and facial), breast enlargement, adult facial features, voice deepening (especially in males) due to vocal cord thickening, and increasing fat deposits (particularly in females) (summarized in Table 3-1). Despite their bad reputation, fat deposits insulate the uterus as well as the entire body. Fat cells play an important role in a female's ability to carry a fetus and produce breast milk. Increased activity of the sebaceous (oil) glands increases the likelihood of skin disorders such as acne (Brooks-Gunn, 1987). All of these changes reflect increased production of gonadal steroid hormones (Savin-Williams & Weisfeld, 1989).

## What Is the Secular Trend?

Over the past 150 years, the rate of biological maturation in Western societies has increased to the point that children today reach puberty several years earlier than their ancestors (Eveleth & Tanner, 1976). This phenomenon of earlier sexual maturation, called the **secular trend** (*secular* means "present"), is illustrated in Figure 3-2. Not only do children today mature more quickly than their counterparts of previous centuries, people today also are notably larger and taller (Eveleth & Tanner, 1976).

What is responsible for this trend toward earlier maturation? Since the human gene pool has not changed very much for thousands of years, improvement in the conditions of child rearing is the likely cause. The secular trend is most marked in societies where children enjoy adequate nutrition and good health care (Malina, 1985). Children raised in poverty have later onset of puberty and do not grow as tall. Thus, improved diet, health, and living conditions

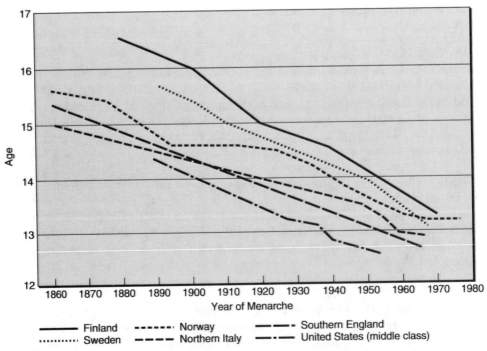

**FIGURE 3-2 Secular trend in age of first menstruation (menarche) from 1860 to 1970 in industrialized nations. Data for Norway, which extend to 1980, suggest that secular change has recently leveled off. (From Berk, 1997)**

apparently have allowed our human genes to maximize their potential for growth (Eveleth & Tanner, 1976).

One result of early puberty is that adolescents today are sexually mature but unmarried for a much longer period than in previous centuries. One unfortunate consequence of early fertility is the large number of unwanted pregnancies during the teenage years, a topic we will return to in Chapters 9 and 10.

Humans achieve reproductive maturity at a proportionally later age than any other primate species. Ethologists view our prolonged childhood as biologically expensive for parents in terms of food, nurturance, and protection. Most parents would agree that child rearing requires a large commitment of resources. But an extended childhood is necessary for "basic training" in the skills that allow successful reproduction and parenting (Savin-Williams & Weisfeld, 1989).

## What Triggers the Onset of Puberty?

Something in our biological makeup delays fertility until we are capable of raising our children to maturity. Actually, puberty is a reactivation of intense hormonal activity that begins before birth. Physical development is controlled by the nervous system but is regulated mainly by endocrine glands that secrete biochemical substances called **hormones** into the bloodstream. Prenatal hormones promote fetal growth and differentiate male and female reproductive organs (Kaplan, Grumbach, & Aubert, 1976). In effect, hormones "organize" the fetal reproductive system. The prenatal hormonal environment also influences the timing of puberty and resulting fertility. The exact mechanisms are not yet known (Sanders & Reinisch, 1990). We do know that sexual maturation is inhibited during early infancy, probably by brain centers that regulate the hypothalamic-pituitary-gonadal axis (Hopwood et al., 1990).

The always-ticking genetic clock reactivates the reproductive endocrine system in the preadolescent, apparently through increases in sex steroid hormone secretion. It is not known whether this increase is triggered by current biological or emotional events or whether the inhibition of sexual maturation that began during infancy is itself inhibited, a process known as **disinhibition** (Sanders & Reinisch, 1990).

As discussed in Chapter 2, the onset of puberty can be accelerated or retarded by biological factors such as heredity and nutrition, emotional factors such as depression and coping resources, and situational factors (for girls, the quality of family relationships and participation in vigorous activities) (Graber, Brooks-Gunn, & Warren, 1995). These factors interact with each other, making it difficult to predict when puberty will begin for a particular individual (Hopwood et al., 1990). A best guess would be based upon the pubertal ages of close relatives, especially same-gender parents and siblings (Graber et al., 1995).

The specific genetic and environmental mechanisms responsible for the onset of puberty are complex and are still being studied (Fishman, 1980; Graber & Brooks-Gunn, 1995; Graber et al., 1995; Hopwood et al., 1990; Marano, 1997). Frisch and Revelle (1970) hypothesized that attaining a critical body weight stimulates sexual maturation, at least for females. This **critical weight model** was modified by Frisch and McArthur (1974), who hypothesized that the critical factor in triggering the onset of puberty is attaining a minimum percentage of body fat. (Fat cells store estrogen, affecting ovulation and menstruation.) The findings of several studies contradict these two hypotheses (e.g., Graber et al., 1995; Kulin, Buibo, Mutie, & Sorter, 1982), although nutrition and weight very early in life may be relevant (Liestol, 1982). Crawford and Osler (1975) suggested that in young females, changes in metabolism initiate the maturational sequence.

A large increase in hormone secretion begins in girls between the ages of 10 and 11 years and in boys about 2 years later. Within each gender, there is considerable variation regarding hormonal secretion, growth, and behavioral effects. Rising hormone levels trigger a sequence of bodily changes that result in fertility, secondary sexual characteristics, and rapid growth leading to increased height, weight, and strength (Brooks-Gunn & Reiter, 1990) (Figure 3-3).

Pubertal development is guided by two hormonal systems: the hypothalamic-pituitary-adrenal (HPA) axis and the hypothalamic-pituitary-gonadal (HPG) axis. Puberty begins when genes prompt the hypothalamus to stimulate the **pituitary gland** (located at the base of the brain), which in turn produces **HGH—human growth hormone**. In response to HGH, the ovaries produce estrogen and progesterone (the latter regulates the menstrual cycle). The testes produce testosterone and estrogen. Male and female bodies manufacture **androgens** (male hormones) and **estrogens** (female hormones), but in different proportions according to gender. These **sex hormones** (steroids) affect growth of the sex organs and the development of the secondary sexual characteristics (Brooks-Gunn & Reiter, 1990). The adrenal glands produce androgens and cortisol; the latter is a hormone associated with stress (Figures 3-4 and 3-5).

Given the crucial role that diet plays in growth and development, it is not surprising that poor nutrition delays sexual development. Strenuous physical exertion also delays the onset of puberty. Girls who regularly engage in such vigorous activities as dance, track, or gymnastics typically display delayed menarche. This outcome is probably mediated by the stress and altered metabolism associated with intense training programs (Cameron, 1990). Delay of pubertal onset also is related to fear of obesity, eating disorders such as anorexia, low levels of body fat, intense dieting, food aversions, and other adjustment problems (Hopwood et al., 1990). *Thought Question: Why do girls in China show delayed maturation compared to girls in the West?*

The termination of pubertal growth is even less well understood than its

**FIGURE 3-3 Effects of increasing hormone levels during puberty.**

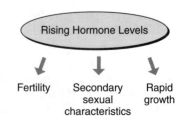

Rising Hormone Levels

Fertility     Secondary sexual characteristics     Rapid growth

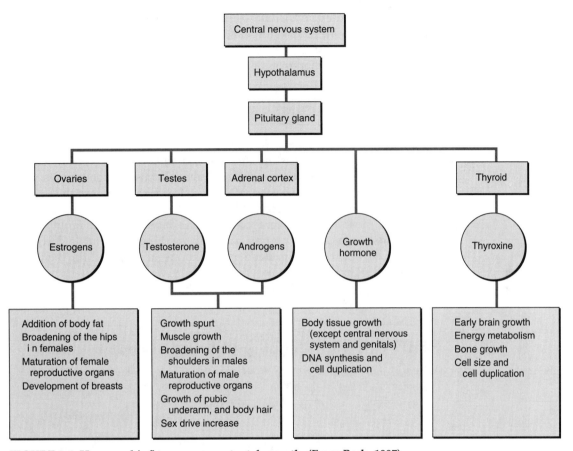

FIGURE 3-4 **Hormonal influences on postnatal growth. (From Berk, 1997)**

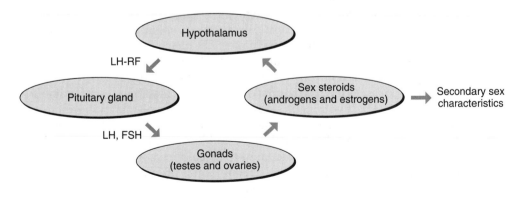

LH-RF: Luteinizing Hormone-Releasing Factor
LH: Luteinizing Hormone
FSH: Follicle-Stimulating Hormone

FIGURE 3-5 **Diagram of the hypothalamic-pituitary-gonadal axis.**

onset. Elevated hormone levels late in adolescence seem to inhibit the production of growth hormones, but the specific mechanisms are not known. Growth ends when "the ends of the growing bones reach and fuse with the joints, leaving no room for further growth" (Richards & Petersen, 1987, p. 36).

## HOW DO ADOLESCENTS FEEL ABOUT THEIR CHANGES?

Girls often report having mixed feelings about their physical and sexual maturation, finding it mildly stressful. They are excited by and take pride in being "feminine," yet many worry or feel upset about menstruation and its well-known side effects (Koff & Rierdan, 1995) (see Spotlight • Preparing Girls for Menstruation). It is not unusual for girls to report feeling self-conscious following menarche. Most have little to say about their development to family members or friends, especially if no one has said anything to them. In fact, self-image seems to suffer only for those girls who are unprepared for menarche (Ruble & Brooks-Gunn, 1982).

### SPOTLIGHT • Preparing Girls for Menstruation

*I sort of didn't want to get it. I remember the day my friend got hers. It was a Sunday. She called me up. It's such a big event when you're 14. "What. Tell me about it. Wow." And everyday I was waiting for mine.*

*(17-year-old girl)*

Girls who are prepared for their first menstrual period typically respond more positively than those who are caught off guard (Koff & Rierdan, 1995; Koff, Rierdan, & Sheingold, 1982). If mothers (who have more personal experience with menstruation than fathers) present useful information in a positive way, an adolescent girl like the one quoted above is likely to develop healthy attitudes and realistic expectations about her period (Ruble & Brooks-Gunn, 1982). Naturally, we prefer that menarche elicit excitement and pride rather than fear, embarrassment, and confusion.

Unfortunately, in not so subtle ways, our culture conveys to girls that menstruation is a "curse," a source of discomfort, moodiness, and irritability (Stubbs, 1982). If nothing is said to the contrary, girls may view menstruating strictly as a burden rather than as a symbol of their femininity or as a sign of impending adulthood (Clarke & Ruble, 1978; Koff & Rierdan, 1995).

The best time for parent and child to discuss menstruation is before its onset. Because early-maturing girls begin to menstruate as early as 10 years of age, it is a good idea to introduce the topic by that time. School health or sex education courses usually are available in middle school or high school, but the information they provide often is too little, too late.

Parents should not limit the exchange to menstruation or fertility. They should present the reproductive process in a more general context that allows discussion of relationships and intimacy. At menarche, most girls look

**It can be helpful for parents to share their own experiences of physical and sexual maturation with their children, preferably before the onset of puberty, including mothers talking to their daughters about menstruation.**

to their mothers for emotional support and ways of avoiding embarrassment and discomfort. They also expect their privacy to be respected. Girls want their mothers to be involved but not too involved. Some girls prefer that their peers be sources of information and advice. As noted, fathers should speak only when spoken to (Koff & Rierdan, 1995). *Application Question: How should single fathers approach the sensitive topic of menstruation?*

Mothers can reassure their daughters that their experiences are normal, provide information about why menstruation occurs, and give practical advice. It is important that parents provide enough information so that a child understands what is happening during a first period and is able to handle most eventualities. For example, mothers should mention that early periods usually involve minimal flow of blood and are irregular, and that cramps and headaches sometimes accompany menstrual bleeding (Lansdown & Walker, 1991).

Mothers can show their daughters tampons and sanitary napkins, and discuss how they are used and disposed of. It is helpful for mothers to share their own experiences of first menstruation—what happened, how they responded, and how they felt (Koff & Rierdan, 1995). Naturally, the connection between fertility and pregnancy should be discussed and questions should be encouraged, unless the child indicates unwillingness to participate in such an exchange. Girls may ask about **premenstrual syndrome** or problems involving difficult or painful menstruation. It is helpful for parents to be educated about these topics. Many excellent books about puberty and reproduction are written exclusively for young adolescents (Lansdown & Walker, 1991).

Girls often report believing that their fathers have a negative attitude toward their changes or are just not helpful (Brooks-Gunn, 1987; Greif & Ulman, 1982; Holmbeck & Hill, 1991b; Koff & Rierdan, 1995; Petersen, 1983; Ruble & Brooks-Gunn, 1982). *Thought Question: What might lead girls to believe that their fathers have negative feelings about their changes?*

Ambivalent reactions are consistent with Freud's claim that adolescents have conflicting feelings during puberty, perhaps reflecting the connection between puberty and sexuality. However, girls' discomfort with menarche typically is mild. Most girls become more accepting over time (Petersen, 1983; Ruble & Brooks-Gunn, 1982).

Boys generally like their physical changes, although those who are not prepared for **semenarche** (first ejaculations of semen) are somewhat perplexed (Stein & Reiser, 1994). In Stein and Reiser's study of Jewish middle-class camp counselors (average age 18.4 years), the average age of semenarche was about 13 years. Reactions to first ejaculation included surprise, curiosity, pleasure, embarrassment, guilt, and confusion. Some boys whose first ejaculation occurred during a "wet dream" confused ejaculation with urination ("It reminded me of peeing in my pants—that was my first reaction even though I'd never done it" [p. 377]).

Some boys said they were surprised at how good the first ejaculation felt. One boy who first ejaculated while masturbating said, "I think I was trying to masturbate—I didn't really—it was—the actual ejaculation came as a surprise—I knew what I was doing but didn't know what would happen—I-I remember—I remember—realizing what had happened but not really knowing exactly until later" (Stein & Reiser, 1994, p. 377).

Like early-maturing girls who do not expect their first period, some boys experienced ejaculation before they had ever heard of it. Ejaculation usually was not discussed until an eighth-grade health education class, long after many of the boys in the study had had their first ejaculation. Those who felt that they were prepared reported more positive feelings about the event and coped better. Boys are unlikely to discuss their emissions (perhaps because of the link to masturbation) but usually are willing to joke about them (Gaddis & Brooks-Gunn, 1985). For boys, social opportunities such as dating or "making out" are more meaningful than any particular bodily change (Stein & Reiser, 1994).

For most girls, the first indication of puberty is breast budding, soon followed by the appearance of pubic hair. Jeanne Brooks-Gunn and her colleagues (1994) interviewed 30 white middle- to upper-class sixth- to eighth-grade girls about their feelings regarding breast and pubic hair growth. They also asked a separate sample of 80 white sixth- to ninth-grade girls to tell a story about a picture of an adolescent female, an adult male, and an adult female. In the picture, the adult female was removing a bra from a shopping bag. **Projective tests** like this one involve the presentation of an ambiguous situation onto which individuals presumably project their feelings and assumptions in the form of a story they tell about the picture. The investigators hoped that the girls' responses to the photograph would shed light on their feelings about their mothers' and fathers' participation in pubertal discussions.

During the interviews, the first sample of girls maintained that breast growth was more important to them than pubic hair growth, partly because breast development is more public. Few girls reported having very negative feelings about either bodily change. Responses to the ambiguous picture were revealing. The girls were more likely to attribute negative feelings to the father character in the story than to the mother character (again suggesting that girls believe that their fathers have negative feelings about their changes).

Almost all girls attributed a feeling of embarrassment to the girl in the story. The girl and father characters were perceived as feeling much more uncomfortable than the mother character. One girl put it this way: "The mother brought out the bra in front of the father. And the girl is embarrassed, and it wasn't a considerate thing to do. And the father is embarrassed" (p. 559).

These findings suggest that girls, at least those who live with both parents, would prefer that their fathers not know about, or be involved in, discussions about their sexual maturation. Fathers' wariness about their daughters' emerging sexuality may reflect their awareness of this preference or perhaps may reflect fathers' own discomfort with the topic.

In their stories, some girls suggested that insensitive mothers embarrass their daughters by sharing private information with their husbands. "The mother, she's going around displaying her daughter's presumable first bra in this way; she [the mother] probably doesn't have any feelings" (p. 560). Many girls interpreted their parents' comments about breast growth as teasing, which made the girls angry or embarrassed. *Application Question: How might par-*

How adolescents feel about their changes depends partly on the feedback they get from their peers and partly on how they feel about what they see in the mirror.

*ents take into account adolescent sensitivity about bodily changes in order to encourage parent–adolescent dialogue about such changes?*

As discussed in Chapter 2 (Figure 2-7a), adolescents' reactions to their bodily changes reflect several factors—the information that they were given before the changes began, prevailing cultural attitudes about puberty and adolescence, what the physical changes mean to them, and the varied reactions of parents and friends (Gargiulo, Attie, Brooks-Gunn, & Warren, 1985; Havens & Swenson, 1988; Rierdan, Koff, & Stubbs, 1989; Ruble & Brooks-Gunn, 1982; Skandhan, Pandya, Skandhan, & Mehta, 1988).

## HOW DOES THE TIMING OF MATURATION INFLUENCE DEVELOPMENT?

Although pubertal changes are inevitable and universal, their timing and sequence vary substantially from one adolescent to another (Eichorn, 1975; Graber et al., 1995). If you look at pictures of yourself and your friends at about age 12, you'll probably see that you and your age-mates differ in facial development, bodily shape, height, and weight. **Pubertal timing** refers to whether pubertal status is on time, early, or late relative to some reference group— usually one's age- or grade-mates. Timing mainly reflects genetic differences among children but also varies with nutrition, health, ethnicity, exercise, and stress.

During a period in life when feeling normal is so important, being the first or last member of one's peer group to ''look different'' can be stressful and embarrassing (Berndt, 1979). Adolescents who perceive themselves to be out of step with their peers report feeling different or inferior (Neugarten, 1969, 1979). To some, it is a blow to their self-esteem (Buchanan, 1991).

As important to adjustment as **objective timing** (actual age and grade when changes occur) is **subjective timing**, adolescents' personal assessment of whether their changes are perceived as on time or off time compared to their peers (Blyth, Simmons, & Zakin, 1985; Downs, 1990). Subjective timing of menarche, for example, is a better predictor of girls' initial menstrual experience than is objective timing (Rierdan et al., 1989). Since early maturers are not likely to publicize their menstrual status, it is easy for young girls to think that they are the first or only ones in their peer group who menstruate.

On the average, girls begin puberty 1 to 2 years before boys, depending on the specific characteristic examined. For girls, pubertal change can begin as early as 7 years of age or as late as age 13 (Gilbert, 1997). Sexual maturity usually is achieved between 13 and 18 years (Dubas and Peterson, 1993; Marshall & Tanner, 1969, 1986). The entire pubertal sequence can occur in as few as 1.5 years or take as long as 6 years. Menarche occurs toward the latter part of puberty, typically before the 13th birthday. Fertility begins with the onset of ovulation, about a year after menarche (Dubas & Petersen, 1993).

For boys, age of onset of puberty ranges from 9.5 to 13.5 years. The attainment of sexual maturity occurs between 13.5 and 17 years of age (Marshall &

During early adolescence, age is a relatively poor predictor of physical and emotional development.

Tanner, 1970). Note that late-maturing boys begin puberty at almost twice the age of early-maturing girls. The pubertal sequence for boys may take as little as 2 years or as long as 5 years.

We can define **early maturers** as the first 20% of their cohort group to reach puberty and **late maturers** as the last 20% to reach puberty. Early-maturing girls and boys will start to show physical changes about 6 years before very-late-maturing girls and boys. The psychological effects of timing are mediated mainly by three factors: preparation, how adolescents feel about their changes, and how the significant people in their lives react to the changes (Petersen & Crockett, 1985; Richards et al., 1993; Richards & Petersen, 1987). Off-time maturation can affect adolescents' self-concept and self-esteem, behavior (including sexual behavior), and relationships.

## Early-Maturing Girls

Early-maturing girls, 7 to 10 years old, are in elementary school when they begin to develop. Obviously, given their age, they are the least prepared for the changes they undergo. It is unlikely that they have discussed puberty with parents or friends, and elementary schools rarely provide useful information about puberty (Brooks-Gunn & Ruble, 1982). Girls report either feeling proud, embarrassed, or having mixed feelings about being the first in their peer group to look different. They almost never report feeling indifferent.

Menarche is a unique pubertal event for girls in that it occurs suddenly, without warning. Psychologically and physically, the onset of menstruation is emotionally charged and somewhat threatening (Koff & Rierdan, 1995; Rierdan et al., 1989). Early-maturing girls, beginning to menstruate while in the fourth or fifth grade, find menarche particularly distressing, especially if they have not discussed it with anyone (Greif & Ulman, 1982; Petersen, 1983; Stubbs, Rierdan, & Koff, 1989).

Unlike later-maturing girls, most early maturers do not talk to their mothers or to anyone about their experience. Rather, they attempt to deny or conceal their development, sometimes through bizarre behavior. To avoid the embarrassment of purchasing a bra, some girls wear several layers of T-shirts and sweat shirts to conceal their developing breasts. It is not unusual for young girls to report being teased about breast growth, particularly by their peers, by their siblings, and, most disturbingly, by their parents (Brooks-Gunn, 1984; Brooks-Gunn et al., 1994; Petersen, 1983; Ruble & Brooks-Gunn, 1982). Negative reactions such as teasing heighten their discomfort (Brooks-Gunn, 1984; Greif & Ulman, 1982).

Most early-maturing girls prefer that their changes not be noticed or commented on. Although there is prestige to be gained by acquiring a feminine form, girls who develop very early usually report feeling self-conscious. Being the first of their peer group to change, they are the least prepared emotionally and socially. Girls who are informed about pubertal changes, and who discuss them with their mothers and girlfriends, usually report positive experiences (Brooks-Gunn & Ruble, 1982; Skandhan et al., 1988).

The stress of changing schools heightens sensitivity to bodily changes. Girls who develop when attending middle school are less likely to feel different because most of their peers (girls and boys) are also growing (Nottelmann & Welsh, 1986). Adjustment problems such as depression and antisocial behavior occur more frequently during times of multiple transitions (Magnusson, Stattin, & Allen, 1986; Rutter, 1986). *Thus, adolescents who experience puberty and who are changing schools at the same time merit special attention and support from their families and teachers.*

Some early-developing girls enjoy the attention that they get from boys and the admiration or jealousy expressed by their friends. Attractiveness and popularity soften the impact of early puberty, particularly for girls. Girls who believe that they are overweight (whether they are or not) or who have a poor body image are more likely to report dissatisfaction with their changes (Alsaker, 1992; Fowler, 1989; Rauste von Wright, 1989; Richards & Petersen, 1987). Given our culture's preoccupation with the female form, it is not surprising that so many females report feeling self-conscious about their bodies well into adulthood.

Early-maturing girls tend to date earlier than their later-maturing peers (Flannery, Rowe, & Gulley, 1993). As they are likely to be socially immature and somewhat naive, romantic contacts with boys are problematic. Young girls who are treated as sex objects by older boys lack the experience to know how to interpret or handle encounters when boys "come on" to them. They may be coerced into unwanted sexual encounters. Some early-maturing girls have older girlfriends and boyfriends and, in trying to act more "grown up," become susceptible to deviant peer influence (Magnusson et al., 1986). Those who enjoy good communication with their parents seem to be less vulnerable to peer pressure (Silbereisen, Petersen, Albrecht, & Kracke, 1989).

Viewing the remarkable development of their early-maturing daughters, parents report feeling both proud and concerned. They worry about how their daughters will handle social and sexual overtures from boys. Some developing girls who expect more freedom find instead greater restrictions. Their parents (especially fathers) become overly restrictive or suspicious, and this increases parent–child tensions (Noller, 1994).

Because of evidence linking early maturation to adjustment and body image problems (Downs, 1990), we should not consider early maturation to be an advantage for girls (Brooks-Gunn & Reiter, 1990; Graber & Brooks-Gunn, 1995). An exception may be those girls who have opportunities to discuss and celebrate their changes with supportive friends and family members (Richards & Petersen, 1987). For most early-maturing girls, negative effects are temporary and relatively minor (Brooks-Gunn, 1987; Paikoff, Brooks-Gunn, & Warren, 1991). Most adjust well, despite the sometimes stressful circumstances surrounding their precocious development (Peskin, 1973).

### Late-Maturing Girls

Just as some early-maturing girls are embarrassed by their increasingly feminine appearance and the attention it attracts, late-maturing girls often report discomfort about a lack of shapeliness. Beginning puberty between 13 and 14 years of age, they envy the changes of their early-maturing peers. They are deprived (temporarily) of the sexualized attention of their male peers and the accompanying prestige. Some parents decide to send their daughters to all-girl schools to minimize this type of pressure. Maturing at the same time as average-maturing boys, late-maturing girls avoid the stresses and strains of precocious development (Brooks-Gunn, 1988).

Later-maturing girls eventually develop "pubertal behaviors" such as marathon telephone sessions, preoccupation with boys, and dating. Inevitably, they catch up to their peers and adjust well to their long-awaited physical transformation. Generally, girls who are on-time maturers report more positive reactions to puberty than early or late maturers (Dubas, Graber, & Petersen, 1991).

### Early-Maturing Boys

Unlike early-maturing girls, most early-maturing boys are enthusiastic about their changes (Petersen, 1988; Petersen & Crockett, 1985). Boys are more likely to react negatively to late maturation than to early or average maturation (Alsaker, 1992; Simmons & Blyth, 1987). Early-maturing boys are developing at about the same time as average-maturing girls, thus avoiding the stigma of being first or different from grade-mates. They are taller, stronger, and better coordinated than their later-maturing peers. These qualities are highly valued by most males, partly because they create opportunities for successful athletic performance and prestige (Hensley, 1994). Boys who develop early are more likely to become leaders of their peer groups and to steer group activities (Clausen, 1975). They appear to be more adult-like to girls, and have earlier and more frequent social and sexual experiences than later-maturing boys.

Potential advantages of early maturation depend on how physical changes are evaluated and how developing adolescents are treated by family members and friends. Like many early-maturing girls, boys who develop earlier than their peers may become self-conscious about their changing appearance. This is likely when almost everyone they encounter comments on how tall they are ("How you've grown!"). Many report feeling awkward about being the first to change. Most boys are happy about their changes and adjust well (Downs, 1990; Gaddis & Brooks-Gunn, 1985).

Because of their increasingly masculine appearance, early-maturing boys are given more freedom sooner than their later-developing peers. More frequent opportunities (in and out of school) for attention, success, and privileges promote positive self-esteem, which persists over the course of adolescence and into adulthood. One down side of early maturation is having to meet higher standards of behavior set by parents and teachers. These expectations are not always realistic.

Young teenagers are considerably more vulnerable and self-conscious than older teens (Rauste von Wright, 1989). Based on his study of Norwegian adolescents, Alsaker (1992) reported that early-developing boys are more depressed and produce more negative self-evaluations than on-time or late-maturing boys. Alsaker notes that in Norway, masculine values are not emphasized as much as they are in the United States.

## Late-Maturing Boys

Of the four groups under consideration, late-maturing boys (who are about 15 to 16 years old when they begin puberty) have the hardest time adjusting (Alsaker, 1992). Compared to their more masculine-looking high school peers, they look child-like. Being 8 inches shorter and 30 pounds lighter than their age-mates often brings sarcastic remarks, teasing, and other blows to their sensitive egos. Even being told that they are ''cute'' or ''cuddly'' by more developed female age-mates does not compensate for their feelings of isolation and humiliation (Brooks-Gunn, 1988).

Their smaller stature is a disadvantage athletically and socially, and their popularity suffers. Some late-maturing boys overcompensate for their delayed development by showing off and displaying other immature behaviors. This brings even greater dishonor. To deal with their anguish, some acquire coping and interpersonal skills that remain useful long after their belated physical development. Depending on individual circumstances, late-maturing boys might display the benefits and drawbacks of delayed maturation well into adulthood (Peskin, 1972).

# SPOTLIGHT • Adolescent Girls' Body Image

*My body is too big for me—too old—too mature—too voluptuous. I don't fit it yet.*

(15-year-old girl quoted by Rosenbaum, 1993, p. 64)

Adolescents all over the world are conscious of and sensitive about their appearance (Downs, 1990; Schlegel & Barry, 1991; Simmons & Blyth, 1987). Schlegel and Barry mention reports of "young people running off to the river to bathe and beautify themselves when their parents would rather have them home working in the garden, or the careful attention given to body painting and decoration before some village festivity. It does seem however, that Western adolescents, and perhaps American adolescents in particular, are inordinately conscious of their appearance and overwhelmingly dissatisfied with it" (p. 205).

As can be seen in Figure 3-6, of all age and gender groups, preadolescent and early adolescent girls report the most dissatisfaction with their appearance, especially their shape and weight (Rauste-von Wright, 1989; Tobin-Richards, Petersen, & Boxer, 1983; Wood, Becker, & Thompson, 1996). Bodily development during puberty provides a powerful incentive for reappraisal, especially in a society that so highly values physical attractiveness (Rosenbaum, 1993). In most Western societies, during the courtship years, looks play a disproportionate role in popularity, dating, and in self-concept (Downs, 1990; Mendelson, White, & Mendelson, 1996; Simmons & Blyth, 1987). Women who are anxious about their appearance as adults report that they did not like the way they looked when they were teenagers and that they did not have satisfying encounters with age-mates (Keelan, Dion, &

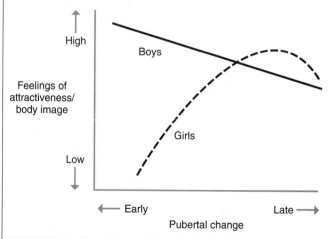

FIGURE 3-6  The relationship of pubertal change to body image and feelings of attractiveness. (From Richards et al., 1992)

Dion, 1992). Middle-class girls are led to believe by fashion magazines, friends, TV, and sometimes parents that slenderness achieved through dieting, exercise, and weight management strategies will bring them personal and professional success (Emmons, 1996; Levine, Smolak, & Hayden, 1994).

Adolescent girls evaluate their appearance partly on the basis of standards that vary according to their culture and subculture (Richards & Petersen, 1987). Cultures and subcultures differ regarding what qualities are considered attractive (Fallon, 1990). A study of West German girls (Silbereisen, Petersen, Albrecht, & Kracke, 1989) reported that early maturers had relatively high self-esteem, suggesting that there may be cultural differences regarding what is considered attractive. For example, African-American and Asian-American girls who live in integrated communities are hard-pressed to satisfy white standards of what is beautiful, especially regarding hair and skin color (Phinney, 1989). Given the importance of feeling accepted by one's crowd, deviating from cultural ideals of attractiveness can be a blow to an adolescent's self-esteem. There is evidence that appearance (or at least body shape and size) matters less to African-American and Asian-American girls than it does to white girls (Flynn & Fitzgibbon, 1996; Murray, 1996e). Those who are self-conscious about racial characteristics may resort to cosmetics in an attempt to conform to a cultural ideal (Sarigiani, Camarena, & Petersen, 1993).

Based on her study of Norwegian adolescents, Alsaker (1992) concluded that early-maturing girls who are overweight develop more negative self-evaluations than normal-weight early-maturing girls. Whereas adolescent boys usually take pride in their changing bodies and abilities, adolescent girls often have difficulty thinking of anything that they like about their bodies (Rosenbaum, 1993). This is disturbing because, as Havighurst (1972) noted, accepting one's physique and using one's body effectively is a key task of adolescence. Given the relationship between body image and attitudes about eating (Brooks-Gunn, Attie, Burrow, Rosso, & Warren, 1989), we must be aware that girls and boys with poor body images diet excessively and many develop serious eating disorders (Keel, Fulkerson, & Leon, 1997) (discussed in Chapter 13). (See Box 3-1.)

Rosenbaum interviewed 30 adolescent girls ranging in age from 11 to 17 years. Most of the girls saw themselves as average regarding their bodily development. About one-third felt that they were less attractive than they thought their peers viewed them. Although they were very influenced by other people's perceptions of them, they generally discounted their mothers' judgments. "She thinks I'm gorgeous—that I have a perfect figure—but that's a lie. That's what all mothers say" (p. 69). *Thought Question: Are parents capable of viewing their children objectively?*

When asked what they liked about their bodies, the girls looked perplexed and troubled. Many mentioned the absence of flaws like pimples, freckles, or being fat. Two-thirds of the girls said that their hair—the one part of their body over which they had some control—was their best feature. Half of the sample of girls said that they liked their eyes. However, the girls had much more to say about what they didn't like about their bodies. They were most concerned about their weight and size, citing pudgy thighs, hips, and faces. Those who felt that they were too thin were afraid that they would never develop features desirable to boys. The girls expressed ambivalence about the growing fat cells that provided curves but also dreaded weight. Many girls complained about their complexions, their noses (too long), their breasts (too small), and their body hair ("messy, too dark, not feminine, something boys were supposed to have").

Rosenbaum gave the girls three magic wishes: if they could, what would they change about their bodies? The most common wish was to lose weight and keep it off. The girls also longed for blonder hair, blue eyes, a clear complexion, a perfect figure, and straighter noses.

It is not surprising that most young girls compared themselves unfavorably to society's image of ideal feminine beauty—Barbie dolls, movie stars, magazine models, and Miss America. Older girls had more realistic body images and were more comfortable with their bodies than younger girls. But all the girls "were continually revising their body image as they reacted to, learned about, accepted, and integrated bodily change" (p. 78).

## Summary

Timing of maturation clearly affects the behavior and emotional adjustment of off-time adolescents. Pubertal change is most stressful when adolescents feel out of step with their peers and when they receive negative feedback. The specific effects of timing depend on their level of preparation for puberty, the type of feedback they receive, and their own assessment of physical changes. In Western culture at least, early-maturing boys benefit from the extra time they have to work on social developmental tasks, but some suffer from the pressure of heightened expectations.

Regarding body-image satisfaction, early-maturing boys benefit more than early-maturing girls from developing qualities (such as size and strength) that confer status and privilege on males. In fact, many young male adolescents want to gain weight, presumably to become stronger and more muscular (Abell & Richards, 1996). For many girls, the weight gain associated with pubertal status conflicts with their desire to be thin (Swarr & Richards, 1996) (see Spotlight • Adolescent Girls' Body Image). Early-maturing girls usually like looking more feminine, but many encounter pressure to date, and some experiment with drugs and alcohol.

No obvious relationship between self-esteem, self-consciousness, and pubertal timing for girls has been identified (Blyth et al., 1985; Downs, 1990; Simmons & Blyth, 1987). The specific qualities and circumstances of each child, including social life and social stressors, must be included in any meaningful account of timing of maturation (Cauffman & Steinberg, 1996). Finally, gender differences in the effects of timing may be culture specific (Blyth et al., 1985; Richards et al., 1993; Simmons & Blyth, 1987).

Parents and pediatricians often express concern about the junk-food diets of teenagers. Adolescent girls in particular are susceptible to dieting patterns that threaten their health (Emmons, 1996). The effects of poor nutrition on development are greatest during periods of rapid growth, including prenatal development, infancy, and early adolescence.

Malnutrition during adolescence usually reflects one of the following: poverty, an eating disorder such as anorexia, a metabolic disorder such as phenylketonuria (PKU), overzealous physical exertion in sports or dance, or excessive dieting for a fashionable appearance or modeling (Rees & Trahms, 1989). Some effects of malnutrition can be permanent. Overnutrition can lead to a sedentary lifestyle, a hopeless outlook, and lifelong obesity. Effective interventions require family participation and nutrition education (Chapman, Toma, Tuveson, & Jacob, 1997; McCullum & Achterberg, 1997). "Parents need to learn how to support efforts of their adolescent children to modify their habits or sustain modifications that require them to eat differently from their peers" (Rees & Trahms, 1989, p. 213).

**Box 3-1
Nutrition and
Growth**

## UNDERSTANDING PUBERTAL HORMONES

*Study Question: How true is the common belief that "raging hormones" are at the root of adolescent mood swings, depression, attitude problems, and parent–adolescent conflict?*

There is a significant increase in hormone secretion as children approach and undergo puberty. Pubertal hormones play a crucial role in growth, fertility onset, and the development of secondary sexual characteristics. Because so many changes in adolescent behavior and life coincide with pubertal change, it is tempting to attribute irritability and problem behavior to increases in hormonal activity. As we shall see in a later section, we can attribute some moodiness to hormones, but young people are irritated by a lot of things—especially by what they see as restrictive parents, demanding teachers, annoying siblings, and many other life hassles.

One problem in understanding the role that hormones play in behavior involves the complexities of the endocrine system. Hormones sometimes act individually, but usually they act in combination. Warren and Brooks-Gunn (1989), for example, observed that a combination of high progesterone and low testosterone is associated with impatience in girls. Further, hormones can exert their effects over short or long periods of time. They affect different people in different ways. Early adolescents may be affected differently from middle and late adolescents (Halpern & Udry, 1992; Paikoff & Brooks-Gunn, 1990).

Gender differences in hormonal action are also likely (Nottelmann, Inoff-Germain, Susman, & Chrousos, 1990). Some studies, for example, have identified direct relationships between hormones and delinquent behavior in boys but not in girls. This suggests the existence of mediating factors that we have not yet identified (Bancroft, 1987; Buchanan, Eccles, & Becker, 1992; Nottelmann et al., 1987; Nottelmann, Inoff-Germain, Susman, & Chrousas, 1990; Paikoff, Brooks-Gunn, & Warren, 1991).

### Models of Hormone Influence

Psychodynamic models such as those offered by Sigmund and Anna Freud attribute primary significance to the role of increased hormone levels during puberty, not only in promoting growth and maturation but also in evoking changes in adolescent behavior and mood (Hamilton, 1984). As noted in Chapter 2, the interactional-contextual perspective integrates biological and psychosocial models of development (Lerner, 1992, 1996). The model implies that the specific effects of hormones on an adolescent's behavior depend partly on personal, social, and situational (contextual) variables.

An adolescent who is experiencing fluctuating hormone levels while working on a difficult math problem might respond to being teased by a younger sibling with a friendly, silly, or aggressive response. If she had received a good grade on a math test that day, she might respond to the teasing by smiling or joking. If she had failed the math test she might retaliate angrily with nasty comments. The effects of hormonal fluctuations on her behavior are mediated by current situational factors, in this case her math grade and how she feels about it. The point is that specific elements of a situation determine how hormonally induced arousal will guide behavior. Figure 3-7 compares the direct, indirect (mediated effects), and bidirectional effects models of hormonal influence on adolescent emotions.

Bidirectional models allow for the possibility that pubertal development (including hormonal activity) not only affects behavior but is itself affected by behaviors such as dieting and exercise and by stressful events. Stressful life problems apparently lead to chronic increases in circulating hormones that can produce maturational delays and behavioral effects (Nottelmann et al., 1990).

**FIGURE 3-7  Direct and mediated hormonal effects. (Adapted from Graber & Brooks-Gunn, 1995)**

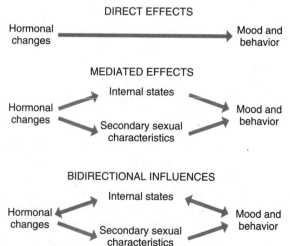

*The fact that almost all studies in this area are correlational makes it hard to interpret the direction of influence between hormonal and behavioral events* (Rubin, 1990).

Like all other developmental changes, the effects of puberty are guided by contextual variables. For example, the relationship between puberty and weight gain in adolescent girls depends on the type of school that they attend (Tobin-Richards et al., 1983). Girls who attend schools with fewer opportunities to exercise are more preoccupied and less satisfied with their weight and appearance. Keep in mind that events such as starting middle school, getting a job, and dating occur at different ages for different adolescents. They are likely to have different effects, depending on the specific age and maturity level of the individual. *Thought Question: Why would starting middle school affect an early-maturing girl differently than an average- or late-maturing girl?*

## Does Aggressive Behavior Increase During Puberty?

One of the most clear-cut gender differences involves aggressive behavior; males are considerably more aggressive than females (Beal, 1994). Because adult males have about 10 times the concentration of testosterone that females do, it is tempting to attribute male aggressiveness to this hormone. (See Box 3-2.)

One group of investigators (Inoff-Germain et al., 1988) studied the relationship between hormone levels and aggressive behavior in 60 boys and girls between the ages of 9 and 14 years. Parent–child interactions were videotaped during problem-solving tasks. The investigators were able to measure circulating levels of male and female hormones associated with growth and sexual development. They wanted to see whether hormone levels are related to adolescents' expressions of anger, dominance, and defiance toward their parents. The researchers did not observe a link between hormones and aggression for the boys but did observe correlations between hormone concentrations and aggressive behaviors of girls.

It is possible that, rather than having a direct effect on aggression, hormones lead to arousal, which in turn triggers an emotional response (Graber & Brooks-Gunn, 1995). Fluctuating levels of testosterone *and* estrogen are associated with increases in adolescent impatience, irritability, and lowered frustration tolerance (Angier, 1995). These emotional states, *under conditions of provocation*, sometimes lead to aggressive behavior (Olweus, Mattsson, Schalling, & Low, 1980, 1988). The specific reaction or emotion may reflect how the individual interprets the emotional arousal. In any case, hormone levels are not likely to induce aggression or other emotions unless some situational factor provides justification (Graber & Brooks-Gunn, 1995).

## The Role of Hormones in Adolescent Sexual Behavior

During early adolescence, fluctuations in testosterone and estrogen levels are associated with heightened sexual arousal and behavior (Nottelmann et al., 1987; Udry & Talbert, 1988; Udry, Talbert, & Morris, 1986). Pubertal hormones, especially testosterone, are associated with sexual arousal and behavior in males and sexual behaviors other than intercourse in females, including sexual

**Box 3-2
What's the
Deal with
Testosterone?**

In male adolescents, pubertal development of the testes includes increasing secretions of the hormone testosterone, which in turn promotes the growth of the male genitals and development of masculine body hair patterns, including facial hair and baldness (Cameron, 1990). Testosterone also builds up muscle cells, including those in the larynx, evoking the impressive low pitched vocal sounds we associate with young adolescent males. These observations are not controversial. But what role does testosterone play in promoting aggression?

Sapolsky (1997) reviews the evidence linking testosterone to aggressive behavior. Males have higher testosterone levels than females and are generally more aggressive. Male aggression peaks after puberty, when testosterone levels are highest. For many species, testes produce high rates of testosterone during the mating season, when male-male aggression is most common. Because these observations are correlational, we are reluctant to make inferences about cause and effect. Experimental evidence, however, would appear to support the connection. Castrating male monkeys (removing the source of testosterone) greatly diminishes aggression. Inject synthetic testosterone back into these animals, and aggressive behavior returns.

Although it seems obvious that testosterone energizes aggressive behavior, there is another possible explanation for the above observations: Aggressive behavior elevates testosterone levels! There is impressive evidence supporting this view. Interindividual differences in testosterone level *do not* predict subsequent differences in aggressive behavior. Fluctuations in testosterone level over time in individuals *do not* predict changes in aggressive behavior. "Study after study has shown that if you

thoughts and masturbation (Paikoff & Brooks-Gunn, 1990; Udry & Billy, 1987). (Once again, correlational studies make it difficult to interpret the direction of influence. Hormonal fluctuations may drive sexual arousal; sexual arousal might trigger hormonal fluctuations.)

Udry (1988) maintains that testosterone level is related to sexual arousal in young female adolescents, but its effect on behavior may be modified by social controls, by girls' participation in sports, and by having a father living at home. *Critical Thinking Question: How might these social factors lessen sexual activity in teenage girls, regardless of hormonal levels?*

## Puberty and Cognitive Development

Is the surge in physical growth we associate with puberty accompanied by a corresponding spurt in mental development? Since the growth spurt at puberty includes growth of the brain and cerebral reorganization (Thatcher, Walker, & Guidice, 1987), it is plausible that new cognitive abilities also emerge. In the next chapter, we will consider the possibility that cognitive advances mediate the effects of pubertal change on moods, family relationships, and adolescent behavior in general.

Over 30 years ago, Tanner (1962) hypothesized that an increase in mental

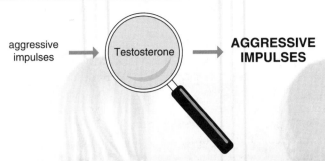

aggressive impulses → Testosterone → **AGGRESSIVE IMPULSES**

FIGURE 3-8 **Testosterone magnifies aggressive impulses that are already present.**

examine testosterone levels when males are first placed together in the social group, testosterone levels predict nothing about who is going to be aggressive. The subsequent behavioral differences drive the hormonal changes, rather than the other way around" (p. 46).

Castrating males typically leads to a decline in aggressive behavior, but it doesn't eliminate it, especially in socially experienced individuals. "In the right context, social conditioning can more than make up for the complete absence of the hormone" (p. 50). Based on studies of dominance hierarchies in male monkeys, Sapolsky concludes that "testosterone isn't causing aggression, it's *exaggerating* the aggression that's already there. . . . Violence is more complex than a single hormone, and it is supremely rare that any of our behaviors can be reduced to genetic destiny" (pp. 47, 50).

ability at puberty would be manifested as an IQ advantage in early-maturing adolescents. Subsequent research revealed a small but reliable advantage in IQ and other measures of intellectual and academic achievement for early maturers. Surprisingly, the IQ advantage was found to precede puberty and to persist into adulthood (Newcombe & Baenninger, 1989; Newcombe & Dubas, 1987).

Tanner (1970) reported that even before they reach puberty, early maturers develop faster than late maturers and are therefore taller and heavier. Since early maturers show a cognitive advantage before puberty, it is possible that there are social factors related to their enhanced physical growth that also stimulate cognitive and intellectual development. For example, due to early maturers' more grown-up appearance, adults and friends might treat them more like adults. This, in turn, could stimulate intellectual growth.

It is also possible that larger preadolescents are perceived as being more attractive than their smaller peers. Perhaps they are also judged to be smarter. If that's the case, they may be given more cognitive stimulation than their less mature-looking peers. Thus, the advantages that we ascribe to early-maturing boys, often attributed to their mature appearance or abilities, might instead reflect cognitive and verbal abilities that precede adolescence (Newcombe & Baenninger, 1989). The cognitive changes of adolescence will be explored at length in the next chapter.

### Is There a Connection Between Hormones, Moods, and Behavior?

Studies of adolescent mood do not support G. Stanley Hall's and Anna Freud's (1946) depiction of teenagers in turmoil (Greene, 1990). The story is somewhat more complicated than they imagined (Larson & Ham, 1993; Simmons & Blyth, 1987). Early adolescence is not a particularly turbulent time for most children, although there is more moodiness, nervousness, and restlessness (Buchanan, 1991; Buchanan, Eccles, & Becker, 1992). Is irritability caused by heightened hormone levels, by stressful circumstances, or by some combination of the two?

Adolescents report "more swings in mood, more intense moods, lower or more variable energy levels, and more restlessness than people at other points in development" (Buchanan et al., 1992, p. 98). These investigators allow for a possible hormonal role in anxiety, self-consciousness, and family conflict. They caution, however, that many nonhormonal factors—for example, gender, age, and timing of maturation—also influence adolescent behavior and probably mediate the effects of hormonal activity.

Moderate concentrations of **sex steroids** (testosterone and estradiol) are associated with positive mood, alertness, and happiness (Buchanan et al., 1992). Low levels of estradiol correlate with depression and unstable mood. Very high concentrations of sex steroids are associated with anxiety and depression. But these hormone–behavior associations apparently require emotional circumstances that heighten arousal, such as a celebration or an argument (Paikoff et al., 1991).

**Adolescent moodiness and the so-called attitude problem probably reflect multiple life stressors and limited coping resources more than hormonal fluctuations.**

Sigmund Freud assumed that the hormonal surge of early adolescence triggers intense sexual feelings, which might be directed toward family members. As discussed in Chapter 2, he assumed that these feelings are threatening to the adolescent because they are unfamiliar and socially unacceptable. Anna Freud (1966) used this idea to account for adolescent irritability, depression, and parent–adolescent conflict. Non-Freudian theorists counter that adolescent moodiness is a reaction to changes in adolescent appearance and self-concept and to heightened expectations from parents and teachers (Brooks-Gunn, 1984).

As we have seen, early adolescence is a distinctive life period in that a variety of potentially stressful life events occur almost simultaneously, including puberty, dating, and school transitions (Simmons, Burgeson, Carlton-Ford, & Blyth, 1987). Larson and Ham (1993) attribute the heightened moodiness of young adolescents not to hormones but rather to the "pileup" of negative life events. They interviewed 483 fifth to ninth graders and their parents to gain hour-by-hour reports about the adolescents' daily emotional states. This was done for 1 week. They also requested information from parents and children about recent major events in the children's lives.

They found that the average young adolescent encounters a greater number of unexpected, stressful life events than does the typical preadolescent. Negative life events include problems involving peers (e.g., fight with a friend), school (e.g., change of school) and family (e.g., fight with parents). The study revealed a correlation between the number of negative life events and adolescent moodiness.

Adolescents' heightened distress reflected both real increases in negative life events and changes in adolescents' interpretation of these events. Preadolescents who experienced multiple life stressors did not seem to get as upset by them. Larson and Ham surmise that the moodiness we observe in many young adolescents is at least partly attributable to the increasing number of stressors these children encounter.

## Are Parent–Child Relationships Affected by Puberty?

During early adolescence, interpersonal relationships are in transition (Alsaker, 1995, 1996). Sigmund Freud (1936) hypothesized that hormonally induced sexual tensions during puberty motivate adolescents to seek greater distance from their parents. Puberty is associated with increased parent–child distance and conflict, particularly between adolescent girls and their mothers (Anderson, Hetherington, & Clingempeel, 1989; Greif & Ulman, 1982; Montemayor, 1986). This may reflect mothers' confusion or distress about their daughter's attempts to become more independent (Holmbeck & Hill, 1991b). *Thought Question: Why would we expect mothers rather than fathers to receive the brunt of adolescent irritability?*

Early adolescents spend less time with their parents and begin to resist or at least question parental restrictions. Investigators report more expressions of negative feelings and fewer expressions of positive feelings by early adolescents (Csikzentmihalyi & Larson, 1984; Steinberg, 1981, 1987b, 1989). Family relationships become more tense and conflicted. Non-Freudians attribute the *distancing effect* to either adolescents' increasing desire for independence (Papini,

Clark, Barnett, & Savage, 1989), to increasing peer influence, or to the difficulty parents have in dealing with moody, unpredictable teenagers (Buchanan, 1991).

To determine how puberty is related to parent–child distance, Steinberg (1988) asked 157 male and female first-born adolescents between the ages of 11 and 16 years and their parents to complete questionnaires measuring autonomy, conflict, and parent–child closeness. All participants completed two questionnaires a year apart. Independent raters assessed each child's pubertal status. The results confirmed that during puberty, adolescent desire for self-regulation increases, especially for boys. Steinberg found modest increases in parent–child distance and parent–child conflict, particularly during the early stages of puberty. Early-maturing boys reported more conflict with mothers. Girls also reported more conflict with mothers, regardless of the timing of their maturation.

Steinberg's results support his **acceleration hypothesis**, that parent–child distance accelerates pubertal maturation. Girls who reported more conflict with their mothers matured earlier than their counterparts. Boys' maturation timing was not influenced by their relationships with their parents. Girls' maturation does seem to be accelerated by conflict with their mothers. Ellis (1991) suggests that stress increases girls' estrogen levels, which, in turn, leads girls to experience more distance from their mothers. Steinberg cautions that adolescents are more likely than their parents to report feeling distant.

In summary, pubertal change is related to adolescents' **subjective** sense of emotional distance from their parents. Pubertal maturation in boys and girls foretells a desire for greater autonomy and less perceived closeness to parents, at least in intact, white, middle-class families (Anderson et al., 1989; Paikoff et al., 1991). Other family configurations and ethnic groups have received relatively little attention from researchers. Regarding family configuration, there is evidence that adolescent girls feel distant from their grandfathers (Clingempeel, Colyar, Brand, & Hetherington, 1992). Comparing Mexican-American and non-Hispanic white families, Molina and Chassin (1996) report that ethnicity moderates the effects of pubertal status on parent–adolescent relationships. For the most part, however, parent–child relationships are positive during early adolescence (Greene & Grimsley, 1990).

## SUMMARY

**1.** The onset of puberty is a convenient marker for the end of childhood and the beginning of adolescence. During puberty we observe remarkable changes in children's size, shape, and other body features. Changes in appearance have social stimulus value in that they influence how adults and peers view and treat young people. Adolescents who look more adult-like may have to cope with heightened expectations and pressures at home and at school. Those who are physically attractive receive more attention and are perceived more positively by peers and adults.

**2.** Parents in Western societies usually have mixed feelings about their children's physical and sexual maturation. They may feel excitement and pride but also concern. Too many adolescents do not receive the emotional support that they need from their families and friends. Nor are they given information that would help them prepare for and understand their physical and social metamorphosis. As a result, there is often a discrepancy between adolescents' emotional and social adjustment and the expectations of parents and teachers.

**3.** Researchers can measure pubertal status using rating scales based on physical examinations of children. Self-ratings also provide useful information about adolescents' perceptions of their bodily development and social status. Early adolescence provides researchers with an ideal opportunity to study the interplay of biological, personal, and social changes.

**4.** Puberty is a period of transition from reproductive immaturity to reproductive maturity. Changes in hormone levels, bone structure, fat deposits, and sex organs begin almost simultaneously. Secondary sexual characteristics include growth of body hair, breast development, adult facial features, voice deepening, and increasing fat deposits.

**5.** The growth spurt for girls begins at about age 10 and for boys about a year later. Boys and girls grow about 10 inches and gain about 40 pounds during a 4-year period, on the average.

**6.** Adolescents today mature more quickly than their ancestors did. By late adolescence, they are larger and taller. The secular trend toward earlier maturation presumably reflects improvements in children's nutrition and health. One troublesome consequence of early fertility is an increased number of unwanted pregnancies.

**7.** Puberty is a reactivation of hormonal activity that began during the fetal period of development. Sexual maturation is inhibited during infancy, but the specific mechanisms that lead to inhibition and disinhibition are not known. Social-environmental factors such as family stressors interact with hormones to determine the onset and course of pubertal change.

**8.** Children who are prepared for their physical and sexual changes before the changes occur usually respond more positively and cope better. Girls who are given little or no information about menstruating may come to view their periods as a burden rather than as a symbol of femininity. Most boys enjoy their growth and sexual maturation, but those who are not prepared for their first ejaculation may experience embarrassment and confusion.

**9.** The timing and duration of physical change have important psychological consequences for how adolescents view and feel about themselves. Although timing effects could have a direct biological origin (early maturers show different changes from late maturers), they usually reflect the interaction between timing of puberty relative to that of one's peers and adolescents' feelings about their own changes.

**10.** Early and late maturers may consider themselves abnormal unless they are given information about the wide range of variations in growth. Early maturation generally is advantageous to boys and is either disadvantageous to or has minimal effect on girls' adjustment. Of the four maturation groups studied, early-maturing boys adjust best and late-maturing boys adjust worst. Timing has modest, temporary effects on early- and late-maturing girls. Gender differences in the effects of timing may be culture-specific.

**11.** Adolescent girls in particular are dissatisfied with the way the look. They tend to be self-conscious about their body shape and weight. It is almost impossible for most girls to attain the slender, shapely body advertised in fashion magazines, in movies, and on television.

**12.** Although we can attribute some moodiness to hormonal fluctuations, it is probably the combination of hormonal arousal and stressful or annoying life events that triggers irritable moods and aggressive behaviors. It is unusual for adolescents to behave aggressively or antisocially without provocation. Since most studies in this area are correlational, it is hard to interpret the direction of influence between hormones and behavior.

**13.** There is still much that we do not know about the physiological mechanisms that initiate and regulate growth and sexual maturation, how biological changes interact with environmental factors to promote or impede maturation, and the extent to which individual differences in maturation and behavior reflect gender, ethnic group membership, and cultural factors.

## GLOSSARY

**Pubescent** Entering puberty

**Social stimulus value** Individual qualities that attract attention

**Pubertal status** Current level of pubertal development

**Pubertal Development Scale (PDS)** A brief self-report instrument that rates maturational status using five pubertal markers

**Puberty** The period of transition from reproductive immaturity (nonfertility) to reproductive maturity (fertility)

**Menarche** The onset of menstruation

**Growth spurt** A period of rapid skeletal growth during puberty

**Sexual maturation** Achieving fertility; the bodily changes that support reproduction

**Primary sexual changes** Changes in the testes and ovaries

**Ovulation** The monthly release from the ovaries of a ripened egg

**Spermatogenesis** The manufacture of sperm

**Secondary sexual characteristics** The growth of body hair, breast enlargement, adult facial features, voice deepening, and increasing fat deposits

**Secular trend** The trend toward earlier sexual maturation

**Hormones** Chemical messengers manufactured by the endocrine glands that help regulate bodily processes

**Disinhibition** The inhibition of inhibition

**Critical weight model** Hypothesis that the critical factor in triggering the onset of puberty is attaining a minimum percentage of body fat

**Pituitary gland** Gland located beneath the brain that produces the largest number of hormones

**HGH** Human growth hormone

**Androgens** Hormones that predominate in males

**Estrogens** Hormones that predominate in females

**Sex hormones (steroids)** Hormones that influence sexual maturation and behavior

**Semenarche** The onset of sperm production

**Projective tests** Personality tests consisting of ambiguous figures

**Premenstrual syndrome** Recurrent emotional and physical problems surrounding menstruation

**Pubertal timing** Whether pubertal status is on time, early, or late relative to some reference group, usually one's age- or grade-mates

**Objective timing** Actual age when puberty begins

**Subjective timing** Adolescent's personal assessment of when puberty begins

**Early maturers** The first 20% of a cohort group to begin puberty

**Late maturers** The last 20% of a cohort group to begin puberty

**Sex steroids** Sex hormones that appear to affect mood

**Acceleration hypothesis** The hypothesis that parent–child distance accelerates pubertal maturation

## THOUGHT QUESTIONS

**1.** Many parents have little to say to their children that would prepare them for the physical changes of puberty (Brooks-Gunn & Reiter, 1990). What do children need to know before puberty begins that will help them adjust to their changes? What would you tell your child?

**2.** Many young adolescents feel awkward or self-conscious about their bodily changes during puberty. How do peers, parents, and the media contribute to these feelings? How could parents and teachers be more sensitive?

**3.** Why is it unfair to attribute teenagers' moodiness or irritability to their "raging hormones?" How might adolescent females feel when their assertive behavior is attributed to premenstrual syndrome (PMS)?

# SELF-TEST

1. The one aspect of adolescence that appears to be inevitable and universal is

   a. educational transitions

   b. vocational preparation

   c. separation from one's parents

   d. puberty

2. Which one of the following probably has the greatest social stimulus value for adolescents?

   a. adolescents' clothing

   b. adolescents' speech

   c. adolescents' bodies

   d. adolescents' abilities

3. Researchers can gauge an adolescent's pubertal status using

   a. blood, saliva, and urine tests

   b. a physical examination

   c. adolescent self-reports

   d. all of the above

4. The main factor influencing physical growth and development is

   a. nutrition

   b. heredity

   c. stress

   d. health

5. During the growth spurt, boys and girls gain an average of how many pounds?

   a. 20

   b. 40

   c. 60

   d. 80

6. For males, a primary sexual change is

   a. body hair

   b. maturation of the testes

   c. deepening of the voice

   d. all of the above

**7.** For females, the first indication of puberty usually is

**a.** the growth spurt

**b.** menarche

**c.** development of breast buds

**d.** changes in muscle and fat composition

**8.** The secular trend refers to generational differences in

**a.** age of onset of fertility

**b.** body size

**c.** body weight

**d.** all of the above

**9.** According to the critical weight model of puberty onset, the key factor instigating puberty is

**a.** percentage of body fat

**b.** steroids

**c.** health and diet

**d.** hormones

**10.** Menarche in females corresponds to _____ in males.

**a.** anarche

**b.** semenarche

**c.** archeology

**d.** nocturnal emissions

**11.** Compared to early-maturing boys, late-maturing boys are considered

**a.** more masculine

**b.** more attractive

**c.** better groomed

**d.** more childish

**12.** Early-maturing girls typically tell _____ about their bodily changes.

**a.** their mothers

**b.** their friends

**c.** their older siblings

**d.** no one

**13.** Which group appears to benefit the most from the timing of their physical changes?

   **a.** early-maturing boys

   **b.** early-maturing girls

   **c.** late-maturing boys

   **d.** late-maturing girls

**14.** During adolescence, hormonal fluctuations appear to influence

   **a.** feelings of frustration and aggression

   **b.** sexual feelings

   **c.** mood

   **d.** all of the above

# FOUR

# COGNITIVE DEVELOPMENT IN ADOLESCENCE

## Preview Questions

1. What do we mean by the term *cognition*?
2. In what ways do adolescent thinking and reasoning differ from that of younger children?
3. How can we account for gender and ethnic differences in intelligence test performance?
4. How do psychologists define and attempt to measure intelligence?
5. What cognitive abilities do adolescents apply when reasoning about social encounters?
6. In what sense is adolescent thinking distorted?

◆

## Disclosures

I wish I could make my parents listen to me. I also wish that I could do better. I wish I was easier to get along with. It's hard to get along with my parents. It's hard to understand things about life. I just refuse to be understanding. I always want things to be my way. Lately, I realize that not everything can be my way.

*(17-year-old male)*

Anywhere we [teenagers] go, we are always being watched. People think that we're going to be doing something bad.

*(16-year-old male)*

<h1>Contents</h1>

## BEN AND ELYSE

Ben's parents invite him to accompany them to a neighborhood movie theater. Ben has been looking forward to seeing this movie, but at age 14 he's self-conscious about being seen with his parents in public. What if one of his friends sees him sitting in the theater with them? While checking himself out in the bathroom mirror, he thinks, "This is very uncool. Well, if any of my friends see me, I'll just ignore them. Or I'll pretend that I'm there by myself. Anyway, the theater will be dark, and I'll sit a few rows in front of Mom and Dad. They won't mind."

Fourteen-year-old honor student Elyse Meredith believes that she has the right to bring her backpack to her classes each day. How else can she carry around all her books and materials? Her principal, the district superintendent, and some teachers at her school disagree. They see her bulging backpack as a threat to the health and safety of students and teachers and believe that it should be banned from classrooms, hallways, and the school cafeteria.

After teachers complained of tripping over backpacks stuffed with cans of hair spray and stuffed animals, her school imposed a backpack ban. Unlike her peers, Elyse refused to store her backpack in her locker, complaining that the 3-minute break between classes was not enough time for her to go to her locker and get her belongings. Having read Thoreau's essay "Civil Disobedience" and being an admirer of Martin Luther King, Elyse viewed her situation as "a question of liberties. I feel it's important to stand up for liberties you have, to keep them. I feel [the backpack ban] is taking away students' rights to property." Despite 10 days of suspension and a lack of peer support, Elyse and her lawyer father carry on the battle for her civil liberties. A judge eventually decides this issue—not in Elyse's favor (Hanley, 1996).

During the early adolescent years, young people like Ben and Elyse not only begin to think for themselves, they also spend far more time thinking *about* themselves. As a preadolescent, Ben never gave a second thought to being seen with his parents. He jumped at any chance to accompany them to the movies, to restaurants, or to the mall. But something has changed. Ben's self-consciousness reflects his newfound concern about how others (especially his peers) see him and what they think about him. His desire to maintain his cool image in public reflects emerging self-evaluation and reasoning abilities that we don't ordinarily find in younger children.

Elyse's willingness to defy powerful authority figures who challenge her rights stands in dramatic contrast to the compliance and conformity we usually observe in school children. Her defiant behavior is propelled by her heartfelt belief that she has rights that cannot be compromised. Somehow, Elyse has begun to create for herself a world view based on abstract principles of justice and fairness.

Over the course of childhood and adolescence, our behaviors and feelings become increasingly guided by situations as we perceive and interpret them (Mahoney, 1991). Ben's concerns about how his friends evaluate him may or may not be valid. After all, he occasionally sees his friends accompanied by their parents, and he doesn't think less of them. But like his peers, Ben is guided more by his self-conscious interpretation of events than by the events themselves. As we shall see, advances in adolescent thinking and reasoning do not preclude the existence of glaring misconceptions and distortions about the world of people and things (Klaczynski, 1997). Psychologists use the term **cognition** to refer to the various ways in which we know the world and try to make sense out of our life experiences. New **cognitive abilities** involving perception, logical thinking and reasoning, planning, memory, language, and problem solving emerge and extend into each and every domain of adolescent life (Siegler, 1991). Of particular importance are **critical thinking skills** that allow young people to analyze, evaluate, and occasionally challenge the information that they are given from teachers, parents, peers, and the media (Keating, 1990; Murray, 1997a).

Appearing more adultlike in body size and shape, Ben and Elyse are becoming better able to think for themselves, to understand their own and other people's thoughts, motives, values, and points of view. Their increasingly sophisticated reasoning abilities play a major role in shaping their beliefs about what constitutes acceptable behavior. We study cognitive development for many reasons, but mainly because *how we think about and know the world colors our every decision and action.* Over the next several years, Ben and Elyse will have to think long and hard about issues concerning their health and safety, their relationships, their goals and values, and their future.

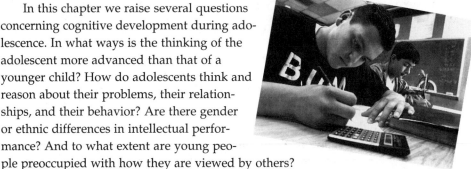

In this chapter we raise several questions concerning cognitive development during adolescence. In what ways is the thinking of the adolescent more advanced than that of a younger child? How do adolescents think and reason about their problems, their relationships, and their behavior? Are there gender or ethnic differences in intellectual performance? And to what extent are young people preoccupied with how they are viewed by others?

## ADVANCES IN THINKING DURING ADOLESCENCE

For a majority of adolescents, a transformation in thinking and reasoning begins at about the same time (age 11 to 14) as the bodily changes we studied in Chapter 3. Although there are marked individual differences in when and how *higher-order thinking* emerges, almost all adolescents show dramatic improvement in their ability to think rationally and to reason systematically. In fact, there are surprisingly few differences between adolescent and adult thinking (U.S. Office of Technology Assessment, 1991). The cognitive transformation that we study in this chapter allows adolescents a richer, more reflective understanding of themselves, their social world, and their future lives (Sternberg, 1990).

Over the course of adolescence, advances in reasoning extend to different domains of adolescent life and problem solving, including self-concept, interpersonal understanding, values, and decisions about education, careers, and romance. However, having an ability doesn't mean that it will be exercised correctly or at all. Cognitive advances represent *potential* rather than typical everday thinking and problem solving (Keating, 1990). Experience, education, and training support the application of intellectual abilities to increasingly diverse areas of adolescent life (Box 4-1).

## WHAT IS INTELLIGENCE?

If my cocker spaniel Maxie wants to know what something is, she smells it. She smells everything: that's her job as a dog. I love my dog, but I have to admit that, because of her obsession with scent, she has a severely limited knowledge base. According to Piaget, an infant can only know something, for example a rattle, by sensing it (e.g., touching, tasting, or looking at it) or by acting on it (e.g., shaking or throwing it)—not so different from a dog. Dogs and babies know the world mainly by sensing it and acting on it. But in a relatively short time, the child will be able to know what a rattle is *conceptually* (i.e., "plastic

*Thought Question: Why bother looking for gender and ethnic differences in intelligence in the first place? (Eagly, 1995)*

**Box 4-1
Are There
Gender
Differences in
Cognitive
Development?**

Over this century, psychologists have tried to determine whether males and females differ in cognitive abilities, intelligence, achievement, and even wisdom (Orwoll & Achenbaum, 1993). Despite the duration of the search, clear-cut gender differences have been few and far between. Perhaps due to more equal opportunities in education, the slight to moderate gender differences that were reported earlier in the century (e.g., in verbal ability or spatial visualization) have become much smaller or disappeared. What we observe today is substantial overlap in the intellectual performance of male and female adolescents (Dubas & Petersen, 1993).

Most reviews of research on general intelligence report few if any gender differences (e.g., Hyde, 1994; Maccoby & Jacklin, 1974; Neisser et al., 1996). Girls receive slightly higher grades than boys at all grade levels and in all academic areas and typically display greater verbal fluency (Halpern, 1992). Although girls perform better than boys in math until puberty, boys generally do better than girls (e.g., on the math SAT and PSAT) throughout adolescence (Halpern, 1992; Linn & Hyde, 1991).* (See Figure 4-1 on page 118.) Male adolescents are more likely than females to apply formal operational thinking. Whether this is due to biology, socialization, opportunity, or some combination remains to be seen (Dubas & Petersen, 1993), although parents and teachers appear to have higher expectations regarding math performance for boys (Keating, 1990). We will return to this issue in Chapter 11.

*Regarding the College Board's advanced placement and achievement tests, male students attain moderately higher scores in physics, chemistry, and computer science. Females show a slight advantage on language examinations. Gender differences in scores appear to be narrowing, especially in American History and Computer Science (Stumpf & Stanley, 1996).

baby toy that makes a noise"). The child will experience an awareness and understanding of the world and herself that even a professional dog such as Lassie could only dream of. So, what is this *intelligence* that allows only humans (as far as we know) to create a world of ideas and concepts?

Although there is general agreement among psychologists that intelligence exists and can explain individual differences in achievement behavior, there is no widely accepted definition of the term (Shobris, 1996; Weinberg, 1989). We do know that people differ in their ability to learn from experience, adapt to their environments, understand complicated subject matter, and solve every-day problems by reasoning about them (Neisser et al., 1996). In everyday life, we consider someone to be intelligent if he or she is knowledgeable or creative, can learn new materials or skills quickly, or can adapt quickly to changing circumstances. Older people generally know more than younger people, but that doesn't mean that older people are more intelligent. They simply have had more time (and experience) to learn about the world.

Traditional models of intellectual development assessed *how* we know the world (cognition) by measuring *what* we know about it (knowledge). Skirting the issue of what intelligence really is, most cognitive scientists have accepted an **operational definition**: Intelligence is whatever intelligence tests measure. This practical definition has allowed valuable research, but real-life skills and competencies that go beyond those measured by academically oriented intelligence tests have received much less attention (Matthews & Keating, 1995).

If we accept that there is such a thing as intelligence, is it one ability (known as *global* or *general intelligence*) or many? After all, most of us are good at some things and not at others. Do people in successful relationships, for example, have *interpersonal intelligence*? Today, psychologists consider the possibility that there are multiple intelligences that, for the most part, are not tapped by standardized intelligence tests. Psychologist Robert Sternberg maintains that creativity and practical intelligence are not measured by mainstream intelligence tests (Sternberg, 1985; Sternberg, Wagner, Williams, & Horvath, 1995). *Thought Question: Are some types of intelligence more adaptive than others?*

The idea of *practical intelligence* echoes popular notions of "street smarts" and "common sense" (Neisser, 1976; Neisser et al., 1996). To do well in school, students need to be "book smart" (demonstrate logical and verbal abilities), but can they solve ordinary life problems such as programming a VCR or balancing a checkbook? How well do they get along with a difficult sibling? Can they avoid a hostile confrontation with a bully or figure out the best route for driving to Grandma's house? Surprisingly, there seems to be little correlation between academic and practical intelligence (Sternberg et al., 1995). Further, different ethnic groups and cultures have their own conception of what intelligence is and how it should be measured (Heath, 1983; Rogoff & Chavajay, 1995).

Psychologist Howard Gardner (1983, 1993) claims that traditional models of intelligence are too narrow. They are oriented only toward logic and academic knowledge. Gardner proposes seven different types of intelligence: musical, spatial, linguistic, logic-mathematical, kinesthetic (body movement), interpersonal (understanding others), and intrapersonal (understanding oneself) (Table 4-1).

According to Gardner, performance in any one of these domains is independent of performance in the others, challenging the idea of general intelligence. Further, each type of intelligence shows improvement with age and has its own "language" or coding system. At any particular moment, whether we are organizing a party or playing a video game, we are displaying several types of intelligence. Gardner maintains that students find instruction more meaningful when it is geared to their personal and artistic sides. He advocates the use of portfolio assessments as a way of assessing students' competencies. Portfolios include students' artwork, creative writing, musical recordings, interviews, and any other materials that indicate mastery of a concept (Murray, 1996b).

Each individual shows relative strengths and weaknesses in each of the seven domains of multiple intelligence, resulting in a unique intellectual profile. Such a profile would be useful in vocational counseling. Counselors could ad-

**Table 4-1 Gardner's Multiple Intelligences**

| Intelligence | Processing Operations | End-State Performance Possibilities |
|---|---|---|
| Linguistic | Sensitivity to the sounds, rhythms, and meanings of words and the different functions of language | Poet, journalist |
| Logico-mathematical | Sensitivity to, and capacity to detect, logical or numerical patterns; ability to handle long chains of logical reasoning | Mathematician, scientist |
| Musical | Ability to produce and appreciate pitch, rhythm (or melody), and aesthetic-sounding tones; understanding of the forms of musical expressiveness | Violinist, composer |
| Spatial | Ability to perceive the visual-spatial world accurately, to perform transformations on these perceptions, and to re-create aspects of visual experience in the absence of relevant stimuli | Sculptor, navigator |
| Bodily/kinesthetic | Ability to use the body skillfully for expressive as well as goal-directed purposes; ability to handle objects skillfully | Dancer, athlete |
| Interpersonal | Ability to detect and respond appropriately to the moods, temperaments, motivations, and intentions of others | Therapist, salesperson |
| Intrapersonal | Ability to discriminate complex inner feelings and to use them to guide one's own behavior; knowledge of one's own strengths, weaknesses, desires, and intelligences | Person with detailed, accurate self-knowledge |

*Sources:* Gardner, 1983, 1993. (From Berk, 1996.)

vise students to pursue vocational areas that are consistent with their intellectual strengths. Gardner and others (Matarazzo, 1992; Mathews & Keating, 1995; McClelland, 1973) contend that there are multiple pathways to intellectual and social competence. They urge schools to support student development in domains of expertise and competence (including practical intelligence) that go well beyond math, verbal, and spatial items on general intelligence tests.

Many elementary and middle schools have adopted some of Gardner's ideas, but there have not been enough outcomes assessment studies to allow evaluation of their success. Critics maintain that Gardner's seven intelligences are better understood as special talents that may or may not reflect general intelligence (Neisser et al., 1996). Others worry that attention to students' creative and interpersonal skills might detract from basic instruction in math, reading, and writing (Murray, 1996b).

## THREE APPROACHES TO STUDYING INTELLECTUAL DEVELOPMENT

Most psychologists studying cognition and intelligence have adopted one of three quite different strategies: the psychometric approach, the information processing approach, and the stage developmental approach. The three approaches have in common the goal of describing and explaining age-related changes in children's and adolescents' ability to know and understand the world. None of the approaches provides a complete picture of intellectual functioning (Bjork-lund, 1997). Whereas the information processing and stage developmental approaches look for universal patterns in adolescent thinking abilities, the psychometric approach focuses on individual differences. All three approaches depend heavily on *hypothetical constructs* (abstract concepts) such as intelligence and knowledge to accomplish this goal.

## Psychometric (Mental Abilities) Approach

Based on the pioneering work of psychologists Alfred Binet (1916) and Raymond Cattell (1971), the **psychometric approach** to intellectual development emphasizes statistical measurement of individual differences in mental constructs, the quantifiable aspects of what and how much we know. It is the earliest model and the most practical of the three approaches we consider (Keating, 1990).

The psychometric approach views intelligence as a set of hypothetical mental abilities on which people differ. Its main premise is that the higher one scores on an intelligence test, the more intelligence one has. For most of this century, psychologists have defined and attempted to measure intelligence using standardized tests of verbal and mathematical skills, memory, spatial cognition, and problem-solving skills (Sternberg & Powell, 1983). Standardized tests of intelligence such as the **Stanford Binet Intelligence Scale** and the *Wechsler Scales* assess an individual's mental abilities at a given age. The resultant **intelligence quotients (IQs)** can be used to compare an individual's intellectual status to that of his or her cohort group (usually age-mates).

During their construction, intelligence tests are administered to large, representative samples of people. Test scores of individuals in each age group form a bell-shaped curve in which most scores fall near the center and progressively fewer scores fall at the extremes. Using this so-called normal distribution of scores, test designers calculate **norms**, standards against which future test takers are compared (Berk, 1996).

Intelligence test scores usually are converted to a scale in which the average score is 100. Thus, the average IQ score for each chronological age group is always 100. Scores below 75 indicate mental retardation and those above 130 represent "superior intelligence" (Azar, 1996b). The average of 100 is maintained by periodically recalibrating the test. If Uma achieves a score of 120 on an intelligence test, we can conclude that she is a brighter-than-average 15-year-old. Only about 11% of her age-mates have an IQ higher than 120. In some IQ tests, an individual is given separate verbal and performance scores and an overall IQ score.

IQ scores remain relatively stable over adolescence; that is, adolescents who score higher than their peers during early adolescence continue to do so throughout middle and late adolescence. The stability of IQ scores does not reflect the absence of intellectual growth. Intellectual ability improves for virtually all adolescents, but their relative standing does not change very much

Intelligence tests are useful in determining whether or not students are working up to their potential, but they do not predict vocational success or personal happiness.

over time. IQ scores have risen in developed countries over this century, about 3 points a decade (Azar, 1996b), but we don't know why.

The **Scholastic Assessment Test (SAT)** (administered by the College Board) is used by most colleges to make decisions about admissions and financial aid. About 41% of graduating high school seniors take the SAT, representing 90% of the seniors applying to 4-year colleges (Arenson, 1996a). Because grading standards vary considerably from one school to another, most colleges and universities heavily weigh performance on standardized tests. The SAT combines verbal and math scores into one global measure. Used in conjunction with high school grades and class ranking, the SAT is a fairly good predictor of how well a student will perform in college, at least during the first year. Revision of the exam in 1994 included a recalibration of the scoring system and the inclusion of more critical thinking and practical problem-solving items than were contained in the older version of the exam (Figure 4-1).

The *Preliminary Scholastic Assessment Test (PSAT)* helps students prepare for the SAT and is also used in the selection of semifinalists for National Merit Scholarships (awarded to students deemed most likely to succeed in college). Critics have charged that both tests discriminate against females, who do

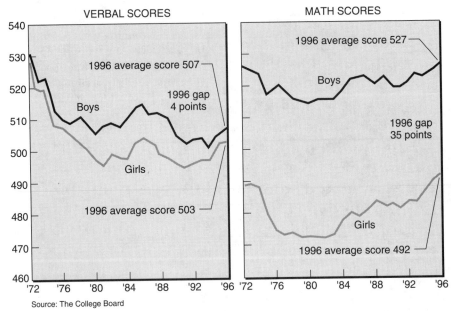

**FIGURE 4-1** Average scores on the verbal and math section of the SAT, 1972–1996.

slightly worse on the tests even though they get better grades in high school and college. The addition of a multiple-choice writing component to the PSAT in 1997 is expected to improve the test's ability to predict college performance and help female students win their fair share of National Merit Scholarships (Arenson, 1996a).

Intelligence test results are helpful in determining whether a given student is working up to his or her potential. If a student scores well on an intelligence test but does poorly in school, we try to make sense of the student's "under-achievement." IQ tests also can be used to place students in appropriate academic tracks or classes. In fact, this is what Alfred Binet had in mind when he created the first intelligence tests. Although there is a modest correlation between IQ tests and school grades, IQs do not predict vocational success or personal happiness (Trotter, 1986).

It is important to remember that school performance reflects many factors: ability, motivation, preparation, persistance, encouragement, and, importantly, the quality of instruction. Although fairly stable over time, IQ scores can change significantly, reflecting the anxiety or motivation of the test taker, major life changes, malnutrition, stressful live events, and the specific tests being used (Aiken, 1987).

Intelligence testing remains one of the most controversial topics in developmental psychology, perhaps reflecting the impact that intelligence tests have on educational and vocational opportunities. As noted earlier, Howard Gardner (1993) contends that standardized tests do not capture the richness and diversity of real-life intellectual abilities. Many educators regard standardized tests as a backward, even discriminatory tool for measuring intellectual ability.

As noted earlier, some educators prefer portfolios, collections of students' work that are graded individually, rather than relative to national standards or norms (Mosle, 1996). According to Gardner, multiple intelligences should be assessed directly, using real-world criteria in natural settings, that is, settings where learning and creativity actually occur. Other critics contend that IQ tests are culturally biased and often misused or misinterpreted (Anastasi, 1988). Youngsters who grow up in poverty or under other less than optimal conditions have fewer opportunities to learn what they need to know in order to perform successfully on an intelligence test. As a result, they may be assigned a label or track that implies a lack of ability.

Performance on intelligence tests reflects the verbal skills of the test takers more than their cultural or economic background (Box 4-2). Differences among ethnic and racial groups in IQ test scores tend to be slight on items that require minimal language proficiency (Bock & Moore, 1986). Although the relative contribution of biology and experience to IQ performance is still debated, most psychologists accept an interactional model. That is, performance on intelligence tests reflects a complex interaction between heredity, intellectual stimulation, and educational opportunity.

Although IQ tests allow comparison of one adolescent's general intellectual development to another's, they reveal little about how adolescents think or how their thinking differs from that of younger children or adults. (Some researchers do compare and analyze the items that children, adolescents, and adults score correctly in order to compare their thinking abilities.) If we took a group of adolescents, all with the same IQ, and compared them, we would still find considerable diversity in their mental abilities (Keating, in press). The information processing model addresses this topic.

## Information Processing Approach

Like computers, human beings receive loads of information (input), process it quickly, and then act (output). In and out of school, young people are bombarded with information concerning academic subjects, friends, chores, news events, sports, popular culture, and so on. At this very moment, you are "processing" the flow of verbal information on this page (I hope). The **information processing approach** to cognition (Figure 4-2), based on our understanding of how computers process complex data, analyzes intelligence in terms of how we receive, interpret, organize, store, and apply information (Flavell, 1985). Its main goal is to describe the cognitive activities (mental strategies) we engage in when we are reasoning and problem solving (Harrison & Turner, 1995). Note that the psychometric approach discussed in the previous section analyzes only "output"—solving problems—and not the input, processing, or storage of information.

Fourteen-year-old Maxine, on the phone with her best friend Frances, *pays attention* to her friend's vocal sounds and thus *receives* the following information: "There is going to be a Spanish test tomorrow." She *perceives* (interprets) her friend's words and *thinks* about them. "Oh, my God," she responds, "I'm not at all prepared." After the phone call, she *remembers* the information, *reflects*

**Box 4-2
Performance
on
Intelligence
Tests by
Ethnic Group
Membership**

Although intelligence tests are designed so that there will be minimal gender differences in scores, the same is not necessarily true for the scores of different ethnic groups. Keep in mind that intelligence tests are scored so that the average IQ for any age group is 100. Although as a group Asian-Americans have performed exceptionally well academically and professionally, their scores on achievement tests are about average. Although Japanese and Chinese children perform much better in math than U.S. children, no significant IQ differences have been found for children in Japan, Taiwan, and the United States (Neisser et al., 1996; Stevenson et al., 1985).

The mean intelligence score for African-Americans is about 15 points below that of whites, although differences in achievement test scores have been decreasing as educational opportunities have become more equitable. Average intelligence scores for Hispanic-Americans (Latinos) fall between those of African-Americans and whites. Linguistic factors may be partly responsible for their less than average test performance. On the average, Native American children attain relatively low scores on tests of verbal intelligence. Again, for many of these children, English is a second language.

Ethnic group differences in IQ scores have been attributed to genetics, child rearing, educational opportunity, nutrition, test bias, or some combination. According to Neisser and his colleagues (Neisser et al., 1996), none of these factors has been proven to be responsible. In effect, ethnic group differences in IQ scores remain a mystery. Although intelligence tests are biased in the sense that advantaged children usually obtain higher scores than disadvantaged children, the tests are fairly good predictors of school performance. This is what they were designed to do.

Researchers who compare the behavior and abilities of minority children to those of mainstream children try to avoid a **deficit model** assumption that "mainstream skills and upbringing are normal and that variations observed with minorities are aberrations that produce deficits" (Rogoff & Chavajay, 1995, p. 870). They do this by viewing cognitive development of minority children as a sociocultural process that cannot be separated from the cultural and historical aspects of children's lives. Each child's cognitive development is viewed in the context of the activities and practices of his or her community or subculture (Harrison, Wilson, Pine, Chan, & Buriel, 1990). "Surviving in the ghetto may require verbal negotiation and a show of bravado, but these same skills may be seen by a middle class white teacher as disruptive and counterproductive to learning in the classroom. By understanding how skills are influenced by culture, however, teachers will be in a better position to capitalize on the performances students do exhibit" (Driscoll, 1994, p. 222).

*Source:* Based on a review of the literature by Neisser et al. (1996).

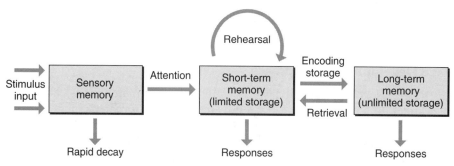

**FIGURE 4-2  Overview of information processing system**
**Based on Atkinson & Shiffrin, 1971.**

on it, and conscientiously *applies it* by opening her Spanish book and *studying*. Each new Spanish phrase is *rehearsed* until Maxine can *retrieve* (recall or recognize) each item on her study list. Throughout her study period, Maxine is *monitoring* and *regulating* her understanding of the material.

As Maxine matures, her ability to receive, process, organize, and store information improves. Her intellectual processing of information becomes faster, more efficient, and more automatic (Case, 1985; Harrison & Turner, 1995). Compared to younger children, adolescents like Maxine spend more time planning how to approach a problem and generate strategies. They are better at organizing diverse types of information into categories (Hale, 1990; Sternberg, 1984). For example, they can hear a new song and immediately classify it as pop, folk, rap, heavy metal, or alternative.

When answering reading comprehension questions on the Student Assessment Tests, they can identify and ignore useless information, recognize the relevant information in a paragraph, retrieve it when needed, and thus extract the main idea of the essay. Compared to younger children, adolescents are better at organizing information, integrating it with what they already know, understanding what they need to know to solve a problem or to make a decision, shifting problem-solving strategies when necessary, and applying previously learned material to a wide range of new situations. This advanced reasoning style allows adolescents to monitor and reflect on their own thoughts, in effect, to think about thinking (this is known as **metacognition**) (Ryan, 1990; Siegler, 1991; Sternberg, 1988, 1990).

By understanding the sequence of events by which adolescents acquire information, memorize it, and retrieve it to solve problems, educators can provide instructional experiences that give learners practice at each step. "Teachers can also help children analyze their own acts of perceiving, storing, and recalling so that they gain greater conscious control over each stage of the process. For instance, children can be taught such memory-enhancing strategies as rehearsal, grouping items, key-word associations, acronyms and rhymes as mnemonic devices, and multiple associations. In other words, teachers can help [children] 'learn how to learn'" (Thomas, 1996, p. 337).

Despite their practical value, information processing models ignore emotional and social factors in intellectual development. Information processing models also have been criticized for implying that people of all ages process information in the same way. Recently, attempts have been made to understand how information is processed during different life periods (Thomas, 1996).

### Stage Developmental Approach

The third model of intellectual development, associated mainly with Jean Piaget (1926, 1950, 1952), is called the **stage developmental approach**. Unlike proponents of the perspectives described previously, Piaget had little interest in individual differences in mental abilities. He was more interested in how intelligence develops from infancy to adulthood, that is, changes in how children and adolescents make sense of their experiences. Therefore, he focused on qualitative changes and universal patterns in intellectual development.

Piaget's model views children and adolescents as passing through predictable and identifiable stages in how they think and reason about the world. Each stage consists of increasingly sophisticated ways of knowing the world. As noted in Chapter 2, stage models assume that individuals remain in a given stage for a period of time and then move fairly rapidly to the next stage. In other words, stage models predict periods of cognitive stability punctuated by spurts of cognitive growth (Andrich & Styles, 1994).

Although the credibility of stage models of intellectual development does not rest solely on biological data, their plausibility would be boosted if we could identify a biological basis for such changes—for example, spurts of growth or other changes in the brain that precede or accompany advances in reasoning ability (Waber, 1977; Case, 1992). What is happening in the brain when the rest of the adolescent body is undergoing a growth spurt? Is there comparable growth in the nervous system that could explain broad advances in core logical competence during the teenage years (Keating, 1990)?

Thatcher et al. (1987) reported two weak bilateral growth spurts in the cerebral cortex, one at about age 12 years and one between the ages of 16 and young adulthood. Do these cortical growth spurts lie behind the impressive cognitive advances we see in many adolescents? Or do the challenging curricula of middle and high school promote brain growth? Although we cannot yet answer these questions, the relatively rapid gains in reasoning ability during the adolescent years support Piaget's contention that intellectual growth occurs in stages. *Critical Thinking Question: Would a lack of growth in the brain during periods of intellectual advancement disprove Piaget's stage model?*

## HOW DID PIAGET VIEW COGNITIVE DEVELOPMENT?

Jean Piaget (1896–1980) was a Swiss epistemologist best known for his studies of cognitive development in children and adolescents. **Epistemology** is the branch of philosophy that studies the nature and origin of knowledge—what is knowledge (how do we know that something is true?), and where does knowledge come from (is it innate, acquired, or created?)?

Perhaps the most impressive cognitive change in life is children's transformation from naive believers in magical beings like Santa Claus and the tooth fairy into rational, strategic thinkers who cope with and solve real-life problems. Piaget was interested in how this happens—specifically, the emergence of logical strategies during childhood and adolescence. Using a variety of materials, he posed logical problems to children of different ages (including his own children) and interviewed them to assess their reasoning abilities. Based on their responses, Piaget identified four qualitatively different "ways of knowing" that emerge gradually over the course of infancy, childhood, and adolescence. Each new stage consists of a more advanced way of knowing the world than existed during previous stages. Piaget considered the four stages and the transitions between them to be universal (observed in all children), although he recognized that children progress through these stages at a significantly different pace (Inhelder & Piaget, 1958). Eventually, cross-cultural studies indicating that formal operational thinking is not universal led Piaget to accept that the fourth stage is culturally variable (Rogoff & Chavajay, 1995).

Piaget emphasized the role of process knowledge in adolescent thinking and reasoning. **Process knowledge** refers to knowledge about the logical strategies that underlie reasoning and that account for the qualitative changes in adolescents' ability to know their world (Linn, 1983). According to Piaget, each stage of cognitive development is characterized by an underlying (hypothetical) logical structure called a **schema** that is shaped and modified by a child's interaction with the physical and social world. When what we know about the world (**cognitive content**) is not sufficient to solve a problem, we must modify our existing schema or acquire new ones.

Piaget defined intelligence mainly in terms of biological **adaptation**, or the need to resolve discrepancies and inconsistencies between what we perceive and what we believe to be true. Adaptation is accomplished by two complementary processes—**assimilating** new information into existing cognitive structures (i.e., using what we already know to learn new material) and **accommodating** existing structures to the new information (i.e., changing what we know) (Neisser et al., 1996). A young child assimilates a zebra as a "striped horse," using existing knowledge (stripes, horse) to understand the zebra. Her parent's correct labeling of the animal ("Honey, that's a zebra") allows her to change what she knows, thus accommodating her perception of the zebra. Piaget used the term *equilibration* to refer to our attempts to maintain a state of balance between our cognitive structures and daily experiences.

As noted earlier, Piaget hypothesized that infants know the world primarily by sensing it and by acting on it. Hence he labeled the first stage of cognitive development **sensorimotor**. Lacking conceptual knowledge, infants cannot think or reason about a rattle. However, they can "know" a rattle by grasping it, looking at it, shaking and hearing it, sucking on it, throwing it, and so on. These ways of knowing the rattle are called **action schemas**, mental structures that know the world by acting on it. Some are innate, but most are learned.

Between the ages of 2 and 6 years, children depend mainly on mental imagery and language to understand the world and to mentally represent (think about) objects and events. However, they are not yet capable of systematic logical thinking. A 4-year-old who is demanding to go to the toy store is not easily dissuaded, even when told that the store is closed. Piaget used the term **operation** to refer to logical thinking. Toddlers are prelogical in their cognitive development, so they are said to be in the **preoperational stage** of cognitive development.

Between the ages of 6 and 12 years, children become increasingly committed to logical thinking. They are more flexible in their reasoning than preschool children. Elementary school children exhibit skill at counting and naming objects. They can classify objects or people into hierarchies (e.g., human, animal, alive), recognize dissimilar objects as members of the same class (e.g., meat and bread are both food), and place objects in serial order according to some dimension (standing in size places). However, they still find it easier to reason about observable objects and events than to analyze hypothetical concepts. They have difficulty analyzing abstract concepts and ideas such as democracy, truth, and mortality.

Although they repeat the Pledge of Allegiance each day in school, it is unlikely that most school children are capable of grasping abstract concepts such as allegiance, republic, liberty, and justice. The third stage of cognitive development is called **concrete operations** because children in this stage are capable of thinking logically, but only about concrete objects and relatively simple ideas. Their understanding of the world remains heavily dependent on immediate, hands on experience (Inhelder & Piaget, 1958) (Table 4-2).

## What Is Formal Operational Thinking?

For most adolescents, between the ages of 11 and 14 there is a metamorphosis, not only in body shape and size, but also in thinking and reasoning ability. Piaget (1950) observed that adolescent thinking is more adult-like than child-like. Again, preadolescents are reasonable, but they tend to think about events in relatively simple, black-and-white terms. A person is either good or bad; an action is either right or wrong. Their thinking is still dominated by perception, intuitive understanding, and naive theories about the world (e.g., "All women

### Table 4-2  Piaget's Four Stages of Cognitive Development

**Sensorimotor** (birth to 2 years)—Infants know the world by sensing it and acting on it (hence sensorimotor).

**Preoperational** (2–6 years)—Toddlers and preschool children know the world intuitively, basing their judgments on perceptions and magical thinking. They are able to use symbols (e.g., words) to represent the world but their thinking is not yet logical.

**Concrete operational**—School-age children can think logically about the "here-and-now" world and organize objects into hierarchies of classes and subclasses.

**Formal operational**—Adolescents are capable of thinking logically about abstract and hypothetical events. They can reason about the world using symbols (words and numbers) that are not necessarily linked to real objects and events.

are mothers"). They conveniently distort or ignore information that contradicts their beliefs (Keating, 1990).

Adolescent thinking is more flexible; adolescents can view events and concepts in relative terms. For example, good people can have bad qualities. A short man can be taller than his wife. Children's thinking frequently is rigid, especially when they are asked to consider information that is contrary to what they believe. They are more likely than adolescents to misinterpret what they see or to jump to conclusions (Siegler, 1991). Keep in mind, though, that the precursors of formal operational thinking are found in the three previous stages (Overton, Steidl, Rosenstein, & Horowitz, 1992).

Piaget called the fourth (and presumably final) stage of cognitive development **formal operations**, because the complex *form* or style of adolescent thinking defines this stage more than its content. Piaget (1972) held that formal operational thinking affects every area of adolescent life. Adolescents can better gauge the accuracy of their ideas, decide whether their thinking is internally consistent, and notice whether there are gaps in their understanding. However, even college students and adults have difficulty integrating every bit of relevant information into a coherent framework (Keating, 1990).

Higher-level thinking frees adolescents somewhat from their immediate experience, so that they are better able to think about their future and eventually create a realistic and meaningful life plan. Adolescents come to realize that there are countless pathways that their lives could follow. This insight apparently requires the ability to hold several complex mental representations of their future simultaneously (Keating, 1990). They can evaluate each pathway (finish school, go to college, enter the military, get married) and then set personal goals based on their evaluations (Table 4-3).

According to Piaget, most teenagers are capable of thinking and reasoning about abstract and hypothetical ideas, including those found in mathematics, religion, literature, politics, and everyday moral dilemmas. For example, adolescents are more capable than younger children of grasping that the Pledge of Allegiance is a promise to be loyal to one's country (symbolically represented

## Table 4-3  Characteristics of Formal Operational Reasoning

*Formal operational thinking allows adolescents to:*

think more flexibly

view events and concepts in relative terms

reflect on their own thinking (metacognition)

notice flaws and inconsistencies in thinking

reason about abstract and hypothetical ideas

distinguish what is possible from what is impossible

distinguish what is real from what is hypothetical

think through several different solutions to a problem

appreciate metaphor, analogy, satire, and parody

by the flag). They can appreciate that in a democracy, freedom of speech is a person's right, not a privilege granted by a government. Sophisticated reasoning abilities allow young people to think critically about themselves, about their families and friends, and about issues in their own lives and in world events (Siegler, 1991). Formal operational thinking allows adolescents to ponder the mysteries of life and the paradoxes of human behavior.

*Thought Question: What is the trade-off in being able to reason critically about one's own behavior and motives?*

In 1991, the United States and other countries formed an international coalition to extricate Iraqi soldiers from Kuwait, the country Iraq had just invaded. There was considerable concern about how children of different ages would react to reports about the war, including news stories about bombings and civilian casualties (Covell, Rose-Krasnor, & Fletcher, 1994). Most preadolescent children I spoke to viewed the war in concrete terms: the United States and its allies are good, Iraq is bad, and the Iraqi leader Saddam Hussein deserves to be punished or killed. Adolescents I spoke to analyzed the war and the conduct of the parties involved in more complex ways.

Regardless of their specific opinions about the justification for the war, adolescents reflected on the implications of using war as a means of resolving international disputes. As they analyzed the reasons given for military action, they wondered whether the reasons were valid. They could consider competing points of view and keep them in mind while formulating their own views. They expressed cynicism about the media's role in glorifying military combat. They were better able than younger children to take into account the devastating effects of the war on the people involved, including soldiers, civilians, and children. More than younger children, adolescents expressed ambivalence (support and reservations) about their country's participation in sanctioned violence. Denholm (1995) reports similar views held by gifted Canadian adolescents.

Piaget (1926, 1950) also observed that adolescents are more capable than younger children of distinguishing what is possible (e.g., world peace) from what is impossible (e.g., flying dogs) and what is real (e.g., death) from what is hypothetical (e.g., life after death). In relation to the war with Iraq, adolescents were more likely than younger children to reason about alternative ways of resolving international conflicts. One 17-year-old offered: "Why not negotiate first, and if that fails, we can try sanctions" (Table 4-4).

Like scientists, adolescents can use **systematic observation** (verification and disconfirmation) to determine how events are related to each other. **Hypothetical-deductive thinking** consists of testing several different possible solutions (hypotheses) to a problem. For example, if an 8-year-old puts a videocassette into a VCR, pushes the "Play" button, and sees only "static" on the TV screen, she might jump to the conclusion that the videocassette or the TV is broken. An adolescent would be more likely to apply **systematic thinking** (inductive and deductive logic) in considering multiple possible causes—is it the videocassette, the VCR, the TV, a connection, the cable, or something else that is at fault?—and then test each hypothesis, one at a time (Foltz, Overton, & Ricco, 1995).

### Table 4-4  What Constitutes Good Reasoning?

Using evidence skillfully and impartially

Organizing thoughts and articulating them concisely and coherently

Suspending judgment in the absence of sufficient evidence

Understanding the difference between reasoning and rationalization

Anticipating the probable consequences of alternative actions before choosing among them

Understanding the idea of degrees of belief

Knowing how to seek information

Seeing similarities and analogies that are not superficially apparent

Learning independently

Applying problem-solving techniques appropriately in domains other than those than in which they were learned

Listening carefully to other people's ideas

Understanding that most problems have more than one solution

Representing differing viewpoints without distortion or exaggeration

Looking for unusual approaches to complex problems

Recognizing the fallibility of one's opinions

(Adapted from Nickerson, 1987, pp. 29–30)

**Adolescents are more likely than younger children to apply systematic thinking when solving a problem with many possible solutions.**

Adolescents' impressive but untrained reasoning abilities sometimes lead to false or inappropriate conclusions (Baron & Sternberg, 1987; Klaczynski, 1997). Misinterpreting other people's behaviors and motives and observing their own contradictory thoughts and behaviors can contribute to adolescent confusion and anxiety. Some parents express frustration about what they consider to be faulty judgment by their teenage children. "How could he make an obscene gesture just when the photographer was snapping the high school class picture?" asked one perplexed father. It takes time and experience to learn how to anticipate and think through the consequences of one's actions and decisions. In a later section, we will consider why adolescents, more than any other age group, act in ways that could jeopardize their own health and safety. The tendency to exaggerate or oversimplify matters, as in idealistic or cynical thinking, further distorts adolescent thinking and reasoning (Table 4-5).

Their newfound ability to think critically about society, its values and its contradictions, encourages adolescents to challenge or at least question what they are taught and to think for themselves. Teenagers are more likely than younger children to notice flaws and inconsistencies in their parents' reasoning and to build a logical case for their own point of view. They also are prone to argue for its own sake, enjoying opportunities to exercise their newfound cognitive tools. Intellectually, young people like Elyse (the backpack girl) are ready to take on their teachers, parents, friends, and "the system" (Elkind, 1994a; Piaget, 1972).

Another important facet of formal operational thinking is an improved ability to **think symbolically**. A symbol is something that stands for or represents something else. The word *cat* stands for actual cats. In the Pledge of Allegiance, the flag represents the United States. We mainly use words (spoken, written, signed, and thought) to refer to objects and events. Greater flexibility in lan-

### Table 4-5 Potential Flaws in Adolescent Reasoning

Self-centeredness and self-consciousness—Two manifestations of adolescent egocentrism, reflecting adolescents' preoccupation with their own needs and thoughts

Misinterpreting other people's behaviors and motives—Perhaps reflecting a failure in perspective taking and in exploring alternative explanations

Faulty judgment—A failure to anticipate the possible consequences of one's actions

Exaggerating or oversimplifying matters—Thinking in extremes, perhaps reflecting idealistic or cynical thinking

Argumentative behavior—Practicing new cognitive abilities, including building a case for one's position

Indecisiveness—Reflects improved awareness of possibilities but difficulty in choosing among them

Finding fault with authority figures—Noticing discrepancies from past idealization of adults

Hypocrisy—Not yet applying newly realized ideals to one's own behavior

Drawing self-serving conclusions while maintaining the illusion of rationality

guage helps adolescents appreciate figures of speech and literary devices such as metaphor (describing one thing as another, as in "I was shattered"), irony (when a result is the opposite of what was expected), analogy (implied similarity), satire (*The Simpsons, Beavis and Butthead*) and parody (*Saturday Night Live*). Compared to school children, most adolescents would have little trouble analyzing a poetic sentiment such as "Let me compare thee to a summer's night."

Changes in how we think lead to changes in what we think about. Hacker (1994), an existential psychologist, suggests that a greater capacity for abstract thought allows adolescents to gain a deeper and more profound awareness of who they are (their self-concept) and of their existence in the world. They can grapple with issues like isolation, death, the meaning of life, and individual responsibility. "An adolescent can awaken one morning with the insight that, for the first time in his or her life, an incredible feeling of isolation and loneliness stemming from a sense of not belonging has invaded his or her thoughts. An adolescent also can gain, in a moment, the insight that who he or she is no longer depends on what others believe but rather on who he or she wants to become" (p. 304). We will consider the effects of advanced reasoning abilities on adolescent self-concept in Chapter 6.

## Evaluation of Piaget's Model

Many of Piaget's hypotheses about cognitive development have been confirmed, at least for white middle-class children, but evidence suggests that his theory underestimates younger children's ability to grasp concepts and ideas (Siegler, 1991). Some of Piaget's basic assumptions about intellectual development have been challenged, including his fundamental premise that all children proceed through comparable stages of cognitive development (Beilin & Pufall, 1992; Harris, 1983; Rogoff & Chavajay, 1995). Many of the changes in thinking that Piaget described can be interpreted as being part of a gradual progression rather than occurring in stages. He also had little to say about individual differences in cognitive development (Sternberg & Powell, 1983). Intellectual development appears to be somewhat more complicated and less predictable than Piaget anticipated (Bjorklund, 1997; Guerra, 1993; Siegler, 1991), although some criticisms of his model are based on misinterpretations of his ideas (Lourenco & Machado, 1996).

Critics also challenge Piaget's assumptions about the role that formal operational thinking plays in adolescent behavior and personality. First, it does not appear that formal operational thinking emerges during early adolescence (Lapsley, 1990). Not all college students display formal reasoning (Blasi & Heoffel, 1974; Gray, 1979; Keating & Clark, 1980). In fact, many adults never display advanced reasoning skills. But that's no great handicap. Most of us can balance a checkbook and plan a graduation party with practical, informal thinking and reasoning. The educationally advantaged youth of Geneva whom Piaget studied apparently were not representative of other children, especially those who receive limited intellectual stimulation and encouragement (Rogoff & Chavajay, 1995).

**Box 4-3**
**An**
**Evolutionary**
**Perspective**
**on Cognitive**
**Development**

According to David Bjorklund (1997), none of the three models described in this chapter provides a plausible overview of cognitive development or even one that is consistent with the current research literature. He calls for a new model of cognitive development based on developmental biology and evolutionary theory. Specifically, Bjorklund maintains that a theory of cognitive development must be consistent with what we know about the relationship between the brain and behavior and especially must take into account the adaptive nature of intelligence. "For stage theorists, knowledge of how the brain develops can be correlated with qualitative changes in cognitive abilities, giving the hypothesized discontinuities some basis in physical reality" (p. 145).

Bjorklund's premise is that natural selection operates on the cognitive level. The brain evolved information-processing capacities to solve current real-world problems. Thus, children's cognitive abilities (e.g., object permanence, conservation, social perspective taking) evolved not in anticipation of literacy skills needed for some future technological society but to allow ancestral children and adolescents to deal with the problems that they faced in specific environments at particular times in their development. Thus, Bjorklund views modern children's difficulty in learning reading and math as the norm, not as an exception. He poses the key question, how are modern children's and adolescents' cognitive abilities adaptive for their *current* cultural contexts, not for an adult world that they will someday inhabit.

Second, formal operational thinking may not be a prerequisite for the social and emotional changes we associate with young adolescents, as Piaget implied. Concrete operational thought, not formal operational thought, may lie behind such adolescent concerns as ideological orientation, life plans, and political commitments (Lapsley, 1990).

Several investigators challenge Piaget's claim that we should wait until young people show adultlike reasoning abilities before teaching them logical and critical reasoning skills. Piaget assumed that providing such training before children are biologically ready for it would be counterproductive. However, it may be precisely this type of instruction that promotes the development of reasoning skills in the first place (Baron & Sternberg, 1987; Keating, 1990; Selman & Demorest, 1984) (Table 4-6).

Piaget's model generally ignores the content of learning and the social and instructional context in which learning usually occurs. This helps explain why attempts to teach formal reasoning (process knowledge) independently of content and social setting have failed (Baxter Magolda, 1992; Perry, 1970). The Russian teacher and psychologist Lev Semenovich Vygotsky (1896–1934) maintained that all intellectual abilities are social in origin. Since conceptual thinking is transmitted to children through words, language becomes a critical tool for teaching children how to think. According to Vygotsky, thinking and speaking are two separate functions. However, a language environment that contains

### Table 4-6  Criticisms of Piaget's Model

His theory may underestimate young children's ability to grasp concepts and ideas.

He did not explore the possibility of individual differences in cognitive development.

Intellectual development seems to be more complicated and less predictable than Piaget anticipated.

Formal operational thinking may not emerge during early adolescence; many adults never display advanced reasoning.

The advantaged Swiss youth that Piaget studied may not be representative of children in other cultures, especially those who receive limited intellectual stimulation and encouragement.

Formal operational thinking may not be a prerequisite for the social and emotional changes we associate with young adolescents.

Piaget's claim that we should wait until young people show adultlike reasoning abilities before teaching them logical and critical reasoning skills is questionable; it may be this type of instruction that promotes the development of reasoning skills.

Piaget's model generally ignores the content of learning and the social and instructional context in which learning usually occurs.

complex and varied concepts teaches children to think in complex and varied ways (Faubert, Locke, Sprinthall, & Howland, 1996; Thomas, 1996).

Vygotsky (1930/1978) viewed children and adolescents as active participants in the learning process. The **cognitive socialization approach** he pioneered attributes a key role to social and instructional interactions in shaping cognitive structures (Harrison et al., 1990; Keating, 1990). For example, some teachers present students with points of view that match the teachers' own thinking and reward students for thinking the way they do. Other teachers involve students in the learning process and help them relate what they are learning to their own experiences. Faubert and her colleagues (1996) conducted a 5-month intervention called *deliberate psychological education (DPE)*, which they used to promote conceptual thinking in African-American rural high school students. Using contributions of African-American scientists as their curriculum, 10th-grade students learned science by doing science and by serving as mentors to 9th-grade mentees. Students' goals included choosing a research topic, searching the research literature, reporting their findings orally and in writing, and participating in a science research celebration. Playing the role of scientist (designing and performing research projects) and serving as mentors to younger peers resulted in significant gains in the students' abstract thinking. *Thought Question: Does the lecture method of instruction that most teachers use accommodate the way most children and adolescents actually think and learn?*

How can we encourage independent thinking in young people? "Placing students in a situation where they have to solve problems, discussing problems with them, probing their thinking by presenting them with questions and conflicting situations, and encouraging them to analyze their own thinking either individually or in groups may foster formal operations reasoning" (Mwamwenda, 1993, p. 102).

# ADOLESCENT DECISION MAKING

As teenagers spend more time away from home and assume new responsibilities, the quality of their judgment and decision making takes on added importance. Decisions regarding academic, career, and interpersonal commitments can and will have lifelong consequences (Galotti & Kozberg, 1996; Gordon, 1996). Parents no longer are looking over their shoulders and guiding their every move. To the extent that adolescents develop good decision-making skills, they are better able to act in ways that promote their own goals and aspirations (Holmbeck & O'Donnell, 1991).

We have already seen that emerging cognitive abilities such as thinking about possibilities, distinguishing what is real from what is possible, testing hypotheses, and reflecting on their own thoughts contribute to adolescents' thought and reasoning. Other cognitive factors involved in decision making include concrete versus abstract thinking, present versus future orientation, and consideration of only some options versus all options. Further, as they mature, adolescents are able to retain larger amounts of information, making it possible to "intercompare" this information and build up bodies of knowledge. Knowledge and retrieval of knowledge usually improve with age and grade (Gordon, 1996).

Social and psychological factors that affect adolescent decision making include egocentrism, identity, intimacy, risk taking, locus of control, gender, family, peers, and life events (Gordon, 1996). As Vygotsky pointed out, children's interpretive styles and decision-making strategies are socialized by family members and peers (Jacobs, Bennett, & Flanagan, 1993; Klaczynski, Laipple, & Jurden, 1992). Cultural and societal factors in decision making include race, ethnicity, religion, political, health, and educational systems, and socioeconomic conditions (Gordon, 1996).

## Role of the Family

As they move from early to late adolescence, young people become aware that they are capable of making good decisions and that they are expected to do so. As their confidence increases, they expect and request more autonomy in decision making but still choose to confer with parents when making important decisions about college attendance, finances, and employment (Collins, 1990; Eccles et al., 1993; Galotti & Kozberg, 1996; Silverberg & Gondoli, 1996; Smetana, 1988a).

Joint decision making is common during midadolescence (Collins, 1990; Fuligni & Eccles, 1993). Through discussion and negotiation with their parents, young people learn about the different types of information that are needed to make specific decisions, such as what athletic team to try out for or what major to pursue. Whereas parents are likely to emphasize health and safety concerns, teenagers often are guided by the opinions of their peers. Whereas parents cite their prior experiences with similar problems, teenagers often overemphasize the specifics of the current situation (Galotti, Kozberg, & Appleman, 1990; Jacobs et al., 1993).

Although adolescents prefer to think for themselves, most are willing to consult with their parents when making important decisions.

It is through family discussions that attentive parents can hone their children's reasoning skills by asking good questions and by pointing out sources of relevant information. During family discussions, parents have the opportunity to model sensible (or irrational) decision-making strategies. The basics of competent decision making include defining the problem, generating options, taking multiple perspectives on a problem, anticipating long-term positive and negative consequences of a given decision, and evaluating different sources of information (Keating, 1990; Mann, Harmoni, & Power, 1989).

During discussions, family members should keep in mind that each participant has different priorities. For example, regarding the question of what college to attend, in a two-parent family Mom might emphasize academic rigor, Dad might be concerned about the cost of tuition, and the prospective student might want to investigate the dormitory and cafeteria. Indeed, so many factors are relevant to making a good decision that the parties may feel confused, frustrated, or overwhelmed. A common deficit in adolescent decision making, probably reflecting inexperience with complex life problems, is "underexploration" of possible solutions to problems (Galotti et al., 1990). Most teenagers resist sustained discussion and research, especially when they feel that their point of view is not being taken seriously. *Thought Question: What can parents do during family discussions to encourage independent thinking in their adolescent children?*

## Role of the School

The classroom is another excellent setting for encouraging independent and critical thinking skills. Teachers can provide instructional materials that are meaningful and stimulating to students, embed the training of reasoning skills in the presentation of course content, give students hands-on experience with real problems, value critical thinking, and encourage meaningful discourse with class members (Keating, 1990). We will return to this topic in Chapter 11.

## SOCIAL COGNITIVE DEVELOPMENT

It is probably not possible to understand people's behavior without knowing how they think about themselves and the social world. **Social cognition** refers to how we think about ourselves in relation to others and about others in relation to ourselves. One of the most challenging life tasks is managing personal encounters with family members and friends, trying to maximize harmony and minimize conflict and hurt feelings.

Improved reasoning abilities enhance adolescents' **social understanding** (understanding what others think and feel) (Selman, 1976, 1980). Mainly through interpersonal experience, not always pleasant, young people learn the "rules" that govern relationships, rules that touch on trust, intimacy, reciprocity, caring, loyalty, self-disclosure, and compromise. Learning how to navigate the choppy waters of close peer relationships is a lifelong task that begins for most of us in early adolescence. *Thought Question: How might improved understanding of people's motives lead to increased interpersonal conflict?*

If advanced reasoning is the up side of formal thinking, then adolescent egocentrism (discussed in the next section) is the down side (Overton et al., 1992). As a result of their self-centered thinking, preadolescents may act without considering the effects of their behaviors on others. With greater maturity, adolescents are able to coordinate a variety of different perspectives at one time (Tisak & Tisak, 1996). They can temporarily "step outside" of an ongoing social interaction and view it as though they were a third party rather than a participant. They can also step outside of a relationship and evaluate it more objectively (e.g., "I'm not acting like a good friend"). **Perspective taking** allows young people to present or defend their own point of view while considering a different opinion and understanding how both views influence each other. **Social role taking** helps adolescents empathize—that is, understand what they

**Adolescents are more likely than younger children to use situational cues to infer motives about other people's behavior.**

might be feeling if they were in someone else's shoes (Selman, 1980). ***Thought Question: How might these changes in adolescent thinking affect their relationships with their parents?***

Over time, young people become a little less rigid and a little more tolerant of opinions with which they do not agree (although they still may challenge what they see as unfair adult authority). Middle adolescents, as they gain more appreciation of the complexity of human personality (including their own), are generally less likely to jump to conclusions about people's feelings and motives. This is quite a change from the time when, as early adolescents, they acted as though they knew it all, contributing to adults' perception of an "attitude problem."

Adolescents also are better able than younger children to use situational cues to infer and reason about other people's motives, a process social psychologists call **attribution** (Collins, 1990). For example, a teenager might infer that Mom is disappointed about not being promoted at her job even when she denies it. They are better able to take into account motivational and situational factors in judging someone's actions. Abstract thinking helps adolescents infer personality traits like credibility or insecurity on the basis of observing an individual's actions over time. Naturally, this ability contributes to their own self-understanding. They can describe or understand aspects of their own personality by citing personal traits such as shy, generous, lazy, or conscientious ("I'm shy with strangers but confident around my friends").

## ADOLESCENT EGOCENTRISM

Each of us is the star of our own life movie. Particularly during childhood, each of us is by far the most important and interesting character in life's daily drama. Young children are reputed to be self-centered—stubborn, selfish, impulsive,

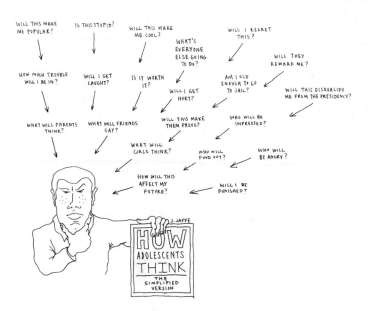

and demanding. They rarely express gratitude for their parents' unceasing efforts and sacrifices. Freud's concepts of the *id* and its creed, the **pleasure principle**, represent our self-centeredness, our preoccupation with satisfying our own needs and desires.

Piaget used the term **egocentrism** to refer to the difficulty children have distinguishing between their own behavior and thoughts and those of others. Children especially have difficulty adopting a perspective that is different from their own. The term *egocentrism* also refers to the tendency to view life events in terms of how they affect us. Piaget noted that as we mature, our thinking becomes less self-centered and more *relativistic*. That is, through maturation and socialization, we become better able to view situations from a variety of perspectives. Eventually, we become capable of seeing ourselves "through other people's eyes" and standing "in other people's shoes."

Adolescents are more likely than younger children to view people as individuals, each of whom has his or her own personality, motives, and points of view. "In many ways, this new objectivity mirrors the young person's emerging sense of her own individuality and separateness, a sense of uniqueness that she now extends to others as well as to herself" (Elkind, 1994a, p. 227). Egocentrism is a continuum. Most of us are preoccupied with our own needs and desires, but adolescents are more willing and able than younger children to consider and respond to a variety of points of view.

Although adolescents are somewhat less self-centered than younger children, they are still very concerned about how others see them. Psychologist David Elkind (1967, 1978, 1994a) and others define **adolescent egocentrism** mainly as heightened self-consciousness. Many studies have identified egocentric thinking patterns in adolescent behavior and relationships (e.g., Adams &

**From an adult perspective, adolescents are preoccupied with how they appear to others.**

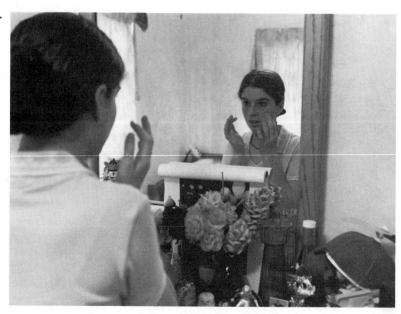

Jones, 1982; Peterson, 1982). Physical changes during puberty and the varied reactions they evoke from peers and parents fuel adolescent self-consciousness.

Elkind described two forms of adolescent egocentrism: the imaginary audience and the personal fable. According to Elkind, the **imaginary audience** reflects a failure to distinguish between an adolescent's own thoughts and the thoughts of others. It is manifested in young people's preoccupation with how they are viewed and evaluated by peers and adults. At the beginning of the chapter, we read that Ben was concerned that his friends would see him accompanying his parents to the movies and that this would detract from his image of being grown up. Naturally, this feeling of being subject to the scrutiny of his peers increased Ben's discomfort, although some adolescents bask in the imagined attention. It is a cognitive advance for adolescents to be aware of and care about how others see them, but the overgeneralization of this perspective could be seen as a flaw in social cognition (Keating, 1990). A 14-year-old girl told one of my students, "People think they have me down pat, but they really don't know me at all." How would you intepret this comment using the concept of the imaginary audience?

Elkind's idea of the **personal fable** refers to the tendency of many teenagers to overdifferentiate their thoughts and feelings from those of others (the other side of the coin from the imaginary audience). According to Elkind, adolescents' belief in their own uniqueness leads to a feeling of invulnerability. The personal fable specifically refers to an overly dramatic story line or fantasy that adolescents create about their lives and the accompanying belief that they have a special destiny. Many young people act as though they are living in a soap opera, with almost hourly episodes of excitement, heartbreak, suspicion, and betrayal. ("He said that? Oh my God, I don't believe it. What did you say? You said that? Oh my God.")

According to Elkind, adolescents believe that their motives and life experiences are unique or so unusual that no one could possibly understand or appreciate what they go through ("Mom, you just don't know what it's like"). Elkind cautions that teenagers' sense of having a unique destiny encourages some of them to take foolish risks sexually, with drugs, or in other ways that endanger their health and safety (see Spotlight • Adolescent Risk Taking). *Thought Question: How should parents handle adolescents' preoccupation with themselves if it is motivated by distorted thinking rather by than selfishness or disrespect?*

Two scales commonly used to measure adolescent egocentrism are the *Imaginary Audience Scale (IAS)* (Elkind & Bowen, 1979) and the *Adolescent Egocentrism Scale (AES)* (Enright, Lapsley, & Shukla 1979; Enright, Shukla, & Lapsley, 1980). IAS measures the extent to which adolescents are willing to reveal various aspects of themselves to others. The AES consists of three subscales that assess the imaginary audience, the personal fable, and self-focused concerns. Imaginary audience and personal fable scores generally peak at about age 10 or 11 years and then decrease gradually (Enright, Lapsley, & Shukla, 1979). According to Elkind, adolescents' sense of uniqueness lessens as they learn that their peers and their parents do understand and even share many of their concerns.

### Perspectives on the Adolescent Egocentrism Concept

Despite the fact that the imaginary audience and personal fable are widely cited as valid descriptions of adolescent behavior, there is evidence both supporting and contradicting Elkind's model (Quadrel et al., 1993). Theorists debate whether adolescent egocentrism is universal, whether it is gender-related, whether it lessens over the course of adolescence, and whether its emergence depends on formal operational thinking or other emerging cognitive abilities (Buis & Thompson, 1989; Lapsley, 1990; Vartanian & Powlishta, 1996).

The imaginary audience and personal fable thinking patterns usually materialize during early adolescence and decline by late adolescence, but not for all adolescents (Lapsley, 1990). Peterson and Roscoe (1991), for example, report that female college freshmen displayed more imaginary audience behavior than did younger teenagers. They hypothesize that the transition stress of entering college produces a temporary increase in self-consciousness. Ironically, there is more evidence of adult feelings of invulnerability than of adolescent feelings of invulnerability (reviewed by Quadrel et al., 1993). In Quadrel's study, low-risk teenagers showed less perceived invulnerability than did their parents!

Adolescents who think egocentrically do not always display formal operational thinking (Lapsley, 1990). Concrete operational thinking can explain many of the behaviors we associate with early adolescence, including adolescent egocentrism (Buis & Thompson, 1989; Gray & Hudson, 1984). Although adolescents are sensitive about how others perceive them, it has not been demonstrated that adolescent egocentrism is universal, inevitable, or even related to formal operational thinking (Goossens, 1984). Lapsley and Murphey (1985) offered a social-cognitive model of adolescent egocentrism that attributes the imaginary audience and the personal fable to changes in adolescents' social perspective-taking skills and interpersonal understanding. An adolescent's ability to understand other people, combined with expanding opportunities for social experiences, seem to be better predictors of the personal fable than is formal operational thinking (Jahnke & Blanchard-Fields, 1993; Vartanian, 1997; Vartanian & Powlishta, 1996).

Finally, several investigators maintain that the "cognitive immaturity" of children and adolescents is adaptive (e.g., Bjorklund & Green, 1992). In other words, self-centeredness and self-consciousness, often seen as deficiencies in young people's thinking, may have benefits related to adolescent learning, exploration, and autonomy. For example, self-centeredness apparently encourages children to relate new information to themselves and therefore improves retention. Vartanian and Powlishta (1996) suggest that overestimating the extent to which one is being evaluated by others (the imaginary audience) could be adaptive during adolescence, for example, engendering a "better safe than sorry" approach to social interaction. Feelings of invincibility (the personal fable) may encourage risk-taking behavior, which can have negative or positive consequences (Bjorklund & Green, 1992). *Thought Question: In what other ways might adolescent egocentrism be adaptive?*

## SPOTLIGHT • Adolescent Risk Taking

Parents worry about children of any age, but adolescents are particularly susceptible to dangerous, sometimes life-threatening situations (Bell & Bell, 1993; Dryfoos, 1990; Thompson, Anderson, Freedman, & Swan, 1996). Parents wonder, "What were they thinking?" Vehicles often are involved. In Canada, teenage drivers comprise 21% of all drivers but account for 58% of traffic accidents (Jonah, 1986). In 1993, two Pennsylvania teenagers were struck by vehicles and killed when they laid down in the middle of two different highways at night. They were copying the behavior of a college football hero in a movie they had just seen. Friends of the two dead boys reported that about 30 other teenagers were "playing the same game" in another town that night (*The New York Times*, October 19, 1993). What were they thinking?

Has engaging in risky behaviors, such as stage diving, crowd surfing, and slamming into each other while dancing in "mosh pits" at hard rock shows become one of the developmental tasks of adolescence (Baumrind, 1991; Jessor, 1987; Maggs, Almeida, & Galambos, 1995; Pogrebin, 1996a)? Feelings of invulnerability ("It can't happen to me") and simplistic thinking about negative consequences ("I can always get an abortion") lead some to make decisions that jeopardize their health and even their lives (Hubbs-Tait & Garmon, 1995; Lavery, Siegel, Cousins, & Rubovits, 1993).

This presents a paradox. A majority of adolescents engage in risk-taking behaviors that they know can jeopardize their health and safety, yet most grow up to be competent, productive adults (Maggs et al., 1995). An article in *The New York Times* caught my attention (Butterfield, 1996a). On the way home from playing in a ballgame, 31 members of the Duxbury (Massachusetts) High School baseball team, dressed in their uniforms, stopped at a convenience store and helped themselves to $100 worth of candy, baseball cards, and soda. Without paying, they got back on the team bus. Later that week, the team's left fielder admitted that "It was a really stupid thing to do. . . . It wasn't premeditated. It was more of a prank, with kids stealing things to see what they could get away with. These kids are not criminals. They just made a stupid adolescent mistake." After questioning all of the students involved, the school's principal concluded that the team members really did not understand why they had taken part in the incident.

Several theories address the prevalence of risk taking during the adolescent years. The **sensation-seeking model** attributes the appeal of shoplifting, loud music, fast cars, unprotected intercourse, cigarette smoking, and illegal drug use to the excitement (novel and intense sensations) provided by these experiences (Arnett & Balle-Jensen, 1993). The **problem behavior theory** recognizes important developmental functions in risk-taking behavior, for example, as a way of gaining peer acceptance or promoting self-esteem (Jessor, 1987). (Many of the baseball team players, when asked why they shoplifted, offered the explanation that they were in a group.)

**Risk-taking behavior during adolescence seems to be rooted in a desire for excitement and social status.**

The **prototype model of risk behavior** (Gibbons & Gerrard, 1995) maintains that young people have an image (prototype) of adult-like risk-taking-behavior, for example cigarette smoking, and an image of the type of person who engages in such behavior. According to the model, adolescents whose self-concepts match their romanticized image of cigarette smokers are more likely to engage in the behavior. Those who have negative images of cigarette smokers are less likely to acquire the habit. One implication of this model is that teenagers might adopt a risk-taking behavior as a way of identifying with or joining a particular peer group or crowd. "The closer the match between the self (concept) and the prototype, the greater the interest in joining the group" (Gibbons & Gerrard, 1995, p. 505).

The **decision-making model** of risk taking cites the costs (e.g., getting caught, possible injury) and benefits (e.g., fun, peer approval) of engaging or not engaging in risk-taking or antisocial behavior (Furby & Beyth-Marom, 1992; Moore & Gullone, 1996). One survey of adolescents revealed that low-risk teenagers perceived more costs to these behaviors than did high-risk teenagers. This is important because, as we saw in a previous section, adolescents don't always appreciate the limits of their knowledge. The two groups did not differ, however, regarding perceived benefits of these activities (Small, Silverburg, & Kerns, 1993).

These findings suggest that parents and teachers should emphasize to adolescents the perceived costs of risk-taking behavior. Of course, it is possible that high-risk adolescents understand the potential danger but choose to ignore it, concentrating instead on the perceived benefits of excitement and social status (Beyth-Marom, Austin, Fischoff, Palmgren, & Jacobs-Quadrel, 1993). In this case, adults might decide to limit adolescents' freedom or simply to let young people reap the painful consequences of their questionable choices (Quadrel, Fischhoff, & Davis, 1993).

Quadrel and her colleagues had low-risk and high-risk adolescents and their parents judge the probability that they (children and adults) would experience various risks (e.g., auto injury, unplanned pregnancy, mugging). Low-risk teenagers *and* their parents viewed the parents as being less vulnerable than the teens. In other words, feelings of invulnerability were more prevalent among adults than among teenagers! Both groups agreed that teenagers face more risk from auto accidents and unwanted pregnancy. The study found few differences in the cognitive decision-making processes of the adults and adolescents. The investigators express concern that some adults underestimate adolescents' reasoning competence and become overprotective or unnecessarily restrictive.

Nevertheless, the desire for peer approval and a fear of peer rejection are potent factors in adolescent decision making. Many teenagers place the social consequences of not participating in a questionable group activity ahead of health and safety considerations. When parents like those of the shoplifting baseball players ask in amazement, "How could you?" hapless teenagers respond, "Everybody was doing it. How could I not?"

A 15-year-old boy told one of my students during an interview, "I'm not as adventurous as my friends, but sometimes they pressure me into doing things. They pressured me into smoking weed. That was pretty cool. They pressured me into stupid stuff like sneaking out of my house when I didn't want to. It was cool—as long as I didn't get caught." When asked whether he ever pressures other people, he replied, "Sometimes, yeah, pretty much the same things that people pressured me into doing. I pressure them. Idiot stuff." Note that this young man makes risk taking sound like fun—it's cool as long as you don't get caught. At the same time, he can characterize his own coercive behavior as "idiot stuff." ***Thought Question: Which of the above risk-taking models is supported by this adolescent's personal account?***

Such contradictory reasoning is not unusual during adolescence. It is likely that young teenagers are guided more by the potential for fun than by potential dangers when making decisions about risk behaviors (Maggs et al., 1995). To be fair, many teenagers claim that they would never be persuaded by others to engage in risky activities. When asked why not, many cite family values, not wanting to disappoint their parents, and not wanting to get into trouble (Arnett & Balle-Jensen, 1993).

To avoid stereotyping all adolescents as risk takers, we also must acknowledge that countless young people actively campaign against drug abuse, drunk driving, unsafe sex, and so on. By providing guidance and supervision and by modeling good judgment and rational decision-making behavior, responsive parents help their children not only survive and prosper throughout a particularly hazardous life period, but also become involved in efforts to create a safer world.

## *SUMMARY*

**1.** Adolescents show remarkable advances in thinking and reasoning abilities. Compared to younger children, adolescents can think about themselves and their world more flexibly, more abstractly, and more hypothetically. They are better able to generate and evaluate hypotheses, to think ahead, and to plan for the future.

**2.** There is considerable overlap between the intellectual abilities of male and female adolescents, presumably reflecting comparable socialization of the two genders and increasingly equitable treatment and opportunity.

**3.** Most cognitive psychologists have adopted one of three approaches to studying intellectual development. The psychometric approach views intelligence as a set of mental abilities in which people differ. The information processing approach analyzes intelligence in terms of how people receive, interpret, organize, store, and apply information. The stage developmental approach views individuals as passing through identifiable stages in how they think and reason about the world.

**4.** Piaget described the cognitive advances during adolescence in terms of formal operational thinking. He claimed that formal reasoning is partly responsible for the social and emotional changes we observe during the adolescent years. Other investigators claim that concrete operational thinking plays a larger role in these changes. In either case, cognitive advances allow young people to question and challenge much of what they had previously accepted as factual. One of the most important shifts that occurs is improved perspective taking, the ability to view an encounter from a variety of points of view.

**5.** Despite improvements in reasoning, adolescent thinking remains somewhat flawed. Adolescents tend to be self-conscious about their appearance and personal qualities and overly concerned about how other people view them (the imaginary audience). Many create a dramatic story line (a personal fable) that suggests a unique destiny. Some have difficulty accepting that their parents understand what they are going through.

**6.** Advances in reasoning help adolescents become better decision makers. Joint decision making with parents helps young people become aware of the kinds of information they need to make good decisions and the various strategies that are important in effective problem solving.

**7.** Risk-taking behavior is more common during adolescence than during any other life stage, although most young people actively avoid placing themselves in harm's way. Feelings of invulnerability, the desire for peer approval, and unrealistic thinking about consequences cause some to jeopardize their safety and health.

**8.** Cognitive change also leads to improvements in social cognition—how adolescents reason about their own behavior and the behavior of those who inhabit their social world. Perspective taking, in particular, allows young people to consider their opinions in relation to other people's views. Role playing helps adolescents take other people's feelings into account.

# GLOSSARY

**Cognition** The mental abilities and processes by which we know the world

**Cognitive abilities** Include learning, perception, logical thinking and reasoning, planning, memory, language, and problem solving

**Critical thinking skills** Allow people to analyze, evaluate, and challenge new information

**Operational definition** Defining something in terms of how you measure it (e.g., equating intelligence with IQ scores)

**Psychometric approach** Emphasizes statistical measurement of individual differences using constructs such as intelligence or temperament

**Stanford Binet Intelligence Scale** Assesses individuals' mental abilities

**Wechsler Scales** Assess individual mental abilities

**Intelligence quotient (IQ)** A numerical value given to intelligence based on intelligence test scores

**Norms** Average ages at which some aspect of development occurs

**Scholastic Assessment Tests (SAT)** Standardized tests used by colleges for selecting students

**Preliminary Scholastic Assessment Test (PSAT)** Helps students prepare for the SAT

**Deficit model** Idea that mainstream skills and upbringing are normal and that variations observed in minorities are aberrations that produce deficits

**Information processing approach** Analyzes intelligence in terms of how we receive, interpret, organize, store, and apply information

**Metacognition** Thinking about thinking

**Stage developmental approach** Piaget's approach to studying intelligence, focusing on qualitative changes and universal patterns in intellectual development

**Epistemology** The study of knowledge, its nature and origin

**Process knowledge** Knowledge about the logical strategies that underlie reasoning and that account for the qualitative changes in our ability to know the world

**Schema** Piaget's term for the mental representations one uses to organize experience

**Cognitive content** What we know about the world

**Adaptation** The need to resolve discrepancies and inconsistencies between what we perceive and what we believe to be true

**Assimilation** Understanding something by using what we already know

**Accommodation** Understanding something by changing what we know

**Sensorimotor stage** Piaget's first stage of cognitive development; infants know the world by sensing it and acting on it

**Action schema** Mental structures that know the world by acting on it (e.g., the sucking reflex)

**Operation** A logical action carried out mentally

**Preoperational stage** Piaget's second stage of cognitive development; toddlers can represent the world symbolically (in language) but mainly understand the world intuitively

**Concrete operational stage** Piaget's third stage of cognitive development; school-age children use logic to understand the world of people and objects

**Formal operational stage** Piaget's fourth stage of cognitive development; adolescents use logic to understand ideas and concepts

**Systematic observation** Studying the world objectively and carefully (i.e., using the scientific method)

**Hypothetical-deductive thinking** Testing several different possible solutions to a problem

**Systematic thinking** Inductive and deductive logic

**Symbolic thinking** Thinking in words and numbers

**Cognitive socialization approach** Vygotsky's model, which attributes a key role to social and instructional interactions in shaping cognitive structures

**Sensation-seeking model of risk-taking behavior** Attributes the appeal of risk-taking behavior to the excitement (novel and intense sensations) provided by these experiences

**Problem behavior model of risk-taking behavior** Recognizes important developmental functions in risk-taking behavior, for example, as a way of gaining peer acceptance or promoting self-esteem

**Decision-making model of risk-taking behavior** Cites the costs and benefits of engaging or not engaging in risk-taking behavior

**Social cognition** Reasoning about the social world

**Social understanding** Understanding people's thoughts and feelings

**Perspective taking** Considering one's opinions in relation to other people's views

**Social role taking** Understanding what someone else might be feeling

**Prototype model of risk behavior** Attributes adolescent risk-taking behavior to romanticized images (prototypes) of adult behavior

**Attribution** How people explain the causes of behavior

**Pleasure principle** Freud's idea that behavior is partly governed by pleasure

**Egocentrism** Self-centeredness

**Adolescent egocentrism** Self-consciousness in adolescents

**Imaginary audience** The exaggerated belief that one's behavior is being watched or discussed

**Personal fable** An overly dramatic story line or fantasy that adolescents create about their lives

## THOUGHT QUESTIONS

**1.** How would knowledge about cognitive change during adolescence help parents understand the following adolescent behaviors?

   **a.** noncompliant behavior

   **b.** spending an inordinate amount of time in front of the mirror

   **c.** experimenting with cigarettes or alcohol

   **d.** questioning parents' religious beliefs

   **e.** anxiety about commiting to a career

   **f.** emulating the lifestyle of popular musicians

**2.** If it were your job to determine whether applicants to your school were intellectually pre-pared for college, what skills or abilities would you look for and how would you assess them?

**3.** Relate David Elkind's concepts of the imaginary audience and the personal fable to your own thinking during adolescence. Do you recall feeling self-conscious or thinking that other people were judging you? Do you remember creating a dramatic story line for your own life experiences? If so, describe.

**4.** As a parent, would you rather have your children be obedient or think independently? Explain.

# SELF-TEST

**1.** In which domain of developmental change do thinking and reasoning fall?

    **a.** physical

    **b.** cognitive

    **c.** psychosocial

    **d.** existential

**2.** Advances in thinking and reasoning affect adolescent

    **a.** self-concept

    **b.** relationships

    **c.** decision making

    **d.** all of the above

**3.** Traditional models of intelligence are oriented to

    **a.** logic and academic knowledge

    **b.** interpersonal understanding

    **c.** musical and artistic ability

    **d.** practical knowledge

**4.** Statistical measurement of individual differences in mental constructs defines what approach to the study of intelligence?

    **a.** stage developmental

    **b.** information processing

    **c.** psychometric

    **d.** multiple intelligence

**5.** The information processing model of intelligence grew out of the study of

    **a.** the brain

    **b.** the telephone system

    **c.** computers

    **d.** epistemology

**6.** In Piaget's model of cognitive development, the fourth and final stage of cognitive development is called

    **a.** final operations

    **b.** formal operations

    **c.** concrete operations

    **d.** metacognition

**7.** According to Piaget, at about what age do children begin to think logically?

   **a.** 4 years

   **b.** 6 years

   **c.** 9 years

   **d.** 12 years

**8.** Adolescent thinking differs from that of younger children in that it can be more

   **a.** abstract

   **b.** hypothetical

   **c.** flexible

   **d.** all of the above

**9.** "You don't know what it's like" exemplifies

   **a.** the personal fable

   **b.** the imaginary audience

   **c.** hypothetical thinking

   **d.** relativistic thinking

**10.** Social cognition refers to

   **a.** how we reason about relationships

   **b.** thinking about thinking

   **c.** analyzing one's thoughts

   **d.** adopting someone else's point of view

**11.** Adolescent egocentrism refers to

   **a.** self-centeredness

   **b.** self-consciousness

   **c.** distorted thinking

   **d.** all of the above

**12.** Risk-taking behavior is most common during

   **a.** childhood

   **b.** adolescence

   **c.** adulthood

   **d.** final exams

# FIVE

# MORAL DEVELOPMENT IN ADOLESCENCE

◆

## Preview Questions

**1.** To what extent do the cognitive advances of adolescence guide the development of moral and prosocial values?

**2.** Do all children and adolescents go through the same sequence of moral development?

**3.** Are there gender or ethnic differences in moral reasoning?

**4.** Do moral beliefs always lead to moral behavior?

**5.** How can parents and teachers promote prosocial behavior in adolescents?

◆

## Disclosures

My mother's generation had it much easier in terms of values and what is expected of a teenager. My mom tells me she did not sleep with any man before she got married, she was 23 years old then. She didn't even sleep with my father, before marriage, and she loved him. But nice girls didn't. And it was just like that! With us, you have all these different things—someone like my mom would be weird. Sometimes I wish I knew what I should do and not do. I can't listen to how my mother was, it does not help me. But when I listen to my friends I'm also confused.

*(A 17-year-old quoted by Perlmutter & Shapiro, 1987, p. 199)*

# Contents

The young woman quoted above admits that she is confused: the old-fashioned values that served her mother's generation do not seem to apply to her world. Almost all adolescents know the difference between right and wrong, yet some occasionally "do the wrong thing" (Schab, 1991). In doing so, they risk hurting members of their community, their parents, and themselves. Adjustment to society requires playing by the rules, but most cultural rules (e.g., "Keep your hands to yourself") are open to interpretation. Life doesn't usually provide clear-cut guidelines to help young people navigate the unanticipated situations and temptations that they face each day. *Thought Question: Does society have higher standards of prosocial behavior for adolescents than it does for adults?*

Daily life provides ample opportunities to make good or bad decisions. Some decisions, such as choosing a major, deciding whether or not to use a condom, or whether to drive under the influence of alcohol, can change the course of one's life. A glance at a daily newspaper reveals stories about angry or alienated youngsters stealing cars, vandalizing property, gambling, using drugs, even assaulting peers, teachers, or parents. Because the news media are inclined toward sensational stories, we don't see as many headlines about adolescents who tutor their classmates, help support their families financially, and work with the homeless. As you surely have noticed, most adolescents do act responsibly most of the time (Offer, 1984). Nevertheless, young people need help to learn how to distinguish between right and wrong, resist temptation and peer pressure, treat other people kindly, and learn to care about and address some of the complex issues in today's world. This is the domain of moral development.

Most educated people embrace the idea that people should think for themselves. If we extend this value to children and adolescents, we need to cultivate in young people *moral strategies* such as questioning what they are told, forming their own opinions and goals, and clarifying their own values. Many teachers, attempting to cultivate critical, reflective thinking, teach students how to consider evidence and how to judge arguments on their merits (Nickerson, 1987). *Thought Question: Do most parents really want their children to be independent thinkers?*

The study of moral development raises many challenging questions for researchers. How is the moral reasoning of adolescents different from that of younger children? How does moral reasoning change over the course of adolescence? Are these changes in moral reasoning rooted in the cognitive advances we discussed in the previous chapter or in socialization and educational practices? Are there cultural or gender differences in how adolescents view moral dilemmas? What can teachers and educators do to facilitate the development of independent thinking and moral reasoning? Finally, and perhaps most importantly, how can we help adolescents make good moral decisions?

Once again, there is no consensus among psychologists about how to answer any of these questions (Kagan, 1987). However, research provides valuable insight into how adolescents think and reason about what is right and wrong. This chapter on moral development follows the previous chapter on cognitive development because of the assumption that *higher-level reasoning guides such moral actions as honesty, helpfulness, resistance to temptation, and other prosocial behaviors* (Eisenberg, Carlo, Murphy, & Van Court, 1995). In the next few sections we explore the cognitive and social influences on adolescent moral judgment and behavior.

As children develop, they become increasingly likely to display prosocial behaviors such as sharing, donating, cooperating, comforting, and offering assistance. What underlies such changes? Cognitive models of moral development attribute prosocial behavior mainly to improved social and moral reasoning (e.g., "If I don't help her, who will?") and to adolescents' caring about others (Eisenberg et al., 1995; Hubbs-Tait & Garmon, 1995; Perry & McIntire, 1995). Advances in perspective taking and feelings of empathy help adolescents notice opportunities to offer aid and comfort (e.g., "Are you okay?") (Eisenberg, 1990).

Jean Piaget and Lawrence Kohlberg observed that level of moral reasoning is but one of many factors that can influence moral behavior. Most studies find only a modest relationship between moral judgment and moral behavior, suggesting the presence of other moderating factors, especially socialization (Eisenberg, Miller, Shell, McNalley, & Shea, 1991; Kasser, Ryan, Zax, & Sameroff, 1995). Most theories of moral development emphasize one or more of the following factors: higher-level (prosocial) reasoning, perspective taking, social problem-solving skills, attributions (inferences about the causes of people's behavior), and feelings of empathy (Eisenberg, 1990; Perry & McIntire, 1995; Selman, 1980).

## MORAL DEVELOPMENT DURING ADOLESCENCE

### Piaget's perspective

Piaget (1932) provided the first comprehensive study of children's moral reasoning. He posed hypothetical situations to children of different ages and asked them questions about their reasoning. He watched children play games (and sometimes played with them) so that he could study their rule-following and rule-breaking behaviors. He also interviewed children about the rules of the games they played so that he could understand their strategies. In other studies, Piaget read stories to children in which people had to make difficult moral decisions. On the basis of his findings, and borrowing some of the ideas of the educator John Dewey (1916), Piaget (1932) constructed a three-stage model of moral judgment.

Children younger than 4 years of age, during the **premoral stage**, show no sense of feeling obligated to obey rules. Children in the **heteronomous stage**, aged 4 to 8 years, obey rules and submit to authority. They take rules and regulations at face value, viewing them as fixed and absolute. This is called **moral realism**. Since rules are posed by adults or some higher authority, children consider them to be unchallengeable.

Children in the **autonomous stage**, aged 8 to 12 years, are more flexible in their reasoning than younger children. Piaget noticed that preadolescents' moral reasoning shifts from blind obedience to considerations of people's motives and intentions. This is called **moral relativism**. Children in this stage take into account the consequences of following or not following rules. They express more flexible opinions. They also understand that rules are important to societal functioning, but that rules can be challenged and changed when the situation requires it.

### Kohlberg's Cognitive-Developmental Model

Inspired by Piaget's findings, Lawrence Kohlberg (1927–1987) continued the investigation of children's moral reasoning. In the process of clarifying and expanding Piaget's initial formulations, Kohlberg generated an influential (and controversial) theory of moral development. Like Piaget, Kohlberg presented to children hypothetical vignettes that described moral dilemmas involving rules, laws, ethics, authority, and obligations (Kohlberg, 1958, 1975). In most moral dilemmas, one person's needs or desires conflict with those of another person.

The best-known dilemma involved a man named Heinz who needed special medicine to save his dying wife. The drug's inventor is selling it for such an inflated price that Heinz cannot afford to buy it. The inventor refuses to lower his price or wait for the money. Should Heinz steal the drug? Kohlberg asked children of different ages questions about how they or the people involved in the moral predicaments should respond. Like Piaget, Kohlberg was more interested in the children's reasoning than in the correctness of their response.

Kohlberg studied the moral reasoning of boys and girls from several cultures, mainly using clinical interviews. On the basis of children's responses to moral dilemmas, Kohlberg identified three levels of moral reasoning that are roughly age related: preconventional, conventional, and postconventional. Each of these levels is further divided into two stages. Thus, in Kohlberg's theory, there is a total of six stages of moral development corresponding to six different ways of reasoning about moral issues. Kohlberg agreed with Piaget that stages of moral reasoning are universal across cultures and, reflecting cognitive maturation, develop in a fixed sequence for everyone.

Although moral reasoning depends mainly on cognitive development, according to Kohlberg children learn to distinguish between right and wrong based on their daily life experiences. Each day they must make decisions about how to behave in specific situations. Should they share their candy with friends, be honest with their parents, return a found calculator? However, their ability to do the right thing is limited by their reasoning ability. A person's logical stage sets limits on the moral stage he can attain (Kohlberg, 1975). The law takes this limitation into account by not holding children under the age of 18 years legally accountable for their actions.

Let's consider Kohlberg's three levels of moral reasoning, remembering that each level consists of two stages. Level I in Kohlberg's model is called **preconventional morality**. During stage 1 (*punishment and obedience orientation*), children judge events as good or bad on the basis of how their actions affect them (rewards or punishments) or in terms of the power of those who state rules. They assume that they must obey without question the rules and regulations of higher authorities such as parents, teachers, and God. Young children claim that it is wrong to lie or to steal because you might get caught and be punished. Justice is viewed in terms of "an eye for an eye, a tooth for a tooth" (Kohlberg, 1958, 1975).

This level of moral reasoning is called *preconventional* because children do not yet see themselves as participants in society's rule-making processes. Something is right if it feels right (as in Freud's pleasure principle) or if an authority tells them so. During stage 2 (*naive hedonism*), children's moral reasoning is more relative, less absolute. Right and wrong are defined by one's own needs and, occasionally, by the needs of others. Children recognize that people have different opinions about what is right and wrong. When making moral decisions, children take into account their own interests and the mutual benefits of certain actions for the people involved. "If you're nice to me, I'll be nice to you" (Kohlberg, 1975).

By 14 years of age, most children achieve Level II moral reasoning, which Kohlberg called **conventional morality**. (This stage corresponds to Piaget's stage of moral relativism.) There is a shift in moral reasoning away from preoccupation with one's own need to get along with and gain approval from others. During stage 3 (*"good boy–nice girl" orientation*), teenagers accept existing rules and group standards. They believe that people should show concern for others, be trustworthy, obey rules, and respect society's laws. High school freshmen might consider upper classmen who use drugs to be "nuts."

Level II morality stresses the importance of living up to other people's expectations, being helpful—in effect, being nice. Good intentions and motives are taken into account and used to justify actions that might otherwise be considered inappropriate or rule-breaking (e.g., "His heart was in the right place").

During stage 4 *(law-and-order orientation)*, the highest level attained by most adolescents and adults, individuals are concerned that society's codes of conduct be respected. People are expected to do their duty and maintain the social order, not challenge it. Most teenagers understand that if everyone violated laws and regulations, even with good intentions, there would be chaos. Thus, authority should be respected and all citizens should act responsibly (Kohlberg, 1975). Note that adolescent reasoning in stage 4 is more abstract ("law and order") and more ideological ("My country right or wrong") than that of younger children. Kohlberg did not consider the possibility that egocentric and hedonistic thinking in middle adolescence might lead to a temporary regression in moral reasoning (Eisenberg et al., 1995).

Kohlberg referred to Level III moral reasoning as **postconventional morality**. This level of reasoning rejects the principle, adopted during previous stages, that authority and laws must be obeyed automatically. Ethical standards of conduct are determined not by subjective feelings, self-interest, social pressure, or even by legal authority. Rather, in this mode of moral reasoning, human behavior is guided by higher principles of human conduct, such as those described in the U.S. Constitution or the Ten Commandments. Kohlberg noted that the druggist in the moral dilemma described previously is not breaking the law by charging an exorbitant price for his drug. However, he is violating an *ethical* principle by taking advantage of a sick person (Kohlberg, 1975).

Individuals achieving stage 5 *(social contract, legalistic orientation)* are capable of viewing moral decisions more abstractly than they did previously. Concepts such as justice, fundamental rights, and democracy guide moral reasoning. Laws generally should be respected but, as Elyse (the backpack girl quoted in Chapter 4) maintained, unjust laws and unfair rules should be challenged and renegotiated in a democratic fashion.

Most late adolescents have the ability to think like moral philosophers, that is, to consider how a truly just society would function (Eisenberg et al., 1995). They can discuss thoughtfully difficult issues such as the ethics of capital punishment and the availability of abortion on demand. Most middle and late adolescents can reflect on moral questions such as what constitutes an ideal society, what types of unfairness exist in our society, and how we achieve social justice for all (Kohlberg, 1975).

Individuals in stage 6 *(individual principles of conscience orientation)* search their own conscience for universal ethical principles to guide their actions. Mohandas Ghandi and Martin Luther King intentionally violated laws that they regarded as unjust, laws that did not provide equal treatment for all people. Unfair laws must be challenged, they believed, regardless of the personal consequences. So few individuals achieve moral judgment stage 6 (about 1% or 2% of those tested worldwide) that Kohlberg eventually dropped it from his manual and considered it to be a theoretical stage (Table 5-1).

## Table 5-1 Moral Development

| Age | Moral Internalization | Moral Construction | Self-Control |
|-----|----------------------|--------------------|--------------|
| 1½–2 years | Concern with deviations from standards first appears<br><br>Modeling of a wide variety of prosocial acts begins. | | Compliance and delay of gratification emerge. |
| 3–6 years | Guilt reactions to transgressions first appear.<br><br>By the end of this period, internalization of many prosocial standards and prohibitions has occurred. | Sensitivity to intentions in making moral judgments is present.<br><br>Differentiated notions about the legitimacy of authority figures are formed.<br><br>Distinction between moral rules and social conventions develops.<br><br>Distributive justice and prosocial moral reasoning are self-serving.<br><br>At the end of this age period, distributive justice is based on equality. | Delay of gratification improves.<br><br>Adult-provided strategies assist with self-control; children can generate only a few strategies on their own.<br><br>Self-control is transformed into a flexible capacity for moral self-regulation. |
| 7–11 years | Internalization of societal norms continues. | Notions about the legitimacy of authority become more complex.<br><br>Preconventional responses to Kohlberg's hypothetical moral dilemmas, focusing on rewards, punishment, and the power of authority figures, are common.<br><br>Distributive justice reasoning includes merit and, eventually, benevolence; basis of fairness is adapted to the situation.<br><br>Prosocial moral reasoning reflects concern with others' needs and approval. | Generation of self-control strategies increases in variety.<br><br>Awareness of effective self-control strategies and why they work expands. |
| 12–adulthood | | Conventional responses to Kohlberg's hypothetical moral dilemmas, emphasizing human relationships and societal order, increase.<br><br>Moral thought and action become integrated as individuals move toward Kohlberg's higher stages.<br><br>Postconventional responses to Kohlberg's hypothetical moral dilemmas, reflecting abstract principles and values, appear among a few highly educated individuals in Western cultures.<br><br>Prosocial moral reasoning reflects empathic feelings, norms, and abstract values. | Moral self-regulation continues to improve. |

*Note:* These milestones represent overall age trends. Individual differences exist in the precise age at which each milestone is attained.

*Source:* Berk, 1997.

## Summary and Evaluation of Kohlberg's Model

Kohlberg's three levels of moral development correspond to three different ways philosophers have defined moral behavior. An action can be considered moral because it's good for me (preconventional level); because it's good for others or because there are no rules against it (conventional level); or because it conforms to certain universal principles of conduct (postconventional level).

Elementary school children are concerned mainly about acceptance and disapproval. Kohlberg contended that as children mature, their moral judgment becomes more "reasonable," that is, more rationally defensible. As children become more reasonable, they adopt cultural norms such as being truthful, not stealing, and helping other people. From middle school on, adolescents' moral reasoning still reflects conformity to social conventions. However, it allows consideration of abstract principles ("All people are created equal") and the ability to appreciate or at least respect other people's points of view. Relatively few adolescents or adults proceed to the third level, where behavior is guided mainly by principles of justice and fairness. The assumption shared by Piaget and Kohlberg that cognitive and therefore moral growth are stage-like, invariant, and universal is still being debated (Beilin & Pufall, 1992). Kohlberg's key assumption that cognitive advances in perspective taking and abstract thinking underlie advances in moral reasoning has received considerable research support. Cognition appears to be a necessary but not sufficient factor for many types of moral reasoning (Eisenberg et al., 1995). *Critical Thinking Question: What factors that influence moral judgment might be overlooked by strictly maturational models?*

Kohlberg's theory has been criticized on several accounts. One major criticism concerns the hypothetical moral problems that he presented to subjects. Almost all of the dilemmas involved abstract problems of justice and fairness, life and death. They have little to do with the real-life problems that most adolescents face (Carlo, Koller, Eisenberg, Da Silva, & Frohlich, 1996). When given the opportunity to generate and analyze moral situations that reflect their own life experiences, adolescents describe issues involving family and peer relationships, cheating, lying, drug use, career decisions, and money (Colangelo, 1982; Yussen, 1977).

In a study asking adolescents attending private boarding schools to describe their own real-life moral dilemmas, 91% of the girls and 64% of the boys described their moral conflicts in a social context (Johnston, Brown, & Christopherson, 1990). They did not cite abstract principles, rules, or rights. Wark and Krebs (1996) found that "females were inclined to report different kinds of real-life moral dilemma from males. In particular, females were more inclined than males to report prosocial types of dilemma, and males were more inclined than females to report antisocial types of dilemma" (p. 228). Reminding us of Sternberg's criticism of standardized intelligence tests (Chapter 4), Kohlberg's moral dilemmas do not appear to tap the typical everyday reasoning patterns of adolescents. Adolescent and adult moral reasoning is more social and situation-specific than Kohlberg believed (Carpendale & Krebs, 1992; Hart & Fegley, 1995).

How children and adolescents think about a problem depends partly on how the problem is presented. The social context and the consequences to the adolescent are key factors in moral reasoning that generally are ignored by Kohlberg's scales (Galotti, Kozberg, & Farmer, 1991; Johnston et al., 1990; Willits & Crider, 1988; Yussen, 1977). This helps us understand why so many early and middle adolescents score at the preconventional level on Kohlberg's scales (Colby & Kohlberg, 1987; Lapsley, 1990).

Despite Kohlberg's assumption that levels of moral development are universal, people in different cultures differ somewhat in their social and moral reasoning (Cousins, 1989). For example, Gustavo Carlo and his colleagues reported that American children scored higher than Brazilian children on internalized moral reasoning, possibly reflecting the degree to which American children's education reflects critical reasoning skills (Carlo et al., 1996). No differences in moral reasoning were found for adolescents in the two cultures. Asian social reasoning is more group oriented ("How do my actions affect the group"?), whereas Western reasoning is more focused on the individual ("How will my actions affect me?") (Hart & Fegley, 1995; Michel, Thomas, & Maimbolwa-Sinyangwe, 1989; Schweder, Mahapatra, & Miller, 1987).

The fact that people in some cultures achieve higher scores on Kohlberg's moral development scales than people in other cultures raises the possibility of cultural bias in the test. It is likely, however, that some professional groups (e.g., mathematicians and physicists) reason at higher levels than others, at least

**People in different cultures have different ideas about what constitutes appropriate behavior.**

when addressing problems in their special area. So few people demonstrate postconventional reasoning on Kohlberg's scales that some critics question his interview methodology and the logic of his model (Schweder et al., 1987).

Kohlberg's model is criticized for underestimating social influences on moral development. Kohlberg and Piaget assumed that children advance to higher levels of reasoning when their present levels are inadequate to accommodate their experiences. This is probably true to some extent, but it seems likely that children's sense of right and wrong is rooted at least partly in their discussions with parents, teachers, and friends about moral transgressions (Walker & Taylor, 1991).

Piaget (1932) acknowledged that peers play an important role in moral development. Disagreements with peers force children to take another perspective into account and to use reasoning to integrate the alternative perspective. This is less likely to occur in discussions with adults because children tend to defer to the adult perspective and reasoning is not activated. Kruger (1992) confirmed this hypothesis in her observation of children's discussions of moral dilemmas with peers and parents. Hoffman's (1983) socialization theory attributes moral development to the transmission of cultural norms and values from parent to child. We will return to this view shortly.

## ARE THERE GENDER DIFFERENCES IN MORAL REASONING?

Might the gender of the theorist influence the assumptions of the theory? Freud (1925) portrayed females as more emotional and less rational than males, implying that females have less moral conviction (weaker superegos) than males. Piaget (1932) and Erikson (1974) held that females are more concerned about relationships and feelings than about abstract ideas of fairness and justice. The two male theorists concluded that females are less advanced than males in their moral judgment.

It is possible that because Kohlberg used all-male samples, his original measures of moral development are biased against females. "This sex difference has commonly been explained as a deficiency in the female's ability to apply advanced principles of moral judgment. Kohlberg's system penalizes women for their caring attitude and rewards males for their preference for citing abstract principles of justice" (Muuss, 1988b, p. 230). Adolescent boys typically score higher than same-age girls in Kohlberg's stage 3. More male than female adolescents move beyond stage 4 to higher levels of moral judgment. When given the opportunity, girls generate more personal real-life dilemmas than boys and boys generate more impersonal (abstract) real-life dilemmas than girls (Skoe & Gooden, 1993).

In the view of Freud, Piaget, and Kohlberg, moral advancement occurs when adolescents judge situations based on universal principles of justice rather than according to personal or situational factors (Linn, 1991). Because females more than males emphasize caring relationships and mutual obligations in their moral reasoning, they generally score lower than males on Kohlberg's scales. Kohlberg acknowledged that males score higher than females on his moral scales. He rationalized that if women were given equal opportunity in employment and education, they would score as highly on his scales as men do (Kohlberg & Kramer, 1969). But would they?

## Carol Gilligan's Views

Carol Gilligan (who at one time collaborated with Kohlberg) maintains that male and female adolescents display different **styles of moral reasoning** but that neither style is more advanced than the other. Whereas males tend to view moral dilemmas mainly in terms of justice and fairness, females are more concerned about maintaining friendships and not hurting others. This distinction is particularly important during adolescence when teenagers are dealing with interpersonal issues such as autonomy, disconnection from parents, and romance (Eisenberg, 1990).

In one study, Gilligan presented two bright, articulate 11-year-olds, one boy and one girl, with Kohlberg's moral dilemma about the man named Heinz. Whereas the boy, seeing virtue in the action, was sure that Heinz was justified in stealing the medicine, the girl reasoned that if Heinz were caught, the theft would deprive Heinz's ailing wife of his company and his help. The girl felt that Heinz and the druggist should discuss the problem and agree to a solution. According to Gilligan, both children recognize the need for agreement but "see it as mediated in different ways: he impersonally through systems of logic and law, she personally through communication in relationship" (Gilligan, 1982).

Based on their different reasoning styles, the girl would score a full stage lower than the boy on Kohlberg's morality scale. Gilligan contends that the girl believes in communication as the proper mode of resolving conflict. Males tend to view morality abstractly as a *contest* of rights and values. Females typically see themselves as part of a concrete **network of relationships** that is valued more than abstract principles of justice and law. Again, Gilligan suggests that neither the male nor the female style of moral judgment should be considered better or more advanced than the other. They are simply different. *Critical Thinking Question: Do you agree with Gilligan that personal considerations, including a feeling of empathy, are a form of moral reasoning, even when they do not reflect abstract principles such as fairness or justice?*

## Evaluation of Gilligan's Views

Gilligan contends that Kohlberg's model is more applicable to the abstract, rational analysis practiced by males than to the more compassionate, relationship-oriented analysis preferred by most females. Gilligan allows that most people incorporate both patterns of reasoning but suggests a significant gender difference in moral judgment that has so far not been demonstrated. Gilligan's complaint of gender bias applies to all the major developmental theories created from a male perspective and based almost exclusively on research using male participants (Muuss, 1988b). She has demonstrated how male theorists and philosophers unfairly denigrated women's intellectual abilities and moral judgment. Such gender bias limits women's social, legal, political, and economic opportunities (Gilligan, 1982; Muuss, 1988b).

Modest gender differences in moral reasoning style occasionally are reported (Garmon, Basinger, Gregg, & Gibbs, 1996). For example, as a group, females may be more adept than males at social perspective taking (Santilli & Hudson, 1992). Some studies report that girls are more concerned than boys about approval and acceptance and are more attentive to relationship details (Cohn, 1991; Skoe & Gooden, 1993; Wren, 1997). Carlo and his colleagues, however, reported that girls are less likely than boys to display approval-oriented reasoning (Carlo et al., 1996). Adolescent girls are a little more likely than boys to view their problems in a relationship context (Galotti, 1989; Johnston et al., 1990) and to show greater prosocial reasoning (Eisenberg et al., 1991). *Thought Question: How would different styles of moral reasoning affect male–female relationships?*

Most research based on the use of real-life problems instead of hypothetical dilemmas reveals few if any gender differences in level or type of moral reasoning (Eisenberg & Lennon, 1983; Ford & Lowery, 1986; Friedman, Robinson, & Friedman, 1987; Galotti et al., 1991; Smetana, Killen, & Turiel, 1991; Walker, 1984). Adolescent males and females usually consider both justice and sensitivity in their moral reasoning (Johnston, 1985; Linn, 1991). In fact, Carlo and his colleagues (1996) report that the only gender difference in moral maturity that they found using Kohlberg's scales favored females. Wark and Krebs (1996) object to characterizing people as morally mature or morally immature and to labeling people as having a care-based or justice-based moral orientation on the basis of their responses to contrived moral dilemmas. "As children acquire new cognitive structures, we would expect their moral judgment to become increasingly inconsistent and, in an important sense, less developmentally based . . . what develops is moral competence—the capacity to make increasingly sophisticated moral judgments" (p. 229).

## SOCIAL INTERACTIONAL THEORY

Although Kohlberg and Piaget acknowledged the social foundations of moral reasoning (e.g., Piaget, 1926), their cognitive-developmental models attributed primary importance in moral behavior to cognitive development. Social interactional theorists disagree. They suggest that prosocial behavior emerges neither from cognitive maturation nor from a parent's level of moral reasoning, but from children's routine daily interactions with other people, especially their parents and peers (Eisenberg & Mussen, 1989; Hoffman, 1983).

(Carol Gilligan [1982] agrees. She suggests that gender differences in moral reasoning have their roots in socialization. Empathy and relationship values, Gilligan maintains, are passed from mother to daughter, whereas valuing independence over connectedness is cultivated in sons by mothers and fathers.)

Social interactional theorists give children credit for recognizing the moral implications inherent in everyday social encounters. They give parents credit for teaching proper behavior. "It is, of course, day-by-day family interactions, not the 1-hour sampling of discussion in the lab, that is responsible for children's moral development" (Walker & Taylor, 1991, p. 280).

Unlike cognitive theorists, social interactionists assume that even young children understand that actions such as hitting and stealing are wrong. They understand that conventions like washing one's hands and being polite are desirable because people agree that they are desirable, not because of underlying moral principles. According to social interactionists, children understand that social conventions are necessary for society to function. They learn that their actions are wrong when parents express anger, disappointment, and hurt feelings following a transgression.

Research confirms that prosocial behaviors are associated with close parent–child relationships and with flexible parental childrearing practices (those that emphasize reasoning and empathy rather than power and punishment) (Baumrind, 1987; Cohen & Strayer, 1996; Eisenberg & Mussen, 1989; Schweder et al., 1987; Walker & Taylor, 1991). Walker and Taylor (1991) reported that parents adjust their level of reasoning when discussing moral issues with their children. Apparently, parents who are able to discuss real-life moral problems at a level that the children can understand have children who show the greatest moral growth. Other family interactional patterns that foster prosocial behavior in adolescents include being open to and respecting other people's ideas, beliefs, and feelings (Cooper, Grotevant, & Condon, 1983). *Thought Question: Does it follow from the social interactionist model that immoral parents inevitably have immoral children?*

## PROSOCIAL BEHAVIOR

Are adolescents more helpful than younger children? Not necessarily (Seppa, 1996a). Although college students and adults are more helpful than early adolescents, there are only slight differences in helping behavior between adolescents and younger children (Eisenberg, 1990). Perhaps this is because younger children are already quite helpful. Some studies (e.g., Bar-Tal & Nissim, 1984) report that younger adolescents are more likely than older adolescents to offer help, especially when they anticipate a reward. *Thought Question: Based on what we know about adolescent egocentrism, what risk would an adolescent be taking in offering help in an ambiguous situation?*

Understandably, young children believe that they are not capable of helping. But why would adolescents be reluctant to offer help? Reflecting egocentric reasoning, many report fearing embarrassment or disapproval for intervening in someone else's business ("Butt out"). When they do help, adolescents typically state motives that are more altruistic than those of younger children. According to one study, teenagers are more likely than younger children to donate money and exhibit appropriate comforting behavior, although they are not more likely to offer emotional support (Burleson, 1982). Eisenberg (1990) notes that there are few changes in most kinds of prosocial behavior during adolescence, although reasons for helping may change during the transition to adolescence. Depending on the specific circumstances, helping behavior in adolescents is motivated by feelings of sympathy and caring for someone in need, by understanding the moral implications of not helping, and, occasionally, by selfish (hedonistic) reasons (Blasi, 1980; Eisenberg, 1986; Eisenberg & Miller, 1987; Perry & McIntire, 1995).

Prosocial moral reasoning has been linked theoretically and empirically to prosocial behavior. "The higher levels of prosocial moral reasoning often reflect other-oriented concerns with the needs of distressed individuals and are consonant with helpfulness and generosity toward others. Moreover, cognitively sophisticated individuals may be more apt to understand and consider the relevant situational and personal factors necessary for engaging in helping behaviors" (Carlo et al., 1996, p. 235).

## The Role of Socialization

What can parents do to help children become less self-centered and more oriented toward helping others? Modeling altruistic and caring behaviors throughout childhood is very important. Children learn how and when to be helpful mainly by observing their parents offer help to them and to nonfamily members. Prosocial behavior is also encouraged by strategies that focus children's attention on other people's needs rather than their own ("Do you think your sister can use some help with her math homework?"). Parents who begin teaching and modeling how to be helpful when their children are very young probably will enjoy the fruits of their labor when their children come of age.

A mother and father brought their 17-year-old son into family counseling after the teenager was caught shoplifting. He was a bright boy and had not

Adolescents who have good relationships with their parents are likely to view them as role models regarding what is considered appropriate behavior.

previously been in serious trouble. When I asked him whether he thought it was all right to steal, he responded that he thought he could get away with it, and, anyway, the store owner would never miss the items he took. He spoke as though he believed that what he had done was no big deal. However, when I asked him how he would feel if his father were caught shoplifting, he said he would be shocked and embarrassed. Somehow, he applied quite different standards to his father's behavior and his own.

As children mature, their increasingly advanced reasoning abilities make it harder for them (but not impossible) to justify selfish actions (Eisenberg et al., 1995). Because violating rules and even laws is not uncommon during adolescence, parents should attempt to (1) monitor their children's activities, (2) help them to understand the reasons for their actions, and (3) help them to predict the consequences of their actions. In my experience, parents who ask questions ("How would you feel if you were caught?") are more successful at instilling values than parents who criticize, lecture, or threaten. Keep in mind that adolescents who enjoy close relationships with their parents usually are reluctant to disappoint their parents with displays of irresponsible behavior.

## MORAL EDUCATION

How do we educate children and adolescents to distinguish between right and wrong and to act accordingly? It is one thing to know the difference between right and wrong and another to be guided by moral values and principles. I may believe that cheating is wrong, but it certainly is tempting to get the answers to the math test from someone who took it this morning (see Spotlight • How Common Is Cheating on Tests?). Although advances in reasoning ability help children and adolescents understand the value of fairness and of expressing caring, socialization and education appear to be the keys to translating values and beliefs into actions (Nickerson, 1987).

Kohlberg (1985) emphasized the importance of providing children with social and cognitive stimulation to enhance what he considered to be the natural developmental process of moral reasoning. His premise was that children's moral reasoning advances when it is challenged by those who reason at higher levels. He believed that exposure to controversial issues and challenging established ideas generate cognitive tensions in children and adolescents that allow them to reorganize their thinking about moral issues. He suggested that role-playing moral arguments fosters moral reasoning.

Adolescents often discuss issues of fairness and sensitivity with each other in and out of school. In classrooms, discussions of moral issues among peers are more fruitful when they are "facilitated by humor, listening responses, praise, and encouragement to participate. These supportive interactions set a positive atmosphere for discussions, whereas hostility, sarcasm, and threats inhibit the meaningful exchange of ideas" (Walker & Taylor, 1991).

Discussions of moral issues may become heated, with disagreement occasionally leading to defensiveness or personal attacks. Young people should be encouraged to evaluate their reasoning when it is challenged or criticized by others rather than become defensive. "As children interact with others, they

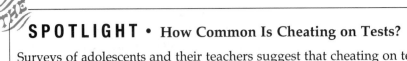

## SPOTLIGHT • How Common Is Cheating on Tests?

Surveys of adolescents and their teachers suggest that cheating on tests and plagiarizing term papers and homework are common occurrences during the adolescent years. A 1990 Harris Poll of over 5,000 high school students revealed that 65% of those surveyed admitted that they would cheat on an important exam. Schab (1991) surveyed 4,020 high school students in 1969, 1979, and 1989 about cheating. Most students reported believing that a majority of their fellow students did indeed cheat occasionally.

Over the 20-year period surveyed, there was an increase in the number of students who admitted cheating on tests and homework. Many acknowledged that their parents occasionally helped them break school rules. The most common reason given for cheating was "fear of failure," followed by "too lazy to study," "parents demanding good grades," "desire to keep up with others," and "it's easy to cheat."

Cheating occurred most often in math, science, history, English, and foreign language courses. The three most often mentioned penalties for cheating were failing the test, calling in parents to discuss punishment, and failing the course. Where did the students believe that children should be taught honest behavior? The majority said they believed that the home was the primary place. Church was mentioned as second most influential, and school was considered the least effective place.

A confidential survey administered at an English university asked students about 21 cheating behaviors (Newstead, Franklyn-Stokes, & Armstead, 1996). Reported cheating was common, with certain types of cheating occurring more frequently than others. Male, younger, less competent, and science students reported cheating more frequently than female, older, more competent, and non-science students. Students who felt that they were in school to learn rather than to obtain good grades were less likely to violate school policies. *Thought Question: Are situational factors, such as competition for grades, or personality factors, such as motivation to learn, more important determinants of cheating?*

learn how viewpoints differ and how to coordinate them in cooperative activities. As they discuss their problems and work out their differences, they develop their conceptions of what is fair and just" (Crain, 1992, p. 142). This is different from simply eliciting cognitive conflict, as Kohlberg recommended.

In the tradition of educator John Dewey, Kohlberg (1985) advocated that classrooms become participatory democracies, which he called **just communities**. Each member of the community, both teacher and student, has the right to express an opinion. In discussions with their peers, students can be encouraged to express and defend their varying points of view. With the teacher asking pointed questions and modeling mature moral reasoning, children's reasoning advances. Teachers must "understand, stimulate, and encourage, rather than directly teach, moral values" (Harding & Snyder, 1991, p. 323).

Harding and Snyder (1991) describe an approach to moral instruction based on teachers' use of films and literature that portray fictionalized and real-life moral dilemmas. Films such as *Serpico* and *Wall Street* and books like *The Adventures of Huckleberry Finn* are entertaining, have interesting characters, and depict problems to which most adolescents can relate. The researchers suggest that provocative films "can provide excellent stimulation for advanced moral reasoning when viewed and discussed by adolescents with the aid of adults who are able to advocate mature moral principles" (p. 326). They suggest that parents participate in the selection of films and that teachers ask open-ended questions without conveying that there is a right or wrong answer. Harding and Snyder caution that children are not likely to apply automatically what they learn from watching and discussing a film in class to real-life situations. Jurich and Collins (1996) describe a similar program that uses movie videos and small-group discussion led by adult facilitators to enhance adolescents' interest in and understanding of their world.

The success of such interventions in raising moral awareness depends on students' ability to comprehend and discuss moral dilemmas in class, analyze arguments, evaluate them critically, and then generalize their conclusions to real-life events outside the classroom. The ability to think for themselves makes them less susceptible to manipulation, peer pressure, and irrational authority (Nickerson, 1987).

Cognitive and emotional factors are important. A parental discussion style that supports the highest level of moral development in children requires eliciting children's opinions and asking them to clarify the issue and their position (Walker & Taylor, 1991). Cognitive ability and communication skills are important mediators of moral development. Adolescents' ability to listen, ask questions, and express themselves during discussion of moral issues is crucial (Santilli & Hudson, 1992) (Table 5-2).

## Table 5-2  Steps in Moral Training

**To help young people internalize prosocial standards of moral conduct and sharpen their moral reasoning:**

State moral rules clearly and explain their rationale.

Enforce moral rules consistently and fairly.

Ask empathy-inducing questions based on your or their actual experiences.

Help them understand how their behavior affects others.

Pose moral dilemmas based on real and hypothetical situations.

Role-play different moral positions.

Provide opportunities to engage in helpful behavior.

Model warmth, empathy, and prosocial behavior.

Practice the authoritative parenting style (see Chapter 7).

Model the highest level of moral reasoning the child can grasp.

Use group discussions and films to help children clarify their own values while actively considering other people's views.

## SUMMARY

**1.** Even when they know the difference between right and wrong, adolescents occasionally violate rules and social norms. Although their reasoning abilities are maturing, they don't automatically use their sophisticated reasoning skills to make decisions. Nevertheless, it does become more difficult for reasonable adolescents to justify selfish or antisocial behaviors.

**2.** Kohlberg maintained that as children mature, their moral judgments become more rationally defensible. He described three levels of moral development that correspond to advances in cognitive development. Kohlberg has been criticized for using moral dilemmas that are far removed from children's and adolescents' real-life concerns and for underestimating social and contextual influences on moral development.

**3.** Gilligan criticized Kohlberg's scales as being biased against females. She proposes that there are gender differences in moral reasoning styles. According to Gilligan, males focus on justice and fairness, whereas females emphasize feelings of connectedness and caring. However, neither style is used exclusively by males or females.

**4.** It is likely that cognitive maturation, socialization, and contextual factors all play an important role in the development of prosocial behavior during childhood and adolescence. Asking children their opinions and helping them clarify moral issues support a higher level of moral development. Parental modeling of altruistic and caring behaviors is especially powerful. Adolescents should be encouraged to evaluate their reasoning when it is challenged by others and to try to entertain several different viewpoints.

## GLOSSARY

**Premoral stage of moral development** In Piaget's model, children younger than 4 years of age showing no sense of feeling obligated to obey rules

**Heteronomous stage of moral development** In Piaget's model, children aged 4 to 8 years obeying rules and submitting to authority

**Moral realism** When children take rules and regulations at face value, viewing them as fixed and absolute

**Autonomous stage of moral development** In Piaget's model, children aged 8 to 12 years showing greater flexibility in their reasoning than younger children

**Moral relativism** The shift in preadolescents' moral reasoning from blind obedience to considerations of people's motives and intentions

**Preconventional morality** In Kohlberg's model, the stage of moral development when children do not yet see themselves as part of society's rule-making processes

**Conventional morality** In Kohlberg's model, the stage of moral development when adolescents stress the importance of living up to other people's expectations and being helpful

**Postconventional morality** In Kohlberg's model, the stage of moral reasoning when behavior is guided by higher principles of human conduct rather than by immediate personal or social considerations

**Styles of moral reasoning** Carol Gilligan's contention that males tend to view moral dilemmas mainly in terms of justice and fairness, whereas females are more concerned about maintaining friendships and not hurting others.

**Network of relationships** Refers to Gilligan's idea that females tend to view themselves as embedded in a social network

**Just community** A classroom environment in which all people have the right to express their point of view

# THOUGHT QUESTIONS

**1.** Who should have primary responsibility for teaching children values?

**2.** If there are gender differences in moral reasoning, how can we understand their origin?

**3.** Are adolescents or adults more prone to rule-breaking behavior?

**4.** Why do people tend to evaluate their own behaviors more leniently (e.g., invoke rationalizations or excuses) than other people's behavior?

**5.** If you were a teacher and discovered that one of your students cheated on a test, how would you handle the transgression? Would you punish or use some other means to teach the student a lesson?

# SELF-TEST

1. Adolescents are less likely to offer help when
   a. they don't expect a reward
   b. they feel self-conscious about "intruding"
   c. they believe that they are not capable of helping
   d. all of the above

2. Adolescent helping behavior is facilitated by
   a. feelings of sympathy
   b. understanding the moral implications of not helping
   c. selfish motivation
   d. all of the above

3. Parents encourage prosocial behavior mainly by
   a. rewarding it
   b. modeling it
   c. lecturing about it
   d. punishing selfish behavior

4. Taking other people's motives and intentions into account during moral reasoning is called
   a. moral realism
   b. moral relativism
   c. empathy
   d. metacognition

5. Piaget and Kohlberg related advances in moral reasoning mainly to
   a. family influences
   b. cognitive growth
   c. emotional development
   d. education

6. Children at Kohlberg's Level I stage of moral reasoning judge events as good or bad mainly on the basis of
   a. rewards and punishments
   b. intuitive beliefs
   c. what authorities tell them about good and bad
   d. all of the above

**7.** People at Kohlberg's Level II stage of moral reasoning judge events as right or wrong mainly on the basis of

   **a.** respect for rules

   **b.** rewards and punishment

   **c.** intuition

   **d.** abstract moral principles

**8.** People at Kohlberg's Level III stage of moral reasoning judge events as right or wrong mainly on the basis of

   **a.** subjective evaluations

   **b.** self-interest

   **c.** legal authority

   **d.** universal principles of conduct

**9.** Kohlberg's moral dilemmas have been criticized for being

   **a.** unrealistic

   **b.** culturally biased

   **c.** gender biased

   **d.** all of the above

**10.** According to Gilligan,

   **a.** there are minimal gender differences in styles of reasoning

   **b.** males usually achieve a higher level of moral reasoning

   **c.** males usually view morality in terms of justice and fairness

   **d.** males are more concerned than females about approval

**11.** Social interactional theory emphasizes the role of _____ in moral reasoning

   **a.** children's everyday experiences

   **b.** cognitive growth

   **c.** rewards and punishments

   **d.** discussion groups

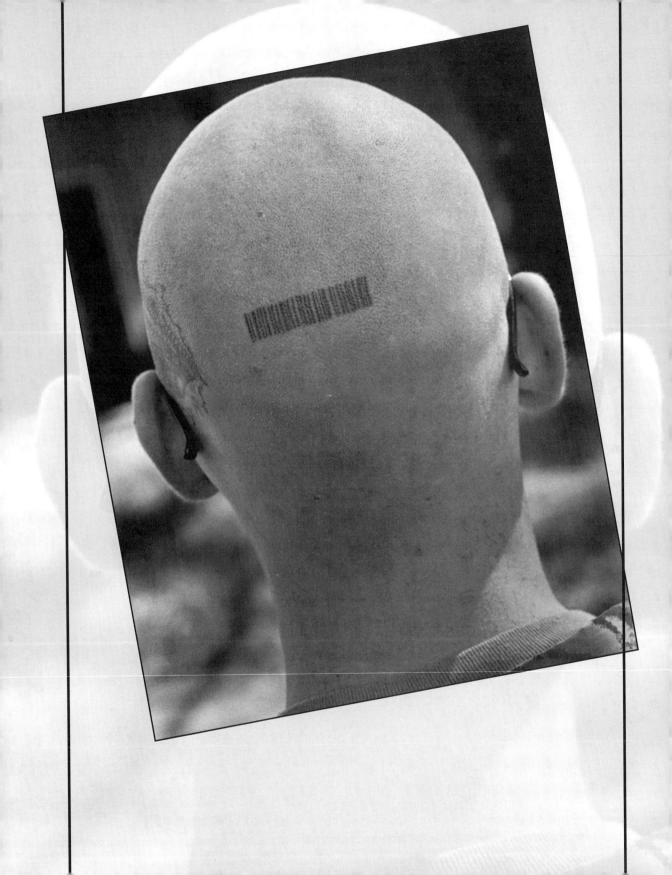

# SIX

# ADOLESCENT IDENTITY, SELF-CONCEPT, AND SELF-ESTEEM

◆

## Preview Questions

**1.** Why did Erik Erikson consider the key challenge facing adolescents to be creating an adult identity?

**2.** Of what use is a self-concept?

**3.** How do adolescents go about creating an adult self-concept?

**4.** What is meant by different types of selves?

**5.** Why are adolescents so self-conscious?

**6.** Why are adolescents more likely than adults to compare themselves to their peers?

**7.** How does self-esteem change over the course of adolescence?

**8.** How can parents promote self-esteem in their children?

**9.** What can parents and teachers do to promote self-esteem in ethnic minority adolescents?

◆

## Disclosures

I'm 5 feet 8 inches and 150 pounds. I have brown hair. I'm Irish, Swedish, English, Polish, and German. I'm a very outgoing person. I like children. I'm usually very hyper. I'm your average typical teen. I'm not anything spectacular. I like being with my friends. I like physical activity: hiking, boating, climbing, dancing. I like the color of my eyes, my personality. I'm pretty happy with myself. I'm all right.

*(17-year-old female)*

They told me to tell you that they want me to be my own person. My mother *told* me to tell you that. I do want to be my own person, but it's like you're interviewing me about who I am and she's telling me what to say—that's not my own person, is it? *(8th-grade girl interviewed by Orenstein, 1994, p. 6)*

Who am I? My name is Joseph Bruchac. The given name is that of a Christian saint—in the best Catholic tradition. The surname is from my father's people. It was shortened from Bruchacek—"big belly" in Slovak. Yet my identity has been affected less by middle European ancestry and Christian teachings (good as they are in their seldom-seen practices) than by that small part of my blood which is American Indian and which comes to me from a grandfather who raised me and a mother who was almost a stranger to me. I have other names, as well. One of those names is Quiet Bear. *(Bruchac, 1993, p. 238)*

# Contents

**W**hat am I like as a person? Complicated! I'm sensitive, friendly, outgoing, popular, and tolerant, though I can also be shy, self-conscious, and even obnoxious. Obnoxious! I'd *like* to be friendly and tolerant all of the time. That's the kind of person I *want* to be, and I'm disappointed when I'm not. I'm responsible, even studious every now and then, but on the other hand I'm a goof-off too, because if you're too studious you won't be popular. I don't usually do that well at school. I'm a pretty cheerful person, especially with my friends, where I can even get rowdy. At home I'm more likely to be anxious around my parents. They expect me to get all A's. It's not fair! . . . I really don't understand how I can switch so fast. I mean, how can I be cheerful one minute, anxious the next, and then be sarcastic? Which one is the *real* me?

*(Composite self-description of a 15-year-old girl, from Harter, 1990a)*

"Which one is the *real* me?" she asks. Good question. In this composite self-description of a real teenager we will call Lydia, we hear sincerity, disappointment, frustration, and confusion. Compared to members of other age groups, adolescents are overly sensitive about their appearance and behavior. They give a lot of thought to who they think they are, who they want to be, and how others judge them.

In Chapter 4 we learned that Piaget and Elkind linked "distortions" in how adolescents view themselves to the emergence of abstract and conceptual reasoning. For example, egocentric thinking leads adolescents to place themselves at the center of other people's attention. Not only does this increase their sense of importance and uniqueness, it also heightens their self-awareness and, occasionally, their discomfort. Adolescent egocentrism, according to Piaget and Elkind, underlies several of the changes we observe in teenagers: insensitive behavior, idealistic thinking, feelings of invulnerability, and desire for privacy (Elkind, 1967; O'Connor & Nikolic, 1990).

Parents who do not understand adolescents' preoccupation with status and peer approval are likely to be puzzled or put off by their children's behavior, language, and tastes in friends, music, and fashion. A psychologist I know well (okay, it's me) was startled one day when his younger son (then 12) came home with an almost shaved head. My son's friend generously had offered to give him a fashionable haircut at no cost. What were they thinking? Such behavior makes sense to adults only when we view adolescence as a time of exploration and reinvention. The process of becoming an adult requires extensive experimentation with different ways of appearing, sounding, and acting. Viewing my son's questionable judgment as a preadolescent experiment with his "look" softened the blow (a little).

Many parents have mixed feelings when their children begin to experiment with makeup, earrings, and hairstyles or express unconventional political opinions and unorthodox spiritual beliefs. Although young people vociferously defend their evolving personal styles, they are not yet terribly confident about them. Note Lydia's attempt to consolidate what would seem to be a variety of sometimes contradictory selves into one coherent self-concept (Harter, 1990b).

Is it a contradiction to want to distance oneself from one's family and still desire to be accepted as a family member? How does one remain true to oneself while satisfying the expectations of parents and friends? Whether we become our own person or the creation of others depends partly on our self-confidence and partly on the opportunities we have to explore alternative roles and lifestyles. As we shall see, some adolescents have more opportunities to explore and more resources available to them than others. Fortunately, most adolescents eventually succeed in defining themselves in their own terms, albeit with some compromise along the way.

A few succumb to powerful social pressure to be the way others want them to be. One 15-year-old girl put it this way: "I myself can't say no to peer pressure. That's bad. You should be able to say no. I give in to peer pressure." As with Lydia, it's almost as if we're listening to two different people, the actor and the observer. Intense conflict or confusion about what kind of person to be can set the stage for a host of adjustment problems, including eating disorders, depression, and antisocial behavior (Damon & Hart, 1988).

In this chapter we consider several related constructs that operate at the core of adolescent personality: personal identity, self-awareness, self-evaluation, self-concept, and self-esteem. We are particularly interested in how young people view themselves as individuals in society, how they feel about themselves, and how eventually, most come to appreciate the richness and complexity of their increasingly adult-like personalities. Although we pay considerable attention to gender and ethnic variation in identity formation, please keep in mind that there is substantial variation *within* each gender, ethnic group, and culture regarding identity formation and self-esteem. We begin our examination of these topics by considering Erik Erikson's views regarding how adolescents formulate the self-definition known as *personal identity*.

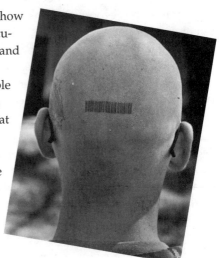

## ERIK ERIKSON'S MODEL OF IDENTITY ACHIEVEMENT

*Study Question: Who are you?*

Erik Erikson (1950, 1960, 1968) proposed that during each stage of life we face distinctive developmental tasks or challenges. He described eight life stages, each defined in terms of a developmental task that he deemed crucial for that period. Erikson proposed that, because of the almost endless opportunities to explore different ways of being, adolescence is the optimal time for deconstructing one's childhood identity and reconstructing a viable adult identity.

According to Erikson, identity resolution during adolescence is most likely to be achieved by those who have successfully negotiated four earlier psychosocial stages. Erikson's **epigenetic principle** states that every stage in development contributes something to future stages and reframes all the earlier ones, a sentiment captured by the saying, "The child is the father to the man."

**Ego identity**, as defined by Erikson (1968), refers to that aspect of who we are that we perceive as having continuity over time (Erikson, 1963). It enables me, for example, to look at pictures of myself as a cute and adorable child and sigh, "That's me" and to imagine my future self as retired or even (gasp) dead and buried. Although I expand daily, I feel that I am basically the same person I was yesterday, last year, even 50 years ago. Thus, who I am has continuity over time and distinguishes me from everyone else. In Erikson's words, "The wholeness to be achieved [during adolescence] I have called a sense of inner identity. The young person, in order to experience wholeness, must feel a progressive continuity between that which he has come to be during the long years of childhood and that which he promises to become in the anticipated future; between that which he conceives himself to be and that which he perceives others to see in him and to expect of him" (Erikson, 1968, p. 87). *Thought Question: Having difficulty conceptualizing one's continuity over time has been linked to adolescent suicide. Why might this be so?*

## Table 6-1 Components of Personal Identity

**Ego identity:** that aspect of who we are that has continuity over time

**Personal dimension of identity:** personal history, abilities, ideology (beliefs about religion, politics, and philosophy), values, perceived strengths and weaknesses, personal goals, vocational aspirations, sexuality, nationality, gender, and ethnicity

**Social dimension of identity:** social roles, relationships, perceived similarities to and differences from others

The **personal dimension of identity**, according to Erikson, includes one's ideology (beliefs about religion, politics, and money, for example), vocational aspirations, sexuality, nationality, gender, and ethnicity. The **social dimension of identity** includes the many roles people play in life, such as student, parent, citizen, gang member, pet owner, consumer, and employee. Joining a church choir, being captain of the girl's tennis team, or achieving Eagle Scout rank in the Boy Scouts each adds a new dimension to how we think of ourselves. The more one values a new role, the more it becomes part of one's identity. Many diverse roles eventually are integrated into a uniquely self-defined person (Archer, 1989a).

Our identity allows us to distinguish between who we are (including all of the above) and who we aren't (possible beliefs, roles, and ways of being we reject). Identity also produces "a sense of psychosocial well-being . . . a feeling of being at home in one's body, a sense of 'knowing where one is going'" (Erikson, 1980, p. 127). Not all aspects of identity are chosen. Some, such as being adopted, Latino, or female, are *assigned* (Grotevant, 1992) (Table 6-1).

As is the case for all eight psychosocial stages described by Erikson, during adolescence there is the possibility of a positive, negative, or mixed resolution. Most adolescents eventually achieve a realistic adult personal identity (positive outcome). Some enter adulthood uncertain about their place in the world (a negative outcome known as **identity confusion**). Some adolescents experience a combination of personal identity and identity confusion (a mixed outcome). Someone who is committed to an occupation but confused about a romantic relationship also exemplifies a mixed outcome.

James Marcia (1994), whose clarification and elaboration of Erikson's model is discussed in the next section, maintains that individuals construct their own particular form of resolution for each stage, incorporating both positive and negative aspects of the stage (Table 6-2).

## Table 6-2 Possible Outcomes in Erikson's Fifth Stage

**Identity:** Fully functioning, unique adult personal identity with a meaningful role in life (positive outcome)

**Identity confusion:** Confusion and aimlessness regarding one's future roles; uncertainty about one's place in the world

**Mixed outcome:** Having direction in some life domains (e.g., vocation) but not in others (e.g., relationships)

Achieving a meaningful adult identity requires exploring and experimenting with a wide variety of roles (e.g., babysitter, Girl Scout, employee, athlete), comparing oneself to others, and identifying with significant people in one's social environment. What role do parents play in adolescent identity formation? "The strengths a young person finds in adults at this time—their willingness to let him experiment, their eagerness to confirm him at his best, their consistency in correcting his excesses, and the guidance they give him—will codetermine whether or not he eventually makes order out of necessary inner confusion and applies himself to the correction of disordered conditions. He needs freedom to choose, but not so much freedom that he cannot, in fact, make a choice" (Erikson, 1960, p. 49).

At least until the late high school years, young people typically lack the experience, perspective, and motivation needed to commit to long-term life goals, such as employment and marriage. Their more immediate concerns are school, social life, and having fun. Some adolescents commit to a career or life goal prematurely (without sufficient exploration), perhaps in response to parental or peer influence.

Erikson coined the term **identity crisis** to refer to adolescents' serious questioning of their essential personal characteristics, their view of themselves, their concern about how others view them, and their doubts about the meaning and purpose of their existence (Erikson, 1960). A 20-year-old female illustrates this concept. "I'm a very confused person, lazy, unhappy, unable to make decisions. Always depending on others. I was a late maturer. I thought I was ugly. Made fun of by the boys. Insecure. I'm not able to deal with my feelings." Erikson maintained that an individual's success with adult developmental tasks involving marriage and career depends on whether and how such an identity crisis is resolved. *Thought Question: Does the girl quoted above appear to be in crisis, or is that term overly dramatic?*

Resolution of the identity crisis is most likely when the three dimensions of identity cited above (ego, personal, social) merge, that is, when a young person's capabilities and interests match the opportunities for expression available in his or her social environment (Markstrom-Adams, 1992). One of the unfortunate features of adolescence in Western cultures is that relatively few young people are given meaningful opportunities to be in charge of a worthwhile project or community service. This limits their ability to develop the responsibility and competence necessary for taking on demanding adult roles. On the other hand, modern society does provide young people with a variety of protective environments (e.g., family home, college campus) for exploring different roles and different arenas in which to clarify their vocational aspirations (Adamson & Lyxell, 1996; Waterman, 1985). Minority children and adolescents generally have fewer opportunities to explore and excel (Spencer & Markstrom-Adams, 1990).

Grotevant and his colleagues (Grotevant, Bosma, De Levita, & Graafsma, 1994) note that there is a fundamental ambiguity in the meaning of *personal identity*. Sometimes the term refers to the essence of one's individuality (my continuing sense of self); at other times it refers to the means by which an individual can be identified by others (the roles that one takes on). Erikson himself used the term in different ways on different occasions, but all of his meanings imply mutual regulation between the individual and society (Graafsma, 1994b).

## MARCIA'S ELABORATION

*Study Question: What role does exploration of alternatives play in identity formation?*

Erikson's theoretical model of identity achievement has been clarified and empirically tested by James Marcia (1966, 1967, 1980, 1994) and others. Marcia's identity status model has dominated the field over the past two decades (Berzonsky, 1992). He developed an extensive interview protocol and a rating manual for studying the different ways that adolescents construct a personal identity. "The interviewer asks individuals about decisions that they may or may not have made, the process by which those decisions were arrived at, and the extent to which they are committed to . . . those decisions. The topics the interview covers vary from culture to culture and from time to time" (Marcia, 1994, p. 72). Interviews contain questions about vocational choice, ideology, religious and political beliefs, and interpersonal values, including sex role attitudes and sexuality.

On the basis of such interviews, Marcia identified four ways (identity statuses) in which late adolescents (approximately 18–22 years of age) may be expected to resolve the identity–identity confusion conflict. The four identity statuses vary according to two dimensions: exploration of and commitment to adult roles.

Generally speaking, the older an adolescent, the more exploration and the greater the commitment we usually observe (Markstrom-Adams & Adams, 1995). **Exploration** refers to a process of active questioning of, and searching for, adult roles and values in the various domains of adolescent life cited above. **Commitment** refers to firm decisions regarding the above domains ("I am going to be a musician") and includes specific strategies for achieving personal goals and a desired life path. In combination, the two dimensions of exploration and commitment yield four potential identity statuses (Table 6-3).

**Table 6-3  Marcia's Four Identity Statuses**

|  | Commitment | |
|---|---|---|
|  | Present | Absent |
| **Exploration** Present | Identity achievement | Moratorium |
| Absent | Identity foreclosure | Identity diffusion |

With each of the four identity status definitions below, we'll include a typical answer to the following question in the occupational area of Marcia's interview: "How willing do you think you'd be to give up going into [specified field of study] if something better came along?" (from Marcia, 1966).

**1. Identity diffusion.** Adolescents in identity diffusion status are not actively exploring or committing to adult roles and values. They may or may not have engaged in exploration in the past, but if so, unsuccessfully. Typical answer to the occupation question: "Oh sure. If something better came along, I'd change just like that." Adolescents in this identity status have no internally consistent set of values and goals and are not searching for any. People in identity diffusion may appear to have a carefree lifestyle or may admit to being unfulfilled (Patterson, Sochting, & Marcia, 1992).

The prototypical high school underachiever who is uninterested in school and who has limited prospects elsewhere provides an example of identity diffusion. Identity diffusion also is seen in the alienation of juvenile offenders and drug abusers. Many disaffected adolescents have strained relationships with their parents (Adams, Dyk, & Bennion, 1987).

**2. Identity foreclosure.** Adolescents in identity foreclosure have committed to specific goals, values, roles, and beliefs but without having first thought through or investigated realistic alternatives. Their commitment is sincere but not the result of meaningful exploration. Rather, they are accepting the guid-

Identity diffusion, or lack of direction in one's life, can be seen in the alienation of juvenile offenders and drug abusers.

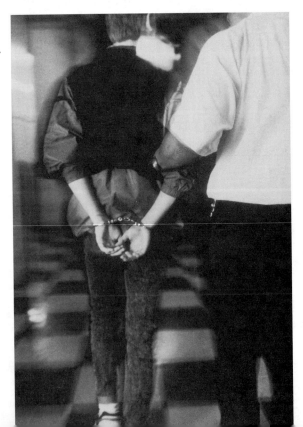

ance of others or submitting to social pressures, usually from parents or other authority figures. Typical answer to the occupation question: "Not very willing. It's what I've always wanted to do. The folks are happy with it, and so am I."

A student in my graduate adolescent psychology course reported that he comes from a long line of police officers. His grandfather and father were policemen, and he and his brother were expected to continue in that tradition. Although this might be a reasonable choice of career for them, we can't help but wonder how much encouragement they had to consider other alternatives. Exploration of roles remains a possibility following premature foreclosure. Adolescents in foreclosure status typically have close relationships with their parents (Adams et al., 1987).

**3. Moratorium.** Adolescents in moratorium status are considering different points of view and experimenting with various adult roles but have not yet made final commitments. College students who take courses in several different disciplines before deciding on a major exemplify moratorium status. Adolescents in moratorium are busy exploring alternatives, but not without some anxiety. Their goal is to narrow their options so that they can commit to occupational, interpersonal, and ideological goals (Patterson et al., 1992). Moratorium status is associated with positive parent-adolescent relationships (Adams et al., 1987). Typical answer to the occupation question: "I guess if I knew for sure I could answer that better. It would have to be something in the general area—something related."

**4. Identity achievement.** Individuals in identity achievement status already have experienced identity diffusion. After investigating a variety of adult roles, they have committed to a life plan. Typical answer to the occupation question: "Well, I might, but I doubt it. I can't see what 'something better' would be for me." The commitment usually is a compromise between personal needs (e.g., to enjoy one's job) and social demands (e.g., to earn a living). For middle-class adolescents, identity achievement usually occurs during the later college years. Vocational commitment occurs when an academic major is declared, although decisions can always be modified. Interpersonal goals such as marriage are set during this period, and ideological (political, religious) opinions intensify. Although it is a relief to commit to an occupational goal and a lifestyle, often there is lingering doubt about whether one has chosen wisely ("Do I really want to spend the rest of my life cleaning people's teeth"?) Some in this status "regress" into periods of crisis and confusion (Marcia, 1976). Adolescents in identity achievement status usually have good relationships with their parents (Adams et al., 1987).

These identity statuses are not necessarily consistent across different domains of an adolescent's life. For example, an adolescent may be in diffusion regarding career goals, in foreclosure regarding sexuality, and in identity achieved regarding family roles. At a later time, after considerable exploration and reassessment, the individual might show a different combination of statuses for these domains (Archer, 1989a).

Most adolescents experience more than one of these statuses. From middle school through the college years, more adolescents attain the status of identity achievement and fewer remain in the identity diffusion stage, particularly for vocational choice (Waterman, 1985).

Adolescents differ in the strength of their investment in any particular domain of identity (Bosma, 1992; Waterman, 1992). Some are invested mainly in career planning, others in sports, music, relationships, or academics. They also differ in the extent to which their chosen identity (e.g., athlete) dominates their lifestyle. Waterman worries that many adolescents who commit to a life path have unrealistic expectations or goals. Pressured by practical or social considerations, they are not too comfortable with their choices. Marcia (1994) urges educational institutions to refrain from requiring hasty decisions from students regarding declaring a major area of study. Rather, high schools and colleges should support occupational and ideological experimentation (e.g., changing majors when appropriate, double majors, minors) and then validate commitment when it emerges.

Other investigators (e.g., Flum, 1994; Valde, 1996) have proposed additional identity statuses, suggesting that there are many possible paths to identity achievement. Newer models of identity formation take into account the diverse personal qualities and abilities of adolescents and the various social contexts and circumstances that affect their opportunities to explore their options (Grotevant, 1987, 1992; Josselson, 1987) (Figure 6-1).

## Criticisms

Erikson and Marcia have been criticized for slanting their theories toward high school and college males in the United States. The contextual model described in Chapter 2 implies that identity formation will vary according to age, gender, ethnic group, and culture, *with considerable variation within each demographic category*. Côté (1996) notes that "it is possible that race is more important for certain dimensions of identity formation than gender, such that depending on their class and age, women of a given race may subjectively experience more in common with men of their own race than with women of another race as they form their sense of identity" (p. 151).

Some theorists (Archer, 1992; Bosma, 1992) criticize Marcia for trying to squeeze all adolescents, regardless of their personal qualities or particular life circumstances, into one of his four identity categories. Further, large numbers

**FIGURE 6-1 Factors influencing opportunities to explore. (Adapted from Grotevant, 1987, 1992)**

of youth do not conform to the developmental pathways that Marcia describes. For example, only between 30% and 40% of college seniors can be classified in the identity achievement category. Do Marcia's status categories miss the boat regarding how youth in the United States actually proceed to identity achievement (Côté, 1996)?

Bosma (1992) contends that by emphasizing individual differences in identity achievement, Erikson and Marcia overlooked something more interesting—the pattern of developmental change that takes an individual adolescent from identity diffusion through identity achievement. This is a familiar issue in developmental psychology: should we focus on individual differences in *outcomes* or on *developmental processes*, "internal and external factors that enhance or restrict development" (Goossens & Phinney, 1996, p. 494)? These include individual personality variables, the exploration of alternatives, and the commitment to choices in different domains of life (Kroger & Green, 1996; Nurmi, Poole, & Kalakoski, 1996).

Archer (1992) maintains that each adolescent constructs an adult identity in his or her own way. She proposes that the content of Marcia's interviews with adolescents be examined for "patterns in the narratives that might enrich our understanding of the content that might coincide with the identity statuses" (pp. 33–34). Archer is suggesting that there is a "story" behind each adolescent's identity status, and that the story is more interesting and informative than the status category itself. McAdams (1987, 1989) maintains that the stories we create to lend coherence to our lives are really what is meant by *identity*.

The narrative approach to the study of identity and self has been adopted by Ruthellen Josselson (1987, 1994) and others (Neisser & Fivush, 1994). Josselson's interviews with female adolescents go considerably beyond the three identity domains that Erikson and Marcia considered essential—vocation, ideology, and family. Interviews conducted by Josselson, Carol Gilligan, and others explore identity domains such as religious beliefs, politics, sexuality, values, dating, friendship, ethnicity, parenting, and others. Their studies confirm that there are identifiable patterns of identity formation that go beyond simple categorization.

Another criticism of both Erikson's and Marcia's models is that they portray identity as "an autonomous, bounded, independent entity created by the individual" (Oyserman, Gant, & Ager, 1995, p. 1217). According to Oyserman and her colleagues, this view of identity formation ("Who am I?) virtually ignores the social context in which identities are constructed. These investigators maintain that identities are negotiated within the framework of one's personal relationships and interpersonal encounters. In effect, we define ourselves partly in relation to others and partly in the context of the wider society and culture. The next two sections elaborate this point.

## BALANCING IDENTITY AND RELATIONSHIPS

Erikson (1968) did not ignore the role that parents and peers play in adolescent identity formation, but he certainly did not emphasize social context to the extent that current theorists do. Carol Gilligan (1982, 1988), Ruthellen Josselson (1994), Sally Archer (1992), and others maintain that Erikson's model of personal identity, stressing separation and individuation, lends itself more to males than to females. Indeed, almost all of the original research on which the identity model is based involved white male university students.

The traditional model's premise is that adolescents must **individuate** (see themselves as unique and separate but not alienated from others) in order to establish their identity and gain the maturity they need to take on adult roles and relationships (Mazor, Shamir, & Ben-Moshe, 1990; McCurdy & Scherman, 1996). As previously discussed, Erikson viewed adolescent identity mainly in terms of individuation, vocational aspirations, and ideological commitments. Feminist theorists do not entirely disagree. "Adolescents, to be sure, do undergo a separation-individuation process on the road to identity. But at the same time, they are not becoming 'lone selves' needing no one, standing to face the forces of life alone. Rather, they are editing and modifying, enriching and extending their connections to others, becoming more fully themselves in relation. . . . [W]omen's sense of self is organized around the ability to make and maintain relationships" (Josselson, 1994, p. 83).

Archer (1992) maintains that Erikson's view of identity achievement during adolescence is overly narrow and negative—"rugged individualism, isolation, separateness, a turning away from community, selfishness, maleness" (p. 27). She invokes a common feminist criticism of Erikson's work: "that it portrays a primarily Eurocentric male model of normality" (p. 29).

Allowing that the traditional model is helpful in understanding male identity formation, Gilligan (1982), Josselson (1987, 1988, 1994), and others question its relevance to female identity development. For male and female adolescents, they claim, identity achievement requires an interplay between separateness and connectedness, that is, meeting one's own needs while satisfying those of the people we care about (Gilligan & Wiggins, 1987; Grotevant, 1992; Mellor, 1989; Perosa, Perosa, & Tam, 1996). An example of this is the way working parents try to balance their careers and family life with their personal needs.

Gilligan hypothesizes that individuation and separation are especially conflictual for girls because girls are more invested than boys in their relationship with their mothers. How do you separate from your mother while remaining emotionally in touch with her? Similar issues arise in girls' relationships with their age-mates, especially boyfriends. Many young girls learn to suppress their beliefs and opinions. Instead of individuating, they seek identity through their relationships, reflected in the tradition of married women taking on their husband's last names.

Archer (1992) maintains that identity theorists have created a false dichotomy—the belief that male identity is based on individualism and separateness and that female identity is based on connecting and caring. (A slightly different version of this dichotomy is that male adolescents are busy achieving an identity, while females are preoccupied with relationships and intimacy.)

For adolescents of both genders, establishing a stable identity usually precedes or accompanies exploration of intimate relationships (Dyk & Adams, 1990). Adolescents are addressing both tasks (identity and intimacy) simulta-

Adolescent girls face the daunting task of separating from their mothers while remaining emotionally close to them.

neously but perhaps with somewhat different priorities (Archer, 1992). This formulation also sheds light on the observation that sons and daughters seek, or at least tolerate, more closeness with parents as they approach adulthood (Weinmann & Newcombe, 1990). Gradually, they renegotiate their psychological and physical ties to their families while remaining emotionally connected to them. This, in turn, enables them to have relationships with parents that are equitable and satisfying (Crespi & Sabatelli, 1993, 1997). *Thought Question: How does being in a romantic peer relationship help adolescents balance individuality with connectedness?*

## OTHER CONTEXTUAL INFLUENCES ON IDENTITY DEVELOPMENT

Given the importance of the interactional-contextual model in understanding development (discussed in Chapter 2), it is surprising that relatively little research attention has been paid to social and other contextual factors in adolescent identity development (Phinney & Goossens, 1996). Cultural differences in identity formation also remain largely unexplored (Goossens & Phinney, 1996). Erikson (1968) acknowledged the mutual influence between individuals and their social context in identity formation. In this vein, Baumeister and Muraven (1996) note that society plays "an important causal role in creating and shaping identity. Then again, it is also clear that identities are not merely created by society and foisted willy-nilly on helpless, hapless individuals. People clearly do exert considerable choice and influence on their identities" (p. 405).

Baumeister and Muraven (1996) portray identity as an adaptation to one's social and cultural context. Individuals choose and modify their identities on the basis of what will enable them to function best in their particular social world. Adolescent identity formation thus can be understood only in the context of (1) historical changes in the roles that adolescents play in society (discussed in Chapter 1); (2) changes in cultural values and beliefs, for example, how the absence of strong values in modern life has led to the elevation of self-interest as a major value orientation; and (3) personal issues in relationships, for example, the conflict between separation from one's family and remaining emotionally connected to them (Baumeister & Muraven, 1996; Goossens & Phinney, 1996).

Investigators have begun to identify the processes that link identity formation to its sociocultural setting (Goossens & Phinney, 1996). Shorter-Gooden and Washington (1996), for example, discuss the challenges facing African-American female adolescents growing up in the United States, especially integrating their ethnicity with their femaleness. The investigators maintain that African-American women struggle to develop a healthy identity in a society that devalues both blacks and women. African-American female adolescents "are often ignored or invisible; both their strengths and their problems receive little attention" (p. 466).

Shorter-Gooden and Washington, using a semistructured interview, questioned female African-American community college students about various identity domains, including race, gender, sexual orientation, relationships, beliefs, and career. Racial identification was the most salient domain as a source of identity. Facing sexism and racism contributed to these women's development of personal strength and was a key factor in their self-definition and survival (Goossens & Phinney, 1996). (We will return to the topic of ethnic identity later in this chapter.)

## SELF-CONCEPT AND TYPES OF SELVES: WHICH ONE IS THE REAL ME?

Erikson (1968) claimed that self-concept and self-esteem exist before personal identity forms and eventually become part of it. According to James Marcia (1994), the self is the "deepest" structure in personality, deeper than identity. "A solid sense of self is a necessary, but not sufficient, condition for an identity" (p. 72). Gecas and Burke (1995) equate self with self-awareness. Clearly, concepts such as identity and self need to be "more sharply defined and theoretically better situated" (Graafsma, 1994a, p. 24).

Presumably, our sense of feeling separate from others and being in relationship with others arises very early in life and eventually merges with our identity—our sense of having continuity over time. The functions of self include lending meaning and organization to one's experiences and motivating action by providing standards, incentives, strategies, and scripts for behavior (Oyserman et al., 1995). In contrast to the concept of identity (the sense of who I am

over time), the concept of self often is used synonymously with the concept of personality, which includes all observable personal traits and behaviors that distinguish one from others (Grotevant et al., 1994).

The simplest way of assessing someone's self-concept is to ask "Who are you?" or to say "Tell me about yourself" and then classify the response using a content coding system (Damon & Hart, 1988). Ruthellen Josselson (1994) began her interviews with the question "If there was someone who you wanted to really know you, what sorts of things would you tell them about yourself?" (p. 81). Lydia's response to such a question began this chapter. Based on her response, we would try to make predictions about her behavior and personality. Although theorists originally thought of self-concept as a single entity, it is more helpful to view a self-concept such as Lydia's as multidimensional (Marsh, 1989).

Children usually have a firm sense of who they are, partly based on the feedback they receive from their parents and other caregivers. In other words, children see themselves mainly through adults' eyes. Self-concept begins to transform during the early adolescent years as abstract reasoning skills and a desire for autonomy begin to emerge. "Adolescents begin to see through their idealized images of their parents, upon whom their own identity has been anchored, and perceive them more accurately and critically" (Larson, 1995, p. 537).

Psychologists consider a self-concept to be healthy if it is realistic, self-generated, and integrated across the many roles that most adults take on (Harter, 1990a). An analogy for a healthy self-concept would be an outfit or uniform that is specifically designed for the wearer rather than one taken off the bargain rack. Compared to adolescents of previous centuries, who had relatively few "uniforms" to try on, it is more difficult for modern adolescents to create an identity that is a good fit (realistic and comfortable) (Baumeister & Tice, 1986). Because it is hard for us to know whether our self-conceptions are realistic ("Am I being a good friend?"), we depend on feedback from others to make adjustments as necessary. In this way, we attempt to create adult selves that are realistic *and* comfortable (Curry, Trew, Turner, & Hunter, 1994).

Because adolescents report varied, opposing, and even contradictory attributes in themselves, some theorists have found it useful to distinguish among a variety of different selves: the true (or private) self, the ideal (or desired) self, the possible (or future) self, the false (or presented) self, and the public self (Harter, Marold, Whitesell, & Cobbs, 1996; Hooker, Fiese, Jenkins, Morfei, & Schwagler, 1996; Oyserman et al., 1995). We can also speak of different role-related selves—for example, a sexual self, a social self, an academic self, and a family self (Shavelson, Hubner, & Stanton 1976; Van Boxtel & Monks, 1992). Such constructs are semantic creations invoked by theorists to explain interpersonal and prosocial behavior (Hart & Fegley, 1995).

Our **true** (private, actual) **self**, equivalent to the **self-concept**, is who we believe we are "deep down inside" (reread Lydia's self-statement at the beginning of this chapter). Adolescents describe their true selves as "the real me inside," "my true feelings," and "what I really think and feel" (Harter et al., 1996). As we do not often reveal this part of our self to others, it is sometimes called the *private self*.

The **false self** is who we want people to think we are, perhaps to impress or please them, as on a college interview or first date. Adolescents report that sometimes they feel pressured to act in ways that do not reflect their true selves. In her self-statement, Lydia claims that "if you're too studious you won't be popular." Many young people report being afraid to reveal their actual selves to others, especially peers, anticipating rejection or ridicule (Harter & Lee, 1989). Such feelings may engender displays of "phony" behavior or "putting on an act" (Harter et al., 1996; Wren, 1997). Harter and her colleagues observed that a low level of social support drives some adolescents to engage in false self behavior in an attempt to please parents and peers. False behavior is maladaptive when it is practiced excessively or when it is motivated by fear of disapproval or rejection. *Thought Question: Is phony behavior ever adaptive?*

The **ideal** (or **desired**) **self** is who we would like to be. Lydia declares, "I'd *like* to be friendly and tolerant all of the time. That's the kind of person I *want* to be, and I'm disappointed when I'm not." The ideal self usually includes qualities we observe in people we admire. Adolescents sometimes draw on prepackaged media images when fantasizing about a private sense of self (Larson, 1995).

The **public self** refers to how others actually see us, although we should not necessarily expect a consensus among those who know us well. The way we present ourselves to others presumably reflects how we want to be evaluated (see Spotlight • Adolescent Dress and the Public Self).

# SPOTLIGHT • Adolescent Dress and the Public Self

*There's nothing extraordinary about me. I have six earrings. That's the only
thing that makes me not normal from everyone else. Besides that, I fit in with
everyone else.*

*(17-year-old male)*

Do their clothing styles affect how young people perceive each other? Investigators interviewed 11 high school students in the students' homes about their personal dressing style and that of their schoolmates (Eicher, Baizerman, & Michelman, 1991). Students responded to questions such as "Do you dress to emphasize something about yourself?" and "Do you dress to hide something about yourself?" Students also answered questions about their perceptions of other students' dressing styles and body markings, for example, "In your school, how do the most popular kids dress?"

The investigators visited school lunchrooms, classrooms, and hallways and studied pictures in the school yearbook. The most common style of dress was casual unisex clothing: loose tops and jeans or pants. Boys and girls were distinguished more by hairdos than by what they wore. The majority of students did not display unusual or extreme clothing styles.

Despite the small sample size (11 students), the students' perceptions of their schoolmates' dressing styles shed light on their own understanding of personal identity. Although the high school students identified a variety of

**What does style of dress reveal about an adolescent's self concept?**

social types, including jocks, freaks, preppies, nerds, and punks, they did not necessarily agree on the criteria for membership in each group. Descriptions of male and female jocks ("jockettes") referred to athletic clothing and inexpensive, casual dress items. So-called nerds wear out-of-style clothing, including unfashionable sweaters and hand-me-downs, and have unkempt hair. Punks and freaks prefer black leather jackets, jeans with holes, and strange makeup and have different-colored dyed hair. Both groups wear their hair long, although they differ in how they color and shape their hair. Preppies wear well-ironed, "expensive, nice clothes" and prefer name brands.

In their interviews, the students used the above social categories to help identify the average or "mainstream" adolescent. Extreme forms of dress ("punk" and "freak") provided dramatic contrast to more conventional fashions. Some students expressed a desire to try the less conforming clothing and hair styles. The investigators concluded that the extreme social types provide a valuable reference point for "average" adolescents who are busy formulating their public selves. *Thought Question: Are there other ways of interpreting the style of adolescent dress than as a form of creative expression?*

The representation of a **possible self,** for example, as parent or worker, helps adolescents organize and make sense of their past and present experiences. Reflecting advances in cognitive development, including an improved ability to view themselves along multiple dimensions, the possible (or future) self motivates teenagers to stay focused on specific career and personal goals and persevere in pursuing them (Cross & Markus, 1991; Curry et al., 1994). "As possible selves are elaborated and become more explicit, the actions and strategies necessary to achieve these identities are anticipated and simulated in preparation for actual performance" (Call, 1996, p. 65).

The possible self refers to who we think we could be. This includes both the *ideal self* (who we would like to be) and the **dreaded self** (who we are afraid of becoming—in Lydia's case, someone who is unpopular). Adolescents have little difficulty envisioning possible selves (Crystal, Kato, Olson, & Watanabe, 1995; Harter & Lee, 1989; Markus & Nurius, 1986; Secord & Peevers, 1974) (Table 6-4).

## Table 6-4 Types of Selves

**True self** (same as self-concept)—Who we think we really are

**False self**—Who we want people to think we are

**Ideal self**—Who we would like to become

**Possible self**—Who we could become

**Dreaded self**—Who we are afraid of becoming

**Public self**—How others see us

"Possible selves are particularly important for understanding changes in self-concept that are likely to occur at transition points in people's lives because new contexts and relationships can be an integral part of self-generated new images" (Hooker et al., 1996, p. 542). Possible selves very much depend on adolescents' experiences with other people: (1) as models for how they can be, (2) for information about what characteristics of self are important, and (3) to provide them with opportunities to practice a variety of adult roles (Oyserman et al., 1995). Oyserman and her colleagues observed that possible selves predict different achievement outcomes for African-American and white university students and for males and females.

For optimal functioning, our various selves must become integrated into one internally consistent, unified self commonly referred to as "me." Lydia wonders, "Which one is the *real* me?" She doesn't yet realize that each of her personal qualities is part of the real her. During midadolescence, contradictory self-attributes (for Lydia, being both responsible and a goof-off) sometimes cause confusion and frustration. Boys seem to be a little less troubled than girls by self contradictions (Harter, 1990b; Strachen & Jones, 1982).

Change in self-concept becomes likely when adolescents perceive discrepancies among their various selves, especially a discrepancy between the actual and desired selves (Markus & Nurius, 1986). In other words, we are motivated to change ("improve") in the direction of how we would like to be. However, large discrepancies may discourage change in those who can't imagine being different. Lydia's response to all of this? "It's not fair!"

## SELF-CONCEPT AND COGNITIVE DEVELOPMENT

As noted previously, self-concept refers to how we view ourselves, to who we think we are. Eventually, most of us view ourselves as fairly consistent, unified personalities that incorporate our personal qualities, intentions, opinions, values, goals, and so on. At birth, of course, we have no concept of self or of anything else. We do not even know that we exist. Over the course of childhood we gradually become somebody special—an individual possessing a unique combination of personal qualities, opinions, beliefs, goals, and aspirations. We are continually reinventing ourselves, at least in our own eyes.

When describing themselves, younger children cite their behaviors and physical characteristics. A 5-year-old girl might answer the question "Who are you" this way: "My name is Frances, I'm a girl, I'm 5 years old, I'm in kindergarten, I'm strong, and I have blues eyes and a cocker spaniel." Note that these **self-descriptors** (terms used to describe oneself) are concrete yet disjointed, exemplifying what Piaget called *preoperational thinking* (Harter, 1990b).

Erikson (1968), Piaget (Inhelder & Piaget, 1958), and Kohlberg and Gilligan (1971) agreed that formal reasoning is a prerequisite to adolescent identity formation, especially for considering personal and vocational possibilities. Perspective taking, social comparison, and increased self-awareness allow adolescents to view themselves in a new light (Harter, 1990b; Selman, 1980). Partly because self-understanding is rooted in understanding others (Enright & Deist,

1979), egocentric (self-centered) thinking would be expected to have an inhibiting effect on identity achievement (Markstrom-Adams, 1992).

Identity formation during adolescence differs from identity formation during childhood in several ways, but mainly because *adolescents are much more aware of their identity and the infinite number of possible identities they can adopt.* When asked to describe themselves, most preadolescents display concrete operational thinking. They refer to general traits and feelings ("I'm smart in math and I am happy most of the time") and begin to add interpersonal qualities that imply social comparison ("I'm friendly, kind of popular, but not super popular"). Whereas younger children can combine specific behaviors into trait labels like *friendly* and *shy*, adolescents can integrate trait labels into higher-order abstractions like *sensitive* and *talented* (Lu, 1990). "I am 17 years old, 5 foot 3, Irish and Italian. I have brown hair and brown eyes. I consider myself to be a very outgoing person, with a lot of dreams and goals. I consider myself to be a very sensitive person. I have a talent for writing poetry and short stories, and I play the piano. I let people take advantage of me. I'm too nice, which makes me vulnerable. I have a problem sticking up for myself." *Study Question: In the preceding quote, distinguish between the concrete and abstract self-descriptors.*

After providing a few concrete self-descriptors (age, height, ethnic group membership), this adolescent characterizes herself as "too nice." Qualities such as *sensitive* and *nice* blend into the higher-level trait *vulnerable*. The more removed from specific qualities abstract self-descriptors become, the greater the risk that an adolescent will possess a distorted self-image. Abstract self-descriptors ("too nice") make self-concept more difficult to verify and less realistic (Harter, 1990b). Unrealistic appraisals of their ability lead some adolescents to avoid opportunities for success and lead others to risk almost certain failure. *Thought Question: Why do so many adolescents seem to enjoy depicting themselves as weird or strange?*

Although we observe more thoughtful and elaborate self-descriptions as children mature into adolescence, newer views of the self usually do not replace older views but include and expand on previous versions. Most adolescents acknowledge having contradictory traits (e.g., *conscientious* and *lazy*, *tolerant* and *prejudiced*). Self-descriptors such as *lazy*, *sarcastic*, and *moody* emphasize the adolescent's "psychological interior, his or her emotions, attitudes, beliefs, wishes, motives. At this stage, the self-reflective gaze is turned inward toward those internal, private attributes of the self" (Harter, 1990b, p. 207). Not yet able to integrate self-descriptions into a coherent and consistent self-theory, adolescent self-reports (like Lydia's) often convey confusion and self-doubt (Harter, 1990b).

## SELF-EVALUATION AND SOCIAL COMPARISON

Although they desire to be accepted and liked by their peers, elementary school children are not particularly interested in or capable of evaluating themselves with any precision. Compared to teenagers, younger children spend minimal time in front of mirrors worrying about what people think of them. Their self-concepts are fairly simple and stable, with little distinction between a public and a private self (Selman, 1980).

A 13-year-old girl named Karen described herself to one of my students as petite, slightly overweight, as having pretty hands and being athletic. She viewed herself as kind, outgoing, kind of popular, and loyal. When asked what she would change about herself, she mentioned her freckles, her hair, and her weight. She said she hates her freckles and finds her hair hard to manage. Her friends were beginning to experiment with cosmetics, but Karen said that when she puts on makeup it doesn't look like her. Although Karen likes herself, she is preoccupied with her appearance and is beginning to explore different ways of presenting herself to others.

Self-evaluation is a mixed blessing, especially for those who are hard on themselves. "Ever since I can remember, I have felt a fraud. I usually surpassed my schools' and my parents' expectations and failed to achieve my own. . . . The more 'successful' I become, the more inadequate I feel: why can people not see my limitations when I find it so easy to fault myself and not live up to my own expectations?" (19-year-old female, quoted by Garrod et al., 1992, p. 21).

This young woman expresses feelings of failure and inadequacy. She wonders why other people don't see her as harshly as she sees herself. We must wonder, is she seeing herself realistically? Why is she having such difficulty satisfying her expectations about herself? Many adolescents engage in similar self-analysis, sometimes to the point of distraction.

As noted in Chapter 3, a crucial factor contributing to adolescents' self-concept is their evaluation of their appearance (body image). This is a little disturbing to adults, most of whom have learned that appearance reveals little or nothing about a person's character. Nevertheless, it is hard to ignore what we see in the mirror, being well aware of the link between physical appearance and popularity (Granleese & Joseph, 1993).

Pledger (1992) administered a self-monitoring scale to 490 adolescents ranging in age from 12 to 18 years. She found that self-monitoring (observing one's thoughts, behaviors, and feelings) steadily increases until the high school years, along with social perspective taking and more sensitive communication skills. Compared to younger children, adolescents are better able to "read" other people and to use the information gained to have more effective interactions. Creating a public self requires that adolescents experiment with how they look and how they act. The goal is to make a good impression, to appear "cool." This is not easily accomplished because it is not clear how others see us or how they want or expect us to be.

During childhood, most of us begin to compare ourselves to our friends, a process known as **social comparison**. On report card day, for example, we hear everyone asking, "What'd you get, what'd you get?" Social comparison requires that children be able to notice similarities and differences between their personal qualities and abilities and those of their peers. By the fourth grade, children are drawing conclusions about their relative popularity, achievement, and personal appeal (Damon & Hart, 1988; Harter, 1987).

**Adolescents frequently compare themselves to their peers to see how they measure up.**

Adolescents frequently compare themselves to their peers. They may be reluctant to admit it because it is not usually socially acceptable to feel superior to someone or to put oneself down. As they become aware of the large number of qualities people have, they realize that everyone (including themselves) has strengths and weaknesses. Nevertheless, young people often are confused about what reference groups they should compare themselves to and on what basis (Harter, 1990b).

Over the course of childhood, children internalize the standards by which their parents, teachers, and peers evaluate them. Most apply these standards to their own behaviors (Selman, 1980). Feedback from peers is so important that some young people try to adjust their desired selves in the direction of increased popularity or likeability (despite conventional wisdom to "be yourself"). In the extreme, this leads to the dubious strategy of doing whatever is necessary to be popular or accepted.

Summarizing, adolescent self-concepts reflect three main factors: feedback about personal qualities ("You're kind of cute"), social comparison ("I'm more popular than my sister"), and self-evaluations of their own qualities and accomplishments based on internalized standards of performance ("I'm disappointed in my French grade").

As adolescents mature, their self-evaluations become more independent of parental influence (Isberg et al., 1989). Similarly, increasing confidence in self-evaluation allows young people to challenge or at least cope with occasional negative feedback from peers. In the long run, social comparisons, sensitivity to the opinions of others, and realistic performance standards help most teenagers construct realistic self-concepts (Harter, 1990b). Toward late adolescence, social comparisons become less influential than internalized standards and personal beliefs in the evolution of self-concept (Damon & Hart, 1988). *Thought Question: What family or life circumstances might hamper the development of a self-concept?*

## INTEGRATION OF THE ADOLESCENT SELF

Two aspects of cognitive complexity, **differentiation** and **integration**, facilitate identity achievement (Markstrom-Adams, 1992). Self-concepts become more differentiated over time. That is, we view ourselves in increasingly varied and complex ways. Whereas a 5-year-old may see herself as "smart," a 10-year-old may see herself as smart in some subjects and not in others. A 13-year-old may discern a range of strengths and weaknesses even within one performance area, such as tennis. Younger children, not terribly reflective to begin with, are less bothered by apparent inconsistencies (Harter, 1990a). Preadolescents notice that their behaviors change in different situations or when they are with unfamiliar people. Sometimes they acknowledge having "mixed feelings" or being of "two minds," but they do not seem to be upset by it.

A more reflective 15-year-old, however, might be troubled by the fact that he feels both brave and timid, sometimes at the same moment. Middle adolescents notice inconsistencies in their thoughts and feelings, and occasionally they are troubled by them (Harter, 1990b). They also realize that how they act and feel and even how they see themselves depend partly on who they are with. The imaginary audience concept captures adolescents' preoccupation with their behaviors, thoughts, and motives. "What would people think of me if they knew my real thoughts and feelings?"

Some teenagers "cannot reconcile the fact that they are cheerful with their friends or depressed with their parents; that they are rowdy or laid-back with friends, but up-tight and self-conscious on dates; or that they are angry around their dads, but comfortable with their moms. Many of these adolescents expressed confusion over how they could be the same person, yet act so differently with different persons, leading them to ponder which was the 'real me'" (Harter, 1990b, p. 214). Sound like someone we know?

As important as differentiation to personality development is integration, taking all facets of our personality and consolidating them in a consistent, ongoing personality. In the following remarkable account of self-discovery, we share the moment at which a young woman accepts her body and her appearance as valued parts of her entire adult self. "That night my faith in the world was unshakable. I stood before the mirror with my glasses gone, my hair sleek and sophisticated, teeth proud and white, and that wonderful dress hugging me close in all its glory. Somehow, without my acknowledging it, I had become someone reasonably all right to look at after all. I stood there for several minutes: gradually it dawned upon me that that strange figure in the shadows was a woman, and that woman was me. There was no longer any need to separate my psychological and physical selves" (19-year-old female, quoted by Garrod et al., 1992, p. 27).

By the late teenage years, most young people are applying their self-reflective abilities more effectively. They are better able to come to terms with their personal inconsistencies and contradictions. They realize that different situations call for different behaviors and feelings. Using their ability to form higher-order abstractions, they view contradictory qualities (e.g., cheerful and depressed) as consistent ("I'm moody") (Fischer, 1980; Harter, 1990b). Older adolescents appreciate that to be ambivalent and indecisive is to be human. Like adults, they feel comfortable revealing different sides of themselves on different occasions to different people when playing different roles.

## ADOLESCENT SELF-ESTEEM

*How much do I like the kind of person I am? Well, I like some things about me, but I don't like others. I'm glad that I'm popular since it's really important to me to have friends. But in school I don't do as well as the really smart kids. That's O.K., because if you're too smart you'll lose your friends. So being smart is just not that important. Except to my parents. I feel like I'm letting them down when I don't do as well as they want. But what's really important to me is how I look. If I like the way I look, then I really like the kind of person I am.*

*("Lydia," from Harter, 1990a, pp. 364–365)*

As far as we can tell from her self-disclosure, Lydia appears to have positive self-esteem—she seems to like and accept herself. If self-concept is who we think we are, then **self-esteem** is how we *feel about* who we think we are. That is to say, self-esteem is the evaluative component of self-concept, with both cognitive and emotional factors (Baumeister, 1993; Harter & Jackson, 1993). Some investigators (e.g., Schweitzer, Seth-Smith, & Callan, 1992) contend that self-concept also is evaluative and that there is no need to distinguish between self-concept and self-esteem. However, research confirms the usefulness of maintaining the distinction. For example, the closer we are to how we want to be, the more we like ourselves (Block & Robins, 1993).

Traditionally, self-esteem has been measured using a single score (**global self-esteem**) that reflects how we feel about our selves. However, as a single measure of feelings of worthiness or adequacy, global self-esteem masks important distinctions between what we like and don't like (Harter, 1990b). Like self-concept, self-esteem is a more useful concept if we consider it to be multidimensional (Baumeister, 1993; Kernis, Cornell, Sun, Berry, & Harlow, 1993; Schweitzer et al., 1992).

In order to predict and understand people's self-esteem, it helps to know the personal qualities that they value and how they rate themselves on these qualities (Block & Robins, 1993). Like most of us, Lydia values some of her qualities more than others. In her self-evaluation, she plays down the importance of intelligence and emphasizes her looks. Her feelings of worthiness appear to be based mainly on her positive evaluation of her appearance. *Thought Question: What types of social experiences lead some teenagers to value popularity more than intelligence or character?*

Psychologist Carl Rogers (1961) considered positive self-esteem to be at the core of a healthy personality. People who like themselves typically have positive feelings about other people and about their lives in general. "The adolescent who likes himself or herself as a person will invariably be quite cheerful, whereas the adolescent with low self-esteem will be affectively depressed.... Those who report happy or cheerful affect report much greater energy levels than those who appear to be depressed" (Harter, 1990b, p. 231).

People with low self-esteem frequently are insecure in their relationships and feel anxious about their futures. Their self worth constantly is "on the line" (Kernis et al., 1993). Low self-esteem during adolescence is associated with conformity, drug abuse, delinquency, depression, and suicidal thoughts (Bolognini, Plancherel, Bettschart, & Halfon, 1996; Harter, 1986). Thus, feelings of unworthiness and shame are associated with psychological maladjustment (Baumeister, 1993; Reimer, 1996; Schweitzer et al., 1992) (Table 6-5).

## Stability of Self-Esteem During Adolescence

Although self-esteem (whether positive or negative) is fairly stable over time for most people (e.g., Bolognini et al., 1996), it does fluctuate to some extent according to circumstances (Tevendale, DuBois, Lopez, & Prindiville, 1997). Instability of self-esteem is more common for those who are overly sensitive to evaluation or who are self-conscious—such as adolescents (Kernis et al., 1993).

We would expect fluctuations in adolescent self-evaluations based on the physiological, cognitive, and emotional changes described in previous chapters. In fact, there is evidence of a *curvilinear* relationship between age and self-

**Table 6-5 Signs of High and Low Self-Esteem During Adolescence**

| High Self-Esteem | Low Self-Esteem |
| --- | --- |
| Cheerful | Depressed |
| More energetic | Less energetic |
| Feel secure | Feel insecure |
| Confident about future | Doubts about future |
| Less conforming | More conforming |
| Feel worthy | Feel inadequate |
| Realistic expectations of self | Unrealistic expectations |
| Like appearance | Dislike appearance |
| Accept compliments | Reject compliments |
| Express point of view | Withhold point of view |
| Friendly | Shy |

evaluation. Self-esteem typically becomes more negative during preadolescence and early adolescence, is stable during middle adolescence, and then improves during late adolescence and early adulthood (Marsh, 1989).

This means that positive feelings about oneself occur more frequently among children, late adolescents, and young adults and less frequently among early and middle adolescents. Self-evaluation disturbances are most common during early adolescence, around the ages of 12–13 years (Rosenberg, 1985).

Self-esteem for boys and girls is at its lowest ebb at about age 13. For most boys, feelings of worthiness improve gradually over the course of the teenage years (Mullis, Mullis, & Normandin, 1992; O'Malley & Bachman, 1983; Rosenberg, 1986; Zimmerman, Copeland, Shope, & Dielman, 1997). Why do some boys and girls think less of themselves during early adolescence? Perhaps it is because they have unrealistically high estimations of themselves when they are younger (Marsh, 1989). In a study of first graders, all 96 children interviewed claimed that they were among the smartest students in their class (Stipek & Tannatt, 1984). With their sharper cognitive abilities and more extensive life experiences, teenagers view themselves more critically than they did when they were younger.

Other factors that could deflate self-concept during early adolescence include negative feedback from peers, feeling socially isolated, challenging school work, and pressure to conform to gender role stereotypes (known as **gender role intensification**). We have already seen that many early-maturing children, particularly girls, react negatively to their precocious physical changes. Many boys want to gain weight so that they can be stronger and look more muscular (Abell & Richards, 1996). Given the important role that appearance plays in self-evaluation, dissatisfaction with their appearance temporarily depresses some teenagers' self-concepts (Bolognini et al., 1996; Granleese & Joseph, 1993). *Review Question: How does the timing of maturation affect the self-esteem of late-maturing boys and girls?*

Further, many students have difficulty adjusting to the transition to secondary school. The so-called top-dog phenomenon suggests that the transition from being high-status sixth graders in a familiar elementary school to being low-status seventh graders in a new school environment is a blow to self-esteem. Many freshmen in middle or junior high become more anxious about school. This is not surprising, given the greater pressure to perform, stricter grading standards, and a disruption of their primary school social networks (Berndt, 1987; Eccles & Midgley, 1989; Eccles, Midgley & Adler, 1984; Harter 1987; Hill & Lynch, 1983; Wigfield, Eccles, MacIver, & Midgley, 1991). We will discuss school-related adjustment problems at greater length in Chapter 11.

Fortunately, the deflation of self-concept is relatively short-lived. Self-esteem usually increases during the seventh grade but may be depressed again during the transition to high school. This is especially true of students who are not performing well academically (Simmons & Blyth, 1987; Wigfield et al., 1991). Why does level of self-concept improve again during late adolescence? Most late adolescents and young adults become more accepting of the personal flaws and inconsistencies that so upset them a few years earlier. Their more sophisticated social skills assure greater interpersonal success and satisfaction with themselves.

Several studies (e.g., Chubb, Fertman, & Ross, 1997; O'Malley & Bachman, 1983) report stability of self-esteem over fairly long periods, but some of these studies averaged self-esteem scores over large numbers of adolescents. A finding of little or no average change is misleading because some individuals may increase in self-esteem, others may decrease, and still others may show little or no change at all. Averaging across individuals could very well mask these differences.

For example, Block and Robins (1993) performed a longitudinal study to identify developmental changes in self-esteem for 47 girls and 44 boys from early adolescence (age 14) until young adulthood (age 23). The mean level of self-esteem did not change appreciably for the combined sample. Those who scored high (or low) in self-esteem during early adolescence tended to score high (or low) in early adulthood. Although the average individual in the total sample showed no change, there was a tendency for males to increase and females to decrease in self-esteem over the course of the study. When averaged, the two groups canceled out each other's changes. Thus, it is more informative to monitor changes in individuals rather than in groups.

Another longitudinal study of 128 adolescents moving from six different elementary schools to the same junior high school revealed four different self-esteem "trajectories" (Hirsch & DuBois, 1991). Thirty-five percent of the students displayed consistently high self-esteem over a 2-year period, whereas 13% displayed chronically low self-esteem. Thirty-one percent showed a small increase and 21% displayed a steep decline in self-esteem.

Those adolescents displaying consistently high self-esteem performed well in school, said that they liked school, and received high levels of peer support. Those with consistently low self-esteem displayed average competence in school but didn't enjoy school and had little peer support. The group showing the largest decline in self-esteem over the 2-year period (about one-fifth of the total group) was the only group that conformed to the "turbulence" model of adolescence. The varying self-esteem trajectories in both studies (and Zimmerman et al., 1997) illustrate the usefulness of monitoring changes in self-esteem in individual adolescents rather than averaging over large numbers.

## Factors Influencing Self-Esteem

*There's another thing about how much I like the kind of person I am. It matters what other people think, especially the other kids at school. It matters whether they like you. I care about what my parents think about me too.*

*("Lydia," from Harter, 1990a, pp. 364–365)*

Lydia likes herself partly because of what she sees in the mirror and partly because she feels accepted and appreciated by the people who are important to her. Much of what we internalize as self-concept reflects feedback from the important people in our lives. Children almost constantly hear positive and negative evaluations such as "Good girl," "Big boy," "You jerk," "You're my favorite," and "What's wrong with you?"

According to the interactional-ecological model presented in Chapter 2, each of us has countless opportunities at home, in school, and in the community to "strut our stuff" and to accumulate a track record of success and failure. Report cards, grade-point average, SAT scores, and extracurricular activities are part of our academic track record and therefore influence self-esteem (Holland & Andre, 1994; Leonardson, 1986). Feedback from respected teachers affects both global and academic self-esteem (Hoge, Smit, & Hanson, 1990). *Thought Question: Would we expect adolescents to be more vulnerable or less vulnerable than younger children to negative feedback from peers?*

The self-concept of older children reflects feedback from the important people in their lives, but also their own self-evaluations (e.g., "I'm a good student," "I'm clumsy," "I have big feet") and their own evolving standards of behavior. Many adolescents give more credibility to feedback from classmates than to the presumably biased opinions of parents and close friends (Harter, 1989).

Adolescents with low self-esteem usually report that their parents accept them conditionally. They are "worthy" as long as they achieve or satisfy their parents' expectations. Carl Rogers (1961) urged parents to express **unconditional acceptance** of their children: "I love who you are without condition, although I do not always approve of your behavior." Rogers was convinced that the feelings of inadequacy and unworthiness so common in human personalities are rooted in the conditional messages we receive from parents, teachers, and peers—"I would like you more if you were nicer, smarter, prettier, more cooperative," and so on (Harter, 1987; Rosenberg, 1979). Indeed, supportive child rearing, parent affection, and healthy family relationships all foretell positive self-esteem during adolescence (Holmbeck & Hill, 1986; Isberg et al., 1989; Lackovic-Grgin, Deković, & Opacic, 1994; Nielson & Metha, 1994; Parish & Necessary, 1994). (See Figure 6-2.)

Feedback from others is not the only factor that influences self-esteem. Once we internalize performance standards, we apply them to see whether we measure up to our peers, siblings, and culturally mandated, gender-appropriate norms (Josephs, Markus, & Tafarodi, 1992; Suitor & Reavis, 1995). Positive regard from peers and opportunities to demonstrate competence and gain recognition are particularly potent factors in self-confidence. However, it is not easy to predict what criteria a given adolescent will use to evaluate the self.

**FIGURE 6-2 Factors influencing self-esteem and self-confidence. (From Jaffe, 1997)**

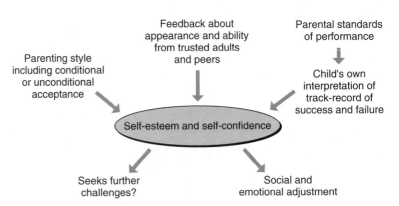

Many young people are down on themselves despite being attractive, popular, and bright. Some pick a real or imagined flaw and magnify its significance. Who would imagine that the musician Eric Clapton, nicknamed "God" by his fans, suffered from an intense feeling of self-contempt? "Like being backstage and hearing the crowd out there, and thinking, 'I'm not worth it. I'm a piece of garbage. And they're fools: if they knew what the truth was about me, they wouldn't like me.' I've identified with that a million times" (Clapton, quoted by Strauss, 1994, p. 32).

As psychologist Williams James noted in the last century, not all successes are evaluated equally. Our self-esteem is particularly boosted or deflated when we succeed or fail in a domain that is important to us. The domain may be academic, vocational, athletic, social, physical, and so on (Covey & Feltz, 1991; Harter, 1986). Even within, say, the academic domain, grades and teacher feedback affect discipline-specific (e.g., math, social studies) self-esteem more than academic or global esteem (Hoge et al., 1990). These investigators found that for sixth and seventh graders at two Midwestern middle schools, special programs aimed at providing recognition to achieving students were not as effective in raising self-esteem as feedback directly provided by teachers. *Critical Thinking Question: What flaw can you identify in programs that attempt to raise self-esteem simply by providing children and adolescents with unconditional praise?*

## Gender Differences in Self-Evaluation, Self-Concept, and Self-Esteem

*I hated my hair, detested my glasses, and was ashamed of the braces on my teeth. For several months, much of my energy was devoted to feelings of physical inadequacy. I defined myself by how others would regard me—and since I was sure that to others I was ugly, awkward, and gawky, I didn't end up with a very strong self-image. Those were days of torment and despair. . . . I wanted, and needed, to belong.*

*(19-year-old female, quoted by Garrod et al., 1992, p. 25)*

As discussed in Chapter 3, body image has a large impact on self-esteem, especially for girls in the United States (Abell & Richards, 1996). Girls value their physical attractiveness even more than boys do, report feeling unattractive more frequently, and are more self-conscious about their appearance (Granleese & Joseph, 1993; Simmons & Blyth, 1987). Facial attractiveness appears to be a good predictor of social functioning for boys and girls (Perkins & Lerner, 1995). In the quote beginning this section, we can see clearly the connection between perceiving oneself as unattractive and feelings of unworthiness and inadequacy. Many studies report that adolescent girls have lower global self-esteem than adolescent boys (e.g., Blyth, Simmons, & Carlton-Ford, 1983; Bolognini et al., 1996; Chubb et al., 1997; Dukes & Martinez, 1994; Simmons & Rosenberg, 1975), although a few studies report minimal gender differences (e.g., Jaquish & Savin-Williams, 1981). Teenage boys usually express more confidence in their abilities than teenage girls do, and most report believing that they are good at a lot of different activities. Girls, on the other hand, often report feeling unsure of themselves, their bodies, and their abilities (Bolognini et al., 1996; Freiberg, 1991; Orenstein, 1994). "Oh, I want to be more confident. I have no confidence at all. I'm extremely insecure and it prevents me from doing a lot of things I should be doing—going out and meeting people—but I don't. I'm shy and antisocial. It's something about myself that I really hate. I'm afraid of being rejected" (20-year-old girl).

We also observe gender differences in certain dimensions of self-evaluation. For example, by middle adolescence, boys have higher sports and math self-evaluations than girls. Girls have higher verbal self-evaluations than boys. However, boys and girls do not differ in self-evaluation of social ability (Marsh, 1989; Meece, Parsons, Kaczula, Goff, & Futterman, 1982; Wigfield et al., 1991). Gender differences in specific dimensions of self-evaluation such as achievement, leadership, and sociability generally are consistent with traditional sex stereotypes (Marsh, 1989), presumably reflecting boys' and girls' distinctive childhood relationships and different socialization norms (Gilligan & Wiggins, 1987; Peters, 1994).

Gender differences in self-esteem could be explained by pressure to conform to traditional male and female sex roles, by society's valuing maleness more than femaleness, or by boys being given more opportunities to succeed. The role conflicts experienced by adolescent girls who want to be both feminine and high-achieving might temporarily dampen self-esteem during middle adolescence and limit their career aspirations (Harper & Marshall, 1991).

Boys and girls also differ in their personal issues and in some of the criteria they use to assess their worthiness (Block & Robins, 1993; Maccoby & Jacklin, 1974; Mullis et al., 1992). For example, masculinity, individuation, and achieve-

**Girls may be at a competitive disadvantage with boys in a coed classroom setting.**

ment are closely linked to male self-esteem, whereas female self-esteem is more related to "the self in relationship" (Brown & Gilligan, 1992; Holland & Andre, 1994; Josephs et al., 1992). *Thought Question: During the middle school and high school years, are males given more opportunities to succeed than females?*

Williams and McGee (1991) asked 15-year-old boys and girls in New Zealand to describe their strengths and weaknesses. Over 70% of the sample of 976 adolescents perceived themselves as kind, trustworthy, easygoing, helpful, having a sense of humor, reliable, being good with pets, friendly, and careful. The average adolescent cited 14 or 15 strengths, and most of them appeared to have positive self-concepts. Boys gave more positive responses than girls to items focusing on their activities, such as sports and hobbies. Girls were more likely than boys to emphasize their positive personal qualities, such as being reliable, kind, independent, and affectionate.

Studying gender norms throughout the 1980s, Suitor and Reavis (1995) observed that boys acquire prestige through sports, grades, and intelligence and that girls gain prestige mainly from their appearance, sociability, and achievement in school. Some have put it this way: females are socialized to get along and males are socialized to get ahead (Block & Robins, 1993). Within each gender, individual qualities such as sex role orientation and temperament influence how each adolescent interprets his or her social encounters. This interpretation, in turn, influences feelings of worthiness or worthlessness (Holland & Andre, 1994; Klein, 1992). *Thought Question: Is there a link between what adolescents boys and girls like about themselves and the role that close relationships play in their lives?*

Other factors that have been shown to influence adolescent self-esteem include popularity, social support, academic achievement and recognition (particularly for girls), athletic performance (for girls and boys), commitment to one's ethnic identity (for minority adolescents), and number of life problems reported (Harper & Marshall, 1991; Harter, 1987; Hirsch & DuBois, 1991; Lackovic-Grgin & Deković, 1990; Phinney & Alipuria, 1990; Steitz & Owen, 1992) (Table 6-6).

## Table 6-6  Parenting Qualities and Behaviors Associated with Children's Self-Esteem

| Positive Self-Esteem | Negative Self-Esteem |
| --- | --- |
| Sensitive, caring parenting | Overprotective |
| Recognizing and valuing achievement | Neglectful |
| Unconditional acceptance of child | Use punitive discipline practices |
| Positive regard (praise, affection) | Overly critical, rejecting |
| Clearly defining and enforcing limits | |
| Respect for child's desire for autonomy | |
| Modeling self-assurance | |
| Encourage and validate child's expression of feelings | |

African-American adolescent girls may have higher self-esteem than white or Asian-American girls, according to a study by psychologist Sumru Erkut and colleagues at Wellesley College (Murray, 1996e). "African-American girls considered themselves the most socially accepted and romantically appealing, areas where Chinese-American girls scored lowest. . . . Although good grades mattered to all the girls, high academic achievement was the strongest predictor of high self-worth among African-American girls" (p. 42).

## Promoting Positive Self-Esteem

Most teachers and parents believe that there is a connection between self-esteem, achievement, and adjustment. Feelings of self-worth often accompany accomplishment of some kind, but most teachers are reluctant to praise mediocre performance to help young people feel better about themselves. Accurate appraisal of one's abilities is necessary for adaptive functioning (Bandura, 1986).

Psychologist Roy Baumeister (1996) and his colleagues (Baumeister, Smart, & Boden, 1996) are concerned that students in the United States think *too highly* of themselves. They criticize the common practice of praising students for achievements that are substandard. They warn that unearned praise undermines children's willingness to work hard. Providing adolescents with opportunities to develop interpersonal skills, perhaps through role playing and behavioral rehearsal, enhances their self-esteem and encourages greater self-acceptance. Positive self-esteem usually is found in individuals who perform competently in areas *that are important to them* (Harter, 1990b). Most people learn to seek opportunities in those areas in which they are likely to succeed and to avoid areas of perceived weakness (Bandura, 1986).

This is not to suggest that young people should have to prove themselves in some way in order to feel good about themselves. Carl Rogers noted that one's worth as a person should not have to be earned. Unfortunately, the assumption of inherent self-worth does not come easily to those who have been raised on conditional acceptance and who base their self-evaluations on their track record or on social comparisons.

During the high school years, most adolescents develop increasingly positive views of themselves. As they adjust to high school and begin to receive more validation from parents and peers, they come to view themselves as more socially adept. Eventually, most learn to seek out and spend time with people who help them feel good about themselves and learn to minimize contact with those who they find to be excessively disapproving (Hines & Groves, 1989; Juhasz, 1989)

One word of caution. It is important that parents of adolescents distinguish between low self-esteem and depression. Depression is more dangerous because of its association with drug abuse and suicide. Children with low self-esteem feel bad about themselves, but most are not depressed. Children who are clinically depressed usually require professional attention (Kutner, 1993a).

# IDENTITY FORMATION IN MINORITY YOUTH

*Study Question: How might membership in an ethnic minority group both enhance and interfere with identity formation?*

> *Everyone knows that no adolescent wants to stick out in a crowd. The desire to be "normal" may just be the [essential ingredient] of adolescence. Being a member of a minority group made it hard for me, as an adolescent, to avoid feeling like I "stuck out." Being Korean was a liability that I felt I had to overcome; I thought that others were constantly conscious of the fact that I was Korean and therefore different in some way. . . . I didn't want to be different, but because I couldn't do anything about it I avoided calling attention to myself.*

> *(Korean-born American male, from Garrod et al., 1992, p. 96)*

In this world, people may be given a hard time for almost any reason—size, weight, gender, skin color, religion, disability, sexual orientation, and so on. Simply looking different or acting differently from the norm is bound to complicate the life of an adolescent. "It is not uncommon for the police to hassle innocent young black men just because they are young black men. Some kids become thoroughly discouraged by the school experience because of how teachers treat them and decide to opt out because it is too difficult" (psychologist Anderson Franklin, quoted in Burnette, 1995, pp. 1, 32). Dr. Franklin points out that some teachers misinterpret or overreact to African-American males' culture-specific behaviors, including style of dress, body language, and eye contact. Asian, Native American, African-American, and Hispanic adolescents and members of other minority ethnic groups must come to terms with incidents of mindless rejection and hostility at the very time that they are trying to accept themselves as they are (Burnette, 1995). In a later chapter, we will see that members of another socially stigmatized group, gay and lesbian adolescents, are involved in a similar struggle.

Exploration and self-discovery are an important part of achieving a healthy identity. As indicated earlier, for most young people, the social environment provides a variety of educational, economic, and social resources that enable them to gain the skills and personal qualities that they will need to become the type of adult who is accepted and valued in their community (Oyserman et al., 1995). Racial discrimination severely limits opportunities for exploration for large numbers of ethnic minority adolescents (Markstrom-Adams, 1992).

Many of these adolescents are struggling to overcome language, educational, and vocational barriers (Florsheim, 1997; Nwadiora & McAdoo, 1996). Those who are rejected or harassed because of their ethnic, racial, or language differences and who are repeatedly exposed to stereotypical views of their ethnic group (e.g., alienated blacks, achieving Asians) need more support and have to work harder to realize what we previously have called a desired self and to avoid the dreaded self (Burnette, 1995; Phinney & Chavira, 1992; Phinney & Rosenthal, 1992; Spencer & Dornbush, 1990; Spencer & Markstrom-Adams, 1990; Tajfel, 1978).

Oyserman and her colleagues (1995) note that urban African-American youth are at increased risk of school failure, dropping out of school, arrest, and incarceration. To avoid these outcomes, they must search for "positive possibilities for the self within a stark social context of ever-shrinking employment opportunities.... More African-American young men are in jail and prison settings than in college or university settings" (pp. 1216–1217). The social settings that many urban youth inhabit provide minimal opportunities to construct a future in which success in school leads to vocational success during adulthood. To formulate a positive sense of self, they must recognize and reject the negative qualities and stereotypes attributed to them. Identifying themselves as members of a larger group that historically has been subject to discrimination helps minority youth make sense of the exclusion, discrimination, and limited opportunities that they may face as individuals and the efforts necessary to overcome these obstacles (Jagers, 1996; Oyserman et al., 1995).

## Ethnic Identity

When individual adolescents commit to their ethnic group, usually during the college years, they are said to achieve **ethnic identity**. They have a secure sense of themselves as members of their ethnic community (Phinney & Rosenthal, 1992). Ethnic identity also refers to one's sense of belonging to a particular ethnic group. One may identify with an ethnic group ("I am Italian-American") or commit to an ethnic heritage ("I'm going to raise my children as Jews"). Even for adolescents who express mixed or competing feelings about their group membership, ethnic identity becomes an important component of adult self-concept (Phinney & Chavira, 1992) and predictor of self-esteem (Phinney, Cantu, & Kurtz, 1997).

One might develop positive attitudes such as pride, negative attitudes such as embarrassment, or have mixed feelings about one's heritage. As a result of negative stereotypes about their ethnic group, some minority children and adolescents come to prefer the majority group (Spencer & Markstrom-Adams, 1990). Others become "raceless," that is, they adopt the attitudes, behaviors, and values of mainstream, majority culture (Arroyo & Zigler, 1995; Fordham, 1988; Fordham & Ogbu, 1986). In a TV interview, for example, actress Whoopi Goldberg disclosed that she prefers to view herself as an American rather than as an African-American.

Ethnic identity includes shared values, traditions, and practices. Although individuals express their ethnic identity in various ways, heritage, religion, language, and skin color are part of one's cultural or biological "packaging." Early in life, it becomes clear that people affiliate with each other partly on the basis of similarity in age, gender, ethnicity, race, and language (Hutnik, 1991; Phinney & Rosenthal, 1992).

Ethnicity is less central to achieved identity for adolescent members of majority or privileged groups (Phinney & Alipuria, 1990; Waterman, 1985) although for white students in America, American identity is a strong predictor of self-esteem (Phinney et al., 1997). In their study of white and African-American college students, Judd and his colleagues (1995) found that African-Amer-

**For many adolescents, ethnic and religious identity becomes an important component of their self concept.**

ican students were more stereotypical in their views of whites than white students were of African-Americans. The researchers speculated that the white students had been socialized to achieve a "color blind perspective" in their ethnic judgments, whereas African-American students had been socialized to respect and value their ethnic heritage and to believe that ethnicity makes a big difference in the United States. *Thought Question: How might experiences with intolerant peers intensify racial identification in ethnic adolescents?*

Some members of minority groups that do not display any overt signs of minority status, such as Jewish-American adolescents, find it easier to assimilate. In the absence of blatant ethnically directed hostility or rejection, most adolescents remain relatively indifferent about ethnic issues. Exceptions include those who strongly identify with their group and those who occasionally clash with parents whom they perceive as too traditional or strict in their religious beliefs and practices (Patel, Power, & Bhavnagri, 1996; Pawliuk, Grizenko, Chan-Yip, Gantous et al., 1996).

But to members of ethnic minority groups who face discrimination and poverty, issues of ethnic identity are inescapable (Burnette, 1995; Mendelberg, 1986; Tizard & Phoenix, 1995). Indeed, studies of high school and college students in the United States reveal that members of ethnic minority groups, especially African-, Native-, and Mexican-Americans, report greater identity search and commitment than whites (Phinney, 1989; Phinney & Alipuria, 1990; Riley, 1993).

Phinney (1990) described three theoretical frameworks of ethnic identity research: identity formation, acculturation, and social identity. *Identity formation* models describe the psychological phases or stages involved in establishing an ethnic identity. *Acculturation models* emphasize the individual's adjustment to the dominant society. A unified ethnic identity reflects individuals' commitment to or separation from their ethnic ties. *Social identity theory* maintains that individuals develop an identity reflecting both their own ethnic group and the dominant group.

Based on their study of 87 Asian-American undergraduates, Yeh and Huang (1996) conclude that all three models are inadequate for understanding ethnic identification for Asians and Asian-Americans. The three models cited above describe a process that is "linear, intrapersonal, and individualistic; the individual is typically motivated by internal forces such as anger and frustration" (p. 654); "Asian-Americans are largely influenced by relationships and external forces . . . the avoidance of shame was found to be a strong motivating factor in determining their ethnic identification" (p. 645). Yeh and Huang describe ethnic identification in Asians as a "dynamic and complex process, emphasizing collectivism, the impact of external forces in defining one's sense of self, and the power of shame as a motivating force in ethnic identity formation" (p. 654).

Ethnic identity usually is achieved through a process of exploration and commitment "that results in a confident sense of self as a member of an ethnic group" (Phinney & Alipuria, 1990). Based on their studies of African-American identity, Oyserman and her colleagues (1995) suggest that three components of what they call "African-American identity"—a sense of community embeddedness, awareness of racism, and individual effort as an African-American—improve the school persistence and performance of African-American youth. "For males, African-American identity seems more likely to focus on action, struggle, and survival, whereas for females the focus seems to

**By late adolescence, most biracial children learn to emphasize the positive aspects of their subculture and express ethnic pride.**

be on school attainment and attention to kin and the wider African-American community and its traditions and institutions" (p. 1220).

## Biracial Children

In the past, it was not unusual for **biracial children** (children of interracial unions) to feel torn between selecting one parent's racial identification or the other's (Gibbs, 1987; Winn & Priest, 1993). However, with an increasing number of interracial unions and liberalization of white attitudes, children with mixed parentage are receiving less overt rejection (Tizard & Phoenix, 1995). Still, questions like "Who am I?" and "Where do I fit in?" are more pressing for biracial adolescents than they are for ethnically mainstream adolescents, as are questions about choice of romantic partners and professional aspirations (Overmier, 1990).

Tizard and Phoenix (1995) interviewed adolescents with one white and one African-American or African-Caribbean parent. Although a fifth of their sample expressed a feeling of "marginality," preferring to be either one or the other race, the majority of the adolescents "were very positive about their mixed heritage. They stressed the advantages of being accepted by both black and white people, of seeing things from both perspectives, or of being 'special'" (p. 1407).

Parents of biracial children can discuss their racial heritage with their children, acknowledge that their racial/ethnic heritage is different from their children's (and recognize that as being positive), and give their children opportunities to develop relationships with peers from many different backgrounds (Poston, 1990). By late adolescence, most biracial children learn to emphasize the positive aspects of their subculture and express ethnic pride (Grove, 1991; Phinney, 1990; Phinney & Chavira, 1992; Phinney & Rosenthal, 1992).

It is misguided to assume that exposure to prejudice automatically translates into academic failure or low self-esteem (Arroyo & Zigler, 1995; Dukes & Martinez, 1994; Spencer & Markstrom-Adams, 1990). How (and whether) young people come to terms with their ethnic heritage depends partly on family attitudes and practices, including parents' commitment to their ethnic tradition (Gibbs, 1987; Sam, 1995). Children of parents who model positive attitudes toward their ethnic group and who are warm and accepting usually express pride in their ethnic heritage. Expressions of pride from parents, peers, teachers, and mentors to some extent counteract negative stereotypes and discrimination from the larger society (although rejection always hurts) (Barnes, 1980; Burnette, 1995).

## Biculturalism

> While I stubbornly denied my "Korean-ness" throughout adolescence, I felt almost compelled to examine it once I got to college. I needed to know whether being Korean really was an essential part of my own being, or whether that part of me could just be boiled off. I ended up going back to Korea for a summer to find out. . . . That summer, aside from learning to speak Korean a lot better, I learned a great deal about what Korean-ness meant to me. . . . The important point for me

*was that I had finally put an end to contending that being Korean meant noth-*
*ing to me.*

*(Same Korean-American quoted above,*
*in Garrod et al., 1992, p. 98)*

Accommodating a larger culture while retaining the characteristics and values of one's own culture of origin is called **biculturalism** (Harrison et al., 1990). Individuals inhabiting two cultures usually strive to develop and maintain competence in both worlds (LaFromboise, Coleman, & Gerton, 1993). Harrison and her colleagues (1990) note that by integrating two cultural systems (and often two languages), bicultural children and adolescents develop greater cognitive and social sophistication than children who inhabit one culture or speak only one language. The choices that adolescents make about the extent to which they identify with one or the other ethnic group (or both) affects their ethnic behaviors, attitudes, and awareness (Kvernmo & Heyerdahl, 1996).

## SUMMARY

**1.** At birth there is no awareness or concept of self, but over the course of childhood and adolescence we gradually become "somebody." Self-concept refers to who we believe we are, including our beliefs, values, roles, and aspirations.

**2.** According to Erikson, the key developmental task facing Western adolescents is achieving an adult identity. Identity is the part of self-concept that provides a feeling of personality coherence and that gives us a sense of continuity or connectedness between past, present, and future. Adolescents construct a sense of identity in the process of making decisions, commitments, and choices in their everyday lives.

**3.** During the early adolescent years, young people attempt to distinguish themselves from their family members and peers, to define themselves in their own terms. This attempt at individuation is occurring at about the same time that adolescents are trying to be accepted by their peers. Many are torn between being true to themselves and succumbing to pressure to conform to the peer group.

**4.** The process of achieving an adult self-concept is propelled partly by the physical, cog-

nitive, and social changes that accompany and follow puberty. Erikson maintained that these changes provide opportunities for adolescents to explore different ways of being and to consider alternative life paths. Adolescents who are confused about their choices are said to experience identity confusion.

**5.** James Marcia described four identity statuses according to an individual's exploration of and commitment to the roles and values that comprise personal identity. Adolescents in identity diffusion are not actively exploring or committing. Those in identity foreclosure status have committed without having explored different roles and values. Those in moratorium status are exploring different adult roles but have not yet made commitments. Those in identity achievement have explored a variety of adult roles and have then committed to a life plan. Waterman and other theorists suggest other dimensions of identity formation, such as personal expressiveness. Critics claim that Marcia's identity statuses conceive identity formation too narrowly in adolescents.

**6.** Traditionally, male identity has focused more on achievement and vocation, whereas female identity has been more strongly linked to feelings of connectedness to others. Individuation and separation appear to be more conflictual for females. Gilligan contends that for optimal development, male and female adolescents must balance independence with caring and connectedness. There is considerable variation *within* each gender regarding gender identity and self-esteem.

**7.** Self-evaluation becomes more negative during early adolescence. Cognitive changes lead teenagers to be somewhat more confused and critical of themselves. The stresses of early adolescence, including greater social and academic pressures, usually are cited as causing the decline. However, many young people continue to feel good (or bad) about themselves throughout the adolescent period.

**8.** Self-awareness and self-consciousness peak during the adolescent years. Social comparisons (noticing similarities with and differences from others) become more frequent. Many early adolescents are unhappy about their appearance and worry about popularity and rejection. For most adolescents, self-evaluations eventually become more realistic and their track records become more impressive. This boosts self-confidence and self-esteem.

**9.** One crucial task of adolescence is integrating various "selves" into one internally consistent, unified personality. Discrepancies between who we think we are and who we want to be motivate change. Large discrepancies between ac-

tual and desired selves may discourage those who can't imagine themselves changing.

**10.** Self-esteem refers to how we feel about who we believe we are. Positive self-esteem is an important predictor of healthy personality development and the ability to have close relationships. Newer models view self-esteem as less global and more multidimensional.

**11.** To understand self-esteem, we need to know what personal qualities people value and how they rate themselves on those qualities. Different self-esteem trajectories are described in the chapter, with girls having more difficulty accepting themselves and their bodies than boys do.

**12.** Self-esteem usually is enhanced by opportunities to excel at activities that are meaningful to the individual. Children who are raised with unconditional acceptance from family members usually feel less pressured to prove their worthiness.

**13.** Committing to an ethnic identity is an important part of creating a healthy adult self-concept. It can be difficult to accept oneself as a member of a group that is subject to discrimination and derogatory labels. Young people adjust better when they are given opportunities to explore their ethnic traditions by family members who model ethnic pride and dignity. Biculturalism refers to an individual's ability to inhabit and become competent in two cultures at one time.

# GLOSSARY

**Epigenetic principle** Every stage in development contributes something to future stages and reframes all the earlier ones

**Ego identity** According to Erikson, that aspect of who we are that we perceive as having continuity over time

**Personal dimension of identity** One's ideology, vocational aspirations, sexuality, nationality, gender, and ethnicity

**Social dimension of identity** The many roles people play in life, including student, parent, citizen, and employee

**Identity confusion** Uncertainty about one's place in the world

**Identity crisis** Erikson's term for adolescents' serious questioning of their essential personal characteristics, their view of themselves, their concerns about how others view them, and their doubts about the meaning and purpose of their existence

**Exploration** The process of considering alternative ways of being and of living one's life

**Commitment** In Marcia's model, firm decisions about relationships and employment, including specific strategies for achieving personal goals and a desired life path

**Identity diffusion** One of Marcia's identity statuses, in which individuals are not actively exploring or committing to adult roles and values

**Identity foreclosure** In Marcia's model, committing to a life plan without adequate exploration

**Moratorium** In Marcia's model, considering different points of view and experimenting with various adult roles but not yet making a final commitment

**Identity achievement** In Marcia's model, the identity status in which adolescents have explored and committed to a life plan

**Individuate** To become "one's own person"

**True self** Who we think we really are

**Self-concept** Who we think we are (same as true self)

**False self** Who we want people to think we are

**Ideal (desired) self** Who we would like to become

**Public self** How others see us

**Possible self** Who we could become

**Dreaded self** Who we are afraid of becoming

**Self-descriptors** Terms we use to characterize ourselves

**Social comparison** Comparing ourselves to a reference group

**Differentiation** Becoming increasingly complex and unique

**Integration** Consolidating all facets of our personality into a consistent, ongoing whole person

**Self-esteem** How we feel about ourselves

**Global self-esteem** A single measure of our feeling of worthiness

**Gender-role intensification** Pressure to conform to gender-role stereotypes

**Unconditional acceptance** Accepting someone regardless of his or her behavior or accomplishments

**Ethnic identity** Committing to one's ethnic group

**Identity formation** Models describing the psychological phases or stages involved in establishing an ethnic identity

**Acculturation models** Emphasizing the individual's adjustment to the dominant society

**Social identity theory** Theory that individuals develop an identity reflecting both their own ethnic group and the dominant group

**Biracial children** Children of parents of different races

**Biculturalism** Accommodating a larger culture while retaining the characteristics and values of one's own culture of origin

## THOUGHT QUESTIONS

**1.** Given the changes in family life during this century, is it harder today than in the past for young people to "find themselves" (i.e., construct a meaningful personal identity)?

**2.** Relate Marcia's concepts of exploration and commitment to your own life goals in regard to education, vocation, or relationships. Do you feel your present commitments are based on sufficient exploration of alternatives?

**3.** To what extent do you measure up to your own standards of performance in the areas of your life that are most important to you. Are your standards realistic?

**4.** Imagine waking up one morning and being of the other gender. How would this transformation affect your self-concept? How would your relationships, goals, and aspirations be affected?

**5.** What role, if any, does your ethnic group membership play in your self-concept?

# SELF-TEST

1. According to Erikson, adolescence is the optimal time to
   a. begin investing in mutual funds
   b. apply to college
   c. have fun and enjoy life
   d. construct an adult identity

2. Psychologists consider a self-concept to be healthy if it is
   a. realistic
   b. self-generated
   c. integrated across roles
   d. all of the above

3. Uncertainty about one's place in the world is called
   a. identity confusion
   b. identity crisis
   c. identity foreclosure
   d. an adjustment reaction

4. Marcia's four identity statuses reflect different combinations of
   a. personal identity and social identity
   b. exploration and commitment
   c. self-concept and self-esteem
   d. the true self and the false self

5. According to Marcia, adolescents usually display identity achievement by
   a. the beginning of middle school
   b. high school graduation
   c. the later college years
   d. their mid-20s

6. Gilligan, Archer, and others criticize Erikson's and Marcia's identity models for
   a. stressing individuation over connectedness
   b. being biased against minorities
   c. overlooking the secular trend
   d. not using appropriate control groups

7. The possible self refers to
   a. who we think we could be

   **b.** who we would like to be

   **c.** who we are afraid of becoming

   **d.** who we want other people to think we are

8. Self-concept reflects

   **a.** self-evaluation

   **b.** social comparison

   **c.** feedback from significant others

   **d.** all of the above

9. The evaluative component of self-concept is

   **a.** self-efficacy

   **b.** identity

   **c.** self-esteem

   **d.** achievement

10. Self-esteem often is depressed during

   **a.** childhood

   **b.** early and middle adolescence

   **c.** late adolescence

   **d.** young adulthood

11. Female self-esteem appears to be most tied to

   **a.** achievement

   **b.** individuation

   **c.** popularity

   **d.** the self in relationship

12. How young people come to terms with their ethnic heritage depends largely on

   **a.** family attitudes and practices

   **b.** peer group support

   **c.** individual temperament

   **d.** exposure to discrimination

13. Individuals inhabiting two cultures

   **a.** usually strive to develop and maintain competence in both worlds

   **b.** ultimately choose one culture over the other

   **c.** experience cognitive and social deficits

   **d.** tend to identify with the mainstream culture

# SEVEN

# ADOLESCENTS IN FAMILIES

◆

## Preview Questions

1. How are families "training grounds" for having relationships?
2. How do mother–adolescent relationships differ from father–adolescent relationships?
3. What life issues do most parents of adolescents face?
4. Is there a generation gap?
5. What is the relationship between parenting style and personal qualities of adolescents?
6. What role does family conflict play in adolescents' striving to be more independent?
7. What are sources of conflict between adolescents and their parents?
8. What stressors do adolescents face when their parents divorce?

◆

## Disclosures

Okay. My family life. Well, I'm not too close with my family. With my father, we joke around. He's very funny, easygoing, makes me laugh, but we're not really close-close. He's like a buddy but he's still my dad. And my mom—well, she tries to be my best friend, but I'm not like that. She wants me to tell her everything, but I never would. She's older and really not in tune with my life. She wants me to go to her all the time, and she tries to get me to talk and tries to ask me questions a lot, but it's not like I have anything to tell her anyway, and I'm not gonna go to her if I did.     *(17-year-old female)*

I get along well with my mother. It's weird because she thinks we have this great relationship and that I can talk to her, but I feel so far away and that I can't, so I know that her perception of the relationship is different from mine. She thinks that I tell her everything. I wish I could be totally honest with her. I have a different relationship with her sister, my aunt. She's awesome. I feel I can tell her everything. She's proven to me that I can trust her and my Mom has proven to me that I can't trust her.

*(17-year-old female)*

I'm thankful for a loving family, people that always care about me, a place to stay when I need to.

*(17-year-old male)*

# Contents

**I**t is my pleasure to introduce you to my daughter Marianne through the pages of my journal. At 16, Marianne is the youngest of our four children. In my very prejudiced view, Marianne is a very special young lady. She represents everything that is good about youth and is the kind of young person anyone would be proud to have for a daughter. She is warm, caring, and very sensitive of other people. She is easygoing and undemanding. She is very unselfish and often puts other people before herself. She tends to be quiet and usually doesn't assert herself. Marianne is a very happy person. She has a cute sense of humor and loves to laugh and make others laugh as well.

All this praise probably makes her sound unreal, but actually she is very typical. She loves pizza, the movies, clothes, the phone, shopping, music, her dog, and school. Marianne is popular with her peers and has just begun to "go out" with her first boy friend. Her hair is brown and she has a face full of freckles.

*(Marianne's mother)*

Marianne's mother obviously enjoys her daughter and is proud of her, sentiments that most parents of adolescent children share. In a textbook, there is a danger of paying too much attention to problems surrounding the adolescent period and not enough to everyday, healthy adolescent behavior. If we are not careful, we see adolescence as pathology—as a period of maladjustment, risk, and parental worry. I chose this particular excerpt from Marianne's mother's journal to emphasize three points: (1) an excellent reason for having children is to enjoy raising them, (2) parents and children feel deeply about each other and enrich each other's lives, and (3) most adolescents live in harmony with their parents most of the time (Offer, Ostrov, & Howard, 1989; Offer & Schonert-Reichl, 1992). It is interesting that Marianne's mother hears her own praise of her daughter as "unreal" but still sees her daughter as a typical teenager.

There is no consensus among parents regarding whether adolescents are easier or harder to live with than younger children. Both points of view are defendable. Certainly, teenagers require less parental care, are more adult-like in their judgment and behavior, and are more cooperative than younger children. However, it's easy to see why so many parents view adolescence as a period of "storm and stress." As a group, teenagers are somewhat more quarrelsome and irritable than when they were younger. Parents' expectations of obedient, respectful behavior often go unfulfilled as their children request (and occasionally demand) more self-regulation and a greater role in decision making. The 17-year-old girl quoted at the very beginning of this chapter makes it clear that, her mother's attempts to the contrary, her life is no longer an open book for her parents to read. Compared to the preadolescent years, there is more family tension and disagreement (Larson & Richards, 1994; Steinberg, 1987a).

During the early teenage years, adolescents' and parents' feelings about each other become more intense. They report fewer positive and more negative emotions when they are in each other's company (Collins & Russell, 1991; Montemayor, Eberly, & Flannery, 1993). And the amount of time parents and children spend with each other lessens dramatically between the 5th and 12th grades, at least for European-American working- and middle-class families (Larson, Richards, Moneta, Holmbeck, & Duckett, 1996). In a national poll of 1,055 teenagers conducted in 1994 by *The New York Times* and CBS News, 40% of those polled claimed that their parents sometimes or often did not make time to help them. During follow-up interviews, many said that their parents did not spend much time with them or communicate well with them. "Even when my parents are here, it's like they're not because they don't have any time," said one 16-year-old (Chira, 1994, p. 16).

Adolescents generally view family events and interactions more negatively than their parents do (Callan & Noller, 1986), perhaps reflecting their need to separate from their families and become "their own person." Having a greater stake in harmonious family interactions, parents usually view their parenting and everyday family encounters more positively (Bengston & Kuypers, 1971; Noller, 1994; Noller & Callan, 1988; Paulson & Sputa, 1996). Fortunately, despite this temporary deterioration in family life, parents and teenagers continue to reinvent the parent–child relationship and enjoy each other's companionship (most of the time) (Ackerman, 1980; Holmbeck & Hill, 1988; Larson & Richards, 1994; Montemayor, 1983).

**Adolescents often interpret family events and encounters more negatively than their parents do.**

However, after so many years of almost total compliance from their children, some parents see their increasingly assertive children as rebellious or even out of control. Some parents overreact when discussing mundane issues such as household chores or homework with their children. Instead of giving their children slack ("If you like, I can check your homework when you're finished"), many parents resort to coercive practices ("If your homework is not finished by dinner time, I will not allow you to leave this house"). Coming on too strong often provokes unnecessary resistance and defiance (Hill, 1987; Hill & Holmbeck, 1987; Montemayor & Hanson, 1985; Patterson, 1982; Steinberg, 1981, 1990).

Frequent power struggles with parents impede adolescents' ability to address developmental tasks, including becoming self-regulating and making good decisions (Patterson, 1982). Parents risk alienating their older children when they attempt to control their problem solving and decision making (Noller, 1994). The adolescent wonders: "How can I become more independent when I'm constantly being told what to do? How do I learn to make good decisions if I'm never given the opportunity?" The parent wonders: "How do I maintain my authority while supporting my child's desire for more freedom?" Not a few parents, out of frustration and anger, throw up their hands in defeat and moan, "I give up. Do what you want." They characterize their children as "unmanageable."

Abdicating control is not the answer. Underinvolved and neglecting parents increasingly have become targets of media critics who blame absent or permissive parents for all kinds of social problems. Despite the apparent freedom that they gain when their parents withdraw from caregiving, children of minimally involved parents report feeling uncared for. Thus, too much or too little parental control bodes ill for adolescent adjustment (Dornbusch et al., 1985; Mason, Cauce, Gonzales, & Hiraga, 1996). Overly controlling and inconsistent parenting is associated with lower academic motivation, lower self-esteem, misconduct, and greater susceptibility to peer influence during adolescence (Conger & Conger, 1994; Eccles et al., 1993; Paulson, 1994; Simons, Johnson, & Conger, 1994; Wentzel, 1994).

Adolescents function best in environments that take into account their developmental needs, including their desire for greater participation in decision making, their need for emotional support and understanding, and their self-consciousness (Eccles, Buchanan, Flanagan, Fuligni, Midgley, & Yee, 1991; Eccles, et al., 1993). Fortunately, most parents learn how to adjust their parenting practices, especially their level of control, so that they respond according to their child's current developmental status and needs (McNally, Eisenberg, & Harris, 1991).

Family life shapes and encourages children's social nature. Regardless of their family configuration or economic circumstances, adolescents benefit from a stable and supportive family climate (Frey & Röthlisberger, 1996). Children's abilities, values, beliefs, self-esteem, and character develop mainly within a family context (Jaffe, 1997). As parents adjust to adolescent changes, most families provide "a strong base for the testing and consolidation of these changes" (Walsh & Scheinkman, 1993, p. 151). For better or for worse, children learn how to have relationships and how to treat people mainly by observing and interacting with family members. Ironically, it is within the family unit that most adolescents establish their individuality (Grotevant & Cooper, 1986; Martin, 1990; Yildirim, 1997).

In this chapter, we consider the nature of relationships in families with adolescents. How do parents respond to increasing requests from their children for self-regulation? How do middle-aged parents balance their own needs with those of their maturing children? Is there a generation gap in values between parents and teenagers? Do different styles of parenting encourage different personal qualities in children? Can teenagers distance themselves from their parents and still remain emotionally connected to them? And how do adolescents cope when their parents fall out of love with each other?

## WHAT IS THE NATURE OF RELATIONSHIPS IN FAMILIES?

Obviously, life does not begin at puberty. It is during the formative years of childhood that children learn what it means to be "in relationship" with, or feel close to, someone else. Children who are fortunate enough to belong to stable, cohesive two-parent families have countless opportunities to watch their parents enjoy each other's company and provide emotional support to each other as they wend their way through their hectic daily lives. Less fortunate children's "education" about adult relationships consists of watching their parents annoy, criticize, and undermine each other. Too many children witness hostile, even violent interactions between their parents. What are they learning about communication and relationships?

The key relationship in any two-parent family is the parental relationship (usually a marital relationship). Children's knowledge of how people are supposed to treat each other reflects mainly their cumulative observations of their parents' interactions and encounters with each other and with other family members (Larson et al., 1996; Necessary & Parish, 1996; Parish, 1993; Parke & Ladd, 1992). Do parents respect each other and take each other seriously? During conflict, are they willing to negotiate and compromise? Children watch their parents closely and are sensitive to their moods and actions partly because they know that their care and well-being are largely in their parents' hands (Feldman & Gehring, 1988).

Parent–child relationships are particularly important because they provide the main context in which socialization is supposed to occur (Alsaker, 1995; Crouter, Manke, & McHale, 1995; Jaffe, 1997). A 15-year-old female high school freshman told a student of mine during an interview, "I have trouble sticking up for myself because I feel that no matter what I say it will always be proven wrong, so don't bother. A lot of people [in my school] hate me because I'm a freshman or because of the person I'm seeing. They really don't know me."

When I first read this interview, I was puzzled. Why does this young girl feel so discouraged and rejected? Perhaps there is a clue in the following excerpt from the same interview. "My mother can be two different people. In front of other people, she's so nice. She tries to be the perfect mother, even though she's not. And when she's around me she'll just be herself. I always feel that no matter what I do, I can never make her happy. That's why I try so hard to get good grades. Not for myself but for her." We can't know for sure from an interview, but these two quotes suggest the possibility that this girl's feelings of helplessness and inadequacy in her peer relationships are linked to similar feelings in her relationship with her mother (Gavin & Furman, 1996; Parke & Ladd, 1992). If she can't please her own mother, who can she please?

Young people are more likely to approach and solicit advice and consolation from people who are sensitive and caring than from those who are critical and distant (Frey & Röthlisberger, 1996). A study of junior high school students in Hong Kong revealed that students' perceptions of their relationship with their parents were the best predictor of their life satisfaction (Leung & Leung, 1992). *Thought Question: Would you predict the same finding for students in the United States?* This is a bit troubling because adolescents often have more negative views of family functioning than parents do (Noller & Callan, 1986; Ohannessian, Lerner, Lerner, & von Eye, 1995).

The **family systems model** provides an interesting framework for viewing interactions and relationships in families (e.g., Jacobvitz & Bush, 1996; Walsh & Scheinkman, 1993). Whereas Sigmund Freud and Erik Erikson viewed families as collections of individuals, the family systems model views families as multigenerational systems of interconnected relationships with shifting alli-

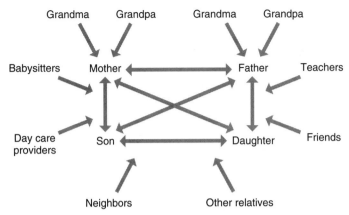

FIGURE 7-1 A family systems diagram of a nuclear family with six dyads (two-person relationships) indicated by double-headed arrows. (From Jaffe, 1997)

ances and changing roles (Jacobvitz & Bush, 1996). Each relationship within a family consists of specific exchanges between participants and displays characteristic interaction and communication patterns (Carter & McGoldrick, 1988; Feldman & Gehring, 1988).

According to the family systems model (Figure 7-1), any important change in one individual or relationship reverberates throughout the rest of the family system. Pubertal adolescents, awash in changes, challenge a family's values, roles, and the family communication system (Alsaker, 1995; Brown, 1988; Jory, Rainbolt, Karns, Freeborn, & Greer, 1996). More than younger children, adolescents desire opportunities to make decisions for themselves and insist on providing input regarding decisions and rules that affect them (Amato, 1989). The entire family system must transform itself (albeit gradually) to allow maturing children greater self-regulation. The family systems model also helps us appreciate how parent factors such as midlife dissatisfaction and marital conflict contribute to parent–adolescent relationships and conflict. *Thought Question: What typical adolescent behaviors might destabilize a family system?*

## PUBERTY, SOCIALIZATION, AND PARENTAL INFLUENCE

Alsaker (1995) raises the intriguing question of whether puberty is a critical period for socialization. A **critical period** is a specific time in development when a life event has its greatest impact (Papalia & Olds, 1996). **Socialization** refers to the process by which children are raised and educated to become social beings through their adoption of the values, norms, roles, and customs of their community. The main goal of socialization is to produce competent, well-behaved, and well-adjusted adults (Alsaker, 1995). Parents report more satisfaction with child rearing when they view their adolescent children's behavior as appropriate for their age (Henry & Peterson, 1995). Alsaker wonders whether pubescent children are especially susceptible to socialization and whether their parents have the resources to promote psychological independence in their children while maintaining emotional connectedness.

According to Alsaker (1995), many parents are confused about what to teach their pubescent children because they, the parents, grew up at a much different time and there are no cultural guidelines about how today's adolescents are supposed to act. With no formal rites of passage in most Western societies, adolescents and their caregivers are not clear about what to expect from each other. Norms differ according to a family's social class, ethnicity, religion, and community (Brody, Stoneman, & Flor, 1996). Even if they have strong values and specific childrearing goals, parents may, through their own behavior (e.g., by smoking or drinking too much), contradict what they tell their children, contradict each other, or communicate mixed messages to their children (e.g., conform, be yourself).

Further, parents may have difficulty adjusting their parenting style to take into account their child's current level of maturation. As we shall see, some parents, beset by worries, fears, and misconceptions, overreact to their children's requests for more freedom. These are just a few of the ways that parents can lose credibility in their children's eyes. Reduced closeness with parents, increased conflict, and more time spent alone in one's room may reflect parents' diminishing influence as agents of socialization in Western and Third World societies (Alsaker, 1995; Mboya, 1995).

## Relationships with Mothers

Mothers are the primary caregivers in most families, whether or not they are employed. They spend more time with their children than fathers do and usually are more in tune with their children's emotional needs (Larson et al., 1996; Paulson & Sputa, 1996; Youniss & Smollar, 1985). Participants in a study of Scottish secondary school students reported that their mothers and same-gender friends were the most significant people in their lives (Hendry, Roberts, Glendinning, & Coleman, 1992).

Young adolescents report that they spend more time with and feel closer to their mothers than to their fathers (Larson & Richards, 1994; Miller & Lane, 1991; Papini, Roggman, & Anderson, 1991; Paulson, Hill, & Holmbeck, 1991; Youniss & Smollar, 1985). They find their relationships with their mothers more satisfying (Noller & Callan, 1990; Thornton, Orbuch, & Axinn, 1995). Mothers usually are seen as being more understanding, open, and accepting than fathers (Barnes & Olson, 1985; Imbimbo, 1995; Klein, O'Bryant, & Hopkins, 1996). Teenagers also view mothers as being more interested than fathers in their day-to-day lives. With their mothers, daughters discuss sex, relationships, and other common interests (Gavin & Furman, 1996; Noller & Bagi, 1985). Feeling close to one's mother appears to be a better predictor of positive adolescent outcomes than any other factor (Field, Lang, Yando, & Bendell, 1995). Nevertheless, boys and girls begin to distance themselves from their parents when puberty begins (Papini et al., 1991). Girls apparently have more difficulty than boys telling their mothers to back off (Smith & Forehand, 1986). By the age of 16 to 17, happily, most teenagers apparently have resolved their conflicts with authority figures and perceive greater warmth and empathy from the significant adults in their lives (especially parents) (Drevets, Benton, & Bradley, 1996).

Mothers in Larson and Richards' (1994) study reported that, despite their hectic work schedules, they strove to be very involved in their children's lives. They talked more to their adolescent children than fathers did, although the average amount of talk time for mothers was only 7 minutes a day. Adolescents in the study said that they enjoyed talking to their parents, at least when conversations occurred on their terms (i.e., time, place, topic). Teenage boys and girls agreed that they speak more to their mothers than to their fathers about friends, family, and feelings. "Because the fathers had longer work hours, the mothers spent more time with their children than the fathers did on weekdays, especially during the difficult transitional times when everyone was getting ready at the start of the day, or when supper had to be prepared at the end of the day" (p. 135).

Because mothers spend more time with their children and usually are the "parent in charge," they find themselves asserting their authority by setting limits, turning down requests, or disapproving of misbehavior (Holmbeck & Hill, 1991b; Steinberg, 1987c). Since mothers are more likely than fathers to back off when challenged, adolescents are more likely to challenge them (Steinberg, 1990). Even though mothers reach out to their sons and daughters more frequently than fathers do (Jory et al., 1996), because mothers usually are more invested in the parenting role, they receive the brunt of adolescent wrath (Ellis-Schwabe & Thornburg, 1986; Montemayor et al., 1993). Ironically, this is particularly true of mothers whose lives revolve around their children (Larson & Richards, 1994).

Many mothers report that their need to feel close to their adolescent children and to enjoy their company often goes unfulfilled. During the early teenage years, a mother "suddenly finds herself caring for an adolescent who is more withholding, more prone to negative moods, and who sometimes directs the brunt of his or her displeasure at her" (Larson & Richards, 1994, p. 131). As these investigators note, adolescents often make it hard for their parents to give them the extra support and approval that they need during social and emotional hard times. This is unfortunate because teenagers (especially girls) who remain close to their mothers usually are better adjusted and less depressed than those who completely shut their parents out of their lives (Canetti, Bachar, Galili-Weisstub, De-Nour, & Shalev, 1997; Larson & Richards, 1994; Simons et al., 1994). *Thought Question: Why do so many fathers not provide their children with the same level of closeness that most mothers offer?*

## Relationships with Fathers

When their children are young, most fathers try to be warm and available. Over time, at least from their children's viewpoint, fathers become less accepting, more demanding, and less interested in the details of their children's daily lives (De Luccie & Davis, 1991). Fathers of teenagers usually are preoccupied with their careers and are less aware than mothers (including working mothers) of children's school work and social lives (Collins & Russell, 1991; Youniss & Smollar, 1985). Fathers in poor and welfare families are still less involved in their adolescent children's lives, even though father involvement appears to be more critical for the development of disadvantaged children (Harris & Marmer, 1996). *Thought Question: How might fathers' increasing emotional distance from their children contribute to adolescent autonomy?*

When they do spend time with their children, many fathers prefer to stay in role (e.g., authority figure, problem solver) rather than be in relationship (e.g., express interest by asking questions and listening). Dad might be having a good time telling stories or giving a driving lesson, but the teenager is not always enjoying the experience. Many adolescents (especially daughters) report that their fathers do not try hard enough to understand them. Thus, like the young woman quoted below, they have little incentive to risk sharing their true feelings (du Bois-Reymond & Ravesloot, 1996; Larson & Richards, 1994; Youniss & Smollar, 1985).

> *My father still sees me as a little girl. I'll always be a little girl to him. A lot of things that I do, I do for my father. Not exactly the best reason. I think that's one of the reasons I'm such a perfectionist. Everything I accomplish, I accomplish for his approval. My father holds me on a pedestal. Everything I do is so I don't fall off the pedestal. My mother I can tell things that I shouldn't have done. I would never tell my father.*
>
> *(19-year-old female)*

Men typically view fathering as a voluntary activity. "A father can enjoy playing a game of ping-pong with his child, but if he does not feel like being engaged, he may withdraw behind the newspaper or retire to watch sports or work in the yard" (Larson & Richards, 1994, p. 164). Most fathers view themselves not as primary caregivers, but as assistants to their partners. Most fathers prefer not to provide care or nurturance when mothers are available. Instead, they assist the mother–child relationship. Single fathers parent more like traditional mothers than like traditional fathers (Risman, 1989), suggesting that role is stronger than gender.

Under certain conditions, fathers assume responsibility for managing their children, lessening pressure on mothers. In the face of conflict, fathers are more likely than mothers to act assertively. Their children usually defer to them (Steinberg, 1990). There is evidence that a father's presence increases a child's responsiveness to a mother (Gjerde, 1986). This is an important finding because it suggests that father involvement improves the mother–adolescent relationship. *Thought Question: Why might father approval be more highly valued than mother approval to adolescents in two-parent families?*

In most families, parent–adolescent contact is guided partly by gender: mothers spend more time with daughters and fathers with sons (Crouter et al., 1995). Some theorists attribute gender differences in achievement, sex-role attitudes, and self-esteem during adolescence to this pattern. Many adolescent boys and girls report having warm relationships with their fathers and enjoying their company (Kurdek & Fine, 1993; Paulson et al., 1991; Thornton et al., 1995). Fathers seem to derive more satisfaction from their sons than from their daughters (Henry & Peterson, 1995). Boys talk to their fathers about their interests, sexual issues, and general problems (Noller & Callan, 1990). Not surprisingly, boys appear to be affected more than girls by their fathers' personal qualities and adjustment (D'Angelo, Weinberger, & Feldman, 1995).

Adolescent girls often complain of an absence of emotional involvement with their fathers (Moser, Paternite, & Dixon, 1996). There is evidence, however, that after puberty some girls rebuff attempts by their mothers and fathers to get closer (Holmbeck, 1987; Salt, 1991; Vuchinich, Hetherington, Vuchinich, & Clingempeel, 1991). Perhaps compared to mothers, who spend more time with their daughters and usually are emotionally expressive, fathers seem distant. Many do not converse seriously with their children on a regular basis, as mothers try to do (see the disclosure that begins this chapter). Girls are more influenced by their mother's opinions and boys are more influenced by their father's opinions (Poole & Gelder, 1985).

Fathers usually feel closer to their daughters than their daughters feel to them (Larson & Richards, 1994; Miller & Lane, 1991). Most children understand that their fathers love them (Paulson et al., 1991), but they still feel closer to their mothers. Boys and girls report that their mothers know them well and treat them fairly, but many girls report that their fathers do not (Harris & Morgan, 1991; Miller & Lane, 1991; Youniss & Ketterlinus, 1987). Some fathers (and mothers) who are trapped in emotionally distant marriages become overly involved with their daughters to the point of exploitation (Jacobvitz & Bush, 1996). *Thought Question: Why might early-maturing girls find their relationships with their fathers particularly unsatisfactory?*

Despite their children's feelings of emotional distance, fathers do play a significant role in helping their children solve problems, think for themselves, and make decisions (Newman, 1989; Schulman & Collins, 1993). Positive treatment by fathers and their active involvement in their children's lives foretell healthy adolescent functioning in intact and divorced families (Holahan, Valentiner, & Moos, 1994; Miller & Lane, 1991; Thomas & Forehand, 1993). All the more reason for fathers to stay in touch with their teenaged children's activities, thoughts, and feelings (Ginsberg, 1995).

## SPOTLIGHT • Adolescents, Unrelated Adults, and Mentors

*In a society in which prepubertal ideals are conveyed to girls in the media, in which young bodies are the norm for the clothing and fitness industry, and in which adults try to remain as young as possible as long as possible, what models do adolescents really have in this transition period?*

(Alsaker, 1995, p. 441)

Who were the three most significant people in *your* life? When asked to name adults who are important influences, adolescents usually list family members, including parents, older siblings, grandparents, and other extended family members. But most also mention at least one adult to whom they are not related (Blyth, Hill, & Thiel, 1982; Galbo, 1984, 1986; Hamilton & Darling, 1996).

Familiar adults whom young people look up to and trust, for example coaches, teachers, neighbors, and Scout leaders, are an important part of most young people's social network (Galbo, 1986; Philip & Hendry, 1996; Scales & Gibbons, 1996), especially for children who live in single-parent families (Zimmerman, Salem, & Maton, 1995). Unrelated adults provide information, reinforce prosocial behavior, and serve as role models. They may even provide care when parents are unavailable (Darling, Hamilton, & Niego, 1994). Girls and adolescents of color seem to benefit the most from close involvement with unrelated adults whom they perceive as accepting them (Galbo & Demetrulias, 1996; Scales & Gibbons, 1996).

Most adults who come into contact with adolescents occupy formal roles such as teacher, clergy, youth worker, or coach (Galbo & Demetrulias, 1996). These roles require "highly scripted behaviors" by adults who are sanctioned by parents or society to administer rewards and punishments to young people (Gottlieb & Sylvestre, 1995). Unrelated adults usually instruct adolescents in groups, which limits one-to-one contact and dialogue.

Many adults are reluctant to give the appearance of violating family boundaries by intruding too deeply into a child's family affairs. They also worry about being accused of sexual or other forms of youth exploitation. Some adults are ill prepared for their helper role (Sleek & Burnette, 1996). Some adults who coach baseball, soccer, and other sports, for example, know a lot about their sport but not enough about children and adolescents. They may inadvertently cause emotional or physical harm by making insensitive comments or applying intense pressure to perform.

Young people may perceive unrelated adults as unavailable or uninterested in having a personal relationship with them. There are adults, however, who adopt a style of communication that lets young people know that they can be trusted and are interested in mutual dialogue. They share their own experiences and encourage adolescents to examine their own motives and personality (Gottlieb & Sylvestre, 1995). Cochran and Bø (1989) found that Norwegian boys who had casual interactions with unrelated adults displayed more positive social behavior and did better in school.

Some highly motivated adults serve as *mentors*, that is, teachers or role models who establish a personal connection with young people, help them acquire practical skills or information, provide encouragement and emotional support, and guide them through unfamiliar situations (Murray, 1995c; Queen, 1994; Rhodes, 1994; Roberts & Cotton, 1994). "I really opened his eyes to computers in photography. I showed Reggie the photo lab at Ciba and the different equipment. I gave him ideas on how he could take his photography and make a career out of it. And I loved doing it" (Shariff Lee, mentor, quoted by Dencker, 1996, p. CE-8). Ms. Lee participates in the Black Achievers Program in Summit, New Jersey (Dencker, 1996).

Mentoring programs typically are designed to help disadvantaged youth gain skills and responsibility by placing them with caring and competent adult volunteers. Mentoring programs are particularly beneficial when parents are unable or unavailable to provide their children with mentoring-type support and instruction (Hamilton & Darling, 1996; Queen, 1994).

Mentors offer adolescents the opportunity to gain support and encouragement from an adult in a one-to-one relationship.

According to Hamilton and Darling (1996), "mentors encourage young people to set goals and to set them high. They help proteges to make plans for achieving their goals and help them evaluate their actions in terms of their contributions to meeting those goals" (p. 202). Mentoring programs are most effective when the mentor and the adolescent participate in a challenging activity with a shared goal (Darling, Hamilton, & Niego, 1994; Hamilton & Hamilton, 1992). "When a particular teacher or coach becomes important to an adolescent, it is either because the adolescent sees in that person qualities the adolescent admires and wants to emulate or because the person holds a vision of the adolescent that the adolescent wants to share" (Darling et al., 1994, p. 229). Praise from the mentor is especially meaningful to an adolescent because it is based on accomplishment or personal qualities rather than on kinship. *Thought Question: What changes during early adolescence might make young people more receptive to the influence of an adult other than a parent?*

Given that most adolescents have minimal opportunities for one-to-one contact with unrelated adults (Bø, 1996), mentoring offers them the opportunity to have such contact with someone they can learn from and confide in. Mentors typically are more involved in children's lives than are teachers or counselors in that they offer instruction and support in the context of an ongoing one-to-one relationship. They "exemplify how mature, thoughtful adults think about issues, solve problems, and confront challenges . . . the purpose of exemplification is not to teach specific values to young people but to demonstrate to them one way to be responsible and competent adults'' (Hamilton & Darling, 1996, p. 203).

Hamilton and Darling's (1996) study of third-year students at Cornell University revealed the following activities that students frequently engaged in with mentors: discussing personal matters the young people cared deeply about, including family, friends, ideas, politics, and the future; listening to music and attending cultural events; and other activities in and out of school. *Thought Question: What domains of adolescent development are likely to be enhanced by such encounters with mentors?*

## PARENTS AT MIDLIFE

*Today Laura is at odds with the world. I say "up" and she says "down." Just because I asked her to do some insignificant thing, she said, "You are the world's meanest mother. No real mother would treat their child like you do." I'm beginning to feel like maybe it's true, she says it so often. As Laura goes through adolescence, I am going through life changes too. We are both moody. I know that mood swings are a big part of adolescence, but just how much of this is normal?*

*(Mother of 15-year-old Laura)*

Parents of teenagers usually are approaching or have achieved middle age (their 40s and 50s). Despite popular stereotypes about "change of life" and the "midlife crisis," middle age is not a time of upheaval and misery for most adults (Azar, 1996c). Middle age typically is a time of normal life stress and reappraisal. However, for parents like Laura's mother, changes in their children's lives can easily magnify their midlife issues (Conger et al., 1991; Steinberg & Steinberg, 1994).

Midlife issues focus on work, marriage, and parenting. Parental well-being can be undermined by a variety of stressful life circumstances that generate a sense of one's life being out of control: poverty, unstable employment situations, racism, conflicted marriages (Azar, 1996c; Elder, Eccles, Ardelt, & Lord, 1995; McLoyd, 1990). As implied by the interactional-ecological model we encountered in Chapter 2, stress and dissatisfaction in any one of these arenas are likely to spill over into the others (Grolnick, Weiss, McKenzie, & Wrightman, 1996; Kurdek, Fine, & Sinclair, 1994; Lempers & Clark-Lempers, 1997; Steinberg & Steinberg, 1994). For example, parents in a less than perfect marriage, after a hard day's work, may not feel particularly tolerant of back talk from a teenager or what they perceive to be a lack of appreciation for their efforts and sacrifices. Mothers confess that living with adolescents is, if not the low point of their parenting experiences, a challenging adventure. The decline in marital satisfaction that began with the arrival of a first child may continue unabated during the teenage years (Steinberg & Steinberg, 1994).

Mothers who have a large emotional investment in their children's lives (as most do) but few outside interests may have mixed feelings about their children's increasing independence. Traditional mothers were said to suffer from the "empty nest blues" when their grown children left home. Research suggests the opposite: most mothers express relief when the last child leaves the family nest (Rubin, 1979; Steinberg & Steinberg, 1994).

It is not unusual to hear parents protest that they are getting back less from their adolescent children than they (the parents) are giving. Mothers often express sorrow about lessening closeness with their daughters; fathers typically lament lessening companionship with their sons. (These sentiments are more often expressed by those who are dissatisfied with their marriages.) Parents of adolescents frequently report feeling unappreciated, especially when their sacrifices are ignored or criticized (Steinberg & Steinberg, 1994).

A mother who had put a lot of effort into decorating her house for her son's party described her hurt feelings when he "took one look at the decorations and then gave me this really disgusted look, like I had done something horrible, just terrible" (Steinberg & Steinberg, 1994, p. 116). He casually told her that he was taking "all this junk" down and then headed to the bathroom. "You know, I was furious, but I didn't want to say anything, not then at least, not right before the party. But I can't imagine ever saying something like that to my mother when I was his age. So disrespectful. So unappreciative. I mean, I had really knocked myself out for him. And for what? For nothing" (p. 116).

Would teenagers be surprised to learn that their insensitive comments cause so much pain? Laura's mother (quoted at the beginning of this section) says, "I show my emotions easily. When she hurts me, she asks, 'Did I hurt your feelings?' When I answer, 'Yes' she says, 'You're just feeling sorry for yourself.' She makes me feel that she doesn't want me for her mom, and I love her so much!" *Critical Thinking Question: What role might adolescent egocentrism play in such encounters?*

Steinberg and Steinberg's (1994) interviews with families with adolescent children revealed that many parents, especially those who are overworked or

Parents who are dissatisfied with their own lives often resent or feel envious of their children's apparently carefree lifestyle.

stressed out, compared themselves unfavorably to their apparently carefree, fun-loving sons and daughters. Many parents admitted feeling envious of their children's popularity and sexuality. Naturally, they felt guilty for having such feelings. Their children's youthfulness and freedom reminded parents that they, the older generation, were no longer young and free. Some parents reported desiring a second chance at adulthood, implying dissatisfaction with the way their lives had turned out. *Thought Question: Who has more freedom of lifestyle, adolescents or their parents?*

It is hard to predict how parents will react to their teenagers' increasing assertiveness. Children's requests (or demands) for more self-regulation can easily intensify existing family and marital tensions. Adolescents give parents who bicker more to bicker about (Steinberg & Silverberg, 1987; Steinberg & Steinberg, 1994). Some parents interpret their children's increasing autonomy as disobedience or as a lack of respect for parental authority. Rather than becoming more flexible, these parents become increasingly restrictive and disapproving (Steinberg & Steinberg, 1994). However, violations of expectancies and heated family discussions, painful as they are, can help parents and teenagers develop more realistic expectations about each other (Collins, 1990; Dickerson & Zimmerman, 1992; Steinberg & Silverberg, 1986).

Parents who understand the stresses and strains of adolescent life are likely to feel pride in their children's physical and social maturity. They provide needed emotional support rather than rigid opposition (Chu & Powers, 1995; Eccles et al., 1993). It is helpful for parents to view their children's increasing independence not as a loss of parental authority but as an opportunity to spend more time pursuing other avenues of satisfaction (Silverberg & Steinberg, 1990). Meaningful activities outside of the family, such as a challenging job or volunteer work, boost parents' self-worth and lessen the threat of an empty nest.

## IS THERE A GENERATION GAP?

Like Marianne, described by her mother at the beginning of this chapter, most teenagers are reasonably happy, have good relationships with peers, and take school and their future seriously. They admire, respect, and are concerned about their parents, feel appreciated by them, and seek their advice (Hill, 1985; Offer, 1987; Youniss & Ketterlinus, 1987). Similarly, most parents report warm, pleasant relationships with their adolescent children. Fewer than 10 percent of families experience chronically strained relationships between parents and adolescent children (Steinberg, 1990).

Then why do we still hear talk of a "generation gap?" Since the late 1960s, our media, especially newspapers, television, and films, have emphasized tensions and conflict between parents and teenagers. To this day, you will rarely come across news stories about teenagers doing their chores, getting good grades, or being nice to their siblings. This bias in reporting stories about crime, drugs, and youth suicide reinforces the impression that most teenagers feel alienated and reject adult roles and values (Bandura, 1964).

Parents who raised their children during the 1960s and 1970s were disturbed by reports of recreational use of marijuana and other illegal drugs. They were upset by campus protests against militarism during the Vietnam War and felt threatened by their children's interest in "countercultural" lifestyles and values. Although reports of widespread intergenerational conflict were not supported by empirical research (Conger, 1981), media perpetuation of the storm and stress myth of adolescence keeps alive the concept of a generation gap (Steinberg, 1990).

Some observers insist that there is a **values gap** between adolescents and their parents. Traub and Dodder (1988), for example, suggest that because adolescents spend so much time with each other and have relatively few meaningful encounters with adults, adolescent norms, values, and behaviors emerge that are objectionable to adults. Do Beavis and Butthead ring a bell? Traub and Dodder use as an example the higher incidence of marijuana smoking among high school and college students compared to adults.

For the most part, close relationships between parents and their adolescent children were the rule in the 1960s and are still the rule. True, during early adolescence we observe increased tension among family members and less automatic compliance by teenagers. Nevertheless, for most families these disturbances are temporary and probably necessary for healthy realignment of family roles (Sessa & Steinberg, 1991). And they almost always occur in the larger context of affectionate feelings (if not expression) between parents and children (Collins, 1990; Hill, 1987; Johnson & Collins, 1988). "For the majority of families, warm and pleasant relationships in which parents continue to influence their children's development appear to be the norm" (Collins, 1990, p. 86).

**Close relationships between adolescents and their parents are the rule, not the exception.**

## PARENTING STYLES

There is evidence that more than anything else, adolescent adjustment reflects the quality of family relationships during childhood and adolescence (Canetti et al., 1997; Coombs & Landsverk, 1988; Lamborn, Mounts, Steinberg, & Dornbusch, 1991). In effect, by observing and interacting with their parents day in and day out for so many years, children come to emulate their parents' emotional expressiveness, communication styles, and relationship skills (Bronstein, Fitzgerald, Briones, Pieniadz, & D'Ari, 1993; Jaffe, 1997). Adolescents who grow up in chronically distressed families are likely to develop serious social and emotional problems (Ohannessian, Lerner, Lerner, & von Eye, 1994). (Sexual abuse of adolescents is covered in Chapter 13. The relationship between maladaptive parenting styles and deviant behavior in adolescents also is discussed in Chapter 13.)

Although no two adults approach parenting in exactly the same way, it is possible to identify distinctive patterns of child rearing and characteristics of children that are associated with each pattern. What we call a **parenting style** refers to the combination of rearing strategies and personal qualities of an individual parent. Psychologist Diana Baumrind (1966, 1967, 1968, 1971, 1975, 1989, 1991a, b, c) distinguished four parenting styles that vary on the dimensions of parental warmth, control, and willingness to grant autonomy: authoritarian, permissive, rejecting-neglecting, and authoritative. (Paulson and her colleagues [1991] define *warmth* as "the extent to which a positive, benevolent attitude permeates child rearing" (p. 277). Warmth is distinguished from closeness, although the two dimensions typically covary.)

**Authoritarian** (punitive) parents are demanding but not particularly responsive to their children's point of view. Valuing preservation of order and tradition, they do not encourage independent thinking. Although they closely monitor their children, authoritarian parents discourage the development of self-regulation by imposing demands that they strictly enforce. They favor punitive, forceful measures and are willing to use coercion to gain compliance. This exercise of power is exemplified by the parental exhortation "Because I said so."

**Permissive** parents are responsive but not very demanding. They are lenient, avoid confrontation with their children, and allow considerable self-regulation. There are two kinds of permissive parenting. **Enmeshed** parents are warm, accepting, and overly involved with their children. They are willing to use guilt to gain compliance ("Look what you're doing to me"). **Indulgent** parents also are warm and emotionally involved with their children but avoid "rocking the boat." Either they do not establish standards of conduct or they set standards that are below those that their children can meet. This style is represented by the parental lament "I try to talk to them but they just don't listen to me."

**Rejecting-neglecting** parents disengage from their children's lives. They are disorganized and do not monitor or supervise their children. They are neither demanding nor responsive to their children's needs. In fact, they are the least emotionally involved of the four parenting groups. This style is represented by the statement "Do what you want. I don't care."

**Authoritative** (democratic) parents are warm, firm, and involved, three key ingredients of competent parenting (Forehand & Nousiainen, 1993; Kurdek et al., 1994). Sensitive to their adolescent children's changing needs, they use reasoning and persuasion to gain compliance. They explain rules, discuss issues, and encourage verbal give-and-take (Chu & Powers, 1995). They encourage independent thinking ("What do you think?") and are respectful of opposing points of view. Note how this approach accommodates adolescents' advancing reasoning abilities (Amato, 1989; Baumrind, 1968).

Authoritative parents set realistic standards, state clear rules, and provide their children with opportunities to feel competent and worthy. They are not permissive. When reasoning does not prevail, they are willing to assert their authority and make demands to gain compliance. Enforcing rules fairly and rationally, authoritative parents gain their children's respect and acceptance of their parental authority (Baumrind, 1989).

Each of these four parenting styles (authoritarian, permissive, rejecting-neglecting, authoritative) is associated with distinctive behavioral patterns and qualities in children and adolescents. Baumrind's studies and those of other investigators demonstrated that different parenting styles predict differences in children's self-reliance, self-control, achievement, mood, and aggressiveness (Baumrind, 1987, 1991b; Glasgow et al., 1997; Maccoby & Martin, 1983; Steinberg, Elman, & Mounts, 1989; Weiss & Schwarz, 1996).

Authoritarian (punitive) parents, the most restrictive of the parenting groups, have children (particularly sons) who are obedient yet likely to act defiantly or give in to peer pressure. They tend to be less self-reliant and self-confident than children of authoritative parents (Lamborn et al., 1991). They also report being more unhappy, unfriendly, fearful, and moody (Baumrind, 1968). Children of punitive parents display less competence in school (Amato, 1989). The absence of parental warmth associated with punitive parenting foretells social skills deficits and low self-esteem (e.g., Klein et al., 1996). Not surprisingly, children of punitive parents often become harsh parents themselves (Lamborn et al., 1991; Maccoby & Martin, 1983; Simons, Whitbeck, Conger, & Chyi-In, 1991; Steinberg & Steinberg, 1994).

Permissive parents typically have children (particularly sons) who are not very self-controlled. Children of indulgent parents have difficulty relating to authority figures. Many are self-confident, but their academic performance is not impressive. Children of enmeshed parents are prone to emotional distress and depression (Capaldi & Patterson, 1991; Kurdek & Fine, 1994; Lamborn et al., 1991).

Children of rejecting-neglecting parents are the least independent and least achieving of the various groups. A disproportionate number have poor self-concepts and drug and school problems (e.g., Weiss & Schwarz, 1996). Inadequate supervision and low parent involvement contribute to problems in self-regulation and poor adjustment in young adolescent boys.

Parents who have an authoritative style (warm and firm) usually have children who are well adjusted, have positive self-concepts, and are socially and academically competent (Amato, 1989; Baumrind, 1991b; Hetherington & Clingempeel, 1992; Klein et al., 1996; Parish & McCluskey, 1992; Shucksmith, Hendry, & Glendinning, 1995; Steinberg, Lamborn, Darling, Mount, & Dornbusch,

1994). Children of highly demanding and highly responsive, authoritative parents are least likely to engage in risk-taking behaviors such as drug and alcohol abuse and vandalism (Baumrind, 1991c). The advantages for adolescents of authoritative parenting appear to increase over time (Steinberg et al., 1994).

Notice that authoritative and authoritarian parents are more controlling than permissive and neglecting parents. (The prefix *authori*, as in the word *authority*, implies a willingness to take charge.) They differ, however, in how they control their children. Authoritative parents are firm, and occasionally strict, but they prefer to gain compliance through acceptance, discussion, reasoning, and persuasion. Authoritarian parents, on the other hand, demand obedience and are unwilling to negotiate or compromise with their children.

Feeling close to one's parents is more conditional during middle adolescence than during the preceding years (Larson & Richards, 1994). For example, teenagers who feel accepted by their parents report feeling closer to them and are more helpful around the home (Eberly, Montemayor, & Flannery, 1993; Forehand & Nousiainen, 1993; Russell, Brewer, & Hogben, 1997). Adolescents who report close and secure relationships with their parents also express higher self-esteem and greater emotional well-being (Greenberg, Siegel, & Leitch, 1984). In the next section, we will see evidence of positive adjustment in adolescents whose parents punish harshly but who also are accepting, consistent, and involved (Simons et al., 1994).

Baumrind (1991a, b) theorizes that the authoritative parenting style helps middle-class adolescents feel securely attached to their parents. Secure attachment encourages self-regulation, individuation, and exploration. Individuation is enhanced when adolescents feel free to speak their minds in a family context of emotional connectedness (Grotevant & Cooper, 1986). These findings suggest that children raised by authoritative parents are in an excellent position to explore life path alternatives and to create an adult identity.

Many parents display, at different times, some combination of the parenting styles described above, partly depending on their mood and the specific circumstances. Although there is evidence that parenting style is important, we must remember that most studies of parenting style are correlational. The direction of causality cannot be inferred from correlational studies (see Appendix). It is possible that children's behavior evokes distinctive parenting styles rather than vice versa (Lamborn et al., 1991; Lewis, 1981). Perhaps authoritative parents can afford to be flexible because their children are well behaved. Restrictive parents may believe that they need to be coercive because their children are defiant and they expect them to remain so (Freedman-Doan, Arbreton, Harold, & Eccles, 1993). *Critical Thinking Question: Describe the self-perpetuating cycle wherein unmanageable teenagers evoke restrictive parenting behaviors and vice versa.*

Although Baumrind endorses authoritative parenting, it is not clear that this style is optimal for all types of families (Darling & Steinberg, 1993; Fauber, Forehand, Thomas, & Wierson, 1990; Julian, McHenry, & McKelvey, 1994; Steinberg et al., 1989; Taylor, Casten, & Flickinger, 1993). No two families are alike (Fine, 1993). The relationship between a given parenting style and adolescent adjustment varies according to ethnic, socioeconomic, and cultural factors and even according to a parent's gender.

Regarding the latter, mothers and fathers socialize their adolescent children somewhat differently. Compared to fathers, mothers talk more to their teenagers, are more emotionally involved, and have more strained relationships with them (Almeida & Galambos, 1991; Wierson, Armistead, Forehand, Thomas, & Fauber, 1990). Ironically, mothers are both more accepting and more controlling of their adolescents than fathers are. However, mothers and fathers usually adopt similar parenting styles, which apparently blend in response to specific areas of adolescent functioning (Forehand & Nousiainen, 1993).

Based on their study of Scottish youth, Shucksmith et al. (1995) concluded that parenting styles are somewhat age-related in that parents of older adolescents tend to be more permissive and parents of younger adolescents tend to be more controlling (authoritative or authoritarian). But they found support for Baumrind's basic model of four distinct types of parenting styles in their Scottish sample. In the same vein, Yau and Smetana (1996) report that conflict between parents and adolescents in Hong Kong is remarkably similar to parent–adolescent conflict in the United States. The investigators found Chinese parents to be relatively warm and controlling (i.e., authoritative).

Chao (1994), on the other hand, contends that the meanings of concepts such as *warmth*, *controlling*, *authoritarian*, and *restrictive* are ethnocentric, that is, embedded in Western culture and not necessarily relevant to other cultures. According to Chao, these concepts do not capture the essential features of Chinese child rearing. For example, for Asian parents, control "may not always involve 'domination' of children per se, but rather a more organizational type of control for the purpose or goal of keeping the family running more smoothly and fostering family harmony. Thus, these concepts may have very different implications when considered in the light of the culture, and may not be as useful for understanding Asian parenting" (p. 1112). Timimi (1995) makes the same point for understanding parent–adolescent relationships in immigrant Arab families.

There is no single parenting style that characterizes a particular cultural group; parents in all cultures and ethnic groups adapt their socialization practices to sociocultural values and life circumstances (e.g., Mason et al., 1996; Taylor, 1996; Taylor & Roberts, 1995). At one time, researchers assumed that Latino parents are more authoritarian than European-American parents. However, recent research reveals that Latino parents exhibit a broad range of parenting styles comparable to that of their European-American counterparts (Julian et al., 1994).

When considering the stricter parenting styles of some Latino and Asian parents (e.g., placing greater demands and expectations on their children), it is possible that ethnic parents are preparing their children to cope with racism in the larger society (Oyserman et al., 1995). In one study, Asian-American college students reported "a less cohesive and more conflictual overall family environment, more conflict between themselves and their parents, and less parental warmth and acceptance than did their European American peers" (Greenberger & Chen, 1996, p. 714). Julian and her colleagues note that exercising control and teaching coping skills for survival in a hostile environment may be distinctive features of child rearing among African-American parents (Julian et al., 1994; Mason et al., 1996).

Adolescents who live in high risk neighborhoods require close supervision.

---

## SPOTLIGHT · Corporal Punishment

Apparently, most parents in the United States and other societies support the use of **corporal punishment** in discipline—physical punishment inflicted directly on the body, as in slapping, spanking, or flogging (Gelles & Straus, 1987). Straus and Donnelly (1993) report that about half of adolescents are hit by their parents. Those who are struck are struck frequently, an average of six to eight times a year. Boys are hit more frequently than girls. Fathers hit girls less often than mothers do. *Thought Question: Spanking is a legal form of corporal punishment (Giles-Sims, Straus, & Sugarman, 1995). How do we distinguish between corporal punishment and child abuse?*

Corporal punishment is associated with children's hostile feelings about parents, an increased likelihood of adolescent violence and other crimes, alcohol abuse, suicidal thoughts, depression, alienation, and lowered achievement (Baumrind, 1971; Deyoung & Zigler, 1994; Noller, 1994; Straus & Donnelly, 1993; Straus & Kantor, 1994). However, one must question the direction of causality when interpreting such findings. Do parents hit because their children misbehave or do children misbehave because their parents hit them?

Based on a study of 332 rural Midwestern families, Simons and his colleagues (1994) report that corporal punishment is not related to adolescent maladjustment in families where parents are otherwise involved and consistent. "Once the effect of parental involvement was removed, corporal punishment showed no detrimental impact on adolescent aggressiveness, delinquency, or psychological well-being. This indicates that it is not corporal

**About half of adolescents are occasionally struck by their parents.**

punishment per se, but the disregard, inconsistency, and uninvolvement that often accompanies harsh corporal punishment, that increases a child's risk for problem behaviors" (p. 603).

The investigators caution that they do not condone the use of coercive discipline (insults, instilling guilt, the silent treatment), as it elicits strong feelings of anger and defiance in a teenager and may well subvert the parent–child relationship. Coercive parenting, including sarcasm, encourages teenagers to lie to their parents about their actions.

## PARENTAL ISSUE: CONTROL VERSUS LETTING GO

**Question**: *Do you keep things to yourself?*
**Answer**: *Yeah, a lot of the time. Even little problems like a bad day in school. I'll just keep it to myself. Because I don't like telling my parents. Because they'll get mad. "Why didn't you do this? You would've had a better day."*

*(16-year-old-girl)*

Over the course of childhood, parents become accustomed to managing their children's time and behavior. It's as though parents believe that they have the answers to all of their children's problems. Finding their parents to be overly involved or controlling, many teenagers disclose as little as possible about their private lives. The above quote conveys a common sentiment of teenagers who feel that their parents give them a hard time. "Whenever I tell you something, you go nuts."

As their children mature, many parents experience a sense of loss regarding the parenting role. One mother, on seeing her 14-year-old daughter wearing a strapless gown, expressed her feelings this way: "She is beautiful and looks so grown up. I feel such bittersweetness. I see her future ahead of her and I see her past 14 years in a flash. I'm not ready to let her go, yet it is out of my hands." Marianne's mother expressed similar sentiments: "I'm happy, but sad. I'm losing the little girl I once had."

Despite their misgivings, most parents eventually accept the inevitable—letting go of their roles as nurturer and protector and launching their children into lives of their own. An important factor parents must consider in deciding how much self-determination to grant their children is community stability—how dangerous is the world that their children will inhabit? In order to become self-regulating, adolescents not only require freedom to explore and experiment, they also need to be protected from potentially dangerous situations (Baumrind, 1991). *Thought Question: Bronfenbrenner (1985) suggests that the amount of freedom that parents grant their children is proportional to the amount of stability that children experience in their community. What special precautions must be taken by parents of teenagers who live in high-risk communities?*

## ADOLESCENT AUTONOMY

> *I noticed how Debby asked her mother's opinion about what to wear to school tomorrow. She's getting her class pictures taken, and evidently it's important to her to look her best. The other day she seemed annoyed when her mother suggested something to wear to church. When her mother suggests, Debby resists. When nothing is said, she wants advice. Maybe she isn't as independent as she thinks.*
>
> *(Father of a 13-year-old female)*

> *I used to do what my parents always told me, but now I have a mind of my own. I spend more free time in my room and less time downstairs with the family.*
>
> *(15-year-old male)*

There is no question but that middle-class teenagers like Debby associate growing up with increased freedom and more frequent opportunities to make their own decisions. They want to decide who their friends are, what movies to see, how they dress, and what constitutes a reasonable curfew. This is not surprising in a culture that so emphasizes independence and self-reliance. At the same time, they are becoming more aware that increasing maturity brings additional responsibilities and heightened expectations from adults.

Ironically, many adolescents have mixed feelings about their parents' changing role in their lives. A 17-year-old girl was asked what she would change about her parents. "Have them be more understanding with some things, like my boyfriend John. Like, it's my life, give me some support instead of being, like 'He's annoying. He's annoying.' I mean, duh, I know that. Just leave me alone and help me."

The ambivalence expressed in her last sentence is telling. "Just leave me alone and help me." When you have to make a tough decision, it's almost a relief to have someone else tell you what to do or what not to do. Admitting that one needs help can be a little embarrassing. Adolescents eventually realize that giving up the "luxury" of parental supervision is part of the price they pay for greater freedom.

When asked by one of my students, "What would you change about your parents," a 16-year-old boy responded, "For them to leave me alone, give me more privacy, and not be so concerned with my life." He might be surprised how difficult that would be for his parents (probably impossible). When asked whether he would like to live completely free of parental authority, he responded, "No, because I'd probably fall apart. I'd have nothing to complain about."

As discussed in Chapter 6, autonomy, individuation, and separation are crucial elements in the process through which adolescents explore their world and forge an adult identity. As they mature, adolescents idealize their parents less, feel more like individuals, and do more things for themselves (Smollar & Youniss, 1989; Steinberg & Silverberg, 1986). Greenberger (1984) maintained that self-reliance (the absence of excessive dependence on others) is at the core of adolescent autonomy. Adolescents who are self-reliant are more successful in separating from their parents (Delaney, 1996; Moore, 1987). *Thought Question: Why might adolescents become more self-reliant and feel more self-confident in families where members are neither too close nor too distant?*

Newman and Newman (1997) define **autonomy** as "the ability to behave independently, to do things on one's own" (p. 730). Autonomy refers to self-determination in thinking, feeling, and behavior (Collins & Repinski, 1994). Autonomous individuals are self-governing and self-regulating. They do not depend on others to satisfy their basic needs or to tell them how to behave. They select the clothes they wear and decide what kind of music they listen to, how to spend their money, and who their friends will be (Collins & Repinksi, 1994).

Autonomous behavior becomes more common as young people increasingly think for themselves. They acquire interests and goals that are less family centered. Preadolescents occasionally express points of view that differ from those of their parents and siblings. They begin to challenge the beliefs, values, and decisions of their elders. Going to school, visiting and sleeping over at a friend's home, and attending sleepaway camp provide young people with opportunities to learn how to cope with longer and longer periods away from their parents (Fichman, Koestner, & Zuroff, 1997). Residing in a college dormitory is a whole other story (see Spotlight • Living Away from Home). The reasoning and self-understanding that accompany the desire for self-determination seem to be based partly on daily encounters and discussions with par-

**SPOTLIGHT** • Living Away from Home

*At first, the complete lack of an adult presence was a revelation to me. My parents, who insisted on a midnight curfew up until the day I left for school, had been constantly involved in everything I ever did. They even helped me pick out my prom dress. At college, however, I can stay out until 3 A.M. ("school nights" aren't an issue), oversleep, and miss my economics lecture. Nobody's watching. If I do poorly on that week's set of economic problems, I have no one to blame but myself.*

(College freshman Chana Schoenberger, 1995)

One of the biggest challenges of late adolescence and young adulthood is living apart from one's parents. Over the course of childhood, separations between children and parents become increasingly common. Eventually, like Chana Schoenberger, many adolescents live in dormitories on college campuses and reside with their parents only a few weeks a year.

When they first occur, extended separations engender marked anxiety and a sense of loss in all parties. However, living apart from one's parents gives adolescents greater privacy and provides countless opportunities to make decisions and to become more independent. Parents who are overly attached to their children also benefit from short-term separations (McBride & Belsky, 1988). Physical distance helps the parent–adolescent relationship become more mutual. Somehow, physical separation helps parents stop treating their children like, well, children (Flanagan, Schulenberg, & Fuligni, 1993).

Berman and Sperling (1991) were curious about how residential status affects freshman college students' attachment to their parents. They hypothesized that living away from home would heighten residential students' attachment to their parents compared to that of commuting students who continued to live at home. They administered questionnaires to 89 students taking an introductory psychology course at an East Coast university. The students were twice questioned about their attachment to their parents, during the first 3 weeks of their first semester at college and at the end of the semester. Contrary to their expectations, parental attachment *weakened* in residential students but was stable in commuting students. Living separately from parents and establishing new bonds with peers apparently lessened attachment to parents for the students who lived on campus. Not surprisingly, living apart improved relations between parents and adolescents, at least from the adolescents' perspective.

A study of Midwestern college students revealed that compared to students who lived at home, those who lived on campus reported more independence and higher levels of mutuality in their relationships with parents (Flanagan et al., 1993). College students who lived at home felt that their parents underestimated their maturity. Many complained that their parents treated them as though they were still in high school.

Living away from home usually improves relationships between college students and their parents.

"When adolescents and parents lived together, they tended to deal with their disagreements by avoiding one another rather than attempting to discuss and resolve differences of opinion. Conflicts with parents in terms of both minor hassles and major disagreements were exacerbated by living together. Even students who resided at college said they had more conflict with their parents during semester breaks when they lived at home" (Flanagan et al., 1993, p. 183). Keep in mind that even (or especially) when parents and their children live separately, parents' emotional support continues to play a crucial role in their children's adjustment (Holahan et al., 1994; Valery, O'Connor, & Jennings, 1997).

ents, friends, and others (Larson et al., 1996; Piaget, 1965; Youniss & Smollar, 1985).

In Western cultures, the adolescent years provide children with endless opportunities to reduce their dependence on caregivers and to accept greater responsibility for themselves. In fact, socialization in the United States and other industrialized societies can be viewed mainly as preparation for independence and self-regulation during adulthood (Silverberg & Gondoli, 1996). Parents of adolescents in Asian and African cultures (and many Asian-American and African-American parents) expect more obedience and compliance with their views than do middle-class white parents in the United States (Chao, 1994; Cooper, 1994; Feldman & Rosenthal, 1991; Poole, Cooney, & Cheong, 1986). However, even within middle-class white families, most adolescents try to strike a balance between autonomy and connectedness with other family members (Delaney, 1996; Silverberg & Gondoli, 1996).

## FAMILY CONFLICT AND COMMUNICATION

Sitting before me uneasily was Kenny, a bright, 16-year-old 11th grader. His mother, Annie, was telling me that her relationship with her husband was being destroyed by their problems with Kenny. Kenny's father, Steve, no longer wanted Kenny in his house. He rarely spoke to him except to criticize or argue.

Kenny's parents voiced the following complaints: He drove their car without permission. He had 11 cavities because of his candy-laden diet. He was extremely uncooperative. He never washed or put away his dirty clothes. He left his school books on the kitchen table despite his parents' repeated protests. He occasionally missed school because he woke up too late for the bus. He performed poorly in school. He talked back to his parents, cursed in their presence, and even had fist fights with his father. As a result, Kenny was not allowed to use the family car, his television, or the family phone. These punishments, in turn, enraged Kenny, and he responded with even greater defiance.

Kenny's father, Steve, admitted that he did not handle Kenny well. He claimed that he "went crazy" when Kenny provoked him and that he sometimes hated his son. He yearned to have Kenny move out. He also reported feeling guilty about their terrible relationship. In counseling, he was struggling to show good faith. He hoped they could learn to get along. He also felt that his wife was too sympathetic to Kenny. His own "strategy," he realized, was to hurt Kenny as much as Kenny was hurting him. Surprisingly, Kenny told me that his father was a "good guy" but unable to overcome their years of constant antagonism.

Annie agreed that Kenny was trying harder than her husband to improve their relationship. With tears streaming down her face, she told me that she was being torn apart by their endless displays of hostility toward each other. Steve, bitter and frustrated, was doing very little to improve what was certainly his own greatest personal failure. Kenny's behavior certainly was obnoxious, but not that unusual for someone his age. I was sure that this bit of information would not help Steve become more patient with his son (from Jaffe, 1997, p. 328).

Trapped in an escalating, occasionally violent pattern of mutual distrust and hostility, Kenny and his father could barely communicate with each other. They would go out of their way to annoy and hurt each other. Such high levels of parent–adolescent conflict are stressful for teenagers and associated with drug abuse, juvenile delinquency, and school failure (Emery, 1982; Hall, 1987; Neighbors, Forehand, & McVicar, 1993).

How could parents who lack knowledge of the adolescent period know that teenagers' emotional needs are so different from those of younger children (Amato, 1989; Fuligni & Eccles, 1993)? When parents and adolescents have unrealistic expectations about each other or view each other stereotypically ("obnoxious teenager," "unreasonable parent"), trivial annoyances may quickly escalate into major battles.

Their children's transition from childhood to adolescence is stressful for many parents and probably heightens their irritability (Silverberg & Steinberg, 1990). It takes parents a while to realize that their children are becoming better decision makers and need opportunities to sharpen their reasoning skills (Dickerson & Zimmerman, 1992). Temperamental teenagers like Kenny provoke hostile rather than sympathetic reactions, especially when parents are uninformed about what constitutes normal adolescent behavior (Talwar, Nitz, & Lerner, 1990).

At one level, Kenny was testing his parents, seeing what he could get away with. At another level, through his outrageous behavior, he also was letting them know that he was not happy. In most families, even when relations are strained, parent–adolescent conflict does not reach this level of intensity. Most teenagers can tolerate occasional negative interactions with family members if they are balanced by frequent positive encounters (Montemayor, 1986). Kenny's relationship with his mother, although shaky, was close and supportive. Annie tried to understand Kenny's anger. She urged her husband to be more tolerant. Many parents, like Steve, are too easily provoked into mindless bickering, futile arguments, and hurtful confrontations (Silverberg & Steinberg, 1990).

One of the closely guarded secrets of successful parenting is overlooking as much annoying behavior as possible. Children who feel rejected by their parents generally have lower self-esteem than children who feel close to their parents (Bretherton, 1987; LeCroy, 1988; Ryan & Lynch, 1989). By the late teenage years, most children shed their adolescent quirkiness and become more cordial and pleasant (Larson et al., 1996). However, Kenny's parents would be seriously mistaken to overlook his offensive behavior. Extreme parental responses, whether ignoring or retaliating, do not bring family members closer. Kenny and his parents needed to reconnect with each other emotionally for there to be any hope of addressing and resolving their differences. Parents and teenagers who view each other's opposition as malicious are most prone to conflict (Grace, Kelley, & McCain, 1993).

In families with good communication skills, adolescents share their feelings and seek guidance from their parents (Hortaçsu, 1989; Hunter, 1985; Papini, Farmer, Clark, Micka, & Barnett, 1990). Adolescents usually are willing to seek counsel from parents who listen instead of lecturing or criticizing. If their parents show interest in their opinions, most young people are willing to talk about themselves. Fortunately, most parents and adolescents get along and communicate well with each other most of the time (Hunter, 1985; Larson et al., 1996; Montemayor, 1983). A close relationship with a parent is worth preserving because it serves as a buffer for the pressures and problems that almost all young people experience (Bronstein et al., 1993; Neighbors et al., 1993).

## MODELS OF PARENT–ADOLESCENT CONFLICT

The term **conflict** suggests an inability to resolve differences, sometimes accompanied by tension, hostility, or aggression (Hall, 1987). Intense conflict occurs when adolescents' desire for freedom clashes with parental attempts to regulate their behavior. This dynamic sets the stage for occasional but heated intergenerational conflict, as with Kenny and his father (Holmbeck & Hill, 1991a; Laursen & Koplas, 1995; Montemayor, 1983; Pardeck & Pardeck, 1990).

Must children distance themselves from their parents in order to become their own persons? Although theoretical models usually focus on conflict and emotional distance between parent and adolescent, adolescent autonomy does not have to be rooted in family tensions and disharmony (Larson et al., 1996; Steinberg, 1990). By striking a healthy balance between independence and connectedness, adolescents can learn to rely less on their parents and still feel emotionally close to them (Cooper et al., 1983; Larson et al., 1996; Steinberg & Silverberg, 1986). "Indeed, individuation is not something that happens from parents but rather *with* them" (Ryan & Lynch, 1989, p. 341).

Theoretical models of parent–adolescent relationships differ regarding the relative roles played by biology, conflict, stress, search for identity, desire for autonomy, and cognition (Montemayor, 1983). Lawrence Steinberg (1987a, 1988) offers a provocative sociobiological perspective. He hypothesizes that parent–teenager conflict is a "vestige of our evolutionary past, when prolonged proximity between parent and offspring threatened the species' genetic integrity" (p. 38).

Steinberg contends that in primates like us, heightened parent–adolescent tension at puberty encourages adolescents to leave their natal group to seek mates elsewhere. This practice improves reproductive fitness because it minimizes inbreeding and promotes genetic diversity. According to Steinberg's model, parent–adolescent conflict encourages autonomy and the formation of relationships outside of the family. Larson and his colleagues (Larson et al., 1996) observed, however, that for working- and middle-class adolescent males, family conflict did not appear to be related to reduction in time spent together by family members.

We may also recall from Chapter 2 that psychoanalytic theory, particularly the work of Anna Freud (1958, 1969), asserts that puberty and sexual maturation trigger an extended period of rebellion and antagonism. Conflict and detachment supposedly characterize daily life during this period. Some Freudians viewed harmonious family relations as counterproductive to the development of adolescent autonomy. This view, rejected by most current theorists (Silverberg & Gondoli, 1996), may have deterred interest in the maintenance of close family ties during the teenage years despite considerable evidence that harmony rather than conflict is the rule (Frank, Avery, & Laman, 1988; Kenny, 1987; Montemayor, 1983; Steinberg, 1990).

Neo-Freudians like Peter Blos (1979) describe a more peaceful individuation process during which adolescents develop a new view of themselves and their parents. According to Blos, emotional autonomy allows adolescents to rely more on their own resources and take responsibility for their actions. This view implies that feelings of emotional autonomy are adaptive, that adolescents who have these feelings are in some sense more competent and well adjusted than their peers. Long-term longitudinal studies are needed to shed light on the relationship between emotional autonomy and adjustment and the extent of individual differences in adolescents on this construct (Silverberg & Gondolin, 1996).

According to social-psychological models, family tensions reflect the multiple transitions that families with adolescents experience during the early teenage years (Simmons & Blyth, 1987). Smetana's (1988b, 1989, 1995) cognitive-behavioral formulation, discussed below, views conflict between parents and adolescents as an inevitable result of changes in adolescents' social reasoning.

Parents and adolescents disagree about what domains of teenage life should fall under the jurisdiction of parental authority. Teenagers wonder why they should have to satisfy their parent's "arbitrary" rules and expectations ("Let me make up my own mind"). According to the cognitive-behavioral perspective, conflict lessens when older adolescents start to reason like adults ("I can satisfy my parent's concerns without sacrificing my own desire for self-regulation").

Thornton and his colleagues (1995) optimistically note that "as young people begin to experience adult roles and have more independence, there are increases in respect, understanding, affection, confidence, and enjoyment between them and their parents. These parent–child relationships may continue to be important as the children establish their own careers and families and the parents mature into old age" (p. 560).

## DOMAINS OF ADOLESCENT AUTONOMY

Most parents grant more freedom as their children mature. Relationships become more mutual. Younger adolescents, however, report dissatisfaction with parental regulation in domains that they consider personal. Throughout this century, parent–adolescent conflict has revolved around such mundane matters as personal hygiene, schoolwork, disobedience, friendships, chores, spending money, conflicts with siblings, and what constitutes appropriate dress (Csikszentmihalyi & Larson, 1984; Hill & Holmbeck, 1987; Montemayor, 1982, 1983, 1986; Papini et al., 1989). Mothers and adolescents argue about personal matters, clothes, and choice of friends. Fathers and adolescents argue about school, money, and use of leisure time (Ellis-Schwabe & Thornburg, 1986).

Adolescents and their parents may disagree on content issues (e.g., chores, personal hygiene, homework) or process issues (e.g., how decisions will be made) (Hall, 1987). Typically, parents are dissatisfied with some behavior; they make an issue of it, and the teenager responds with an autonomy defense—"It's my room, it's my hair, it's my life." By keeping their affairs to themselves, adolescents attempt to avoid anticipated parental disapproval in predictable domains of conflict. In other words, "What they don't know they can't prohibit or disapprove of."

Judith Smetana (1988a, 1989) investigated how adolescents and their parents interpret the domains of parental authority. She interviewed 102 adolescents, ranging in age from 10 to 18 years, and their parents. She found that parents of preadolescents and young adolescents view all events in their children's lives as being under parental jurisdiction. Although most parents agree that teenagers should have some say regarding personal issues (those that affect only the child), parents do not view their children's hygienic practices, grooming, and homework as personal issues. Rather, they are viewed as conventional behaviors that must be performed (Smetana, 1989). To a parent's assertion, "You must dress appropriately," the adolescent replies, "It's my body; I should be able to dress the way I want." The parent replies, "But what will people think?" and so it goes.

As children mature, parents generally lessen their control regarding personal and friendship issues but not moral issues (entailing fairness and the rights or welfare of others), conventional issues (agreed-on norms that structure social interactions), or prudential issues (relating to a child's safety and health). Moral rules especially are seen as obligatory, and adolescents typically offer little resistance to parental input regarding moral conduct (Smetana & Asquith, 1994).

The adolescents in Smetana's studies agreed that their parents should help them make important, longer-term, and difficult life decisions, those that involve educational, moral, financial, and vocational decisions. They also accepted that parents should retain jurisdiction over moral and conventional issues throughout adolescence. However, they differed from their parents in whether or not they viewed certain issues as personal or conventional. "Adolescents appear to view an increasing range of issues that were once viewed as legitimately subject to parental control as now under personal jurisdiction" (Smetana, 1988a, p. 321).

Such issues involve family obligations and chores, getting along with other people, diet, cleanliness, appearance, dating and other social activities, choice of friends, and, of course, homework (Hill & Holmbeck, 1987; Smetana, 1989). Because of their concerns about peer pressure, parents feel obligated to make rules regarding friendships. Adolescents feel that their friendships definitely should be a matter of personal choice. Parents see themselves as having greater authority over these and safety and health issues, but as adolescents grow older, almost all issues become subject to negotiation (Smetana & Asquith, 1994).

By late adolescence, serious topics such as sex and drugs are discussed more frequently with peers than with parents (Hunter, 1985; Wilks, 1986). Older adolescents report fewer "hassles" with parents. However, they continue to disagree with parents about such matters as drinking and dating (Carlton-Ford & Collins, 1988; Wilks, 1986). To some extent, issues are gender-related, with parents reporting more intense conflicts with sons than with daughters over serious offenses—drugs, cursing, and drinking (Papini et al., 1989). However, families with adolescent daughters usually are more restrictive, having more rules regarding personal issues (Smetana & Asquith, 1994).

Smetana (1995) also reports that parents' judgments about the legitimacy of their authority vary according to their parenting style. Authoritative parents, for example, view the domain of adolescent personal jurisdiction more narrowly than do permissive or authoritarian parents. Permissive parents (not surprisingly) are more permissive than other parents about what constitutes a personal issue and take their children's personal choices into account more frequently. They are not more lenient, however, regarding judgments of issues pertaining to their children's health and safety.

## AVOIDING AND RESOLVING CONFLICT

There is an emerging consensus among theoretical models that the eventual result of parent–adolescent conflict is a realignment of the parent–child relationship. New interactional patterns emerge that help teenagers stay connected to their parents while allowing them to become self-regulating (Cooper & Carlson, 1990; Grotevant & Cooper, 1986; Laursen & Collins, 1994; Sessa & Steinberg, 1991). Most adolescents are able to separate from their parents without severing emotional ties (Crespi & Sabatelli, 1993). As noted earlier, parent–adolescent disagreement and conflict can encourage autonomy by teaching conflict-resolution skills and by hastening exploration and independence (Montemayor, 1986; Pardeck & Pardeck, 1990).

The strategies that adolescents use to resist or challenge parental power vary as a function of a parent's compliance strategy and a child's gender. White, Pearson, and Flint (1989) asked 118 9th through 12th graders to identify the resistance strategy they use when their parents try to gain their compliance. When mothers used personal rejection or empathic understanding to gain compliance, adolescents responded with nonnegotiation. When mothers used emotional appeals, adolescents resorted to their desire for autonomy ("It's my life"). When fathers tried to persuade their children with an emotional appeal, adolescents justified their actions. Adolescents were more likely to use identity management ("It's my life") with their mothers and justification ("I have a good reason") with their fathers.

Boys generally were more controlling, particularly with their mothers. Boys and girls preferred to negotiate with their mothers than with their fathers. We have seen in a previous section that during conflict mothers are more likely to back off (stay in relationship) while fathers continue to assert their authority (stay in role). As teenagers learned a variety of strategies, negotiation replaced confrontation (see Spotlight • Disagreeing with a Teenager).

## SPOTLIGHT • Disagreeing with a Teenager

*We have our bad times and good times. We can be close friends one time and the next minute they'll change. They'll find out something I did wrong, and they'll get really mad. I'm not always innocent. . . . I'm not the kind of person that will just sit there and be yelled at. I'll yell right back and say, "What's yer problem? Why are you yelling at me?" In the past two weeks it's been better. We talk things out a lot. Less fighting. I give them their space and they give me my space. Things are better now.*

*(17-year-old male)*

Parents and children, disagreeing over everyday matters like homework and chores, sometimes miss the more important relationship issues at stake (Laursen & Koplas, 1995). "Battles that seem to center on friends or curfews are often reflections of much deeper issues like privacy and trust. That's why focusing simply on how late your child may come back from seeing a movie misses the points" (Kutner, 1991c, p. C2). Similarly, children and adults may argue when they feel insecure or are upset. Family members are relatively safe and convenient targets for each other's frustrations and disappointments. It is also not unheard of for adolescents to be oppositional or defiant as a way of getting noticed (Kutner, 1991c).

Caring, empathic communication is the key to healthy family functioning (McFarlane, Bellissimo, & Norman, 1995). Young people from all ethnic groups show more positive adjustment when they engage in joint decision making with their parents (Lamborn, Dornbusch, & Steinberg, 1996). All family members deserve the opportunity to express themselves, which requires listening, asking questions, explaining one's point of view, negotiating, and compromising. This is particularly important because adolescents and their parents tend to evaluate relationships and events quite differently *and usually don't realize it* (Thornton et al., 1995). It also may help parents to remember that during family disagreements, adolescents are practicing their newfound intellectual skills.

Realizing that parents are not all-powerful and not always right adds fuel to adolescent fire. Some parents enjoy adolescents' clever, although imperfect reasoning as the latter try to persuade, coerce, or manipulate. It is a good idea to avoid overinterpreting each other's thoughts and feelings. Differences of opinion should be respected (Worden, 1991). It is helpful to distinguish between anger, which needs to be expressed, and hostility, which elicits defensiveness and counterattacks.

Although parents should be flexible in granting greater freedom, setting and enforcing limits also is an important ingredient of responsible parenting (Smetana, 1995). When refusing a request, parents should offer a good reason but should not feel obligated to present their position over and over again. The essential message that parents need to communicate to their adolescent children is that *freedom is earned through good judgment and responsible behavior* (Jaffe, 1997).

With their improving perspective-taking skills, adolescents become better at persuading and convincing other people (including their parents) to accept their point of view. Older adolescents are more knowledgeable and more skillful in expressing their views and making a case for themselves (Houchins, 1991). By late adolescence, most parents and adolescents are treating each other almost as equals (Cooper & Carlson, 1990; Flint, 1992; White et al., 1989).

## ADOLESCENTS AND PARENTAL DIVORCE

*My mother had to sell the house and make some money. It was cheaper to live in New Jersey. I felt terrible. I didn't understand what happened. My brother, sister, and I didn't know where our father went. We just knew he was gone. We didn't know what to feel. He left, and he wasn't there for me. If I needed something, I wouldn't know how to call him. I don't see him much anymore. I call him about three times a month.*

*(17-year-old boy whose parents divorced when he was 13)*

*I'll probably get married. But I'll probably get divorced. Everybody gets divorced in this country.*

*(17-year-old female)*

In most Western countries, including the United States, the divorce rate hovers around 50%. This means that about half of all marriages each year eventually will end in divorce. About 60% of divorces involve children and adolescents. Thus, each year, over a million children in the United States witness the dissolution of their parents' marriage. About one-fifth of them will experience a second parental divorce, and some a third (Brody, Neubaum, & Forehand, 1988; Furstenberg & Cherlin, 1991). At least half of all children in the United States live with a single parent for at least part of their childhood (Glick & Lin, 1986). Many of them will spend time in a stepfamily when their parents remarry (Hetherington, Stanley-Hagan, & Anderson, 1989).

How does divorce affect children? There is no simple answer to this question. Each child reacts differently. The effects of family disruption depend on a child's developmental status at the time of divorce or remarriage (Sim & Vuchinich, 1996). Some children cope with stress better than others. Also, some effects do not become apparent until a later developmental stage (the **sleeper effect**). For example, the impact of divorce on girls' relationships and sexuality may not become apparent until they reach adolescence (Wallerstein & Blakeslee, 1989). Not surprisingly, marital conflict and father absence affect boys more negatively than girls (Beaty, 1995; Harold, Fincham, Osborne, & Conger, 1997). Although adult children often have great difficulty coming to terms with the dissolution of their parents' marriage (Cooney, Hutchinson, & Leather, 1995), only a small number of young adults develop serious mental health problems (Chase-Lansdale, Cherlin, & Kiernan, 1995).

With their heightened awareness and more advanced reasoning skills, adolescents are in a better position than younger children to appreciate the complexities of failed adult relationships (Harold & Conger, 1997). They are less parent dependent than younger children and more capable of finding emotional support outside of the family. However, adolescents in unstable families undoubtedly experience more distress and life disruption (sometimes continuing into adulthood) than children in intact families (Aro & Palosaari, 1992; Barber, 1995; Frost & Pakiz, 1990; Hetherington & Clingempeel, 1992; White, 1992).

Relationship disruptions almost always increase the risk of adjustment problems (Fauber et al., 1990; Osborne & Fincham, 1996). During stressful times, children usually approach their parents for comfort and reassurance. When parents' lives are in turmoil, they usually are less physically and emotionally available to their children and sometimes are more hostile toward them (Harold & Conger, 1997). Children must then solicit support from other family members or friends.

Adolescents in unstable families display a variety of academic and emotional problems and antisocial behaviors that interfere with normal adolescent transitions (Frost & Pakiz, 1990). Generally, the more frequent and intense the conflict, the greater the adjustment problems (Rogers & Holmbeck, 1997). Some adolescents (especially girls) who have experienced parental divorce become wary of entering new relationships, believing that they are doomed to follow in their parents' footsteps (Wallerstein & Corbin, 1989). They may resent either parent's pursuing a social life of his or her own.

Adolescents are less likely to have adjustment problems when their parents adjust well to their marital dissolution and when family members treat each other civilly (McCombs & Forehand, 1989). Most adolescents do well if they can maintain a close relationship with the residential parent and if they do not feel pressured to choose sides (Buchanan, Maccoby, & Dornbusch, 1991; Forehand, 1992; Maccoby, Buchanan, Mnookin, & Dornbusch, 1993; Thomas & Forehand, 1993).

Each successive transition in the divorce process (Figure 7-2) takes its toll on all family members (Kurdek et al., 1994). Forehand, Middleton, and Long (1987) interviewed 58 young adolescents and their teachers. About half of the children were from intact families and about half had parents who were recently divorced. The authors found that the level of adolescent functioning in school was related to the number of stressors in the adolescent's life. Adolescents who experienced three stressors (parental divorce, poor relationship with their mothers, and poor relationship with their fathers) reported more adjustment problems than adolescents who experienced zero, one, or two of these stressors.

Long and Forehand (1987) concluded that it is not divorce per se but rather frequent displays of hostility between parents that most distress children. These investigators questioned teachers about adolescents' academic and social performance. Half of the children had parents who had recently divorced and half belonged to intact families. Teachers were not able to distinguish between teenagers from broken homes and those from intact families on the basis of their behavior in school. However, they could distinguish between children whose parents displayed high levels of conflict and children whose parents got along.

Thus, it seems to be awareness of parental conflict rather than parental separation or family structure that is most closely associated with poor adjust-

**FIGURE 7-2 The divorce process. (From Jaffe, 1997)**

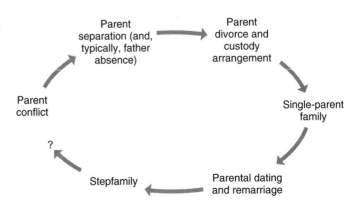

Grandparents generally prefer contact with their grandchildren when the children are very young. Although adolescents spend relatively little time with their parents and grandparents, they consider their family elders to be important members of their social networks and value contact with them. Many adolescents report that their grandparents are more sympathetic and nurturant than their parents (Kornhaber & Woodward, 1981).

Kornhaber (1996) notes that some adolescents use their grandparents as a "safety valve" when they are feuding with their parents. They may view a grandparent as a confidant and use the grandparent's home as an emotional sanctuary during troubled times. Adolescents (especially girls) report feeling close to their grandparents and talk to them (mainly grandmothers) on the phone several times a month. More frequent visual and phone contact with grandparents is associated with supportive relationships and greater attachment (Creasey & Koblewski, 1991). Unfortunately, children of divorce lose access to some of their grandparents just when they need them most. Although they may acquire new stepgrandparents when their parents remarry, adolescents often have more difficulty than younger children in bonding to new family members.

**Many adolescents report that their grandparents are more sympathetic and nurturant than their parents.**

**Box 7-1
Adolescents
and Their
Grandparents**

Adolescents are adversely affected more by frequent exposure to parental conflict and hostility than by parental separation or divorce.

ment in adolescents (Bickham & Fiese, 1997; Cummings & Davies, 1994; Harold & Conger, 1997; McFarlane et al., 1995). Conflict between parents disturbs the parent–child relationship, especially when there is reduced parental emotional and physical availability (Beaty, 1995). Divorced parents who cooperate with each other help their children avoid feeling "caught between parents" (Buchanan et al., 1991).

## ADOLESCENTS LIVING IN SINGLE-PARENT FAMILIES AND STEPFAMILIES

Parental divorce and all that precedes and follows it can have positive, negative, or mixed effects on children. Because of the uncertain effects of divorce on children, it is important that we view divorce not as a tragedy but as a sequence of stressful family transitions (Abelsohn & Saayman, 1991; Kurdek et al., 1994; Neighbors, Forehand, & Armistead, 1992). How children adjust to these transitions depends partly on the number of transitions experienced, children's gender, their parents' adjustment, available social support, and children's coping resources (Hetherington, 1989; Kurdek et al., 1994).

Perhaps the most unfortunate consequence of divorce for children is losing daily contact with one parent, usually the father (Beaty, 1995). Many nonresidential fathers become increasingly less available after the divorce, although some fathers maintain meaningful contact with their adolescent children (Furstenberg & Nord, 1985; Maccoby et al., 1993).

Adolescents living with single mothers and in stepfamilies usually report receiving less supervision and warmth from their fathers or stepfathers than those living with both parents (Beaty, 1995; Kurdek & Fine, 1993). One improvement for most children after parental separation is enduring fewer hostile encounters between the two most significant people in their lives. Following divorce, many parents make a concerted effort to get along with each other for their children's sake, but not all succeed (Buchanan et al., 1991).

Divorce research has given rise to a negative impression of single parenting by emphasizing the difficulties children encounter during the first few years following their parents' divorce. Although studies (cited in the previous section) find poorer academic performance and lower self-esteem in adolescents from divorced families, the differences usually are small and sometimes disappear when moderator variables are controlled. Negative stereotypes of single-parent families create additional problems for parents and children in such families. In addition, terms such as *broken home* have negative connotations that lead to stereotypical views of families (Barber & Eccles, 1992). *Thought Question: Does parental divorce promote or interfere with an adolescent's attempts to separate emotionally from his or her parents?*

Parental divorce and remarriage lead to substantial changes in family life, including the need to renegotiate family relationships and responsibilities. We have already seen that renegotiations of family relationships play an important role in the development of adolescent autonomy. Sessa and Steinberg (1991) suggest that children of divorce grow up faster. They are pushed into the realm of self-reliance whether or not they are ready for it. Adolescents in divorced families usually are granted more freedom and argue less with their parents (Smetana, Yau, Restrepo, & Braeges, 1991), perhaps because they have less contact. Developmental status, however, makes a big difference in how children handle the succession of taxing events that await them. They must give up what most of their age-mates still can take for granted—images of infallible parents and the belief that family life guarantees them security, emotional stability, and financial support.

The lessened availability of parents in crisis may lead young people (especially boys and early-maturing girls) to disengage from the family system and seek support from peers much earlier than they would have if their family had remained intact (Beaty, 1995). Children who live with both parents receive more adult supervision and are less susceptible to deviant peer influence (Steinberg, 1987d). Parents' diminished capacity to parent after divorce accelerates their children's behavioral autonomy. Diminished parenting is characterized by "decreased parental affection, communication, control, and monitoring [and] requires increased independence and self-reliance from the adolescent" (Sessa & Steinberg, 1991, p. 44).

Single parents carry a special burden. A single mother of three children expressed her parental burden this way: "As a single mother, I made financial sacrifices. I assumed full responsibility for my children's growth and development. I had no one to depend on for emotional support. I made all decisions alone. I had sole responsibility for providing home, security, love, discipline, and religious training" (from Jaffe, 1997, p. 122).

As a group, single mothers are more permissive, less restrictive, and less supervisory than married mothers (Hetherington, 1989). Their teenage children usually are more responsible, independent, and self-regulating, presumably because they are given more freedom in decision making and more responsibility for household chores (Hetherington, 1987). In their study of maternal employment, Duckett and Richards (1995) found that adolescent children of mothers who were employed full time had higher self-esteem and more positive experiences than children of nonemployed mothers, perhaps because the employed mothers felt less stress or felt better about themselves.

Smetana and colleagues (1991) hypothesized that there is less parent–adolescent conflict in families with single mothers than in dual-parent families. After all, adolescents in households led by single mothers are granted more privileges and greater freedom. These investigators interviewed family members individually about family conflict and then observed them interacting during a structured task. Supporting the hypothesis, married mothers of early adolescents had more conflict with their children than did divorced mothers. Divorced and married mothers did not differ, however, in the types of conflicts they had with their children. They fought about everyday matters, including chores, homework, and relationships.

The investigators note that less conflict does not necessarily mean that children of divorced parents have more positive interactions with them. Further, if parent–child conflict is a necessary part of the struggle for autonomy, lower levels of conflict could undermine adolescent development. "Indeed, our results indicated that early adolescents from divorced families had poorer communication [and lower grades] than same-age adolescents from married families" (Smetana et al., 1991, p. 1008).

When single parents remarry, their children become stepchildren. Early adolescents in remarried households have a slew of normative and nonnormative issues to address: creating new family rituals and routines; dealing with unresolved anger, grief, and crises from earlier families; continuing relationships with parents not living in the household; sexuality issues involving stepsiblings and stepparents; building new family relationships, and much, much more (Bray & Harvey, 1995; Henry & Lovelace, 1995).

Busy distancing themselves from their parents, young adolescents typically have mixed feelings about their new stepparents. Strained parent–adolescent relationships, although not the norm, are more prevalent in single-parent families and stepfamilies than in intact households (Montemayor, 1986; Ryan & Lynch, 1989). Adolescents do better in remarried households when parents are both consistent and flexible, when adolescents have predictable household routines, and when there is meaningful parent–child communication (Bray & Harvey, 1995; Collins, Newman, & McKenry, 1995; Henry & Lovelace, 1995).

## ADOLESCENTS AND THEIR SIBLINGS

*The person I admire most is my oldest brother Ronnie. Ever since I was allowed to go outside, I would always follow him around because I thought he was the greatest, and he still is in my eyes. I used to dress like him, listen to the same music, and I always tried to talk like him. I still use certain phrases that I learned from him many years ago. I admired him so much because he understood everything I was going through. I've always wanted to be just like him when I grew up, and I think I am.*

*(Freshman college student; from Jaffe, 1997, p. 204)*

Is it an advantage to have an older sibling? As usual, the answer depends on many factors. These include the personal qualities (e.g., temperament) of the particular older brother or sister, the age difference between siblings, the number of siblings, whether or not they are the same gender, and how their parents treat each sibling (Brody, Stoneman, & Gauger, 1996; Newman, 1991).

When siblings perceive preferential treatment, they may develop an adversarial relationship (Dunn & Plomin, 1990). Montemayor and Hanson (1985) found that almost half (44%) of all family conflicts occur between siblings. Most parents recognize the love-hate nature of sibling relationships and try to encourage sibling closeness by not showing favoritism. Sibling relationships usually are more intense and possibly most influential during early childhood, when there is more contact, more conflict, and more expressed warmth and affection than during later years (Burhmester & Furman, 1990). As siblings mature, their relationship usually becomes more positive (Newman, 1991).

Because of the relative closeness in age, some adolescents become surrogate parents to their younger siblings. A younger adolescent feels more comfortable

**Older siblings can be positive or negative role-models for social skills and responsible behavior.**

discussing topics such as sex and drugs with a sympathetic older sibling than with a rigid, old-fashioned parent (Buhrmester & Furman, 1990; Dunn & Plomin, 1990). Because of the closeness in age, siblings sometimes are more influential than parents. Older siblings can be positive or negative role models for social skills and responsible behavior.

Adolescents and younger siblings report feeling closer during the older sibling's adolescence even though (or maybe because) there are fewer interactions. Sibling relationships typically are closer and more harmonious for adolescent girls than for boys (Kurdek & Fine, 1993; Moser et al., 1996). Despite the decreased contact and companionship and occasional conflict, emotional attachment between siblings remains surprisingly strong (Buhrmester & Furman, 1990; Newman, 1991).

## LEAVING THE NEST

Earlier in the chapter, we considered the important life transition of living away from home. In the past, marriage, not college attendance, was the most common route out of the parental home. Although many nonfamily living arrangements are available today, such as living alone, with a partner, or with housemates, most college graduates who live away from home eventually return to the nest. Factors responsible include the high cost of housing, divorce, and unemployment. Many older children (especially sons) leave home and return repeatedly before their final departure (Da Vanzo & Goldscheider, 1990; Thornton, Young-DeMarco, & Goldscheider, 1993).

As much as they love their children, most parents look foward to launching their children into lives of self-sufficiency. Although college-age adolescents rarely request support from their parents, when they ask for it, they almost always get it (Valery et al., 1997). Remarried and single parents in particular report feeling less supportive of and less financially obligated to their grown children than do first-marriage parents (Marks, 1995). Parents (especially mothers, who usually are the primary caregivers) are happier and more satisfied with their lives and marriages when their children depart. Although parents usually are willing to provide a temporary "safety net" to help children become self-supporting, living with older children (**coresidence**) can be taxing. This is especially true when parent–child relationships are tense or conflictual, when the adult child is unemployed, or when the child has never left home. Coresidence most commonly involves unmarried and never-married children. About half of coresident children have never left home. Returning coresidents are older and are more likely to have been married. Most expect to leave within a year, although their parents are skeptical (Ward & Spitze, 1996b). There are relatively few gender differences among coresident children, although daughters are more likely to do housework and sons are more likely to pay room and board (Ward & Spitze, 1996a).

Some parents interpret their adult child's continuing dependence on them as a personal failure. Most parents who live with their adult children, however, get along with them and are satisfied with the arrangement (Aquilino, 1991; Ward & Spitze, 1992).

## SUMMARY

**1.** Parent–child relationships provide the main context in which children's socialization occurs. Much of what children know about getting along with people is learned by observing and participating in family relationships. Parents exert optimal influence by staying emotionally in touch with their children, taking their concerns seriously, and setting firm limits on their behavior.

**2.** Children are affected by changes in their parents' lives and vice versa. The life transitions that occur during adolescence and middle age require adjustment by the entire family system.

**3.** Close parent–adolescent relationships are associated with adolescents' self-disclosure, cooperation, and acceptance of parental values. Adolescent boys and girls report feeling especially close to their mothers. Because mothers usually are the primary caregivers, they usually receive the brunt of adolescent wrath. Mothers typically are more flexible than fathers and more likely to back off (or compromise) during conflict. Thus, adolescents are more willing to confront them.

**4.** Fathers typically spend much less time than mothers with their adolescent children. When dealing with their children, they are more likely to stay in role, that is, assert their authority, correct behavior, and engage in problem solving. Many adolescent daughters report feeling distant from their fathers and believe that their fathers do not know them very well, but most teenagers respect their fathers and enjoy their company.

**5.** Parents of adolescents are dealing with midlife issues in the areas of work, marriage, and parenting. Dissatisfaction in one area often spills over into the other areas. Many middle-aged parents report feeling left out of their children's lives. Some feel unappreciated or jealous of their children. Parents who have a very high investment in their children's lives but few outside interests are most vulnerable to the "empty nest blues."

**6.** Adolescents occasionally challenge certain aspects of their parents' opinions, beliefs, and lifestyles. But there is little evidence of a generation gap in values. Most young people live in harmony with their parents and feel close to them most of the time.

**7.** Each parent develops a parenting style that is a combination of childrearing strategies and personal qualities. Diane Baumrind identified four parenting styles, each of which is associated with distinctive behaviors and personal qualities of children. Parents who are warm and firm (the authoritative parenting style) typically have children who are socially and academically competent. Authoritarian parenting is associated with more troubled parent–child relationships. High support and low to moderate control provide an ideal family environment for most middle-class adolescents in Western cultures.

**8.** About half of adolescents are occasionally struck by their parents. Corporal punishment is associated with a variety of adolescent problems, including aggressive behavior, drug abuse, suicidal thoughts, and poor achievement in school. Adolescents apparently can tolerate occasional harsh punishment if it is tempered by consistent and involved parenting.

**9.** There is a trade-off for adolescents between being able to seek comfort and assurance from their parents and being free of their authority. The corresponding issue for parents is controlling their children versus letting go. A sensible guideline is that freedom is earned through good judgment and responsible behavior.

**10.** Parent–adolescent conflict contributes to a realignment of family relationships as adolescents gain a greater role in family decision making. Gains in autonomy often lead to a decrease in the time that adolescents spend with their parents and reduced emotional closeness. Rather than abdicating control or overreacting to adolescent provocations, parents can maintain relatively harmonious relationships with their children by listening to them, taking them seriously, and negotiating new ways of living together. Family disagreements are normal and healthy. However, most teenagers will occasionally test their parents' resolve to stay in relationship.

**11.** Families are destabilized, at least temporarily, by the series of stressful transitions that accompany parental conflict and divorce. Each child reacts differently, depending partly on age, gender, and coping resources. Each successive life stressor takes its toll on adolescent functioning. Frequent conflicts between parents disturb the parent–adolescent relationship.

**12.** Although negative stereotypes of single-parent families and stepfamilies are misguided, adolescents in such families do appear to have more adjustment problems than those in intact families. They are pressured to grow up faster and become more autonomous, whether or not they are ready.

**13.** It is not unusual for children to "return to the nest" following college attendance or divorce. Although parents usually report relief when their children leave, most are willing to support their children until the latter are self-sufficient. Most late adolescents and young adults who live with their parents get along with them and are satisfied with the arrangement.

# GLOSSARY

**Family systems model** A theoretical model that views families as multigenerational systems of interconnected relationships with shifting alliances and changing roles

**Critical period** A specific time in development when a life event has its greatest impact

**Socialization** The processes involved in raising and educating children and adolescents

**Values gap** Adolescent norms, values, and behaviors that are objectionable to adults

**Parenting style** A combination of childrearing strategies and personal qualities of an individual parent

**Authoritarian style** A power-based parenting style that is rigid and demanding

**Permissive style** A parenting style involving parental detachment from or indulgence of children

**Enmeshed style** A style of parents who are warm, accepting, and overly involved with their children

**Indulgent style** Parenting style in which parents do not set or enforce limits on their children's behavior

**Rejecting-neglecting style** Parenting style in which parents are minimally involved in their children's emotional lives

**Authoritative style** Parenting style in which parents are warm and firm, preferring reasoning and persuasion to power and coercion

**Corporal punishment** Physical punishment inflicted directly on the body, as in slapping, spanking, or flogging

**Autonomy** Self-regulation

**Conflict** An inability to resolve differences, sometimes accompanied by tension, hostility, or aggression

**Sleeper effect** When the effects of a stressful experience do not become apparent until a later developmental stage

**Coresidence** Grown children living with their parents

# THOUGHT QUESTIONS

**1.** Using the family systems model, describe the parent–adolescent relationships in a family that you know well.

**2.** In what ways did your family have to adjust to your changes during early adolescence?

**3.** As a teenager, how successful were you in balancing your desire for greater self-regulation with your need to stay connected to family members?

**4.** What generational differences in values, roles, and beliefs can you identify in your family?

**5.** How are individuation and separation more challenging tasks for adolescents in single-parent families and stepfamilies?

**6.** In what ways did you become more independent during your adolescence? In what ways are you still dependent on your parents?

**7.** Describe your parents' parenting style based on chapter material. How do you think your parenting style might differ from that of your parents?

**8.** How do parental separation and divorce affect developmental tasks such as identity formation, individuation, and separation from parents?

## SELF-TEST

1. The key relationship in any two-parent family is the
   a. mother–son relationship
   b. father–daughter relationship
   c. sibling relationship
   d. relationship between the parents

2. The family systems model views families as
   a. a collection of individuals
   b. a multigenerational system of shifting alliances and changing roles
   c. inherently stable social units
   d. all of the above

3. In most families, the primary caregiver is
   a. an unemployed mother
   b. an employed mother
   c. an employed father
   d. a hired employee

4. Most adolescents report feeling closest to their
   a. peers
   b. same-gender parent
   c. mother
   d. siblings

5. Compared to mothers, fathers usually are
   a. less accepting
   b. more demanding
   c. less involved
   d. all of the above

6. Most mentors
   a. are related to the children they work with
   b. help youngsters acquire practical skills and information
   c. work with economically advantaged children
   d. work with children in groups

**7.** For most parents, middle age is a time of

   **a.** crisis

   **b.** normal life stress and reappraisal

   **c.** heightened marital satisfaction

   **d.** feeling appreciated by one's children

**8.** The key childrearing issue faced by parents of adolescents is

   **a.** security versus freedom

   **b.** autonomy versus shame and doubt

   **c.** intimacy versus isolation

   **d.** control versus letting go

**9.** The greatest gap between parents and adolescents appears to be in the area of

   **a.** achievement

   **b.** religious beliefs

   **c.** values

   **d.** tolerance

**10.** Authoritative parents are

   **a.** warm and firm

   **b.** rigid and coercive

   **c.** lenient and detached

   **d.** overly involved (enmeshed) with their children

**11.** Authoritarian parents mainly value

   **a.** achievement

   **b.** obedience

   **c.** independent thinking

   **d.** none of the above

**12.** Permissive parents generally are the least

   **a.** involved

   **b.** controlling

   **c.** interested

   **d.** all of the above

13. The most desirable child outcomes are associated with which parenting style?

   a. authoritative

   b. authoritarian

   c. permissive-neglecting

   d. permissive-indulgent

14. About what percent of adolescents are hit by their parents?

   a. 20

   b. 30

   c. 40

   d. 50

15. Adolescents who live apart from their parents

   a. are less attached

   b. get along better with them

   c. feel more independent

   d. all of the above

16. Occasional conflict between adolescents and parents ultimately

   a. increases adolescent autonomy

   b. decreases adolescent autonomy

   c. increases parent–adolescent distance

   d. is destructive

17. Adolescents seem to be harmed most by

   a. parental divorce

   b. frequent displays of hostility between parents

   c. father absence

   d. living with a single parent

# EIGHT

# THE WORLD OF ADOLESCENTS:
# PEERS AND YOUTH CULTURE

## Preview Questions

**1.** How do adolescents benefit from belonging to peer groups?

**2.** What is the difference between cliques, crowds, and gangs?

**3.** What personal qualities motivate friendships during adolescence?

**4.** How do members of adolescent peer groups influence each other?

**5.** How do adolescent friendships compare to those of younger children?

**6.** How do parents influence their children's choice of friends?

**7.** Why are some adolescents rejected by their peers?

**8.** What role does popular music play in adolescent identity formation?

**9.** How do teenagers spend their leisure time?

## Disclosures

New friendships with women which I developed in college did not replace or mimic the relationships I had with [earlier friends], but there are elements of sameness. I see my relationships with women as continuing to be places where I develop and define myself, where through interaction and shared experience I become more and more comfortable with who I am, where I have come from, and where my life is going. I am supported in these relationships; in them I feel comfortable and safe and loved.

*(Young woman quoted by Garrod et al., 1992, p. 210)*

I think I'm a pretty good person, I do the right things when it comes to my friends. But because I don't go along with what they do, I feel like I'm not as cool as they are. . . . I never tell anyone this but I sometimes want to try the things my friends do. I mean, I'm 16 and never been drunk or high. My friends sneak out at night, like at 2 A.M., and meet somewhere. If I ever got caught, my parents would be disappointed.

*(16-year-old female)*

Yeah, I feel pressure to do what my friends do, but it's not like they pressure me. They really can't pressure me that much. If they're doing it, I *want* to do it.

*(16-year-old female)*

◆
———

# Contents

Sixteen-year-old Rita describes the students in her suburban high school. The so-called popular group is outgoing, the nerds are smart, and the Asian group is bound by its members' ethnicity. Rita is proud that her group is not labeled, although she admits that they conform in dress, interests, and academics. She reports that her friends dress for comfort, not fashion. Members of her crowd are interested in athletics and are enrolled in college prep courses. Most drink alcohol and some are sexually active, but Rita quickly adds that she is not.

According to Rita, friends are "people you have fun with and with whom you can be yourself. You do not have to worry about acting a certain way." She met her friends in school and in summer camp. They come from various ethnic and religious backgrounds. She has a male and a female best friend, both of whom are "extremely open" with her. However, there are certain topics she can discuss only with her girlfriend.

Fifteen-year-old Mike attends the same high school as Rita. He describes a peer as someone with whom he associates on a regular basis. The crowds in his school, he advises, are metalheads, the alternative group (who listen to progressive music), the rappers (who listen to, you guessed it, rap), and the eastsiders and westsiders (depending on where they live). Mike is an eastsider but, like Rita, prefers not to be classified. Mike's group likes progressive music, dresses casually, and does not use drugs. His friends are fun to be with, assist him with personal problems, and help him avoid feeling lonely. He met most of them at school, and they are from different cultural backgrounds. All except one are male.

Interviews with teenagers like Rita and Mike confirm that close friends and friendship groups contribute to several different domains of adolescent development. Children and adolescents use their friendships as cognitive and social resources for developing moral judgments and values (Hartup, 1996). It is mainly in peer groups that adolescents hone their social skills and rehearse the social roles that they will adopt as adults (Erikson, 1960). Perhaps the main theme of this chapter is that, although peer influence can be positive or negative, it is more likely to be positive (McIntosh, 1996).

In their endless conversations, friends rely on each other for companionship, feedback, practical information, and emotional support (Seltzer, 1989; Sullivan, 1953). One 17-year-old girl put it this way: "My friends. What can I say? They are always there for me. They know just what to say when I need advice. They are great."

The peer group is a source of powerful social rewards, including prestige, acceptance, status, and popularity, that can enhance an adolescent's self-esteem (Bishop & Inderbitzen, 1995; Muuss, 1988a). Friendship also plays a key role in constructing a personal identity (Berndt & Savin-Williams, 1993; Erikson, 1960; Youniss & Haynie, 1992). For adolescents, affiliating with peer groups and crowds is a "way station in their development between early identification with family and self-identity as an individual" (Dornbusch, Herman, & Morley, 1996, p. 201).

Friendships provide adolescents with "opportunities to express, test, and verify alternative views freely with someone who shares similar life experiences" (Hunter, 1985, p. 439). Friendships allow adolescents to learn the importance of reciprocity, self-disclosure, trust, caring, and conflict resolution skills in close relationships (Collins & Repinski, 1994).

Most adolescents turn to their friends more than to their parents for recreation, companionship, and understanding (Blyth et al., 1982; Furman & Buhrmester, 1992). This is not to say that friends replace parents in adolescents' social network; they don't (Blyth et al., 1982; Bø, 1996). Rather, there is a temporary shift in the hierarchy of relationships. For most adolescents, closeness to peers increases as closeness to parents decreases. Those who are accepted by their peers and who have reciprocal friendships usually have higher self-esteem and do better in school (Bishop & Inderbitzen, 1995; Savin-Williams & Berndt, 1990).

Young teenagers, somewhat insecure and vulnerable, crave acceptance and validation from their age-mates. For a few, this need elicits thoughtless conformity to the values and behaviors of their companions. A 20-year-old female disclosed: "If my friends are going somewhere, I want to go too. I don't know why. It just seems that I should be doing it too, to be like them."

Children who are deficient in interpersonal skills are more likely to be rejected by their peers and must settle for friendships with other "social rejects" (Brown, 1996; Dishion, Andrews, & Crosby, 1995; Dodge, 1983; Merten, 1996a, 1996b). Interpersonal problems during childhood and adolescence are especially worrisome because they set the stage for relationship and other difficulties during adulthood (Hansen, Giacoletti, & Nangle, 1995; Parker & Asher, 1987; Patterson, 1986).

In this chapter, we examine the nature of friendships and other peer relationships during adolescence. We consider how peer groups form, how they function, and the diverse ways in which peers influence each other. We also raise the following questions: Why do so many adolescents come to prefer the company of their friends to that of their parents? What role do parents play in the selection of their children's friends? What personal qualities lead to popularity with one's age-mates? How do adolescents spend their leisure time? Are cultural media such as popular music, television, and video games potentially harmful to adolescents, are they merely sources of amusement and pleasure, and what role, if any, do they play in adolescent identity formation?

## PEER RELATIONSHIPS AND COGNITIVE DEVELOPMENT

The changes of early adolescence profoundly alter the nature of adolescents' interpersonal relationships. Advancing cognitive and verbal abilities, in combination with physical and emotional growth, change the way adolescents view and interact with their peers. Selman (1980) noted that the cognitive advances of early adolescence, especially perspective taking, enhance young people's understanding of how relationships work. They understand that relationships are guided by certain standards of conduct, including honesty, cooperation, and sensitivity.

According to Selman, empathic understanding allows and encourages teenagers to become strongly attached to peers, to value friendships, to seek exclusive relationships, and to achieve intimacy with others through kind treatment and self-disclosure. Peer relationships raise several issues that young adolescents did not have to think about when younger, issues involving availability, trust, and loyalty. In order to succeed at relationships, one has to monitor the other party's needs and expectations. I think most adults would agree that this type of learning is lifelong.

Parker and Gottman (1989) relate friendship to the process of identity formation. More than younger children, adolescents are capable of relating to and identifying with their friends' daily experiences. Conversations with friends that involve mutual self-disclosure ("That happened to me") elicit a wide range of emotions and perspectives that help adolescents view themselves in a relationship context. This includes the insight that who I am as a person is defined partly by my relationships with family members, friends, teachers, employers, and many others. Over the course of adolescence, interpersonal understanding continues to expand in the direction of greater empathy and less self-centeredness. *Thought Question: What elements of formal reasoning might contribute to adolescents' ability to value and participate in close peer relationships?*

## FAMILY VERSUS PEER RELATIONSHIPS

*My friend Carla. We're really the same person. We think alike, we act alike. We get along very well. I go to her for everything.*

*(17-year-old female)*

Most teenagers come to prefer the companionship of peers to that of their family members (Blyth et al., 1982; Csikszentmihalyi & Larson, 1984; Larson et al., 1996; Montemayor & Hanson, 1985; Reisman, 1985). To some extent, this reflects their realization that parents dominate parent–child relationships. Friends are less likely than parents to coerce, criticize, and lecture and are more willing to give each other what they really want—validation and status. More than younger children, teenagers recognize and begin to challenge parental control. Like adults, they desire equality in their relationships. Peer relationships are more egalitarian than adult–child relationships (e.g., Laursen, Hartup, & Koplas, 1996). Explanations and understanding are more balanced (Hunter, 1985).

As discussed in Chapter 7, most adolescents have no desire to torment their parents or withdraw from their families. Decreased frequency of contact in itself does not necessarily mean lessened closeness or poorer-quality relationships (Blyth et al., 1982; O'Koon, 1997). Most adolescents acknowledge that some of their closest relationships are with family members, including parents, step-

Peer relationships are more egalitarian than parent-child relationships, making them more attractive to adolescents.

parents, and grandparents (Bø, 1996; Field et al., 1995). Parental influence continues to prevail in future-oriented domains such as education and career, although peers have greater influence regarding current events and leisure-time activities. Adolescents consult parents and friends about relationship and personal problems (Meeus, 1989).

We can't attribute the reduced amount of time adolescents spend with their families solely to the push of family conflict or to the pull of the peer group. Much of the diminished family time is replaced by time spent alone at home (Larson, 1997; Larson et al., 1996; Smith, 1997). Nevertheless, for most adolescents, the pull of the peer group and other outside interests (job, car, romance) is stronger than the enticement of playing Monopoly with family members (Larson et al., 1996).

## TYPES OF PEER GROUPS

Adolescents become embedded in a complex network of relationships with best friends, close friends, acquaintances, cliques, crowds, and romantic relationships. Based on his study of Australian youth, Dunphy (1963, 1969, 1972) distinguished three groupings of adolescents: cliques, crowds, and gangs. These three types of groups differ in structure and function, but all three provide members with a sense of belonging (see Table 8-1).

The basic functional unit of adolescent group life is the **clique**, usually four to six close friends who spend much of their leisure time together. Members typically are of the same gender and social class, of similar age, attend the same school, and live in the same community. Group members exert pressure on each other to conform to group norms, using social rewards and sanctions to keep members in line. Members of a clique do not necessarily consider all other

THE CLIQUE

The basic unit of adolescent social life is the clique, four to six close friends who enjoy spending their leisure time together.

clique members to be friends, and not all of one's friends are members of one's clique (Urberg, Degirmencioglu, Tolson, & Halliday-Scher, 1995).

Dunphy (1972) observed that during early adolescence, teenagers move from same-gender to mixed-gender cliques. During middle adolescence, a loosely connected network of dating couples emerges. Adolescents in middle school and high school usually leave their close-knit cliques to become members of larger and more diverse crowds of boys and girls. This provides them with an even greater sense of belonging (Brown, Mory, & Kinney, 1994).

Brown (1990) distinguished between activity-based cliques, such as a wrestling team, and friendship cliques, which consist of self-chosen friends. He noted that young people typically identify with a reference group to which they may or may not belong. "A nerd who hopes to become a popular may be more heavily influenced by the popular peer culture than by the norms of nerd culture" (p. 178).

**Crowds** are larger than cliques (Dunphy, 1969, 1972). They usually are school-based and have male and female members. Most common during mid-adolescence, crowds range from 15 to 30 members, with an average of 20 members (at least in Dunphy's Australian sample). The main function of the crowd, according to Dunphy, is to facilitate contact between the two genders so that heterosexual behaviors can be learned and practiced. Crowds are created when two to four cliques come together. Thus, clique membership is a prerequisite to crowd membership. Whereas cliques usually are activity-based, crowds are reputation-based. Membership implies certain attitudes and activities associated with crowd members. Whereas clique norms develop within the peer group itself, crowd norms sometimes are imposed by outsiders who view the crowd stereotypically (Brown et al., 1994).

Crowds are characterized by general dispositions or shared interests—their clothing, preferred music and activities, interest in achievement, and type and

extent of drug use. Over the years, my students have apprised me of the following crowds from their high school days: normals, populars, unpopulars, loners, partyers, brains, nerds, jocks, punkers, druggies, greasers, metalheads, freaks, and many others. Social class and ethnicity play a role, as evidenced by crowds labeled black, Hispanic, or Asian. Note that crowd labels ignore the diversity within each group and give the impression that Asians, for example, cannot be jocks or freaks.

Druggies are viewed as alienated students who use drugs and have little interest in achievement. Nerds presumably have few friends and low self-esteem. Jocks concentrate on sports and beer. It is not yet clear how the individuals so named perceive themselves or end up identifying with or joining one crowd or another. Students do not join a crowd "so much as they are thrust into one by virtue of their personality, background, interests, and reputation among peers" (Brown, 1990, p. 183). Thus, your crowd membership tells you something about who you are in the eyes of your peers. ***Thought Question: Do members of crowds view themselves stereotypically or as individuals?***

Each crowd has a set of hard-core members, a set of peripheral members, and those who "float" from one crowd to another (Brown, 1996). Not everyone is pleased about the crowd with which he or she is identified, particularly those who aspire to belong to a higher-status crowd. Many high school students report belonging to several crowds. And every school has students who defy categorization. Even though schools differ in the existence and size of their crowds, it is impressive that the core groups (brains, jocks, normals, nerds, druggies) are identified by students from so many different high schools. Nevertheless, in the later years of high school, the boundaries that separate different crowds begin to break down as members of different crowds adopt a new

**An important function of the crowd is to facilitate contact between adolescent boys and girls.**

perspective—they realize how much they have in common (Brown, 1990; Youniss, McLellan, & Strouse, 1994).

Crowds provide high school students with frequent opportunities to experiment with their identity while maintaining a sense of group belonging (McIntosh, 1996; Pombeni, Kirchler, & Palmonari, 1990). For example, some groups display a subtle yet distinctive style of dressing and hairstyle (the crowd "uniform") that indicates both their membership in a particular crowd and their aloofness from other crowds (Eicher et al., 1991). (Some adolescents apply cosmetics or change their "uniform" in school to avoid detection by disapproving parents.) Given that students in large high schools cannot know all of their peers individually, crowds help clarify the "rules of engagement" for same-sex and opposite-sex peers, for example, who can date each other (Brown, 1996).

The dominant crowds in most schools, the populars and normals, are perceived as socially and academically competent. Groups with the lowest level of involvement in school activities (usually the druggies and metalheads) are viewed negatively by other groups (Brown, Mounts, Lambert, & Steinberg, 1993; Downs & Rose, 1991).

Crowd membership is somewhat related to family configuration and ethnicity. A study of 3,781 high school students (Brown et al., 1993) revealed that students from intact families were overrepresented among the brains and underrepresented among the druggies. The opposite pattern was true of students from stepfamilies. White students were overrepresented among the popular

### Table 8-1  Cliques, Crowds, and Gangs

**Clique**
- basic unit of adolescent group life
- four to six same-gender friends
- similar age, attend the same school, live in the same community

**Crowd**
- school- and reputation-based group with male and female members
- ranges from 15 to 30 members, with an average of 20 members
- provides high school students with frequent opportunities to experiment with their identity while maintaining a sense of group belonging
- membership implies certain attitudes and activities shared by crowd members
- not everyone is pleased about the crowd with which he or she is identified, particularly those who aspire to belong to a higher status crowd

**Gang**
- larger and more highly organized than cliques
- commonly found in working class urban areas
- provide protection to group members and define a territory to prevent incursion by other gangs
- members typically reject the values of their families and society

crowd (in predominantly white schools), Asian-American students were over-represented among the brains, and African-American students were overrepresented among the jocks. Students who are members of ethnic minorities usually are less connected to school peer networks than ethnic majority students (Urberg et al., 1995). Why do you think this is so?

A crowd often creates its own vocabulary, "a language by which to understand and express the complicated and sometimes confusing patterns of social relationships with peers" (Brown, Mory, & Kinney, 1994, p. 162). (The sentiment "cool" has persisted for decades and has even achieved dictionary status as slang. My son tells me that, at least in his high school, if something is

Gang members typically reject family and societal values and believe that they have little to lose through antisocial behavior.

"the bomb" it is the best.) Crowds partly determine who a teenager's friends will be and what their relationships will be like. Over the high school years, loyalty to a particular crowd usually weakens.

**Gangs** are similar to cliques in that they usually are unisexual, but they are larger and more highly organized (Dunphy, 1969, 1972). More commonly found in working-class urban areas, gangs provide protection to group members and define a territory to prevent incursion by other gangs. Gang members typically reject the values of their families and society. Illegal activities provide excitement and adventure for gang members while isolating them from the larger community. Gang members are likely to believe that they have no stake in society and thus have little to lose by challenging social conventions. Keep in mind that teenagers feel pressured to conform to group norms whether the norms are prosocial or antisocial (e.g., Jenkins, 1996).

## PEER RELATIONSHIPS AND DELINQUENCY

Not surprisingly, the single best predictor of delinquent behavior is associating with delinquent peers. It is misguided, however, to attribute antisocial behavior solely or mainly to deviant peer influence. Many young people are disposed toward antisocial behavior long before they reach adolescence (Fergusson & Horwood, 1996).

When social theorists try to understand the origins of deviant behavior, they look first to the family of origin (Patterson, 1986). Although some people speak of a genetic disposition toward antisocial behavior, most theorists assume that family factors guide children's interpersonal style and values. As we shall see in Chapter 13, children who behave antisocially frequently come from families with parents who share that characteristic (Patterson & Dishion, 1985). *Thought Question: Does this observation help us distinguish between a nature and a nurture model of antisocial behavior?*

Children who practice coercive strategies are disruptive in school and usually are rebuffed by nondeviant peers, who see them as selfish and obnoxious. Rejection drives some children into the arms of troubled peers, many of whom share unfortunate family histories (Simons, Whitbeck, Conger, & Conger, 1991). Delinquent peers model and reinforce coercive strategies (Fergusson & Horwood, 1996; Patterson & Dishion, 1985).

Dishion and his colleagues (1995) interviewed and assessed 186 13- and 14-year-old boys and videotaped them during a problem-solving task. Compared to interactions among prosocial boys, the interactions of antisocial adolescents were of lower quality, shorter duration, marginally satisfactory, and often ended with hostility. This was due less to a lack of positive behaviors than to the *frequent occurrence of bossiness and coercive behavior*. Based on his review of studies comparing the friendships of delinquent and nondelinquent adolescents, Marcus (1996) concluded that friendships among delinquents have more conflict and aggression, poorer attachment quality, less ability to repair relationships, more cognitive distortions, and poorer social-cognitive problem solving.

Although it is tempting to view gang members as social outcasts who are unable to have meaningful relationships, the dynamics of youth gangs are not entirely different from those of ordinary peer groups, especially regarding self-disclosure and loyalty (Cairns, Neckerman, & Cairns, 1989). Aggressive adolescents select each other and have relationships that are no less meaningful to them than those of their less alienated peers. Within their deviant groups, they establish social bonds that can be quite satisfying. Thus, those who reject social norms and values can find acceptance within a like-minded peer group, as long as they are willing to tolerate lower-quality relationships and more conflict (Dryfoos, 1990; Marcus, 1996).

## FORMATION OF PEER GROUPS

Close friendships are the rule during the teenage years. Almost all young people are eager to participate in shared activities and to exchange ideas and opinions with their age-mates (Youniss & Smollar, 1985). This propensity leads to the formation and maintenance of fairly stable peer groups that foster the development of mutual similarity (synchrony) in group members (Savin-Williams & Berndt, 1990).

Dunphy (1972) suggested that youth groups form in societies where families or kinship groups cannot provide young people with the social skills and roles that they need to function outside of the family setting. Adolescents must be resocialized by their peers, according to Dunphy, because the values they learn in their families are not relevant to the educational or vocational settings that they inhabit. Dunphy maintained that participation in a youth group is necessary for becoming self-regulating and for constructing an adult identity.

During early and middle adolescence, most children have at least one primary peer group. Personal needs and social pressures compel adolescents to identify with at least one friendship group. The alternative is loneliness and isolation. Although friends typically live in the same community and are similar ethnically and socioeconomically, friendships occasionally cross barriers of gender, race, age, and social class (Savin-Williams & Berndt, 1990).

Younger children usually select friends on the basis of availability and shared preferences for play activities rather than feelings of closeness or safety. Competitiveness is a significant element in preadolescent friendships among boys, although excessive competitiveness inhibits friendly behavior and can damage friendships. *Proximity* is a crucial factor in adolescent group formation in that we can only spend time with someone who is present and available. Frequent and pleasing contact promotes close relationships. Close friendships promote frequent and pleasing contact (see Table 8-2).

At least until teenagers get their driving licenses, they spend most of their leisure time with friends who live within walking or biking distance of their homes and who attend the same school. Although friendships usually begin in school, time spent together outside of school strengthens the bond. Some children fail to establish out-of-school friendships because they lack confidence or the skills needed to initiate or maintain contact. Lack of transportation and race and gender differences are potential obstacles to out-of-school friendships (DuBois & Hirsch, 1993).

According to U.S. Census Bureau statistics, each year more than 9 million children are displaced as 17% of families in the United States relocate. Family relocation is stressful to young adolescents, who are very concerned about leaving close friends behind (Seppa, 1996b). Peer networks become more exclusive with increasing age (Urberg et al., 1995). Compared to younger children, who usually are more flexible and less self-conscious about social encounters, many adolescents feel awkward about meeting and joining established social groups. Vernberg (1990b) compared 36 early adolescent boys and girls who recently moved and began the academic year in a new school year to 37 early adolescents who hadn't moved regarding their contact with friends. The teenagers were asked to name their best friends and to indicate how often they interacted with each friend in various situations. Those who had recently moved reported fewer contacts with friends and less intimacy and sharing in relationships with best friends. Boys who had moved reported receiving more rejection (being hit or teased in a mean way) from peers compared to boys who were stable. It took at least a year for many of the boys to re-establish close relationships with peers. *Thought Question: What can parents and teachers do to help teenagers who relocate when their families move?*

**Table 8-2  Factors Influencing the Formation of Peer Groups**

Availability

Proximity

Goodness of fit in personal qualities

Shared interests and preferences

Race, gender, ethnic group similarities

Frequent and pleasing contact

Transportation

## DYNAMICS OF PEER GROUPS

At any age, some children are better prepared than others to get along with their age-mates. How well children get along with friends partly reflects what they have learned about close relationships at home. Every day family life provides children with countless opportunities to learn about self-disclosure, trust, loyalty, conflict, compromise, and respect (Collins & Repinski, 1994).

Like married couples, friends become increasingly alike over time (Berndt & Keefe, 1995; Dinges & Oetting, 1993). They reinforce in each other common behaviors and values, whether it be an interest in music or sports or learning the proper way to inhale marijuana. High-achieving children compete for good grades, while uninterested students mock those who make an effort (Epstein, 1983).

One of the first tasks of any group is to form a dominance hierarchy of leaders and followers. The leader of a group is the one who is imitated and followed by other group members (Dunphy, 1972). Group leadership is not necessarily stable across activities. The athletic leader and social leader may be two different members. However, each individual influences and is influenced by the larger group. Some group members are more influential than others. Because most young people feel awkward in a role of authority, peer group members usually deny that any one of them is the leader. Nevertheless, it is not hard to find differences in the prestige status of group members (Dunphy, 1972).

Dunphy (1969, 1972) observed that although dominant members of cliques and crowds do not overtly exercise authority, they control communication and decision making. Leaders initiate action via coordination of activities rather than by using power and control. Certain clique members become leaders because they represent to their peers the ideal personality type at this stage of development. Admired traits such as friendliness, athletic ability, intelligence, and popularity qualify one for being a dominant member of an adolescent peer group.

Clique leaders initiate new ideas and activities, are usually the first to date, and are regarded by group members as essential to the group's existence (Dunphy, 1969, 1972). Qualities that are admired (e.g., looks, sense of humor, strength) may change from one phase of adolescence to the next. To some extent, high-status members are role models to their peers in their ongoing efforts to construct a personal identity.

## MECHANISMS OF PEER INFLUENCE

Although peer influence during the teenage years usually is positive and constructive, "peer pressure" remains a convenient (if simplistic) way for adults to explain antisocial or self-destructive behavior during adolescence. *Members of peer groups usually are similar to begin with and influence each other in the direction of greater similarity* (Mounts & Steinberg, 1995). Prosocial peers model and reinforce prosocial behaviors such as consideration for others, while deviant peers may encourage antisocial or self-destructive behaviors (Brown, Lohr, & McClenahan, 1986; Epstein, 1983; Kaplan, Johnson, & Bailey, 1987). It is unusual for a troubled adolescent to lead well-meaning peers down the road to ruin (Brown, 1990; Steinberg & Silverberg, 1986). Most adolescents, even those who get into trouble, are attracted to peers who do not get into trouble (Gillmore, Hawkins, Day, & Catalano, 1992).

The tendency of group members to have similar characteristics is called **homophily**. For example, adolescents tend to associate with peers who report similar levels of emotional distress (Hogue & Steinberg, 1995). We can attribute similarities among peer group members to the following processes: (1) **sociodemographic conditions** that bring children into proximity with each other; (2) **differential selection**, whereby individuals seek out as friends those who already are similar to them; (3) **reciprocal (mutual) socialization**, whereby peers become similar to friends by interacting with them; (4) **a contagion effect**, whereby people in highly cohesive groups sometimes do things that they would not do on their own; and (5) **selective elimination**, whereby nonconforming group members are forced to leave the group or leave voluntarily. These processes may operate simultaneously or at different times during a group's existence (Cairns, Neckerman, & Cairns, 1989; Hartup, 1996; Hogue & Steinberg, 1995; Kandel, 1978). All of these processes indicate the active nature of friendship selection during adolescence (see Table 8-3).

It would be misguided to assume that all young people are equally susceptible to peer influence. Most are somewhat susceptible to a given type of peer influence at certain times under specific conditions. For example, a 15-year-old might succumb to pressure to experiment with cigarettes but not to get a tattoo or have her head shaved. Adolescents are more likely to experience subtle pressure to conform to group values and standards than blatant attempts to control or manipulate them (Brown, 1990). *Thought Question: Why might children of authoritative parents be less susceptible to peer pressure (Mounts & Steinberg, 1995)?*

There is increasing evidence that small groups of close friends wield more influence on adolescent behavior than individual friends (McIntosh, 1996). Theorists propose the following mechanisms to understand how groups affect individual members (Kelly & Hansen, 1987): (1) **observational learning** (mod-

## Table 8-3 Factors That Increase Peer Similarity

**sociodemographic conditions:** bring individuals into proximity with each other

**differential selection:** individuals seek out as friends those who already are similar to them

**reciprocal (mutual) socialization:** peers become similar to friends by interacting with them

**contagion effect:** people in highly cohesive groups sometimes do things that they would not do on their own

**selective elimination:** nonconforming group members are forced to leave the group or leave voluntarily

### Table 8-4  Mechanisms of Peer Group Influence

**observational learning (modeling, imitation):** adolescents observe and may imitate some of the qualities or behaviors of their peers

**reinforcement:** behavior can be modified by peer positive and negative feedback, including agreement, encouragement, criticism, teasing, and coercion

**negative sanctions:** including rejection and exclusion

**participation in group activities:** provides opportunities for practice of skills and feedback

**social comparison:** comparing one's thoughts, feelings, and actions to those of one's peers

**transmission of skills, values, and behaviors:** from older to younger group members

eling, imitation)—adolescents observe and then imitate some of the qualities of their peers; for example, we observe fads in verbal expressions, haircuts, and footwear; (2) **reinforcement**—prosocial and antisocial behaviors are modified by peer feedback, including encouragement, criticism, teasing, and mild coercion; (3) **negative sanctions**, including rejection and exclusion; (4) *participation in group activities* that provide opportunities for practice and feedback; (5) **social comparison**—comparing one's thoughts, feelings, and actions to those of one's peers; favorable comparisons lead to positive feelings (pride) about oneself, whereas negative evaluations are painful, often leading to attempts to measure up to or withdraw from the group; and (6) *transmission of skills, values, and behaviors* from older to younger group members. Overlapping membership in several crowds allows social skills to filter down from older to younger members (see Table 8-4).

How these factors affect adolescent behavior depends partly on specific patterns of peer interaction (Hartup, 1996), including the amount of time spent with friends, the length of the relationship, and an individual's susceptibility to peer influence. Regarding the last, 16-year-old Francesca, a high school sophomore, told one of my students that she doesn't experience any direct pressure from her friends. She did admit that she goes along with whatever they propose, never taking her own opinions into account. She disclosed that she could not make any decision on her own. First, she must consult with her best friends. She values her friends' opinions more than her own. She claims that she is not happy about this but is afraid of "messing up." *Thought Question: What family factors might dispose an adolescent like Francesca to be susceptible to peer pressure?*

Berndt and Keefe (1995) wondered whether friends' behaviors (e.g., participating in extracurricular activities) or qualities of friendships (e.g., intimacy) exert greater influence on adolescent school adjustment. They performed a short-term longitudinal study of the behaviors of adolescents' friends and the features of their relationship during the fall semester of a school year and then again during the following spring semester. Seventh and eighth graders were asked to report their involvement and disruption at school (behaviors) and the positive and negative features of their best friendships (friendship qualities). Teachers also reported student involvement and disruption, as well as grades.

Results of the study indicated that adolescents' adjustment to school depended on both factors—their friends' behaviors and specific features of their relationships. For example, students whose friends in the fall semester described themselves as more disruptive increased in their own reports of disruption during the spring semester. Girls' self-reports of disruption were more influenced by their best friends than were boys' self-reports. Students whose best friendships in the fall had more positive features increased in self-reported school involvement in the spring. Students whose friendships had more negative features increased in self-reported disruption, but only when the relationships also had many positive features. (Presumably, friendships that have mainly negative features do not last.) The results suggest that close friendships increase adolescents' likelihood of adopting their friends' behaviors, positive or negative.

## PEER RELATIONSHIPS

Peer influence is mainly positive (Ball, 1981; Brown, Clasen, & Eicher, 1986; McIntosh, 1996). Realizing this, most parents encourage their children to develop friendships and to spend time with age-mates. Spending more time outside of the family environment allows young people to explore the world of nonfamily relationships and become comfortable in the larger community (Collins & Repinski, 1994). Surprisingly, despite the importance of social skills in adult work and relationships, social achievement in adolescence usually is not perceived as a major influence on occupational achievement or family life (Dornbusch et al., 1996).

Self-concept is broadened when we see ourselves through the eyes of others, especially those whom we deem credible. Peers offer valuable feedback that helps shape adolescents' self-perceptions. Parents offer feedback, but most children understand that their parents cannot view them objectively. Although negative feedback from friends can be painful, it helps all but the most vulnerable adolescents to develop a thicker skin. With friends, we hone our ability to disagree, argue, negotiate, resolve conflict, and cope with strong feelings (Collins & Repinski, 1994; Savin-Williams & Berndt, 1990).

Like younger children, some adolescents create imaginary companions, invisible name-bearing persons whom they can communicate with or write about on a daily basis. Seiffge-Krenke (1997) studied 241 German adolescents ages 12 to 17. She found that imaginary friends were similar to their ''creators'' and appeared to play a meaningful role in identity formation. Imaginary companions did not substitute for family members or friends. In fact, they were more likely to play a role in the lives of socially competent and creative adolescents with good coping abilities.

Peer groups also provide a relatively safe haven for trying out new beliefs and behaviors and for experimenting with adult roles and values. Typically, friends are more accepting than family members, at least for unconventional ideas. Our parents can't help but correct our behavior (''Brush your teeth,'' ''Clean up your room,'' ''Untie your sister''). Friends are more willing than family members to overlook our personal flaws—after all, they don't have to live with us. We've noted previously that adolescents would rather discuss their personal life with friends (or older siblings) than with parents. Presumably, they avoid discussing topics with their parents that in the past led to their parents "getting hyper" (Wilks, 1986). *Thought Question: How might parents inadvertently discourage self-disclosure in their children?*

Boys and girls report having about the same number of best friends, although findings are inconsistent regarding whether boys or girls belong to larger social networks. In friendships, boys generally are more activity-oriented and girls are more relationship-oriented. Girls typically are more positive about their close relationships, report more intimacy than boys do, and report getting more intensive social support from their peers (Frey & Röthlisberger, 1996; Jones & Costin, 1995; O'Koon, 1997). Boys judge each other on attributes related to group functioning. These include athletic and academic ability, interests, and following rules that allow the group to function. Girls prefer as friends peers who are sensitive, cooperative, and willing to share (Benenson, 1990; Karweit & Hansell, 1983; Youniss et al., 1994). *Thought Question: How might some of these gender differences reflect the earlier maturation of girls?*

## ADOLESCENT FRIENDSHIPS

We can define **friendship** as a relatively enduring, affectionate relationship between two people who enjoy each other's company. (Although friendship and popularity are overlapping domains of peer relationships, they are different phenomena with different correlates [Hanna & Berndt, 1995; Oldenburg & Kerns, 1997].) Friendships vary in level of intimacy. There are casual friends, close friends, and best friends. The number of best friends peaks at about five during early adolescence and then gradually declines until adulthood. (Adults report having an average of one best friend and a few close friends [Reisman & Shorr, 1978].)

The developmental significance of friendship varies from one child to another, although for all children supportive relationships certainly are advantageous (Hartup, 1996; Sullivan, 1953). No two friendships are alike. Each friendship reflects the personal qualities of each participant (e.g., temperament), each child's history of early relationships, a child's status and reputation among other children, and the specific environmental conditions that prevail. "Along with knowing whether or not children have friends, we must know who their friends are and the quality of their relationships with them" (Hartup, 1996, p. 10).

Claes (1992) administered questionnaires about friendships to 349 adolescents ranging in age from 12 to 18 years. Approximately half of the older adolescents reported that they had successfully maintained close contact with their best friend for at least 3 years, suggesting that adolescent friendships are fairly stable. Three-quarters of the respondents reported meeting their best friend at school. The number of best friends peaked during early adolescence and then declined gradually. Males and females agreed that loyalty, frankness, and trust are highly valued traits in friends. Confirming the findings of previous studies, girls expected more from their friendships than boys did. Communication deficits and the number of conflicts between friends were slightly related to adjustment.

How do friends spend their time together? Boys and girls enjoy going out with their friends—to the movies, for example. More than girls, boys prefer recreational activities such as sports and opportunities to use alcohol. More than boys, girls prefer simply talking (Fitzgerald, Joseph, Mayes, & O'Regan, 1995; Smith, 1997). Teenagers talk to their friends about relationships, their families, school, dating, and plans for the future. Older adolescents are more likely to discuss social issues (Youniss & Smollar, 1985).

Although adolescent boys and girls value same-gender companionship, girls generally desire more emotional closeness than boys do (Gilligan, 1982; Windle, 1994). Boys bond with each other more through shared activities than through self-disclosure (Savin-Williams & Berndt, 1990). Girls in particular confide in their girlfriends and in their mothers if they view these relationships as supportive (Monck, 1991). Boys often turn to their mothers for emotional support (Frey & Röthlisberger, 1996). Although teenage girls report wanting and having more intimacy and self-disclosure in their same-gender friendships than do boys, their expectations are so high that frequently they are disappointed (Bakken & Romig, 1992; Claes, 1992; Clark & Ayers, 1993). *Thought Question: What significance is there, if any, in the fact that most males and females learn to seek emotional support from females?*

What behaviors do adolescents believe will lead to success in peer relationships? Jarvinen and Nicholls (1996) questioned 266 ninth-grade students about their social goals and beliefs. The students identified six beliefs about circumstances or behaviors that lead to social success: being sincere, having status, being responsible, pretending to care, entertaining others, and being tough. In this sample, prosocial beliefs about relationships were associated with satisfying peer relations.

As children mature emotionally and cognitively, they come to expect more from relationships—loyalty, intimacy, and sympathetic understanding (Berndt & Perry, 1990). An 18-year-old college student told one of my students that she considers trust and honesty to be the most important characteristics of a good friend, along with the ability to "stick together in bad times when you really need them."

For most adolescents, interactional qualities such as intimacy (sharing, caring, validation), nurturance, dependability, and interpersonal skills play an increasingly important role in maintaining closeness (Claes, 1992; Hartup, 1989; Jarvinen & Nicholls, 1996; Savin-Williams & Berndt, 1990; Seltzer, 1989; Zarbatany, Ghesquiere, & Mohr, 1992). During early adolescence, "friends are no longer simply good playmates, but also must be psychologically similar and compatible, must trust each other with personal revelations, and must be willing to stand by and support each other through problems" (Burhmester, Goldfarb, & Cantrell, 1992, p. 75). Compared to friendships of younger children, adolescent friendships are more intense, richer, and more adultlike.

Berndt and Perry (1990) describe additional differences between childhood and adolescent friendships: (1) early adolescent relationships, especially between girls, are more intimate and supportive than those of earlier childhood, with greater sharing and understanding of personal problems; (2) early adolescents, especially girls, value loyalty or faithfulness more than do younger children—friends stick up for each other in a fight and don't talk about each other behind their backs; and (3) early adolescents compete with each other less and share with each other more than do younger children (see Table 8-5).

Warning: Friendship can be hazardous to your emotional health. Honest self-disclosure is risky. Occasionally, we learn that certain "friends" cannot be trusted. Adolescents complain about disloyalty, betrayal, disrespect, and insufficient attention from their friends (Wentzel & Erdley, 1993; Youniss & Smollar, 1985). An eighth-grade girl confirmed that close relationships are a mixed bag: "I can tell Karen things and she helps me talk. If we have problems in school, we work them out together. And she doesn't laugh at me if I do something weird—she accepts me for who I am." Things do not always go smoothly in this friendship. "When she's in a bad mood, she ignores you and yells at you and sulks. I hate it when people sulk. And she likes to be everybody's boss. She puts herself above other people that aren't as good as she is" (quoted by Berndt & Perry, 1990, p. 269).

## Table 8-5 Characteristics of Adolescent Friendships

The number of best friends peaks at about five during early adolescence and then gradually declines.

The developmental significance of friendship varies from one adolescent to another.

Adolescent friendships are fairly stable over time.

Most friends first meet at school.

Early adolescents, especially girls, value loyalty or faithfulness more than do younger children.

Early adolescents compete with each other less and share with each other more than do younger children.

Males and females agree that loyalty, frankness, and trust are highly valued traits in friends.

Girls expect more from their friendships than boys do, especially emotional closeness.

Girls' friendship expectations are so high that frequently they are disappointed.

As they mature, boys and girls come to expect more from relationships.

Boys prefer recreational activities such as sports; girls prefer talking.

Adolescents discuss with their friends relationships, families, school, dating, plans, and goals.

Older adolescents are more likely to discuss social issues.

Interactional qualities play an increasingly important role in maintaining closeness.

Early adolescent relationships, especially between girls, are more intimate and supportive than those of earlier childhood.

Adolescents complain about disloyalty, betrayal, disrespect, and insufficient attention from their friends.

Another risk of friendship is having to adjust to the loss of a close friend, not an uncommon phenomenon during adolescence. Whether the loss is due to an argument, family relocation, or death, adolescent grief is as deep and enduring as an adult's (O'Brien, Goodenow, & Espin, 1991).

## FRIENDSHIP AND ETHNICITY

Most of what we know about adolescent friendships has come from the study of white (European-American), middle-class teenagers. These findings do not necessarily apply to adolescents of African descent or to other ethnic groups (Clark, 1989; Giordano, Cernkovich, & DeMaris, 1993). Partly due to racism and different cultural opportunities, the socialization experiences of African-American youth in the United States differ to some extent from those of white youth (Coates, 1987). Since African-American and white peer groups often exist in relative isolation from each other, differences emerge in friendship patterns, preferred activities, and the importance of different settings (e.g., neighborhood versus school) to friendship networks (DuBois & Hirsh, 1990; Hallinan & Smith, 1985; Urberg et al., 1995).

We noted previously that adolescents gradually become more socially involved with their friends than with their parents. It is tempting to assume that adolescents of African descent are even more peer-oriented than their white counterparts because family fragmentation is more common in the African-American community. Indeed, DuBois and Hirsh (1990) found that the African-American middle school students in their sample reported having more close neighborhood friends than did white students. Yet, the investigators also found evidence of a strong bond between African-American adolescents and their parents, especially their mothers (Martin & Martin, 1978).

Based on interviews with 942 African-American and white adolescents, Giordano et al. (1993) concluded that African-American youths are more emotionally connected to their families than are white youths. African-American adolescents reported significantly higher levels of parental control and family intimacy compared to white youths. Friendships were described as somewhat less intimate than appears to be the case for white adolescents. The African-American adolescents perceived less peer pressure and reported having less of a need for approval from peers than did the white youths in the sample.

DuBois and Hirsh (1990) also reported differences in friendship patterns between young African-American and white adolescents. These investigators examined the school and neighborhood friendships of 292 children of both races who attended an integrated junior high school. The school's enrollment was predominantly white. Although 80% of the students reported having a close school friendship with a child of another race, only a quarter had regular contact with this friend outside of school. African-American students and students who lived in integrated neighborhoods were the most likely to have interracial school friendships that extended to nonschool settings. In fact, African-Americans were about twice as likely as whites to report having a close other-race friendship outside of school, probably reflecting the predominantly

In one study, African-American adolescents were about twice as likely as whites to report having a close other-race friendship outside of school.

white community in which the students lived. Neighborhood contact appears to be an important factor in encouraging cross-race friendships outside of school.

White girls in the study reported having more peer support than did white boys, but no gender difference was found for the African-American students. Coates (1987), however, found several differences between the social networks of young African-American male and female adolescents. Boys reported having more best friends, but girls appeared to feel closer to their friends. These and other findings confirm that we need to be cautious about generalizing the findings of studies of white adolescents to other ethnic or racial groups. *Thought Question: Why might efforts to encourage other-race friendships be more successful at the elementary school level than at the middle or junior high school level?*

## PARENTS AND FRIENDS

Many parents are concerned that as their children spend more time away from home, they will "fall in with the wrong crowd." As we have seen, children do tend to be similar to their friends, but not necessarily because of peer pressure or imitation. Young people actively select friends on the basis of similar interests, characteristics, and behaviors. Similarity among friends in cigarette smoking and drinking alcohol, for example, depends more on selection than on mutual influence (Berndt & Savin-Williams, 1993; Fisher & Baumann, 1988).

Fear of deviant peer pressure leads some parents to attempt to restrict their children's choice of companions. Parents can easily manage the social life of a preschooler, but such attempts are likely to backfire during adolescence. Most teenagers resist having their social lives regulated by their parents ("Why don't you trust me? Do you think that just because Julia smokes cigarettes, I am going to?"). It would help parents to understand that peer influence usually is consistent with parental influence. Parent and peer influence complement each other in ways that prepare adolescents for adultlike relationships with friends and family members. Family relationships during childhood provide a strong emotional foundation for peer relationships during adolescence. *Peers usually model and reinforce in each other the same behaviors and values that they learn from their parents* (Gavin & Furman, 1996). For example, children of parents who have difficulty expressing negative emotions are likely to bring that problem into their peer relationships. Children of parents who act collaboratively and who show caring by considering their opinions are likely to bring these skills into their peer relationships (Brown et al., 1993; Deković & Meeus, 1997; Fuligni & Eccles, 1993; Hunter, 1985; Levitt, Guacci-Franco, & Levitt, 1993; Parke & Ladd, 1992; Steinberg & Silverberg, 1986; Wilks, 1986).

Encouraging children to bring their friends home results in parents knowing more about their children's friends and friendships. Parental awareness of children's friendships serves several purposes (Steinberg, 1986). First, children who are having trouble making or keeping friends often need adult help. Second, showing interest in their children's friendships helps parents stay involved in their daily lives. Third, parents can anticipate or respond to any negative pressure applied to their child.

Outright parental rejection of a friend usually is counterproductive. It challenges teenagers' sense of autonomy and leads to defensive behavior. When parents criticize their children's friends, they often hear, "I don't tell you who your friends should be." One of my students interviewed a 13-year-old girl named Alice and her mother, Sandra. Sandra objected to one of Alice's friends, claiming that the friend was selfish and that she would "control" Alice. Alice was aware of her mother's concerns about her friend but felt that her choice of friends should be hers alone. She believed that her mother didn't really know the girl and that she was judging her on "surface actions" only. Rather than banning the relationship, Sandra encouraged Alice's other friendships, a sensible strategy.

Parents are better off asking direct questions about friends' personal behaviors and qualities ("Is she pressuring you to smoke cigarettes with her?") than issuing ultimatums. It makes more sense to help children clarify their attitudes about smoking or drinking than to try to restrict their friendships. If restrictions are necessary, they should be placed on behaviors such as smoking and drinking rather on specific friends. If a child's health or safety is at stake, parents should not hesitate to act quickly and decisively (Berndt & Savin-Williams, 1993; Feldman & Wentzel, 1990).

Feiring and Lewis (1993) investigated how much mothers know about their children's friends. They concentrated on mothers rather than fathers because mothers usually are more involved in their children's social lives. They hypothesized that mothers of younger children would be more in touch with their children's social lives than mothers of adolescents. They suspected that, compared to younger children, adolescents have more friends that their mothers do not know about. The investigators also hypothesized that mothers would know more about their daughter's social lives than about their son's. They interviewed 110 children of ages 9, 13, and 15 years and their mothers.

Most mothers were well informed about their children's best friends, regardless of the children's age. Mothers of the 13-year-olds knew as many friends as they did when their children were younger, although there were more friends that the mothers were not aware of. This reflects adolescents' larger social network. During early adolescence, mothers also knew less about opposite-sexed friendships than about same-sexed friendships. The closer the parent–child relationship, the more mothers knew about opposite-sexed friendships.

Importantly, the more mothers knew about their children's social lives, the less likely the children were to be cigarette smokers at age 15. "Mothers who more closely monitor opposite-sexed friends may have teenagers who are more concerned with living up to adult standards and acceptable behavior" (p. 351). The researchers suggest that parent–child discussion and agreement about friends are important in maintaining connectedness at a time when adolescents are striving to become freer of parental control. (Schneider and Younger [1996] found that parents who were seen by their adolescent children as close and trusting had *negative* opinions of their children's best friends! This could be still another source of parent–adolescent conflict that fosters parent–child distance.)

As noted in Chapter 7, children who feel close to their parents usually resist deviant influences. Their parents take the time to learn and talk about their friends and help them solve friendship-related problems (Gauze, Bukowski, Aquan-Assee, & Sippola, 1996). By using authoritative parenting practices, such parents demonstrate to their children how to get along with other people. Adolescents are more prone to mindless conformity when their parents are permissive and inconsistent or if they simply don't monitor their children's activities (Feldman & Wentzel, 1990).

## CROSS-GENDER SOCIALIZATION IN THE PEER GROUP

Before adolescence, most peer groups are unisexual. The composition of peer groups reflects more an affinity for same-gender peers than a dislike of the other gender. This inclination, in turn, is based mainly on preferences for similar activities, those sanctioned for their gender (Dunphy, 1972). Boys usually prefer competitive, rough-and-tumble play, a type of activity that most girls shun. During early adolescence, clusters of same-gender peers remain common. Children who are not liked by the other gender are unlikely to be chosen by them as friends. Thus, caught in a self-perpetuating cycle, they have few opportunities to learn behaviors that appeal to the other gender (Bukowski, Gauze, Hoza, & Newcomb, 1993; Cairns, Perrin, & Cairns, 1985; Maccoby, 1988).

Most children enter adolescence as members of unisexual cliques that have reinforced their identification with maleness or femaleness. For boys, this often takes the form of punishing an interest in girls. Female peer groups often reinforce such sex-typed behaviors as shopping, domestic role playing, and wearing attractive clothing. "Thus, the preadolescent peer group functioned to stamp in each individual's social sex identity. It is as if society separates the sexes at that stage so that the individual will make few mistakes in learning the basic attitudes considered desirable in this society for males or for females" (Dunphy, 1972, p. 178). *Thought Question: Has early adolescent behavior become less sex-typed in the present generation?*

For heterosexual adolescents, physical and sexual maturation and heightened sex drive increase interest in the other gender. "Now the cliques of boys and girls begin self-consciously to approach one another, to pester, tease and make mock attacks instead of quietly and systematically ignoring each other" (Dunphy, 1972, p. 178). It is usually the leaders of the male and female cliques who make the first tentative forays into "romantic" territory. Initially awkward in their efforts, group leaders eventually adopt and model a more mature, sociable stance.

"Leaders of boys' and girls' cliques begin to form stable relationships with each other and these relationships lead to dating and the first romantic encounters in which the participants are not supported by the immediate presence of other group members" (Dunphy, 1972, p. 178). Other group members follow their leaders' romantic inclinations, with considerable sharing of experience. During middle adolescence, dating gradually replaces clique activity. Romantic partners become an important source of social support at this time (Furman &

During middle adolescence, romantic partners become an important source of social support and self-confidence.

Buhrmester, 1992). Sexuality and romantic relationships will be examined at length in subsequent chapters.

## POPULARITY

Being popular is a highly valued goal during adolescence, often more valued than being successful in school. Whereas friendship refers to a close bond between two or more people, popularity reflects the way an individual is regarded and treated by a crowd. It is possible, although not common, for one to be popular and have few or no close friends (Bukowski & Hoza, 1989).

Popular individuals typically are friendly, sensitive, and have a sense of humor. Children who are sociable and cooperative are more popular with peers (e.g., Coie, Dodge, & Kupersmidt, 1990). Being physically attractive doesn't hurt. Attractive individuals benefit from a "halo effect." They are assumed to have pleasing personalities that match their pleasing appearance. A disadvantage of the halo effect is that popular adolescents, assumed to be competent and self-reliant, often find it harder to elicit support from peers when needed (Munsch & Kinchen, 1995).

Sensing what behaviors are offensive to others is important for avoiding peer rejection. In an earlier section we noted that adolescents believe that being sincere and pretending to care contribute to successful friendships (Jarvinen & Nicholls, 1996). These social strategies require the ability to recognize people's needs and interpret people's verbal and nonverbal behavior. Other attributes that contribute to adolescents' popularity include being smart, wearing fashionable clothing, and having a late model car. Successful athletes gain consid-

**Attractive adolescents are assumed to have pleasing personalities that match their pleasing appearance.**

erable prestige in communities that value competition and winning (Lerner et al., 1991; Wentzel & Erdley, 1993)

Eder (1985) noted that friendship with a popular girl gives less popular girls access to the popular crowd. Thus, having high-status friendships contributes to one's popularity (Perry, 1987). However, the number of friends or admirers one has does not necessarily reveal much about the closeness of these relationships. Jealousy of very popular girls sometimes leads to accusations of their being conceited. One can be popular and lonely at the same time. Frequent contact with peers does not guarantee satisfying interactions (Savin-Williams & Berndt, 1990). *Thought Question: Accusations of conceitedness are common during early and middle adolescence. How can we relate this judgment to adolescent egocentrism?*

## REJECTION AND ISOLATION

Children and adolescents who are actively disliked and rejected by their peers may be deficient in social skills and thus difficult to get along with. Or they may just be perceived as being different (nerdy, geeky, doofus) by intolerant peers (Merten, 1996a). Rejected adolescents have few if any friends in their neighborhood or school. Most suffer from loneliness and low self-esteem. Some develop a reputation for nasty or unfriendly behavior, which solidifies their rejected status (Asher & Coie, 1990; Coie & Dodge, 1983).

Desperately trying to connect with peers, socially unskilled teenagers often withdraw or "come on too strong." Some are unable to maintain cooperative, friendly relations with anyone. Their interpersonal problems often are rooted in less than optimal family relationships that leave many of these children unable to "read" social cues and adapt their behavior to group activities. Without supportive family or peer relationships, these children become increasingly isolated and alienated (Asher, 1983; Berndt & Perry, 1986, 1990; Buhrmester, 1990; East et al., 1992; Levitt et al., 1993; Reisman, 1985; Savin-Williams & Berndt, 1990; Vernberg, 1990a).

Lacking adequate social support, unpopular adolescents are particularly vulnerable to stress. Many feel resentful toward their classmates, which may lead to hostile behavior at school and at home. Some rejected children are antagonistic, some withdraw, some attempt to dominate peers, and others act appropriately but are rejected anyway (French & Waas, 1985; Merten, 1996a).

Adolescents who are spurned by their age-mates are at risk for a host of adjustment problems, the seriousness of which depends on the intensity and frequency of rejection. Adjustment problems include absenteeism from school, lower achievement, and aggressive or withdrawn behavior, or both. Even a single rejection experience can lead to excessive absenteeism in school, which in turn depresses achievement and increases the risk of dropping out of school (DeRosier, Kupersmidt, & Patterson, 1994; Parker & Asher, 1987).

Bronfenbrenner (1979, 1989) and others (Erikson, 1968) allege that the breakdown in adolescents' social networks leads to impairment in their mental health, social behavior, and academic performance. Social isolates typically drop out of school before graduation and engage in aggressive or other anti-social behaviors that continue into young adulthood. As adults they are at high risk for marital, sexual, psychological, and vocational problems (Parker & Asher, 1987; Reisman, 1985).

At the extreme end of the unpopularity continuum are **social isolates**. They have few if any friends and are perceived as withdrawn, hostile, aggressive, or nerdy. Making and keeping friends requires personal qualities and skills that most of these children lack. They are caught in a cycle of rejection, harassment, and aggression that usually begins during early childhood. Lacking appealing personal qualities, social isolates try too hard to gain attention or admiration, often through obnoxious behaviors like boasting or bullying. When their peers reject them, some become angry and overreact, offending other children. Relationships that they manage to establish are conflictual. Unlike adolescents in satisfying relationships, they have few opportunities to learn the very skills that they need to develop close friendships (Bierman, Smoot, & Aumiller, 1993; Savin-Williams & Berndt, 1990).

Once they are labeled as nerds or dweebs, it is virtually impossible for rejected children to improve their situation, at least until they change schools (Evans & Eder, 1993; Kinney, 1993). Merten (1996a) quotes Morton, a junior high school student. "For some reason they just hear about me and say, 'Hey let's bug the kid or let's chase him.' I don't know, that always seems to amaze me—like kids that I've never seen before know my name, know half the things about me; some of them I don't know" (p. 12). *Thought Question: How might rejection and isolation affect identity formation during early and middle adolescence?*

Attempts by rejected and neglected adolescents to reach out to peers during stressful times sometimes are successful (Munsch & Kinchen, 1995), but trying to change their behavior to please their peers usually doesn't work. When interviewed, tormentors claim that they don't know why they reject or harass some of their peers (Merten, 1996a). One wonders how many of them have been victims of such harassment in their own families or peer groups.

By teaching rejected youngsters assertiveness and other social skills and giving them opportunities to practice these skills, training programs provide promising interventions for teenagers who are overlooked or rejected by their peers (Christopher, Nangle, & Hansen, 1993).

Some adolescents do not match the profile of the aggressive or alienated social isolate. Instead of being rejected, they simply are unpopular (neglected or ignored) (George & Hartmann, 1996; Parkhurst & Asher, 1992). Many are just shy. Shyness, self-consciousness, and social anxiety usually are rooted in a fear of negative evaluation. Because of their avoidance of social encounters, they miss out on the very experiences they need to become more skillful in social situations. Although they date less, spend more time alone, and are lonely, they do not have the serious adjustment problems associated with rejected adolescents. However, when they try to interact with peers, the quality of the interaction often is not satisfying to either party (Hansen et al., 1995; Kelly & Hansen, 1987; Roscoe & Skomski, 1989). Adolescent shyness and loneliness are discussed further in Chapter 13.

Some adolescents are actively rejected by their peers while others are simply neglected or ignored.

## ADOLESCENTS AND LEISURE TIME

Unlike their predecessors of previous eras, middle-class adolescents in the United States today do not have to support themselves financially. Rather, their days are occupied mostly by a whirlwind of rushed meals, schoolwork, chores, lessons, and sports activities (Stewart, 1996). About 40% of the waking hours of adolescents in the United States are spent in leisure (nondirected) activities compared to 29% spent in "productive" time and 31% in "maintenance" activities such as eating and performing chores (Csikszentmihalyi & Larson, 1984; Larson & Richards, 1989).

Teenagers in other countries spend far more time than those in the United States doing schoolwork and family chores (Csikszentmihalyi & Larson, 1984; Larson & Richards, 1989). How adolescents spend their free time depends partly on their family configuration. For example, girls who live in single-parent families are more likely to have a part-time job and thus less leisure time (Zick & Allen, 1996).

How young people spend their free time is not a trivial matter. Although the intended purpose of leisure-time activities is to relax and have fun (Brake, 1985), such activities can be an important source of learning. "A child slumped in front of a TV watching Tom and Jerry cartoons is absorbing different messages about him/herself and the world than a child doing a homework assignment or wrapped up in an art project" (Larson & Richards, 1989, p. 502). Meaningful leisure activities can also provide a sense of accomplishment and

### Table 8-6  Adolescent Leisure Pursuits

*Leisure pursuits that (a) interested girls most; and (b) interested girls least*

(a)

| | |
|---|---|
| 1. Listening to music | 81% |
| 2. Going to parties | 80% |
| 3. Visiting friends | 79% |
| 4. Listening to the radio | 77% |
| 5. Having friends to visit | 76% |
| 6. Going to a disco/dancing | 67% |
| 7. Sitting around and talking | 60% |
| 8. Going to pop concert | 57% |
| 9. Watching TV/video | 55% |
| 10. Reading paper/magazines | 53% |

(b)

| | |
|---|---|
| 1. Gardening | 3% |
| 2. Playing hockey | 4% |
| 3. Playing cricket | 4% |
| 4. Playing rugby | 4% |
| 5. Going to evening classes | 5% |
| 6. Going to "time zone"/amusement arcade | 6% |
| 7. Skateboarding | 6% |
| 8. Playing with toys or video games | 7% |
| 9. Playing golf | 8% |
| 10. Knitting/sewing/making clothes | 9% |

*Leisure pursuits in which boys (a) participated most; and (b) participated least*

(a)

| | |
|---|---|
| 1. Watching TV/video | 95% |
| 2. Listening to music | 95% |
| 3. Listening to radio | 93% |
| 4. Visiting friends | 85% |
| 5. Read papers/magazines | 83% |
| 6. Having friends to visit | 82% |
| 7. Sit around and talk | 79% |
| 8. Hang around/talk to friends in the street | 77% |
| 9. Hobby | 71% |
| 10. Play soccer | 71% |

(b)

| | |
|---|---|
| 1. Surfing/wave-skiing | 2% |
| 2. Boardsailing/windsurfing | 2% |
| 3. Play hockey | 2% |
| 4. Knitting/sewing/making clothes | 3% |
| 5. Play cricket | 4% |
| 6. Sailing | 5% |
| 7. Go to museum art/gallery | 6% |
| 8. Go to evening classes | 6% |
| 9. Dance classes | 7% |
| 10. Water-skiing | 7% |

(From Fitzgerald et al., 1995)

mastery. Misuse of time is associated with educational, social, and economic deficits (Bruno, 1996; Widmer, Ellis, & Trunnell, 1996).

According to Nielsen Media Research (1993), the average teenager in the United States watches about 22 hours of television a week, not including movies and video games. Strasburger (1992) estimates that by the time they reach age 70, today's children will have spent 7 to 10 years of their lives watching television. Preferred programs are news, comedy shows, and movies. Females watch more soap operas, and males watch more sporting events on TV. We will have more to say about the potential influence of television on adolescent behavior in the next section.

Many young people are active in sports, but like adults, they are more content than younger children to spend time alone reading, sleeping, or listening to music. Boys are more likely than girls to engage in sports and other vigorous activities, to play video games, and to spend more time alone. Girls spend more time than boys shopping with and talking to their friends and reading magazines that address their current interests (Bruno, 1996; Garton & Pratt, 1987).

Time at home usually is spent privately—alone in one's bedroom (perhaps behind a closed door with a sign that says "Keep Out" or "Do Not Disturb"). Spending a moderate amount of time alone can be beneficial (see Box 8-1). "The cognitive changes associated with this age period may give young adolescents the capacity to deliberately employ solitude for relaxation, self-renewal, and exploration of a newly discovered private self" (Larson & Richards, 1991, p. 295).

During early adolescence, boys and girls spend much more leisure time with their friends than with their parents. This continues into middle adolescence, presumably because parents are less restrictive (Fine, Mortimer, & Roberts, 1990; Larson & Richards, 1989, 1991). The most preferred leisure-time activities for adolescents in the United States include watching television, spending time with same- or opposite-sex friends, talking, and listening to music, and going to parties (Garton & Pratt, 1987). Much interaction occurs on the telephone (Anderson et al., 1995) or wandering through malls and shopping centers with friends, waiting for something to happen (Readdick & Mullis, 1997).

Fitzgerald and his colleagues (1995) interviewed adolescents in Dublin, Ireland, about their leisure pursuits. The most popular activities of boys and girls matched those of adolescents in the United States: watching television and listening to the radio, visiting friends, listening to music, having friends visit, and reading newspapers and magazines. In both countries, boys were more likely than girls to spend time in solitary activities such as watching TV; girls spent considerably more time than boys with their friends (see Table 8-6). In their study of Canadian high school seniors, Van Roosmalen and Krahn (1996) found that Canadian youth culture is heavily gendered regarding household chores, part-time jobs, and athletic participation.

In a similar vein, Laura Kamptner (1995) questioned high school students about their treasured possessions. Males' most treasured possessions included vehicles, sports equipment, and music equipment and recordings. Girls trea-

**Box 8-1
Adolescent
Solitude**

Adolescents in the United States and Europe spend about a quarter of their waking hours alone (Larson & Richards, 1991; Montemayor, 1982; Smith, 1997), more time than they spend with family members and about the same amount of time that they spend with peers. Larson (1997) suggests that, although solitude appears to be a negative experience for elementary school children, voluntary choice of solitary time plays a constructive role in adolescent adjustment. Even though teenagers may feel lonely and less happy when alone, solitary time can be spent constructively: relaxing, reflecting, creating, and coping with negative feelings.

In Larson's (1997) study, 483 fifth through ninth graders of European-American descent provided experience-sampling reports on their companionship and subjective states at random times over a week. Participants came from four suburban Chicago neighborhoods, two in a working-class community and two in a middle-class community. Using the time-sampling technique described in Chapter 1, participants carried electronic pagers for 1 week and provided reports on their experience when signaled at random by the pagers. Seven signals were sent each day, and each participant carried a booklet of identical self-report forms that they filled out immediately after the signal. Data were also obtained from teachers, parents, and school records. Each participant was paid $8.00 upon completion of the study.

The study revealed that time alone becomes more voluntary over this age period (10–15 years). That is, the older participants reported more frequent desire to be alone. For seventh through ninth graders but not fifth and sixth graders, time alone ultimately had a positive effect on emotional state. The older adolescents reported feeling somewhat better after being alone, even though they may have felt lonely and not as happy while alone.

Adolescents, but not preadolescents, who spent a moderate amount of time in solitude were better adjusted and received better grades than those who spent a little or a great deal of time alone. Larson wonders, What developmental changes during early adolescence might be responsible for the "therapeutic" functions of solitude? "As a whole, the findings suggest that, while continuing to be a lonely time, in early adolescence solitude comes to have a more constructive role in daily life as a strategic retreat that complements social experience" (p. 80).

sured their jewelry, stuffed animals, and vehicles. Kamptner interprets boys' possessions as embodying personal enjoyment and practical utility, whereas girls' possessions embody mainly interpersonal meanings. *Thought Question: What do adolescents' prized possessions tell us about their self-concept?*

Having too much unstructured and unsupervised time leads some youngsters to get into trouble. Many teenagers report that there is nothing else for them to do between school and bedtime except hang out. "When I'm off, I'm at home saying, 'Cool, I have a day off.' I'll be watching TV and my friends

**SPOTLIGHT** • Adolescent Subcultures: Teenagers United Against Adult Values?

In Chapter 1, we evaluated common stereotypes and myths concerning adolescents—for example, that teenagers are obnoxious, lazy, and rebellious. One view that we did not consider is that young people today stand united in a worldwide pleasure-seeking subculture that rejects adult values and goals.

According to Havighurst (1987), a **subculture** is a culture shared by a group within a larger society. It is true that compared to adults, adolescents display somewhat distinctive social values, activities, language, dress, hair styles, and musical preferences. However, just as the idea of a generation gap in values does not pass muster, there is little evidence to support the idea of a single, organized youth subculture standing in opposition to adult authority (Youniss et al., 1994).

In any particular community, such as a high school, we observe a variety of groups with distinctive values, interests, and goals. For example, how much in common do college track youth have with disaffected druggies or metalheads (Brown, 1990; Havighurst, 1987)? Our consumer society reinforces the idea of a unified youth subculture by marketing products and images directly to young people (Palladino, 1996). Although the 1960s' hedonistic theme of sex, drugs, and rock'n'roll still appeals to large numbers of adolescents, it doesn't follow that they will drop out of school, become addicted, or hate their parents. If there is one common thread that does unite almost all adolescents, it is the attempt to strike a balance between staying connected to their family and friends while searching for a place of their own in adult society (Brown, 1990; Havighurst, 1987).

call me up and say, 'Michelle, come and hang out.' And I say, 'Where are you?' And they say, 'I'm at the mall.' And I say, 'Oh, okay.' So after a while, I just became a mall rat'' (17-year-old girl in a Danbury, Connecticut, mall quoted by Glaberson, 1992, p. 31). Her friend Scooby reported, "We do have status. We own the mall. 'Cause we know so many people—so many mall rats come around. The more people you know, the more status you have."

## ADOLESCENTS AND THE MEDIA

In this century, adolescents have become massive consumers of media products and materials: films, television programs, CDs, tapes, records, computer games, comic books, magazines, newspapers, and the Internet (Brake, 1985; Klein et al., 1993; Murray, 1997b; Palladino, 1996). Arnett (1995) views this transformation in our cultural environment as a new and important source of socialization for adolescents. Since adolescents select their own media materials and programming, they are to some extent self-socializing (Mifflin, 1997). Arnett contends that adolescents use media for entertainment, identity formation, stimulation, coping, and as a way of identifying with youth culture. Roe (1995) extends this list to include "killing time," atmosphere creation, and mood control.

All of these uses except entertainment, Arnett maintains, have particular developmental significance for adolescents. Gender role identity is partly guided by media images of what it means to be a man or a woman and by depictions of male–female relationships. Action films and heavy metal music are especially appealing to male teenagers, many of whom are high in sensation seeking. Adolescents depend on media, particularly music, to relieve negative emotions such as anger and anxiety. Media depictions of adolescents and their popular culture heroes reinforce young people's identification with youth culture (Arnett, 1995). Much of their contact with media occurs in the privacy of adolescents' own bedrooms, a place where the private self and the public self are woven together (Larson, 1995; Steele & Brown, 1995).

Adolescents do not react passively to music videos, movies, television, or other pathways on the information highway. Rather, they are "active makers of media choices" (Arnett et al., 1995, p. 514). Adolescents seek and select media according to their particular personalities and needs. The media materials they choose "reflect important aspects of themselves and their views of the world. They choose certain media as a way of demonstrating (and for some protesting) their current status in school. They [seek out] media from diverse sources in their pursuit of information about the possibilities of life" (Arnett, Larson, & Offer, 1995, p. 514). Arnett and his colleagues emphasize that teenagers are active selectors, users, and interpreters of media content. They paste media images on their bedroom walls. They discuss TV and music with their friends. They use media to moderate their moods, explore their identities, and create meaning in their lives. Parents, of course, are concerned about their children's exposure to "socially disvalued media" and worried that their children might become "media delinquents" (Roe, 1995) on the Internet or elsewhere (Murray, 1997b).

## Television

Although TV watching is a major leisure-time activity for adolescents, overall viewing time decreases during early adolescence. By seventh grade, adolescents become less interested in cartoons (except for "hip" cartoon programs like *The Simpsons*) and more interested in MTV and cable programming (Comstock, 1991; Larson, Kubey, & Colletti, 1989).

Larson (1995) suggests that adolescents tune into music more than television because popular music speaks directly to adolescents' developmental issues. Watching television becomes "an opportunity to turn off the self . . . by turning on the TV adolescents are able to turn off the stressful emotions they experience during a long day of school and interactions with peers. I suspect that, compared to children, adolescents begin to use TV viewing more deliberately as a response to negative emotional states" (p. 544).

Aside from MTV and *The Simpsons*, there are relatively few TV shows aimed directly at teenagers. Teenagers generally watch the same prime-time sitcoms (e.g., *Seinfeld*, *Home Improvement*) that adults watch (Mifflin, 1996), despite the fact that advertisers want to reach the teenage audience and tap its discretionary income. What do adolescents see and hear when they turn on the TV? Television programs in the United States are more violent than those in any other country (Rothenberg, 1975; Strasburger, 1995). On television, aggressive and antisocial behaviors often gain immediate rewards rather than disapproval or other sanctions. Even cartoons designed for young children glorify the use of firearms and gratuitous violence.

Television provides viewers with an enormous amount of information, including information about sexual norms and expectations. By watching television, adolescents learn about attracting and selecting partners, dating, and sexual decision making. "Watching is an eager audience of children and adolescents who may have little experience of their own and minimal input from other sources to which they can compare these portrayals" (Ward, 1995, p. 596).

Louis Harris and Associates (1988) report that children and adolescents in the United States witness 14,000 sexual references, behaviors, or allusions each year. Afternoon talk shows feature heated, often irrational discussions about premarital sex, marital affairs, prostitution, sexual abuse, homosexuality, rape, and incest. Relatively little attention is given to topics such as abstinence and sexual responsibility. On prime-time TV shows, sexual messages emphasize a recreational orientation toward sex far more often than a procreational orientation (Ward, 1995).

Ward (1995) analyzed the sexual content of the top 10 prime-time television programs watched by adolescents. "For some programs, nearly 50% of the interactions contained statements related to sexuality, which is not only exceptionally high, but paints a false impression of the degree to which sexuality is discussed in everyday life. Regardless of what characters were doing or saying, references to sexuality often worked their way into the conversation" (p. 610). The content of sexual discussions emphasized the importance of physical appearance for women and of "scoring" for men. Sex was portrayed as an exciting competition involving strategies and manipulations. Looking good and being cool were treated as major assets. According to Ward, some of the information presented could be valuable to romantically naive teenagers. For example, adolescents learn what prospective partners might expect from a romantic relationship, and they learn that close relationships can be problematic and painful. The bottom line is that we really don't know how children and adolescents are affected by such programming. R-rated and X-rated movies broadcast on cable stations are much more sexually explicit and violent than network programming. How young people respond to these media also is not known. There is evidence that teenagers use the new rating system to seek out violent and sexually explicit programs (Mifflin, 1997).

How are adolescents influenced by TV commercials? According to the Centers for Disease Control (1994), by glamorizing smoking, cigarette advertising increases the likelihood that teenagers will experiment with cigarettes. "Studies show that young people attend to cigarette and alcohol ads, are influenced by them, and that consumption decreases in the absence of such ads. Additional evidence exists that tobacco and beer companies actually target young people with particular advertising" (Strasburger, 1995, p. 73). Given that adolescents watch TV for an average of 3 to 4 hours a day, it is not surprising that TV advertising exerts considerable influence over adolescent spending (Carruth, Goldberg, & Skinner, 1991; Garton & Pratt, 1987). "The preponderance of evidence suggests that the tobacco and alcohol industries profit illegally and irresponsibly from marketing their products to children and teenagers" (Strasburger, 1995, p. 73).

We also must acknowledge the stereotypical way teenagers (and almost everyone else) are depicted on television. Steenland (1988) analyzed over 200 episodes of programs featuring female adolescent characters. Looks were emphasized more than intelligence and other personal qualities, very intelligent girls were portrayed as social outcasts, and girls were portrayed as being more passive than boys. Most girls were obsessed with shopping, grooming, and romance. *Thought Question: How might teenagers' body image be influenced by television's emphasis on physical appearance and sexuality?*

Are young people adversely affected by daily exposure to violence, sexual innuendo, and stereotypical depictions of women, minorities, older people, and teenagers? Polls suggest that adults and adolescents believe that the media

**The entertainment media often portray adolescents stereotypically—as materialistic, irresponsible, and arrogant.**

affect adolescent behavior and attitudes and are a major source of information. But surveys and questionnaires do not prove a connection between media exposure and adolescent behavior. Liebert and Sprafkin (1988), in their extensive review of television's effects on children, concluded that TV violence is only one of many possible causes of aggressive behavior. There are many other factors, notably family violence, that are much more influential than TV viewing. Studies of the effects of sexually explicit materials usually report no antisocial effect (e.g., Donnerstein, Linz, & Penrod, 1987), but attitudes and values might be affected through repeated exposure. Hagborg (1995) divided 152 9th and 10th graders into three groups based on total daily TV viewing time—light, medium, and heavy. He found that the three groups did not differ in school performance, educational plans, school attitudes, or motivation.

Acknowledging the power of the media to influence adolescents' beliefs and behavior (and the need for more research on this topic), Strasburger (1995) recommends the following: (1) that broadcasters adopt voluntary guidelines regarding portrayals of violence and sex on TV; (2) that deceptive and misleading advertising directed to young people be banned; (3) that children and adolescents need to become more "media literate" so that they can put into perspective the unreality of TV violence, media stereotypes, misleading advertising, and the like; (4) that the media be used to expose young people to prosocial behaviors, including respect for human life and tolerance for people who are different; and (5) that parents and health professionals become more involved in shaping public policy related to the media.

## Video Games

Most video games have violence as their major theme. Thus, millions of children and teenagers gain pleasure each day from symbolic acts of violence. One survey of seventh and eighth graders revealed that boys spent over 4 hours a week and girls spent about 2 hours a week playing these games (Funk, 1993). Some teenagers spend 15 or more hours a week playing video games at home

64-BIT ARCADE FISHING

or in arcades. Video games allow the modeling and practice of symbolic violent behavior and constantly reward such behavior. Women often are portrayed as helpless victims (Strasburger, 1995). Violent games sometimes increase players' hostility, anxiety, and aggression (Anderson & Ford, 1987).

## Rock Music

If there is a universal youth subculture, its voice is heard in the lyrics of rock music (Holland, 1995). What we call rock music is an extremely diverse collection of musical styles and themes rooted in rhythm and blues, folk music, and country and western music. One hesitates to refer to rock and roll as teenage music because musical tastes today are multigenerational and somewhat more sophisticated than those at midcentury. Rock music consists of a variety of sounds: hard rock, soft rock, punk rock, rap, soul music, heavy metal, salsa, grunge, and reggae (Strasburger, 1995). Whatever we call it, today's popular music expresses adolescent values, conflicts, attitudes, and emotions (Palladino, 1996; Plopper & Ness, 1993).

Solitary music listening provides countless opportunities for adolescent self-exploration and stress management (Larson, 1995; Seelow, 1996). "Because music listening does not tie up attention as much as TV, it leaves the mind and 'heart' free to wander or ruminate on the universal conundrums and pain expressed in these lyrics" (Larson, 1995, p. 545). Larson maintains that solitary music listening "is a fantasy ground for exploring possible selves. Sometimes this involves pumping oneself up with images of power and conquest; other times it may involve fantasies of merger and rescue by an idealized lover; yet other times, it may involve intense worry about shortcomings and their significance for one's future. The images and emotions of popular music allow one to feel a range of internal states and try on alternate identities, both desired and feared" (p. 547). This effect is magnified by music videos, with their combined video and audio presentations (Strouse, Buerkel-Rothfuss, & Long, 1995). The effect is retarded by the presence of disapproving family members (Thompson & Larson, 1995), but since music typically is listened to privately, it is somewhat outside the realm of parental control (Raviv, Bar-Tal, Raviv, & Ben-Horin, 1996).

Rock music emerged in the 1950s. Its major themes are alienation, romantic longing for an ideal partner, and frustrated sexuality. "There were songs for dancing, songs for necking, songs for just hanging around, and songs that drove parents crazy. There were songs that captured the crazy mixed-up emotional spirit of adolescence" (Palladino, 1996, p. 132). Early performers such as Little Richard and Elvis Presley were more overtly sexual in appearance and behavior than the more subdued idols of previous eras. At midcentury, rock music was featured in movies about gangs and juvenile delinquents, reinforcing an association between teenage music and alienation. Lyrics of contemporary hard rock and heavy metal music generate images of power, potency, and sexual conquest, but it is the raw emotion of the rhythm and beat more than the imagery that strikes a chord with most adolescents. Listeners tend to imbue lyrics and images with their own private meanings (Larson, 1995). Many young adolescents, especially girls, idolize pop singers and, to some extent, use personal information about idols in the construction of their self-identity (Raviv et al., 1996).

"With its origins in the music of slaves and other downtrodden groups, rock music has always spoken to values and points of view outside the mainstream, values frequently divergent from or in opposition to adult culture. . . . Rock music offers an antidote to and an escape from the unrelenting socialization pressures that emanate daily from family and school. Popular music does not tell its listeners to delay gratification and prepare for adulthood. Rather, it tells young people that the concerns they have today are of importance, that they merit expression in music, and that one ought to value one's youth and not worry so much about the future" (Larson, Kubey, & Colletti, 1989, pp. 584, 596–597).

As Strasburger (1995) points out, rock music's antiestablishment lyrics (and those who sing them) continue to be problematic to parents. In the 1950s, many parents feared popular music because it espoused values that were unconventional and sometimes antisocial. Parents and teachers are annoying, school and work are a drag, romance and partying are cool. Popular music of the 1960s was more overtly defiant, some songs openly advocating political revolution and drug use, containing sexually explicit lyrics, and condemning war, inequality, and materialism. It is not surprising that adolescents, many of whom feel at least somewhat alienated from the adult world, embrace this music (Roe, 1995). At the same time, most continue to take school seriously and get along with their parents and siblings.

Eventually, most of those who were teenagers in the 1950s and 1960s became parents. Much of the popular music they embraced during their adolescence intrigues today's young people. Parents' taste in music is not so different from that of their children, with the probable exception of adult revulsion at sexist and racist lyrics of some heavy metal and rap songs. To be fair, many rap songs advocate traditional values and present antidrug messages. The popularity of heavy metal and rap music among teenagers partly reflects the fact that mainstream rock music has been coopted by adult society (Strasburger, 1995).

There is a large audience (known by their peers as *metalheads* or *headbangers*) for hard rock or heavy metal music played by groups like Motley Crue, Poison, Iron Maiden, and Metallica. In 1989, the Grammy Awards added a special category just for this type of music. Arnett (1991a) describes heavy metal music as "distorted electric guitars, pounding rhythms, and raucous raw vocals, all typically played at an extremely loud volume" (p. 573). "The extremely intense sensation of this, which is so abrasive and offensive to adults with their generally lower capacity for sensation, is precisely what makes it attractive to (some) adolescents" (p. 589). The lyrical themes of heavy metal music usually are bleak and hopeless compared to the more optimistic music of the 1960s that promised a brighter future. More than most other media, popular music continues to test the boundaries of what society considers to be socially acceptable (Arnett, 1991b).

Parent groups and members of Congress occasionally voice concern about the content of music that seems to advocate sexual promiscuity, drug use, Satan

Compared to the relatively optimistic music of earlier decades, the lyrical themes of heavy metal music usually are bleak and hopeless.

worship, and suicide. Opponents of this music claim that heavy metal music crosses the boundary of good taste. They urge that warning labels be placed on recordings to indicate offensive lyrical content. During Senate hearings on the "Contents of Music and the Lyrics of Records" held in 1985, parent groups and members of Congress clashed with music industry officials, some of whom claimed that the hearings were an attempt by a puritanical society to censor creative self-expression (Arnett, 1991b).

What do we know about teenagers who like this music? Arnett (1991a) compared high school students in Georgia who like heavy metal music (Metallica, Megadeth, Anthrax, and Ozzy Osbourne) to those who don't. The attitudes of the two groups were different. Boys who preferred such music reported an attraction to sensation-seeking behaviors, including drunk driving, casual or unsafe sexual behavior, minor criminal activity (e.g., shoplifting), and marijuana use. They also reported lower satisfaction with family relationships. Girls who said they liked heavy metal reported being more likely to shoplift, use drugs, and engage in vandalism. They displayed lower self-esteem than girls who said they did not like heavy metal. The lower self-esteem of girls who said they liked this music is interesting because heavy metal songs often contain themes that denigrate females. Girls with high self-esteem usually reject music with antifemale themes (Arnett, 1991a).

In a related study, Arnett (1991b) asked the boys who like heavy metal music what the attraction is. The boys said that they liked the musical talent of the groups, especially the guitar playing. One boy felt that each member of Metallica "is a virtuoso of his instrument" (p. 81). The boys said that they liked the lyrics, especially those that expressed social consciousness (themes of ecology, injustice, child abuse, and nuclear war). The themes that they found appealing involved the dismal state of the world and personal emotional crises. The also cited the raw, intense quality of the music and the fact that the music provided a strong bond among their close friends.

Most said they liked either the music (48%) or the combination of music and lyrics (41%). Only 11% of the participants said that they liked the lyrics most. The songs they listened to often depended on their mood. They listened to "harder" heavy metal music when they were annoyed. Most described heavy metal concerts as opportunities to release pent-up anger and aggression—as "violent fun." About a third of the participants, when asked what they saw themselves doing in 10 years, said they expected to be doing something related to music, hopefully heavy metal music. Many of their heroes were heavy metal guitarists, and most of the boys were inspired to learn how to play the guitar. More than half of the participants said their parents disliked their music, although very few parents placed restrictions on their listening (other than regarding loudness). More than half reported a conventional religious affiliation.

Based on his interviews, Arnett (1991b) concluded that heavy metal music plays an important role in these boys' lives. "It is not just a music preference to them, but an intense avocation that shapes their view of the world, their spending habits, their moods, their friendships, their notions of who and what is admirable, and their hopes for what they might become. . . . It is not difficult to understand the lure of this fantasy for male adolescents: riches, fame, and the adulation of millions" (p. 92).

Does listening to music about reckless behavior or sensual gratification increase teenagers' feelings of alienation or cause them to act self-destructively? Or are disaffected teenagers attracted to music that reflects their troubled state of mind? Consistent with Larson's (1995) point that solitary music listening allows adolescents to explore their possible selves, Took and Weiss (1994) contend that heavy metal and rap music empower male teenagers and provide them with an identity "complete with clothes and hairstyle. [Rap and heavy metal music] also offer a peer group that has few requirements for entry. They do not need to be scholars or athletes, or even have musical talent" (p. 620). Ballard and Coates (1995), under the guise of administering a memory for lyrics test, examined the impact of homicidal, suicidal, and nonviolent heavy metal and rap songs on the moods of male undergraduates. They found no effect of song content or music type on adolescent mood but did find that rap songs elicited more angry responses than heavy metal songs.

Arnett suggests that teenagers' fascination with the despairing lyrics of heavy metal music is a *symptom* of alienation, not its cause. For a small number of these boys, drug use and reckless behavior provide an escape from a chaotic family environment. Such behaviors also reflect an absence of parental supervision. For most of the boys who are fans, heavy metal music serves not as a source of anger and frustration but as a release. "They listened to it especially when they were angry, and it consistently had the effect of making them less angry, of calming them down" (Arnett, 1991b, p. 93). Thus, for many adolescents, popular music provides a means of identifying with a particular group or performer (Seelow, 1996) and a way of releasing pent-up feelings (Larson, 1995).

Parents and adolescents often share an interest in popular music. Only by listening to their children's music carefully can adults understand its appeal, as well as clarify their objections to some of its themes and lyrics. Some popular music challenges parents' tolerance but also provides countless opportunities to discuss values, ethics, and morality with teenagers (Took & Weiss, 1994; Trzcinski, 1992).

Although at the time of this writing there is no evidence that violent or sexual lyrics in themselves provoke antisocial or self-destructive behavior, preferences for explicit lyrics during the early teenage years may serve as a marker for alienation, substance abuse, and risk-taking behaviors. There is some evidence that violent music videos desensitize viewers to violence (Rehman & Reilly, 1985). Regarding music's potential effect on young people, Strasburger (1995) asks, "Which music? Which adolescents? At what stage of development? With what coping abilities and environmental stresses?" (p. 82).

## Analysis

Popular music serves many functions during adolescence: entertainment, self-expression, construction of one's identity, learning about sex roles, shaping values, coping with stress, and providing social status. Should we be concerned about the potentially corrupting influence on children's development of these cultural media? Despite the considerable amount of research devoted to this topic, it is almost impossible to predict how a given adolescent will respond to a particular program, movie, song, or advertisement (Arnett et al., 1995). Despite the research indicating that children and adolescents are especially vulnerable to media influences, it would be a mistake to conclude that our cultural media are irresponsible or harmful to young people. For example, television programs such as *Beverly Hills 90210*, *The Wonder Years*, and *Growing Pains* present fairly realistic depictions of the joys and sorrows of teenagers in the 1990s (Strasburger, 1995). Parents and teenagers who watch these programs together have frequent opportunities to discuss issues that they might not otherwise broach.

## Teenage Magazines

Television advertisers and magazine publishers pay a lot of attention to the teenage market. Most adolescents have money of their own. In dual-career or single-parent families, many are responsible for significant family purchases. Although television and music are the dominant media in most adolescents' lives, since the 1940s magazines have provided young girls with information and advice about dieting, fashion, beauty care, feminine hygiene products, birth control information, dating, and the latest fads (Evans, Rutberg, Sather, & Turner, 1991; Palladino, 1996).

Teenage magazines have been around for decades. *Seventeen*, a magazine for teenage girls, was first published in September 1944 and still dominates the field (Palladino, 1996). Recent additions, such as *Sassy* (first published in 1988), *YM* (formerly *Young Miss*, first published in 1955), and *'Teen*, are more irreverent than *Seventeen*, carrying articles on celebrities, music, and cosmetics. "Magazines for teenagers have not changed much: they continue to expound upon the best bubble-gum lip gloss, to offer tips on how to wear a bikini and get the boy, to trumpet cover lines such as 'Zit-free forever!,'" 'Should you cut your hair?' and "What's up with him? Your guy questions answered'" (Pogrebin, 1996b, p. D8). Teenage boys prefer to read comic books and magazines about sports, computers, and cars and magazines that have racy pictures (Carmody, 1993).

Evans and his colleagues (1991) sampled three widely circulated, female-oriented magazines (*Seventeen, Sassy,* and *YM*) to identify the messages directed to teenage girls and to see how these messages relate to female identity development. Ten issues of each magazine published between January 1988 and March 1989 were analyzed. The investigators found that these magazines were hardly feminist in their philosophy. The theme of self-improvement was approached mainly through fashion, dressing, and beautification, with somewhat less attention paid to female–male relationships. According to these magazines, the road to happiness for girls "is attracting males for successful heterosexual life by way of physical beautification" (p. 110).

Many articles implied that female self-esteem should be related to body image, physical attractiveness, and satisfaction with one's weight. As with women's magazine such as *Glamour* and *Vogue*, the magazine advertisements portray slim, blue-eyed, white females as enchanting sex objects. Relatively few articles considered "problems of future orientation, longer-term consequences of behavior, and issues associated with transitions to adult roles. . . . The few career articles in these magazines revealed no substantial orientations for personal enhancement through professional development and leadership . . . the most salient career emphasis was modeling" (p. 112).

Few if any articles promoted intellectual pursuits, sports, educational advancement, or social issues that most young women face. Minorities were drastically underrepresented. The investigators are concerned that the self-concept of girls who read these magazines might suffer when they realize that they will

Articles in magazines for teenage girls relate self-esteem to body image, physical attractiveness, and satisfaction with one's weight.

never achieve the ideal of beautiful slimness depicted in the articles and advertisements. Although most people read magazines for entertainment, not enlightenment, girls might benefit more if their parents and teachers provide them with interesting reading materials that do not reinforce materialistic values, stereotypical views of women, or the belief that cosmetic changes will make one's life more fulfilling.

## SPOTLIGHT • Adolescents and Athletics

It is not surprising that there is massive interest in sports in our ultracompetitive society. Although excessive competition can overshadow prosocial values, athletics serve many desirable functions. They provide adolescents with opportunities for (1) learning about sportsmanship and teamwork, (2) building character and self-esteem, (3) making friends, (4) fostering task orientation and perceived competence, (5) gaining prestige and popularity, (6) intrinsic enjoyment, and (importantly) (7) vigorous exercise (Boyd & Yin, 1996; Burnette, 1996; Kirshnit, Ham, & Richards, 1989).

Sanford Dornbusch and his colleagues (1996) view athletics as a great opportunity for "extracurricular achievement," especially in small schools. They describe several levels of achievement: making the team, representing one's school, accumulating substantial "playing time," and, for a lucky few, becoming "stars." "Athletic teams are often the only aspect of school life that is widely discussed and observed by members of the larger nonschool community" (p. 197).

The social rewards for athletic success usually outweigh those for academic achievement, at least for boys. Many high school boys claim that they would rather be a star athlete than a brilliant or popular student. Girls, however, generally maintain that they would rather be popular or brilliant than intramural (Chandler, 1990; Hultsman, 1992; Kirshnit et al., 1989).

A survey of high school students in upstate New York (Goldberg & Chandler, 1989) found that high school boys highly valued the status of student athlete—the athletic All-American. Unfortunately, very few teenage boys have both the academic ability and the physical prowess to achieve this status. "When the performance expectations associated with both roles

### Table 8-7  Benefits of Participation in Sports

- Learning about sportsmanship and teamwork
- Building character and self-esteem
- Making friends
- Fostering task orientation and perceived competence
- Gaining prestige and popularity
- Intrinsic enjoyment
- Vigorous exercise
- Extracurricular achievement

are unrealistic or beyond the adolescent's reach, the result may be role confusion, lowered self-esteem, and increased susceptibility to peer group pressures" (p. 247).

About 20% of early adolescents participate in team sports, many more males than females. Girls generally prefer individually oriented sports such as running and swimming (van Roosmalen & Krahn, 1996). Reflecting traditional values, some adolescent girls see a conflict between being female and being an athlete. Compared to males, there are limited opportunities for female star athletes to become professionals in their sports. Some female athletes are denigrated for violating gender stereotypes (Dornbusch et al., 1996; Engel, 1994). African-American football and basketball players on campuses with low enrollment of African-American students report racial isolation and discrimination. Athletes in particular have more difficulty getting to know other students and being liked by others (American Institutes for Research, 1988).

Males and females tend to drop out of informal sports (and other organized activities) during the early teenage years, to some extent because they are no longer satisfied with their level of skill relative to competent peers. Believing that one excels in a sport is a major contributor to sport enjoyment (Boyd & Yin, 1996). Participation in formal competition is also time-consuming, reducing time available for other activities (Hultsman, 1992; Kirshnit et al., 1989).

Adolescents give the following reasons for their lack of participation in sports and other organized activities (Hultsman, 1992; Seppa, 1996b): (1) the cost of the activity, (2) parents denying permission to join or participate, (3) lack of transportation, (4) not being old enough to participate, (5) the time commitment, and (6) the pressures of competition. Many teenagers report losing interest in an activity, moving, or discontinuation of the activity. Losing interest might reflect the greater attraction of time spent with friends after school. Given the value of participation to adolescents, service providers should minimize the obstacles cited above. Parental involvement, carpooling, using centralized locations, and using sliding fee scales promote participation in activities, which, in turn, helps adolescents engage in meaningful pursuits and stay out of trouble (Hoyle & Leff, 1997; Hultsman, 1992).

## SUMMARY

**1.** Adolescents inhabit a complex, overlapping network of relationships consisting of family members, peers, teachers, coaches, counselors, employers, and many others. Although their parents remain the most important people in their lives, teenagers increasingly turn to their peers for companionship, support, understanding, and fun. Adolescent peer networks include best friends, close friends, acquaintances, cliques, crowds, and, eventually, romantic relationships.

**2.** Friendship and other peer relationships are an important source of resocialization—learning how to get along with people who are not family members. Friends also rely on each other for feedback, information, and emotional support.

**3.** Cognitive changes during early and middle adolescence enhance young people's conceptions of how relationships work. Perspective taking, social comparison, and empathic understanding help adolescents understand their friends' motives and personalities. They become more sensitive to their friends' needs and better able to see themselves through the eyes of others.

**4.** Dunphy described three types of peer groups. Cliques usually consist of four to six same-gender friends who spend their leisure time together. Crowds are larger than cliques and usually are school-based. Crowds help adolescents develop an identity and regulate their social interactions. Membership in a crowd implies shared attitudes and interests. Gangs are larger than cliques and more organized. Most gangs reject conventional values but provide protection to members and a sense of belonging.

**5.** Most adolescents identify with at least one peer group. Proximity is an important factor in peer group formation, but frequent and pleasurable contact is necessary for the maintenance of close relationships.

**6.** Most adolescent peer groups have a dominance hierarchy of leaders and followers. Leaders are admired for possessing valued personal qualities and dominate communication and decision making. They coordinate group activities and initiate new activities.

**7.** Group members typically have similar qualities and interests. This is because individuals seek out friends who are already similar, adopt each other's behaviors, and reject members who don't tow the line. Most teenagers are somewhat susceptible to peer influence, but those who have the poorest relationships with their parents usually are the most vulnerable.

**8.** Most parents realize that peer influence is mainly positive and encourage their children to

have friendships. Peer groups usually function as a normative reference group for early and middle adolescents. Peer groups provide a safe haven for acquiring new beliefs and behaviors and for experimenting with adult roles and values. Close friendships appear to be crucial to adolescents' social and emotional development. Within close relationships, teenagers learn how to trust, self-disclose, express positive and negative emotions, and become intimate with others. Close friendships also are risky but help teenagers learn how to cope with strong feelings such as anger and rejection.

**9.** Research findings concerning white, middle-class adolescents do not necessarily apply to other ethnic or socioeconomic groups. Racial differences in friendship patterns appear to reflect different socialization experiences. African-American youths are more emotionally connected to their parents and less susceptible to peer pressure than white youths, at least in predominantly white communities. Neighborhood contact seems to be an important factor in out-of-school cross-race friendships.

**10.** Parents influence their children's choice of peers indirectly by raising their children to have certain values. Adolescents usually seek out as friends peers who share their (and thus their parents') values. Direct parental intervention in peer selection usually is resisted and resented by teenagers. It is helpful for parents to express interest in their children's relationships without being intrusive.

**11.** Most adolescents highly value being popular. Popularity is served by being physically attractive, having a good personality, wearing fashionable clothing, and achieving in athletics or academically. Having popular friends contributes to one's popularity.

**12.** Young people who are deficient in social skills and difficult to get along with may suffer the rejection of their peers. Peer rejection is very stressful and self-perpetuating. Rejected children have few opportunities to learn the skills they need to be accepted. Social isolates tend to be withdrawn, hostile, and low in self-esteem. Without corrective experiences, they are likely to have relationship and other problems well into adulthood.

**13.** About 40% of adolescents' waking hours are spent in leisure activities. They enjoy watching television, listening to music, and hanging out with friends. Leisure-time activities can promote healthy development or expose teenagers to excessive amounts of violence and sexual material.

**14.** It is not always easy to distinguish media that are merely entertaining from those that are detrimental to healthy development. Well-adjusted adolescents are not likely to engage in antisocial or self-destructive behavior as a result of exposure to overly violent or sexual music or materials. For those who are "close to the edge," it is conceivable that an intense media experience can push them over. Adolescents depend on media such as TV and music to relieve negative emotions and as resources in identity formation.

**15.** Many adolescent girls become voracious readers of teenage magazines that provide information and advice about fashion, dieting, and romance. Girls' self-esteem may be damaged when they realize that they will never achieve cultural ideals of slimness and beauty.

## GLOSSARY

**Cliques** The basic functional unit of the adolescent group; usually four to six same-gender friends who spend much of their leisure time together

**Crowds** School-based peer groups ranging from 15 to 30 boys and girls, with an average of 20 members

**Gangs** Deviant peer groups that provide protection to group members and define a territory to prevent incursion by rival gangs

**Homophily** The tendency of group members to have similar characteristics

**Sociodemographic conditions** Bringing children into proximity with each other

**Differential selection** Seeking out as friends persons who already are similar to oneself

**Reciprocal (mutual) socialization** The process by which members of a peer group become increasingly similar by interacting with each other

**Contagion effect** People in close groups sometimes do things they would not do on their own

**Selective elimination** The process by which nonconforming group members are forced to leave the group or leave voluntarily

**Observational learning** Learning a behavior simply by observing someone engage it

**Reinforcement** Increasing the probability of a behavior by following it with a desirable outcome

**Negative sanctions** Negative action affecting an individual by a group such as rejection and exclusion

**Social comparison** Comparing oneself to a reference group

**Friendship** A relatively enduring, affectionate relationship between two people who enjoy each other's company

**Subculture** A culture shared by a group within a larger society

**Social isolates** Children who have few if any friends and who are perceived as withdrawn, hostile, aggressive, or nerdy

## THOUGHT QUESTIONS

**1.** Under what social conditions might peer influence compete with parental influence?

**2.** Describe your clique during your high school years. What attracted you to this particular group of teenagers?

**3.** Is the teenage subculture antiadult? Explain.

**4.** What developmental needs are satisfied by peer recognition and acceptance?

**5.** Describe any social isolates whom you remember from your middle or high school years. What was their problem?

**6.** What does an adolescent's musical preferences tell us about his or her personality or self-concept, if anything?

**7.** Is there a down side to adolescent participation in organized competitive activities?

# SELF-TEST

1. Compared to parent–child relationships, adolescent friendships are more
   a. equitable
   b. emotional
   c. stressful
   d. conflictual

2. The basic functional unit of adolescent social life is
   a. the clique
   b. the crowd
   c. the gang
   d. the boyfriend/girlfriend

3. Crowds usually are composed of
   a. same-gender adolescents
   b. the most popular teenagers
   c. several cliques
   d. white, middle-class students

4. Peers usually affiliate on the basis of
   a. proximity
   b. similarity
   c. common interests
   d. all of the above

5. Seeking out as friends those who are already similar is called
   a. homophily
   b. differential selection
   c. reciprocal socialization
   d. conformity

6. Peer influence usually is
   a. coercive
   b. negative
   c. positive
   d. unpredictable

**7.** More than do girls, adolescent boys prefer

   **a.** recreational activities

   **b.** reading magazines

   **c.** going to the movies

   **d.** going shopping

**8.** Compared to white adolescents, African-American adolescents

   **a.** feel closer to their parents

   **b.** are less controlled by their parents

   **c.** have more intimate relationships

   **d.** report more peer pressure

**9.** Social isolates

   **a.** are perceived by peers as nerdy

   **b.** try too hard to gain attention

   **c.** usually have conflictual relationships with peers

   **d.** all of the above

**10.** The best predictor of delinquent behavior is

   **a.** drug use

   **b.** permissive parents

   **c.** having delinquent peers

   **d.** having a learning disability

**11.** The average teenager in the United States watches about _____ hours of TV weekly

   **a.** 14

   **b.** 18

   **c.** 22

   **d.** 26

**12.** The developmental task most likely to be satisfied by listening to heavy metal music is

   **a.** autonomy

   **b.** identity

   **c.** separation

   **d.** achievement

**13.** Parents are most likely to complain about a song's

    **a.** loudness

    **b.** lyrics

    **c.** video

    **d.** bass track

**14.** In most high schools, the highest social status goes to

    **a.** the best looking

    **b.** the highest achievers

    **c.** the most talented musicians

    **d.** the star athletes

# NINE

# ADOLESCENT SEXUALITY

♦

## Preview Questions

1. What consequences of careless sexual activity can occur during adolescence?
2. How have adolescent sexual behaviors and values changed over the course of this century?
3. What moral dilemmas face adolescent girls concerning their desire to be sexually active?
4. Why might adolescents have sex for the wrong reasons?
5. What is the relationship between adolescent sexual attitudes and sexual behaviors?
6. What social dilemmas face gay and lesbian adolescents?
7. What factors predict early sexual intercourse?
8. What role does cognitive development play in adolescent sexual decision making?
9. Why don't many adolescents use contraceptives during intercourse?
10. What is meant by a *comprehensive* approach to sex education?

♦
_____

## Disclosures

A 15-year-old unmarried woman becomes pregnant. If she is a rural Iraqi girl, her father may kill her. If she is a Kalahari bushwoman, she may marry quickly and comfortably. If she is a middle-class U.S. high school student, she may stay unmarried and attend a special class for expectant mothers.

*(Hotvedt, 1990, p. 157)*

It doesn't bother me that I am gay. I don't know why shrinks should get so upset about it. What bothers me is that people should have such a hard time believing it. This is a new time and society has to learn to accept us as no different from anyone else. My roommate and friends understand that. My biggest problem is with my parents and my high school teachers who never understood that teenagers can be gay but no different from anyone else.

*(First-year college student quoted by Boxer, Cohler, Herdt, & Irvin, 1993, p. 249)*

_____

# Contents

Physical growth and sexual maturation are the most distinctive and universal features of adolescence. Romantic feelings and desires are normal, natural, and healthy. In Western culture, sexual behavior is a powerful way of achieving intimacy in romantic relationships. The bad news is that careless sexual activity can alter the course of an adolescent's life. It can set the stage for unwanted pregnancy and parenthood, family conflict, abortion, and sexually transmitted diseases such as herpes and AIDS.

The age at which young people begin to engage in sexual activities with others has been gradually decreasing (Katchadourian, 1990; Miller, Christopherson, & King, 1993; Pestrak & Martin, 1985; Wyatt, 1990). Approximately half of the teenagers in the United States are sexually experienced by the age of 19, with age of first intercourse averaging about 16 years. At least 80% of boys and 70% of girls report having had sexual intercourse by age 20 (Hayes, 1987; Murstein & Mercy, 1994). One in five teenagers reports having four or more sex partners. Since most teenagers do not use contraceptives consistently when having sex (Morrison, 1985), it is not surprising that teenage pregnancies account for about 13% of all births in the United States (Kean, 1989).

The United States has the highest rate of **sexually transmitted diseases** of any developed country. One-quarter of the estimated 12 million new cases each year involve adolescents, a population at greater risk because of engaging in unprotected sex and other high-risk sexual behaviors. In the United States in 1995, the most frequently reported infectious diseases were chlamydia, gonorrhea, syphilis, and herpes, all sexually transmitted and potential causes of infertility, cancer, birth defects, miscarriages, and death (Leukefeld & Haverkos, 1993; *The*

*New York Times,* October 20, 1996, p. A28; *The New York Times*, November 20, 1996, p. D20).

In the past, people knew that sexual indiscretions would be severely punished. All authorities—family, church, and state—strongly condemned premarital sexual behavior, even in the form of masturbation ("self-abuse"). Today, adolescents are given mixed messages about expressing their sexuality—wait, don't wait. Confusion about how and when to express their sexual feelings makes it more likely that young people will seek sexual intimacy before they are emotionally ready.

Perhaps it was easier to not think or feel sexual in the past, before popular music, television, magazines, movies, and advertising commercialized sexuality. As described in the previous chapter, young people today are exposed to an incessant flow of sexual images and information. In 1995, fashion designer Calvin Klein was forced to withdraw billboard advertisements featuring young adolescents in such sexually suggestive poses and attire that critics claimed the ads bordered on child pornography. Dramas on commercial television and cable TV include nudity, profanity, and increasingly explicit sexual situations. Sex appeal and sexual activity are glamorized to the point that many teenagers are embarrassed to admit that they are still virgins.

Unfortunately, much less attention is paid by the broadcast media to the potential consequences of casual sexual behavior. Despite all the sexual content of

**Teenagers are exposed to an incessant flow of sexual images and information.**

their programming, until 1995 the major TV networks refused to carry ads for condoms or other contraceptives (Blau & Gullotta, 1993; *The New York Times,* May 3, 1995).

Sexuality is an especially challenging topic for researchers to study, partly because of people's discomfort in discussing their own intimate feelings and behavior. Although we know a lot about what adolescents do and don't do sexually, we know relatively little about what sexual experience means to adolescents and how it relates to other areas of their lives (Brooks-Gunn & Furstenberg, 1989). What we have learned about the sexual practices of previous generations may or may not apply to the current generation of adolescents.

Research methods (such as direct observation, verbal inquiry, and experimental manipulation) that can be used to study other aspects of human behavior are not easily applied to the study of sexuality, especially that of children and adolescents. Reliable information on sexual behavior is hard to come by because of differences in how researchers collect data, difficulty in interpreting what adolescents say, and the **social desirability effect** (study participants giving socially acceptable rather than truthful responses) (Zani, 1991). Males tend to exaggerate their sexual experiences and females sometimes underreport theirs. Retrospective reports from adults about their teenage sexual experiences are not necessarily reliable. Further, research involving underage adolescents requires parental consent and the cooperation of the participants (Katchadourian, 1990; Oliver & Hyde, 1993).

In this chapter and the next, we raise many questions about adolescents' transformation into fertile, sexual beings, including: How has society's view of adolescent sexual behavior changed during this century? What is the relationship between puberty, fertility, and sexuality? How do gay adolescents cope with social rejection at a time when they most crave peer acceptance? What factors influence the timing of first intercourse? Why do so many sexually active teenagers decide to not use contraception despite the potentially serious consequences of casual sex? Perhaps the key question we address in this chapter is: How do we provide adolescents with the knowledge and skills that they need to make good decisions regarding intimate relationships and sexual behavior? As we consider these and other questions, it becomes clear that teenagers need to understand how the decisions they make, especially during passionate encounters, can alter the course of their lives and the lives of the people who care about them.

# PERSPECTIVES ON ADOLESCENT SEXUALITY

Until recently, two quite different models of adolescent sexuality coexisted: a biological model that emphasizes sexual urges seeking genital expression and a sociocultural model stressing the importance of social learning and cultural sanctions (Miller & Fox, 1987). Newer so-called biosocial models appeal to biological, personal, and social factors to explain the timing and variation of sexual behavior during adolescence (Miller et al., 1993; Schmitt & Buss, 1996).

A reasonably complete understanding of human sexuality requires consideration of evolution, genetics, the role of the nervous system and hormones, cultural mores and prohibitions, religious and ethnic traditions, an individual's family and sexual learning history, peer influences, and resultant attitudes and values (Downs & Hillje, 1993; Tiefer, 1995). (See Table 9-1.)

During this century, the pendulum has swung from austere, moralistic pronouncements about human sexuality to objective, scientific study. Freud (1920/1965) was the first modern theorist to view sexuality as an important motivator of behavior (a *biological imperative*). Freud viewed infants and children as sexual beings who derive considerable pleasure from self-stimulation, who display curiosity about sexual organs (their own and others'), and who express a primal longing for those persons they feel close to, including family members. Although young children exhibit sexual curiosity and feel pleasure when touching their sex organs, it is not until puberty that powerful hormones intensify sexual desire. *Thought Question: Why did Sigmund Freud get so much flak from his contemporaries for suggesting the obvious—that children have sexual feelings?*

Although children gain pleasure from self-stimulation, sexual feelings become more pronounced during early adolescence. Freud characterized early adolescents as being in the **genital stage of psychosexual development**. According to Freud, adolescence is the life period when sexual orientation is initially confused and ultimately finalized. Intense sexual desire is a new, exciting, and possibly threatening experience to adolescents. To avoid feeling uncom-

**Table 9-1  Factors Associated with Adolescent Sexual Behavior**

Sexual identity

Family values

Ethnicity and socioeconomic status

Religiosity

Commitment to academics

Cultural attitudes

Peer and media influences

Sex education

Opportunity for sexual encounters

The meaning that adolescents attribute to their biological maturation and bodily sensations

fortable, Freud conjectured, adolescents must direct sexual desire away from family members and toward their peers.

Although impressive as a pioneering effort, Freud's psychosexual model overemphasized biological determinants and overlooked many social, situational, and cognitive factors that we now know guide sexual conduct. As noted earlier, current models of adolescent sexuality take into account family values, socioeconomic status, religiosity, peer and media influences, opportunity, and, importantly, the meaning that adolescents attribute to their biological maturation and bodily sensations (Billy, Brewster, & Grady, 1994; Zani, 1991).

Concurrent with Freud's theorizing, G. Stanley Hall (1904) attempted to provide a scientific rather than a moralistic or religious context for understanding adolescent sexuality. He was only partly successful. Like Freud, Hall raised important issues but was hindered by a scarcity of good information about human sexuality. Hall noted correctly that menstruation is a normal biological function and that boys' nocturnal emissions probably are universal. Like Freud, he considered homosexuality and bisexuality to be degenerate practices, a view at odds with most current psychological thinking. He also contended that masturbation is evil and is caused mainly by laziness, erotic pictures, and springtime (Downs & Hillje, 1993).

Downs and Hillje (1993) reviewed changes in adolescent sexual behaviors and attitudes during this century. At about the time of the First World War, there was an increase in premarital sex and a decline in the age at which adolescents began to date. During the Roaring Twenties, the availability of automobiles and a weakening of the chaperone system were associated with increased intimacy in adolescent relationships. At midcentury, the availability of safe, reliable contraception set the stage for sexual experimentation (*free love*). The Supreme Court's *Roe* v. *Wade* decision in 1973 reduced the stigma and removed the penalties tied to abortion. The media continued to exploit the marketability of sexual gratification in advertising and TV programming.

Within the last 15 years, the most threatening factor associated with teenage sexual behavior has been acquired immunodeficiency syndrome (AIDS), a topic we will address later in this chapter. About one-third of those with AIDS are children. At the same time, increased social awareness, education, and laws protecting adolescents have reduced (but hardly eliminated) the sexual victimization of adolescents that was so common in previous eras. Today, most adults agree that sex education for adolescents is a good idea (Reuters News Service, 1991). Because adolescent sexuality often is discussed in relation to one or another social problem, there is the danger of viewing it as pathological or as something to be discouraged (McConaghy, 1995). We rarely if ever hear of adolescents being encouraged to explore and enjoy their sexuality, whether through self-stimulation or in the confines of an exclusive relationship. Being sexually mature in a sexually ambivalent society translates into psychological conflict for many young people (Rodman, 1990).

Preindustrial cultures celebrated the transition from infertile child to fertile adult. Many tribes encouraged premarital sex and practiced sexual initiation rites, both homosexually and heterosexually (Hotvedt, 1990). Although we understand why parents today prefer that their children delay marriage and pregnancy, a balanced view recognizes both positive and negative consequences of adolescent sexual activity.

## SEXUAL MATURATION

Children are capable of sexual arousal before puberty. Infants and toddlers gain gratification from self-stimulation, and older children express sexual curiosity and engage in sex play. During childhood, penile erection, vaginal lubrication, and even orgasm can be elicited by manual stimulation or other erotic stimuli. The dramatic increase in hormone production during puberty energizes the sex drive and eroticizes it. Sexual behavior becomes more varied and more frequent (Miller et al., 1993).

As described in Chapter 3, hormones initiate the development of secondary sexual characteristics. For boys, testosterone level is correlated with sexual behavior and sex drive. For girls, it is correlated mainly with sexual interest. Female sexual behavior, less impulsive than that of males, appears to be more easily inhibited by social prohibitions. Hormones produce secondary sexual changes that increase the sexual stimulus value (appearance) of boys and girls. Young male adolescents experience erections, often at night. Sometimes erections occur spontaneously; at other times they reflect erotic stimulation. Although arousal usually is pleasurable, some boys who are not comfortable with their sexual changes feel embarrassed or guilty (Katchadourian, 1990).

**SPOTLIGHT** • Pseudosexuality

*Thought Question: Why are adolescents so vulnerable to sexual exploitation by peers and adults?*

Although our society is still debating what the right reasons are for having sex, it is clear that adolescents sometimes engage in sex for the wrong reasons. Hajcak and Garwood (1988) use the term **pseudosexuality** to refer to adolescents' need for acceptance and closeness, which leads some of them into unwanted sexual encounters. "Adolescents have sex when, in fact, they primarily want and need something else, such as affection, to ease loneliness, to confirm masculinity or femininity, to bolster self-esteem, to express anger or escape from boredom. In short, during adolescence, sex becomes a coping mechanism to express and satisfy nonsexual needs" (p. 755).

Behaviors such as holding hands and kissing are potentially stimulating sexual experiences. Young teenagers are capable of having intercourse; by age 15, most females can conceive. "However, many teenagers are not psychologically, emotionally, or socially ready for sexual intercourse, or for oral

**Some teenagers have sex for the wrong reasons.**

sex, anal sex, or mutual masturbation. Although the latter sexual practices will not result in pregnancy, they may be frightening, confusing, or even traumatizing to an unsophisticated adolescent" (Shaughnessy & Shakesby, 1992, p. 476).

To many teenagers, being sexual is a way of demonstrating one's normality or proving one's love. It is also a way of confirming that a relationship is serious and that the participants are "grown up." Having sex also is a way of avoiding the embarrassment and conflict that result from simple refusal. Thus, sexual activity often meets one partner's needs at the expense of the other's. "Guilt, fear of pregnancy, and fear of parental disapproval often accompany sexual activities. There is limited communication, and love and passion are often confused" (Weinstein & Rosen, 1991, p. 332).

For some young people, orgasm becomes a quick fix for any uncomfortable feeling or situation. "Eventually, sex becomes a general coping mechanism, a drive to get relief, through orgasm, from emotional tension or discomfort" (Hajcak & Garwood, 1988, p. 757). When affection and esteem needs are met nonsexually, adolescents are better able to develop mature sexual relationships. However, when these nonsexual needs are linked to pleasurable sexual feelings, mature levels of sexuality and emotionality become harder to achieve.

# ATTITUDES ABOUT SEX

Over the past century, thanks to people like Sigmund Freud, Alfred Kinsey, Masters and Johnson, and Dr. Ruth, sex has become less mysterious. Analysis of popular music, TV, movies, and fashion confirms that as a society we are fascinated by matters sexual. Sexual messages pervade our entertainment media and advertising. Popular talk shows dwell on themes such as promiscuity, infidelity, rape, incest, sexual abuse, harassment, and abortion, topics avoided in the past as too controversial for daytime television (Strasburger, 1995). *Thought Question: Do TV talk shows and dramas present young viewers with realistic or distorted accounts of close adult relationships?*

Changes in sexual attitudes and values have occurred so rapidly since mid-century that some observers proclaim the movement toward individual freedom and choice to be a *sexual revolution*. Indeed, attitudes about sex-related practices such as masturbation, premarital sex, and abortion have become more liberal. With the availability of safe, effective birth control technology, sexual activity and reproduction are no longer inextricably linked, leading to increasingly permissive sexual values and attitudes. Discussion of sexual topics occurs more frequently, and self-disclosure is more explicit than in previous decades (Zani, 1991).

If there has been a sexual revolution, it probably has affected females more than males. The victimization of females throughout history via forced marriages, prostitution, rape, and sexual abuse is well documented (Boswell, 1980; Downs & Hillje, 1993). Over the past few decades there has been a slight lessening of the **sexual double standard**, society's greater tolerance of premarital sexual activity for males than for females. The double standard presumes that males ("studs") have almost uncontrollable sexual needs that must be satisfied as opportunities arise. The double standard downplays female sexual desire (even in marriage) and provides sanctions for females who are sexually active outside of a marriage relationship ("sluts") (Oliver & Hyde, 1993; Wilson & Medora, 1990).

Although not as conspicuous as it used to be, the double standard still exists. Early sexual activity still is considered less deviant for boys than for girls (Crockett, Bingham, Chopak, & Vicary, 1996). According to a Harris Poll conducted in 1994 and published in May 1995, 70% of American men do not think they can be counted on to choose a method of birth control; 73% of the women polled shared that view (Steinhauer, 1995). Men and women agreed that men are uninvolved in birth control decisions because they don't care and because they consider birth control to be the woman's responsibility.

Still, female sexual desire no longer is denied or condemned. Female college students have become more like male college students in initiating and being comfortable during sexual encounters, at least in close relationships. Sex within an affectionate relationship rather than within a committed relationship has become the norm for adolescents. Females remain more conservative sexually than males, are less interested in having extramarital sex, and are more disposed to long-term relationships (De Gaston, Weed, & Jensen, 1996; Murstein

& Mercy, 1994; Salts, Seismore, Lindholm, & Smith, 1994; Wilson & Medora, 1990; Zani, 1991).

Sexual attitudes typically are more conservative than sexual behaviors. Further, adolescents often condone behaviors for others that they would not engage in themselves. College students generally disapprove of homosexual behavior but are becoming more tolerant of gays and lesbians (Wilson & Medora, 1990). Most adolescents report believing that they should wait to have intercourse, but most don't wait (de Gaston, Jensen, & Weed, 1995). *Critical Thinking Question: Why would we expect sexual attitudes to be more conservative than sexual behaviors?*

## SEXUAL ORIENTATION AND SEXUAL IDENTITY

Among the myriad developmental tasks of adolescence are discovering, coming to terms with, and, for most people, enjoying one's sexuality (Erikson, 1968; Havighurst, 1972). Indeed, "sexual exploration is critical to sexual identity formation. Sexual exploration offers adolescents opportunities to integrate their own arousal with learning to care for and respect their partners and attain the physical competence needed to engage in the behaviors" (Herold & Marshall, 1996, p. 76).

For at least the past several hundred years, virtually all social institutions considered heterosexuality to be the only acceptable form of sexual expression (Savin-Williams, 1994). Partly because we have a limited understanding of the origins of sexual attraction (Bailey, Bobrow, Wolfe, & Mikach, 1995; Bem, 1996; Meyer-Bahlburg et al., 1995), the question of what constitutes normal or healthy adult sexuality is still debated. When this question is applied to children and adolescents, the debate is even more intense (Savin-Williams, 1994). As far as we know, sexual orientation is involuntary and a weak predictor of an individual's mental status or moral virtue. Thus, the implications of defining oneself as homosexual or bisexual are more social and psychological than biological or cognitive (Boxer et al., 1993; Edwards, 1996a).

Sexual preferences can change before one's orientation stabilizes in adulthood. It is important for teenagers to know that sexual feelings and behaviors during adolescence do not necessarily predict their final sexual orientation (Bell & Weinberg, 1978; Savin-Williams, 1990). Sexual experimentation with peers or with younger or older people is common during adolescence. Most adolescents who have homosexual encounters during their teenage years eventually consider themselves to be heterosexual. Most lesbians and gay men explore heterosexual sex during adolescence (Bell & Weinberg, 1978; Marano, 1997b). Because of the stigma attached to any nonnormative sexual preference (including celibacy and virginity), there is pressure on teenagers, regardless of their feelings or desires, to seek romantic relationships with members of the other gender.

As in society, in research gay, lesbian, and bisexual adolescents have been almost invisible. Most prefer to remain unnoticed because they anticipate or have experienced hostility regarding their sexuality. They are considered " 'sexual outlaws' in a society that assumes heterosexuality of all its members and institutions. . . . All youths are considered innocent and straight until proven guilty and gay" (Savin-Williams & Rodriguez, 1993, pp. 77, 79). One problem with invisibility is that it fosters denial both for society and for the conflicted adolescent.

In addition to having to deal with the rejection of family and friends, gay teenagers are vulnerable to humiliation and physical violence (known as **gay-bashing**) (Freiberg, 1995; Zera, 1992). In 1989, the U.S. Department of Health and Human Services reported that gay, lesbian, and bisexual young people are more likely to be physically and verbally abused than their peers and more likely to attempt suicide.

Many of those who participate in homosexual encounters rationalize their actions by attributing them to loneliness or curiosity, or they dismiss their desires as temporary. Some label themselves bisexual because bisexuality is less unacceptable (Savin-Williams & Rodriguez, 1993) or simply pass as heterosexuals (Edwards, 1996a).

Accepting one's sexuality is difficult when one's feelings are denigrated or despised. Almost all children hear derogatory terms like *faggot* and *dyke*. No wonder that only a tiny percentage of adolescents who experience homosexual attractions or behavior label themselves gay or lesbian, let alone say it out loud (Coles & Stokes, 1985; Remafedi, Resnick, Blum, & Harris, 1992; Savin-Williams, 1994).

Many gay, lesbian, and bisexual adolescents in the United States belong to minority ethnic or racial groups that are subject to discrimination (De Angelis, 1996b; Edwards, 1996a). Homosexuality usually is incompatible with the conservative values of these ethnic subcultures. This makes it especially difficult to merge one's homosexual identity with one's racial or ethnic identity, magnifying adolescents' sense of isolation and despair (Hetrick & Martin, 1987). What must life have been like for homosexual adolescents in the days before anyone ever dreamed of a concept like *gay pride*?

Gay and lesbian identity develops gradually, usually beginning with confusion and denial and ending with self-affirmation, a redefinition of group membership, and **coming out** (voluntary disclosure to others) (Fassinger, 1991; Fontaine & Hammond, 1996; Savin-Williams, 1995; Savin-Williams & Rodriguez, 1993; Waldner-Haugrud & Magruder, 1996). (See Table 9-2.) McCarn and Fassinger (1996) describe four phases of lesbian identity formation: (1) *awareness* of being different and of having a different sexual orientation; (2) *exploration* of erotic feelings for women and of one's attitude toward lesbians; (3) *deepening commitment* to self-knowledge and to personal involvement with one's reference group; and (4) *internalization* of one's identity as a member of this group.

Many gay, lesbian, and bisexual adolescents report that during childhood they felt different from their peers. Males in particular say that they felt isolated, alienated, and more easily hurt emotionally than their age-mates. They usually shied away from aggressive and competitive activities, although a large number report trying to fit in by participating in sports and by dating girls. Some girls are surprised to find themselves identifying with supposedly male traits like competitiveness. Many lesbians report feeling and acting heterosexual before

**Table 9-2 Stages of Sexual Identity Development and Suggested Counseling Interventions**

| Identity Stages | Possible Feelings/Behaviors | Counseling Interventions |
| --- | --- | --- |
| 1. Confusion | Feeling "different"<br>Same-sex attractions, dreams, fantasies | • Provide support<br>• Provide readings<br>• Explore strengths in "differentness"<br>• Discourage premature self-labeling |
| 2. Comparison | Continued sense of difference from peers<br>Strong same-sex attractions, preoccupations<br>Anxiety about fitting in<br>Social isolation, alienation, shame | All of above, plus:<br>• Explore fears, anxieties, shame<br>• Identify positive role models<br>• Locate age appropriate peer support resources |
| 3. Tolerance | Actively seeking out bi/homosexual peers or adults<br>Living "double life" with secret bi/gay self<br>Denial of sexuality | All of above, plus:<br>• Maintain safe, supportive relationship w/adult<br>• Discourage inappropriate sexuality w/adults<br>• Encourage gay/lesbian/bi peer social activities<br>• Address fears of exposure |
| 4. Acceptance | Increased contact with g/l/bi peers<br>Severe loneliness/alienation if peers not available<br>May be scapegoated at home/school | All of above, plus:<br>• Encourage "safer sex" if sexually active<br>• Explore coming out issues<br>• Affirm basic self-worth<br>• Explore & build self-esteem |
| 5. Pride | Us/them attitude about heterosexuality<br>Belief in superiority of g/l/bi lifestyle<br>Aggressively "out" stance<br>Sexually active to bolster identity<br>Anger at prejudice, discrimination | All of above, plus:<br>• Support self-acceptance & pride<br>• Encourage bridging w/supportive heterosexuals<br>• Caution about "crashing out" |
| 6. Synthesis | Rejoining supportive heterosexuals<br>Increased empathy<br>Renewed emphasis on work, school, family roles | • Support efforts to bridge gay/lesbian/bisexual self with aspects of identity |

(From Fontaine & Hammond, 1996, pp. 824–825.)

they discover or acknowledge their true orientation. As discussed in Chapter 8, boys and girls are drawn to peers who seem to be like them (Isay, 1989; Newman & Muzzonigro, 1993).

With the onset of puberty, vague feelings of attraction become eroticized and are experienced as desire for same-gendered peers, but they are accompanied by fears of being rejected or physically harmed. Among gay and bisexual teenagers, at least initially, there is painful confusion, denial, guilt, shame, conflict, and self-hatred regarding their fantasies and feelings. Taken together, these reactions are called **homosexual panic**, and reflect fear of rejection and attack more than discomfort about erotic feelings. In their distress, many youngsters hope and pray for these feelings to go away. In the face of denial or rejection, some turn to drugs, feigned heterosexuality, orthodox religion, or counseling (Goff, 1990; Savin-Williams & Rodriguez, 1993).

In Rodriguez's (1988) study of white gay men in Utah, awareness of same-sex attractions was reported to occur at about age 11, followed by same-sex erotic fantasies at about age 14, labeling these feelings as homosexual at about age 16, labeling oneself as homosexual at about age 20, and labeling oneself as gay (including lifestyle) at about age 23. It has not been demonstrated that this sequence is the same for females, nonwhites, or other groups.

In Newman and Muzzonigro's (1993) small multiethnic sample of gay male adolescents (aged 17–20 years), the average age reported for realizing that they were gay was 12.5 years. Most study participants reported feeling different from other boys between the ages of 4 and 9 years. In this sample, about half reported feeling little or no guilt or shame when they first realized that they were gay. By the time of the study, most had incorporated their gay identity into a positive sense of self. About a third expressed negative or mixed feelings about being gay and about themselves. In Savin-Williams' (1995) study of 83 gay and bisexual males, being gay or bisexual did not reduce young people's self-esteem relative to that of a comparable sample of heterosexual youth.

Before homosexual adolescents can come out to the world, they must come out to themselves—that is, admit their true feelings and attractions. This requires overcoming not only societal hostility and social stigma, but also denial, self-devaluation, self-blame, and hostile feelings toward other gays (Sleek, 1996). Even more prevalent and damaging is the attempt to "pass" as heterosexual, that is, to hide one's true sexual identity (Edwards, 1996a). This includes lying to others about oneself, concealing information, and avoiding being seen with other homosexuals. Naturally, such strategies contribute to feelings of loneliness and of being a fraud (Newman & Muzzonigro, 1993; Savin-Williams & Rodriguez, 1993; Zera, 1992).

Parents of gay and lesbian teenagers also experience homosexual panic, engaging in denial, guilt, and self-blame, all of which leave them emotionally unavailable to their children. One mother of a gay son disclosed, "I found out my son was gay when he was 16. And when I did, I was very, very upset. I thought there were few things in the world that would happen to me that would be worse" (quoted by Tabor, 1992a). Since that time, she has participated in Gay Pride marches and speaks about her experiences at local high schools. (What about parent's sexual orientation? Contrary to many researchers (e.g., Golombok & Tasker, 1996), Cameron and Cameron [1996] contend that homosexual parents disproportionately have homosexual children.)

Some parents verbally or physically abuse their children or expel them from the family (Zera, 1992). A young woman from Brooklyn, New York, reports that she was driven out of her house when she told her mother that she was a lesbian. "Now she calls me a freak and says she wishes I was never born" (quoted by Tabor, 1992a). It is a terrible feeling for most adolescents to so disappoint their parents or to feel that they are not living up to the religious or moral ideals that they were taught.

Remafedi (1987) interviewed 29 homosexual and bisexual teenagers who were mainly white, middle class, and Christian. About half reported losing

Some gay and lesbian adolescents are rejected by their own parents.

friends and receiving negative or mixed responses from their parents. Most said they experienced verbal abuse, physical brutality, religious condemnation, and rejection because of their sexual orientation. Family rejection fuels their own confusion and self-blame, leading many gay adolescents to lives of conflict, isolation, despair, and hopelessness. A report by the U.S. Department of Health and Human Services in 1989 concluded that 30% of teenage suicides occur among homosexuals and lesbians. Gay males in particular are susceptible to practices—drug use, multiple partners, high-risk sex—that increase their chances of contracting AIDS (Youngstrom, 1991). Although victimization compromises gay adolescents' mental health, family support and self-acceptance of their sexual orientation help them deal with occasional verbal abuse and harassment (Hershberger & D'Augelli, 1995).

There is no one strategy for coping with prejudice and rejection that will work for all homosexual and bisexual adolescents. Coming out to oneself at a relatively early age appears to be important to the development of a healthy self-concept and adjustment, even if it means being deceptive with most others. "The adolescent can disclose only to those who will provide support, understanding, and growth. The youth has an opportunity to learn crisis management and an internal sense of self-respect and ego integrity that will prove beneficial in the adult homophobic world that most will soon be entering" (Savin-Williams & Rodriguez, 1993, p. 91).

Despite the rejection and abuse that they encounter, many of the developmental concerns homosexual adolescents grapple with are similar to those of heterosexual adolescents (Fontaine & Hammond, 1996; Savin-Williams, 1995). Bisexual, gay, and lesbian adolescents crave acceptance from their peers, some of whom are tolerant and some of whom are homophobic. **Homophobia** (antihomosexual prejudice) is a serious social problem rooted in myths and stereotypes about gay and lesbian culture (Van de Ven, 1995). It is most destructive when it occurs in school and is ignored or, worse, condoned by teachers. In 1993 student leaders at a high school in Seattle voted to prevent any openly gay or lesbian student from serving in student government "to preserve the integrity and high moral standards" of the school (*Time*, May 24, 1993).

Homosexual student organizations exist in hundreds of high schools throughout the country. Some openly gay and lesbian teachers support students' efforts to dispel myths, build self-pride, and create safe or separate school environments for sexual minorities (Gurney, 1993; McCarron, 1996). More and more schools have counseling programs that provide emotional support, information, and referrals to gay, lesbian, and bisexual youth.

A governor's task force in Massachusetts recommended that schools formulate policies to protect homosexual students from harassment. This was the first statewide effort to train teachers to prevent harassment of and violence toward gays and lesbians. Some parents fear that too much attention is being paid to homosexuality and bisexuality in high school and that their children's sexual orientation might be affected (Marano, 1997b; *Newsweek*, November 8, 1993). Opponents of programs that teach tolerance contend that such programs encourage teenagers to experiment with their sexuality, but there is no evidence that sexual orientation can be changed by exposure to educational messages.

All adolescents need loving parents, caring friends, a supportive peer group, proud role models, and validation for their thoughts and feelings. Homosexual and heterosexual adolescents ask themselves the same questions: Who am I? What kind of life can I lead? Where do I fit in? and, Is my life worth living?

## SPOTLIGHT • Sexual Confusion in College-Age Males

Homophobia takes its toll in other ways. Goff (1990) describes a syndrome of **sexual confusion** in heterosexual college males who have failed to achieve a close relationship with females. Many males this age desire intimacy and are looking for a life partner. Because most of their peers date successfully or at least claim that they do, these young men begin to wonder whether something is wrong with them.

Failure to establish a heterosexual relationship encourages feelings of inadequacy and confusion about their sexuality. They fear that they might be gay, not because they are attracted to males but because of their apparent failure with females. Their sexual feelings have no available target, and they are frustrated. A fear of being homosexual elicits many of the feelings and actions that gay and lesbian adolescents report—anxiety, depression, shame, isolation, denial, drug abuse, same-sex exploration, fear of AIDS, even homophobia. Supportive counseling can help these young men understand and accept their sexual feelings (Goff, 1990).

## SEXUAL BEHAVIORS OF ADOLESCENTS

### Self-Stimulation (Autoerotic Behavior)

Most adolescents and adults gain pleasure and relief from sexual tension by stimulating their genitals manually, usually while engaging in erotic fantasies. Such experiences are almost never discussed with anyone and have received minimal research attention. Thus, we know relatively little about the sexual development of adolescents who do not engage in intercourse (Herold & Marshall, 1996).

Self-stimulation episodes initially are exploratory of one's sexual self and can provide a sense of control over one's body and sexual needs. However, feelings of guilt about masturbation or accompanying fantasies undermine self-esteem and, for some, inhibit the development of intimacy. Although widely practiced, masturbation apparently is not necessary for normal sexual development (Weinstein & Rosen, 1991).

In their study of autoerotic behavior, Coles and Stokes (1985) found that 72% of the teenagers they sampled reported having erotic fantasies about celebrities, rock stars, boyfriends and girlfriends, and imaginary people. Such fantasies presumably reflect hormonal and cognitive changes during puberty, as well as frequent exposure to popular media.

Sexual fantasies produce pleasurable arousal and enhance enjoyment of other sexual activities, including masturbation. They also serve as substitutes for sexual behaviors that may not be attainable. Sexual fantasies allow adolescents to explore their sexuality in safety and privacy. They also provide opportunities to practice sexual behaviors as preparatory to real-life sexual encounters. Sexual fantasizing is considered problematic only if it is obsessive or guilt-ridden or if it substitutes for age-appropriate interactions with peers (Katchadourian, 1990).

Nocturnal orgasms begin to occur in males and females at about age 12 or 13. Boys may be embarrassed or frightened by their ejaculations when they occur unexpectedly. Thus, providing boys with information about their emerging sexuality can help them feel more comfortable. The dynamics of self-stimulation and fantasizing differ somewhat for the two genders (Wilson & Medora, 1990).

Initially, teenagers experience a combination of feelings regarding masturbation, including a release from tension, pleasure, fear, and guilt. Those who know that self-stimulation is neither unusual nor harmful are less prone to feeling guilt and shame. It is beneficial for young adolescents to view self-stimulation as an alternative to intercourse. Masturbation is a safe and convenient way for young teenagers to explore their bodies and their sexuality. Like sexual fantasy, masturbation should be considered a problem only if it is compulsive. In Coles and Stokes' study, about half of the boys and a quarter of the girls said they masturbated. Frequency of masturbation remains one of the few significant gender differences in sexuality (Oliver & Hyde, 1993).

## Heterosexual Behavior: "Seven Minutes in Heaven"

The continuum of normative heterosexual behaviors for white adolescents includes holding hands, kissing, embracing, fondling, petting (fondling above and below the waist), and, eventually, intercourse (Smith & Udry, 1985). These sociosexual behaviors represent a maturational advance over autoerotic behaviors in that they require social skills (such as negotiation and compromise) that are not necessary for self-stimulation. The intensity of sexual activity, for white adolescents at least, increases with age and the seriousness of a relationship and decreases with religiosity (Miller et al., 1993; Thornton, 1990).

African-American teenagers apparently follow a different sequence, with intercourse occurring at an earlier age and with no predictable sequence of precoital behavior (Furstenberg, Morgan, Moore, & Peterson, 1987; Smith & Udry, 1985). Oral sex is commonly performed by adolescents, boys preferring it more than girls. Some adolescents refuse to engage in oral sex even if they have had intercourse. Others use oral sex as an alternative to intercourse (Newcomer & Udry, 1985), perhaps believing (incorrectly) that they need not take precautions against AIDS and other sexually transmitted diseases (Lewin, 1997). (See Table 9-3.)

Adolescents report that they initially engage in sexual behavior for a variety of reasons—pleasure, opportunity, curiosity, because their friends are doing it, as proof of their desirability and popularity, to feel grown up, and as a way of proving their love for their partner. Sexual behavior also serves as a means of defying parental and religious authority. For boys, sexual behavior is a way to establish masculinity. For teenagers, it can be a way of achieving intimacy in a meaningful relationship (Weinstein & Rosen, 1991).

## Premarital Intercourse: "Going All the Way"

Intercourse during the middle teenage years has become common in the United States and Canada, and at earlier ages for many African- and Hispanic-Amer-

**Table 9-3  Percentage of Adolescents Engaging in Heterosexual Behaviors at Various Dating Stages**

| | Stage of Dating | | |
| --- | --- | --- | --- |
| | **First Date** | **Several Dates** | **Going Steady** |
| Behavior | % | % | % |
| Hand holding | 90 | 93 | 95 |
| Light embrace | 93 | 94 | 97 |
| Necking | 47 | 82 | 88 |
| Deep kissing | 46 | 84 | 90 |
| General body contact | 40 | 79 | 94 |
| Mutual masturbation | 18 | 45 | 64 |
| Simulated intercourse | 16 | 44 | 60 |

(From McCabe & Collins, 1984)

ican youth (Furstenberg, Morgan, Moore & Peterson, 1987; Hofferth, 1990; King et al., 1988; Paikoff, 1995; Stanton, Black, Kaljee, & Ricardo, 1993). Cross-cultural research suggests quite different patterns in Asia and Latin America, where girls are likely to remain virgins until marriage and males' first sexual partners are likely to be prostitutes (Herold & Marshall, 1996).

People who speak of a sexual revolution in Western cultures are referring both to a decrease in the age of first intercourse and to an increase in the frequency of intercourse and in the number of sexual partners during the teenage years (Alan Guttmacher Institute, 1994). Premarital intercourse has become more common since the beginning of this century (Gagnon, 1990), although the trend toward casual sex abated in the 1980s due to fear of AIDS. We can assume that for many teenagers, lack of opportunity rather than lack of interest is the limiting factor in frequency of intercourse. Once teenagers establish a steady dating relationship, there usually is a rapid transition to sexual encounters (de Gaston et al., 1995; Miller & Dyk, 1993; Thornton, 1990).

Why has premarital sex become normative in the West over the past few decades? No one theory can account for adolescent or adult sexuality. Although family socialization appears to be important, many factors work in combination to dispose young people toward early intercourse (Crockett et al., 1996). With the advent of safe, effective birth control, sex and reproduction no longer are inextricably linked. Unwanted pregnancies can be aborted, although it would be misguided to view abortion (as some young people do) as "no big deal." Certainly there are fewer social sanctions nowadays regarding premarital sexual activity, especially when it occurs within a loving or committed relationship (Herold & Marshall, 1996). Constant references to and depiction of sexual behavior in the media keep sex on people's minds (Strouse et al., 1995; Ward, 1995). And the long interval between puberty and marriage makes it more difficult for sexualized adolescents to wait.

First intercourse is a milestone, a rite of passage representing a significant step toward independence and adulthood. In the past, losing one's virginity signified an emotional commitment between two people and a degree of intimacy not easily achieved by other means. Today, many adolescents (and some preadolescents) view first intercourse as an achievement or as a way of gaining adult status (Netting, 1992; Paikoff, 1995; Pratt & Eglash, 1990), although guilt is not an uncommon reaction (Donald, Lucke, Dunne, & Raphael, 1995).

Most males and females have their first intercourse during the late teenage years, before marriage. Results from two 1995 government surveys (released in 1997) indicated that the proportion of American teenagers (15 to 19 years old) who have had sexual intercourse at least once dropped for the first time in 20 years (*The New York Times*, May 2, 1997, p. A20). Fifty percent of girls reported having sex, compared to 55% in a 1990 survey. In 1970, only 29% of the girls reported having had sex. Fifty-five percent of the boys surveyed in 1995 reported having sex at least once, a drop from 60% in 1988. Seventy-five percent of the girls said they used birth control the first time they had sex, up from 64% in 1988. Decreasing sexual activity and greater use of condoms may be responsible for the recent decline in the teenage birth rate.

The age of first intercourse is significant. Adolescents (males and females) who become sexually active at younger ages typically display a variety of problem behaviors and are at greater risk for outcomes such as alcohol abuse, unwanted pregnancy, academic failure, and sexually transmitted diseases, including human immunodeficiency virus (HIV) infection (Bingham & Crockett, 1996; Capaldi, Crosby, & Stoolmiller, 1996; Crockett et al., 1996; Sonnenstein, 1986; Tubman, Windle, & Windle, 1996).

We have already seen that early-maturing girls experience intercourse before later-maturing girls (Billy & Udry, 1985). By the time they are 19 years old, males and females who have had early first intercourse have had more partners and more regular sexual intercourse than those who become sexually active later. The negative outcomes associated with early intercourse persist over the adolescent years (Koyle, Jensen, Olson, & Cundick, 1989; White & DeBlassie, 1992).

Early sexual experiences usually are unplanned, infrequent, and rarely involve close relationships with good communication between partners. The effect of alcohol and other drugs on adolescent judgment cannot be ignored (Crockett et al., 1996; Leigh & Aramburu, 1996; Warzak, Grow, Poler, & Walburn, 1995). Harvey and Spigner (1995) surveyed male and female high school students. They found that alcohol consumption was the strongest predictor of sexual activity for males and females, although drinking may provide an anticipatory excuse (Leigh & Arambaru, 1996). We should not interpret an initial sexual encounter as a transition to a new stage of sexual involvement or think that the sexual patterns of nonvirgin adolescents resemble those of married adults. Most teenagers are neither permanently nor continuously sexually active (Olsen, Jensen, & Greaves, 1991, p. 420). Older adolescents (17 or older) engaging in intercourse are more likely to be in committed, affectionate relationships and to use contraceptives (Faulkenberry, Vincent, James, & Johnson, 1987; Thornton, 1990).

Many females report that their first intercourse was not what they hoped for or expected (Guggino & Ponzetti, Jr., 1997). Instead, they felt exploited and guilty. Nancy Darling and her colleagues (1992) questioned 304 never-married undergraduates at a Midwestern state university about their sexual histories. Sixty percent of the females and 84% of the males reported experiencing sexual intercourse. The mean age of first sexual intercourse was 17.7 years for the females and 17.8 years for the males. The females were more likely than the males to be in committed relationships when first intercourse occurred. Due to a lack of planning, most did not use contraceptives. Females reported feeling less satisfied than males sexually and psychologically. They found first intercourse to be painful (41.4%), unsatisfying (22.2%), and uncomfortable (11.1%). Only 27.8% of the males reported being dissatisfied, although 22.2% said that they were drunk and didn't remember.

Boys' apparently greater enjoyment of sex may reflect the high rate of failure in girls to achieve orgasm during sexual intercourse. Despite their high motivation, most teenage girls rarely if ever achieve orgasm during intercourse and apparently do not get as much physical satisfaction as they would like. Females generally become increasingly orgasmic with increasing age, suggesting a lessening of learned inhibitions over time (McConaghy, 1995).

In 1988, Roche and Ramsbey (1993) surveyed 268 mostly white, Roman Catholic students attending a state college in southern New England. Most lived at home with their parents and commuted to school. The students were asked what they considered to be proper sexual behavior at five stages of dating, what they told their peers about their sexual activities, and what they thought their peers were doing. They were also questioned about cohabitation, AIDS, and their views about premarital sex. The results were compared to those of a similar study done in 1983.

Females in the 1988 sample reported lower levels of intercourse at all five dating stages than did those in the 1983 sample. Males in the 1988 sample reported higher levels of sexual intercourse than did those in the earlier survey. Attitudes of males and females were more conservative, apparently reflecting fear of contracting AIDS. Attitudinal change was greater than behavioral change. As hypothesized, in both samples, male and female students showed an increase in permissive attitudes at each succeeding dating stage. Males displayed more permissive attitudes than females about what is proper during the early stages of dating (before love and commitment) and toward cohabitation.

Partly because of the risks associated with unprotected, casual sexual behavior, most female adolescents prefer sex within a committed, affectionate relationship. Casual sex, more acceptable to males (Leigh & Aramburu, 1996), is becoming less common. The current trend is toward males and females sharing responsibility for sexual encounters. Most teenagers report that their first intercourse experiences were with older partners. As noted previously, more than males, females are likely to feel exploited after sex, especially when they were drunk or high or had sex with someone who was not a steady partner (Donald et al., 1995; Warzak et al., 1995).

Age of first intercourse is related to ethnic group status. African-American males have intercourse about 2 years on the average before white and Hispanic males (Paikoff, 1995). Early first intercourse is associated with lowered college attendance for white females and lower school grades for white males (Billy, Landale, Grady, & Zimmerle, 1988).

Girls are less likely to be sexually active at a young age if they are religious or more career or academically motivated, or if they live with their fathers. Having a less educated mother and being the daughter of a teenage mother are associated with early sexual activity. Adolescents who reside in unstable families and who have mothers who were teenage parents become sexually active at earlier ages, perhaps reflecting reduced parental monitoring and exposure to permissive sexual norms (Crockett et al., 1996; Forste & Heaton, 1988).

## COGNITIVE ABILITY AND ADOLESCENT SEXUAL DECISION MAKING

Understanding and making decisions about relationships and sexual behavior involves complex cognitive and emotional processes. Many of the elements of formal operational thinking and moral reasoning discussed in Chapters 4 and

**Table 9-4  Reasoning Abilities Involved in Sexual Decision Making**

- generating and evaluating hypothetical scenarios
- generating and evaluating alternative actions
- decision-making abilities
- perspective taking
- thinking about the future and anticipating consequences
- being concerned about the welfare of oneself and one's partner
- adolescent egocentrism, including feelings of invulnerability

5 are necessary for responsible sexual decision making (Gordon, 1996; Hubbs-Tait & Garmon, 1995). These include generating and evaluating alternatives, engaging in perspective taking, reasoning about probability, thinking about the future, and being concerned about the welfare of oneself and one's partner (Gordon, 1996; Jadack, Hyde, Moore, & Keller, 1995).

Adolescent reasoning and judgment also play an important role in thinking about commitments, having sex, using contraceptives, and deciding whether or not to abort an unwanted pregnancy. Adolescent reasoning is limited by immature decision-making abilities and adolescent egocentrism, including a sense of invulnerability (Foster & Sprinthall, 1992; Franz & Reardon, 1992; Galotti, Kozberg, & Appleman, 1990; C.P. Gordon, 1996; D.E. Gordon, 1990; Green, Johnson, & Kaplan, 1992; Schecterman & Hutchinson, 1991).

Adolescents who become pregnant typically are not prepared to analyze their alternatives or to anticipate the consequences of their sexual behaviors. The ability to generate and evaluate hypothetical situations promotes good decision making. Asking oneself questions like "What types of birth control are available to me?" or "What might happen if I engage in unprotected sex?" set the stage for more responsible behavior. Engaging in perspective taking and reasoning about probable occurrences also allow adolescents to make informed judgments about the consequences of various sexual actions. Providing adolescents with tasks that stimulate formal operational reasoning, such as role playing being pregnant or caring for an infant, might improve sexual and contraceptive decision making (C.P. Gordon, 1996; D.E. Gordon, 1990).

When presented with an opportunity to be sexual with another person, adolescents must make hard choices (see Table 9-4). Material we have covered previously suggests that adolescent judgment is not equivalent to that of an average adult. Often there is inconsistency in young people's values and attitudes. Impulsive behavior might result. As we have seen, adolescents are prone to have sex for the wrong reasons, including peer pressure, wanting to feel more grown up, or simply surrendering to intense desire. They weigh the anticipated discomfort or inconvenience of birth control too heavily and its effectiveness too lightly (Loewenstein & Furstenberg, 1991).

## CONTRACEPTION

Sixteen-year-old Fran claims that if a condom is close at hand, she uses it. But if it is inconvenient to obtain, she'll have sex without one. She feels regret after not taking precautions, but the feeling quickly passes. She has had scares, as have her friends. She admits that she almost never uses birth control when she has sex.

Sexual risk takers like Fran have multiple partners and rarely if ever use contraception. Careless sexual behavior is but one element of the cluster of high-risk behaviors observed in many adolescents, perhaps reflecting the feeling of invulnerability with which many adolescents face their everyday lives. According to the Centers for Disease Control (1992), about one out of five high school students (twice as many males as females) have had four or more sex partners. High-risk youths are not necessarily more likely than those at low risk to use condoms (Stiffman, Dore, & Cunningham, 1994). Lower-risk adolescents have one mutually faithful, uninfected partner and use condoms consistently and correctly. No-risk adolescents abstain from sexual activity (Centers for Disease Control, 1988; Luster & Small, 1994). Most sex education programs emphasize **abstinence** as a viable alternative to reluctant sexual activity.

Pregnancy risk is determined by two clusters of risk-related behaviors: sexual activity and contraceptive behavior. Sexual activity includes not only sexual behavior, but also the timing of first intercourse, the frequency of sexual encounters, and the number of sexual partners. Contraceptive behavior includes contraceptive decision making at first intercourse and during subsequent sexual encounters and the effectiveness of contraceptives employed (Jorgensen, 1993).

Like Fran, most young people are sexually active whether or not contraceptives are available. Almost half (47%) of sexually active youths admit that they never use contraceptives (Centers for Disease Control and Prevention, 1995). Murstein and Mercy's (1994) study of sexual behavior at a Northeastern college revealed that only one-third of the sexually active students reported practicing safe sex consistently, with male students feeling less concerned about safety than female students. A study of Mexican adolescents revealed that about one-third of the male adolescents (students and workers) used contraception and about a quarter of the female students and a tenth of the female workers used contraception (Huerta-Franco, Diaz de Leon, & Malacara, 1996). Although the percentage of adolescents using contraceptives (especially condoms and pills) has increased over the past decade, most of those who use birth control methods do not use them consistently (Hayes, 1987; Jorgensen, 1993; McCormick, Izzo, & Folcik, 1985; Poppen, 1994). If there is discussion about contraception, it usually occurs after sex rather than before (Poppen, 1994).

Those who admit to themselves that they are sexually active are more likely to use contraceptives. As emotional commitment to a relationship and frequency of intercourse rise, teenagers become more willing to employ contraceptives (Thornton, 1990). Being involved in an affectionate relationship apparently motivates partners to minimize the chance of pregnancy and AIDS. This is an important point because partners seem to have more influence than parents or peers regarding whether contraception is used (Jorgensen, 1993).

Many parents give their children a straightforward, two-part message: "I prefer that you delay intercourse, but if you are sexually active, make sure you take proper precautions." Stated more directly, if you do not want to become pregnant or get AIDS, either avoid intercourse or use contraceptives. That 1 out of 10 teenage girls becomes pregnant each year suggests that many adolescents are not buying this advice (Green et al., 1992). Because we mistakenly associate pregnancy with females rather than with males, most research on contraceptive use has focused on females. Sonenstein (1986) concluded that the factors that influence contraceptive use do not differ for the two genders, although female sexual self-concept is more oriented to contraceptive responsibility than is male sexual self-concept (Breakwell & Millward, 1997).

It is not hard to understand why adolescents avoid using contraceptives during their early, unplanned intercourse experiences. It usually takes several months for teenagers to admit to themselves that they are sexually active. It is harder to understand why so many sexually active teenagers continue to take chances in the face of serious negative consequences (Loewenstein & Furstenberg, 1991). Why do so few sexually active teenagers use contraceptives consistently when they have so much to lose by becoming pregnant or by contracting a sexually transmitted disease?

When we ask teenagers about their reasons for not using birth control, (1) many reveal a poor understanding of fertility, (2) some contend that they're too young to become pregnant, (3) many are confused about the menstrual cycle, (4) they claim that they don't know how or where to get contraceptives, (5) they do not plan ahead for sexual encounters, (6) they have negative attitudes and feelings (including embarrassment) about using contraceptives, and (7) some want to become pregnant (Gordon, 1996; Green et al., 1992; Levinson, 1995; Pleck, Sonenstein, & Ku, 1990).

Thus, they don't think about it, don't want to use contraceptives, don't know much about them, or have none available. Consistent with the personal fable concept, many adolescent risk takers convince themselves that they cannot or will not get pregnant. Passion apparently overrides rational decision making (Darling et al., 1992).

However, cognitive factors such as beliefs about contraception do play an important role in sexual decision making (C.P. Gordon, 1996; D.E. Gordon, 1990; Green et al., 1992; Johnson & Green, 1993; Rosenthal, Cohen, & Biro, 1996; Stiffman et al., 1994). Planning for future sexual activity is inconsistent with the here-and-now thinking of some adolescents. Teenagers who have higher educational and vocational aspirations and better school performance are more consistent users of contraceptives. Many researchers note a link between alcohol and drug use and the onset of intercourse and contraceptive use (e.g., McLean & Flanigan, 1993). Those who do not drink during early sexual encounters are more likely to use contraceptives.

Conception and contraception are not simple topics. Lacking a good understanding of reproduction and contraception, many teenagers become pregnant accidentally, that is, using luck, rhythm, douching, or withdrawal as a birth control method. To act responsibly, adolescents must admit to themselves that they are sexually active and face the delayed consequences of pregnancy and sexually transmitted diseases when they have unprotected intercourse. Being able to analyze the probability of becoming pregnant or seriously ill without contraceptive use and considering alternative courses of action allows adolescents to inhibit impulsive actions that they might later regret (Arnett, 1990).

Socialization and social learning models of contraceptive use emphasize the role of learned attitudes and values, particularly through family relationships (e.g., Huerta-Franco et al., 1996). Girls are more likely to use contraceptives when parents support this action (Balassone, 1991; Brooks-Gunn & Furstenberg, 1989; Handler, 1990; Keith, McCreary, Collins, Smith, & Bernstein, 1991; Luster & Small, 1994; Morrison, 1985; Murstein & Mercy, 1994).

Offering contraceptives to adolescents remains controversial. Should teenagers have the right to obtain birth control devices (or abortions) without their parents' knowledge and consent? Do parents have the right to be notified about any decision their child makes that could affect the child's health? Will adolescents even try to obtain contraceptives if they must first get their parents' permission?

Unless teenagers are guaranteed confidentiality regarding their birth control practices, many will avoid contraception and still be sexually active. Although courts so far have upheld adolescents' rights to obtain birth control without parental consent or knowledge, about half of the states now require some notification or consent from parents before a judge will allow an abortion. Optimally, parents and schools will provide young people with information about reproduction and contraception and create meaningful programs that address sexual responsibility. Such an approach has been successful in Canada, Sweden, and England, where sexually active adolescents are much more likely to use contraceptives (Forrest, 1990). Adolescents' stated willingness to use contraception is not enough, as it is not likely to be translated into behavior (Lagana & Hayes, 1993).

---

## SPOTLIGHT • Early Intercourse, Contraception, and Pregnancy among African-American Adolescents

Although pregnant teenagers come from all socioeconomic, racial, and ethnic groups, premature coital activity and pregnancy occur proportionately more frequently among minority youth (Stanton et al., 1993). African-American teenagers make up about 14% of the adolescent population in the United States but account for 28% of all births and 47% of births to unwed teenagers. In 1995, the percentage of African-American babies born out of wedlock slipped to 69.5% from 70.4% the previous year. The African-American teenage birth rate has dropped 17% since 1991 (U.S. Census Bureau, National Center for Health Statistics, 1996).

Many disadvantaged youth regard sex as a way of achieving intimacy in an environment that is frequently hostile and depressing. About half of all African-American females conceive outside of wedlock; most choose to have and raise the child. Their families generally are tolerant of early sexual behavior and pregnancy. Teenage pregnancy and parenting by African-American adolescents occur so commonly that some consider the role of mother normative and developmentally appropriate for this population. Pregnancy for many of these girls is complicated by a variety of serious

**About half of African-American females conceive out of wedlock.**

health problems (such as premature labor) that threaten the health of mother or child (Hayes, 1987; Sandven & Resnick, 1990; Smith & Udry, 1985; Stanton et al., 1993; Zabin & Hayward, 1993).

Pete and DeSantis (1990) interviewed five recently delivered or pregnant African-American 14-year-olds to learn what led them to initiate sexual activity and to maintain their pregnancy. The girls had difficulty describing the factors that influenced their actions. They did not plan to have intercourse, they maintained, and were not prepared for motherhood. Several expressed a desire to have a trusting and loving relationship with a boy. They said they did not believe that at age 14 they could become pregnant or they relied upon their partners to use contraceptives. Their knowledge of contraceptives was limited.

Most of the girls reported having a lot of unsupervised time, watching TV or "hanging out" with their boyfriends. None was involved in extracurricular school activities. Although the girls described having good relationships with their mothers, they did not feel that they could discuss sex with them. Their main reaction to their pregnancies was denial, typically for several months. One girl said that "as long as I did not tell anyone I was pregnant, as far as I was concerned, I wasn't pregnant" (p. 151).

Because of the girls' ages, none of the mothers suggested marriage. All the teenage fathers provided some financial support and child care. The girls decided to keep the infant and raise it, citing their friends who did the same, the participation of their male partner, and their mother's approval. These girls' mothers blamed themselves, not their daughters, for the unfortunate turn of events. Compared to white adolescent mothers, African-American adolescent mothers are more likely to receive welfare, probably because they live independently as single parents. Marriage reduces the likelihood of being on welfare for both groups (Rudd, McKenry, & Nah, 1990).

## ADOLESCENTS AND AIDS: THE SILENT EPIDEMIC

Given their propensity for trying new things and living for the moment, adolescents are at risk for contracting sexually transmitted diseases, including AIDS (Thompson et al., 1996). (See Table 9-5.) AIDS is a disease characterized by the gradual loss of the immune system, the body's main defense against disease. The virus is spread through unprotected sexual contact, sharing of intravenous needles, and transfusions of infected blood products. Although they may lack symptoms, carriers can infect their sexual partners with the HIV virus. About 20% of AIDS patients are under 30 years of age, but because the incubation period is at least 8 years, many are believed to be infected as teenagers. By January 1996, 6,600 children under the age of 13 and 2,100 teenagers had been diagnosed with AIDS (Centers for Disease Control and Prevention, 1996; Youngstrom, 1991).

Poor, delinquent, incarcerated, and gay teenagers and those who run away from home are particularly susceptible. Studies of how well informed adolescents are about AIDS and its prevention have not produced consistent results. Over time, teenagers have become more aware of AIDS. However, there is still substantial confusion about certain AIDS-related topics, especially risk factors, transmission of HIV, and the use of condoms (Buysse, 1996). As with knowledge of contraceptives, knowledge of the disease by itself rarely translates into

**Table 9-5  Common Sexually Transmitted Diseases**

| Sexually Transmitted Disease | Symptoms and Comments |
| --- | --- |
| Chlamydia | Pain and burning during urination, discharge; caused by a parasite; most common STD; can cause female infertility |
| Crabs | Severe itching; parasitic infection |
| Cytomegelovirus (CMV) | Fever, fatigue, or no symptoms; symptoms may come and go |
| Genital herpes (Herpes simplex) | Pain or burning during urination; bumps, sores, and blisters on genitals; can be passed to fetus during labor; contagious when blisters appear; incurable |
| Genital warts | Warts on or near genitals or rectum; can lead to cancer |
| Gonorrhea | Pain or burning during urination; most females show no symptoms but all males show genital discharge; can cause heart, liver, and brain damage |
| Hepatitis B | Nausea, vomiting, stomach pain; can cause liver damage; mainly transmitted through sexual contact and by sharing infected needles |
| HIV/AIDS | Swollen glands, open sores, weight loss; incubation period varies widely; treatable but incurable |
| Syphilis | Sores, rashes, genital ulcers; can cause blindness, brain damage, and heart disease; can be transmitted to fetus |
| Trichomoniasis | Itching and rash around genitals |

(Adapted from Burroughs Wellcome Company, 1990)

**Sexually active teenagers underestimate their risk for contracting AIDS.**

safe sexual practices (Boyer, Shafer, & Tschann, 1997; Maticka-Tyndale, 1991; Roscoe & Kruger, 1990). And if AIDS has not become a deterrent to unprotected sex, what would?

A study of over 1,000 heterosexual Australian adolescents aged 17 to 20 years (Moore & Rosenthal, 1991) revealed only occasional use of condoms with regular or casual partners. About three-quarters of those surveyed reported believing that they had a less than average risk of contracting AIDS compared to their peers, despite the fact that at least half of them engaged in risky behaviors. About a quarter of the sample, the "risk and be damned" group, engaged in moderate- to high-risk behaviors with regular or casual partners and admitted that they were at significant risk of developing AIDS. Another quarter of the sample also engaged in high-risk behaviors but perceived themselves to be at low risk. These results suggest that a significant number of adolescents feel invulnerable to the threat of AIDS despite engaging in unsafe sexual practices.

Roscoe and Kruger (1990) interviewed 300 late adolescents regarding their knowledge of AIDS and their sexual practices. Although most were knowledgeable about AIDS transmission, only about one-third reported altering their behavior accordingly. Desiderato and Crawford (1995) surveyed 398 undergraduates about their disclosure of previous risky sexual behavior to current sexual partners. Within a 3-month period, two-thirds of the students had engaged in sexual intercourse, and one-third of these reported having sex with more than one partner. The students generally were not very disclosing to partners about their past risky behaviors. Almost half of the sexually active students reported not using a condom during their last sexual encounter. Only one-fourth said that they used condoms consistently. Alcohol use appeared to inhibit condom use.

Rather than using condoms consistently, many college students base their belief about the need for protection on how much risk they perceive in their current sexual environment and how much they like their partners (Thompson et al., 1996; Williams et al., 1992). They assume that if you know somebody well and trust that person, he or she is safe to sleep with. Some of the male participants in the Williams study explained that they used condoms only with risky partners, such as someone whom they had just met or someone who dressed provocatively. In a long-term relationship, they reasoned, there was much less to worry about (although many were concerned about the possibility of unwanted pregnancy).

Many did not view their college peers as a likely source of AIDS exposure. In reality, the superficial cues the students used to gauge their partner's health (appearance, personality) are in no way related to HIV status. Their potentially fatal belief provides a false sense of security. AIDS prevention efforts must emphasize adolescents' personal vulnerability to HIV infection and the fact that birth control pills, although protecting against pregnancy, provide no protection against sexually transmitted diseases. Prevention programs must help vulnerable teenagers take the consequences of their actions into account. They must also learn how to communicate comfortably with partners about using condoms. The role of alcohol in impairing judgment must also be addressed (Williams et al., 1992).

## SEXUAL HARASSMENT AND ASSAULT

*When I was in the seventh grade, a boy on my bus said nasty, unrepeatable things to me and touched my breasts. Now I wish that I had broken his wrist or at least told someone about it. But back then I thought that if I said anything, everyone would get mad at me or make fun of me, because this boy was very popular. So I kept quiet about it.*

*(15-year-old girl, quoted by Minton, 1994, p. 30)*

*When I was in the seventh grade, a group of boys in my math class would make crude remarks to me every day before class. . . . I felt ashamed of being a girl, and I despised my body and its changes. Even now, I hate to wear anything that draws too much attention to my chest.*

*(19-year-old girl, quoted by Minton, 1994, p. 30)*

*What really bothers me about girls is that they often say, "Why can't guys just like me for who I am, rather than for my body?"—and then they dress as if they want guys to look at their bodies. Wearing tight jeans and shirts isn't the best thing to do when you want guys to stop looking at your bodies. Try dressing modestly.*

*(16-year-old boy, quoted by Minton, 1994, p. 30)*

More than younger children and adults, adolescents are frequent targets of sexual victimization, which includes harassment, coercion, abuse, assault, and rape. **Sexual harassment**, which includes lewd comments, gestures, and un-

**Sexual harassment in schools creates a hostile learning environment.**

wanted sexual contact, is common during early and middle adolescence, especially in school. It is so common that many students accept sexual harassment as a fact of life (Trigg, Davis, Kirschner, Marolis, & Wittenstrom, 1995).

Victimization in school creates a hostile environment, which adversely affects victims' ability to learn or otherwise benefit from being in school. Adolescents are victimized mainly by peers (79%), but also by teachers, relatives, and strangers. Typically, victims are female and perpetrators are male, although many boys report being taunted by peers regarding issues of masculinity (e.g., being called gay). Occasionally, inexperienced males report being harassed by early-maturing girls who come on too strong.

In the past, the vast majority of instances of harassment went unreported, partly because about half of all victims (mainly boys) were not upset by the harassment and partly because students who were upset (mainly girls) believed that there was nothing they could do about it. A high level of exposure to music videos and membership in an unsatisfactory or nonintact family are associated with acceptance of sexual harassment, especially for females (Miller et al., 1993; Roscoe, Strouse, & Goodwin, 1994; Strouse, Goodwin, & Roscoe, 1994).

Alarmed by increasing numbers of lawsuits, school districts are beginning to pay more attention to sexual harassment, including sexual taunting and threats. According to new federal guidelines, schools that do not take appropriate steps to stop harassment could be in violation of a federal law that prohibits sexual discrimination in schools receiving federal funding. In response, some schools have prohibited hand holding or kissing. While some critics claim that schools that suspend students for such actions are overreacting, others complain that most schools still fail to respond adequately to complaints of persistent harassment. School districts feel caught in the middle, as they are not harassers but may be liable to pay heavy damages if it can be shown that students face a hostile learning environment and their school fails to act. Given inconsistent lower court rulings, the U.S. Supreme Court may eventually have to decide whether schools are liable when they are not the source but are the location of the harassment (Lewin, 1996).

Students simply do not feel safe in an environment in which others can offer humiliating suggestions or treat them in an offensive manner. But children and adolescents often are reluctant to report offenders; they are afraid of being rejected by their peers (Kutner, 1994). In a survey of high school students commissioned by the American Association of University Women and conducted by Louis Harris and Associates in 1993, 85% of the girls and 76% of the boys reported experiencing unwanted and unwelcome sexual behavior that interfered with their lives (*NJEA Review*, March 1994). Two-thirds of girls and 42% of boys reported being touched, grabbed, or groped in the hallways of their schools. Significant numbers of students reported being targets of sexual comments, gestures, and rumors and having their clothes pulled at in a sexual way or even having their clothes pulled down or off. Eleven percent said they had been forced to do something sexual other than just kissing. About half the students reported that the first episode of harassment occurred in middle or junior high school.

Girls especially reported that the hostile environment created by unwanted sexual advances and comments in school hallways and classrooms interferes with their ability to pay attention and study and dampens their self-esteem. Harassment sometimes causes them to stay home from school or cut a class. Seventy percent of the girls and 24% of the boys said they were "very upset" or "somewhat upset" after being harassed. A study of Canadian high school girls linked sexual harassment and assault to subsequent emotional disorders and suicide attempts (Bagley, Bolitho, & Betrand, 1997).

To socially immature boys, showing disrespect to ("dissing") girls is a way of demonstrating their manhood. They find that they can gain peer approval by publicly propositioning or touching girls in an offensive manner. Although such actions increase girls' cynicism about boys and about having close relationships with them, about one out of three boys and girls in the study considered such harassment "no big deal."

It is important that teenagers who feel powerless be taught that they should not ignore harassment; they are entitled to a safe and comfortable learning environment. They must be encouraged to notify a counselor or another adult or learn to confront the harasser directly. Most important, they should not blame themselves for the disturbing encounter. Secondary schools need to create grievance policies on harassment that are accessible and understandable to teenagers. Teachers should talk to students about sexual harassment, respect, and sensitivity. Unfortunately, many teachers tolerate sexual harassment and do not take sexist remarks seriously (Minton, 1995b, 1996; Orenstein, 1994). Antioch College's sexual offense policy, requiring that initiators of sexual activities first request a partner's verbal consent for each act, sensitized men on campus to sexual harassment and date rape issues. However, the policy divided the campus and elicited considerable media attention and debate concerning political correctness and adolescent romance (Vest, 1996).

Small and Kerns (1993) sampled 1,149 adolescent females about unwanted sexual activity initiated by their peers. Twenty percent of the sample reported such contact during the past year. One-third of this group said they had been forced to have intercourse, and the remaining two-thirds reported being touched by boyfriends or dates against their will. Most babies born to teenage mothers are fathered by adults, leading many states to enforce their statutory rape laws that prohibit sex between adults and minors (Navarro, 1996). It is not clear how many of these young mothers are victims of sexual abuse (Holmes, 1997). It is important that all adolescents be taught how to identify sexual exploitation, understand the importance of giving consent for sexual advances, and recognize **date rape** for what it is: sexual assault (Hannon, Kuntz, Van Laar, Williams, & Hall, 1996; Kershner, 1996; Mills & Granoff, 1992).

A group of California boys known as the "Spur Posse" received much national attention in early 1993. This group of 20 to 30 teenagers literally scored with every sexual conquest. Some of the girls admitted that they submitted to the boys' overtures because they wanted to be popular. Eventually, charges were dropped for all but one of the boys.

After getting out of jail, unrepentant members of the gang returned to school to a heroes' welcome. The boys and most of their friends defended their actions, accusing the girls of being promiscuous troublemakers and getting what they deserved. Some of their parents expressed pride in their sons' virility and defended their actions with a "boys will be boys" rationalization. Other parents were mortified at their children's actions and attitudes. A 16-year-old member of the gang pleaded no contest to a charge of lewd conduct and was sentenced to 9 months in a juvenile detention center. His 10-year-old victim said, "I have been very upset about what the boys have said about me and what they did to me. It is not a joke. It has hurt me very much." The school planned assemblies on date rape and harassment (Gross, 1993; *The New York Times,* April 29, 1993).

It is not unusual for teenage girls to find themselves involved in abusive relationships with boyfriends (Pipes & LeBov-Keeler, 1997). "When I started going out with him [at age 14], things went really fast. After a week, he was saying 'I love you.' But the deeper we got into it, the more controlling he became. He would tell me, 'You can't be more than an arm's length away.' When we were in a car, I had to be right next to him or on his lap. He isolated me to the point where I had only him and his friends" (18-year-old girl named Janet, quoted by Harris, 1996, p. 4). Janet described how her boyfriend grabbed her violently one night after drinking heavily and threatened to kill her if she didn't spend more time with him. Despite the red welts on her arm, she did not tell her parents about the incident. Eventually, she found the courage to break up with her boyfriend.

Like Janet, fear of violence prevents some girls from ending the relationship. Abusive relationships during adolescence are a precursor to domestic violence in adult households. Many of these girls have been physically, sexually, or emotionally abused by their own families and have low-self esteem or feelings of unworthiness. For some, their insecurities prevent them from confronting their abuser (Kalof, 1995). Often they blame themselves for the abuse. Teenagers need help in recognizing patterns of victimization and abuse. They need to learn that there are rules about how people treat each other, how to leave relationships in which they are not respected, and that they need to seek adult help (Bonate & Jessell, 1996; Kutner, 1991b).

A majority of college men and women report experiencing some form of sexual aggression during high school. Not uncommonly, a female adolescent is assaulted in her own home by a boyfriend or acquaintance of the same age. Many males do not take females' resistance to sexual advances seriously, believing that when women say "no" they really mean "yes" (Mills & Granoff, 1992; Nurius, Norris, Dimeff, & Graham, 1996). Some boys maintain that if they have spent money on a girl, they have the right to pressure her for sex (Miller et al., 1993).

The incidence of rape is higher for teenagers than for any other age group. It is an underreported crime, partly because many teenage girls fear that they will be blamed by their parents or scorned by their peers. In their confusion about appropriate sexual boundaries, some teenage girls who are assaulted by their boyfriends or dates do not realize that they have been raped (Small & Kerns, 1993). They often feel guilty or responsible for the attack (Rickel & Hendren, 1993), perhaps because they initiated the date, went to the boy's apartment, or got drunk (Muehlenhard, 1988). Some males justify sexual coercion by citing various "rape myths," for example, that girls who say "no" don't really mean it or that spending money on a girl entitles a male to sexual favors (Johnson, Kuck, & Schander, 1997). Rape prevention programs must reach out to males and females so that both genders can learn to communicate their expectations and desires to their partners without using coercion (Feltey, Ainslie, & Geib, 1991; Kershner, 1996; Murray, 1995a). (Incest and sexual abuse of adolescents are discussed in Chapter 13.)

A significant number of adult sex offenders initiate their sexual offenses during adolescence. Offenders are obsessed with satisfying their own needs, regardless of the consequences for their victims. They usually have low self-esteem, feel anger toward women, are socially isolated, and lack the social skills necessary to maintain a mutually satisfying relationship (Bolton & MacEachran, 1988; Vizard, Monck, & Misch, 1995). Many have been sexually and emotionally victimized themselves. "Thoughts of building up to a sexual relationship are nonexistent; immediate sexual gratification is the goal" (Lakey, 1994, p. 756).

## SEX EDUCATION: WHAT DO TEENAGERS WANT AND NEED TO KNOW?

Regardless of their parents' wishes, most teenagers are sexually active by their late teenage years. Those who are sexually experienced are not necessarily well informed about fertility, reproduction, and contraception, let alone intimacy, expressing feelings, and close relationships. The bottom line is that, for most adolescents, the immediate consequences of sex (pleasure, peer status, feeling grown up) outweigh the potential long-term risks (pregnancy and disease). Admittedly, it is hard to keep one's mind on safety issues or fertility during the heat of passion (Zabin & Hayward, 1993).

Although parents know that their adolescent children think about sex and have sexual feelings, sexuality is not a topic that most adults are comfortable discussing, at least in personal terms (Lefkowitz, Kahlbaugh, & Sigman, 1996). They feel unprepared, unsure of what to say. After all, who took them aside when they were young and patiently answered their questions? Many parents suspect that they are not particularly well informed about sexual development (Hockenberry-Eaton, Richman, DiIorio, Rivero, & Maibach, 1996). Further, some parents fear that discussing sexual matters with their children gives the appearance of condoning premarital sex. This could be a legitimate concern if parents speak just about birth control and not about values and relationships (Brooks-Gunn & Furstenberg, 1989; Stanton et al., 1993). *Thought Question: What might parents be communicating to their children by not broaching the topics of sex and reproduction?*

Although not necessarily seen as desirable, adolescent sexuality is accepted as inevitable in most industrialized countries (Jones et al., 1985). Policymakers in these countries focus on preventing teenage pregnancy rather than preventing sexual intercourse. In Sweden, sex education begins at age 7. Sexuality is considered to be a natural part of education (Trost, 1985, 1990). Parents and teachers discuss sexual matters openly and honestly. At dinner, Swedish children bring up topics like masturbation, homosexuality, orgasm, abortion, and AIDS. Sex educators emphasize self-respect and respect for others. Even though Swedish teenagers are sexually active at a slightly younger age than those in the United States, the rate of unwanted pregnancies in the United States is three times higher (Lohr, 1987). Like their counterparts in the United States, Japanese parents have little to say to their children about sex. Still, Japanese teenagers are far less sexually active than teenagers in the United States.

This is not to say that parents in the United States should lecture their children about reproduction and fertility or make dramatic moral pronouncements about good and evil. It is more helpful for parents (or a knowledgeable surrogate) to help children explore various scenarios so that they know what their alternatives are and are prepared to make good decisions. Teenagers need to know where they can go for help in a crisis situation. It is also beneficial for parents to share with their children some of their own dating concerns and experiences during their adolescent years. Parents can clearly express their values and let their children know that if they are confused or in trouble, they will not be criticized. It also makes sense for parents to take advantage of opportunities provided by TV shows like *The Wonder Years*, *Melrose Place*, and *Beverly Hills 90210*, which depict dramatically some of the complex issues of adolescent sexuality. Movies and popular songs also raise sexual issues. Such discussions are most useful before children find themselves in awkward situations. (See Table 9-6.)

The most common theme in sex education is abstinence. Although hailed by our ancestors, virginity has acquired a bad reputation among young people.

**Table 9.6  Talking to Adolescents About Sex**

Children usually are more willing to discuss sex and reproduction before puberty.

Ask sensitive questions to determine their knowledge of the consequences of careless sexual activity.

Let your children know what your values are and why you have them.

If you are comfortable doing so, provide accurate information about reproduction in an accepting and matter-of-fact way, but avoid preaching.

If you are not comfortable discussing sex and reproduction with your children, give them a book to read that is appropriate for their age.

Meaningful discussions include topics like dating, relationships, values, and the possible consequences of careless behavior.

Help children view sexual behavior as an expression of love and as a source of pleasure in an intimate relationship.

If it is consistent with your values, consider offering the following message: your (mother, father) and I urge you to not have sex until you are older, but if you do, it is important that you take proper precautions to avoid pregnancy or a sexually-transmitted disease like AIDS.

Teach your child assertiveness skills to avoid being pressured into doing something that he/she does not want to do.

(From Jaffe, 1997)

Teenage virgins find themselves "in the closet" because they are afraid of being judged as nerdy by their presumably more experienced peers. Most parents favor abstinence during adolescence, believing that sex outside of marriage is wrong. Other supporters of abstinence argue that simply preaching chastity without providing accurate information about sexuality and reproduction is naive. In many school systems, various groups wage legal battles concerning what information to provide to teenagers and how to present it.

Providing adolescents with information about sexuality and reproduction is the most widely practiced approach to prevention. Teenagers garner most of their sexual information from peers, many of whom are as poorly informed as they are. For example, girls might believe that they can become pregnant only when they are menstruating or that birth control pills cause cancer. Sex education from parents usually is offered after something bad happens—when someone they know becomes pregnant or is raped. Parents who do discuss sexual matters with their children usually do so after their children are sexually active, which may be as early as 12 years of age. This is a case of too little too late, since half of first pregnancies during adolescence occur within 6 months of the first sexual encounter.

## SEX EDUCATION IN THE SCHOOLS

The initiation of school-based sex education programs in the 1970s generated heated controversy, despite the bare-bones information they provided ("This is how babies are made") and their simple but straightforward messages ("Sex is not dirty but wait until marriage"). Attempts to initiate a family life curriculum in elementary school still meet resistance from parents who feel that teaching about sexuality and reproduction robs young children of their innocence and might confuse or upset them. But a 1991 Gallup poll reported that 87% of Americans favored sex education. Sex education does not encourage students to be sexually active (Blau & Gullotta, 1993; Furstenberg, Moore, & Peterson, 1986). Bringing parents into the process of selecting materials to teach "sexual literacy" reduces some opposition (Shaheen, 1994).

Very few elementary schools have sex education programs. Middle school programs usually are brief (8 to 10 hours) and emphasize the bodily changes of puberty, reproductive anatomy, and dating. Information about family planning, contraception, sexual relationships, and abortion often is part of the high school sex education curriculum. School programs usually are either abstinence focused or comprehensive in nature. The federal government will only fund programs that emphasize abstinence (*The New York Times*, July 23, 1997, p. A19). Critics maintain that abstinence-only programs may do more harm than good because so many high school students are sexually active and need good information about protecting themselves from pregnancy and sexually transmitted diseases (Petersen, 1997). Most programs encourage abstinence and emphasize the benefits of protection and having fewer partners. They try to help teenagers make sensible decisions about sexual behavior (Blau & Gullotta, 1993; Christopher, 1995; Katchadourian, 1990). The comprehensive approach to sex education takes into account personal, social, and cognitive factors (Christopher, 1995; Whitehead, 1994–1995). It presents abstinence as an alternative but recognizes that many or most adolescents are sexually active.

To avoid controversy, some school systems avoid topics such as homosexuality, abortion, masturbation, and sexual pleasure. Some programs include units on puberty, dating, attraction to the other gender, peer pressure, family planning, consequences of teenage pregnancy, and sexually transmitted diseases such as gonorrhea. It is preferable to offer these programs in middle school when students are more open to different ideas (Olsen, Weed, Nielsen, & Jensen, 1992; Olson et al., 1991). Some sex education teachers have their students adopt and care for a raw egg during so-called egg week. Students must supervise their egg or find someone (an egg sitter) to do it for them, thus learning about the burden of providing constant care.

## Recommendations

Are school-based sex education programs getting the job done? Outcome studies concerning the impact of these programs on either abstinence or contraceptive behavior are not that encouraging (Whitehead, 1994–1995). Although students learn about sexuality and reproduction, they are not necessarily more careful (Boyer et al., 1997; Buysse & Van Ost, 1997). Sex education alone does not appear to reduce the rate of teen pregnancy. Still, it is a necessary component of pregnancy prevention programs (Ubell, 1995).

Comprehensive programs that include the family, the school, and peer counselors have been successful in delaying the initiation of coitus, increasing condom use, and thus reducing the rate of unwanted pregnancies (Kirby, 1994).

Because these programs are multidimensional, it is not clear what components are effective. Nevertheless, older teenagers (especially females) who have a stake in their future and who have meaningful goals and aspirations are less likely to jeopardize their futures through careless sexual behavior (Blau & Gullotta, 1993; Rauch-Elnekave, 1994).

Effective sex education requires that teenagers be shown how they will benefit from avoiding disease and unwanted pregnancy. They need to be taught, through role playing, games, and homework, how to obtain and use protection and about alternatives to intercourse, including masturbation (Whitehead, 1994–1995). They need to be able to recognize "lines" intended to manipulate them into having sex and rejoinders to those lines. Depending on the children's age, they must learn either to wait until they are older or to avoid unprotected intercourse.

Basic components of such a policy include easy access to and effective use of contraception, postponing first intercourse, and emphasizing the benefits of abstinence. It is important that teenagers be given basic reproductive information. The interpersonal aspects of sexuality also require greater coverage. Noncoital sexual expression could be presented as an alternative, along with advice on how to refuse unwanted sexual advances and reasons for saying no (Whitehead, 1994–1995).

Many teenagers need problem-solving, assertiveness, and decision-making skills to protect them from their own impulses and peer pressure. "Teenagers must be capable of comprehending and evaluating the consequences of their actions, be assertive in communicating their needs and beliefs, and feel competent regarding their feelings and themselves. Thus, even if a teenager has knowledge, she or he may still cause an unwanted pregnancy because she or he failed to think through a behavioral decision, or because she or he could not emit the behavioral responses necessary for avoidance" (Blau & Gullotta, 1993, p. 191).

Most efforts to prevent teenage pregnancy are directed to females, reflecting the cultural assumption that pregnancy prevention is a female problem. Meyer (1991) suggests that males have greater influence than females on sexual decisions and that male contraceptive behavior is more in need of change. Girls usually depend on "male methods" of contraception, including condom use and withdrawal. Boys generally know little about female reproductive cycles and contraceptives. Because males are more persistent in making sexual advances and sometimes less committed in the relationship, they need to know more about the care and use of condoms (Yesmont, 1992).

Should high schools provide condoms to students? Many school districts provide condoms to students after counseling them about safe sex. Some districts require parental consent. Although such a policy undoubtedly reduces the risks of pregnancy and AIDS, it is not known whether easy access to condoms increases sexual activity. School personnel often report that students who accept condoms already are sexually active but most have not purchased contraceptives. A final point: sex education is helpful, perhaps necessary, but it does not substitute for a family environment in which parents and children feel close to each other and can discuss almost anything.

''We should also make clear to our children that sex is not a weapon or tool, but an intense expression of love and a desire for mutual pleasure. Sex should not be used to enhance one's popularity, keep a boyfriend or girlfriend interested, defy one's parents, counter loneliness, be one of the crowd, prove one's manhood or maturity, or avoid hurting someone's feelings'' (Brody, 1986).

## SUMMARY

**1.** Sexual maturation is one of the most distinctive biological features of adolescence and potentially the most problematic. Fertility and sexual desire are important elements of the process of becoming an adult. Unfortunately, reproductive maturity emerges before most young people develop the judgment and responsibility needed to make good decisions about sexual behavior.

**2.** About half of U.S. teenagers are sexually experienced by the age of 19 years, with first intercourse occurring at about age 16. Relatively few teenagers use condoms consistently during intercourse, resulting in about 1 million unwanted pregnancies each year and increasing the risk of sexually transmitted diseases, including AIDS.

**3.** Biosocial models of adolescent sexuality attempt to integrate biological, cognitive, and social factors in explaining individual differences in adolescent sexuality. Key social factors include family, peer, and media influences. The meaning and the potential consequences of sexual activity are important cognitive factors.

**4.** It is difficult to know when a particular adolescent is ready to become sexually active or is capable of meeting a partner's emotional needs. Pseudosexuality refers to the phenomenon whereby adolescents have sex for the wrong reasons, such as peer pressure or coercion from partners. Adolescents need help in learning how to fend off unwanted sexual overtures.

**5.** In the latter part of this century, partly reflecting the availability of safe and reliable birth control, there has been an increase in premarital sex and a decline in the age at which teenagers begin to participate in romantic relationships. Some people refer to these changes as a sexual revolution. During the past 15 years, the AIDS virus has led to increased conservatism in sexual attitudes, if not sexual behavior, among adolescents.

**6.** Males generally are more liberal in their sexual attitudes than females. For males and females, sexual attitudes are more conservative than sexual behaviors. The so-called sexual double standard has lessened during the past 30 years, but it has not disappeared. Males and females maintain that they should have equal responsibility for sexual activity within romantic relationships, but males avoid participating in decisions about birth control. As relationships become more committed, sexual intercourse becomes more likely.

**7.** Although sexual orientation apparently is involuntary, people with nonnormative orientations often are rejected by family members and peers. It is important for adolescents to know that sexual preferences can change before sexual orientation stabilizes during early adulthood. Gay and lesbian adolescents who receive support from family members and who accept their sexuality cope best with intolerant or hostile reactions.

**8.** Masturbation is a safe and convenient way for adolescents to learn about their bodies and explore their sexuality. Self-stimulation and sexual fantasies usually precede heterosexual behaviors such as kissing, embracing, and fondling.

**9.** Premarital sex has become the norm for young people in the United States. Adolescents say that they engage in sex out of curiosity, for pleasure, to prove their popularity, or as a means of feeling close to a partner. Early sexual experiences usually are unplanned and infrequent. Older adolescents who have intercourse are more likely to be in committed relationships and to use contraception. Casual sex is more acceptable to males than to females.

**10.** Although use of contraceptives has increased over the past decade, many sexually active adolescents report that they rarely if ever use them. Many lack knowledge about conception and contraception, although some report that they do not want to use condoms or don't know where to get them. Admitting to themselves that they are sexually active and in a committed relationship increases adolescents' use of protection.

**11.** Poor, delinquent, and gay teenagers are at highest risk for contracting AIDS. Although most young people are aware of the risks of unprotected sex, knowledge of the disease does not automatically translate into safe sex practices. Many adolescents feel invulnerable to the threat of AIDS or assume that their partners are uninfected.

**12.** Most teenagers, both boys and girls, report that they have been sexually harassed, that is,

touched, groped, or verbally abused. Usually, the perpetrators are males and the victims are female. Victims often do not report harassment, either because they do not think it is important or because they believe that nothing will be done about it. Many teenage girls are abused by their boyfriends. The high incidence of harassment and assault implies that adolescents need instruction about what constitutes appropriate sexual boundaries.

**13.** Most teenagers are poorly informed about fertility, contraception, and reproduction, contributing to high rates of unwanted pregnancy and disease. Most parents have little to say to their children about sexual topics. Parents should start talking about reproduction before children reach puberty. Given the pressure on young people to be sexual, simply preaching abstinence usually is ineffective.

**14.** Most school programs advocate abstinence and attempt to help teenagers make good decisions about their sexual conduct. School programs usually address puberty, dating, family planning, contraception, and disease and typically ignore controversial topics such as masturbation, abortion, and homosexuality. Comprehensive programs that take into account personal, social, and cognitive factors are the most effective in reducing unwanted pregnancies.

# GLOSSARY

**Sexually transmitted diseases** Infectious diseases that are transmitted through sexual contact (e.g., syphilis)

**Social desirability effect** When participants in a study give socially acceptable rather than truthful responses

**Genital stage of psychosexual development** In Freud's model, the life period when sexual orientation is initially confused and ultimately finalized

**Pseudosexuality** Having sex for the wrong reasons

**Sexual double standard** Different standards of sexual conduct and accountability for males and females

**Gay-bashing** Violence and harassment directed toward gays and lesbians

**Coming out** Publicly declaring one's homosexual or lesbian sexual orientation

**Homosexual panic** Confusion, denial, guilt, shame, conflict, and self-hatred on discovering one's homosexual orientation

**Homophobia** Prejudice directed toward homosexuals
**Sexual confusion** Feelings of confusion and inadequacy regarding one's sexual feelings
**Abstinence** Refraining from sexual activity

**Sexual harassment** Lewd comments, gestures, and sexual contact directed toward an unwilling target
**Date rape** Sexual assault that occurs during a date

## THOUGHT QUESTIONS

**1.** What stake does society have in adolescent sexual behavior?

**2.** Why would an unmarried adolescent female want to become pregnant?

**3.** How can we understand the discrepancy between adolescents' sexual attitudes and behaviors?

**4.** Are gender differences in sexuality based more on biological differences or on socialization differences?

**5.** Is adolescence a reasonable time of life to select a life partner?

**6.** How might a homosexual orientation alter the developmental tasks of adolescence?

**7.** How can we tell when someone is ready to become sexually active?

**8.** What is the cost of the sexual double standard to male and female adolescents?

**9.** Given the potential risks of careless sexual activity, why do so many adolescents not use contraceptives?

**10.** If you were a sex education teacher, what methods would you use to help your students make good sexual choices?

# SELF-TEST

1. By what age are most teenagers fertile?
   a. 13
   b. 14
   c. 15
   d. 16

2. Average age of first intercourse in the United States is about
   a. 15
   b. 16
   c. 17
   d. 18

3. Freud referred to adolescence as the _____ psychosexual stage of development
   a. phallic
   b. genital
   c. erotic
   d. latency

4. Pseudosexuality mainly refers to
   a. sexual fantasies
   b. compulsive masturbation
   c. sexual inhibitions
   d. unwanted sexual encounters

5. The sexual revolution refers to changes in
   a. sexual attitudes
   b. sexual activity
   c. discussions of sexual topics
   d. all of the above

6. Usually the last step in homosexual identity formation is
   a. labeling oneself as gay
   b. passing as a heterosexual
   c. joining a homosexual organization
   d. coming out

7. What percent of teenage suicides occur among gays and lesbians?

    a. 15

    b. 30

    c. 45

    d. 60

8. Antihomosexual prejudice is called

    a. homophobia

    b. gay bashing

    c. homosexual panic

    d. the double standard

9. Perhaps the main factor disposing young people to early intercourse is

    a. parental permissiveness

    b. sex education

    c. effective birth control

    d. peer pressure

10. Perhaps the main factor inhibiting promiscuous behavior in adolescents is

    a. fear of AIDS

    b. fear of pregnancy

    c. religious prohibitions

    d. parental monitoring

11. Pregnancy risk is determined by what risk-related behavior?

    a. sexual activity

    b. contraceptive behavior

    c. a and b

    d. neither of the above

12. About what percent of sexually active youths admit never using contraception?

    a. 50

    b. 40

    c. 30

    d. 20

**13.** Sexual harassment includes which of the following?

a. lewd comments

b. obscene gestures

c. unwanted sexual contact

d. all of the above

**14.** The comprehensive approach to sex education

a. takes into account personal, social, and cognitive factors

b. presents abstinence as an alternative

c. recognizes that many or most adolescents are sexually active

d. all of the above

# TEN

# INTIMACY, PREGNANCY, MARRIAGE, AND CHILD REARING

## Preview Questions

1. Why does every society attempt, to some degree, to regulate its members' sexual conduct?

2. What role does dating play in adolescent identity formation?

3. Do adolescent boys and girls date for different reasons?

4. What conflicts do teenage girls face in their romantic relationships?

5. What is the connection between family relationships and romantic relationships?

6. Why might parents let their adolescent children have sex at home?

7. What is the profile of the typical unmarried, pregnant teenager?

8. How well equipped are adolescent mothers and fathers to care for their children?

9. Why are adolescent marriages particularly unstable?

## Disclosures

Having sex for the first time didn't change much. I guess I was still a little nervous, because we did not proceed to have sex all of the time; in the course of the next three months we only made love twice more. What was more important was my discovery of the powerful sexuality within me. In the course of our relationship, I got in touch with my sexual feelings, and was able to express them. In this way, my early sexual experiences helped to shape my future sexuality, which continued to be a powerful force. It takes a powerful force to make me ride my bike six miles uphill to see a girl, as I did in the eighth grade.

*(20-year-old quoted by Garrod et al., 1992, p. 58)*

I cannot say to my children, you must do this . . . but we discuss things openly—and they tell me, if something [sexual intercourse] has happened. I insist on that, or let me say, whatever they do, I want them to tell me. I never could do that with my mother when I was young. We never were able to say anything to our mother and that's what I want with my children . . . I insist.

*(Mother quoted by du Bois-Reymond & Ravesloot, 1996, p. 185)*

## Contents

Sexual maturation brings not only fertility, but also heightened sexual desire and romantic longing. Like romantic love, sexual feelings are an important part of intimacy in close relationships, as well as a source of intense pleasure (Jankowiak & Fischer, 1992). Sexual feelings probably are universal and certainly enrich most people's lives. Prevailing attitudes about sexuality, however, are varied and somewhat contradictory, making it harder for adolescents to come to grips with their emerging sexual identity.

In the United States, each year, over 1 million teenage girls become pregnant, most of them unintentionally. This means that 12% of the children born in the United States each year have teenage mothers, married and unmarried. In 1995 the birth rate, although still high, declined for teenagers for the fourth year in a row (National Center for Health Statistics, 1996). The decline in out-of-wedlock births and teenage births reflects a general decline in the national birth rate.

Premature sexual activity and pregnancy disrupt what society considers to be the normative progression of life tasks for adolescents. Those who delay childbearing to their middle to late 20s are much better prepared biologically and emotionally for the demands of parenting and usually do a better job (Brooks-Gunn, 1988; Zabin & Hayward, 1993).

Sexuality is a small yet essential component of human personality. Without sexual desire and the ability to reproduce, our species could not continue. Since survival is the highest priority of virtually every society, there is pressure on almost all of us to be fruitful and multiply. Western societies grant individuals considerable freedom in selecting partners and deciding when to begin sexual activity. However, the weakening of the traditional link between sexual activity, marriage, and childbearing during the past few decades has created social problems that seem almost insurmountable (Brooks-Gunn & Furstenberg, 1989; Netting, 1992).

To minimize unnecessary suffering and confusion about paternity and inheritance, most societies attempt to regulate the sexual activities of their members.

Reflecting long-standing beliefs about virtue and family life, most cultures discourage sexual intercourse outside of marriage. In sexually charged societies like our own, there is no shortage of views about when people should begin having sexual relations. Some believe that people should be sexual solely for the purpose of reproduction. Some contend that pleasure is reason enough for sexual behavior. Others view sexual relations as an excellent means of achieving intimacy in a close relationship, marriage or otherwise (Zabin & Hayward, 1993). The bottom line is that premarital sex in the context of stable relationships has become normative in most Western societies.

The timing and onset of romantic life vary considerably from one person to another. Some adolescents date frequently, others not at all. Pubertal maturation intensifies sexual desire and interest in romantic relationships. Early romantic experiences influence the course of later relationships, including marriage (Erikson, 1968). Careless sexual activity can have serious repercussions for adolescents, including pregnancy, family conflict, and disease. For some, pregnancy is followed by marriage and child rearing. For others, it leads to abortion or giving up a newborn child for adoption.

Dating and other early forms of romantic behavior provide opportunities for teenagers to become skillful at having close relationships. Acquiring intimacy skills takes time. Parents should be aware and be concerned if their child feels coerced into having a relationship that he or she is not ready for. Teenagers who

**Premarital sex has become normative in most Western societies.**

are immature or who have low self-esteem are vulnerable to emotional and sexual exploitation. Over time, especially with parental help, adolescents learn how, when, and who to trust, how to disclose and share, and how to be intimate with another person. For most adolescents and adults, the absence of intimacy foretells isolation, loneliness, and alienation (Erikson, 1950; Fischer, Munsch, & Greene, 1996).

In this chapter, we continue our examination of adolescent sexuality, highlighting intimacy, romance, pregnancy, marriage, and child rearing. In Chapter 8, we saw that adolescents play an active role in selecting peers, joining crowds, and maintaining friendships. The same is true regarding intimate relationships. Adolescents make decisions about who their romantic partners will be and about how to treat them. They initiate and terminate close relationships. They are responsible for preventing early pregnancy and sexually transmitted diseases. They also must adjust to limitations placed on their sexual behavior (du Bois-Reymond & Ravesloot, 1996).

## SHARON AND KRIS

The emergence of sexuality and fertility is a crucial part of the progression of events that lead to adulthood. Indeed, learning how to function responsibly as a romantic partner is one of the most important tasks of adolescence (Havighurst, 1972; Sullivan, 1953). But what happens when reproductive maturity precedes emotional maturity, judgment, and self-control? Meet Sharon, interviewed by one of my students for a course project.

An 18-year-old high school graduate, Sharon was unemployed and 8 months pregnant. On discovering her pregnancy, she moved in with her boyfriend. After he physically abused her, she left. At the time of the interview, Sharon resided with her mother, stepfather, and stepsister in a suburban middle-class neighborhood in New Jersey.

According to Sharon, her strengths include being happy, having a good sense of humor, and relating well to others. Her weakness is that she is too emotionally and financially dependent on others. Sharon believes that once her baby is born, she will become more responsible because she will be thinking of the baby instead of just thinking about herself.

According to Sharon, all of her friends are sexually active. Most are excited about her pregnancy. Several disclosed to Sharon that they want to be mothers too. One friend didn't agree. She thought that Sharon could make something

**What happens when reproductive maturity precedes emotional maturity, judgment, and self-control?**

of her life and that a baby would only put her life on hold. Her parents had wanted Sharon to go to college. They feel that now college attendance would put too much pressure on her. They no longer comment on how she lives or what she does.

Sharon had thought that she was pregnant for about 2 months before she went for confirmation. After the test proved to be positive, the reality of pregnancy sank in. When she learned that the test was positive, she cried. She is happy about her pregnancy, but part of her wishes that she had waited. She stays home most of the time. Being pregnant, she does not think it appropriate to hang out with her friends. She says that she is "too fat to do anything except stay at home and watch television."

Fifteen-year-old Kris is in no hurry to become sexually active. Although several of her friends have had sex with their boyfriends because "they were in love," Kris will not have sex with her steady boyfriend. She says that she is not ready and that "one never knows what could happen." She added, "I'm too young." At 15, she believes that she is not prepared to handle the whole "sexual situation" and will not be for a few more years. When asked, "What if you were in love?" she replied, "Not unless I'm around 18 or 19. I figure then I could handle it."

Sharon and Kris fall on opposite ends of a continuum of sexual responsibility. Both have sexual feelings and romantic desires, but Kris is the more reluctant of the two to jeopardize her present life and future goals by taking chances. Sharon claims that having a baby will force her to become more responsible, but her present circumstances sound more like a burden than an opportunity.

To a large extent, adult apprehension about adolescent sexuality reflects a lack of confidence in teenagers' willingness to take responsibility for their actions. Some of this concern is unfounded because, like Kris, many teenagers can and do make good sexual decisions. Sharon's plight, however, confirms that adult concerns about adolescent sexuality are not totally off base. With puberty occurring at such a young age and the normative age of marriage shifting upward, many teenagers claim that they cannot or will not wait until marriage to be sexually active. Further, teenagers point out that their parents aren't providing adequate guidance or moral instruction in the sexual arena. Conflicting value systems and discomfort about discussing sexual topics with their children leave most parents with little to say about dating, courtship, and responsibility (Blau & Gullotta, 1993). *Thought Question: Why are some parents reluctant to discuss sexually related topics with their children?*

## COURTSHIP AND DATING

*If a boy asks you to dance, it's not cool to giggle. It's not cool to run away. Say yes.*

> (Adult advice to young girls at a summer camp,
> quoted by Bernstein, 1995)

Most people spend considerable time during the adolescent and early adult years searching for a suitable mate. The ultimate biological function of courtship is mate selection, that is, achieving a long-lasting, perhaps permanent reproductive relationship (Savin-Williams, 1994). The process of courtship includes initial attraction, casual dating, steady dating, establishing an exclusive relationship, and committing to a life partner (Furman & Wehner, 1994) (Figure 10-1). Nevertheless, *many social and identity needs that have nothing to do with sex and reproduction can be satisfied in romantic relationships.* Dating provides young people with opportunities to practice relationship skills and prepare for adult roles while bolstering their peer group status and having fun. Over time, in-

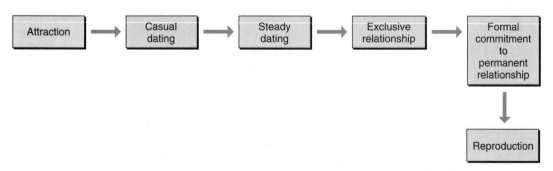

FIGURE 10.1 Courtship sequence.

teractions with romantic partners allow young people to learn about trust, commitment, self-disclosure, dependency, and power (Grauerholz, 1987).

Gay and lesbian teenagers have much less opportunity to date those whom they are attracted to and very little support for forming same-gender romantic relationships. Initially, most attempt dating heterosexually but experience a minimal emotional investment. Whatever one's sexual orientation, a lack of satisfying romantic relationships during adolescence and resultant feelings of inadequacy may impair the development of friendships and other relationships during adulthood (Savin-Williams, 1994).

According to a cross-cultural study of male and female adolescents in the United States and Iceland, the ideal dating partner is fun to be with, good looking, and sexy (Stiles, Gibbons, Hardardottir, & Schnellmann, 1987). Boys and girls desire partners to be at least their age and preferably older (Kenrick, Gabrielidis, Keefe, & Cornelius, 1996). In Smith's (1996) study of 80 African-American inner-city high school students, the students reported valuing personality traits such as being honest, being caring, and having a sense of humor more than material attributes such as nice clothes and a car in describing the qualities of a person they would like to date. This finding contradicts the popular notion that romantic attraction during adolescence is driven mainly by considerations of status and materialism. ***Thought Question: As young people become more experienced romantically, how would we expect their partner preferences to change?***

It might reassure some parents to know that teenage dating is just one more area of exploration and experimentation and a way for young people to assert their independence. Dating also is a way of fitting into one's social network.

**Dating is a way of fitting into one's social network.**

Many children hide their love life from their parents because they are convinced that if their parents knew, they would "go nuts." Parental objections, real or imagined, add fuel to the fire of adolescent romance. Some parents are astounded at their children's choice of romantic partner. Then again, some children are astounded at their parents' choice of romantic partner. Parental disapproval usually is counter-productive. Unless the relationship is abusive, it is better for parents to ask good questions (e.g., "Does he help you feel good about yourself?"), let the romance run its course, and allow it to be a learning experience, painful or otherwise.

In Erikson's psychosocial model of development, the central task of adolescence is to create a meaningful adult identity. As discussed in Chapter 6, the main challenge facing young adults is to form an intimate relationship. In effect, Erikson's premise is that before you can find a partner, you need to find yourself. Dating serves both functions—becoming intimate with someone else while becoming more self-aware (Kroger, 1997; Sanderson & Cantor, 1995). Adolescents who have not yet become "their own person" are still exploring a variety of ways to be an adult. They are ill prepared to satisfy the needs and expectations of someone else (Pestrak & Martin, 1985). *Thought Question: How might limited courtship experience during adolescence be related to the 50% divorce rate in Western societies?*

For some adolescents, popularity and possessions play as large a role in interpersonal attraction as personal qualities and behaviors. Attention solely to superficial traits distracts from personal qualities that are better predictors of satisfying long-term relationships. Apprehensive parents instruct their children that there are "plenty of fish in the sea" and urge them to "play the field" rather than commit prematurely to a partner who does not measure up to parental standards. Yet who among us does not remember our first "crushes" and how they helped us begin to understand ourselves in relationship (Erikson, 1968; Furman & Wehner, 1994)?

## "EVERYONE'S DATING"

Most young people begin to date long before they have any idea about how to be close to another person. Sometimes children as young as 9 or 10 years old announce that they are going to the movies with a person of the other gender. Alarming as this might be to unsuspecting parents, it is more an attempt to act grown up than a desire to settle down and raise a family. A father of a 10-year-old said that he was flabbergasted when his son told him he wanted to double-date with a friend. "When I was young, we started seeing the opposite sex in the seventh or eighth grade, and under supervision. We would go roller-skating and there would be other kids and parents around. But today these 10-year-olds want to be unsupervised, just boy–girl" (Lawson, 1990, p. C15).

In the past, chaperoned dating was the first step in the courtship process. Today, dating is more a gauge of popularity than a step toward marriage. At eighth-grade graduation parties in middle-class communities, we observe young girls in strapless gowns and boys wearing tuxedos taking limousines to

A considerable amount of research documents the existence of gender differences in adult interactional behavior. Women usually ask more questions, smile and laugh more often, gaze at their partners, and engage in self-touching; men usually interrupt more often than women, spend more time speaking, and are more likely to challenge their partner's statements. Are there comparable gender differences during adolescence?

Kolaric and Galambos (1995) hypothesized that verbal and nonverbal gender differences in adults might be learned or exaggerated during adolescence. They were particularly interested in whether there are gender differences in asking questions, interrupting, expressing uncertainty, speaking time, gesturing, smiling, head and facial touching, and gazing. They predicted that when interacting with boys, girls would cast coy looks, flip their hair, tilt their heads sideways, and huddle in a defensive posture (i.e., look smaller). They predicted that boys would more frequently engage in chin stroking and back neck touching. Such *display behaviors* are calculated to impress a partner. The investigators observed 60 predominantly white Canadian adolescents, 14 to 16 years old, from two-parent families. They made sure that the adolescents did not know the partners with whom they would be interacting. Each boy and girl was seated at a table and separated by a removable partition. They were told that the purpose of the study was to gather information about how pairs of individuals communicate about certain tasks they are performing. The boy and girl were given three tasks to discuss (changing car oil, babysitting, caring for a pet) for 3 minutes each and were informed that the interaction would be videotaped. Consent forms were obtained from parents and participants.

What did the investigators observe? "In contrast to the plethora of research revealing consistent and robust gender differences in these behaviors in adulthood, there was little evidence of such gender differences in adolescence. Girls and boys behaved similarly overall in speaking, questions, uncertainty, gestures, head and facial touches, and gazing" (p. 375). Boys did speak more during discussions about changing car oil, and girls spoke more about babysitting (i.e., gender-typed topics). Boys engaged in more chin stroking (to look thoughtful?), and girls engaged in more hair flipping, appearing smaller, and coy looks (to look seductive?). To some extent, verbal and nonverbal behavior reflected the topic discussed—more gesturing and uncertainty during the masculine topic. The lack of adultlike gender differences surprised the investigators, who speculated that the boys and girls might have been nervous or constrained by the contrived laboratory situation. This is one of the relatively few studies that has measured adolescent behavior in a controlled laboratory situation. What other variables can you think of manipulating in this situation (e.g., physical features of the adolescents) to shed more light on display behaviors?

**Box 10-1
How Do Unacquainted Boys and Girls Act During a First Meeting?**

dinner-dances. A busy social life engenders positive feedback that boosts self-esteem. Having a boyfriend or girlfriend becomes an important source of prestige, self-confidence, and relationship training. Although most parents would not permit young children to date at such an early age, some are so eager for their children to be popular that they grant them this status symbol. Children who are not ready to date probably feel relief when their parents turn down their requests. They can blame their parents when they explain to peers that they tried but failed.

Dating becomes more common during the middle school years. It usually takes the form of mixed-gender groups going out together. By the age of 15 or 16, many adolescents begin to date as couples, although they might not view it as dating. Girls are more interested than boys in dating, and they date earlier. Early dating and early going steady signal earlier and more frequent involvement in serious relationships and sexual experiences (Thornton, 1990). Keep in mind that not all romantic relationships are sexual and not all sexual encounters are romantic.

Although modern girls are a bit more assertive than their predecessors, boys usually initiate dating encounters and dominate heterosexual teenage relationships. Teenagers who date for dubious reasons—for example, to impress their friends—find such encounters awkward and stressful. Girls usually are more vulnerable, disappointed, and feel more guilty than boys do about precocious sexual experiences. They don't get the feeling of closeness that they expected. A large number of adolescents do not date at all during their high school years, lacking opportunity or fearing rejection (Gordon & Gilgun, 1987). In college, relationships are more exclusive and more serious (Kutner, 1992a; Long, 1989).

It is important that teenagers and their parents know that the age at which children begin to date is not related to their sexual orientation or to their eventual social competence. However, early dating does predict earlier serious relationships and therefore earlier sexual experiences (Kutner, 1992b; Thornton, 1990).

## HETEROSEXUAL RELATIONSHIPS

For most adolescents, participating in heterosexual relationships is an important part of growing up. Physical growth and sexual maturation occur in an ever-widening context of social roles, cultural expectations, rules of conduct, and sanctions for inappropriate behavior. Boys and girls typically have little to do with each other before puberty and may express discomfort in the presence of opposite-gender peers. With maturation comes greater interest in the other sex and eventually dating, attachment, courtship, and love (Furman & Wehner, 1994; Thornton, 1990).

Lacking formal instruction in the bewildering arena of romance, teenagers learn how to have close relationships on a trial-and-error basis, usually over the course of a series of relationships (Furman & Wehner, 1994). ''Young people become increasingly experienced in dating, the amount of time young couples spend together increases, and often the courtship process intensifies. This emotional and romantic involvement is often accompanied by, and intensified by, expanding levels of sexual involvement" (Thornton, 1990, p. 240).

The traditional norm guiding the intensity of sexual interaction, at least for girls, has been the level of social and emotional investment in the relationship. The more committed the relationship, the greater the intensity of sexual expression. However, the progression from kissing to intercourse was much more gradual in past decades, with a lot of precoital experimentation along the way. Some teenagers move through the dating and courtship process more rapidly than others. For many of today's teenagers, events progress rapidly. Intercourse before marriage is the norm (Thornton, 1990) and is not unheard of on a first date (Buckley & Wilgoren, 1996).

Adolescent girls in particular find themselves bogged down in moral dilemmas in their romantic relations. How can they maintain their sense of self (and their virginity) without losing their boyfriends and their self-respect? One Israeli girl reasoned as follows: "I do not know how to explain it, but I am certain that the reason males do not make anything of sexual intercourse is the fact that it does not change their personality. However, I can assure you, at least from my experience, that we are changed after this experience. And that is why it is so important to us with *whom* we have sex and what the quality of our relationship with him is" (Linn, 1991, p. 66).

Whereas boys usually are more concerned about their pride and performance ("scoring"), girls seek a feeling of connectedness in relationship (being "in love"). Whereas boys are more permissive regarding casual sex, girls usually expect more emotionally (Eaton, Mitchell, & Jolley, 1991). Boys tend to be opportunistic, whereas girls usually are guided by a desire for closeness

**Adolescent girls generally expect more emotionally from romantic relationships than boys do.**

(Schmitt & Buss, 1996). Some boys consistently deny the validity of their partner's feelings. "Women, on the other hand, deny their own feelings and perceptions about intimate encounters, feeling that they have relinquished their right to withdraw consent when the encounter advances beyond a preliminary stage" (Feltey et al., 1991, p. 245). Adolescent boys and girls are inexperienced in communicating their sexual needs and desires (Rosenthal & Peart, 1996). The situation becomes ripe for coercion (Seppa, 1997).

Rosenthal and Peart (1996) examined the rules that young people follow during a sexual encounter. The researchers were interested in how teenagers communicate that they would like to have sex and how they proceed to encourage or discourage a sexual encounter. For example, how does one broach the topic of condom use or whether a sexual encounter is even desired? A sample consisting of predominantly working class, Australian-born 15- to 17-year-old adolescents responded to questionnaire items concerning social rules for giving messages indicating whether they wanted to have sex, strategies for encouraging or avoiding sex, and the acceptability and usefulness of these strategies. Strategies included stating rules about intent at the beginning of the encounter ("I don't want to"), making up excuses, leaving the situation, giving nonverbal cues, and joking your way out of it.

Results indicated that avoiding unwanted sex was a difficult area for this sample of young people. The investigators concluded that "the rules for getting sex appear to be more clearcut than those for knowing how to avoid sex but the strategies that are regarded most favorably are those which are indirect" (p. 329). Boys and girls agreed on a wide variety of predominantly nonverbal strategies for encouraging sex. Four-fifths of the girls and half of the boys reported having to use at least one strategy to avoid unwanted sex. Girls seemed to be better than boys at communicating their sexual needs. Boys apparently learn that being direct does not always pay off.

Serious romantic involvement increases adolescents' vulnerability, particularly for those who have low self-esteem. Feeling wanted and loved helps them feel worthwhile but also makes them susceptible to exploitation. Teenagers wonder, "Am I attractive? Will anyone ever love me?" Some boys put pressure on girls: "What's wrong with you?" "If you really love me, you would have sex with me," "I won't go out with you unless we have sex," "Everybody does it," or "You owe it to me" (Gordon & Gilgun, 1987).

As they mature, boys and girls become increasingly comfortable with self-disclosure, emotional closeness, and feeling cared for in cross-gender relationships (Youniss & Haynie, 1992). Still, most young adolescents have poorly developed intimacy skills. They have few role models in adult relationships who display intimate self-disclosure. Children in single-parent families have fewer opportunities to observe adults trusting and respecting each other. Media depictions of stereotypical adult relationships muddy the relationship waters even more. "Relationships as portrayed on television are generally superficial, and self-disclosure is minimal. For these and other reasons, teenage romances are often based on physical attraction rather than depth of emotionality" (Shaughnessy & Shakesby, 1992, p. 477).

These investigators suggest that adults help teenagers consider the following as they find themselves becoming more attached to a particular peer: (1)

**Table 10-1 Issues in Adolescent Romantic Relationships**

Degree of commitment to the relationship

The relationship "ground rules"

Confidentiality of self-disclosures

Expectations about the relationship

Concerns about being hurt emotionally

Discussing limits of each partner's responsibility

their commitment to the relationship, (2) a discussion of relationship ground rules, (3) confidentiality of self-disclosures, (4) expectations about the relationship, (5) concerns about being hurt emotionally, and (6) the limits of each partner's responsibility toward the other (see Table 10-1).

Partly because these concerns rarely are addressed and partly because most adolescents still are working on their interpersonal skills, teenage romantic relationships are not very stable. When relationships end, teenagers grieve at least as intensely as adults do. It is not clear whether females grieve more intensely than males, but depression and sadness usually are present for both genders. "Grief may result in reduced academic performance and health problems, as well as carelessness about attire, employment responsibilities, and home duties. Adolescents may withdraw and spend more and more time alone, even taking

**When romantic relationships end, teenagers grieve as intensely as adults.**

meals to their room. They may be preoccupied with thinking and fantasizing about the former partner while listening to sentimental music" (Kaczmarek & Backlund, 1991, pp. 256–257).

In their misery, many seek consolation from alcohol and other drugs. Adults should take adolescent grief seriously. It is helpful for parents or counselors to encourage the expression of feelings of sadness and loss and then to validate these feelings ("It's difficult losing someone you feel close to"). The expression of grief is normal following a loss. Adolescents should be given time to heal and the opportunity to rely on friends and family for emotional support (Kaczmarek & Backlund, 1991).

## FAMILY INFLUENCES ON INTIMACY

Although pubertal maturation is hormonally driven, the expression of sexual behavior is guided by a variety of social influences (which may vary from culture to culture). During early adolescence, teenagers in search of companionship and intimacy approach their peers (Furman & Wehner, 1994). Close friends become important counselors and confidants regarding questions like "Do you think he likes me?" and "Should I ask her out?" (du Bois-Reymond & Ravesloot, 1996). Nevertheless, the desire to seek and share intimacy develops mainly within the family. After all, relationships among family members provide the socioemotional context in which bonding and nurturing occur (Romig & Bakken, 1992).

As discussed in Chapter 7, family bonding foreshadows the development of intimacy and identity during adolescence. Through expressions of warmth and support, parents socialize their children into romantically responsible individuals (Barnett, Papini, & Gbur, 1991; Huerta-Franco et al., 1996; Pick & Palos, 1995; Romig & Bakken, 1992). Teenagers' romantic behavior and sexual conduct reflect parental values, expectations, instruction, supervision, and behavior (Rosenthal, Lewis, & Cohen, 1996).

For example, adolescent daughters who report good relationships with their mothers are more likely to delay sexual activity. When they do become sexually active, they are more likely to use contraceptives and have fewer partners (Inazu & Fox, 1980). Teenagers who are more strongly bonded to their parents report higher levels of companionship and affection in their peer relationships (Romig & Bakken, 1992). Young people from religious families are less sexually active than their less pious peers (Thornton & Camburn, 1989).

Parental level of education and aspirations for their children indirectly affect adolescents' sexual attitudes and behavior. The more educated parents are, the less likely that their children will be sexually active (Forste & Heaton, 1988). Presumably, educated parents are in a good position to cultivate a need for achievement and high aspirations in their children that preclude sexual risk-taking (Hayes, 1987).

Good parent–child communication is an essential family resource, especially as a source of knowledge, beliefs, attitudes, and values for children and adolescents. In the healthiest families, adolescents' expressions of autonomy are balanced by a sense of emotional connectedness among family members.

Some adolescents who feel isolated or alienated from their family members compensate by seeking intimacy via premature sexual behavior with peers (Ravert & Martin, 1997). Boyfriends or girlfriends (and babies) serve as substitute companions or love objects (Barnett et al., 1991; Jessor & Jessor, 1977).

Teenagers who communicate well with their parents receive more sex education at home (Baldwin & Baranoski, 1990). However, adolescents get most of their sexual information and misinformation from their friends and the media. Since many parents are either poorly informed about sexual development or reluctant to discuss sexual matters with their children, parental influence on adolescent sexual behavior usually is more indirect than direct (Hockenberry-Eaton et al., 1996). Parent-child communication may be inhibited by parents' fear of condoning sexual activity and adolescents' fear of losing personal freedom (Yowell, 1997).

Relationships between parents and children today are more relaxed than in previous eras. Many more parents are willing to permit, tolerate, or negotiate about premarital sexual activity in serious romantic relationships (du Bois-Reymond & Ravesloot, 1996; Neubauer & Melzer, 1989). Du Bois-Reymond and Ravesloot (1996) interviewed secondary school students (age 15 to 19 years) in Leiden, the Netherlands, and their parents about how these young people experienced the transition to adulthood, including starting sexual relationships. Most of the parents claimed that they did not want to interfere with their children's sexual behavior. "It's their life and their body" and "We're here if they need us" were typical sentiments, especially from fathers. *Thought Question: These parents apparently respect their children's privacy. Can you think of another explanation for their liberal attitude of nonintervention?*

Mothers felt that they were liberal and noninterfering. Daughters saw their mothers as demanding. The mothers thought that they were being supportive, but their daughters did not perceive them that way. Mothers and sons generally agreed that the mothers were noninterfering. One mother said that she hoped that her son would be polite to girls and never go further than the girl wanted, but she, the mother, would not interfere. Fathers preferred either to stay in the background or to negotiate about sexual matters. "We talk until a solution is found," said one father. However, some girls felt that their fathers were authoritarian, even when the fathers reported feeling helpless. Once again we see that parents and adolescents have quite different views of their interactions. Fathers and sons agreed that the fatherly attitude toward their sons' sexual activities was liberal. Like daughters, some sons felt that their fathers were authoritarian.

Research hasn't revealed any simple relationship between parental communication and children's sexual attitudes and practices. In du Bois and Ravesloot's (1996) study, when adolescents discussed sexual matters at all, it was with their romantic partners, rarely with their parents or even with friends. A few did rely on mothers as confidants. Ironically, parents felt that they were much more open regarding discussing sexual topics than *their* parents had been. But discomfort about this topic persisted, and their children sensed it. Parental discomfort and adolescent fear of parental disapproval may partly explain increasingly frequent reports of adolescent girls' concealing their pregnancies from their parents and sometimes killing their offspring (Seelye, 1997b).

Teenage children of permissive and punitive parents have the most liberal attitudes toward sexual intercourse. Some fathers condone or encourage their son's sexual exploration. Parents who practice the authoritative parenting style, who supervise their children's dating, and who teach responsible behavior typically have children who internalize their values. Naturally, this does not guarantee that these children will delay sexual activity or be more sexually responsible, but it helps (Fisher, 1986; Miller, McCoy, Olson, & Wallace, 1986; Sanders & Mullis, 1988; White & DeBlassie, 1992).

Older siblings often play a role in younger siblings' sexual development by serving as confidants and through modeling, shared parenting influences, and shared risk factors (East & Felice, 1992). Younger sisters of childbearing adolescents are more accepting of nonmarital childbearing, have lower school and career expectations, and are more likely to engage in problem behaviors such as smoking and truancy (East, 1996).

Rodgers and Rowe (1988, 1990) found that younger siblings consistently have similar or higher levels of sexual activity at a given age than their older same-sex siblings. Further, younger siblings of virgins are less sexually active than siblings of nonvirgins. The sibling influence was observed for white and African-American teenagers, although it was more pronounced for whites. Ironically, siblings often are more aware of each other's love lives than are parents. *Thought Question: Why are teenagers more willing to confide in older siblings than in parents?*

## FAMILY STRUCTURE AND ADOLESCENT ROMANCE

Some researchers have reported that changing family structure indirectly affects adolescent sexual behavior. Parental divorce and living with a single parent are often mentioned as factors that increase the pregnancy risk in teenagers (Barnett et al., 1991; Hayes, 1987). In most single-parent families, the presence of only one harried supervisor (usually an employed single mother with sole custody) may be partly responsible. Sexually active single parents model permissive sexual behavior to their children (Thornton & Camburn, 1987). Further, single parents may not be able to provide as much emotional support and supervision to children as two parents. Some studies suggest that the financial and emotional stability of two-parent families lessens such risk, especially for males.

Young, Jensen, Olsen, and Cundick (1991) surveyed white and African-American males and females living either in single-parent or two-parent homes. The teenagers were questioned about their sexual behavior. Teenagers from single-parent families reported being more sexually active. For males, being from a two-parent family predicted less sexual activity and older age at first intercourse. For females, belonging to a two-parent family was not as important as race in predicting sexual behavior. White females living with two parents were more likely to be virgins. But once they had intercourse, they tended to be more sexually active than African-American females from two-parent families.

Barnett et al. (1991) studied 124 sexually active female teenagers. Those who were pregnant at the time of the study reported problematic communication with their parents. Many described fragmented families with only one or no parent living at home. Most came from low-income households, did not use birth control, and were more likely to be married than their nonpregnant counterparts.

Coleman, Ganong, and Ellis (1985) questioned 96 males and 81 females at two Midwestern universities about their dating relationships. The students were from intact or nonintact families. Marital happiness of parents was a better predictor of females' number of partners and number of steadies than was family configuration. However, the key factor affecting dating was adolescents' confidence and self-esteem. "The more confidence in interacting with the other sex and the more positively adolescents rated themselves on personality and attractiveness, the more dates generally and the more serious dating relationships the adolescents experienced" (p. 542). Those with the least dating success were those who were the most sensitive to rejection.

Peer influence usually is more direct. For white female teenagers, sexual conduct is very much influenced by best friends (Billy & Udry, 1985; Rodgers & Rowe, 1990). White male teenagers chose friends partly on the basis of sexual activity (Billy & Udry, 1985). Adolescents (girls more than boys) frequently report that pressure from their friends is the major reason for being sexually active (Harris & Associates, 1986). Although girls may view their mothers as experts regarding long-term relationships and marriage, they see best friends as experts in their current romantic relationships (Yowell, 1997b).

---

# SPOTLIGHT • Should Parents Let Their Teenage Children Have Sex at Home?

Most parents would never dream of sanctioning their children's premarital sexual behavior by letting them have sex in their own home, yet there are parents who find themselves reluctantly accepting this arrangement. Ironically, they view allowing sex at home as a way of protecting their children. Once they accept that their children are sexually active, whether they (the parents) like it or not, they would rather have their children be sexually active at home. It also allows them to keep track of their children's sexual partners (Lawson, 1991; O'Connell, 1996).

"It's not that I think this is wonderful. But I don't want my son and his girlfriend hiding in basements or the back seat of a car, getting mugged. I feel better knowing where my child is, so I decided that his room is his territory, his privacy" (mother of a 17-year-old, quoted by Lawson, 1991, p. C1). Parents of sexually active teenagers are caught in a dilemma—they don't want to condone their child's sexual activities, but they don't want their child to have sex with people they don't know and in places that could be dangerous. Thus, against their better judgment, they concede to their child's request or demand to have sex at home.

Psychologist Lawrence Aber responds, "Parents need to set limits, and it is the children's job to push them. But when parents don't set limits, it can be scary and disruptive for children" (quoted by Lawson, 1991, p. C8). A mother who also disapproves of this practice says, "We have raised her to be careful, to know about birth control and AIDS, but if she wants to have sex she has to be responsible for finding the place. She should not expect to have it in my face" (Lawson, 1991, p. C8). Some parents say they accept this arrangement because their child is in a long-term relationship. They don't want their children to lie to them. They want to know where and with whom their children are sleeping. Other parents wonder how younger children react when their older siblings have their romantic partners sleep over. Such are the dilemmas faced by parents today.

## ADOLESCENT PREGNANCY AND CHILDBEARING

Society's treatment of pregnant teenagers has improved considerably since midcentury. Formerly, girls who were pregnant out of wedlock ("wayward girls") were outcasts, banished from their schools, shunned by their peers, often shipped out of town to give birth or to get an illegal abortion. Today, we encourage pregnant teenagers to give birth, keep their babies, and stay in school. Some schools provide day care for their students' offspring. Pregnant young women appear on afternoon TV talk shows justifying their choices and lifestyles, imploring viewers to not judge them. Critics complain that by being "tolerant" of these young mothers, we are condoning irresponsible sexual behavior (Williams, 1993).

In Japan, single motherhood is much more stigmatized. Only 1% of births in Japan are to unwed mothers compared to 30% in the United States (WuDunn, 1996). In Japan, teenagers are much less sexually active and abortions are easily available. But having a baby out of wedlock is considered disgraceful, as it used to be in the United States. Then again, 17-year-old unmarried Amanda Smisek received a court summons in Emmett, Idaho, in early 1996 charging her with fornication (*The New York Times*, October 28, 1996, p. A10).

The United States has one of the highest rates of teenage pregnancy in the industrial world. Of the approximately 1 million adolescents who become pregnant each year, 360,000 have abortions, 500,000 bear their child, and 140,000 miscarry (Alan Guttmacher Institute, 1991, 1994a,b; Hayes, 1987). Of those who bear their child, 72% are unmarried. Teenage mothers are getting younger, especially in the poorer African-American and Latino communities. Early-maturing girls attract boys, including some between 10 and 14 years of age, who have little knowledge of fertility or contraceptives.

Unlike past eras, teenage mothers today usually do not marry and do not give up their children for adoption. Most are unemployed, undereducated, and on welfare. Taxpayers in the United States paid 7 billion dollars in 1996 because of social problems resulting from recent births by girls under the age of 18 (*The New York Times*, June 13, 1996, p. A19). This amount includes welfare payments and the use of publicly financed health care. Having conceived and born children, many teenagers say that they feel responsible for raising them. Their families usually oppose adoption and abortion and may not be upset by the pregnancy (Folkenberg, 1985; Rauch-Elnekave, 1994).

Few unwed adolescent mothers live with their child's father or receive emotional or financial support from their families and community. As mentioned in Chapter 9, babies born to these mothers often are fathered by older men who have little interest in providing for the mother or child (Navarro, 1996). The Alan Guttmacher Institute (1995) reported that 65% of adolescent mothers aged 15 to 19 years had children by men who were 20 years of age or older, sometimes much older (many of the older teenagers *were* married to the child's father [Holmes, 1997]). Usually, the younger the mother, the wider the age gap between mother and father (see Table 10-2).

These circumstances create "an expanding group of economically disadvantaged, single-parent mothers dependent upon welfare support and other costly government-subsidized programs" (Jorgensen, 1993, p. 106). Most pregnant teenage girls lead stressful lives at a time when their coping resources are still developing (Ravert & Martin, 1997). The less support they receive, the more stressful their lives (Camp, Homan, & Ridgway, 1993). It is well documented that lack of social support and stress impair parenting competence (Grolnick et al., 1996; McLoyd, Jayaratne, Ceballo, & Borquez, 1994), especially when adolescent mothers are depressed (Leadbeater, Bishop, & Raver, 1996).

## Table 10-2  Profile of the Adolescent Mother

Although they are a very diverse group, adolescent mothers typically

- are young and unmarried
- are unemployed, undereducated, and economically disadvantaged
- feel responsible for raising their child
- live with their parents
- lead stressful lives
- have minimal occupational aspirations
- have limited social lives
- are out of developmental synchrony with their age group
- are at higher risk than older mothers for premature birth and other complications
- are less socially competent
- have relatively low self-esteem
- are poor problem solvers
- are risk takers, more likely than their nonparent peers to smoke, drink alcohol, and use other drugs
- are ill-prepared for the demands of parenting
- lack the coping resources necessary for successful parenting
- are impatient, insensitive, and uninformed about children
- are inclined toward the use of physical punishment in discipline and have female children who are more likely to follow in their footsteps
- are less prepared than adult parents cognitively and emotionally to meet the demands of childrearing
- have less knowledge about child development and more negative attitudes about parenting
- are less knowledgeable about children, display less empathy and interest toward their children, and provide less overall stimulation than older mothers do

Knowing the plight of the pregnant teenager and single mother might help their peers to think twice about taking sexual risks. Although adolescent mothers are an extremely diverse group, their development is out of synchrony with the developmental norms of their age group (Raeff, 1994). For example, while most teenagers anticipate separating from their families, teenage mothers become more dependent on their mothers or grandmothers. Teenage pregnancy speeds up some and slows down other aspects of social maturation (Buchholz & Gol, 1986; Gilchrist & Schinke, 1987; Schamess, 1993; Schellenbach, Whitman, & Borkowski, 1992).

Some adolescent mothers claim that they wanted to become pregnant. Rodriguez and Moore (1995) asked 341 mostly Hispanic, never-married, pregnant or parenting teenagers (11 to 19 years old) to complete an anonymous questionnaire. Twenty-five percent of the girls were under age 14 when they first had intercourse. (This is important because early first intercourse increases the likelihood of teenage pregnancy.) Thirty percent claimed that they had wanted to become pregnant. Pregnant adolescents offer several reasons for wanting a baby, including keeping a boyfriend, thinking it would be fun, spiting their parents, and wanting to feel loved by someone (Resnick, Blum, Bose, Smith, & Toogood, 1990). "For those who feel isolated, the prospect of a baby offers the possibility of someone to love. Pregnancy also brings attention to a girl who feels neglected. Entrapping a reluctant suitor may motivate some teenagers. Others may see pregnancy as a way to assert their independence from their parents, to become their mothers' equal. Some may want to keep up with their pregnant girlfriends" (Stark, 1986, p. 30).

At least three different models have been offered to explain the high frequency of adolescent pregnancy. The **cognitive model** views adolescent pregnancy as resulting from some cognitive deficit, such as poor problem-solving skills, inability to plan for the future, or lack of knowledge about contraception. There is evidence that many teenage mothers have undetected learning problems that make it difficult for them to succeed academically (Rauch-Elnekave, 1994). The **psychosocial model** attributes pregnancy to faulty social learning experiences or to a lack of social support. The **sexual behavior model** assumes that the only difference between nonpregnant and pregnant females is that the latter are more sexually active and do not use contraceptives (Holden, Nelson, Velasquez, & Ritchie, 1993). (See Table 10-3.)

**Table 10-3  Three Models of Adolescent Pregnancy**

The **cognitive model** views adolescent pregnancy as resulting from some cognitive deficit, such as poor problem-solving skills, an inability to plan for the future, or a lack of knowledge about contraception.

The **psychosocial model** attributes pregnancy to faulty social learning experiences or to a lack of social support.

The **sexual behavior model** assumes that the only difference between nonpregnant and pregnant females is that the latter are more sexually active and do not use contraceptives.

Many of these undereducated girls have minimal occupational aspirations. They believe that life has little to offer them. When sexually active, they have no motivation to avoid pregnancy or postpone parenthood (Jorgensen, 1993). Holden and his colleagues had 69 pregnant adolescents and 58 comparison adolescents fill out a series of questionnaires using a computer. Pregnant teenagers were more likely to be doing poorly in school and less likely to use contraceptives than the comparison group. Pregnant teenagers were more likely to know an adolescent mother. They expected childrearing to be easier than did the nonpregnant adolescents. Some support was found for each of the three theoretical models cited above.

How could these young girls know how drastically pregnancy and single motherhood would change their lives? One 18-year-old mother commented, "I go to school, take care of my baby and go to sleep. If they [sexually active teenage girls] understand that there is no time for parties or even going to a shopping mall, it might help them" (Sullivan, 1987). Their limited social life is not necessarily negative. "I'm off the streets. . . . After me having the baby and having to take care of that child, I don't run it as much as I usually do" (adolescent girl quoted by Theriot, Pecoraro, & Ross-Reynolds, 1991, p. 353).

Very young mothers are at higher risk than older mothers for premature birth and other complications, regardless of their socioeconomic status or quality of prenatal care. Most are ill prepared for the demands of parenting. Some studies report that compared to pregnant adults and nonpregnant peers, teenage mothers are less socially competent, have relatively low self-esteem, are poor problem solvers, and lack the coping resources necessary for successful parenting. Many adolescent mothers are impatient, insensitive, and uninformed about children and inclined toward the use of physical punishment in discipline (Passino et al., 1993; Schellenbach et al., 1992; Theriot et al., 1991).

Young mothers often are risk takers, more likely than their nonparent peers to smoke, drink alcohol, and use other drugs (Zoccolillo, Meyers, & Assiter, 1997). Early sexual activity also is associated with multiple sexual partners and a higher risk of genital infection. Because of these girls' young age and the greater chance of complications during pregnancy and childbirth, their children often have characteristics such as premature delivery, low birth weight, difficult temperament, or disabilities that make them more difficult to raise. Children of adolescent mothers are at disproportionate risk of mortality, cognitive problems, social-emotional problems, abuse and neglect, school failure, and other forms of developmental delay (Camp, 1996; East & Felice, 1990; Rauch-Elnekave, 1994; Sommer et al., 1993). Their female children are more likely to follow in their footsteps—conceive, marry young, divorce, and become adolescent mothers (Schamess, 1993).

Results of studies comparing the parenting behaviors of adolescent and older mothers are mixed. However, many studies confirm the obvious—that teenage parents are less prepared than adult parents cognitively and emotionally to meet the demands of child rearing (Karraker & Evans, 1996; Passino et al., 1993). Cognitive readiness includes wanting to be a parent, knowing how children develop, and knowing how to parent. Adolescent mothers have less knowledge about child development and more negative attitudes about parenting (Karraker & Evans, 1996; Sommer, Whitman, Borkowski, Schellenbach, Maxwell, & Keogh, 1993), but those who are cognitively prepared for parenting generally do a better job (Miller, Miceli, Whitman, & Borkowski, 1996).

Although many studies confirm that teenage mothers are less knowledgeable about children, display less empathy with and interest in their children, and provide less overall stimulation than older mothers do, differences in many other parenting qualities are slight or nonexistent. Researchers caution against a "disease model" of adolescent mothering that focuses only on these mothers' inadequacies and negative child outcomes (Baranowski, Schilmoeller, & Higgins, 1990; Buchholz & Gol, 1986; Garcia-Coll, Hoffman, & Oh, 1987; Passino et al., 1993; Schilmoeller & Baranowski, 1985). Indeed, some studies support the possibility of greater maturity in adolescent mothers than in nonmothers (e.g., Oz, Tari, & Fine, 1992).

The prospects for adolescent mothers and their children are not necessarily poor (Furstenberg, Brooks-Gunn, & Morgan, 1987; Shapiro & Mangelsdorf, 1994). Many young mothers have goals similar to those of peers who are not pregnant—financial security, marriage, school, a better life. Although many are dependent on their own mothers, they desire independence (Theriot et al., 1991). Mothers who are adjusting well, who have temperamentally easy children, and who have varied sources of social support do best (Belsky, 1984; Mulsow & Murray, 1996). Unfortunately, the social support networks (boyfriends, parents, and peers) that are so important in coping with stress often are disrupted by unwanted pregnancy (Sherman & Donovan, 1991; Unger & Wandersman, 1988).

As the ecological model (discussed in Chapter 2) implies, it is not age per se but the situational "package," including the financial, social, and emotional stresses faced by teenage parents, that predicts parent and child adjustment (Bronfenbrenner, 1986). Those lucky enough to have adequate coping resources,

**Many adolescent mothers have goals that are similar to those of their peers who have not had babies—financial security, marriage, school, and a better life.**

a supportive family and peer environment, a stable, sympathetic partner (or partner substitute), and access to well-designed intervention programs that teach parenting skills and help them solve their problems usually adjust better and provide higher-quality parenting (Cooper, Dunst, & Vance, 1990; Mulsow & Murray, 1996; Murray, 1995b).

Completing their education and receiving family support also help young mothers catch up developmentally with their peers, although their children still may have problems. Naturally, the better the mother does, the better the child will do (Buchholz & Korn-Bursztyn, 1993; Cooper et al., 1990; Fulton, Murphy, & Anderson, 1991; Furstenberg, Brooks-Gunn, & Chase-Lansdale, 1989; Luster & Mittelstaedt, 1993; Miller, 1992; Oyserman, Radin, & Benn, 1993; Passino et al., 1993).

## ABORTION AND ADOPTION

The U.S. Supreme Court decision in *Roe* v. *Wade* in 1973 legalized abortion and thus gave rise to heated moral, religious, and political controversies that show little sign of abating. In the United States, abortion currently is the most commonly performed surgical procedure. In effect, it is the leading method of birth control in this country (Foster & Sprinthall, 1992).

Forty percent of adolescent pregnancies end in abortion. However, large numbers of pregnant adolescents and their parents describe abortion as morally unacceptable and contrary to their religious beliefs. Given that so many cannot picture themselves giving up their children for adoption, we can understand why so many adolescents opt to raise their children themselves. Nonwhite adolescents are more likely than whites to choose parenting as an option.

About a quarter of all abortions in the United States are performed on teenagers. Those who seek abortions tend to not be highly religious, have higher educational and vocational aspirations, perform well in school, and have family members or partners who support their decision (Jorgensen, 1993). About two-thirds of unmarried teenage girls who have abortions tell their parents (usually their mothers) in advance, even though the law in most states does not require parental notification or consent. Often the mother suspects that something is wrong and confronts her daughter. Most of those who do not tell their parents fear disappointing them or making them angry (Alan Guttmacher Institute, 1992; Seelye, 1997a).

In one study, about half of the teenagers seeking abortion did not confide in their parents regarding their pregnancy and therefore sacrificed their participation in decision making (Griffin-Carlson & Mackin, 1993). One of the many issues surrounding the abortion controversy concerns who makes the decision to abort a pregnancy when the female is a minor; should parental consent be required? Some states, such as Montana, have a notification law that requires a minor to tell one parent at least 48 hours before an abortion. The U.S. Supreme Court has ruled that such laws are constitutional.

Although most adolescents adjust well following an abortion, a significant number experience guilt and emotional stress. Franz and Reardon (1992) surveyed 252 women from 42 states about their decision to have an abortion. Most were young and unmarried at the time of the abortion and regretted the decision. More than older women, adolescents reported feeling coerced into having an abortion and were dissatisfied with their decision. Perhaps reflecting their cognitive and psychological immaturity, many reported feeling confused and misinformed about their alternatives. Many admitted regretting their decision.

The investigators conclude that it is important that women considering abortion be fully informed and feel that they have enough time to make a good decision. Feeling pressured increases their distress and leads to a negative view of the procedure. Apparently, guided by idealistic notions of parenting, most adolescents would prefer to keep the baby. Those who have reservations about abortion require counseling to help them reflect on acceptable alternatives (Foster & Sprinthall, 1992).

Only about 4% of adolescents choose adoption as an alternative to abortion or parenting. Teenage girls who relinquish their babies for adoption tend to be younger, white, and from more affluent families. They are more religious and have higher educational and vocational aspirations. Their parents and friends usually support their decision (Herr, 1989; Jorgensen, 1993).

The relatively small percentage who choose adoption say that they are guided by what they believe is best for the child and for themselves (Resnick et al., 1990). Yet, they still report a sense of loss, partly due to their lack of participation, even indirectly, in the child's life (Sobol & Daly, 1992).

Informal adoption is common among African-American adolescents. Biological mothers surrender some but not all of their rights to the social mother, known as "mama." Such shared parenting among close kin is believed to reflect the impact of slavery on black families in the United States (Sandven & Resnick, 1990).

As we have seen, adoption generally frees adolescent mothers from a combination of stressful circumstances that hinder their development. Knowledge of adoption and comfort with this choice increase the likelihood of choosing adoption as an alternative to abortion or parenting (Custer, 1993).

## ADOLESCENT MARRIAGE

In previous centuries, early pregnancy and marriage were the norm. Agricultural society allowed young couples to be economically self-sufficient. Today, becoming an employable adult requires much more preparation. Early marriage no longer is typical or desirable. Most pregnant adolescents do not marry the child's father (who may be much older), but those who do are at heightened risk for marital strife, divorce, educational setbacks, and dependence on welfare. Thus, marriages of convenience usually are not to the advantage of the parents or child. Married teenagers generally lack the maturity, financial stability, and relationship skills necessary for a satisfying adult relationship (Gilchrist & Schinke, 1987).

What about teenage fathers? A few conform to the popular stereotype of an irresponsible teenage boy preying on vulnerable females. One pregnant girl said, "A lot of us young girls who get pregnant, and we tell the father, they seem to disappear; like a magic trick, they seem to disappear" (quoted by Theriot et al., 1991, p. 353). Some boys are happy when their girlfriends become pregnant, and they resent family pressure to abort the pregnancy. Many teenage fathers are emotionally attached to their girlfriends and to their babies.

Those who are in ongoing, committed relationships with their girlfriends have more say about how an unplanned pregnancy will be resolved. More than females, males prefer arrangements that allow them and the mother to live with their child. Teenage girls are much more likely than boys to prefer the role of single parent, suggesting that girls are more selective than their boyfriends about choosing a life mate (Marsiglio & Menaghan, 1990).

"For those performing poorly in school, caring for a baby may be their first tangible accomplishment. For those reared in troubled homes, the infant may be the first human from whom they can receive love" (Robinson & Barret, 1985, p. 68). The boys would marry except for the understandable resistance (and contempt) from the girl's parents. After all, most of these boys are very young, poorly educated, and financially dependent on their own parents (Kiselica & Sturmer, 1993; Robinson & Barret, 1985).

Optimally, bringing up children is the responsibility of the mother and father. Like teenage mothers, teenage fathers need help if they are to remain emotionally involved with their child. There is much that can be done to help adolescent boys be more involved in the prevention of pregnancy, family planning, and their children's development (Weinstein & Rosen, 1994). A few programs exist that help young fathers be actively involved in raising their children. A program in Trenton, New Jersey, called First Step provides innercity men with the skills they need to become independent and socially responsible. The curriculum ranges from birth control, finding employment, and making good decisions to feeding, bathing, and diapering babies (Friedman, 1991).

## *SUMMARY*

**1.** Sexual behavior is an excellent way of achieving intimacy in a romantic relationship. It is also a source of pleasure that enriches people's lives and a way of ensuring the continuation of our species.

**2.** Although all societies want their younger members to reproduce, most parents prefer that sex occur within a committed relationship. Today, partly due to the relatively early age of puberty and the relatively late age of marriage, intercourse has become normative in premarital long-term relationships.

**3.** Among young people, dating is a gauge of one's popularity. It provides opportunities for young people to practice the skills and roles that are necessary for successful adult romantic relationships. Dating also allows young people to assert their independence from their families and feel that they fit in with their peer group.

**4.** There is pressure for young people to date before they are emotionally or socially ready. Those who date for the wrong reasons find close encounters stressful. Early daters feel awkward and tentative in their initial attempts to act like adults. Over time, on a trial-and-error basis, adolescents become aware of the personal qualities that they value in a close friend or partner.

**5.** Some young people move through the courtship process much more rapidly than others. Adolescent girls, especially early maturers, find themselves wondering how to maintain their sense of self in relationship without risking losing a boyfriend. Boys generally are concerned about their pride and reputation, whereas girls value feeling emotionally connected to their partner. Most boys and girls are quite vulnerable during this period.

**6.** Adolescents who are close to their parents and who feel comfortable communicating with them usually have more satisfying and less problematic relationships with romantic partners. Several aspects of family life, especially quality of communication, are associated with frequency of dating, sexual activity, and pregnancy.

**7.** Some parents allow their children to have sex at home. Although they do not condone their children's behavior, they claim that their children will be sexually active anyway, and they prefer to know where and with whom their children are being intimate. Most parents are uncomfortable with this arrangement and prohibit it.

**8.** The United States has one of the highest rates of teenage pregnancy in the industrial world. Few pregnant females live with or marry their sexual partner or give up the child for adoption. Most are undereducated, economically disadvantaged, and lead stressful lives, especially if they lack family support. Many claim that they intended to become pregnant, perhaps as a way of gaining love or attention. Although as a group adolescent mothers are emotionally immature and not very competent parents, those with good coping resources and enthusiastic social support usually adjust well and provide adequate caregiving.

**9.** Forty percent of unmarried, pregnant adolescents abort their pregnancies. Some report being coerced into having the procedure. Many are confused and misinformed about their alternatives and regret their decision. A small number of pregnant adolescents, who are younger, white, and relatively affluent, choose adoption, a decision usually supported by family and friends.

**10.** Pregnant adolescents who marry their child's father are at high risk for marital conflict and divorce. Married teenagers usually lack the maturity, financial resources, and relationship skills necessary for a satisfying relationship. Despite the stereotype of the predatory male teenager, boys usually are emotionally attached to their girlfriends and their babies. Although it would be better for an infant to be raised by two caring parents, teenage fathers usually are given limited opportunities to interact with their child.

## GLOSSARY

**Cognitive model of adolescent pregnancy** Views adolescent pregnancy as resulting from some cognitive deficit, such as poor problem-solving skills, inability to plan for the future, or lack of knowledge about contraception

**Psychosocial model of adolescent pregnancy** Attributes pregnancy to faulty social learning experiences or to a lack of social support

**Sexual behavior model of adolescent pregnancy** Assumes that the only difference between nonpregnant and pregnant females is that the latter are more sexually active and do not use contraceptives

# THOUGHT QUESTIONS

**1.** How can we tell when someone is ready to be sexually active?

**2.** Should adolescents be required to obtain parental consent to obtain birth control materials or to get an abortion?

**3.** Can becoming a mother or father ever be the right choice for a teenager?

**4.** As a parent, how would you prepare your child for dating, romance, and sexual decision making?

**5.** For most of human history, females became pregnant almost as soon as they were fertile. Why does modern society reject this practice?

## SELF-TEST

1. Which group of adolescents has the least opportunity to date?
   a. religious
   b. bilingual
   c. bisexual
   d. homosexual

2. Cross-cultural studies indicate that to adolescents, the ideal dating partner is
   a. sexy
   b. fun to be with
   c. attractive
   d. all of the above

3. According to Erikson, the central task of young adulthood is
   a. achieving an adult identity
   b. forming an intimate relationship
   c. supporting the next generation
   d. living independently

4. In romantic relationships, girls generally
   a. are opportunistic
   b. seek a feeling of connectedness with their partner
   c. deny the validity of their partner's feelings
   d. tend to be permissive regarding casual sex

5. Most early adolescents
   a. have poorly developed intimacy skills
   b. have few role models for self-disclosure
   c. grieve when romantic relationships end
   d. all of the above

6. Adolescents get most of their sexual information
   a. at home
   b. from peers
   c. in school
   d. from the media

**7.** Parents who let their children have sex at home

   **a.** condone premarital sex

   **b.** usually provide birth control devices

   **c.** view this practice as a way of protecting their children

   **d.** are confident that they are making the right decision

**8.** What proportion of adolescents who become pregnant each year actually bear the child?

   **a.** one-third

   **b.** one-quarter

   **c.** one-half

   **d.** two-thirds

**9.** Teenage mothers

   **a.** usually marry the father

   **b.** usually complete their education

   **c.** feel responsible for raising their child

   **d.** usually have high vocational aspirations

**10.** Children of adolescent mothers are at disproportionate risk for

   **a.** being abused or neglected

   **b.** school failure

   **c.** social and emotional problems

   **d.** all of the above

**11.** The best predictor for positive adjustment in adolescent mothers is

   **a.** having varied sources of social support

   **b.** living with their child's father

   **c.** living independently

   **d.** quitting school

**12.** Most adolescents who have abortions report feeling

   **a.** regret

   **b.** relief

   **c.** ambivalence

   **d.** angry

# ELEVEN

# SCHOOLING AND ACHIEVEMENT

◆

## Preview Questions

1. What were the original goals of secondary schools?
2. Why are so many high school students disaffected with school?
3. What personal qualities predict academic success?
4. What role does family life play in helping adolescents learn to value academic achievement?
5. How does parental divorce affect adolescent school performance?
6. In what sense is achievement self-perpetuating?
7. How do peers influence each other's academic achievement?
8. How can we account for gender differences in achievement?
9. How can we design more effective secondary schools?
10. Why are school transitions stressful to so many teenagers?
11. What is the profile of the academic underachiever?

◆
___

## Disclosures

I try to do good in school to get into a good college. You need an education so that you can get a job and do something in life. Best thing about school? To see my friends and catch up on all the gossip.

*(Danielle, 15-year-old high school freshman)*

This year, my favorite subject is a toss-up between science and German. In German, our teacher is from Germany and she tells us everything that goes on and different things that a normal German teacher wouldn't tell you. And our science class is like, everything is hands on. My teacher in world history, she's a very boring teacher. Like, she'll give us the book, read this, do this section, and review. She's always screaming at people, throwing them out, and they always make a fool out of her because she doesn't do anything. She's afraid of most of the kids in the class.

*(Jeannine, 14-year-old high school freshman)*

When I check notebooks, it's an atrocity. There are virtually no notes. These students lose their books. They don't bring pens or notebooks to class. When I try to discipline, some of them just pick up and walk out.

*(High school English teacher, quoted by Tabor, 1996, p. A15)*

# Contents

During our first session, eighth grader Chris tells me that school is just a game played by teachers and students. On his last report card, Chris received all C grades, reflecting a decline from previous marking periods when he received A's and B's. He admitted that he did as little school work as possible, but he was still surprised and disappointed by his grades. He knows that he is capable of doing better.

His parents, who "yelled and screamed" at him and punished him in other ways, blamed Chris's poor performance partly on his hanging out with the "wrong people." When they found out that he occasionally smokes marijuana with his friends, they insisted that he come into counseling. He tells me that his parents have almost given up on him because of what they see as his rebellious behavior and rudeness.

When I ask about his goals, Chris tells me that he wants to attend college. He has his eyes on the Coast Guard Academy because of his interest in sailing and "anything aquatic." He says that he knows what he has to do to succeed in school; it's just hard to get himself to take schoolwork or his teachers seriously.

Chris's cynical attitude toward school is not so different from that of many other students in middle and high school. As children grow older, many become increasingly disillusioned about school and learning. The transition from elementary to secondary school is an important milestone, and it is stressful. Most students take time to adjust to a new school, an increased workload, and harder work. Compared to elementary school teachers, middle school teachers have higher expectations and less time to spend with each student. Secondary school teachers usually are less sympathetic than primary school teachers and more demanding. The social network students established in elementary school is disrupted, and new relationships must be formed (Eccles et al., 1991).

Like Chris, some students are less enthusiastic about school than they were in elementary school. Their teachers may view them as having an attitude problem. Although Chris is not typical of secondary school students, his situation reminds us that adolescents' performance in school cannot be separated from their experiences outside of school. As we shall see, family and friends can have a big impact on young people's willingness to take school seriously. Despite their ambivalence about working hard to achieve good grades, most do take care of business, especially those who are confident in their academic and social abilities (Lord, Eccles, & McCarthy, 1994; Patrick, Hicks, & Ryan, 1997).

Why should young people take school seriously? The moratorium arrangement discussed in Chapter 1 requires that they commit to the role of student. Five days a week, 10 months a year, for about 16 years (counting college attendance) they arise at dawn, travel to a large building where they are expected to respect, pay attention to, and obey not always sympathetic adult authority figures, concentrate for several hours on academic subjects that may not be particularly stimulating, and then bring additional material home for further study. What is the immediate payoff for all of this effort? At best, a sense of accomplishment, good grades, and parental approval.

Adults are quick to point out the link between an impressive transcript, occupational opportunities, and material gains (Brooks, 1995), but these outcomes are many years away. From this cynical perspective, it is easy to see why students like Chris display far less enthusiasm about their schoolwork than their parents and teachers would like.

In this chapter, we consider the topics of schooling and adolescent achievement. Why is school attendance mandatory? How do the cognitive advances of early adolescence prepare young teenagers for the increasingly challenging work that they will encounter in high school and college? What role do parents and peers play in adolescent achievement motivation? Why do some students excel academically, while others are disaffected? How do we understand ethnic and gender differences in achievement? And what can parents and teachers do to ease the transitions to middle school, high school, and college?

# COMPULSORY EDUCATION

There are ample rewards for students who work hard in school—appreciation and understanding of the world we live in, pride in one's work, and, eventually, employability. **Literacy**, the ability to read, write, and calculate, is essential for functioning in a competitive technological society. It is difficult to imagine how one could function as a worker, parent, or citizen without literacy skills.

Including college attendance, students like Chris spend about 16 of their first 21 years of life in school. Adolescents spend more hours in classrooms than they do in any setting other than their own bedrooms. About a fifth of the life span is spent in school, but even these 16 years pale in comparison to the amount of time spent in the workplace. Assuming a 21st-century retirement age of 70, the average college graduate will spend about 45 years working, almost three times as long as the time spent in school. *Thought Question: If the average life span doubles in the next century, as it did in this century, how might the moratorium arrangment be affected?*

Compulsory education is society's way of introducing its new members to the culture at large. Although socialization occurs mainly at home, society holds schools primarily responsible for teaching basic literacy skills, passing on cultural traditions, and cultivating traditional social values, including competition and achievement. Schooling is intended to prepare young people to function competently in a wide variety of adult roles (Csikszentmihalyi & Larson, 1984; Jackson & Hornbeck, 1989; Trickett & Schmid, 1993).

It was not always this way. Before this century, it was mainly privileged males who had access to formal education. Although the first high school was founded in 1821, it was not until 1872 that courts decided to let local communities tax themselves to support public education. At the turn of the century, only about 10% of adolescents attended high school. By the 1970s, almost all adolescents between the ages of 14 and 17 years were enrolled in public or private high schools (Murphy, 1987).

Initially, education was intended to prepare children for a vocation. In exchange for their work, they would be granted the privilege of deferring vocational choices and adult roles until they were mature enough to handle adult responsibilities. Today we expect that virtually all children can be and will be educated. (The national high school graduation rate hovers at around 85%.)

There is a consensus that education should prepare children to function as well-adjusted, productive adults in a competitive technological society. Other possible goals of secondary education include (1) preparing children for adult roles such as parent, citizen, and consumer: (2) social reform, for example, integration of the races and equality of the sexes: (3) providing youth with hands-on opportunities to explore and examine the world; (4) preparation for college; (5) vocational training; (6) teaching critical thinking skills; (7) teaching ethics and moral decision making; and (8) providing interventions for antisocial and self-destructive behaviors (see Table 11-1). Not everyone accepts that public schools single-handedly can or should address these goals. Business organizations in particular have been critical of schools' providing nonacademic ser-

**Table 11-1 Possible Goals of Secondary Education**

Preparing children to function as well-adjusted, productive adults in a competitive, technological society

Preparing children for adult roles such as parent, citizen, and consumer

Social reform, such as integration of the races and equality of the sexes

Providing youth with "hands-on" opportunities to explore and examine the world

Preparation for college

Vocational training

Teaching critical thinking skills

Teaching ethics and moral decision-making

Providing interventions for antisocial and self-destructive behaviors

vices such as pregnancy counseling and driver education rather than focusing on literacy and critical thinking skills (Manegold, 1994).

No one denies that schooling affects development. However, children do not automatically benefit from sitting in a classroom, even if they are attentive. Is it realistic to expect that school attendance, no matter how well designed or implemented, can compensate for the family or life problems that so many children face, especially those who lack the resources available to middle-class, able-bodied students? Although schooling can buffer the effects of early exposure to biological, environmental, and cognitive risk factors (Gorman & Pollitt, 1996), it would be naive to expect that education alone can counteract the effects of poverty, discrimination, and abuse (Pungello, Kupersmidt, Burchinal, & Patterson, 1996).

## EFFECTIVENESS OF SCHOOLING

Given its immensity and diversity, it is difficult to evaluate the effectiveness of our educational system. For every statistic indicating a decline in academic performance, there is another statistic that raises our hopes (Applebome, 1995b; Arenson, 1996a; Chira, 1992b). We hear or read reports of students in the United States doing better than they did previously on standardized tests yet not doing as well as students in other industrialized countries, especially Asian countries like Singapore, South Korea, Japan, and Hong Kong (Applebome, 1996a; Stevenson, Chen, & Lee, 1993).

Average scores of students taking the Scholastic Assessment Test peaked in 1963 and 1964 and then dropped steadily until 1980, when math scores began to increase (Ravitch, 1996). Math scores have improved for 5 consecutive years since 1992 (Honan, 1997; *The New York Times*, August 23, 1996), erasing the 5% decline since the 1960s. Verbal scores have not improved much since 1972, perhaps reflecting the facts that fewer students are taking 4 years of high school English and that more students who speak English as a second language are taking the test (Arenson, 1996a). And reading remains a less than favorite leisure-time activity.

A study entitled *Adult Literacy in America* was released in 1993 by the U.S. Education Department. The study concluded that half of the country's adult citizens are unfit for employment. They are not proficient enough in English to write a letter about a billing error or to figure out the length of a bus trip based on a schedule (*The New York Times*, September 9, 1993; *Time*, September 20, 1993). A National Science Foundation random telephone survey performed in 1995 revealed that fewer than half of all Americans know that the earth orbits the sun each year. Only 9% could define the term *molecule*, and only 21% could define DNA (*The New York Times*, May 24, 1996).

Relatively few students realize their full potential and consistently do quality work. Too many students in the United States learn just enough to satisfy their teachers, their parents, and themselves. A long-term study comparing Asian school children with those in the United States (Stevenson, Chen, & Lee, 1993; Stevenson & Stigler, 1992) revealed that only 14.5% of Chinese and 8% of Japanese eleventh graders scored lower on a standardized math test than the *average* score of the U.S. students. Despite a persistent myth that overworked Asian students are on the brink of suicide, the study reported that the superior performance of the Asian students did not come at great psychological cost. U.S. students most reported feeling stress, depression, and other bodily complaints.

There is no shortage of explanations for the achievement gap between U.S. students and their counterparts in many other countries: absence of a common, rigorous national curriculum and national standards, lack of incentives for achievement, inadequate funding for schools, large classes, inadequate time for teachers to prepare their lessons, student tracking, low academic standards, unearned student promotions, diluted course content, too little or unchallenging homework, too much TV, poor attendance, inadequate classroom discipline, unsafe schools, overemphasis on nonacademic goals such as sports, poorly trained teachers, peer pressure, high dropout rates, unstable family life, and on and on (Applebome, 1996a; Bishop, 1995).

Parents, teachers, and students in the United States do have lower expectations regarding achievement than their counterparts in other countries, such as China, Japan, and Germany. Parental satisfaction with student achievement in the United States remains high despite poorer relative performance and lower standards than those of other countries. "Few Chinese and Japanese mothers, but over 40% of the American mothers, expressed high degrees of satisfaction with their children's academic performance" (Stevenson et al., 1993, p. 55). Ironically, a much higher percentage of mothers in the United States than in China or Japan believe that the schools are doing a good or excellent job. Most mothers in the United States believe that innate ability is the key to academic success. Thus, if you fail in math it is because you are "bad" at math. Mothers in Asian countries attribute success to hard work. If you fail in math, it is because you are lazy. Seventy percent of the Japanese students and 60% of the Taiwanese students agreed that studying hard was the reason they did well. Only a quarter of students in the United States cited hard work as the key to academic success. Instead, more than half reported that "a good teacher" is the most important factor. Most educators would agree with the Asians parents and children—learning can occur in the absence of good teaching but not without considerable effort (Welsh, 1992).

Critics of current educational practices such as William Glasser (1990) maintain that too many teachers and school administrators are willing to accept low-quality work. The guiding principle in secondary school seems to be expediency ("get them through"). Many teachers respond to poor performance or poor behavior in class with disapproval, detention, or suspension. They complain about lazy or unmotivated students. Apathetic students rebel through misbehavior, lack of attention, or truancy. Many students claim that their teachers do not care about them or even about the subject matter.

Glasser reports that students tell him that "a good teacher is deeply interested in the students and in the material being taught. They also say that such a teacher frequently conducts class discussions and does not lecture very much. Almost all of them say that a good teacher relates to them on their level; the teacher does not place herself above them and they are comfortable talking with her. They also tell me that a good teacher does not threaten or punish and that they have little respect for teachers who do. . . . Students also tell me that they appreciate teachers who make an effort to be entertaining. To maintain student interest month after month in potentially boring courses, good lead-teachers try to inject humor, variety, and drama into the lessons" (pp. 66–67).

Teachers respond that students are not willing to work hard and expect immediate results. They feel pressure from parents and administrators to lower standards. Parents who encourage teachers to raise their standards complain when their children bring home report cards with mediocre grades. When parents express more concern about grades, transcripts, and college applications than about what their children are actually learning, the *GPA perspective* (grades rule) is passed from one generation to the next (Bishop, 1995; Welsh, 1992). The key question remains: how do we create a parent–teacher–student alliance that fosters meaningful learning in secondary school classrooms (Brophy, 1986; Grolnick & Slowiaczek, 1994; Linney & Seidman, 1989)?

## ACHIEVEMENT MOTIVATION

Chris's parents are disturbed because he doesn't seem to care about his schoolwork. They worry that if he does poorly in the eighth grade, his high school career will be compromised. Chris claims that he wants to succeed, yet he can't explain why academic work has so little appeal to him. He finds much more satisfaction in time spent with friends, listening to music, and playing video games.

It is helpful to distinguish between two very different types of attitudes that students display toward school: **engagement** and **disaffection** (Kindermann, 1993). Engaged students seek and enjoy challenging work, take the initiative when given the opportunity, and exert effort and concentration during learning tasks. In other words, they are ready and eager to learn. Disaffected students are passive, expend little effort, and give up easily when challenged. Like Chris, they would rather be someplace else, doing something else.

What contributes to engagement? This is a difficult question to answer because so many factors are involved, including learning style and biology (Ablard & Mills, 1996; Bouffard-Bouchard, Parent, & Larivee, 1991; Cohen, Beckwith, Parmelee, Sigman, Asarnow, & Espinosa, 1996; Horton & Oakland, 1997; Mwamwenda, 1993). For example, learning-disabled students generally have lower vocational and career aspirations than their nondisabled peers (Rojewski, 1996).

If you examine your own engagement in schooling, you might conclude that *motivation* (wanting to do well), *commitment* (willingness to work hard), and *self-efficacy* (believing that you can succeed) are key factors (Bandura, 1986, 1989; Bandura, Barbaranelli, Caprara, & Pastorelli, 1996). High achievers usually are persistent, task-oriented, and have positive attitudes about learning. "Students who are quick to adapt, stay on task, and eager or willing to approach new tasks or situations may fit into classroom settings more successfully and correspond more closely to teachers' perceptions of ideal students" (Guerin, Gottfried, Oliver, & Thomas, 1994, p. 219). (See Table 11-2.)

Students who expect to do well engage themselves more deeply in challenging material and assignments and seem to gain more intrinsic enjoyment (Pintrich, Roeser, & De Groot, 1994; Skinner, Wellborn, & Connell, 1990; Wigfield & Eccles, 1992). Lack of interest ("It's so boring") and lack of self-confidence ("I'm bad at math") lead to minimal engagement in schoolwork, which in turn produces outcomes that confirm students' low expectations of

**Table 11-2  Factors That Contribute to Achievement Motivation**

Family preparation for and encouragement of learning

Enjoyment of learning

Willingness to work hard

Self-efficacy (belief that one will do well)

Commitment to and positive attitudes about learning

Welcoming challenging material

Realistic expectations about one's ability

Desire to succeed

Mastery goal orientation

Sense of belonging to the social group

High peer standards

Stimulating tasks and materials

Choice regarding subject matter

Cooperative learning opportunities

School size

Quality of instruction

Students' perceptions of teacher

themselves (Haller, 1982; Henderson & Dweck, 1990; Pintrich & De Groot, 1990).

If you continue your academic self-examination, you may identify specific *beliefs and attributions* that keep you in the achievement arena (Strage, 1997; Weiner, 1985). Attribution theory describes how expectancies about success affect efforts to achieve (Dornbusch et al., 1996). Persistence in the academic arena requires the belief that if one works hard enough, one has the ability to succeed. Further, most students believe that doing well in school will gain them recognition from their family and friends and, eventually, economic success.

In your self-examination, you might discover achievement-related *motives* and *feelings*—for example, a desire to be successful, a fear of failure, or a love of learning—that reflect your own personal and educational history. Can you identify *goal orientations* that reflect your desire to master an assigned task or your concern about how your school performance will be evaluated? **Mastery goal orientations** ("What must I do to succeed?") usually foretell high levels of persistence and finding alternative solutions to problems. **Performance goal orientations** ("How am I doing?") are associated with weaker performance on challenging tasks due to anticipation or fear of failure (Dweck & Leggett, 1988; Nicholls, 1984).

Social goals (such as being popular) can motivate or inhibit academic performance (Patrick et al., 1997). Wentzel (1996) found that for students in a suburban middle school, the pursuit of social goals (rather than a performance orientation) was the best predictor of class effort in sixth and eighth grades. "Although speculative, it is possible that a sixth-grade student's interest in being an integral part of the social life of the classroom is a more powerful motivator of academic engagement than is interest in a particular content area" (Wentzel, 1996, p. 402). Ryan and her colleagues (Ryan, Hicks, & Midgley, 1997) observed that 5th graders who worried about how their peers viewed them were less likely to ask for help when they needed it. (See Box 11-1.)

Contextual variables operating in schools shape achievement expectations and values (Dornbusch et al., 1996; Elmen, 1991). Classmates and other peer reference groups set different standards for achievement. How teachers structure their classes makes a big difference in students' willingness to stay engaged when facing difficult, abstract material.

Students report being more interested in course material (1) when they can relate the material to their own life experiences, (2) when they are given some choice regarding learning tasks, (3) when teachers provide good explanations, and (4) when teachers allow students to work with each other. These findings are important because they suggest that rather than writing off some students as "hopeless," teachers can take steps to help students become cognitively engaged in academic work (Brown, 1997; Pintrich et al., 1994) (Figure 11-1).

Other school characteristics play a key role in achievement motivation. School size, for example, is related to achievement, with students from smaller schools generally doing better. (Why do you think this is so?) A 14-year-old high school girl commented to one of my students about the large size of her high school population: "It was positive because you make new friends and

**Box 11-1 Self-Handicapping Strategies in Middle School Students**

*Study Question: How might their concern about how their peers view them affect middle school students' study strategies?*

Several theorists have noted that some people arrange circumstances so that, if they perform poorly on a task, the circumstances can be blamed rather than their ability (Higgins, Snyder, & Berglas, 1990). For example, many students procrastinate, stay up late partying instead of studying, or deliberately do not try to do well on a test or project. These so-called **self-handicapping strategies** apparently are intended to deflect attention away from their ability and toward these circumstances (Midgley & Urdan, 1995).

Such strategies are called *self-handicapping* because they lead to inferior performance. Self-handicapping strategies are different from the attributions described in the previous section in that self-handicapping precedes and impairs performance, whereas attributions follow and rationalize performance. Claiming that you failed a math test because you stayed out late the night before (an attribution) is different from deliberately staying up late to provide an excuse for failing the test. The use of self-handicapping requires the cognitive capacity to understand the relationship between ability, effort, and performance (Midgley & Urdan, 1995).

Midgley and Urdan (1995) hypothesized that males use self-handicapping strategies more often than females and that lower-achieving students use them more often than higher-achieving students. The investigators surveyed 256 eighth-grade students from two middle schools in a Midwestern working-class community. Parental permission was required. The surveys took 40 minutes to complete. Students were asked about a variety of self-handicapping strategies cited by middle school teachers. The strategies were introduced as follows: "Below are examples of things most students do at one time or another. Please be very honest and tell us how true each of these is for you. No one at home or school will ever see your answers" (p. 395).

The investigators' hypotheses were supported. Boys used self-handicapping strategies more often than girls and low achievers more often than high achievers. Although high-achieving girls did not self-handicap, some high-achieving boys did. High achievement apparently doesn't reduce boys' concerns about appearing competent as much as it does girls' concerns.

According to their survey responses, self-handicappers are concerned about appearing academically competent to others, yet they shy away from situations that would allow such comparisons. In other words, they want to appear smart but don't think that they will be. Students who use self-handicapping strategies generally are low achieving, have low regard for themselves, and are anxious when performing in front of their peers. Clearly, these students need help learning positive strategies for improving their performance rather than resorting to strategies that ultimately bring inferior results.

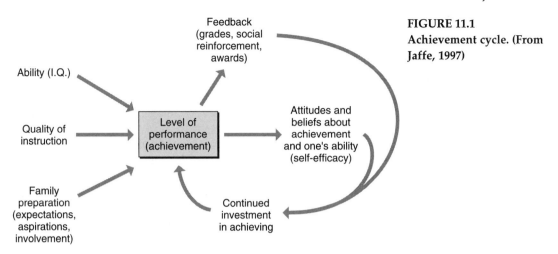

**FIGURE 11.1**
**Achievement cycle. (From**
**Jaffe, 1997)**

have greater opportunities to be involved in activities. It was negative because there are a lot of experiences that you feel afraid to get involved with because you don't know how they will turn out."

Instructional and subject-matter variables also are important (Fraser, 1989). These include the quality of instruction, opportunities to learn and practice skills, and the amount of homework. In Reynolds' study (1991, described below), students who liked their teachers learned more. Motivated students also viewed their classrooms as higher in quality. Reynolds concluded that schools and teachers make a big difference in learning.

Add to the equation the myriad changes of adolescence and the emotional adjustments that they require and you see that we have a complicated story indeed. The bottom line is that some students fulfill their academic potential, while others muddle through (Csikszentmihalyi, Rathunde, & Whalen, 1993).

## ACHIEVEMENT TRAJECTORIES

In a longitudinal study of 3,116 seventh- and eighth-grade public school students, Reynolds (1991) found that prior achievement in the sixth grade, particularly in math and science, was an excellent predictor of students' performance in the seventh and eighth grades. For almost any activity, starting off well gives us the impetus to continue trying. Those who perform well in the early grades usually continue to excel in secondary school and college. (As we have seen, this was not true for Chris, who had done well until middle school. His parents wonder: Was it the "bad crowd," the marijuana, the deterioration in family communication, or something else?)

Reynolds' study confirms that successful early schooling makes middle school success more likely. Classroom behaviors that pay off in school, such as effective use of time, interest in the subject matter, good attention span, and active participation, usually are present by the first grade. Thus, we observe "a 'window of opportunity' in first grade, before achievement trajectories are fully established, when good classroom adjustment helps establish early learning patterns and places children on favorable trajectories that tend to persist" (Alexander, Entwisle, & Dauber, 1993, p. 812).

Although children typically begin formal schooling during their fifth year of life, it is not until adolescence that most recognize the connection between education and their future lives. As adolescents mature cognitively, they realize that their academic track record sets the stage for their adult life path (Brooks, 1995). With the help of parents and teachers, most come to understand that college attendance and access to desirable jobs partly depend on report cards, transcripts, extracurricular activities, and letters of recommendation. "Students who intend to go to college will function better because of that intention, while students who see only a bleak job market ahead may be tempted to drop out" (Entwisle, 1990, p. 198).

Thus, academic performance is anchored both in past performance and in future goals. There are at least two possible side effects of this trajectory. First, extrinsic goals such as employment or college attendance, competition with peers, and evaluations from teachers increase pressure to get good grades and discourage mastery of a subject matter for its own sake (Elmen, 1991). Second, those who flounder in elementary school have to try harder in middle and high school to stay above water.

## THE ROLE OF THE FAMILY

The ecological-contextual perspective, emphasizing a *spillover effect* from one life setting to another, implies that adolescents who function well in one type of environment are likely to do well in other settings (Luthar, 1995). Young people who enjoy supportive, harmonious, egalitarian home environments usually are better prepared to benefit from schooling (Burge, Hammen, Davila, Daley, Paley, Herzberg, & Lindberg, 1997; Hieshima & Schneider, 1994; Kurdek, Fine, & Sinclair, 1995; Updegraff, McHale, & Crouter, 1996; Westerman & La Luz, 1995). It is a cliché, but still true, that parents are children's first and most important teachers, especially because parental influence is felt so early in life. In other words, *family influences are fundamental. They precede and determine other factors that support achievement in and out of school* (Haller, 1982; Reynolds, 1991).

Although we do not yet fully understand the specific mechanisms by which parents help their children to achieve, there is ample evidence that the following factors contribute to progress in school: (1) a close parent–child relationship, (2) positive parental attitudes toward school, (3) realistic expectations about achievement, and (4) parents' displaying interest and involvement in school functions and their children's schooling. Thus, parents' attitudes and expectations are both a cause and an effect of their children's academic achievement (Amato, 1989; Bandura et al., 1996; Fuligni, 1997; Hess & Holloway, 1984; Linney & Vernberg, 1983; Marjoribanks, 1986; Paulson, 1994; Seginer, 1983; Wood, Chapin, & Hannah, 1988; Yee & Flanagan, 1985).

Children of educated and affluent parents generally have more advantages and opportunities for achievement than children of less fortunate parents. To their children, educated parents are role models regarding achievement, responsibility, high aspirations, self-restraint, and good work habits. Educated parents also encourage their children to have relationships with peers who share their values, especially values that support achievement (Baker & Stevenson, 1986; Brown et al., 1993; DeSantis, Ketterlinus, & Youniss, 1990; Dye, 1989; Masselam, Marcus, & Stunkard, 1990; Snodgrass, 1991; Stevenson & Baker, 1987; Wentzel & Feldman, 1993; Williams & Radin, 1993).

Their own success in school enables achieving parents to participate more fully in their children's education rather than assign prime responsibility to unrelated caregivers. This is particularly important during the secondary school years. Recent polls indicate declining involvement of parents as children grow older (Chira, 1994). Earlier, we discussed disengaged students. It is troubling to discover that uninvolved parents and disengaged peers can undermine adolescents' interest in schoolwork (Steinberg, 1996b). When parents show interest in schoolwork and homework assignments, adolescents know that what they are doing is important. (See Table 11-3.)

Young people who have frequent, positive encounters with the significant people in their lives do better in school and feel more self-confident. Good communication and family cohesion (emotional closeness) make it more likely that children will develop feelings of competence even before they begin school.

**To their adolescent children, parents can be role-models regarding achievement, responsibility, high aspirations, self-restraint, and good work habits.**

**Table 11-3  Family Factors Supporting Academic Achievement**

A close parent-child relationship

Positive parental attitudes toward school and schoolwork

Realistic parental expectations about achievement

Parents' displaying interest and involvement in school functions and their children's schooling

Parental participation in parent-teacher conferences and other school-related activities

Parental education and socioeconomic status

Parental modeling of reading, good work habits, and high aspirations

Parental encouragement of friendships with achieving peers

Good communication and family cohesion (emotional closeness)

Parental self-efficacy regarding parenting competence

Authoritative parenting style

Students who feel secure and supported by their parents often transfer these feelings to their teachers. It is as though family life prepares some children more than others for having satisfying relationships with teachers and peers (Masselam et al., 1990; Ryan, Stiller, & Lynch, 1994).

Attending activities such as open houses reinforces the importance of school and provides parents with useful information about how their children are performing and how they can help their children do better. Assisting with homework and studying, expressing high expectations ("I know you can do it"), and attending meetings with teachers and parent–teacher associations are some of the ways parents express interest in their children's schooling (Epstein, 1992).

Making sure that adolescents are prepared for their classes, that they arrive in class on time, assigning reasonable amounts of household chores, and encouraging reading also are effective strategies for promoting achievement. These tasks are not easy to accomplish when parents work full time. But the potential cost of parental indifference to children's schoolwork is high (America's Smallest School: The Family, Educational Testing Service, 1992; Grolnick & Slowiaczek, 1994; Steinberg, 1996b; Stevenson & Stigler, 1992; Wentzel, 1994).

It is crucial that parents understand their potential role in their children's academic performance. Bandura and his colleagues (1996) demonstrated that parents' belief that they can promote their children's intellectual development (i.e., parental self-efficacy) and their educational aspirations for their children are key factors in achievement. In effect, parents who believe that they are good at parenting typically have children who believe in their own abilities.

Parents who doubt their parenting competence are more reluctant to take action, may give up prematurely when they meet resistance, and resort to coercive discipline strategies to manage problem behavior. Parents who are overly controlling and critical often have children with unimpressive academic performance. Parents who are inconsistent or who display a harsh parenting style

**Box 11-2
Home
Schooling**

Although the exact number is not known, more and more students are being schooled at home. The U.S. Department of Education estimates that 500,000 students, 1% of the country's school population, receive home instruction. About one-third of them are adolescents (Lewin, 1995c).

Some of these students attend regular school for specific services, such as a chemistry lab, or for extracurricular activities. A 16-year-old Massachusetts girl named Anna commented, ''I would never want to go back full time but I feel fine going to that [creative writing] class. It's what I want to learn, not what someone told me I was supposed to learn. When I was in school, I didn't like reading or writing. But since I've started home schooling I've read some books that have changed my life. And every day I do a 10-minute writing exercise on an assigned word. It has taught me that I have a million stories in me'' (quoted by Lewin, 1995c, p. D20).

Some parents choose home schooling to instill religious values. Other parents say that they are dissatisfied with public school instruction, feel that public schooling is too competitive, or fear for their children's safety. Although home schooling is legal in every state, school districts across the country differ regarding their willingness to support students who study exclusively at home (Lewin, 1995c). *Thought Question: What are some potential disadvantages of home schooling?*

**National Spelling Bee champion Rebecca Sealfon and her mother. Rebecca was home schooled by her mom.**

may inadvertently discourage children's attentional and exploration skills. Inconsistent and punitive parenting practices contribute to distress, low self-restraint, and low levels of responsible behavior (DeBaryshe, Patterson, & Capaldi, 1993; Ginsburg & Bronstein, 1993; Glasgow et al., 1997; Wentzel & Feldman, 1993; Wentzel, Feldman, & Weinberger, 1991).

As noted in Chapter 7, authoritative parents are flexible, consistent, and prefer reasoning and persuasion to power and coercion. Children of authoritative parents usually have higher self-esteem, greater academic success, and better adjustment than children from punitive families. Many studies confirm that the authoritative parenting style is linked to academic success in middle-class children and adolescents. Perhaps this is because these children are better adjusted or because they get along better with their parents and teachers and receive more support. Adolescent children of authoritative parents typically work harder in school, participate more in classroom activities, have higher aspirations, and do better than children of punitive or permissive parents. Not surprisingly, they like school more (Linver & Silverberg, 1997; Steinberg et al., 1989; Steinberg, Lamborn, Dornbusch, & Darling, 1992).

Lawrence Steinberg and his colleagues (1992) asked a diverse sample of 6,400 adolescents between the ages of 14 and 18 years about their parents' childrearing practices and achievement-related behaviors. The investigators also collected data regarding the students' school performance and commitment. Students who viewed their parents as warm, firm, and fair did better in school and improved more academically than students from nonauthoritative families. The impact of authoritative parenting on achievement depended on the level of parental involvement (e.g., attending school programs, helping with schoolwork). Parental involvement enhances school success for students of authoritative parents, not for students of permissive or punitive parents. Presumably, parents are more pleased with their children when they perform well in school. This creates a self-perpetuating cycle of achievement and parent–child closeness (Grolnick & Slowiaczek, 1994; Smith, 1993). *Thought Question: Why might students of permissive parents perform more poorly in school?*

## FAMILY INSTABILITY AND ACHIEVEMENT

Around the world, in wealthy and poor countries, the structure of family life is changing dramatically. Trends include higher divorce rates, more children being raised by single parents, and the feminization of poverty (Lewin, 1995a). Children's emotional adjustment and school performance are vulnerable to a host of life stressors, especially chronic family conflict (Keith & Finlay, 1988; Nelson, Hughes, Handal, & Katz, 1993).

It is hard to concentrate in school when one's home life is unstable or conflictual. Witnessing heated parental arguments, experiencing separation from a parent following divorce, living with a distressed single parent, and adjusting to parental dating or remarriage all take their toll on children and adolescents. Children in single-parent families receive poorer grades and display more behavior problems in school than children from intact families. They do not get along as well with peers and are more likely to suffer from anxiety and depression. They care less than those from two-parent families about being perceived as smart or as good students by parents and friends (DeSantis, Ketterlinus, & Youniss, 1990; Featherstone, Cundick, & Jensen, 1992).

Neighbors and his colleagues (1992) studied 58 young adolescents, half from intact families and half with divorced parents. Boys recently experiencing a parental divorce did worse in school prior to the divorce compared to boys from intact families and compared to girls whose parents divorced. Boys seemed to be more vulnerable than girls to the heated confrontations they witnessed at home before their parents separated. They appeared to suffer more than girls from the lessened attention and supervision that they received from their preoccupied caregivers. Performance in school began declining for girls before the divorce and continued to decline following the divorce. It is not clear why the girls' decline was more gradual and delayed than the boys.' Perhaps the girls' decline reflected the *added* stress of parental divorce to stressors such as school transition and menarche. In any case, it is important to consider predivorce differences when trying to understand postdivorce differences.

Zimiles and Lee (1991) analyzed academic achievement data from a subsample of high school sophomores living in either intact, single-parent, or remarried families. Although the grades differed only slightly among students in the three groups, larger differences were found regarding the number of students dropping out of school. Students from stepfamilies and single-parent families were almost three times more likely to drop out compared to students from intact families, even when socioeconomic and ability differences were controlled for.

Adolescents living in the custody of the same-gender parent were less likely to drop out if they lived with a single parent but more likely to drop out if they lived with a stepparent. According to the study's findings, "when a mother decides to remarry, the probability that her daughter will drop out of high school rises sharply, whereas the likelihood that her son will drop out is almost halved" (p. 318). Boys are more likely and girls are less likely to drop out when their fathers remarry. Thus, adolescents who do not live with both of their natural parents are at greater risk of not graduating from high school. The gender match between custodial parent and child appears to be a critical determinant of the dropout risk for children of divorce. Children of divorce who go away to college typically report enjoying school, presumably benefiting from the distance between them and their family problems (Austin & Martin, 1992).

## PEER RELATIONSHIPS AND ACHIEVEMENT

Given their strong feeling of connectedness to friends, it is predictable that teenagers exert strong influence on each other's willingness to work hard and participate in school-related activities (Kindermann, 1993). As discussed in Chapter 8, the cultural belief that peer influence competes with parental influence has not been supported empirically. Parental influence is greater than that of peers, at least when parents and adolescents get along. Further, peer influence on achievement usually is positive. In most cases, parents and peers reinforce each other's (usually) positive influence on adolescent achievement (Berndt, Miller, & Park, 1989; Kindermann, 1993).

Good students seek each other out. They provide mutual assistance and share resources and information. Pride in their accomplishments and competition with friends encourage them to work hard (Goodenow, 1993; Kindermann, 1993; Wentzel, 1991). Smith (1990) notes that even if time spent with friends occasionally interferes with study behavior, it is not without redeeming social value.

The role of peer influence in adolescent achievement is indicated by the following empirical findings: (1) some friends encourage and some denigrate academic interest and effort; (2) a given friend may sometimes support and sometimes discourage achievement-related behavior; (3) parents and close friends appear to exert the greatest academic influence; (4) adolescents usually seek out as friends those whom they perceive to be at about the same level of achievement; (5) negative peer influence is magnified by low self-esteem and excessive need to be accepted by one's peers; and (6) peer influence is but one of many concurrent, sometimes conflicting, influences on academic motivation (Bishop, 1989; Brown et al., 1986; Epstein, 1983; Kandel, 1978).

To investigate how friends influence each other's academic decision making, Berndt, Laychak, and Park (1990) asked 118 eighth graders from two junior high schools to discuss with a close friend a series of dilemmas relevant to achievement motivation. A control group of friends discussed topics that were unrelated to school. The discussions were videotaped so that the investigators could observe how friends influenced each other's decisions. In one dilemma, a student has purchased a ticket to see one of the most popular rock groups. The student learns that the concert is on the night before a big exam. The student is not prepared for the exam, and it is for a difficult course. This night is the only time the student can study, and he risks a poor grade on the exam if he is not prepared. What to do?

The experiment revealed that friends' decisions about how to resolve the dilemmas were *more similar* after they discussed them than before. Even brief discussions between friends increased the similarity of their decisions. The stronger the friendship, the greater the increase in similarity. "Adolescents changed their decisions on the dilemmas when their friends gave them new information about those decisions" (p. 669). Thus, *exchanging information seems to be a more potent form of influence than social pressure*. This study confirms that friends influence each other's achievement-related decisions and probably their behaviors. Naturally, such influence can be positive, negative, or mixed.

## GENDER AND ACHIEVEMENT

It is common to observe gender differences in academic performance and self-confidence, with boys usually expressing more confidence about their abilities than girls even when girls perform better. Boys generally do a little better than girls in science and math during the middle school years (Beller & Gafni,

1996). Reynolds (1991) found that while boys performed better than girls in the seventh grade, girls were beginning to catch up in the eighth grade, at least in science achievement. Regarding math, girls often outperform boys in elementary school, whereas boys excel during high school and college (Hyde, Fennema, & Lamon, 1990; Wigfield & Eccles, 1994). In a study of 20,000 high school students, Steinberg (1996b) found that girls, on the average, earned higher grades than boys.

Boys typically do better than girls on tasks involving problem solving, whereas girls excel on computation-type tasks. Since the 1960s, boys have scored an average of 46 points higher on the math portion of the Scholastic Assessment Test (SAT) than girls, although this gender gap has been narrowing (Murray, 1995d). In 1995 and 1996, boys outscored girls by 40 and 35 points, respectively, on the math portion and by 3 and 4 points, respectively, on the verbal portion of the test (Arenson, 1996b; *The New York Times*, August 24, 1995). Investigators have attributed the math gap to socialization differences (parents and teachers treating boys and girls differently), differences in cognitive abilities and self-confidence, gender differences in the number of math courses taken, or some combination of these factors (Casey, Nuttal, & Pezaris, 1997; Murray, 1995d).

Byrnes and Takahira (1993) gave 108 high school students (59 girls and 49 boys) math problems from the SAT and measured their prior knowledge and problem-solving strategies. The boys and girls had taken roughly the same number of math courses, and the girls had a slightly higher math grade point average. They found that although the boys did better on the SAT items, it was not their gender that best predicted differences on math performance but their prior knowledge and strategy.

The investigators were not able to explain why the girls displayed less prior knowledge of math when they had the same number of math courses as the boys and received similar grades. "It could be that male subjects took more advanced math courses than female subjects or were more interested in the content" (p. 810). They concluded that socialization, biology, and cognitive processes all account for gender differences in math performance. It does appear that when boys and girls receive comparable treatment, the differences become smaller (Applebome, 1997a; Gilbert, 1996).

---

## SPOTLIGHT • School Girl or Cool Girl?

Like girls of average intelligence, many gifted girls are conflicted about achievement, gender identity, and social acceptance. We have previously noted a general decline in self-esteem and achievement motivation in girls during early adolescence. Apparently, some girls fear that excelling academically will cause them to be rejected by boys or by their female classmates (AAUW Report: Girls in Middle Grades, 1997). *Thought Question: Would we expect peer relationships to have a greater impact on boys' or girls' feelings of self-worth?*

Girls who differ from their peers in achievement, whether they are over- or underachievers, feel less desirable as friends. Fear of success sometimes motivates self-conscious adolescents, especially girls, to avoid taking challenging courses that they believe will compromise their popularity (Roberts & Petersen, 1992). Some parents inadvertently contribute to girls' ambivalence about achievement by expressing low expectations about their abilities in science and math (Eccles-Parsons, Adler, & Kaczala, 1982). Some parents impose on their children gender stereotypes (such as buying science books or computers for sons but not for daughters) that discourage achievement-related behavior in girls.

Kramer (1991) studied 10 gifted sixth-, seventh-, and eighth-grade girls attending a highly rated middle school in the Southeast. The girls' IQ scores ranged from 131 to 140, all but one were white, and all were from middle- to upper-middle-class families. Kramer conducted formal and informal interviews with the girls. Classroom activities were observed and recorded over a period of 7 months. The investigator identified the teacher–student relationship as being crucial to the girls' feelings of self-worth. Those students who felt close to their teachers perceived themselves as competent in their coursework. Nongifted girls also acknowledge the importance of teacher support for their classroom efforts (Goodenow, 1993).

The girls displayed a strong need to satisfy their parents and teachers. "I try to get good grades because my mom's brought me up right. Some people say, 'Look at the brain! She knows all the answers.' Some of those people could be just as smart as us if they'd study. They just don't want to take the time" (p. 352). Some girls complained that their parents were very hard to please. One eighth grader wrote in her journal, "Up until the last few years my parents have encouraged my growing up. Now they sometimes disagree with my thinking [decision making about the future]. It seems like I can't do anything right in their eyes" (p. 349). The girls were eager to be perceived as socially competent by their peers. They occasionally received flak from their nongifted schoolmates. After missing a question in class, one girl reported that a boy in her class said to her, "I thought you were in gifted [class] and I'm smarter than you" (p. 352). Another remarked, "People think you're a *brain*" (p. 352).

Being able to provide the right answer to a question was central to their view of giftedness. In fact, they learned how to avoid situations where they would be put on the spot. Giving the wrong answer was associated with a feeling of worthlessness. Note the bind these girls are in when giving either the right answer or the wrong answer can lead to embarrassment. "Rather than risk speaking out, arguing points of view, or moving ahead in their class work as did gifted boys, the girls in this study focused on finding the answer acceptable to teachers, and not appearing too smart to peers. . . . As females, they believed that social acceptance was important in itself and that being liked and accepted contributed to greater achievements" (p. 359). Many adolescent girls, gifted and not, struggle to find ways to achieve and to belong to their peer group that won't threaten their fragile sense of self-worth (Orenstein, 1994).

# ACHIEVEMENT AND SELF-ESTEEM

We note a temporary decline in school performance for boys and girls during the early adolescent years, partly because achievement becomes secondary to issues of self-esteem, gender-role identity, and autonomy (Elmen, 1991; Hill & Lynch, 1983; Simmons et al., 1987). Many students become more negative about school and about themselves following the transition to middle school. Adjusting to a new school environment, they are not as self-confident about their academic ability as they were when they were "seniors" in elementary school. Confidence usually returns as they reestablish their social networks (Eccles et al., 1984; Wigfield & Eccles, 1994).

In middle and high school, there are many paths to self-esteem, including academics, athletics, and popularity. Girls especially feel that they must decide which domain, social or academic, is the potential source of greatest satisfaction. Some of these students conclude that the rewards for academic achievement are not as sweet as those for athletic accomplishment and popularity (Kramer, 1986; Orenstein, 1994; Roberts & Petersen, 1992).

Nevertheless, school offers all students opportunities to achieve and to participate in activities that can boost their self-confidence. Achievement promotes self-esteem, while academic failure and dropping out of school depress it. Harder work and higher expectations increase pressure and self-doubts in early adolescents. Advancing intellectual abilities and heightened self-awareness magnify already existing positive and negative feelings (Elmen, 1991).

As noted in Chapter 6, it is helpful to distinguish between global self-esteem (how one generally feels about oneself) from academic self-esteem (feelings about one's academic ability) and self-esteem in specific disciplines such as math or science. Hoge and colleagues (1990), in a longitudinal study of sixth- and seventh-grade students from two schools, measured all three types of self-esteem in the fall and spring of each school year.

Different aspects of self-esteem were influenced by different factors. A supportive school climate and positive feedback from teachers fostered global and academic self-esteem. As expected, grades were the critical factor influencing self-esteem in a particular discipline. Programs designed by schools to provide recognition for student success had little influence compared to direct feedback from teachers. Further, excelling in one subject did not necessarily boost academic self-esteem. Success in one area sometimes led to feelings of inadequacy in other areas if heightened internal standards could not be met ("I'm good in English but I stink in math") (Skaalvik & Rankin, 1992).

Steitz and Owen (1992) studied high school sophomores and juniors who worked part time after school. They did not find any relationship between self-esteem and participation in school activities, but they did find lower self-esteem among students (especially girls) who worked. The more hours the girls worked, the lower their self-esteem. Perhaps girls with low self-esteem seek part-time work to help them feel better about themselves. Boys and girls who participate in athletics usually report higher self-esteem. Why do you think this would be true?

Educators and parents debate which should be the greater priority, achievement or feeling good about oneself. However, there is no obvious reason why schools cannot structure curriculum and programs to accomplish both goals. Some school programs attempt to improve study skills as well as to deal with problems that hinder achievement or weaken self-confidence. It is safe to assume that self-esteem influences and is influenced by academic achievement. Fortunately, students who do not do well academically have ample opportunities to gain recognition in nonacademic areas (Liu, Kaplan, & Risser, 1992).

## SOCIAL COMPETENCE AND ACADEMIC ACHIEVEMENT

Students who are socially skillful do better in school than those who are aggressive and who alienate their classmates and teachers (Wentzel, 1991). In fact, social competence appears to be a better predictor of academic achievement than intellectual ability. Adolescents who lack the ability to gain recognition often settle for negative attention in the classroom rather than getting no attention at all.

Wentzel (1991) hypothesized that socially skilled adolescents get better grades. She administered questionnaires assessing social competence to 423 sixth and seventh graders and their teachers in a Midwestern middle school. She assessed social skills using feedback from peers regarding helpfulness, sharing, rule-following behavior, and other prosocial behavior. Students whose teachers and peers perceived them as socially responsible earned higher grades, even when taking into account IQ, ethnicity, and family structure. Popular children earned higher grades than rejected children. Although it is not obvious how misbehavior and underachievement are related, it is possible that there is a common core of social skills (e.g., working cooperatively) that promote social interaction and successful classroom behavior.

In a subsequent study of sixth and seventh graders, Wentzel (1993b) examined the relationship between classroom behavior and achievement, taking into account teachers' preferences for students. Predictably, teachers prefer students who are cooperative and responsible to those who are disruptive and disrespectful. It is possible that teachers spend more time with and behave more positively toward such students, boosting their achievement. However, findings did not confirm this prediction. Although teachers preferred the better-behaved students, this liking did not automatically translate into higher grades or test scores.

Wentzel proposes that students with prosocial skills have more positive interactions with peers and share intellectual resources, both of which promote cognitive and intellectual development. Perhaps prosocial behavior contributes to academic achievement by promoting positive academic exchanges among peers. Similarly, those who act antisocially (e.g., fighting, rule breaking) alienate peers and thus deprive themselves of valuable social-educational exchanges with classmates and teachers. Wentzel proposes that teachers emulate authoritative parents and promote cooperative, sharing, and helpful behavior among their students.

Tierno (1991) suggests that knowing about the heightened self-consciousness and self-doubts of young adolescents might help teachers understand that silly or obnoxious classroom behaviors are attempts by some adolescents to establish themselves within their peer groups. "Only occasionally are these typically adolescent behaviors intended to upset or anger teachers. In a sense, then, teachers should remember not to take unacceptable behaviors personally. Instead, the teacher might try to help the student to understand how these actions *could* be perceived as personal affronts. In short, do not take it personally, but try to make it personal" (p. 572).

Because adolescents are concerned about how they look to their peers and may be more worried about peer approval than teacher disapproval, teachers should avoid unnecessary personal classroom confrontations. Talking to a distruptive student after class avoids unnecessary humiliation of the student and possible retaliation. Since some adolescents gain prestige from teacher disapproval or detention, teachers would be better off modeling nonpunitive means of gaining compliance.

## STUDENTS' ATTITUDES TOWARD SCHOOL AND SCHOOLWORK

Doing well in school is as much a function of one's attitude about working as it is of one's ability and interest in the subject matter. Even students who excel have been heard to complain that they don't like school or at least schoolwork. Psychologists Csikszentmihalyi and Larson (1984) referred to schools as "part jail, part temple of learning" and as "machines for providing negative feedback" (p. 198). "Schooling is not designed to appeal to what is familiar and instinctively interesting; rather it deals with the abstract, the complex, the unknown—with materials that are inherently difficult and alien. French, mathematics, literature, ancient history.... Assignments and tests follow upon each other regardless of whether the students are ready or not. Hence, of all parts of an adolescent's life, this is the least responsive to spontaneous inclinations" (p. 202). It is safe to conclude that most students prefer social encounters and other leisure-time activities to lectures, tests, and homework (Wigfield & Eccles, 1994).

It is not until middle or late adolescence that most students appreciate the potential benefits of schooling. Anderson and Young (1992) analyzed essays written by 47 college students on the topic "If you could live your high school days over again, what, if anything, would you change?" More than a third (38%) wrote that they would improve their attitude toward high school. Only 36%, not necessarily those who did best, reported that high school was a positive experience. Attitude toward school in general appears to be a more important factor in achievement than attitudes toward specific courses or school characteristics.

"The school is a workplace, the student is a learner, and the learner is a worker. It's as simple as that" (Munson & Rubenstein, 1992, p. 290). Is it really that simple? Probably the most common complaint of teachers is that so many of their students do not commit to schoolwork, that they must be cajoled or coerced into completing their assignments. In Csikszentmihalyi and Larson's study (1984), during class time students reported feeling sad, irritable, and bored. They felt self-conscious and wished that they were doing something else. This is unfortunate. Student interest in course work and pride in accomplishment are important motivators. Students who are genuinely interested try harder to understand the material (Pintrich & De Groot, 1990).

Students have different school-related goals. These include mastering the subject matter, proving one's ability, gaining approval from one's peers or teachers, and preparing for a desired career. Such goals are important motivators of study behavior and persistence. Bishop (1995) notes that U.S. students gauge their academic success in terms of grades and class ranking. Being graded on a curve tells them how well they've done compared to their peers, but unlike student assessment in other countries, there is no external standard of comparison for appraising mastery of the subject matter. However they perform, high school students know that there is a college somewhere that will accept them. "Many simply don't see the point of putting themselves out to get a decent grade in a difficult course when they could take an easy one. [Taking difficult courses] won't help them get a better job or get into college, unless they are one of the few who wants to go to a highly selective school" (p. 12). Those who work hard in school make it more difficult for their peers to get good grades. Some believe that they must mask their efforts and play down their successes to avoid peer disapproval.

To identify student goals, Wentzel (1993a) administered questionnaires to 423 sixth- and seventh-graders in a Midwestern middle school. She found that the pursuit of multiple goals was positively related to achievement. Students with mastery-oriented goals (e.g., learning is fun and exciting) received the highest grades. Students who reported believing that they should get good grades because "that is what you are supposed to do" did not fare as well.

In discussing students' responsibility for learning, it is helpful to distinguish between students who take responsibility and students who are held responsible (Morris, 1961). Responsible students complete their assignments without having to be reminded or prodded. Students who are being held responsible complete their work only when forced to do so. Responsible students, by definition, are self-regulating. They seek out challenges or at least do not back away from them (Bacon, 1993).

Bacon interviewed sixth and seventh graders attending a California middle school regarding their school performance and their perception of schoolwork and responsibility. He concluded that "the students did not appear to do much learning and/or studying. They were more concerned with getting through the assignments and having something to hand in to the teacher" (p. 206).

Consistent with teachers' complaints, the students did not view school as a place for learning. Rather, they valued school as a place to spend time with their friends. Most students reported that they did not find schoolwork challenging. They did what they did in school to satisfy their teachers or because schoolwork was seen as a means of getting something else that they wanted. In effect, their attitude was that you get the same diploma with C's and D's that you get with A's and B's.

Students did what their teachers asked, but no more and sometimes less. This gave them the sense of being responsible for their schoolwork, but Bacon

**Table 11-4  How Teachers Can Motivate Students**

Promote self-determination rather than holding students responsible

Encourage students to enjoy both the challenge of learning and mastery of the subject matter at hand

Demonstrate that what students are learning in school is worth knowing and that they are responsible for what they learn

Provide learning tasks that are interesting and challenging

Arrange immediate, meaningful, and positive consequences

(1993) interprets this to mean that they were "being held responsible." Students did not see much of a connection between school and the rest of their lives. Even college students who "play the academic game" usually are guided by the *GPA perspective*—"a system of learning in which the emphasis is on making a good grade at the expense of deeper, critical, analytic learning" (Rabow, Radcliffe-Vasile, Newcomb, & Hernandez, 1992, p. 73). *Thought Question: To what extent is this perspective encouraged by parents who equate a high grade point average with achievement or success ("How did you do?" instead of "What did you learn?")?*

Students who are externally motivated (by rewards and punishments) seek less challenging tasks. They work to please an adult or to obtain good grades. They expend the least amount of effort necessary to gain the grade or approval they desire and show little interest in the activity after the reward is granted. Doesn't it make more sense for teachers to promote self-determination in students, to encourage them to enjoy both the challenge of learning and mastery of the subject matter at hand (Boggiano & Katz, 1991; Eccles et al., 1991)?

Bacon concludes that educators must demonstrate to skeptical students that what they are learning in school is worth knowing and that they are responsible for what they learn. Students are more likely to become engaged when teachers provide learning tasks that are interesting and challenging (Glasser, 1990). Learning improves when students' efforts have immediate, meaningful, and positive consequences (Anesko & O'Leary, 1983; Pintrich & De Groot, 1990; Skinner, Wellborn, & Connell, 1990). "So long as we allow students merely to 'be held responsible,' they will probably be content to put forth minimal effort in order to get by. If we want students to take some initiative in their own learning, we must enable them to 'be responsible' " (Bacon, 1993, p. 210). (See Table 11-4.)

## STUDENTS' USE OF TIME AND ACADEMIC ACHIEVEMENT

The ability to plan and to use one's time conscientiously gradually improves from the 8th to the 12th grade (Anderssen, Myburgh, van Zyl, & Wiid, 1992). However, many students spend their study time fooling around. Further, there is no guarantee that completing an assignment inevitably leads to learning. Time is a potent factor in meaningful learning only when it is spent on intellectually stimulating activities such as listening, thinking, analyzing, studying, and questioning.

According to a report from the National Education Commission on Time and Learning (1994), secondary school students spend only about 3 hours a day (41% of the school day) on core academic courses. The 2-year study reported that much of school time is devoted to nonacademic pursuits such as shop, driver's education, and athletics. Students in Japan, France, and Germany spend more than twice as much time as students in the United States studying math, science, and history. The relatively poor showing of students in the United States compared to students in many other societies also reflects the amount of time they spend in frivolous activities.

As discussed in Chapter 8, most adolescents spend considerable time involved in leisure-type activities that are neither physically nor mentally demanding, such as watching television, playing video games, listening to music, and spending time with friends (Csikszentmihalyi & Larson, 1984; De Witt, 1997; Garton & Pratt, 1987). A moderate amount of television watching is harmless, but heavy watching seems to be detrimental to some students. As we will discuss below, time spent on homework is a very good predictor of achievement. Time spent with peers reduces time availability for studying (unless they are studying together), although it enhances social skills and the sense of well-being.

Smith (1990, 1992) investigated the relationship between academic achievement and student allocation of time to media (TV, music, radio, reading), homework, friends, parents, and household chores. He administered questionnaires to seventh- and ninth-grade students in 14 selected racially and economically diverse public schools. Only time spent in leisure reading predicted academic achievement. Because so many previous studies suggested that parental involvement in a child's schooling predicts success in school, the lack of association between achievement and time spent with parents was unexpected. Smith suggests that it is what parents do when spending time with their children that affects academic achievement, not the amount of time per se. *Thought Question: Does the type of joint activity or the quality of the interaction between parent and adolescent have a greater impact on the child's school performance?*

For ninth graders, achievement was negatively related to time spent with friends. Smith speculates that how time spent with friends affects achievement depends largely on who the friends are, especially their academic values. The negative effects on achievement of listening to music and spending time with friends suggest either that exposure to the antiacademic subculture discourages academic achievement or that adolescents simply spend too much time nonproductively.

## HOMEWORK

In most adults' lives, homework and housework are necessities. Having children learn to work at home as well as in school prepares them for this reality of adult life. However, important as it is to learn how to work and learn at home, many young people receive little guidance. Presumably, they are supposed to figure out for themselves how to allocate time, choose necessary materials, and study. Teachers promote home working skills by assigning homework regularly, by being specific about their expectations and standards, and by providing students with detailed feedback regarding their performance (Bryan & Nelson, 1994).

Based on their study of 401 public school students in Grades 5–9, Leone and Richards (1989) report that the young adolescents spent about 21½ hours per week engaged in classwork or homework. Compare this figure to that of Japanese and Russian children, who spend over 50 hours a week in school or studying. Despite the fact that we expect employed adults to spend about 40 hours a week working, students in higher grades reported decreasing amounts of time spent on academic tasks.

Acquiring information and skills takes time, but as Smith's studies suggest, it is more the quality than the amount of study time or homework that predicts school achievement. Adolescents in all five grades told Leone and Richards that they did not like doing homework. "Homework was found to be especially noxious in terms of mood, as students reported feeling more unhappy, lethargic, and disinterested during homework than during other activities. Even students performing well academically reported similar negative moods during homework suggesting that they achieve despite their negative moods" (p. 545). As girls move into higher grades and spend more time socializing, their time spent doing homework decreases noticeably. It would appear that the closer students (especially girls) move toward adulthood, the less of an influence school has on their socialization (Orenstein, 1994).

The students studied by Leone and Richards admitted that they rarely paid close attention or concentrated hard on schoolwork. Thus, they don't study much and when they do, they don't study hard. Students are not intrinsically motivated to do schoolwork, and schoolwork does not appear to help them develop work-related values. Students whose parents help them with homework get the best grades. The investigators concluded that there is "a need for increased learning time, increased parental involvement in education, and ap-

Without adequate structure and social support, homework may not contribute very much to adolescents' academic development.

proaches to education that foster greater intrinsic enjoyment of learning as children get older''(p. 547).

## ORGANIZATION AND SOCIAL CLIMATE OF SCHOOLS

*Most American junior high and middle schools do not meet the developmental needs of young adolescents. These institutions have the potential to make a tremendous impact on the development of students—for better or for worse—yet they have been largely ignored in the recent surge of educational reform.*
(Carnegie Council on Adolescent Development, 1989, pp. 12–13)

Schools differ from each other in countless ways—large versus small, public versus private, single-gender versus coeducational, cooperative versus competitive. Research does not suggest that one type of school is necessarily better than another at educating students. Each type of school or school program presents advantages and disadvantages to individual students (Good & Weinstein, 1986).

The social ecology of each school is related to its size (Cotterell, 1992; Glass, Cohen, Smith, & Filby, 1982). Smaller schools (400 students or less) usually have fewer course selections but more opportunities for each student to stand out or at least be noticed. Students in small schools display fewer behavioral problems, have better attendance and graduation rates, and sometimes have higher grades and test scores. Large urban high schools (2,000 students or more) usually have

**Many high school students claim that the best thing about school is being with their friends.**

more services and extracurricular activities, but some students perceive them as impersonal. Big cities like Philadelphia and New York are gradually replacing larger schools with smaller ones (Chira, 1993; Entwisle, 1990).

Each school has its own distinctive organization regarding age grading, curriculum, tracking, standards, attendance policy, beliefs about education, bureaucracy, parent involvement, and so on (Urdan, Midgley, & Wood, 1995). In school, students learn how to deal with authority issues, become increasingly self-regulating, and learn to cope with a formal system of rules and regulations that constrain their behavior (Smetana & Bitz, 1996; Trickett & Schmid, 1993).

Although there is pressure on all students to conform to rules and regulations, roles and expectations differ for students according to their gender, race, grade, family economic status, and ability. It is hard to tell how a given school's organization affects individual students. For example, tracking is likely to have different effects, depending on students' initial ability level. **Tracking** may refer to programs that prepare students for different vocational paths or to subject-by-subject groupings commonly found in high schools (Mansnerus, 1992b). The best students usually get to work with the most skilled teachers, an advantage. Students in the lowest tracks (disproportionately minority students) expect less from themselves, a disadvantage. Although more able students usually gain from high-ability classes, middle-ability students usually have little to show for attending lower-track classes. They are expected to expend less effort and learn less than students in higher tracks. Even high-ability students reduce their level of effort when assigned to a lower track (Dornbusch et al., 1996; Entwisle, 1990; Fuligni, Eccles, & Barber, 1995; Oakes 1985, 1987).

Parents and students seem to be unaware of how tracking affects school performance (Useem, 1992). "When individuals are placed at a level below their academic potential, the entire society, as well as the individual, suffers from the loss of skill and economic productivity" (Dornbusch et al., 1996, p. 192). Tracking should not be confused with **ability grouping**, which regroups students to provide a curriculum aimed at a common instructional level. It involves temporarily placing students with others who have similar learning needs, such as dividing students into groups in a classroom or combining students in a gifted and talented class that meets weekly (Fiedler, Lange, & Winebrenner, 1994).

## SPOTLIGHT • Do Separate Schools Help Students Learn?

*You feel uncomfortable sometimes around boys. You feel more insecure about yourself. You feel like you have to look nice for them. I don't want to go to school to be a model. I want to go to school to learn.*
        (Albeliza Perez, a 12-year-old girl who applied to a new
                single-sex public school in New York City,
                    quoted by J. Steinberg, 1996, p. B1)

During the middle and high school years, when adolescents are busy learning about relationships and exploring various adult roles, does it make a difference whether their education takes place within a single-gender or a coeducational setting? Do girls who are not distracted by the presence of boys place greater emphasis on conduct and achievement and less emphasis on appearance and romance?

It is hard to defend the idea that boys and girls are treated comparably in school since the two genders begin school roughly equal in achievement and self-confidence and girls finish high school trailing boys in both (Orenstein, 1994). For example, boys score an average of 46 points higher than girls on the math SAT. Boys usually dominate class discussions. Girls receive less attention from teachers, face sexual harassment, sometimes are ignored or stereotyped in textbooks, and have fewer opportunities to develop leadership skills (AAUW Report: How Schools Shortchange Women, 1993; Chira, 1992a). In some classes, girls appear to move at a different pace from boys, asking more questions and enjoying lengthy discussions. Some teachers note that boys prefer to barrel forward whether they understand the concept or not (Gross, 1993; Orenstein, 1994).

Even when girls receive higher grades than boys, they report feeling less confident. In mixed-gender groups males usually emerge as leaders, or at least they dominate the conversation (Lockheed & Hall, 1976). Boys are more competitive than girls and more likely to tease them about wrong answers. Girls usually work for the best group outcome. These gender differ-

**Many adolescent girls attending all-girls schools claim that they concentrate better on course material without having to worry about being distracted or harassed by boys, but critics worry that these girls may be unprepared for the male-dominated work world.**

ences sometimes work to the disadvantage of females attending coed schools or courses (Orenstein, 1994).

Females attending single-gender schools are more likely to gain recognition for achievement through awards, scholarships, and leadership opportunities. In single-gender settings, girls are better able to resolve achievement–affiliative conflicts and increase their self-confidence (Monaco & Gaier, 1992). Girls attending schools without boys receive more recognition for their accomplishments. They are more likely than girls attending coed schools to be exposed to high-achievement women. They have more opportunities to lead. For example, they are more likely to be school president and vice-president than secretary or treasurer.

Some public high schools in California segregate boys from girls in math and science courses. Girls claim that they concentrate better on course material without having to worry about being badgered by boys or putting up with their misbehavior. Some boys acknowledge that they pay attention better when not distracted by the presence of girls.

Critics of this policy argue that females have to learn how to work with males because that's what they will face in the real world (Bleeden, 1995). They suggest that rather than segregating students by gender, teachers be trained to discourage gender bias in classrooms by emphasizing cooperative learning, which helps both genders (Gross, 1993). When females learn how to be assertive, they can interact with males on an equal basis (deGroot, 1994).

A similar issue exists regarding the desirability of special schools or programs for male African-American adolescents, many of whom drop out of school or are suspended or expelled (Hudley, 1995; Oakes, 1985). Most programs specifically designed to enhance the academic performance and school adjustment of African-American males emphasize the importance of male role models (Murray, 1995c). They offer a challenging Afrocentric curriculum and a safe, orderly classroom environment (Ascher, 1991; Roth & Constantine, 1995).

Middle school participants in Hudley's (1995) study reported a positive classroom experience, but their grades were not more impressive than those of students in regular classes. Separate schools or classes have been considered or established in several cities, including New York, Baltimore, and Chicago. Critics claim that the idea approximates racial segregation and discriminates against female students (*NEA Today*, October 1991, p. 31). Inner-city girls have problems of their own. Many experience unwanted pregnancy, dropping out, sexual abuse, and gang violence. Perhaps they would benefit from all-girl schools.

## IN THE CLASSROOM

Several investigators (Eccles & Midgley, 1989, 1990; Simmons & Blyth, 1987) emphasize the concept of **person–environment fit**. They contend that middle schools and junior high schools do not provide developmentally appropriate educational environments for young adolescents. Different age groups require different types of educational environments, depending on their developmental status. Because so many adolescents inhabit classroom (and other) environments that do not suit their emotional and social needs, their academic interest and performance declines (Eccles et al., 1993).

Eccles and her colleagues point to dramatic differences in how elementary schools and secondary schools treat young people. Secondary schools usually are larger, less personal, and more formal than elementary schools. They emphasize competition and social comparison at a time when early adolescents are self-conscious. Despite their desire for greater self-regulation, teenagers have minimal opportunities to make decisions about their course work. Middle and junior high school classrooms are less personal and more oriented to ability than are elementary school classrooms. Instruction is less individualized, and teachers are more controlling. There is a greater emphasis on performance ("How did you do?") than on the task at hand ("What are you learning?") (Midgley, Anderman, & Hicks, 1995). Most students try harder and persist longer when they focus on the task at hand rather than on their performance or grade. At a time when young people benefit from close relationships with adults who are not family members, student–teacher relations are increasingly strained (Wigfield & Eccles, 1994).

Perhaps reflecting their acceptance of the storm and stress model of adolescence, seventh-grade teachers in middle school are more likely than sixth-grade teachers in elementary school to believe that students need to be disciplined and controlled. They rate students as less trustworthy and report believing that they themselves are not very effective as teachers (Eccles & Midgley, 1989; Eccles, Midgley, & Adler, 1984; Midgley, Feldlaufer, & Eccles, 1988). *Thought Question: Why would teachers in middle and junior high schools feel less confident than teachers in elementary school?*

Eccles and Midgley (1989) suggest that these factors partly account for the so-called attitude problems of disaffected students. Adolescents are more willing to work hard when they feel that their teachers are supportive. They desire more freedom and fewer restrictions. Unfortunately, too many teachers (and parents) believe that controlling strategies are necessary to get adolescents to take them seriously. Although this might be true for disaffected students, for engaged students this belief creates a vicious cycle of increasing teacher control and increasing student resentment. Overly controlling strategies weaken achievement motivation and promote helpless behavior in the classroom. When teachers are unsympathetic, the classroom ceases to be a safe or comfortable place for learning and self-expression (Eccles, Flanagan, Lord, Midgley et al., 1996; Eccles et al., 1993). *Thought Question: How might a teacher deal sensitively and effectively with a student who is disrupting a class?*

## DESIGNING BETTER SCHOOLS

One obvious problem in measuring school effectiveness is defining what we mean by an effective school. Rutter (1983) proposed that the effectiveness of

**The most effective teachers teach their students how to think both critically and creatively about challenging subject matter.**

schools is best measured by a constellation of factors: scholastic achievement, classroom behavior, absenteeism, dropout rates, attitudes toward learning, employment, and social functioning.

Although there is controversy and confusion about how to create and maintain effective schools, there is agreement that secondary schools and colleges can and must do better in meeting the needs of adolescents (Manning, 1992). Schools that provide a developmentally appropriate learning environment, that recognize adolescents' need for intimacy, autonomy, and intellectual challenge, are more likely to help them achieve their educational and social goals (Urdan et al., 1995). It is also important that middle and junior high schools anticipate

**Table 11-5  Characteristics of Effective Schools**

A principal who is a good leader and who sets high standards

Clearly stated and organized curriculum

Meaningful staff development

Parental involvement and support

Schoolwide recognition for achievement

Maximized active learning time

Collaborative planning and a unified staff

A sense of community

Clearly stated goals and high expectations

Order and discipline

Teachers who cover the curriculum, involve students in class activities, encourage creativity, and are flexible and forgiving

common adjustment problems associated with school transitions and the role strain that accompanies the challenges of secondary schooling (Fenzel, 1989).

Studies of effective schools reveal the following: (1) a principal who is a good leader and who sets high standards, (2) a clearly stated, well-organized curriculum, (3) meaningful staff development, (4) parental involvement and support, (5) schoolwide recognition for achievement, and (6) maximized active learning time. Successful schools display collaborative planning and a unified staff, a sense of community, clearly stated goals and high expectations, order, and discipline (see Table 11-5). Students appear to learn more when teachers (1) cover the curriculum, (2) involve students in class activities, (3) encourage creativity, and (4) are flexible and forgiving. As previously noted, the quality of instruction, amount of homework assigned, and subject interest also influence learning (Entwisle, 1990; Purkey & Smith, 1983; Rowan, Bossert, & Dwyer, 1983; Rutter, 1983). Obstacles to school reform include teachers and administrators viewing adolescents stereotypically ("brain dead," "raging hormones"), resistance to interdisciplinary learning, inappropriate grouping by ability, large school size, and bureaucratic inertia (Urdan et al., 1995).

## SCHOOL TRANSITIONS

Major life changes are stressful, and school transitions are no exception (Fenzel, 1989; Seidman, Allen, Aber, Mitchell, & Feinman, 1994). There are four major school transitions during adolescence: from elementary school to secondary school; from middle or junior high school to high school; from high school to college; and from college to graduate school or to the world of work. Each year an estimated one out of five primary and secondary school students transfer to a new school. Most of these transitions are normative, reflecting graduation to a new school. Social networks usually remain intact. But unscheduled transfers, for example when families move to a new community, disrupt young adolescents' social networks. Students attending a new school may not know a single student. Naturally, they wonder whether or not they will be accepted by their new peers (Custer, 1994).

For many students, especially those with poor social skills, events surrounding the transition to secondary school threaten their self-esteem, especially when they feel unsupported by school personnel and hassled by insensitive peers (Seidman et al., 1994). These students become increasingly disenchanted with their educational setting. Ethnic minority students, especially those in schools with few minority teachers, report experiencing significantly more stressors than do ethnic majority students. They report feeling less bonded to the school culture and experience more frequent discipline encounters (Munsch & Wampler, 1993).

Each school transition carries its own potential burdens and challenges. Each student adjusts differently, depending on his or her personal maturity, temperament, personal coping resources, social support, and the specific stressors and circumstances. How well young people adjust partly depends on how much control they believe they have over the situation and partly on other stressful life changes. The more change, the more pressure. There is a large continuum of student response to stress. It includes mild to extreme discomfort, poor grades, physical illness, and even suicide (Cotterell, 1992; Entwisle, 1990; Grannis, 1992; Talwar, Schwab, & Lerner, 1989).

Although changing schools is stressful for young adolescents and comes at an inopportune time in their development, there is also much opportunity for growth. Compared to elementary school, there are more frequent occasions to interact with other students outside of the classroom and to encounter individuals who are culturally diverse. Secondary schools are more adultlike environments for children than are elementary schools, where teachers are more like surrogate parents. The work is more challenging, and students become increasingly aware of decisions they must make that will affect their education, careers, and adult lives. Schools today offer freshman orientation activities and implement *buddy systems* for new students to facilitate interaction and communication between new and established students. The earlier the intervention, the easier the adjustment (Custer, 1994). It is also important that teachers hold boys and girls to the same standards in class and provide feedback to the two genders equitably (LaBreche, 1995).

## Secondary School

The middle school years are crucial to our understanding of adolescent development. Youngsters are coming to terms with their bodily changes and budding sexuality at about the same time that they are changing schools, advancing cognitively, and entering into more adultlike relationships with their peers. Parents and teachers are not likely to overlook changes in behavior and temperament, particularly disruptive and antisocial behaviors.

Pubertal changes require adjustment by young adolescents, as well as understanding and patience from their parents and teachers. As noted, teachers in middle schools tend to be more controlling and less sympathetic to students than teachers in elementary school. Pupils are tracked according to ability; teachers expect higher-tracked students to work harder (Fuligni et al., 1995; Midgley et al., 1995).

The level of difficulty of the secondary school curriculum rises, as do the expectations of parents and teachers. Perhaps reflecting the increased pressure to perform, average grades drop dramatically during the first year of middle school. Interest in school and self-confidence also diminish. Koizumi (1995) reports that Japanese students, who experience a transition to junior high school very similar to that in the United States, find the transition very stressful and are much more pessimistic about school than they were in elementary school. By the end of the first year, high achievers in both cultures usually regain their composure (and grades), while low achievers often continue to flounder (Azar, 1996a).

Middle school students are given more responsibility for their work, and most become increasingly self-reliant. Whereas elementary school children have one teacher, students in middle and high schools typically have different teachers for different subjects. Changing classes calls for organizational skills that may not yet exist. Unlike elementary school teachers, secondary school teachers identify more with the particular subject area they were trained in than with their students or school. Each teacher has many more students than do elementary school teachers and therefore less opportunity to get to know each student's strengths and weaknesses (Cotterell, 1992; Crockett, Petersen, Graber, Schulenberg, & Ebata, 1989; Midgley et al., 1995).

Middle schools were created to accommodate the changes of early adolescence, especially enhanced intellectual abilities. Whereas junior high school usually includes Grades 7 through 9 (ages 12–14), middle schooling usually encompasses Grades 6 through 8 (ages 11–13). An advantage of the middle school arrangement is that it removes pubertal girls from elementary school at an earlier age and at a time when their self-esteem may be more fragile. Lisa Crockett and her colleagues (1989) compared three groups of adolescents: those making a single early school transition to middle school before the sixth grade; those making a transition before the seventh grade; and those making a double transition before both sixth and seventh grades. Students who faced the double transition fared worst with respect to their course grades. The investigators concluded that "making two, closely spaced school changes is indeed more debilitating than making a single transition prior to seventh grade" (p. 201).

Educators are not quite sure whether it is more beneficial for ninth grade to come at the end of middle or junior high or at the beginning of senior high school. Gifford and Dean (1990), for example, observed that ninth graders in a junior high setting participated in more extracurricular activities and did better academically than ninth graders in a high school setting.

Whether entering middle or junior high school, students experience the so-called **top dog phenomenon**, that is, going from being the seniors, or top dogs, in elementary school to occupying the lowest rung of the new school hierarchy. The effect is particularly noticeable for students who are younger than their classmates (Fenzel, 1992). Some schools place students who are in different grades in different wings or sections of the school building to minimize the chance of negative encounters. We have previously noted a temporary decrease in self-esteem during early adolescence, at least for girls. It appears that it is not so much the transition to secondary school that temporarily suppresses self-esteem in girls as the *timing* of the transition (Simmons, Blyth, Van Cleave, & Bush, 1979). School transition apparently suppresses self-esteem in girls if it occurs when they are adjusting to other changes, such as menarche or starting to date. Boys are less likely to experience such physical and social changes at the same time that they are changing schools. Girls beginning middle school or junior high usually are coping with multiple changes.

Nottelmann (1987) measured the stability of competence and self-esteem in fifth- and sixth-grade boys and girls during a 1-year period when approximately half were making the transition from elementary to secondary school. Both groups (transition and nontransition) showed positive change in perceived competence and self-esteem. Unlike the results of the Simmons study, self-esteem was found to be higher in transition than in nontransition children. Importantly, self-esteem was linked to perceived social, physical, and cognitive competence. Girls' self-esteem was linked particularly to their perceptions of social competence.

Students reported that they liked the bigger school, access to more than one teacher, and instruction in a wider range of topics. They felt good about growing up, having more freedom, and meeting new people. By the end of the first year, most students reported that they were completely used to their new school. Students who had difficulty adjusting to their change in schools usually were experiencing two or more transitions concurrently (e.g., dating, pubertal change, more challenging schoolwork).

Boys seem to be more vulnerable than girls to simultaneous life stressors, with highly stressed boys displaying more learning and behavior problems in school (Goodman, Brumley, Schwartz, & Purcell, 1993). It would be helpful for parents and teachers to be aware that for many young people early adolescence is a difficult time and that children need extra understanding and attention. Fortunately, most teenagers adjust well given the number of challenges they face during the middle school years (Compas, 1987a,b).

## Transition to College

Senior year presents a challenge to most high school students. Given the pressure to gain entry into a competitive college or university, they exist in a state of limbo (Brooks, 1995). Their high school track record is mostly established. If they plan to attend college, their applications must soon be in the mail. Facing an uncertain future regarding school and career, many seniors express anxiety about their choice of college and, for many, ambivalence about living away from home (and friends) for an extended period of time (Brinckerhoff, 1996; Brooks, 1995; Murray, 1996c).

A major challenge of childhood is separating from one's parents for extended periods (Blos, 1979). The separation of parent and child, even under happy circumstances, requires adjustment in the entire family system (Berman & Sperling, 1991). By the time they are 17 years old, most children have experienced extended separations from family members, such as required by attendance at summer camp. Extended separations provide adolescents with opportunities to take responsibility for their actions and well-being and to enhance their self-reliance and judgment (Astin, 1993). There are no parents to advise that bedtime is approaching or that one's room or body requires servicing.

During the first few weeks that my older son was away at college, my wife and I were surprised by his apparent need to check in with us (including his younger brother) almost every day. We experienced a corresponding need to hear from him, at first daily and eventually, every few days. Clearly, coping was occurring at both ends of the phone line. With every compliment or criticism of his new surroundings, our hearts leaped or sank. For those first weeks, we were the only ones that he could confide in.

College administrators advise that about half of new freshmen feel lonely and isolated and sorely miss their homes and families. The freshman year of college is recognized as being the most stressful year, with an average dropout rate of about 20%. Harder schoolwork and spending time with so many new and different classmates in a new environment requires considerable adjustment. Students are afraid of making mistakes; some are overconscientious. Others fear taking on new commitments and responsibilities (Austin & Martin,

1992; Bloom, 1987). Core academic stressors include test taking, competition for grades, time demands, and living arrangements (Murphy & Archer, 1996). Relationships, depression, career worries, loneliness, sleep and health problems, and financial pressures bring large numbers of college students to their campus counseling centers (Murray, 1996c).

As freshmen become better integrated into college and dormitory life, develop supportive social networks, and enjoy the taste of new freedoms, distress gradually lessens (Fagan, 1994). New freedoms include sleeping, eating, and studying when they want to and freedom from inquisitive parents. A significant number rush fraternities and sororities, which, according to some studies, appear to increase students' social involvement but perhaps at a cost to openness to new ideas and art forms (Murray, 1996f).

Rubin (1988) administered a battery of tests to 24 randomly selected college freshmen living on a "small personal campus." He found that most were happy and healthy and had average self-concept scores. "It appeared that this well-nurtured and protected group was not generally experiencing the turmoil of early adulthood, at least not at the beginning of college life. . . . The wealthy, nurturing college environment may be similar to high school and, therefore, these well-travelled students who have had separations before are on familiar turf, and adaptation is relatively easy" (p. 590).

Some freshman students at Rutgers University in New Jersey, a week or two after school began in fall 1993, reported that they missed their mothers, home cooking, security, and towels in the bathroom. Others said they didn't miss their parents or siblings. "The worst thing is just adjusting to the lack of privacy, to having a roommate" said one. "I'm more adjusted than I thought I'd be. But we're all lost together" said another (quoted by Judson, 1993, p. B8). As a group, they must cope with days of orientation, workshops on how to use the library and computer center, how to avoid sexual assault, and how to get along with each other. One student said about drinking, to his friends' amusement, "I'll speak for everyone. I don't do it, but all my friends do."

Which group of adolescents has a harder time adjusting to dorm life, those who feel closer to or more distant from their parents? One might predict that adolescents who are most attached to their parents would experience greater

**As freshmen become better integrated into college and dormitory life, develop supportive social networks, and enjoy the taste of new freedoms, their distress usually lessens.**

*When they are at school, you don't worry as much. But when they are at home, you wait at night for the front door to close. It is a Pavlovian response.*
*(mother of a freshman college student, quoted by Lawson, 1992, p. C1)*

**Box 11-3
Visiting
the Nest**

As stressful as leaving for college are college students' home visits during school breaks. Parents often are surprised by how much their child has changed in the few weeks or months of college (Lawson, 1992).

Returning children anticipate continued emotional and financial support but also expect greater freedom. Sensitive parents try to be less controlling and to speak more respectfully. They have difficulty, however, accepting how little time their children spend at home and their reluctance to share their new experiences with family members. Awkward feelings are the norm for all parties. Life is less complicated when children return to college but, "Two days after the children leave, the parents are lonely again, and the children miss them and being home. The tension dissipates, and both sides forget. Until the next time" (Cantor, quoted by Lawson, 1992, p. C5).

distress during a lengthy separation such as living away at college. Berman and Sperling (1991) hypothesized that extended separation from one's parents heightens the attachment drive of at least some college students. Increased attachment drive, they speculated, would be associated with increased sadness or depression, especially at the beginning and end of the first semester. These investigators examined first-year male and female college students attending an East Coast university. Residential students (those living in dorms) and commuter students (those living at home) participated. Their average age was approximately 18 years. Eighty-nine students completed questionnaires during the first 3 weeks of the semester and again at the end of the semester. The questionnaires assessed the students' depression and anger, as well as their attachment to their parents.

Their study revealed that residential and commuter students were equally attached to their parents at the beginning of the college transition. Females showed somewhat greater intensity of attachment than males, particularly to their mothers. Contrary to their expectations, the researchers found that residential students' attachment to their parents decreased over time but remained unchanged for commuting students. "The attachment bond for residents may decrease slowly during the first semester of college, as the adolescent adjusts to the college environment and forms new relationships among his or her peers. In contrast, those adolescents who maintain close physical proximity with their parents appear to maintain a higher level of attachment, perhaps because they do not establish new bonds to take their place" (pp. 436–437).

Thus, rather than heightening attachment, separation from parents appears to lessen the attachment of residential college students to their parents. However, male students who were very attached to their parents (who thought a lot about them) at the beginning of the semester were most likely to report feeling depressed at the end of the semester. This was not true for females. Although males report feeling less attached to their parents than females do, those males who are strongly attached appear to have the greatest difficulty coping with separation.

## ETHNIC DIFFERENCES IN ACHIEVEMENT

Compared to Asian-American and white students, Hispanic (Latino), African-American, and Native-American students receive lower grades, are more likely to drop out of high school, and receive less education (Fordham & Ogbu, 1986; Mickelson, 1990; Steinberg, 1996a, 1996b; Sue & Okazaki, 1990; Swisher & Hoisch, 1992; Wood & Clay, 1996). African-American students are underrepresented in higher education in relation to their numbers in the population and have higher dropout rates, although attendance and graduation rates had been improving until recently (Applebome, 1996b).

According to a study by the Education Trust, minority students slipped further behind white students in achievement after a long period of narrowing the gap (Applebome, 1996c). The gap between the two groups (white and ethnic minority) declined by about 50% in the 1970s and 1980s but has begun to increase. The study attributes ethnic differences in achievement partly to differences in expectations, which traditionally have been lower for ethnic minority groups, and partly to the poorer training of those who teach poor and minority students (see Table 11-6).

In Steinberg's (1996a) 3-year study of 20,000 high school students, on the average, Asian-American students earned a mixture of A's and B's, white stu-

### Table 11-6  Ethnic Differences in SAT Scores

| | Mean SAT Scores for College-Bound High School Seniors | | | | | |
|---|---|---|---|---|---|---|
| | **Average SAT Scores for Various Groups, 1987\* and 1996** | | | | | |
| | **Verbal** | | | **Math** | | |
| | 1987 | 1996 | | 1987 | 1996 | |
| American Indian | 471 | 483 | ▲ 12 | 463 | 477 | ▲ 14 |
| Asian-American | 479 | 496 | ▲ 17 | 541 | 558 | ▲ 17 |
| Black | 428 | 434 | ▲ 6 | 411 | 422 | ▲ 11 |
| Mexican-American | 457 | 455 | ▼ 2 | 455 | 459 | ▲ 4 |
| Puerto Rican | 436 | 452 | ▲ 16 | 432 | 445 | ▲ 13 |
| Other Hispanic | 464 | 465 | ▲ 1 | 462 | 466 | ▲ 4 |
| White | 524 | 526 | ▲ 2 | 514 | 523 | ▲ 9 |
| Other | 480 | 511 | ▲ 31 | 482 | 512 | ▲ 30 |
| All students | 507 | 505 | ▼ 2 | 501 | 508 | ▲ 7 |

\*First year when College Board broke down ethnic groups in this way.

*Source: College Board*

dents earned more B's than C's, and African-American and Latino students earned more C's than B's. Most Asian-American students (55%) but only a third of white students had grade point averages of A or A−. African-American and Latino students made up one-fourth of the sample but accounted for more than 40% of all students with grade point averages of C− or below. Of all the ethnic groups studied, Asian-American students were the most engaged in school: they spent more time on homework, cut class less often, reported higher levels of attention in class, and felt the most challenged. In other words, they did better because they worked harder. Are Asian-American students brighter? As Steinberg points out, if they were more intelligent than other students, they wouldn't have to work harder to get good grades.

On the verbal part of the SAT in 1993, the average score for white students was 444 and for African-American students was 353. On the math part, whites had an average score of 494 and African-Americans, 388. Asian-American students scored an average of 415 on verbal and 535 on math. Puerto Rican students scored an average of 367 on the verbal part and 409 on the math part (*The New York Times*, August 19, 1993, p. B1). There were slight gains across groups in 1995, but the same ranking held (*The New York Times*, August 24, 1995).

It would be misguided to attribute ethnic differences in achievement solely to ethnic group membership, genetic factors, or even differences in family values or family structure. As we have seen, sociocultural factors such as expectations, teacher training, family income, parent education, students' personality characteristics, and students' perceptions of school as a means of achieving upward mobility in life are all related to achievement motivation (Alva, 1993; DeBlassie & DeBlassie, 1996; Geary, Salthouse, Chen, & Fan, 1996; Honan, 1996; Sue & Okazaki, 1990).

Students with family members and friends who view school as an opportunity to learn how to succeed in life usually value achievement. Children from families with limited educational and financial resources are the least likely to view school positively. Not liking or not being prepared for schoolwork, they are at highest risk for academic failure and dropping out (U.S. Department of Education, 1994). This is unfortunate because in our culture education is viewed as the most promising means of social advancement, especially for the disadvantaged. *Within any ethnic group, there is enormous diversity in ability and achievement* (Kim & Chun, 1994).

Diana Slaughter-Defoe and her colleagues (1990, p. 373) perceive a "troubling stereotype" in achievement research, one that predicts educational failure for Native-, Latino-, and African-Americans and educational excellence for Asian-Americans. They note that little distinction is made regarding different cultural backgrounds, language, immigration, economic backgrounds, and family adaptation in a broader cultural/ecological context.

Most students perform best when their learning environment is congruent with their home environment and family background. Several observers note that ethnic minority students are more likely than majority students to experience cultural discontinuities between their family, neighborhood, and school environments (Harrison et al., 1990; Jagers, 1996; Locust, 1988; Sanders, 1987).

This *cultural discontinuity hypothesis* suggests that the cultural belief systems of some ethnic groups may be incompatible with those of mainstream U.S. society (Wood & Clay, 1996). Further, the interpersonal and achievement skills that allow adaptation to school are not adaptive in an unsafe neighborhood and thus might not be encouraged or modeled by parents. Many minority students do well in school, however, challenging the hypothesis (Ledlow, 1992; Ogbu, 1982). Gifted, high-achieving African-American students in a study by Ford and Harris (1996) reported that school was more interesting to them when they were permitted to study their own ethnic group. Some students confided that they were tired of learning just about white people.

Although Wood and Clay (1996) acknowledge that cultural conflicts can impair academic performance, they attribute the lower academic performance of Native-American (and possibly other minority) students mainly to students' belief that education will not lead to upward mobility (the **"glass ceiling" hypothesis**). They maintain that "the effect of prolonged discrimination at the hands of Anglo-dominated society is manifested in a distrust of Anglo-dominated institutions and in negative perceptions regarding the likelihood of achieving social mobility through educational attainment" (p. 43).

Do Asian-American students believe more than do African-American and Latino students that educational success will improve their chances of getting a decent job? They do work harder and report that their parents would be angry if they received poor grades. "In contrast, African-American and Hispanic students, who do less well in school, are more cavalier about the consequences of poor school performance, devote less time to their studies, are less likely than others to attribute their success to hard work, and report that their parents have relatively lower standards" (Steinberg, Dornbusch, & Brown, 1992, p. 726). Students who believe that effort is not related to success are not willing to work as hard, which in turn leads their teachers to give them lower grades (Fordham & Ogbu, 1986; Spencer, Kim, & Marshall, 1987).

When Steinberg (1996a, 1996b) questioned students in his study about the economic and occupational rewards of school success, he found no ethnic differences in their answers. Students in all ethnic groups reported believing that getting a good education would pay off for them down the road. However, ethnic students differed regarding their perception of the consequences of *failing* in school. Asian-American students were the most likely to equate school failure with vocational failure. Non-Asian ethnic students were cavalier about the potentially negative effects of poor school performance.

Steinberg concludes that it is mainly African-American and Latino students' belief that doing poorly in school will not hurt their chances for decent employment that is behind their poorer performance. Asian-American students had the most realistic attributional style—linking their success in life to how hard they work (Steinberg, 1996b). This finding supports the attribution model of achievement described earlier in the chapter.

Steinberg observed that the longer children of immigrants reside in the United States, the poorer their school performance. Do students become increasingly skeptical about the American system or do they come to view schooling as less important? Steinberg speculates that the latter is true. "It looks as if the longer a family has lived here, the more its children resemble the 'typical' American teenager, and part of this package of traits is, unfortunately, academic indifference, or even disengagement" (p. 45).

Peers seem to play a major role in this process. "Specifically, Asian students' friends have higher performance standards, spend more time on homework, are more committed to education, and earn considerably higher grades in school. Black and Hispanic students' friends earn lower grades, spend less time on their studies, and have substantially lower performance standards. White students' friends fall somewhere between these two extremes on these various indicators" (Steinberg, 1996a, p. 46).

When doing well academically is labeled "acting white," African-American students experience conflict between satisfying themselves and satisfying their peers. Although their parents may be supportive, they have more difficulty joining peer groups that reinforce achievement, unless they are willing to associate with high-achieving students from other ethnic groups (Arroyo & Zigler, 1995). Some have to choose between doing well academically and being popular among their ethnic peers (Fordham, 1988; Luthar, 1995). As a result, African-American students during early adolescence are less inclined than whites to adopt their parents' educational goals (Smith, 1993; Taylor, 1996).

Steinberg and his colleagues (1992) report that urban, minority students are "more influenced by their peers, and less by their parents, in matters of academic achievement. . . . Across all ethnic groups, youngsters whose friends and parents both support achievement perform better than those who receive support only from one source but not the other, who in turn perform better than those who receive no support from either" (p. 727). The congruence of support from both peers and parents, greater for whites and Asian-Americans, is the best predictor of academic success. White students raised by authoritative parents are likely to associate with other students who also value school attendance and good grades.

Using data based on a sample of 15,000 high school students attending nine schools that were diverse socioeconomically, Steinberg and colleagues (1992) concluded that parenting style and peer influence are primarily responsible for ethnic differences in achievement. Based on his study of four ethnic minority groups in Australia, Kevin Marjoribanks (1996) concluded that the learning environments that parents construct for their children (especially parent involvement in teaching) vary according to the family's ethnic background. This is not to say that lack of equal opportunity and lower expectations of teachers play no role (Spencer & Dornbusch, 1990). Yet, there appears to be a strong link between the practices of authoritative parents (who are warm, demanding, and encourage autonomy) and adolescent success in school. Punitive and permissive parenting practices are associated with poorer grades and occur more frequently in ethnic minority families (Spencer & Dornbusch, 1990).

White and Hispanic students are more likely to benefit from authoritative parenting than are African-American or Asian-American students. Asian-American students do better than average and African-American students do more poorly than average, regardless of the parenting style that they are raised with. For ethnic minority students, there is less of a relationship between their parents' parenting style and their peer group membership. White and African-American youths want their parents to see them as smart and as good students, but many try to please their peers by not appearing to be too scholarly or successful in school (DeSantis et al., 1990; Luthar, 1995).

Asian-American students usually depend on peer support and encouragement at school, regardless of how they are raised at home or their parents' involvement in school. Children of immigrants usually lead stressful lives, coping with language problems and pressure from their parents to achieve (Fuligni, 1997). They complain about having to live up to the stereotype of Asian-Americans students as being experts in science and mathematics. Many struggle to meet unrealistically high expectations of teachers and parents and must cope with the resentment or antagonism of non-Asian classmates. The dropout rate for Asian-Americans in the New York City school system is about 15% a year. Because they tend to be smaller and quieter, Asian-American students are easy targets for harassment from peers. Some play down their heritage or their intelligence in order to gain acceptance (Lee, 1990). Nevertheless, those who believe in hard work and have positive attitudes toward achievement and who have a sense of identification with their schools generally succeed (Alva, 1993; Chen & Stevenson, 1995; TerLouw, 1994).

Some minority students (and females) who do well in school complain that teachers and counselors still treat them stereotypically (Steele, 1997). One Puerto Rican girl who had good grades approached her counselor to get a college application. She recalled that her counselor just rolled her eyes. "That's all she did, then just silence. I don't even know how I managed to leave the room. I felt like crying. Actually, I did go the bathroom and just started crying, because I felt completely worthless" (quoted by Chira, 1992c, p. 1). She found a sympathetic teacher to help her with her applications. She eventually attended the University of Connecticut.

It is important that teacher training programs help teachers appreciate cultural diversity and the special needs and personal qualities of individual ethnic students and their parents (DeBlassie & DeBlassie, 1996; TerLouw, 1994). Most Asian-American children, for example, are socialized to listen, not to speak. They are taught to not disagree with adults, especially teachers. Teachers could misinterpret these behaviors as a lack of interest. Asian-American parents may say "yes" when they understand but do not agree with a teacher. Their smiles may be inconsistent with their feelings (TerLouw, 1994). Teachers who are not familiar with their students' cultural backgrounds and traditions risk misinterpreting their (and their parents') behavior and thus lessening their own instructional effectiveness.

## DROPOUTS

Keeping disaffected students in school is becoming one of the greatest challenges confronting educators. Young people cannot benefit from schooling if they are not in school. A dropout is defined by the government as a student who was in Grades 7 to 12 the previous year but is not enrolled in the present year and has not graduated (ill and suspended students are not counted). According to the U.S. Department of Education (1994), 11% of students between the ages of 16 and 24 years are high school dropouts. Approximately 381,000 students drop out each year.

In 1995, about the same proportion (87%) of whites and African-Americans finished high school (U.S. Census Bureau Report, *Educational Attainment in the United States*, March 1995). Those most at risk for dropping out include ethnic minority students (especially Hispanics, whose dropout rate is about 32%), students from low-income families, girls who become pregnant (and their boyfriends), students for whom English is not their first language, and students who abuse drugs and alcohol. The number of middle-class students dropping out for academic reasons or because of personal relationship problems is increasing (Franklin & Streeter, 1995). Students with poor grades and low self-esteem are considered most vulnerable (Rumberger, 1983; Steinberg, Blinn, & Chan, 1984; Tabor, 1992b).

Students' reasons for leaving school before graduation include (1) poor grades, (2) dislike of school (boring and a waste of time), (3) expulsion, (4) financial difficulties and desire to work, (5) home responsibilities, and (6) pregnancy and marriage (Borus, Crowley, Rumberger, Santos, & Shapiro, 1980; Tidwell, 1988; U.S. Department of Education, 1994). To some extent, reasons for dropping out vary according to ethnic group. In a study using nationally representative high school student data (Jordan, Lara, & McPartland, 1996), white dropouts cited alienation from school (failing, not getting along with teachers) more often than African-American and Hispanic dropouts. African-American males reported being suspended or expelled from school more than the other groups. Hispanic and African-American females cited family-related reasons (e.g., providing care) most frequently. Most dropouts planned to resume their education by taking equivalency tests, attending alternative high schools, or returning to regular high school (see Table 11-7.)

Most high school dropouts recognize the value of school and graduating and would recommend to their peers that they stay in school. "Dropouts nearly always experience alienation (rootlessness, hopelessness, and estrangement) from their school, home, neighborhood, and society in general. Such perceptions are grounded in youths' belief that they have suffered great injustices because of their race, language, culture, or religion" (Tidwell, 1988, p. 940). A disproportionate number of dropouts come from nonintact families.

**Table 11-7 Reasons Students Give for Dropping Out**

Poor grades

Dislike of school

Expulsion

Financial difficulties and desire to work

Home responsibilities

Pregnancy and marriage

The National Dropout Prevention Center at Clemson University reports that 83% of all prison inmates dropped out of school. "You have to keep in mind that formally dropping out is the end point of a long continuum in which there are lots of levels of dissatisfaction. What we found was that kids are distanced, alienated, disaffected from the life of schools at every social stratum" (Philip Wexler, educator and author, quoted by Judson, 1992). Naturally, compared to graduates, dropouts have more difficulty getting and keeping a decent job and earn less money. When unemployed, they must learn to cope with time spent alone, since so many of their peers are still in school. Often there is an opportunity to engage in antisocial behavior. Some return to school after getting a taste of what their lives will be like without a diploma (Fisher, 1992).

The government has set as a goal a high school graduation rate of at least 90% by the year 2000. The most successful retention programs bring about 30–40% of students back to school, but how many graduate is not known. Given the nature and extent of the problems that lead to high rates of dropping out and the scarce resources available to schools in disadvantaged communities, we must wonder whether the admirable goal of 90% graduation is realistic. One-quarter of the children in the United States live in poverty; one-third are members of minority groups or recent immigrants, many of whom speak English as a second language (Singh & Hernandez-Gantes, 1996). Half a million children are homeless. The scope of these problems is enormous, and federal aid to schools and model programs continues to shrink (Darling-Hammond, 1991). Nevertheless, some retention programs have had promising results.

Successful programs incorporate some of the following strategies (Dugger, 1995; Jordan et al., 1996; Mahoney & Cairns, 1997; Tabor, 1992b): (1) early intervention for young disadvantaged students, such as provided by the Head Start program, (2) meeting high-risk students' individual needs, perhaps providing them with tutoring or caring mentors, (3) helping students feel that they are part of the school community, for example, through participation in extracurricular activities, (4) helping students link schoolwork to their present and future goals, (5) holding students accountable for their behaviors, (6) using short-term incentives such as small stipends for hours spent studying and monetary fines for missing class, and (7) frequent program evaluations.

Based on their survey of 60 African-American college students attending a predominantly white college in the South, Gardner, Keller, and Piotrowski (1996) suggest the following steps to improve student retention: maintaining support systems (groups, clubs, organizations); training in racial sensitivity for faculty, staff, and students; hiring more minority faculty and staff; improved counseling; and involving more African-American students in organizational functions and activities.

## HIGH SCHOOL UNDERACHIEVERS

High school plays a key role in preparing students to take on adult roles and responsibilities. What happens to *underachievers*—those students who do not seriously engage themselves in the schooling process? The term **underachievement** implies that a student is performing academically at a level below what we would expect based on his or her intellectual ability. Recently, use of the term has been limited to students who do not have any identifiable learning disability, such as short attention span or hyperactivity. There are twice as many male as female underachievers. Underachievers come from all socioeconomic classes, ethnic groups, and racial groups and are quite a diverse group (McCall, Evahn, & Kratzer, 1992).

Underachievers typically have poor self-concepts, as we might expect from a history of academic failure. They display little interest in academics. They annoy teachers, exert minimal effort, or skip school completely. Few participate in class or in school activities. Male and female underachievers are more precocious in their dating and sexual behavior. "The more intense and frequent heterosexual relations by underachievers might be a consequence of few friends and poor self-esteem producing the need for the social support and security that intimate relations sometimes offer" (McCall et al., 1992, p. 136).

Viewing underachievement as a syndrome, rather than as just uninterest in school, is supported by the long-term educational and vocational outcomes of this group. Compared to their achieving peers, they are less likely to complete high school or attend college, and if they do attend college, they are less likely to graduate. Following high school, most hold jobs of low status. They earn less money, change jobs more frequently, and their marriages are much more likely to end in divorce than those of peers who engage academically. "The higher divorce rates may also be associated with the earlier and more intense heterosexual relations that some underachievers displayed, perhaps leading to marriage at a more immature age and subsequent divorce" (McCall et al., 1992, p. 140). Although teachers and principals frequently tell parents that their underachieving children will "get their act together" after leaving high school, sadly, most do not. (See Table 11-8.)

What causes underachievement? We don't know for sure, but consider the profile of a typical low achiever: (1) personal traits or behaviors (e.g., aggressiveness) that alienate their teachers or peers, (2) low self-efficacy and poor self concept (believing that they cannot perform successfully in school or compete with their peers), (3) low achievement motivation, (4) teachers or peers who

**Table 11-8 Profile of the Underachiever**

Has a poor self concept

Displays little interest in academic subject matter

Annoys teachers and disrupts class

Exerts minimal effort in school

Avoids school when possible

Rarely participates in class or in school activities

Is more precocious in dating and sexual behavior

Less likely to complete high school or attend college

Holds low status, poor paying jobs

Changes jobs more frequently

Marriage is more likely to end in divorce

are unsympathetic to their particular needs, and (5) distracting or distressing home conditions, such as poverty or coercive parenting (Hinshaw, 1992; Nunn & Parish, 1992; Sommer & Nagel, 1991).

Underachievement and antisocial behavior during early adolescence appear to be rooted in earlier life problems related to poverty, ineffective parenting, family adversity, subaverage IQ, language deficits, and, occasionally, neurological problems (DeBaryshe et al., 1993; Hinshaw, 1992; Singh & Hernandez-Gantes, 1996). However, many underachieving students come from affluent families with well-educated parents, so family life is not the whole story.

Based on a study of 2,056 secondary school students, Mau (1992) identified four dimensions of alienation in school:

**1. Powerlessness.** Some students set standards for themselves that they have difficulty satisfying. Students doing remedial work feel frustrated and vent their frustrations on their teachers, particularly if their teachers are coercive. They feel they cannot control or change school policies or their own personal status. Many of these students rebel or cut classes, leading to sterner measures from administrators.

**2. Meaninglessness.** Some adolescents do not perceive a link between their present and future roles. That is, they may not see a connection between doing well in school and getting a good job when they graduate. Much or most of what they learn in school is considered irrelevant to their everyday lives.

**3. Normlessness.** Some students reject their school's rules and standards, particularly when peer norms regarding acceptable behavior conflict with those of the school. Cutting or disrupting a class may be applauded by peers.

**4. Social estrangement.** Socially estranged students are loners who do not participate in class or in school activities. They experience school as monotonous, teachers as uninspiring, peers as unfriendly. Because they attend school and class, they are not recognized as alienated.

One trait common to most underachievers is failure to persist. According to McCall and colleagues (1992), "underachievers lack persistence in the face of challenge and adversity. High school academics, college, employment, and marriage all require some self-confidence and the ability to continue when the going becomes difficult. Underachievers do not persist in these activities as long as others [who have] the same mental ability or the same grades. Instead of persevering and attempting to conquer the inevitable difficulties of life, they check out" (p. 143). Unfortunately, special education programs have not helped this population.

## HELPING AT-RISK HIGH SCHOOL STUDENTS

Nunn and Parish (1992) advocate the following strategies to help high school students who are at risk for school failure: (1) provide them with opportunities to demonstrate their competence, both socially and academically; (2) demonstrate to these students that they are not powerless, that they can improve their performance; (3) help them develop positive relationships with peers and others in school who can appreciate their accomplishments; (4) help these students participate in the "fabric" of school life, so that they can feel that they are part of the school community; (5) provide learning experiences that at-risk students can perceive as relevant to their present and future lives; and (6) improve school climate for all students.

## *SUMMARY*

**1.** Adolescents spend more time attending school than they do in any other waking activity. Schools originally were designed to provide children with a vocation. The goals of modern secondary schools are much broader, including passing on cultural traditions and values, preparing students for college, and teaching critical thinking skills.

**2.** We can distinguish two attitudes toward school: engagement and disaffection. Engaged students seek and enjoy challenging work and persist during learning tasks. Disaffected students have little interest in school and avoid difficult subject matter.

**3.** Parental interest and involvement, close parent–child relationships, the quality of instruction, and many other contextual factors usually have a significant impact on adolescents' academic performance. Good teachers present material in ways that students find interesting. Family conflict and instability interfere with school adjustment. Achievement is self-perpetuating in that children who do well in their early schooling usually continue to succeed during secondary school and college.

**4.** Although friends sometimes discourage or distract adolescents, peer influence on school performance usually is positive. Achieving students seek each other out and share resources and information. African-American adolescents may be especially vulnerable to negative peer influence on achievement.

**5.** The sources of gender differences in achievement are not well understood, but when boys and girls are treated equitably, gender differences tend to be small or nonexistent. Some adolescent girls experience role conflict regarding being popular and doing well in school. It is particularly important, therefore, that parents and teachers express high expectations of them. For most students, achievement enhances self-esteem.

**6.** Negative attitudes toward school and schoolwork are common in secondary school, even among those who do well. Although many students enjoy and seek mastery of course material, too many students are disaffected; they are passive, do not try hard, and give up easily when faced with challenging material. A common complaint is that assignments are not sufficiently challenging. Students who find meaning in their assignments have the most positive attitudes. Payoffs for hard work include proving one's ability, gaining approval from others, and preparing for a career.

**7.** Less than half of the time students spend in school is devoted to core academic courses. Students in the United States spend considerably less time in academic pursuits than students in Japan, France, and Germany, perhaps accounting for the former's poorer performance in science and math. Students in the United States spend much less time doing homework and do not study as hard. Parental encouragement is a critical factor in high school students' willingness to work hard.

**8.** It may be advantageous for some girls to attend single-gender classes or schools. Girls move at a different pace than boys in class and report feeling less competitive. Further, some teachers give boys more attention than girls. Many girls complain about being sexually harassed by boys. Girls in single-gender schools usually receive more attention for their accomplishments and have more frequent opportunities to hold leadership positions. Critics of single-gender schools contend that coeducational schools provide a more realistic environment for females, most of whom eventually will have to work with males. However, observers agree that gender bias in the classroom needs to be discouraged.

**9.** Students do better in a developmentally appropriate educational environment, one that takes into account their cognitive, social, and emotional changes. Secondary schools, larger and more impersonal than elementary schools, often do not make the grade. Students are given minimal opportunity to make decisions that affect them and find teachers to be overly controlling and insensitive. The so-called attitude problem of disaffected students partly reflects a restrictive middle school environment and less than sympathetic teachers. The best middle schools try hard to meet the developmental needs of young adolescents.

**10.** Parents, students, and teachers in the United States have lower expectations about achievement than those in many other countries. Whereas Japanese parents attribute achievement to hard work, parents in the United States tend to view achievement in terms of innate ability. Since so many students in the United States complain that they are not being challenged, it makes sense for all parties to raise their expectations.

**11.** Graduating from one level of schooling to another is both exciting and stressful for most young people. School transitions usually involve more work, harder work, and higher expectations. Self-esteem suffers, especially when social networks are disrupted. Adolescents who feel socially competent usually adjust best during school transitions. College freshmen who live on campus must face the additional challenge of living away from home. Many feel lonely and isolated, at least until they establish a network of new friends and enjoy the taste of their new freedom. College students who live at home are more attached to their parents.

**12.** White and Asian-American adolescents tend to get better grades than African-American and Hispanic students. Many investigators attribute ethnic differences in achievement to parenting and peer influences. Students do best in school when their parents and peers support their achievement. Discrimination also plays a role. Students who believe that their hard work will not lead to success are less willing to apply themselves. Some minority students and females feel pressure from their peers to not engage in schoolwork. They feel that they must choose between being liked and doing well in school.

**13.** Between 15% and 30% of adolescents in the United States never graduate from high school. Pregnant students, minority students, and those who simply do not like school are at highest risk for dropping out. They have difficulty finding and keeping a job and earn less money when they do work.

**14.** Underachieving students perform at an academic level below what we would expect given their ability. They have little interest in academic work and rarely participate in class or in extracurricular activities. Most have poor self-concepts, believing that they are not capable of doing well. The essence of underachievement appears to be a lack of persistence in the face of challenge and adversity. Even if they graduate from high school, underachievers typically obtain low-paying, low-status jobs. Although the causes of underachievement are not well understood, many of these teenagers had family and other life problems when they were younger.

# GLOSSARY

**Literacy** The ability to read, write, and calculate

**GPA perspective** Overly emphasizing the importance of grades

**Engagement** Seeking and enjoying challenging work, taking the initiative when given the opportunity, and exerting effort and concentration during learning tasks

**Disaffection** Displaying passivity, expending little effort, and giving up easily when challenged

**Mastery goal orientations** Focusing on the task at hand

**Performance goal orientations** Focusing on the quality of one's performance

**Self-handicapping strategies** Strategies used by some students to provide justification for poor performance by deflecting attention away from their ability and toward circumstances

**Tracking** Programs that prepare students for different vocational paths; subject-by-subject groupings commonly found in high schools

**Ability grouping** Temporarily placing students with others who have similar learning needs

**Person-environment fit** Providing developmentally appropriate educational environments for young adolescents

**Cultural discontinuity hypothesis** The idea that the cultural belief systems of some ethnic groups are incompatible with those of mainstream society

**Top dog phenomenon** Upon graduating, students go from being seniors in one school ("top dog") to freshmen (bottom of the ladder) in the next

**"Glass ceiling" hypothesis** Discrimination in employment against women and minorities that places artificial limits on advancement

**Underachievement** Performing below one's ability

# THOUGHT QUESTIONS

**1.** What do secondary school teachers need to know about adolescents?

**2.** How far should teachers go in making schoolwork more palatable for students?

**3.** What is the link between the parent–adolescent relationship and adolescents' achievement motivation?

**4.** Are boys more achievement-oriented than girls?

**5.** Based on your own middle school and high school experiences, how would you design a better secondary school?

**6.** In what sense are college students better equipped for a school transition than secondary school students?

**7.** How much of a school's limited resources should be geared to motivating underachievers?

**8.** Why should society care about students who drop out?

# SELF-TEST

**1.** At the turn of this century, about what percent of adolescents attended high school?

   **a.** 10

   **b.** 20

   **c.** 30

   **d.** 40

**2.** Engaged students

   **a.** are passive learners

   **b.** expend minimal effort

   **c.** give up easily when challenged

   **d.** are ready and eager to learn

**3.** Disaffected students

   **a.** seek challenging work

   **b.** would rather be someplace else than school

   **c.** are avid readers

   **d.** seek leadership positions

**4.** Believing that one can succeed on a task is called

   **a.** commitment

   **b.** attribution

   **c.** self-efficacy

   **d.** extrinsic motivation

**5.** Which one of the following does *not* predict adolescent achievement?

   **a.** close parent–child relationship

   **b.** realistic expectations about achievement

   **c.** inconsistent, punitive parenting

   **d.** parental interest and involvement

**6.** Parents may prefer home schooling for their children because

   **a.** they want to instill religious values

   **b.** they are dissatisfied with the quality of public school instruction

   **c.** they fear for their children's safety

   **d.** all of the above

**7.** Some gifted girls fear that their achievement will

    **a.** compromise their popularity

    **b.** outshine their athletic ability

    **c.** be overlooked by employers

    **d.** lead to sexual harassment

**8.** Secondary school teachers need to become more sensitive to adolescent

    **a.** self-consciousness

    **b.** identity needs

    **c.** psychomotor deficits

    **d.** music

**9.** Adolescents value school mainly as a place to

    **a.** acquire literacy skills

    **b.** play competitive sports

    **c.** seek vocational guidance

    **d.** spend time with their friends

**10.** Compared to Japanese and Russian adolescents, those in the United States spend _____ doing classwork and homework.

    **a.** less than half as much time

    **b.** half as much time

    **c.** twice as much time

    **d.** the same amount of time

**11.** In high school classrooms,

    **a.** girls usually dominate discussions

    **b.** boys usually dominate discussions

    **c.** girls report feeling more confident than boys

    **d.** boys move at the same pace as girls

**12.** Middle school teachers tend to be overly

    **a.** sensitive

    **b.** tired

    **c.** educated

    **d.** controlling

13. The "top dog" phenomenon applies to
    a. school transitions
    b. classroom behaviors
    c. extracurricular activities
    d. study skills

14. Those most at risk for dropping out of high school include
    a. students who abuse drugs and alcohol
    b. students from low-income families
    c. girls who become pregnant (and their boyfriends)
    d. all of the above are at higher risk

15. The term *underachievement* implies that a student is performing academically at a level below what we would expect based on his or her
    a. socioeconomic level
    b. intellectual ability
    c. previous performance
    d. age

# TWELVE

# VOCATIONAL DEVELOPMENT

◆

## Preview Questions

1. In what sense is career development a lifelong process?
2. What trends in employment will affect today's secondary school and college students?
3. What are the stages in career development?
4. How does vocational development relate to other aspects of adolescent development, such as creating an adult self-concept and striving for autonomy?
5. What are common obstacles to making good career decisions during adolescence?
6. What is meant by *goodness of fit* between a person and a career?
7. Do male and female adolescents have different career aspirations?
8. What role do the family and school play in helping adolescents make good vocational decisions?
9. What vocational options are available to youth who are not college bound?
10. What are the special vocational needs of ethnic minority students?
11. What are the pros and cons of part-time employment for teenagers?

◆

## Disclosures

I don't want to be a bottom man. I want to be someone you can look up to. But a lot of people come out of college with no place to go. Me and my friends, that's the biggest fear that teenagers have.

*(High school senior quoted by Kilborn, 1994)*

Sure, you can tell kids to go out and get a job—your employer will train you. But they can't train you if you can't think on your feet, write a memo, get along with people, and get to work on time. That may sound simple, but there's a whole lot more to it. *(Teacher Kathleen Kirby, quoted by Weiss, 1996, p. 17)*

◆

# Contents

During the middle school years, adolescents begin to make academic and other decisions that could restrict or broaden the types of employment for which they will qualify. The hordes that avoid courses in science and math eliminate almost any possibility of pursuing potentially rewarding careers in medicine, engineering, or computer technology. College students know that declaring a major is a turning point in the vocational process. But do they understand how competitive the world of work is and that even for college graduates there are no guarantees of future employment in their desired field (Patterson, 1997)? Vocationally tracked students hope to obtain employment after graduating from high school. How many of them realize that a high school diploma isn't highly valued by employers and that most will find unskilled, low-paying positions?

During adolescence, the question "How will I support myself as a young adult?" may elicit confusion and discomfort. The idea of having to find a real job is intimidating when there are so many different types of employment and the work world is so competitive. Further, many females experience *role conflict* when trying to decide whether to become wives, mothers, workers, homemakers, or some combination of these roles. Females and members of ethnic minorities become increasingly aware of the *glass ceiling* and other forms of discrimination that they are likely to face in the world of work.

But one doesn't have to wait until graduation to find employment. About 61% of 10th graders and 90% of 11th and 12th graders work part time during the school year (Manning, 1990). A significant number work more than 20 hours a week (Bachman & Schulenberg, 1993). High school students who work become familiar with employment-related concepts such as seniority, job security, promotion, and benefit packages. They are beginning to understand how work, lifestyle, and leisure time are linked.

In Chapter 1, we noted that obtaining paid employment and becoming financially independent are useful markers for adulthood in that earnings signify that an individual can function in the adult world (Shanahan, Elder, Burchinal, & Conger, 1996). According to Havighurst (1972), committing to a career path is one of the most important challenges that adolescents face. Erikson agreed, emphasizing that vocation becomes a crucial part of adult identity. The transition to full-time employment occurs in the context of the physical, social, and emotional changes that we have studied in previous chapters. Advancing reasoning abilities allow adolescents to view their futures more realistically and to contemplate the vast number of options available to them.

In this chapter, we view career development as a process that begins during early childhood with a vague awareness that "grownups" go to work to make money and that ends with a retirement party and a proverbial gold watch. Although vocational development is lifelong, it is during adolescence that young people have the greatest number of opportunities to explore different types of work roles and eventually commit to a particular career path.

Several questions arise when we consider the topics of employment and vocational decision making. Given the large number of employment choices and the uncertainty of the labor market, how can parents and educators help young people make good vocational decisions in preparing for the lifelong role of worker? How do we help adolescents evaluate their strengths and weaknesses and set realistic career goals for themselves? How do we help young people develop positive attitudes toward work and gain the information that they need to make good decisions about career and lifestyle? And how does part-time work affect adolescents' schoolwork, family life, and peer relationships?

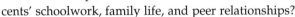

## CAREER DEVELOPMENT: A LIFELONG PROCESS

*Study Question: How are play, school, and employment connected?*

Early family life points us in certain career directions and not others (Finch & Mortimer, 1996). Ryu and Mortimer (1996), for example, maintain that parental work experiences indirectly influence children's work values. According to these investigators, the parental workplace "is one of the most important environments influencing the vocational development of children" (p. 168). The sequence they describe is the following: parental work establishes certain be-havioral demands and payoffs that influence parental personality. Changes in parental personality, in turn, change parenting practices and thus children's personality, including work values. For example, adults who at work have more opportunity for self-direction and decision making will attach greater value to individual responsibility and self-reliance, values that they will culti-vate in their own children.

Although we rarely can identify a direct link between specific childhood experiences and a subsequent career, the *exploration stage* of vocational devel-opment unquestionably begins during childhood. Play, the most common wak-ing activity of young children, is an excellent source of exploration opportu-nities. Play not only provides fun and excitement, it is also a way for children to acquire and practice a variety of cognitive, social, emotional, and coping skills that will serve them well in the classroom (Piaget, 1962). Play is pleasur-able, but by sharpening skills and abilities, it also serves a larger purpose (of which children are blissfully unaware). Household chores usually comprise children's first work experiences. Informal jobs such as babysitting or doing yardwork prepare young people for paid part-time employment. Play, house-hold chores, informal jobs, and part-time employment all can be viewed as an early part of the exploration stage of vocational development. Grusec and her colleagues (1996) report an interesting side effect of household chores: teen-agers who are expected to do housework that benefits other family members (rather than themselves) are more likely to show concern for the welfare of others.

Formal instruction during the school years allows children to master skills and, importantly, feel pride in their performance. Schooling provides countless opportunities to learn good work habits and healthy work attitudes. As stu-dents, children learn how to read, write, and calculate, how to solve practical and hypothetical problems, and how to think critically about information and ideas. We like to think that schoolwork is satisfying to students in its own right, but whether it is or isn't, like play, schoolwork ultimately serves a larger pur-pose—preparation for full-time employment.

The moratorium arrangement of deferred adult responsibility permits most young people to spend considerable time in leisure activities—watching tele-vision, listening to music, socializing with friends, and engaging in hobbies and sports. These activities may occur in a variety of settings—homes, malls, street corners, and schoolyards. Although teenagers engage in leisure activities to relax, have fun, and socialize, such activities influence attitudes, behaviors, and values that can indirectly affect their career development. Leisure-time activi-

**FIGURE 12.1 Career develop-ment as a lifelong process.**

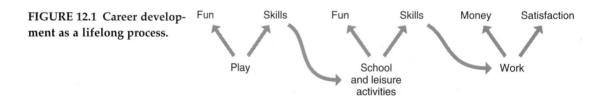

ties prepare adolescents for adult roles that require social skills, persistence, concentration, and challenge (Fine et al., 1990).

Like play, school, and leisure-time activities, employment can be a source of meaning and fulfillment. Its traditional function, however, has been to serve as a way for individuals to support themselves and their families and to contribute to their community. Play, school, and employment are linked in that each activity, potentially satisfying in its own right, orients us to future roles, responsibilities, and potential rewards (Figure 12-1).

It is the rare youngster who grasps the relationship between household chores, schooling, part-time work, and subsequent commitment to an occupation and a lifestyle. How could young people know (until we tell them) that when they choose an academic major, let alone a vocation, they are also acquiring an identification with a profession, a lifestyle, colleagues and friends, organizational ties, and a socioeconomic status? *Thought Question: How prepared is the average high school student to make decisions that might have lifelong consequences?*

## BRIEF HISTORY OF CHILD LABOR

In most Western societies, underage children are not permitted to work full time. Until the advent of child labor laws in the late 19th century, however, working-class families depended on children's financial and household chore contributions (Aronson, Mortimer, Zierman, & Hacker, 1996). Working-class children could expect to labor for long hours, even at a relatively young age. Girls joined their mothers to pick wild fruit, gather wood, care for siblings, and help with cooking and laundry. Boys accompanied their fathers to tend sheep, chop wood, and work the fields. Everyone pitched in at harvest time (Gottlieb, 1993).

Under the command of their parents, most young people had little or no say in the jobs they were assigned. At about age 14, many boys left home to serve as apprentices in unrelated families. The master of the household served as supervisor and teacher to the child. (Apprenticeships came close to what today we call vocational training.) In the 17th and 18th centuries, naval and military officers began their careers at about age 15. "Among all classes, noble, artisan, and peasant, some adolescents left home, to be educated, to learn a trade, or to become servants. The sons and daughters of the nobility were sent to other aristocratic households, often those of relatives, the sons to train as knights, the daughters to learn social graces. When twelve-year-old William Marshal departed from Normandy to become a squire, according to his biographer, he wept at taking leave of his mother and brothers and sisters, 'like an adolescent going off to boarding school' " (Gies & Gies, 1987, p. 209).

Keep in mind that in previous centuries, children began puberty at a relatively late age, perhaps 16 or 17 years. Youth remained under their parents' authority as long as they lived at home. Before children began to be "sentimentalized" in the late 19th century, they were considered to be "economically useful" by their parents (Zelizer, 1985). *Thought Question: Why are parents*

During industrialization, countless children and adolescents worked in factories under barbaric conditions.

*today more lenient than those in previous centuries regarding not having their children earn money through labor?*

When children served as apprentices, they lived under the authority of both their father and the family they served. Only at marriage, usually in their middle to late 20s, could they gain their freedom from family and employers. Apprentices were not allowed to marry. In later centuries, school became a small part of children's lives, but most children "continued to spend the years after ten or so in a household, working and learning to work" (Gottlieb, 1993, p. 168).

It was not until children's labor was no longer needed that the present moratorium arrangement of deferred freedom and responsibilities emerged in industrial societies. Although children have been given fewer household and financial responsibilities during most of this century, the increasing number of poor and single-parent households appears to be reversing this trend (Aronson et al., 1996). About 2.6 million 16- and 17-year-olds worked an average of 19.2 hours a week in 1995, according to the U.S. Labor Department. Only four states (New York, Wisconsin, Washington, and Oregon) set limits on how late teenagers can work (Geoghegan, 1996). Is child labor becoming normative again in the late 20th century? We will return to the issue of part-time employment for adolescents later in this chapter.

# TRENDS AND ISSUES IN EMPLOYMENT

*Study Question: How has the job market changed over the past 25 years?*

Living in a time of rapid, unpredictable economic and technological change presents a serious obstacle to career planning. It is not easy to plan and prepare for a career when the employment picture is so uncertain. How can middle school and high school students anticipate what work life and the job market will be like in 5 or 10 years? New vocations arise in fields such as science, technology, and medicine that require skills that we can only imagine. Jobs that exist today may be sought by far more people than are needed to fill them or may no longer exist in a few years. Fortunately, there are people such as demographers, policymakers, and career development professionals who attempt to predict what the future employment picture will be like based on current trends. Table 12-1 lists several current trends, issues, and problems that affect the career plans of today's students (Hansen, 1993).

Emerging trends over the past 25 years include the globalization of careers and of the economy, proliferation of computer technology and telecommunications, increasing specialization, ecological and environmental considerations, fewer jobs involving manual labor, and an increasing number of jobs in the service sector. The latter require more education and training than the former. We know that to maximize their employability, today's graduates must be flexible and well rounded. They should avoid becoming overspecialized, perhaps pursuing a double major or a major and a minor. Employers expect workers to

## Table 12-1  Current Trends in Employment

Globalization of careers and the economy

Proliferation of computer technology and telecommunications

Increasing specialization

Ecological and environmental considerations

Fewer jobs involving manual labor

A decline in manufacturing and agricultural jobs

Growth in jobs related to retail sales, computers, legal services, engineering, and residential care

Many openings expected in the service sector of the economy (especially health services)

Jobs requiring more education and training

Emphasis on teamwork, practical problem-solving abilities, and a positive work ethic

Increases in self-employment

New technologies require retraining and relocation of current workers

New opportunities and obstacles for women in the workplace

The working population is getting older

The shrinking number of young workers will have to support the increasing number of those over age 65

be literate and to be able to communicate well with their colleagues. They also value teamwork, practical problem-solving abilities, and a positive work ethic (Stern, McMillion, Hopkins, & Stone, 1990). People whose training does not match their job requirements usually are unhappy with their vocation.

The United Nations reported that in 1995 the number of adults worldwide who were either unemployed or underemployed increased to 1 billion—30% of the world's labor force (United Nations International Labor Organization, 1996). About one-third of the jobless were under age 25. In 1995, the jobless rate in the United States was about 5%, a 7-year low (*The New York Times*, November 26, 1996). We know that there are not enough attractive jobs for young people today, even for those who graduate from high school (Kilborn, 1994). In 1993, according to the U.S. Bureau of Labor, 24% of high school graduates who did not attend college and wanted to work were still unemployed by the October following graduation. Many of those who find employment work part time for the minimum wage (less than $6 an hour). Although the U.S. economy creates about 2 million new jobs a year, most are low-paying and without health benefits or job security. Unfortunately, a college degree and a good attitude do not guarantee reasonable employment.

The U.S. Department of Labor predicts a growth rate in jobs of 1.2% annually, a slowdown compared to the last 20 years. Still, the U.S. Bureau of Labor Statistics expects 26 million new jobs to be created over the next 15 years, about half in the service sector of the economy (especially health services). This increase will accompany a decline in manufacturing and agricultural jobs. We can also expect growth in jobs related to retail sales, computers, legal services, engineering, and residential care. The number of self-employed individuals continues to increase (Leftwich, 1992).

Certain types of jobs are becoming more common (e.g., service, health), while others are becoming relatively scarce (e.g., manual labor). New technologies require retraining and relocation of current workers. Changing gender roles provide new opportunities and obstacles for women in the workplace, the latter exemplified by the glass ceiling that limits advancement and equitable pay for female workers. Employers need help in increasing the representation of ethnic minorities and disabled people in the workplace and dealing with difficult interpersonal issues such as sexual harassment and discrimination. White-collar workers, male and female, experience conflict regarding their commitments to work and family (Hansen, 1993).

With an increased life expectancy, the working population is getting older. There are few economic incentives for senior workers to retire early. The shrinking number of young workers will have to support the increasing number of those over age 65. More of these new workers will be undereducated immigrants or their children, minorities, and the poor. These latter populations, especially urban youth living in poverty, will need considerable help viewing themselves as potentially productive workers (Darling-Hammond, 1991; Hansen, 1993).

As noted in the previous chapter, students and their parents have a rosier view of student competence than do teachers and employers. A study conducted by the Harris Education Research Center and sponsored by the Committee for Economic Development questioned these four groups about student preparedness for jobs and college (*American Educator*, Summer 1992, pp. 33–35). Employers and college professors provided almost uniformly negative ratings of recent high school graduates regarding basic skills, understanding instructions, solving complex problems, and having disciplined work habits. Only a third of employers felt that high school graduates can read and understand written and spoken instructions. Only a quarter felt that recent graduates are capable of doing arithmetic. Students and parents gave much higher ratings to the graduates than did employers and teachers. The report concluded that students and parents are deluding themselves about what educators and employers consider to be an acceptable level of performance.

# DEVELOPMENTAL THEORIES OF OCCUPATIONAL CHOICE

How do people go about choosing a vocation? Vocational decision making is a complex process that is still poorly understood. Plausible models of career development must take into account a variety of factors: home and family influences, education and training, job opportunities, and, perhaps most important, individual differences in people's interests, talents, and personal qualities (Lambert & Mounce, 1987; Super, 1953).

Most theoretical models treat adolescents as rational actors moving through predictable stages of reflective decision making. Ideally, adolescents would seek the closest possible match between their personal qualities and the requirements of various types of employment. If there were a discrepancy between their ability and interests, on the one hand, and the requirements of a specific job opportunity, on the other, they would know to look for more suitable employment (Owens, 1992).

That's the theory. But how many young people actually engage in a systematic, logical analysis of their personal qualities, career options, present and future job markets, and so on? The reality is that career exploration and commitment are complex behaviors that span a period of up to 10 or more years, with earlier decisions limiting later options. Decision making usually is far more haphazard and unpredictable than most theorists allow (Holland, 1996). Just as it would be misguided to assume that there is only one perfect mate out there for each of us, it is equally unreasonable to assume that there is just one type of job or career that we would find fulfilling. A reasonable theory of vocational choice must allow for a range of occupations that would be suitable for a given individual.

## Super's Model

Donald Super (1967, 1984), one of the pioneers in career development research and theory, viewed career development as a predictable, orderly process that requires considerable planning and exploration. During the high school and college years, young people explore a variety of roles and activities that reflect their maturing self-concepts. During what he called the **growth stage of vocational development**, children and early adolescents develop increasingly realistic self-concepts and views of work. During the **exploration stage**, which spans middle and late adolescence, individuals make decisions about possible careers that reflect their self-assessment of interests and abilities and their growing knowledge of specific occupations.

As their self-concepts become more differentiated, young people strive to match their self-perceptions to the requirements of jobs that they might consider ("I like arguing issues: maybe I should become a trial lawyer"). During the **establishment stage**, which corresponds to early adulthood, people become accustomed to a particular work routine. During the **maintenance stage**, which spans middle age, most adults persist in their chosen job, but growth and personal advancement are almost inevitable. Some individuals seek higher levels of responsibility and decision making, while others are content to stay put in a comfortable and predictable job situation. Finally, during the **decline stage** in late adulthood, individuals retire from the workplace and search for other meaningful ways to spend their time. Unfortunately, many of Super's propositions have not been operationalized sufficiently to allow empirical testing (Salomone, 1996).

### Ginzberg's Model

Eli Ginzberg (1972, 1990) views vocational development mainly as a series of decisions that reflect increasingly realistic thinking about one's personal goals and career opportunities. Based on his interviews with mainly advantaged boys, Ginzberg identified three stages of occupational choice. During the **fantasy stage**, children imagine themselves in roles and activities that they find pleasing, although unrelated to their actual interests and abilities. They may imagine themselves to be athletes, astronauts, doctors, entertainers, or superheroes. (According to basketball coach Michael Neer at the University of Rochester, of 25,000 athletes who play college football, only 50 eventually are selected by National Basketball Association teams each year [Kutner, 1993c].) During the second, or **tentative stage**, adolescents' thoughts of a career are guided initially by their interests. Subsequently, their choices are governed by their rough impressions of what abilities and values are needed to perform a job competently. A teenager may consider becoming a social worker because of a desire to help people or decide to not go into engineering because of an aversion to math.

The third, or **realistic stage**, begins at about age 18 when older adolescents begin to explore some of the alternatives they are considering, perhaps through volunteer work, through part-time employment, or by taking courses in a special area of interest. Most young people eventually commit to a particular field and sometimes a specialization within that field. Such a commitment reflects their interests and abilities, the education and training required for the occupation, and many other factors.

It is not clear that these stages hold for lower-income or minority youth, for girls, or even for all middle-class boys. For example, girls' career plans tend to be more tentative than those of boys. Ginzberg (1972) acknowledged that people's employment trajectories are more variable than his model allows, and that males and affluent adolescents have several employment advantages. *Thought Question: What role do unforseeable events play in vocational development?*

## Holland's Model

John Holland's (1985, 1996) vocational model characterizes people according to their resemblance to six personality types and categorizes work environments according to six ideal environments. The six personality types include realistic, investigative, artistic, social, enterprising, and conventional. Holland proposes that people seek occupations in which their areas of interest can be expressed. For example, realistic personality types seek and flourish in realistic work environments because such environments provide them with opportunities, activities, tasks, and roles that are congruent with their personalities. He hypothesizes that congruence of personality and job environment leads to job satisfaction, career path stability, and achievement. Incongruence leads to dissatisfaction, career path instability, and low performance (Holland, 1996).

Several empirical studies reveal career stability in nationally representative samples of men and women; that is, when people change jobs, they tend to remain within the same general occupational category. Holland (1996) invokes the construct of **vocational identity** to explain career stability or instability. "For example, a person with a clear sense of identity has an explicit and relatively stable picture of his or her goals, interests, skills, and suitable occupations. Therefore, a person with a clear sense of identity is more likely to accept or find work that is congruent with his or her personal characteristics and to persist in his or her search for a congruent work environment. In contrast, persons with a diffuse sense of identity are more likely to have a work history that is characterized by incompatible choices, frequent job changes, and a diverse set of successive jobs" (p. 403).

Given current downsizing trends in employment, Holland (1996) worries that stable careers will not be the norm in the future and that jobs will no longer be a major source of personal identity or fulfillment in life. If this is the case, he maintains, there will be little left for career models to explain. "Most people will become casualties of vast structural and social changes and take whatever part-time or full-time work they can find. Any job will become more important than a compatible one" (p. 404). *Application Question: If you were a vocational counselor, which one of the above three vocational models would most help you advise high school students?*

## CAREER EXPLORATION AND PREPARATION

*Everyone has a direction. My dad is pounding on my head every time I talk to him. I feel like I have to make some kind of decision and pounce into it, but I just don't know.*

*(Priscilla Stack, 21-year-old psychology major, quoted by Johnson, 1996, p. A22)*

Two familiar concepts that guide our understanding of adolescent career development are *exploration* and *commitment* (Marcia, 1980). Prematurely committing to an academic major or vocation without adequately investigating the alternatives is a common pitfall. Not being ready to commit by one's junior year of college is another. These are two extremes of a continuum in career decision making. Priscilla (quoted above) confirms that parental pressure to commit doesn't help. The best decisions are made by those who explore several suitable fields of study and then select one based on interest and opportunity.

Premature closure, unreflective decision making, and submitting to parental demands or pressure leave many young people unhappy with their vocational choice (Esman, 1991). Such a rude awakening could occur as early as the college years or after working in a field for several years. Naturally, the more time and effort invested in preparing for a particular career, the more upsetting it is to question one's commitment. However, if not corrected, the situation could lead to lifelong dissatisfaction with one's career or repeated changes in employment (Esman, 1991).

Students might discover that their chosen career is no longer feasible because (1) the field has become glutted, (2) they cannot afford or are otherwise unwilling to attain the required education or training, (3) their academic credentials are inadequate, (4) the realities of their job situation may not be what they expected, or (5) office politics or unwanted job responsibilities may create unwelcomed pressure (Mitchell, 1988). ***Thought Question: What reasons might some people give for remaining in a job or career that is not satisfying?***

How prepared are youth for the realities of today's job market, including intense competition, hectic work schedules, and job insecurity? Even when they become more realistic in their vocational thinking, most adolescents have little awareness of what engineers, architects, and accountants actually do or of the education and training such professions require. A career is much more than a job. It involves extended preparation, willingness to expand one's capabilities, working with a variety of people, a distinctive lifestyle, earning a living, and much more.

Most people prefer a career that is consistent with their personal goals and values and, for some, with their spiritual beliefs (Hansen, 1993; Holland, 1996). Whereas our ancestors labored mightily just to survive, people today expect more than economic survival from their work lives. They desire meaningful work, pleasant social encounters, comfortable working conditions, opportunities for advancement, and job security. More than students in other countries, students in the United States link employment to success, achievement, and wealth (Stiles, Gibbons, & Peters, 1993).

Career exploration, which occurs mostly during late adolescence, eventually leads to commitment to and establishment of a career choice. Super (1985) acknowledged "that some people never cease exploring, that some drift, and that some are destabilized by accident, illness, war, politics, recessions, and their own personal development as interests change and values shift with age and experience" (p. 407). Perhaps it is naive to assume that a career that seems exciting to a 20-year-old will necessarily appeal to that same person in 10 or 20 years.

Super (interviewed by Freeman, 1993) described a process he calls **emergent career decision making**. Children don't need to know what they should be when they grow up. What they need to know is what they should *do* so that as each new kind of career-related decision is made, they will be ready for it. "Such decisions include, whether to go to college; which college to go to; what to major in when you are a sophomore; whether to go to graduate school when you finish college; what kind of graduate work to do if you do go" (p. 261).

Super defined **career maturity** as the readiness to make career decisions. Is the adolescent willing to be an *explorer*, someone who asks questions and finds out about opportunities and obstacles? Is he or she flexible regarding what the future may bring? Does the adolescent have knowledge of the work world and of the stages of life? In developing plans and goals, what is the relative importance of work, study, homemaking, leisure time, and community? There is evidence that the plans and goals that students formulate in high school continue to guide them for at least 2 years following high school graduation (Pimentel, 1996).

## VOCATIONAL CHOICE

*Study Question: Is there a "perfect job" for everyone?*

One of the key developmental tasks of adolescence, according to Robert Havighurst (1972), is organizing "one's plans and energies in such a way as to begin an orderly career; to feel able to make a living" (p. 62). To accomplish this task, adolescents require good information about career choices. Today's young people are confronted with more vocational alternatives than any previous generation. The *Directory of Occupational Choice* lists at least 22,000 different job titles. How does one become aware of the possibilities, let alone narrow the alternatives down to a manageable few? Analogously, there are dozens of academic majors listed in a typical college catalog. Doesn't it make sense to sample many different fields of study before committing to a particular one? How do you know that business or occupational therapy is for you if you haven't tried geology, literature, or gymnastics? Despite the pressure to choose a major and make long-term career decisions, most students feel unprepared for the challenging task of making decisions that will affect almost every aspect of their future lives (Murray, 1996c).

Adolescents need good information before they can make sensible decisions about what courses to take, what field to major in, and what career choices would be suitable. They need to be informed about how different careers are associated with different lifestyles and standards of living. Students also need information about career alternatives, education, and training requirements of different careers and their costs in time and money. They require information about projected job demand in 5 and 10 years so that they avoid preparing for an occupation that might no longer exist when they graduate.

Additionally, young people need to learn how to assess their own interests and skills to ensure goodness of fit between their personal characteristics and those required by a particular job. There are many tests and inventories that

**Table 12-2 What Adolescents Need to Make Good Career Decisions**

Good information about career choices

Good information about how different careers are associated with different lifestyles and standards of living

Information about career alternatives, education, and training requirements of different careers and their costs in time and money

Information about projected job demand in five and ten years so that they avoid preparing for an occupation that might no longer exist when they graduate

Help in assessing their interests and skills to ensure goodness of fit between their personal characteristics and those required by a particular job

measure interests and abilities. Counselors can use these measures, as well as grades, to help students narrow the wide range of alternatives within a career. One can have a career in sports, for example, by being a player, coach, journalist, manager, agent, or referee (see Table 12-2).

## WORK ORIENTATION AND WORK VALUES

Most of us have learned that hard work can be rewarding in its own right (Lindsay & Knox, 1984). There is a sense of accomplishment that we experience when we perform competently in or out of school. In past generations, scholars were motivated by their love of learning (**intrinsic motivation**). Today, students work for more worldly purposes—to pass a test, get a good grade, and eventually secure a well-paying job with opportunities for advancement and a comfortable lifestyle (**extrinsic motivation**) (Rosseel, 1989; Ryu & Mortimer, 1996).

With our first serious job we may feel flattered by a generous salary and benefits, but we must not lose sight of the fact that we will be spending thousands of hours of our precious lifetime at work. Young people need to understand that satisfaction with work is as important a consideration as financial compensation. Every job is a "package deal." Would-be employees need to know how to evaluate the pros and cons of any particular job offer.

As noted earlier, many employers are losing confidence in the ability of educational institutions to train young people for the workplace. According to recent U.S. Census Bureau surveys of managers and business owners, in making hiring decisions many employers have been playing down the importance of grades and school evaluations and basing their judgment on such qualities as attitude, communication skills, and previous work experience (Applebome, 1995a). Although conventional wisdom suggests that ability is the key to successful job performance, interpersonal skills and personal traits such as conscientiousness, ambition, creativity, leadership, cooperation, and integrity play a crucial role in determining an individual's employability and job satisfaction (Azar, 1995). (Box 12-1.)

Despite the links between family, school, and work, the workplace is considerably different from home and school. Parents and teachers usually are

**Box 12-1
Credibility**

When I asked 22-year-old Douglas why he had come into counseling, he said he didn't know. His mother and girlfriend told him that he had a problem with money and urged him to get help. As an unemployed undergraduate, Douglas had accumulated $3500 in credit card debt, partly because he liked buying his girlfriend expensive presents. At the time of his first session with me, Douglas hadn't quite graduated from college. Because he rarely attended classes, he had to complete two more courses in summer school. Douglas admitted that he had lied to his girlfriend about his class attendance, contributing to his credibility problem with her. Douglas shared that he resented his college's attendance policy. He didn't see why he had to attend class if he could do the work on his own.

Douglas told me that he was seeking employment so that he could pay off his credit card debt and save enough money to rent an apartment with his girlfriend, whom he desperately wanted to marry. He repeated that he needed help with his spending. I suggested to Douglas that his mother and girlfriend advised counseling for him not solely because of his money problems but because of a more general credibility problem. He had attended few classes during his senior year; he had a mediocre grade point average; had lied to his girlfriend about his attendance; and despite his lack of income, he had accumulated a considerable debt. And he was not graduating on time, with his classmates. How could his girlfriend view him as a responsible partner? Why would she, or a potential employer, or anyone else commit to someone who could act so irresponsibly? Douglas was resistant to the idea that his lack of commitment to his studies in college would be a red flag for employers.

Unhappy with my analysis of his problem, Douglas responded that this was the way he was and that he wouldn't change for anyone. When Douglas returned for a second session, his attitude had softened. Conversations with his mother and girlfriend convinced him that he indeed had a credibility problem and that to earn their trust he would have to change his ways.

---

more sympathetic and less demanding than employers. Many new workers are surprised to discover that the bottom line of business is the profit margin, not concern about employees' feelings. But Ruscoe and his colleagues (1996), in a study of 1,800 working Kentucky high school students, report that employers showed greater interest in and concern for working students' academic life than they expected.

## CAREER ASPIRATIONS AND GENDER

*Study Question: Do parents expect more from their sons than from their daughters regarding vocational achievement?*

One day, in the spring of 1993, thousands of mothers and fathers took their daughters with them to work. Although some sons felt left out of the "Take Our Daughters to Work" campaign, hundreds of thousands of girls aged 9 to 15 got to see firsthand how their parents earn a living. One goal of the campaign was to let teenage girls, so many of whom have low career aspirations, get a glimpse of the adult work world. All children need help in understanding the connections between home, school, and career, but girls in particular have been short-changed regarding encouragement to aspire to meaningful, satisfying employment.

Many women who achieve professional success report having as influential role models their mothers, who demonstrated to them that achievement is not incompatible with femininity or having a family. Successful women often give credit to their fathers, who they say gave them "permission" to realize their potential. High-achieving women generally are self-confident and reject narrow definitions of sex roles (Maier & Herman, 1974; McDonald & Jessell, 1992; Super, 1963; Unger & Crawford, 1992).

Work, achievement, and gender have been linked since the beginning of recorded history. Even during the first half of this century, most girls viewed their futures in terms of marriage and family. Women's work always has been unpaid and undervalued. To this day, few societies provide equal career opportunities and financial compensation to males and females. Jobs are available to men and women partly on the basis of long-standing stereotypes about what constitutes masculinity and femininity. Biologically based differences in size, strength, and reproduction have led to rigid cultural roles and expectations that encourage males to achieve and females to nurture. Stereotypes about emotional and reproductive differences between men and women lead some employers to view women employees as less dependable and less competent than men (Unger & Crawford, 1992).

**Adolescent girls require guidance to help them understand and prepare for difficulties they are likely to face in the world of work.**

For the most part, our ancestors raised their sons to value competition and achievement. Domestic and nurturing skills were cultivated in daughters. When women worked at all, it was in the role of helper or assistant to a man—secretaries served bosses, nurses helped doctors, stewardesses assisted pilots, and so on. The traditional division of labor, wherein men labored while women bore and raised children, made some sense during the agricultural and industrial eras. In modern times, strength and speed rarely are factors in job performance. The traits that employers look for in modern jobs are shared equally by males and females.

Recently, female career development began receiving the same degree of research attention as male career development (e.g., Wulff & Steitz, 1997). Researchers and theorists previously ignored gender differences, partly because they assumed that such differences are minor or nonexistent. An important component of adult identity is seeing oneself as a member of a particular profession or vocation. Traditionally, *vocational identity* has been stronger in males than in females, partly reflecting the conflict that many females feel about choosing between family and career. To some extent, men and women have different needs and different aspirations regarding work and career and achieve their vocational identities through different paths (Grotevant & Thornbecke, 1982). On the average, women commit to career choices later than men do, value job characteristics more than pay and advancement, and place a higher priority than men do on marriage and family (Monaco & Gaier, 1992).

Over the past 35 years, proportionately more women than men have joined the labor force, many occupying positions traditionally held by men. Not all women seek nontraditional employment. For example, religious women are more likely than women with secular orientations to seek employment consistent with traditional sex roles (Rich & Golan, 1992). Flexibility in sex roles doesn't mean that all women must pursue nontraditional careers. Rather, it frees men and women to aspire to whatever life path appeals to them. However, despite expanding opportunities available to women, gender stereotyping of jobs is still widespread.

The U.S. Census Bureau (1994) reports that only about 9% of doctoral degrees in technological fields are held by women. Women are overrepresented in nontechnical, low-wage, low-status jobs. Given the limited number of successful female role models in business and public life, it is not surprising that girls generally have lower career aspirations than boys, especially during the high school years. Compared to males, females are more interested in occupations involving social service, clerical pursuits, and artistic interests and less interested in science, technology, and business (DeAngelis, 1994; Erb, 1983; Gerstein, Lichtman, & Barokas, 1988).

Girls can identify as many occupations as boys, but they see fewer occupations as possibilities for themselves (Stiles et al., 1993). Is this because they have lower aspirations or less self-confidence, or because teenage girls are aware of barriers in certain areas of employment that don't exist for men? In 1988, women represented 30% of scientists and 4% of engineers. In 1960, females comprised only 10% of scientists and 1% of engineers (Brush, 1991). When polled recently about why they thought so few women in the United

States consider entering engineering or the sciences, female college students cited the difficulty of combining technical professional work with home and childrearing responsibilities and the gender bias they expect from men in these fields (Morgan, 1992).

One group of investigators (Schulenberg, Goldstein, & Vondracek, 1991) wondered whether gender differences in career interests are moderated by students' educational aspirations, certainty about careers, and parental educational level. They administered a standardized measure of 14 career interests to a rural sample of 699 junior high and high school students. The investigators found marked gender differences in career interests consistent with the traditional sex role stereotypes mentioned above. The largest stereotypical gender differences occurred among students with low educational aspirations, who reported that they had already decided on a career. Males and females with high educational aspirations were more similar in their career interests, at least in science-related areas. Contrary to the investigators' expectations, stereotypical gender differences were greatest for children of parents with higher educational levels.

Adolescent girls require guidance to help them understand and prepare for difficulties they are likely to face in the world of work. They need to be prepared for the sexism that remains prevalent in the working world, including devaluing women's work, discrimination in hiring, lower-status positions, lower salaries, fewer opportunities for promotion, sexual harassment, and the paucity of role models. Women and minorities still are underrepresented in occupations such as medicine and law. As noted in Chapter 9, little is being done in most high schools and colleges to prepare young women to deal with gender bias either in the classroom or in the workplace (DeAngelis, 1994; Hansen, 1993; Kramer, 1986; Unger & Crawford, 1992).

Self-concept and self-esteem are important factors in vocational development. Adolescents who feel a sense of personal worth are more likely to believe that a variety of careers is possible for them. Adolescents who act decisively and effectively—those who know what they want to do occupationally—typically have greater self-worth than those who are indecisive or confused. Chiu (1990) administered a self-esteem scale to 221 high school sophomores and juniors and asked their teachers to rate these students' self-esteem. Boys who stated career goals scored higher in self-esteem than those who had no idea what they wanted to do after graduation. The effect was not as strong for girls. Boys and girls with career goals were rated as having higher self-esteem by their teachers. Similarly, students with low self-esteem typically came up with a very short list of career choices and had doubts about their ability to succeed.

## THE ROLE OF THE FAMILY

*Study Question: How does parental employment affect children's career aspirations?*

Vocational development begins in early childhood as children learn about work and come to see their parents as workers. Children learn about the world of work by listening to their parents discuss their work lives and through exposure to parental attitudes about work. Children usually turn to their parents first when making career-related decisions. Yet describing vocational development in a family context is problematic for two reasons. First, families are so diverse. Do both parents work? What do they do? Are they satisfied with their work or do they complain about poor working conditions, low salary, or lack of opportunity to advance? Second, family life has changed substantially over the past three decades. Changes include a variety of nontraditional family configurations (e.g., stepfamily, single-parent family), increased rates of maternal employment, equal opportunity legislation, and changing sex-role expectations (Larson & Richards, 1994; Schulenberg et al., 1984).

Parents influence their children's vocational development in several ways: (1) by providing information about jobs and work life, (2) by generating opportunities to learn about and explore their neighborhoods and communities, (3) by modeling activities associated with various professions, and (4) via family processes such as socialization and the quality of parent–child relationships (Leung, Wright, & Foster, 1987; McNair & Brown, 1983; Palmer & Cochran, 1988; Saltiel, 1985; Schulenberg et al., 1984). (See Table 12-3.)

Affluent, educated parents are more likely to have an authoritative parenting style, which in turn promotes good parent-child relationships, academic achievement, and realistic career aspirations (McDonald & Jessell, 1992; Schulenberg et al., 1984). As previously noted, mothers are particularly important role models for their daughters. Career-oriented women usually are well educated, have well-educated mothers, and receive considerable encouragement to achieve from their parents. Typically, they postpone marriage or childbearing until they are established in their profession (Astin, 1974; Monaco & Gaier, 1992).

Fathers who have good relationships with their sons have greater influence on their career paths. Adolescents also are influenced by the job status of the opposite-gender parent. For example, sons of working mothers generally have

**Table 12-3 How Parents Influence Their Children's Vocational Development**

| |
|---|
| By providing information about jobs and work life |
| By generating opportunities to learn about and explore their neighborhoods and communities |
| By modeling activities associated with various professions |
| Via family processes such as socialization and the quality of the parent–child relationship |
| By practicing the authoritative parenting style, which promotes good parent–child relationships, academic achievement, and realistic career aspirations |
| Mothers are particularly important role models for their daughters |
| Fathers who have warm relationships with their sons have greater influence on their career paths |
| Realistic expectations encourage good decision making whereas excessive family pressure often leads to poor decisions |

*"Just because you're Attila the Hun, Dad, doesn't mean
I have to be Attila the Hun."*

higher aspirations and more egalitarian sex-role values than sons of unemployed mothers (Schulenberg et al., 1984).

Adolescents' career aspirations thus reflect a large number of family factors that interact with such child qualities as temperament, ability, attitude toward school, and the parent–child relationship. Not all family influences on career development are positive. Some parents have unrealistic expectations regarding their children's ability or motivation. They may put too much pressure on their child to achieve or to pursue a career goal that the child does not relate to (Levine & Gislason, 1985). The film *Dead Poet's Society* (1989, Walt Disney Studios) depicts dramatically how a rigid father drives his son to suicide by demanding that his theatrically inclined son pursue a medical education (Middleton & Loughead, 1993).

### Parents as Counselors

Parents usually are in a better position than counselors or peers to educate their children about careers because of the strong parent–child bond. Who knows children better than their parents? Parents also have more time than counselors to spend with a given child. Although highly motivated to help their children make good career decisions, most parents lack the information and counseling skills that promote good vocational decision making. Some parents lack a good working relationship with their children.

Structured training, such as *The Partners Program*, teaches parents how to help their children identify personal strengths, interests, and values that are career-related. It is called a partners program because a child's career plan is seen as a family plan, with parents contributing personal support, advice, financing, and more. Parents learn how to guide children in exploring different careers, making tentative choices, and, ultimately, developing a detailed plan for entering a particular profession. Palmer and Cochran (1988) performed an experiment to assess the effectiveness of The Partners Program. They studied 40 volunteer families with children in Grades 10 or 11 in Vancouver, British Columbia. The students who participated in the program demonstrated marked improvement in career development and a strengthening of parental bonding compared to students who did not participate.

Middleton and Loughead (1993) describe a framework for adolescent career counseling that integrates parental influence. The goal is to "empower parents to be active facilitators of their adolescents' career decision-making process" (p. 170). This goal is particularly important for parents who are unsupportive of their children's career development. Counselors make *contact* with the client and establish a *trusting* relationship. A safe counseling environment encourages adolescents to explore personal issues, as well as interests, abilities, and goals.

The next phase involves *exploration* and *intervention*. Counselors inquire about the extent and quality of parental involvement in career decision making by asking questions such as "What do your parents think of your career inclinations?" Parental involvement is classified as positive, negative, or noninvolvement. When involvement is positive, counselors encourage it and provide additional information and support to parents if desired. When involvement is negative, counselors help clients decide whether to confront their parents or to avoid confrontation by acquiescing to their desires. Counselors must be sensitive because some parents perceive counselors as meddling in family issues.

Sometimes clients decide to confront their parents. Confrontations may occur between the parents and the child, between a parent and a counselor, or between all parties. When parents are not at all involved in career planning, the counselor tries to stimulate their interest and involve them in the decision-making process. This is accomplished by meeting collectively and providing the parents with career information, suggestions, and guidance.

## THE ROLE OF SCHOOLS

*Study Question: How does schooling prepare students for the role of worker?*

Family life is not the only source of influence on career aspirations. The family is but one of several *micro-systems* that is embedded in other social systems, including the educational system and an influential peer network (Bronfenbrenner, 1989; Mortimer & Finch, 1996). In many ways, school is an ideal place to learn about work and careers. In the early grades, children have countless opportunities to learn good work habits and develop achievement motivation. Over time, students receive considerable feedback about their strengths and weaknesses and can receive remedial instruction when necessary.

Most secondary schools have guidance departments with personnel trained to provide career education. Mason (1992) describes a middle school activity that promotes career exploration. A teacher lists several careers on the chalkboard. Students think about how they would fit into these careers, how their current hobbies or afterschool jobs prepare them for work. The students discuss the relationship between their extracurricular activities and possible careers. They identify a family friend or relative with an interesting career. They spend a day during spring break with this "mentor" and get a taste of the average work day. They report back to their group what they did during spring break. Thus, they have several opportunities to relate current interests to career choices.

Ideally, career instruction is provided by specially trained counselors in a systematic and comprehensive way. Guidance counselors help students become aware of their alternatives and explore different vocational fields. Standardized tests are available that assess interests, values, and abilities. Most students need help in setting realistic goals. "School counselors can no longer afford to be on the periphery but need to be at the center of the curriculum and the classroom in collaboration with teachers, parents, and community. If business–school partnerships are to become a reality, a career development team must be in operation, and a structure must be created for each student, in consultation with family, to have an individual career plan" (Hansen, 1993, p. 20).

Career development programs in schools were popular in the 1960s and 1970s and then languished in the 1980s during the "back to basics" reform movement. In the present decade, there is renewed interest in blending career development into the core curriculum. One important goal of such programs is to help the United States become more competitive economically. Parents and employers want to see career development programs in the schools, although there is no consensus about what form they should take. There is agreement that economically disadvantaged adolescents need considerable help in developing literacy and technical skills (Gysbers & Henderson, 1988; Hansen, 1993).

Guidance counselors help students to become aware of their alternatives and to explore different vocational fields.

# THE ROLE OF THE GUIDANCE COUNSELOR

*Study Question: Do school guidance counselors know students well enough to recommend specific career paths?*

Ideally, guidance and vocational counselors are well positioned to help high school students make good educational and career decisions. However, the quality of counseling available to students is quite varied. School counselors usually are better prepared to help students make decisions about what college to attend than what type of career to pursue. Some schools provide excellent vocational programs for all students. Other schools provide no counseling at all. Unfortunately, many counselors view students in stereotypic ways based on their race, socioeconomic status, or gender (Yogev & Roditi, 1987).

What information should counselors gather before making specific recommendations? At the least, counselors need to know about students' ability, achievement, interests, and personal qualities, such as persistence and sociability. They also must be knowledgeable about the state of the economy, specific job responsibilities, education and training requirements of various jobs, and trends in employment (Mitchell, 1988).

# LEISURE ACTIVITIES, VOLUNTEERING, AND CAREER DEVELOPMENT

Leisure activities such as reading, computing, sports, and music require intellectual and other abilities that contribute to career development. Sometimes hobbies are transformed into careers. In one study, 48 Israeli students who participated in a study of creative thinking were questioned 18 years later about their employment. The investigators (Hong, Milgram, & Whiston, 1993) hypothesized that there would be a link between the out-of-school activities of these students and their eventual career choice. The hypothesis was confirmed for more than one-third of the subjects. Eleven years after graduation, vocational choice reflected leisure activities for 38.6% of the subjects. "Our findings indicate that leisure activities may be as valid a predictor of occupational choice as personality types" (p. 227).

Volunteer work, although unpaid, provides students with valuable vocational preparation. They learn good work habits, establish contacts for future employment, gain self-confidence, and learn specific skills that may be useful for later employment. Students also can participate in extracurricular activities at school—for example, joining a band or writing for the school newspaper—that might lead to related career opportunities such as music or journalism (Lambert & Mounce, 1987).

# WHAT TO DO AFTER HIGH SCHOOL?

In the past, graduating from high school was almost equivalent to becoming an adult. There were relatively few life paths available to high school graduates or nongraduates. Males could enter military service, go to college, or join the full-time labor force. Parents expected their daughters to marry and have children. Today, people of color and males have a more favorable view of the military than do whites and females. Military service is seen by some as patriotic and as providing leadership training, although adolescents view civilian jobs as allowing more freedom and being more enjoyable (Bartling & Eisenman, 1992).

Owens (1992) compared the personality characteristics of boys who chose the military, college, or employment. Boys' decisions about what to do after high school are influenced mainly by family, school, and peers. Boys from large, low-income families and who were enrolled in high school vocational tracks usually chose work. Boys who chose the military had similar characteristics, but most believed that serving in the military would please their parents. Boys who chose college came from the smallest families and had the highest socioeconomic backgrounds. They had the highest grade point averages, were highly motivated to attend college, and were employed for the fewest hours (in the 12th grade) of all three groups.

### Vocational Education: Need for a Smart, Competitive Labor Force

Left on their own, teenagers looking for employment typically settle for low-paying, low-status, dead-end jobs. They take what is available and feel lucky to have a job at all. Economists recognize that stoking the nation's economy requires not only more and better jobs but also better-trained workers, including those who do not attend college. Although most high school graduates are college bound, students who do not plan to go to college or enter the military, many of them disadvantaged, tend to choose a vocational track in high school

Vocational schools provide an alternative to college attendance.

or attend vocational school. In 1990, about 8% of high school sophomores considered themselves to be vocational students, down from 21% in 1980 (U.S. Department of Education, 1991).

Vocational or trade education is intended to prepare students for work following high school graduation, although many vocational students eventually continue their education. Most high schools track vocational students and college-bound students separately, some say to the disadvantage of both groups. Many schools try to incorporate vocational education into the academic program by adding academic courses to the vocational curriculum or vice versa. Of the 12 million students in 15,000 public high schools in the United States, 97% take one or more vocational courses, such as health care, home economics, or typing (Nordheimer, 1996). Nevertheless, most college track students get minimal exposure to practical, job-oriented courses, and vocational track students find that they are not prepared either for a specific job or for community college if they decide to attend (Mansnerus, 1994).

Attempts to integrate academic and vocational tracks have not been very successful. It is not always easy to find a connection between what schools teach and what employers want from their workers (DeParle, 1992; Mansnerus, 1994; Pearce & Jones, 1992; Williams & Sackley, 1990). Traditionally, vocational schools attracted students who were less academically interested (including troublemakers and truants), contributing to these schools' less than glowing reputation (Nordheimer, 1996).

Prompted by a growing demand for skilled labor, the curriculum in vocational schools is becoming more rigorous. The new labor force is culturally diverse and, to a large extent, composed of those who traditionally have not done well in school. Teachers encourage vocational students, being trained perhaps as plumbers or cosmetologists, to do more reading, writing, and computing and to learn more science and math. Gradually, technological programs are replacing industrial arts. Computer science is replacing electric and metal shops in some schools. The private sector—corporations, business and labor groups—also is playing an increasing role in specifying the knowledge and skills currently required in the workplace and funding vocational programs (Herr, 1991; Silberman, 1991). Due to the need for specialized teaching tools and machinery, it costs about 50% more to educate a vocational student than one who is academically tracked (Nordheimer, 1996).

Many students drop out of vocational programs before graduation. They do not see how school is preparing them for work, and they may be right. Many suspect correctly that employers do not attach much significance to a high school diploma. Disaffected students enter the work force with no special training and drift from one low-paying job to another. Young, unskilled workers suffer financially and are a drag on the economy. But there are also success stories:

> *In the morning, they are two high school girls with big hair, red nails, and bored looks in physics class. Sylvia Velez doodles. Susan Colarusso chews gum. They wonder what they have to gain by memorizing the difference between velocity and acceleration. But in the afternoon they are cheerful exemplars of the job-*

*training approach that economists are endorsing as a tonic for the nation's ailing economy. As members of a youth apprenticeship program here [in Boston], called Project ProTech, they spend part of their high school days cultivating a marketable skill, in their case as hospital technicians.*

*(DeParle, 1992, p. 1)*

Such apprenticeship programs have proved quite successful in European countries. They provide a possible solution to the dropout problem. Expanding industries including health care, printing, and the machine-tool business need well-trained employees. Uninterested students looking for meaningful work prove to be excellent potential trainees. There are only a few thousand students in youth apprenticeship programs. Whether such programs proliferate depends on unprecedented cooperation between schools, businesses, and government (Hamilton, 1990).

## COLLEGE AND CAREER

*Study Question: To what extent should one's choice of major be geared to the marketplace?*

Economically, college attendance makes a lot of sense. Employed college graduates earn significantly more than employed high school graduates. People with professional degrees, such as doctors and lawyers, earn the most. Employees gain an average 8% increase in income for each additional year of schooling, whether it be high school, college, or graduate school (Applebome, 1995a). Nevertheless, fewer than 30% of high school graduates earn a college degree (W. T. Grant Foundation).

In the 1980s, many college students selected majors, such as computer science, that they believed would guarantee well-paying jobs in business and technology. By the end of the decade, however, the job market had become glutted with computer-science majors and many preprofessionally trained students struggled to find employment. With the country's economy in recession, about one in five college graduates were accepting low-wage, dead-end positions that they felt lucky to have (U.S. Bureau of Labor Statistics, 1992). The U.S. Department of Labor predicted that college enrollments would continue to outpace the growth of professional and managerial jobs. This was not good news for college graduates of the early and mid-1990s looking for jobs (Nasar, 1992; Prouse & Dooley, 1997), although the class of 1997 was very much in demand by recruiters (Applebome, 1997b).

Although students should be concerned about the marketability of their hard-earned skills, those with preprofessional majors are not necessarily more attractive to employers than those who major in the liberal arts. Yet students feel pressure to make practical decisions about careers and to take "skills" courses. Given the types of skills that employers value, it makes sense for most students to spend their first 2 years in college pursuing a liberal education, that is, sampling many different courses in different fields of study (Johnston, 1992):

*Liberal education emphasizes a rigorous but broad and open-ended approach to subject matter. It ranges across many disciplines; it exposes the student-poet to physics and technology, and the young accountant or engineer to the history of art. It exploits each subject's potential for posing value questions, and for displaying problems, facts, ideas, events, and situations in their full contexts—cultural, scientific, aesthetic, political, historical, and technological. . . . And at its best, it produces generalists who can think critically and creatively, exercise judgment, sort through complexities, tolerate ambiguities, communicate effectively, and adapt to change.*

(p. 64)

It is almost impossible to anticipate the specific skills and abilities that employers will be seeking 5 and 10 years down the road. But the skills acquired through a broad liberal arts curriculum will always be valued by employers. Employers usually are more concerned that job applicants read, write, and communicate well than with technical skills acquired in college courses. Job applicants are likely to be evaluated on the basis of their communication and relationship skills, and their ability to think critically and be good problem solvers. A 10th course in computer science or a 12th math course yields diminishing returns in employability compared to a diversified curriculum that provides flexibility in career choice.

Fortunately, most colleges and universities offer career counseling. The bad news is that the quality of counseling varies considerably. Some schools provide students with current educational and occupational information using advanced computer systems such as DISCOVER and SIGI Plus. Although most colleges offer courses specifically designed to help students make good decisions, students usually wait until their senior year to seek help in career planning. Although almost all students need assistance, not all colleges place a high priority on career placement (Hansen, 1993). Finally, keep in mind that there are other advantages of a college education besides employment—do you know what they are?

## SPOTLIGHT • Career Needs of African-Americans

Most vocational counseling models are based on the study of white, middle-class males. These models are inadequate when applied to females or people of color. Special career counseling strategies are necessary for African-American students, for example, because as a group they have higher dropout rates and achieve lower grades than white students (Murray, 1996a). While middle-class adolescents have a broad spectrum of vocational opportunities available to them, African-Americans are disproportionately represented in such low-status jobs as sanitation worker, waiter, and domestic and underrepresented in most high-status professions. Apparently, many avoid seeking employment in fields that they believe are not open to them (Kimbrough & Salomone, 1993; Terrell, Terrell, & Miller, 1993).

Parmer (1993) describes the "athletic dream" of African-American youth, especially males—the belief that athletics provides a "quick and easy path to success and mobility" (p. 132). The likelihood of becoming a professional athlete is about 1 in 50,000. In an attempt to describe the career goals of African-American urban high school students, Parmer had 446 11th and 12th graders from three different schools complete questionnaires containing items on demographics, school and family factors, career dreams, and career choices. One item asked, "if you were to enter the occupation of your dreams, what type of job would you be doing?" Students were self-identified as athletes if they represented their school in any sport as a first or second team player.

Parmer found that

> the athletic dream continues to be a career dream for many African-American males. Although intramural male athletes were significantly more likely to perceive themselves as athletes, percentages suggest that some nonathletes may possess the athletic dream. The obvious reason is mobility, status, and fame. However, another explanation is that in a racist and segregated society, sport affords an opportunity for the African-American male to dominate on the field or court, something he is unable to do elsewhere in society.
>
> (p. 140)

A study by Thomas and Shields (1987) confirms that urban students viewed work not only as a means of earning money, but also as a way to achieve independence and self-esteem. Females valued the monetary rewards of work more than males, perhaps anticipating their possible future role as single parents. African-American students in both studies were optimistic about their ability to achieve their career goals. Parmer suggests that counselors educate disadvantaged African-American students about a variety of careers besides athletics and about the education or training that they require.

Counselors also should provide information about the barriers that minorities face in the world of employment. Many of these youth are pessimistic about finding decent employment for good reasons. Counselors can help them find the middle ground between unrealistic dreams of fame and fortune on the one hand and hopelessness on the other. Students who are mistrustful of whites might benefit more from access to and encouragement from African-American role models who have been successful in a variety of careers (Terrell et al., 1993).

## SHOULD STUDENTS WORK?

Employment of high school students during the school year is widespread. From 60% to 75% of high school students report that they have part-time jobs, many in retail and fast-food industries. Juniors and seniors work up to 20 hours a week or more for the minimum wage and receive no benefits like health insurance or vacation pay. Federal law prohibits students under the age of

16 years from working more than 3 hours a day on school days, but these laws are rarely enforced (Geoghegan, 1996). In difficult economic times, jobs for teenagers become scarce. Entry-level jobs, many of which require specialized training, are the first to be eliminated. The paucity of jobs, however, keeps many adolescents in school. This is good because it improves their chances of eventually finding decent employment (Bernstein, 1993; Ramasamy, 1996).

First jobs introduce teenagers to the not always nurturing world of adult work. Part-time jobs usually involve (at least based on adult standards) routine, regimented, nonchallenging activities (e.g., delivering, cleaning, serving, carrying) that require little knowledge or skill and that provide minimum opportunity to learn or practice cognitive skills. Most have no connection to students' career goals or interests, although stores and fast food restaurants with a teenage clientele like having teenage workers with whom their customers identify (Fine et al., 1990; Greenberger & Steinberg, 1986).

For many years, educators and government officials emphasized the virtues of integrating school and work, especially for disadvantaged youth or for those on a vocational track. They assumed that for most students, part-time work fostered the development of good work habits, social skills, a work ethic, money management skills, self-confidence, and good vocational decision making. These qualities are valued by most employers and perhaps can best be learned through appropriate work experience (Stern et al., 1990). It also seemed like a good idea to get uninterested students out of the classroom for a few hours a week so that they could get a taste of the real world. Perhaps being trapped in a monotonous part-time job would help apathetic students appreciate the value of education in finding decent employment. Of course, an undemanding school curriculum allows them the time to work in the first place (Dornbusch, Herman, & Morley, 1996).

Does part-time work actually build character and responsibility or does it sabotage students' academic performance and social life? Does it ease the transition from school to work or does it prevent teenagers from participating in meaningful extracurricular activities? Do working adolescents gain useful real-work experience and financial independence from their parents or are they being deprived of valuable social encounters with their peers? And what are the long-term effects of part-time work on vocational development?

Many studies (e.g., Bachman & Schulenberg, 1993; Greenberger & Steinberg, 1986; Marsh, 1991; McKechnie, Lindsay, Hobbs, & Lavalette, 1996; Steinberg & Dornbusch, 1991) question the value of part-time work, at least for white, middle-class teenagers. They report that intensive part-time work interferes with adolescents' social and family lives and threatens their academic achievement.

> Compared with their classmates who do not work or who work only a few hours each week, students who work longer hours report diminished engagement in schooling, lowered school performance, increased psychological distress and somatic complaints, higher rates of drug and alcohol use, higher rates of delinquency, and greater autonomy from parental control.
>
> (Steinberg & Dornbusch, 1991, pp. 309–310)

Based on their study of almost 4,000 high school students in California and Wisconsin, Steinberg and Dornbusch (1991) report that the harmful correlates of employment increase as a function of number of hours worked each week, especially for students who work more than 15 to 20 hours a week. Students with long work schedules have little time for homework and find it hard to pay attention in class. They are more prone than their nonworking peers to cheating, copying assignments, and cutting classes.

Some studies report that employed high school students like working and benefit from their employment academically, vocationally, and socially (e.g., Aronson et al., 1996). In 1985, Green (1990) surveyed the entire senior class (138 students) of a North Carolina high school. He inquired about students' employment status, type of jobs, and the number of hours they worked each week. He followed up with an intensive, flexibly structured interview of 35 working and nonworking students. Green found that working students generally viewed the workplace positively and developed a work ethic that stressed financial responsibility. According to Green, high school students are "capable of regulating their work experience in accordance with their personal, familial, educational, and social priorities, and have developed a variety of positive interpretations of the work ethic in doing so" (p. 427).

The themes revealed during the interviews included self-reliance, discipline, social cooperation, materialism, and educational achievement. One subject said, "For me, I work because it's a family responsibility and I also think it's important that when I go home in the afternoon that I have some sort of system, something that I have to do, to give me a sense of discipline" (p. 431). Another viewed work as a means to material acquisition: "People here work, and they get their money to go have a good time. You've got your car, and in order to have your car you've got to work to pay for it. The reason you've got a car is so you can go around and have a good time. That's the whole process right there" (p. 431).

Based on their study of adolescent employment in England and Scotland, McKechnie and his colleagues (1996) contend that Green has painted too rosy a picture of part-time employment. "In effect, Green has failed to consider an important variable—job type. The demands and opportunities provided by different jobs can vary widely and it is too simplistic to assume that all jobs offer the same possibilities to develop social skills" (p. 202). About half of McKechnie et al.'s sample felt that their work experience would make them better adult workers, and about half felt that their work had no long-term value.

Greenberger and Steinberg (1986) reported that fewer than 20% of teenagers who work attempt to save more than a few dollars from their paycheck. Teenagers who work in clothing and music stores spend a substantial part of their paycheck where they work. Since most adolescents have few if any living expenses, they can spend their earnings on products their parents are reluctant to pay for, such "teen luxuries" as stereos, compact discs, cars, and clothes. Many high school students spend as quickly as they earn (like their parents?), sometimes purchasing alchohol or gambling. Bachman found that only 5% of students who work contribute most of their income to their families ("I earn it and I spend it on me" is their credo, according to Dr. Bachman).

Studies that report negative outcomes associated with part-time work can be criticized on the basis of what is called their **differential selection** of subjects in the labor force. It is possible that students who are less academically inclined to begin with are more likely to seek part-time employment than students who enjoy school or at least do well academically. (Ruscoe and his colleagues [1996] found that students who work primarily to save for college have *higher* grade point averages.) If this is the case, we would expect to find negative correlates of employment such as those mentioned above. Steinberg, Fegley, and Dornbusch (1993) tested this hypothesis by studying 1,800 high school sophomores and juniors both before and after they entered the work force. They found both significant selection effects and negative consequences of employment:

> *Before working, adolescents who later work more than 20 hours per week are less engaged in school and are granted more autonomy by their parents. However, taking on a job for more than 20 hours per week further disengages youngsters from school, increases delinquency and drug use, furthers autonomy from parents, and diminishes self-reliance. Leaving the labor force after working long hours leads to improved school performance but does not reverse the other negative effects.*
>
> *(p. 171)*

Employed students who work long hours sometimes avoid getting even worse grades by selecting easier teachers and courses or by cheating on tests and assignments.

A similar study involving a national representative sample of 7,000 high school seniors (Bachman & Schulenberg, 1993) also revealed selection effects but concluded that long working hours make it less likely that students will get enough sleep, eat breakfast, exercise, and have a satisfactory amount of leisure time. Students who worked long hours (more than 15–20 hours a week) were more likely to smoke cigarettes, drink alcohol, use illegal drugs, argue with their parents, and get into trouble with the law. Taken together, these two studies suggest that disengagement from school typically precedes entering the labor force, which in turn leads to greater disengagement. Particularly for those who do not want to go to college, working long hours represents an early (and often premature) transition to adulthood. For example, having money allows greater independence from parents and more access to gratification-related activities and possessions.

Clearly, some students benefit from part-time work and others suffer, mainly depending on the type of job and the number of hours worked (Ruscoe et al., 1996). And some adolescents will both gain and lose from paid labor (Shanahan, Elder, Burchinal, & Conger, 1996b). Teachers are wary of student employment but generally do not adjust their teaching to accommodate working students (Bills, Helms, & Ozcan, 1995). The effects of employment on minority and disadvantaged students, younger adolescents, and females require further study. For most adolescents, part-time work involves a set of trade-offs. Unquestionably, many teenagers work long hours, do well in school, and display positive adjustment (Mortimer, Finch, Ryu, Shanahan, & Call, 1996), al-

**Job type and hours worked seem to be the key variables affecting students' perception of their part-time work experience.**

though these investigators report heightened alcohol use by students who work long hours.

Studies have produced contradictory findings regarding whether part-time work is associated with enhanced or lower self-esteem for girls, possibly as a function of the number of hours worked. For almost all students, part-time work reduces the amount of time available for studying, spending time with peers, and being involved in extracurricular activities at school (Fine, Mortimer, & Roberts, 1990; Steitz & Owen, 1992).

Bachman and Schulenberg (1993) conclude that students who choose not to work long hours generally are better off. The key factor is how much time students spend at work and how well parents monitor their children's work lives. Parents should regulate more closely their children's working hours, set limits on their spending, and encourage enforced savings. Parents also can encourage their children to find part-time work that is more challenging and relevant to their career goals or that makes a contribution to society (Greenberger & Steinberg, 1986).

When summer jobs can be found, they have many of the same advantages and disadvantages of jobs taken during the school year. Seventy-five percent of students 16 to 24 years of age in New York and New Jersey who sought summer jobs in 1995 found them, down from 86% the previous summer (Lueck, 1996). Like part-time work, summer jobs bring opportunities to earn extra money, learn about work, and gain self-confidence and self-esteem. Part-time work and summer jobs also can bring pressures and challenges that tax adolescents' coping resources. For example, many adolescent workers are supervised by other adolescents. One of my older son's friends told me that his summer job as chief of staff at a sleepaway camp in Rhode Island was stressful because many of the staff were his friends. Some of them gave him a hard time when he tried to assert his authority. In work life, the role of authority and the role of friend sometimes conflict.

### Table 12-4 Pros and Cons of Part-Time Employment

**Pros**

Learning the value of money

Having extra spending money

Learning about the world of work

Developing good work habits and responsibility

Most working students view the workplace positively and enjoy their jobs

**Cons**

Most part-time jobs offer minimum wage and no benefits like health insurance or vacation pay

Part-time jobs usually involve routine, regimented, non-challenging activities that require little knowledge or skill and that provide minimum opportunity to learn or practice cognitive skills

Part-time jobs usually have no connection to students' career goals or interests

Part-time work reduces the amount of time available for studying, spending time with peers, and being involved in extracurricular activities at school

Students with long work schedules may have little time for homework and may find it hard to pay attention in class

Such students are more prone than their nonworking peers to cheating, copying assignments, and cutting classes

Many high school students spend as fast as they earn, perhaps purchasing alcohol or gambling

Like part-time jobs, most summer jobs carry little responsibility or creativity. They usually are low-paying and involve repetitive work that does not contribute much to adolescents' vocational development. Jeylan Mortimer, a sociologist studying teenage employment, reported that "Teenagers felt best when they had jobs with advancement opportunities and a chance to help others. Bad jobs simply drained them of energy and were highly stressful" (quoted by Kutner, 1993b, p. C12). (See Table 12-4.)

## SUMMARY

**1.** One of the most exciting and intimidating tasks facing adolescents is exploring their vocational options and committing to a career. Cognitive maturation helps teenagers realize that their eventual independence from their families requires them to support themselves financially. But how do they commit to one career when there are so many alternatives to choose from?

**2.** Although career development is a lifelong process and much exploration occurs during childhood, it is during adolescence that young people have the greatest number of opportunities to create a realistic vocational path. In the past, youngsters had far less opportunity to make vocational decisions. Not until marriage did they gain freedom from their parents and employers.

**3.** The moratorium arrangement of deferred financial responsibility provides adolescents with an extended period of time to receive the education and training they need for satisfying employment. Leisure-time activities and socializing also are part of the career exploration process.

**4.** Current trends in employment include a decline in manufacturing and agricultural jobs, the globalization of the economy, increasing specialization and technological development, fewer jobs involving manual labor, more jobs in the service sector, increasing numbers of self-employed individuals, and greater competition for desirable employment. Employment today requires more education and training than ever before, extending the amount of time young people remain financially dependent on their families.

**5.** A plausible model of vocational decision making must take into account individual differences in ability and interests, home and family influences, education and training, job opportunities, and luck. Vocational theorists offer stage models suggesting that young people make increasingly realistic decisions about careers based on their self-concepts and views of work. Most theorists agree that inadequate exploration of options and premature foreclosure are likely to lead to poor vocational choices.

**6.** Adolescents need help from parents, teachers, and counselors in planning for their eventual employment. They need information about the education and training required for different careers and about trends in employment. They need to understand the importance of finding employment that is compatible with their abilities and interests. Importantly, they need to develop good work habits and attitudes that will increase their vocational attractiveness to potential employers.

**7.** Women and members of ethnic minorities tend to be overrepresented in nontechnical, low-wage, low-status jobs. During the high school years, girls generally have lower career aspirations than boys. Girls with higher self-esteem usually are more ambitious. Research is needed to help us understand the career decision making of those who have been short-changed in the employment arena. Even some school counselors make recommendations about college and employment based on gender and racial stereotypes.

**8.** Parents can play a major role in helping their children understand the connection between school, employment, and lifestyle. Children learn about the work world by listening to their parents discuss work and through their exposure to their parents' work values and attitudes. Parents who have good relationships with their children usually are more influential in their career decision making. It is important that parents have realistic expectations of their children and not exert undue pressure on their goals and aspirations.

**9.** School is the optimal setting for educating children about employment and careers. In school, children have unlimited opportunities to learn good work habits and enjoy achievement. Schools also can help students understand their strengths and weaknesses and match them to possible vocations. Unfortunately, most secondary schools do not have exceptional career development programs. Vocational counselors need to take into account students' personal qualities, abilities, and interests. They must also have knowledge about the economy, trends in employment, specific types of jobs, and the training they require.

**10.** Vocational education is intended to prepare students for employment following graduation from high school. In the past, vocational programs were not very successful in producing competent, motivated workers. Vocational education works best when it operates in conjunction with the private sector so that employers can provide input about what type of employee skills they are looking for.

**11.** College graduation increases young people's appeal to employees, although it is not a guarantee of satisfying employment. In most fields today, the job market for college graduates remains highly competitive. College students increase their employability by being flexible in their course work and gaining skills in several areas, including foreign language and computers. Students should not wait until their senior year to seek help in career planning.

**12.** Although part-time jobs teach adolescents about the work world, and give them a chance to earn and spend their own money and contribute money to their households, employment sometimes interferes with their social and family lives and their academic achievement. Young people usually report positive work experiences, but those who work more than 20 hours a week risk becoming disengaged from their school, family, and friends. Although most adolescents report enjoying their employment, especially their income, there is little evidence of long-term positive or negative consequences. Job type and hours worked seem to be the key variables affecting students' perception of the work experience. Parents need to regulate their children's work hours, set limits on their spending, and make sure that schoolwork is not being overlooked.

# GLOSSARY

**Growth stage of vocational development** According to Super, children and early adolescents develop increasingly realistic self-concepts and views of work

**Exploration stage of vocational development** According to Super, adolescents make decisions about possible careers that reflect their self-assessment of interests and abilities and their growing knowledge of specific occupations

**Establishment stage of vocational development** According to Super, during early adulthood people become accustomed to a particular work routine

**Maintenance stage of vocational development** According to Super, middle-aged adults persist in their chosen jobs, but growth and personal advancement are almost inevitable. During this stage, some individuals seek higher levels of responsibility and decision making, while others are content to stay put in a comfortable and predictable job situation

**Decline stage of vocational development** According to Super, the stage when individuals retire from the workplace and search for other meaningful ways to spend their time

**Fantasy stage** In Ginzberg's model, the stage when children imagine themselves in roles and activities that they find pleasing, although unrelated to their actual interests and abilities

**Tentative stage** According to Ginzberg, adolescents' thoughts of a career are guided initially by their interests. Subsequently, their choices are governed by their rough impressions of what abilities and values are needed to perform a job competently

**Realistic stage** According to Ginzberg, older adolescents begin to explore some of the alternatives they are considering. Most young people eventually commit to a particular field or to a specialization within a field

**Vocational identity** According to Holland, a person with a clear sense of vocational identity has an explicit and relatively stable picture of his or her goals, interests, skills, and suitable occupations

**Emergent career decision-making** According to Super, points at which sharper, finer, more specific vocational decisions are made. The ultimate decision emerges from earlier successive approximations

**Career maturity** The readiness to make career decisions

**Intrinsic motivation** Motivation that comes from performing a task

**Extrinsic motivation** Motivation that comes from external incentives, such as grades or money

**Differential selection of subjects in the labor force** Students who are less academically inclined to begin with may be more likely to seek part-time employment than students who enjoy school or at least do well academically

## THOUGHT QUESTIONS

**1.** Recall your own thoughts and fantasies about a possible career during your childhood and adolescent years. How do you evaluate your exploration of career alternatives?

**2.** What helped you finally commit to your major in college? What role if any did your family, friends, and advisors play?

**3.** What type of lifestyle do you associate with the career you have committed to?

**4.** Do you view work as a necessary evil or as a potential source of fulfillment? Explain.

**5.** Based on your own part-time work experiences during adolescence, what are the pros and cons of teenage employment?

# SELF-TEST

1. Employment trends emerging over the last quarter century include
   a. globalization of jobs and the economy
   b. proliferation of computers and telecommunications
   c. increased specialization and self-employment
   d. all of the above

2. According to Don Super's five-stage model of vocational development, during which stage do adolescents tentatively decide on possible careers?
   a. growth stage
   b. exploration stage
   c. establishment stage
   d. maintenance stage

3. According to Eli Ginzberg's three-stage model of career development, during which stage are adolescents' thoughts of a career guided by their interests and abilities?
   a. fantasy stage
   b. tentative stage
   c. realistic stage
   d. latency stage

4. Which theorist attempts to match personality type with ideal work environment?
   a. Ginzberg
   b. Super
   c. Holland
   d. Marcia

5. The two concepts that dominate our understanding of career development are
   a. exploration and commitment
   b. trust and mistrust
   c. assimilation and accommodation
   d. downsizing and recession

6. Super-defined career maturity is
   a. the willingnes to explore
   b. the desire to excel

    c. the readiness to make career decisions

    d. the will to live

**7.** Intrinsic motivation is similar to

    a. a desire to succeed

    b. a love of learning

    c. a commitment to humanity

    d. surrendering to a higher power

**8.** About what percent of doctoral degrees is held by women?

    a. 10

    b. 20

    c. 30

    d. 40

**9.** More than males, females in the workplace need to be prepared for

    a. making less money

    b. sexual harassment

    c. fewer opportunities for promotion

    d. all of the above

**10.** To help students make good career decisions, counselors need to know

    a. their interests and abilities

    b. their age and gender

    c. their sexual orientation

    d. their ethnic group membership

**11.** What percent of high school graduates ever earn a college degree?

    a. 70

    b. 50

    c. 40

    d. fewer than 30

**12.** The effects of student part-time employment depend mainly on

    a. the type of job

    b. the number of hours worked

    c. attitudes toward working

    d. all of the above

# THIRTEEN

# ADOLESCENTS IN CRISIS

## Preview Questions

**1.** How do we distinguish between adolescent adjustment and maladjustment?

**2.** What stressors do most teenagers face?

**3.** What is the difference between coping and problem solving?

**4.** What risk factors increase adolescent vulnerability to psychological disorders?

**5.** What life circumstances encourage antisocial behavior during adolescence?

**6.** Is there a "syndrome" of multiple problem behaviors during adolescence?

**7.** Why are eating disorders so common during the teenage years?

**8.** Why do so many teenagers experiment with drugs?

**9.** What are the most common danger signals of adolescent suicide?

## Disclosures

I've been asked to try drugs and I say no, I don't want to start that. If I was ever using drugs and my mom found out, it would be all over for me, because she's strict. When my mom talks to me about drugs, she really puts a lot of emotion into it. She was choking up when she told me not to use drugs. I think it would really hurt my family.

*(15-year-old boy quoted by Wren, 1996, p. A20)*

I'm trying to disassociate from my family. My parents divorced when I was 4. Yesterday, I took a car ride with my mother and came really close to attacking her because she set me off. She was hassling me, and it got to a boiling point and I really exploded. I said to her, "Shut up or I'll smash your head in." She kicked me out of the car. We haven't talked since then. That used to happen a lot with my father but not anymore. I need to get away from both of them. The best thing would be to separate and see them one half hour a week and leave. I don't know too many people who are not messed up. I'm pretty sure there's something wrong with me.

*(Josh, 19 years old)*

# Contents

Jennifer, a 17-year-old high school student, is angry. She goes to school every day and helps raise her two younger sisters, but she cannot forgive her drug-addicted mother for dying from an AIDS-related illness. Although she herself is not infected, Jennifer struggles with the anger, shame, and loneliness that her mother's death has left behind. "I would like to forgive her, to be free of anger. I started going to church so I can be helped. I've tried and I'm trying, but it's hard." By 1995, about 20,000 children, half of them teenagers, had lost their mothers to AIDS. Many do poorly in school. Some engage in self-destructive behaviors and show signs of clinical depression (Goddard, Subotsky, & Fombonne, 1996; McLaughlin, Miller, & Warwick, 1996). Unfortunately, they do not discuss their loss with friends (Navarro, 1992).

Seventeen-year-old Danny reports that he acts differently at different times, depending on which group of friends he is with. When he is around his "bad friends," he steals bikes, gets into fights, and breaks car windows. Although he likes being around his bad friends, he doesn't expect too much from them because they take drugs. Danny feels that he is a better person when he is around his "good friends." "When I behave normally, I feel good about myself. When I'm bad, I feel bad because I know that what I'm doing isn't right."

Danny lives with his father. His mother lives in Florida. His parents are divorced. He does not get along well with either parent. He says that they yell at him all the time and start arguments about almost anything. His father once said to him, "If you get in trouble one more time and the police come, I'm going to tell them I don't know you." Danny laughed when recalling this exchange, claiming that his father was just trying to scare him. Danny says he wants to be like his father, who has quit drinking alcohol and attends church regularly. Danny's goals are to graduate from high school and become a lawyer.

Darren W., an 18-year-old biracial (African-American/Indian) high school student, participates in the Transitional Opportunities Program (TOP) for youth in urban New Jersey. The program is designed to help troubled teenagers with a history of foster care make the transition to independent living. During an interview, he says that getting his life together and graduating from high school are his main priorities. He feels good about being in TOP since most young people his age either live with their parents or are in trouble. His girlfriend is in the program. According to Darren, some of his friends who are not in TOP are jealous of the privileges and special opportunities Darren enjoys as a member.

The worst part about being in the program, according to Darren, is the stereotyped attitudes that people have about him. He feels that some people will not give him a chance. Just because he is in a youth program, some people see him as a hoodlum. Darren is looking for more acceptance from the community, for the ability to walk down the street without being questioned by the police. Darren is cynical. Society has no meaning; life is a "never-ending battle" among people, with only the fittest surviving.

Darren takes pride in his racial and ethnic origins. What angers him most are police and judges with a negative attitude and people who prejudge others because of the clothes they wear or their skin color. Darren believes that teenagers, especially African-American teenagers, are misunderstood. He worries about his future, especially when he loses the adult supervision and security of the program and has to be self-sufficient.

Partly because of their less than optimal life circumstances, Jennifer, Danny, and Darren are growing up quickly, perhaps too quickly. Although they have not yet had enough time or experience to develop adult problem-solving skills or coping resources, they face adult problems. They are not alone. Large numbers of adolescents have family lives that lack warmth and nurturance. They receive inadequate care and attention from their parents, feel neglected and misunderstood, and have poor self-concepts. Many decide to run away from abusive, violent family life. Some behave promiscuously, using their bodies to gain companionship, money, or drugs. A significant number function poorly or not at all in school, have little ambition, and leave school before graduating. Some have learning disabilities or emotional problems that escape the attention of parents or teachers (Dryfoos, 1990; Kazdin, 1993; Miner, 1991; Pakiz, Reinherz, & Frost, 1992; Terrell, 1997).

Although the vast majority of adolescents are well adjusted (Offer & Schonert-Reichl, 1992), psychological disorders are more common during adolescence than during the preadolescent years (Rutter, 1990). Relationship problems, depression, drug abuse, attempted suicide, eating disorders, schizophrenia, antisocial behaviors, and delinquency peak during the teenage years (Dryfoos, 1990; Rutter, 1985; Teare et al., 1995). Young people who are unable to find meaningful activities in their daily lives and who have no personal investment in their communities may express their despair through violence, theft, or other antisocial acts.

Not all troubled teenagers are as angry at life as Jennifer. Many are isolated, lonely, depressed, and confused. Some get high, join gangs, or suffer abuse at the hands of their parents. More than a few feel hopeless and wish that they were dead. Lacking trust in adults, many teenagers are reluctant to seek help when they need it and refuse help when it is offered (McHolland, 1985; Wassef, Ingham, Collins, & Mason, 1995).

Serious emotional and behavioral problems during adolescence interfere with the learning of academic and social skills that are necessary for a healthy, productive adulthood. Troubled teenagers are at risk of never becoming responsible adults (Dryfoos, 1990; Kaywell, 1993). Psychological disorders during adolescence range from mild (e.g., shyness) to extremely serious (e.g., anorexia). Some problems are unique to adolescence (status offenses), and others occur during childhood and adulthood (e.g., depression). There is a danger that, because adolescence is commonly viewed as a transitional period of life, adults will assume that troubled youth "grow out of their problems" and will not provide adequate prevention efforts or treatment. Many parents of troubled adolescents wait until there is a crisis before seeking help (Kazdin, 1993; Petersen et al., 1993).

The study of adolescent adjustment and mental health raises many difficult questions. How do we account for the striking changes in the frequency and form of emotional and psychological disorders during adolescence? Why do some adolescents have more difficulty than others making the transition to adulthood? Is there a single underlying tendency toward deviant (rule-breaking) behavior or do different problem behaviors reflect different underlying problems? Is there a common developmental pathway for adolescent disorders or does each disorder have its own set of causes? What role do stressful life events play in precipitating various adjustment problems? What can society do to identify and help children in trouble? Finally, how do we prevent problem behaviors from arising in the first place?

In this chapter, we consider a variety of behavioral and emotional problems during adolescence and the conditions of modern life that contribute to these problems. We might think that we would know a troubled adolescent if we met one. Yet, casual conversations with young people like Jennifer, Danny, and Darren often do not reveal their feelings of confusion, frustration, and alienation. How do we identify such children, and how do we help them?

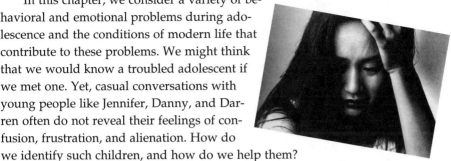

## DO ALL ADOLESCENTS HAVE ADJUSTMENT PROBLEMS?

We have already noted the contention of G. Stanley Hall, Sigmund Freud, and Anna Freud that for most young people adolescence is a time of emotional and psychological instability. According to these influential theorists, youth are alternately moody and stable, cooperative and defiant, self-assured and self-conscious. It is the nature of adolescents, they claimed, to be irritable, impatient, and dissatisfied.

Psychologist Kurt Lewin (1939/1980) suggested that it is adolescents' status as neither child nor adult that contributes to their emotional and behavioral problems. It would be misguided, however, to equate teenage resentment of adult authority with serious psychological disorder. Research findings cited in earlier chapters refute the idea that the normative changes of adolescence constitute dysfunction or disorder (Offer & Schonert-Reichl, 1992). Yes, there is heightened moodiness, testing of limits, family conflict, and, occasionally, inner turmoil. Life is problematic for most people. But for the majority of adolescents, the journey to adulthood occurs without any significant psychological or emotional disorder (Hauser & Bowlds, 1990; Offer, Ostrov, & Howard, 1989; Offer & Schonert-Reichl, 1992; Powers, Hauser, & Kilner, 1989).

As we consider some of the serious problems that adolescents may face, it is important that we not succumb to a so-called **deficit model**, one that assumes that maladjustment during the teenage years is inevitable and universal. As illustrated in preceding chapters, adolescence is more a time of excitement, hope, and aspirations than of fear and uncertainty (Newcomb, 1996). Although there are difficult periods during all people's lives, including moments of despair, confusion, loneliness, and self-doubt, the majority of young people cope with these feelings and try to correct the adverse situations that cause them (Plancherel & Bolognini, 1995). Most eventually acquire a realistic adult identity and accept and live by the rules of society, set reasonable goals for themselves, and have close relationships with friends and family members (Csikszentmihalyi & Larson, 1984; Offer et al., 1989). This is particularly encouraging given the pervasive threats to their health and safety (Takanishi, 1993a,b).

# WHAT DO WE MEAN BY HEALTHY ADJUSTMENT?

According to his parents, Sam is a moody, uncooperative 15-year-old who displays miminal effort in school. He would prefer to sleep away his days and spend evening hours listening to music and fooling around with his friends. Is Sam's behavior normal for children his age or does he suffer from some juvenile disorder? The psychological term **adjustment** implies mastery of one's environment and being at peace with oneself (Sarason & Sarason, 1993). Sam may be at peace with himself, but at least from his parents' point of view, he is hardly mastering his environment.

Given the diversity of adolescent behavior and life circumstances, it is not easy to come up with criteria that would help us distinguish normative behavior from problem behavior. Behavior that we view as deviant or bizarre in our culture may be considered normal or desirable in other cultures (Fabrega, 1989, 1992). There is a wide range of behavioral differences among adolescents that can be considered normal, especially given the rapid pace of development during the early teenage years (Hansen et al., 1995). Attempts to categorize problem behavior during adolescence are made more difficult by the fact that a significant number of teenagers occasionally violate social norms, for example, by skipping school, shoplifting, drinking alcohol, driving under its influence, or experimenting with other drugs (Butterfield, 1996a; Tolan, 1988). Thus, the frequency, seriousness, and variety of involvement must be taken into account when clinicians attempt to diagnose psychological disorders (Tolan & Loeber, 1993) (see Box 13-1: The Clinical Diagnosis of Adolescent Disorders).

In trying to define what we mean by healthy adjustment, we must be careful to not equate unusual or nonconforming behavior such as body piercing, face painting, or head shaving with antisocial behaviors such as shoplifting and vandalism. We have already seen that a key developmental task of adolescence is creating an adult identity. Nonconforming behaviors are best viewed as part of the exploration phase of identity creation. Maintaining an objective stance, we want to avoid applying negative or derogatory labels (e.g., weirdo, nut case) to people's behavior simply because their actions are unusual, unpopular, or annoying. We also want to avoid confusing ordinary adolescent exploration and discovery with behavior that is dangerous to oneself or others (Brack, Brack, & Orr, 1994).

One strategy for deciding what we mean by maladjusted or abnormal behavior is to define what constitutes healthy adolescent behavior. Smith and Rutter (1995) note that it is easier to define psychological disorders or problem behaviors than vague concepts like happiness and well-being. If we adopt this approach, we try to determine how well a given individual is adjusting to his or her adolescent changes and to the circumstances of everyday life. According to Kazdin (1993), the term **mental health** refers to "optimal functioning or well-being in psychological and social domains. Well-being is not merely the absence of impairment; rather it refers to the presence of personal and interpersonal strengths that promote optimal functioning" (p. 128).

Waterman (1992) offers four criteria for deciding what constitutes **optimal psychological functioning**. An individual's behaviors and personal qualities

When diagnosing childhood and adolescent disorders, most clinical psychologists and psychiatrists refer to the *Diagnostic and Statistical Manual of Mental Disorders* (American Psychiatric Association, 1994), currently in its fourth major revision and thus known as *DSM-IV*. DSM-IV includes detailed descriptions of 41 so-called childhood-onset disorders. Each of five DSM-IV axes requires clinicians to assess individuals using different types of information, with the goal of producing a comprehensive psychological evaluation (Mesco, Rao, Amaya-Jackson, & Cantwell, 1995). Ideally, the evaluation (diagnosis) will lead to a prognosis and treatment plan or intervention. The causes of most serious psychological disorders are still debated as are the diagnostic categories themselves (Volkmar & Schwab-Stone, 1996).

Disorders found on Axis I include disruptive behavior and attention-deficit disorders, anxiety disorders, mood disorders, eating disorders, and substance-related disorders. Axis II includes personality developmental disorders, including mental retardation. Axis III includes general medical disorders believed to be relevant to disorders listed in Axes I and II. Axis IV assesses psychosocial and environmental problems, including educational, health care, and economic difficulties. Axis V consists of a global assessment of psychological, social, educational, and occupational functioning (Mesco et al., 1995).

Diagnostic categories most frequently applied to adolescents include conduct disorder, emotional disorder (depression and anxiety), attention-deficit disorder, and substance use disorder. Factors most predictive of psychiatric disorders include education and socioeconomic status, male gender, agressivity, hyperactivity, hostility, chronic health problems, poor family relations, and physical and sexual abuse (Mezzich, Bukstein, & Grimm, 1995).

**Box 13-1
The Clinical Diagnosis of Adolescent Disorders**

should contribute to (1) a sense of personal well-being, (2) the realization of life goals, (3) social acceptance, and (4) the realization of goals that society values. In other words, optimal functioning during adolescence is achieved when individuals feel good about themselves, others feel good about them, and they are able to achieve goals that they and significant others value.

Wagner (1996) offers a multidimensional model of optimal adolescent functioning that addresses six domains of development. His criteria include adolescents being alive and healthy, physically mature, and engaging in proper eating and exercise (*biological domain*); abstract, future-oriented thinking and completion of at least 12 years of formal education (*cognitive domain*); emotional awareness, feeling secure and self-confident, optimistic about the future, and resilient (*emotional domain*); ability to engage in cooperative, genuine, and trusting interactions with friends and romantic partners (*social domain*); internalizing and following a personalized set of abstract moral principles and being responsive to the feelings and needs of others (*moral domain*); awareness of one's

### Table 13-1 What Constitutes Optimal Adjustment?

**biological domain:** adolescents being alive and healthy, physically mature, and engaging in proper eating and exercise

**cognitive domain:** abstract, future-oriented thinking and completion of at least 12 years of formal education

**emotional domain:** emotional awareness, feeling secure and self-confident, optimistic about the future, and resilient

**social domain:** ability to engage in cooperative, genuine, and trusting interactions with friends and romantic partners

**moral domain:** internalizing and following a personalized set of abstract moral principles and responsive to the feelings and needs of others

**vocational domain:** awareness of one's unique potential and displaying career literacy, employable skills, and a life plan

(From Wagner, 1996)

unique potential and displaying career literacy, employable skills, and a life plan (*vocational domain*). Note that these criteria would have to be modified according to an adolescent's age and culture (see Table 13-1).

Summarizing *optimal functioning* models, well-adjusted teenagers are those who do not jeopardize their health and safety, feel comfortable with family members and peers, have reasonably positive self-esteem, perform adequately in school, have realistic goals, participate in close friendships with peers, and cope adequately with the changes (and hassles) that are an inevitable part of their everyday lives (Rutter, 1985; Schweitzer et al., 1992). *Thought Question: How might a typical adolescent respond to this view of optimal functioning?*

## COMMON STRESSORS OF ADOLESCENCE

*Study Question: What do adolescents worry about?*

As children approach adolescence, they encounter an increasing number of stressful life events that elicit negative emotions (Forman, 1993; Henker, Whalen, & O'Neil, 1995; Larson & Ham, 1993). Extreme stressors such as the death of Jennifer's mother typically elicit intense emotional and coping reactions that temporarily depress school performance and interfere with peer relations (Harris, 1991). Multiple stressful events in children's lives often foretell emotional and behavioral problems later in life (Compas, 1987a, 1987b).

**Normative stressors** refer to difficult life circumstances that most teenagers experience, typically in the areas of relationships, achievement, and health (Boldero & Fallon, 1995; Murray, 1996c). Examples include strained relationships and pressure to get into a good college or find a decent job. Many young adolescents report feeling concerned about death and global issues, including homelessness and environmental degradation (Henker et al., 1995). **Nonnormative** stressors refer to stressful life events that are not typical of a particular cohort group. Jennifer's mother died as a result of being infected by AIDS,

Danny's parents are divorced, and Darren feels that people give him a hard time because of his race. Although they are not typical life events for most teenagers, poverty, discrimination, family violence, serious illness, and parental divorce are hardly rare occurrences (Hauser & Bowlds, 1990; Munsch & Wampler, 1993; Sampson & Laub, 1994).

Boys and girls express their adjustment problems somewhat differently, especially during middle adolescence. Troubled boys usually *externalize* their turmoil through rebellious and disobedient behavior (McDermott, 1996). Girls are more likely to *internalize* distress by withdrawing socially, complaining of somatic complaints, or feeling tense, depressed, or moody (Adelman, Taylor, & Nelson, 1989; Forehand, Neighbors, & Wierson, 1991; Ingersoll & Orr, 1989; Petersen, Sarigiani, & Kennedy, 1991; Simmons & Blyth, 1987). Understandably, adolescents are more concerned about feeling better than about changing the external behaviors that annoy other people (Phares & Danforth, 1994; Plancherel & Bolognini, 1995).

Adolescent girls report more fears and life problems than boys do and generally are more vulnerable than boys to stressful life transitions (King, Ollier, Iacuone, & Schuster, 1989; Windle, 1992). Girls express greater concern about their appearance and relationships, whereas boys are more likely to worry about schoolwork, vocational choices, and money. In a study of 201 Australian adolescents aged 14 to 16 years, girls were more worried than boys about their health and physical development, relationships, courtship, sex, and marriage (Harper & Marshall, 1991). (See Table 13-2.)

### Table 13-2  Common Stressors of Adolescence

**Normative Stressors**

Schoolwork and tests

Strained relationships with parents and peers

Pressure to get into a good college or find a decent job

Insecurity about one's appearance and physical development

Finances

Changing schools or moving

Concern about death and global issues, including homelessness and environmental degradation

Concern about the future

**Nonnormative Stressors**

Death of friend or family member

Poor health of self or family member

Physical disability

Poverty

Racial discrimination

Family or ethnic violence

Parental divorce or separation

Going through several important changes at once inevitably takes an emotional toll. Most people can cope with a succession of negative life events if stressors are spread out over time, but each subsequent transition makes coping more difficult (Cohen, Burt, & Bjorck, 1987; Graber & Brooks-Gunn, 1996; Rubin, Rubenstein, Stechler, Heeren, Halton, Housman, & Kasten, 1992; Siegel & Brown, 1988; Simmons et al., 1987; Wierson & Forehand, 1992; Youngs, Rathge, Mullis, & Mullis, 1990).

For most teenagers, positive life events and supportive relationships with family members, other adults, and peers serve as an emotional buffer during hard times (Brack, Brack, & Orr, 1994; Frey & Röthlisberger, 1996; Holahan, Valentiner, & Moos, 1995; Simons, Whitbeck, Beaman, & Conger, 1994; Stice & Barrera, 1995). *Thought Question: What is it about close relationships with friends and family members that protects young people from stressful life circumstances?*

## COPING STRATEGIES

How do you handle a heated argument with your mother, a poor grade on a term paper, or the loss of a close friend? Do you keep your feelings to yourself or do you share them with someone close to you? The transition to adolescence presents young people with a succession of life events and problems that evoke powerful, sometimes overwhelming, emotions (Larson & Ham, 1993). Adolescents vary considerably in their ability to put stressful life events in perspective and take steps to make things better (Morin & Welsh, 1996; Plancherel & Bolognini, 1995).

Two types of abilities distinguish those who struggle almost continually with adverse life circumstances from those who manage: problem-solving skills and coping skills. **Problem-solving skills**, such as defining a problem and generating possible solutions, help resolve difficulties that pose a threat or keep us from reaching our goals (e.g., Greening, 1997). **Coping skills** refer to a set of learned responses (actions and cognitions) that enable us to tolerate, avoid, or minimize stress (Lazarus & Folkman, 1984; Spirito, Francis, Overholser, & Frank, 1996). Learned coping responses include communicating distress, relying on others, seeking and exchanging information with others, exercising self-control, and generally, bringing ourselves back to reality ("Calm down, it's not the end of the world") (Blechman & Culhane, 1993; Plancherel & Bolognini, 1995).

Coping skills help resolve emotional distress and lessen the likelihood of serious psychological disorders (Plancherel & Bolognini, 1995). They are especially important when we face problems that we cannot solve or easily overcome, such as parents' divorce or the death of a close friend (Hauser & Bowlds, 1990; Morin & Welsh, 1996).

Seeking help and advice is a problem-focused coping strategy that is associated with positive adjustment. Social support networks buffer the effects of stress and thus are particularly useful to adolescents in crisis. Schonert-Reichl and Muller (1996) asked 221 adolescents whether or not they sought help from their mothers, fathers, friends, or professionals to cope with a recent stressful event. Previous research indicated that adolescents (especially girls) increase their utilization of friends and mothers for support as they move from early to middle adolescence. In the present study, females were more likely than males to seek help from their mothers. Middle adolescent males were more likely than younger adolescent males to seek help from their fathers. Self-consciousness was a factor in whether or not adolescents approached their fathers, suggesting that adolescents are somewhat shy about seeking help from fathers. (Why might this be so?) Adolescents who sought help from adults were older, had lower self-worth, and were less self-conscious than those who did not. The investigators concluded that mothers, and to a lesser extent fathers, continue to be the key sources of support for adolescents.

Several investigators report gender differences in the perception of stress and subsequent coping. Girls typically adopt emotion-focused solutions, whereas boys more often cite problem-focused strategies (Olah, 1995). Girls are more likely to rely on relationships and social support—for example, talking to a mother or friend—whereas boys are more likely to avoid thinking about their problems or to vent their frustrations by swearing, complaining, or finding alternative activities (Bird & Harris, 1990; Copeland & Hess, 1995). Swiss and American boys cope by using their sense of humor or by practicing a hobby or sport. Girls are more likely than boys to eat or shop (Patterson & McCubbin, 1987; Plancherel & Bolognini, 1995). Adolescent coping strategies are remarkably similar across cultures (Olah, 1995), although Copeland and Hess (1995) report that Hispanic adolescents cope more frequently than Anglos (whites) by seeking social activities and spiritual support. Ethnic minorities are more likely to report stressors such as poverty, unemployment, language differences, and discrimination.

Coping can be adaptive or maladaptive. Adaptive coping includes changing, managing, or reappraising a problem situation. Maladaptive coping—for example, avoiding thinking about an upcoming exam—increases stress in the long run because the problem remains unresolved (Baumrind & Moselle, 1985; Ebata & Moos, 1991; Fromme & Rivet, 1994; Lee & Larson, 1996; Mates & Allison, 1992; Van Buskirk & Duke, 1991).

Since coping strategies are learned, the older we get, the better we cope (Hauser & Bowlds, 1990). Adolescents generally have fewer and weaker coping resources than adults (Nasserbakht, Araujo, & Steiner, 1996; Patterson & McCubbin, 1987). New coping strategies emerge gradually during early adolescence, roughly coinciding with the appearance of formal operational thought (Hoffman, Levy-Schiff, Sohlberg, & Zarizki, 1992).

Social-cognitive models of coping maintain that advancing intellectual abilities such as multiple perspective taking allow adolescents to think about their emotions and relationships in ways that produce effective coping and problem solving (Boldero & Fallon, 1995; Hauser & Bowlds, 1990). Many coping strategies consist of fairly sophisticated cognitive strategies that reduce stress (e.g., rationalizing, reassuring oneself) or generate possible solutions to problems (e.g., seeking help). Further, being able to adopt multiple perspectives on a stressful situation such as peer pressure allows teenagers to view a problem constructively (e.g., "I have to make my own decisions").

Social psychological theories of coping suggest that in addition to minimizing emotional reactions, truly adaptive coping strategies improve the situation that is causing distress (Blechman & Culhane, 1993). Consider two high school students in a similar situation. They both receive a test grade below what they expected. One makes an appointment to discuss the grade with the instructor. The other seethes in anger and rehearses nasty comments to make in class. Which individual would you predict will be more successful in school and in life?

## VULNERABILITY AND RESILIENCE DURING ADOLESCENCE

*Study Question: Why are some adolescents more vulnerable than others to the stresses and strains of adolescent life?*

Naturally, there is a correlation between the seriousness of people's life circumstances and their ability to adjust to them. Children fortunate enough to grow up in stable, affluent, supportive families usually turn out fine. Those who are raised in impoverished, violent, emotionally abusive, or neglecting families are at significantly higher risk of developing serious emotional and behavioral problems (Compas, 1987a, 1987b; Hoge, Andrews & Leschied, 1996; Reese & Roosa, 1991). But there are always exceptions to the rule. Children of well-meaning parents can have serious adjustment problems, especially if their parents have personal or psychological problems that distract them from their children (Ge, Conger, Lorenz, Shanahan et al., 1995; Kurdek et al., 1995; Tannenbaum, Neighbors, & Forehand, 1992).

The concept of **risk factor** implies that certain personal or situational factors increase the likelihood of developing problem behavior or a psychological disorder (Hoge, Andrews & Leschied, 1996; O'Connor & Rutter, 1996). Each individual has a unique constellation of risk factors. **Vulnerability** refers to susceptibility to developing an adjustment or health problem (Garmezy & Masten, 1986). Although adolescence is not a period of pathology, it is a time of heightened vulnerability. Vulnerability increases during times of transition—for example, during puberty or when changing schools (Graber & Brooks-Gunn, 1996). **Resilience** refers to personal qualities and situational factors that allow individuals to adapt to difficult life circumstances. Resilience reflects the existence of **protective factors** that buffer the effects of chronic stressors. Interest in protective factors is based on the observation that some children who are exposed to high-risk circumstances adjust surprisingly well (Jessor, Van Den Bos, Vanderryn, Costa, & Turbin, 1995). Our knowledge of protective factors can be useful in designing programs that prevent adjustment problems from arising in the first place (Corvo, 1997). (We will return to the topic of prevention at the end of this chapter). (See Table 13-3.)

Some children who grow up amid major stressors such as poverty, parental discord, or family mental illness are remarkably well adjusted during childhood

**Table 13-3  Protective Factors of Resilient Children**

**Personality and Dispositions**

Adaptable, recover quickly from upsets

Positive thinkers

Easygoing temperament

Positive self-esteem

High frustration tolerance

Persistence

**Family**

Good relationships with supportive parents

Seeking help from other caring adults

Positive coping model

**Situational**

The fewer the risk factors, the better the adjustment

Supportive school environment

Recognition for some skill or achievement

Non-family support system

(From Jaffe, 1997)

and adulthood (Jessor, 1993; Werner & Smith, 1992). However, children who grow up in poor or unstable families disproportionately show serious learning or behavior problems by the time they are 10 years old. Some display antisocial or maladaptive behaviors during adolescence, but as adults about one out of three high-risk individuals somehow surmount their troubled past and become fully functioning adults. They perform much better during their adult lives than we would expect based on their adverse childhood experiences (Werner & Smith, 1992). Robins and his colleagues report, for example, that resilient white and African-American male adolescents are intelligent, successful in school, and relatively free of psychopathology (Robins, John, Caspi, Moffitt, & Stouthamer-Loeber, 1996).

Coping ability (and thus vulnerability) reflects a balance of risk and protective factors, including (1) how an individual interprets a particular situation; (2) personal resources, including self-esteem and an easygoing temperament; (3) family resources, including strong family bonds, parental guidance, emotional support, and validation; (4) access to a support system outside of the family—for example, teachers, mentors, and peers; and (5) prior experience in coping with controllable and uncontrollable life challenges (Blechman & Culhane, 1993; Gamble, 1994; Grossman et al., 1992; Hardy, Power, & Jaedicke, 1993; Hauser & Bowlds, 1990; Losel & Bliesener,1994; Neighbors et al., 1993; Seiffge-Krenke & Shulman, 1990; Spirito, Stark, Grace, & Stamoulis, 1991; Werner & Smith, 1992). (See Spotlight • Adolescents with Physical Disabilities.)

## SPOTLIGHT • Adolescents with Physical Disabilities

*Since I have been physically disabled all of my life, I have managed to cope with the purely practical problems arising from this with a minimum of fuss on my part; I felt no loss, because I had no feelings of "normality" to compare with. One of my physical problems is that I am short, about four feet, two inches tall. Until I began growing whiskers on my face and driving a car, I was constantly mistaken by strangers as being a little kid. It's a hell of a pain for a 16-year-old boy to be handed a kiddie's menu every time he enters a restaurant. . . . I have high standards for myself, perhaps not as high as many straight-A college students, but I am always impressed when I witness, say, good writing and intelligent conversation in others, and I aspire to such standards of intelligence. During my teen years it was a constant nagging irritation that everyone around me had what I felt were extremely low expectations. I never knew where I stood.*

*(Excerpt from the personal account of a young man born with serious physical disabilities, quoted by Garrod et al., 1992, pp. 263–264)*

If early and later maturers have a hard time coming to terms with being different from their peers, imagine the plight of teenagers like the young man quoted above, who are taunted or pitied by their peers because of physical or cognitive disabilities. About 7% of early adolescents are considered handicapped, living with one or more of the following disabilities: deafness, blindness, chronic illness, emotional problems, psychological disorders, and a variety of motor limitations.

Adolescents with disabilities are an extremely diverse group in terms of specific disability, personal resources, and adjustment. Many are forced to remain dependent on family members or other adults at a time when they are supposed to be developing greater self-sufficiency. One important goal is achieving as much independence as possible, preferably by participating in activities that gain peer acceptance and approval. Disabled teenagers also need opportunities to express their feelings of anger, frustration, rejection, and alienation. These feelings may be directed toward their parents, their peers, their teachers, or life in general.

Partly because of their disability and partly because others perceive them as being different, it is more difficult for them to meet basic developmental challenges such as having close relationships with peers and creating an adult identity. They often lack the very opportunities that they need to develop social skills and self-confidence (Ammerman, Van Hasselt, & Hersen, 1987; Anderson, Clarke, & Spain, 1982).

Those who are not informed about people with disabilities sometimes encourage unnecessary dependence or have unrealistically low expectations. The disabled individual may come to question his or her own worthiness. "Does everybody still think of me as a disability, and not as a person? I don't know. I'll never really know for sure, because I am always suspicious of others' response to me" (Garrod et al., 1992, p. 265).

**One common goal of adolescents with disabilities is achieveing as much independence as possible, sometimes by participating in activities that gain peer acceptance and approval.**

Family members and peers often are not available to provide disabled adolescents with the time and social experiences they need to gain confidence in their social desirability. Overly restrictive parents limit their opportunities to test their abilities or to separate from the family (Lindemann, 1981; Murtaugh & Zetlin, 1990).

Reflecting their increased sensitivity, adolescents with handicaps often manifest serious adjustment problems during adolescence and adulthood. It is hard to tell whether their problems reflect the limitations and stresses associated with the disability, prolonged dependence on others, peer rejection, or some combination of factors. Facing more than their share of peer rejection, many lack self-confidence and have poor self-esteem.

> *Some aspects of adolescence are harder to cope with than others. I often wonder what is to become of my sexuality—I cannot envision (except in erotic dreams) a time when a woman would find me attractive enough to spark a long-term love relationship. . . . I am short, my back curves severely, and because of my rapid metabolism and restricted abdominal cavity, I am skinny to the point of being emaciated. I have had many female friends, but what could possibly provoke them to see me and be sexually attracted to me?*
>
> *(Garrod et al., 1992, p. 270)*

Disabled adolescents report feeling lonely, isolated, and depressed. The greater the disability, the greater the isolation and despair (Ammerman et al., 1987; Anderson et al., 1982).

Acceptance of the disabled teenager by parents and peers probably is the best predictor of adjustment (Godenne, 1978). "In sum, I have come a long way. Because of me and those who have supported me, I have accomplished many things and done a lot of growing up. I am still an adolescent, though. Only an adolescent has the audacity to hope for what I hope for, which is—everything" (p. 271).

## MODELS OF DEVIANT BEHAVIOR

*Study Question: Do antisocial children necessarily become antisocial adolescents and adults?*

Problems manifested during adolescence usually reflect the continuation of problems that first appeared during childhood (Block, Block, & Keyes, 1988; Caspi et al., 1995; Fergusson & Horwood, 1996; Fergusson, Lynskey, & Horwood, 1996b; Masten et al., 1995; Moffitt, 1993). After the fact, it is not hard to trace a sequence of events throughout childhood that disposes a given child to emotional or behavioral problems during adolescence and adulthood. For example, a history of lack of control, aggressive behavior, and school failure during childhood is associated with experimentation with sex, alcohol, and other drugs during adolescence and antisocial behavior (Caspi, Henry, McGee, Moffitt, & Silva, 1995; Moffit, 1993).

A variety of theories attempt to explain why some adolescents are more likely than others to engage in various forms of deviant or self-destructive behavior (e.g., Noam, 1996; Petraitis, Flay, & Miller, 1995). Classic **psychoanalytic theory** maintains that poor early relationships and unresolved issues of sexuality or aggression leave a permanent impression on personality development. Contemporary psychoanalytic theorists emphasize the self as the central organizer of psychological development and the role of distorted interpersonal relationships in maladaptive behavior (McCarthy, 1995).

**Social learning models** emphasize the role of a child's learning history, especially a history of reinforcement, punishment, and observational learning. Children who are frequently punished and who observe deviant or aggressive family behavior are considered to be at higher risk of maladjustment (D'Angelo et al., 1995; Paschall, Ennett, & Flewelling, 1996). Research confirms that troubled adolescents are more likely than well-adjusted adolescents to come from troubled families, although each teenager in turmoil experiences a unique combination of personal qualities and circumstance (Dishion, Patterson, Stoolmiller, & Skinner, 1991; Hagell & Newburn, 1996; Rutter, 1985; Vuchinich, Bank, & Patterson, 1992). Supporting a learning model, juvenile offenders do reinforce antisocial behaviors in their deviant peer group (Fergusson & Horwood, 1996; Fergusson et al., 1996b).

Some observers (e.g., Sigurdsson & Gudjonsson, 1996; Sokol-Katz, Dunham, & Zimmerman, 1997) emphasize the role that personality traits play in the development of deviant behavior, especially an inability to bond with family members. Other models cite poor impulse control (Gottfredson & Hirschi, 1990; Henry, Caspi, Moffitt, & Silva, 1996) and inadequate self-restraint

(D'Angelo, et al., 1995; Feldman & Weinberger, 1994). **Trait theories** recognize the inept parenting experienced by most antisocial children, but these theories hypothesize that the temperamental or noncompliant child induces the ineffective parenting rather than vice versa.

**Cognitive (attributional) models** maintain that aggressive children's faulty thinking styles get them into trouble. For example, they infer hostile intent following an ambiguous or negative interaction with a peer, which leads them to retaliate (e.g., Graham, Hudley, & Williams, 1992). (See Table 13-4.)

Some theorists cite biological factors—for example, heredity (Rutter, 1997), brain disorders (Azar, 1996d), or a difficult temperament—that lead to deviant behavior by inducing negative reactions in parents and peers (Caspi et al., 1995; Chess & Thomas, 1984; Zahn-Waxler, 1996). Henry and his colleagues found that childhood temperament (i.e., impulsive behavior) was a good predictor of being convicted for a violent offense (Henry et al., 1996). Some adolescents suffer from *attention-deficit hyperactivity disorder (ADHD)*, characterized by inattention, impulsivity, hyperactivity, poor peer relationships, family problems, and other learning disabilities (Cantwell, 1996; Evans, Vallano, & Pelham, 1995; Markel & Greenbaum, 1996). The disorder is heritable and almost certainly has a neurobiological basis. Children with ADHD are at risk of low self-esteem, school failure, and peer rejection (Brochin & Horvath, 1996). We noted in Chapter 11 that learning-disabled high school seniors generally have lower achievement and occupational aspirations than their nondisabled peers (Rojewski, 1996).

**Social-psychological and sociological models** focus on the relationship between individuals and their social environments. In explaining deviant behavior, they take into account poverty, exposure to multiple life stressors, and a lack of legitimate opportunity to succeed or find meaningful activities (e.g., Compas, 1987a). Fabrega and Miller (1995) view psychological disorders as products of social and cultural changes (modernization) in Western industrial

## Table 13-4  Models of Deviant Behavior

**Psychoanalytic theory** claims that poor early relationships and unresolved issues of sexuality or aggression leave a permanent impression on personality development.

**Contemporary psychoanalytic theory** emphasizes the self as the central organizer of psychological development and the role that distorted interpersonal relationships play in maladaptive behavior.

**Social learning models** focus on a child's learning history, especially his or her history of reinforcement, punishment, and observational learning.

**Trait theories** hypothesize that the temperamental or noncompliant child induces ineffective parenting.

**Cognitive (attributional) models** maintain that aggressive children's faulty thinking styles are the source of deviant behavior.

**Biological models** hypothesize that neurological disorders or difficult temperaments lead to deviant behavior by inducing negative reactions in parents and peers.

**Social-psychological and sociological models** emphasize the relationship between individuals and their social environments, especially poverty and discrimination.

countries. They attribute eating and identity disorders and antisocial behavior during adolescence to unstable family life, stressful school experiences, occupational competition and uncertainty, and a social philosophy that emphasizes individual freedom and materialism.

## MALADAPTIVE PARENTING STYLE AND DEVIANT BEHAVIOR

*Study Question: Do troubled children always come from troubled families?*

Recent models of adolescent antisocial behavior highlight the role of maladaptive parenting and family disorganization (Jacobvitz & Bush, 1996; Paschall et al., 1996; Reitman, Gross, & Messer, 1995; Sansbury & Wahler, 1992; Vuchinich et al., 1992). It is hard to think of a factor that carries more weight in children's adjustment than their family life. Although there is no single parenting style or family configuration that works best for all children, good parent-child communication, a relatively peaceful home environment, and the core features of the authoritative parenting style described in Chapter 7 predict the best child and adolescent outcomes, at least for white, middle-class children (Clark & Shields, 1997; Nelson et al., 1993; Klein, Forehand, Armistead, & Long, 1997; Sokol-Katz et al., 1997).

There are differences among ethnic groups in how parents socialize their children and in the role that family life plays in adolescent behavior (Gfellner, 1990; Paschall et al., 1996; Smith & Krohn, 1995). However, the socialization and stress factors that affect mental health appear to be quite similar across ethnic groups (Knight, Virdin, & Roosa, 1994).

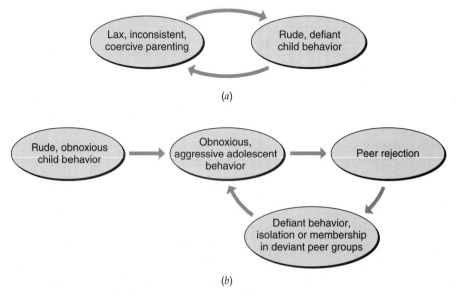

FIGURE 13.1  (a, b) Self-perpetuating trajectories.

Patterson and others have described **developmental trajectories**, fairly predictable sequences of antisocial behavior beginning during childhood and continuing into adulthood (Dishion et al., 1991; Patterson, 1982, 1986; Patterson, DeBaryshe, & Ramsey, 1989). Typically, a history of antisocial behavior begins with lax, inappropriate, or inconsistent discipline during early childhood (Jacobvitz & Bush, 1996; Seydlitz, 1991). Inconsistent parents bring out the worst in their children by threatening them when they are noncompliant, by overlooking deviant actions, and by not following through after discipline encounters (Sansbury & Wahler, 1992). Their children bring out the worst in them through rudeness, defiance, and other annoying behaviors (Stice & Barrera, 1995). Each party uses coercion to control the behavior of the other. One 15-year-old girl reported, "My family is a fighting family, we don't discuss things. Nowadays fighting is the answer. Talking won't solve anything" (quoted by Lee, 1992, p. B8). (See Figure 13-1a.)

In stable families, children learn prosocial skills, such as cooperation and sensitivity, mainly by observing and participating in caring family relationships (Gardner, 1987; Jaffe, 1997). Rather than learning prosocial skills, conduct-problem children learn from their tumultuous family life an obnoxious, aggressive behavior style that spills over into their peer relationships. This pattern of obnoxious behavior interferes with a child's peer relationships and typically leads to peer rejection. Peer rejection, in turn, retards the natural evolution of prosocial skills. It encourages hostile and suspicious feelings in the increasingly isolated teenager (Cohen & Strayer, 1996; Garnefski & Okma, 1996). In school, difficult children usually are tracked together in the same classes, reinforcing and modeling each other's problem behaviors. During adolescence, many of these children join deviant peer groups that continue to encourage and reinforce coercive and other antisocial behaviors (Dishion et al., 1991; Fergusson et al., 1996b; Jenkins, 1996; Simons et al., 1991; Vuchinich et al., 1992). (See Figure 13-1b.)

Mothers and fathers influence their children's adjustment through direct interactions, including emotional displays and punitive parenting, as well as indirectly, via marital conflict and family stress (Emery, 1982; Henggeler, Edwards, & Borduin, 1987; Jacobvitz & Bush, 1996; Peiser & Heaven, 1996; Simons, Robertson, & Downs, 1989). Conger and his associates demonstrated that economic stress demoralizes parents and disrupts parenting behavior and communication in ways that adversely affect the adjustment of early adolescents (Conger et al., 1992, 1993).

Patterson and his colleagues note that parents of children with behavior problems usually have lower educational achievement and are coercive in their parenting. They respond to their children's negative behaviors in kind, that is, they express more anger and use more physical punishment than parents of better-behaved children. They are inconsistent in discipline, sometimes capitulating to their children's demands and at other times being tough (Sansbury & Wahler, 1992). Eventually, a self-perpetuating cycle results "in which both the parent and the child become increasingly coercive in an effort to exert control" (DeBaryshe et al., 1993, p. 796). The role of inadequate parenting in promoting antisocial behavior is supported by studies showing that children have fewer behavioral problems when their parents learn how to discipline them consistently and strategically (Kazdin, 1987).

Given their greater role in child care and discipline, mothers frequently are blamed for their children's emotional problems. However, it is clear that fathers also contribute to children's behavior problems (Phares & Compas, 1992). Children of alcoholic and depressed fathers, for example, have more behavior problems than children of emotionally healthy fathers. The finding that adolescents who live with single parents or with stepparents have more adjustment problems and are less resistant to deviant peer presssure than those in intact families suggests that living with both biological parents is a protective factor (Garnefski & Diekstra, 1997a; Steinberg, 1987d). However, research does not support the conclusion that family configuration (nuclear, single-parent, stepfamily) *in itself* affects adjustment (Shucksmith, Glendinning, & Hendry, 1997; Nelson, Hughes, Handal, Katz, & Searight, 1993; Sokol-Katz et al., 1997).

## MULTIPLE PROBLEM BEHAVIOR SYNDROME

Serious maladjustment during adolescence usually is indicated by what is called **multiple problem behavior syndrome**, a combination of behaviors and personal qualities that includes antisocial conduct, low academic achievement, mood disorders, low self-esteem, truancy and dropping out of school, drug use, and precocious sexual activity (Brier, 1995; Dobkin, Tremblay, Masse, & Vitaro, 1995; Garnefski & Diekstra, 1997b; Jakobsen, Rise, Aas, & Anderssen, 1997; McDermott, 1996). (See Table 13-5.) *Thought Question: Is there a comparable "syndrome" of healthy and adaptive behaviors during adolescence (Newcomb, 1996)?*

Blau (1996a) offers the following as examples of problematic behaviors during adolescence: negativism, rebellion, drug use, school problems, pregnancy, hostility, opposition, defiance, disobedience, and running away. "These behaviors create immediate social and family difficulties for the child and have the possibility, if preventive steps are not taken, of developing into more serious

**Table 13-5  Multiple Problem Behavior Syndrome**

Antisocial conduct

Negativism and hostility

Defiance and disobedience

Mood disorders

Low self-esteem

School failure, truancy, and dropping out

Drug use

Precocious sexual activity and pregnancy

Running away

problems in adolescent adaptation" (p. 65). It is not yet clear how these problem behaviors are related to each other and how they are related to other factors in adolescents' environments. For example, does negative self-esteem lead to relationship conflict or do increasing problems with parents and friends lead to a negative view of the self?

Just as disorders that emerge during childhood tend to persist into adolescence, most individuals who exhibit multiple problem behaviors during the teenage years continue to have mild to severe adjustment problems in adulthood (Brack et al., 1994; Donovan & Jessor, 1985; Ensminger, 1990; Hartnagel, 1996; Jessor, 1982; Jessor, Donovan, & Costa, 1991; Maggs, Frome, Eccles, & Barber, 1997).

Dryfoos (1990) identified four categories of risk for youths 10 to 17 years old. *Very-high-risk youth* comprise about 10% of the adolescent population. This group includes those who have been arrested or who have committed serious offenses. *High-risk youth* include about 15% of the teenage population. They commit less serious offenses, but they abuse drugs, engage in unsafe sexual practices, and don't perform well in school. *Moderate-risk youth* constitute about one-quarter of adolescents. They commit minor delinquent offenses and use "soft" drugs. About half of youth are *low-risk*. They do not commit any serious delinquent acts, do not use drugs, and are not sexually active.

Dryfoos (1990) contends that problem behaviors are interrelated. She identifies six common characteristics that predict delinquency, substance use, school failure, and teenage pregnancy: (1) early onset of high-risk behaviors, (2) poor school performance and low expectations, (3) acting out and antisocial behaviors, (4) low resistance to deviant peer influence, (5) inept parenting, and (6) poverty and an overcrowded neighborhood.

Dryfoos hypothesizes the following "sequence" of events. School failure and minor delinquent offenses like gambling and shoplifting occur first (Yeoman & Griffiths, 1996). When high-risk children grow older, substance abuse and precocious sexual activity are likely, followed by early childbearing, heavy substance abuse, serious delinquency, and dropping out of school. One model suggests that each problem behavior is a "stepping stone" to the next. Other models contend that problem behaviors share common influences or precursors (e.g., Vitaro, Ladouceur, & Bujold, 1996).

It is safe to assume that although problem behaviors usually are correlated, there are many pathways to deviance (Edwards, 1996b; Ensminger, 1990). Investigators looking for the causes of multiple problem behavior syndrome have suggested a variety of underlying factors, including negative attitudes toward school (Browne & Rife, 1991); unwillingness to conform to societal norms (Donovan & Jessor, 1985); disadvantaged and disorganized home environments (Furgusson, Horwood, & Lynskey, 1994; Ingersoll & Orr, 1989); low self-esteem (Ingersoll & Orr, 1989); and poor coping resources (Brack et al., 1994). Most of the studies cited in this section investigated white, middle-class adolescents. Interestingly, Rotheram-Borus, Rosario, Van Kossem, Reid, and Gillis (1995) did not find a multiple problem behavior cluster for gay and bisexual male African-American and Hispanic youths, suggesting that their developmental trajectory differs from that of heterosexual adolescents.

## SELECTED ADJUSTMENT PROBLEMS

### Eating Disorders: In Pursuit of Thinness

*Study Question: Why might eating disorders occur more commonly among females than males?*

About 30 billion dollars are spent each year in the United States by people trying to lose weight and keep it off. Weight loss is one of the most popular topics on TV talk shows and in everyday conversation. Modern advertising implores females to become slimmer and thus more attractive—not an easy task given the limits of heredity, physiology, and the cost of cosmetic surgery. Those with unrealistic expectations about body change and dieting and their imagined benefits may suffer physiological damage and intense disappointment (Brownell, 1991; Bryant-Waugh & Lask, 1995).

Fifty percent of the 462 teenagers that Mueller and her colleagues studied reported having eating concerns (Mueller, Field, Yando, Harding et al., 1995). Emmons (1996) reported that 40% of the white and African-American high school students she questioned had lost 5 or more pounds by dieting. Two-thirds of the African-American girls and three-quarters of the white girls also met this criterion.

About 9 out of 10 teenagers who suffer from eating disorders are female. As discussed in Chapter 3, pubertal females often have mixed feelings about their bodily changes. Because a thin body has become our society's cultural ideal, the thickening layers of fat surrounding the uterus are an unpleasant surprise to many pubescent girls. Two-thirds of the females in one study reported that they had first dieted at age 12 or younger (Moreno & Thelen, 1995). So many girls, dissatisfied with their body shape and size, believe that being thinner will make them happier and more popular (Paxton, Wertheim, Gibbons, Szmukler, Hillier & Petrovich, 1991). Girls who are physically involved with boyfriends generally are very concerned about their appearance and are at higher risk of developing abnormal eating behaviors (Cauffman & Steinberg, 1996).

**Anorexia nervosa**, a strong desire for a thin body and a concurrent fear of gaining weight or being fat, is most likely to appear during early adolescence. Many of those who suffer from anorexia perceive themselves as having excessive body weight. Although some are overweight, even those who are normally weighted or thin report that they "feel fat" (Bryant-Waugh, Hankins, Shafrin, Lask et al., 1996; Eisele, Hertsgaard, & Light, 1986; Halmi, 1987). Halmi (1987) describes a 15-year-old girl, Gloria, who began dieting after being told by a girl she admired that she looked overweight. She gradually eliminated food items from her diet until her caloric intake was less than 600 calories a day. She did 30 sit-ups twice a day to keep her stomach flat. Although refusing to eat the elaborate meals she prepared for her family, she hid candies and sweets around the house. A month after she began restricting her food intake, Gloria developed bulimic episodes, eating large quantities of ice cream. Nevertheless, when she began dieting she weighed 100 pounds. Two months later she weighed 80 pounds.

Most anorectic females perceive themselves as being overweight.

Although anorexia usually is viewed as a female disorder, there has been a steady increase in the number of males who are diagnosed as anorectic, perhaps up to 10% of all anorectics. A significant number of males who are receiving medical attention for gastrointestinal or endocrine problems may be suffering from an undiagnosed eating disorder (Romeo, 1994). Most males who want to lose weight are obese or involved in sports that require leanness. Many report feeling pressured by their fathers to excel in sports. Compared to the general population, male and female athletes are at elevated risk of developing eating disorders (Brownell, Rodin, & Wilmore, 1992; Hamlett & Curry, 1990; Romeo, 1994; Stoutjesdyk & Jevne, 1993; Taub & Blinde, 1992).

Some adolescents are more susceptible than others to developing an eating disorder, especially those who have trouble expressing feelings and whose self-esteem is strongly linked to their body image (Lawrence & Thelen, 1995). They restrict their food intake, and are preoccupied with thoughts of food and with their body size and weight. Death through starvation or heart attack is not unheard of (Bryant-Waugh & Lask, 1995; Muuss, 1985). (See Table 13-6.)

Another severe eating disorder, **bulimia nervosa**, was officially recognized by the American Psychiatric Association in 1980. Like anorectics, bulimics are

**Table 13-6 Multifactorial Model of Eating Disorders**

A possible hereditary component

Pressure on women to be slim

Distorted ideas about nutrition, weight, and appearance

Interpersonal stressors

Low self-esteem

Body dissatisfaction and obsessiveness about one's appearance

Fear of rejection

Poor eating habits and inappropriate dieting

Childhood trauma such as sexual abuse

A chaotic or conflictual family history including family preoccupation with food, conflict during meals, and the use of food as a tool for manipulation or punishment

A precipitating stressful event such as peer rejection

preoccupied with food and engage in uncontrolled binge eating. Unlike self-starving anorectics, bulimics usually are normally weighted, which makes this disorder harder for parents to detect (Pendley & Bates, 1996). Bulimia typically emerges during the college years, at least for middle- or upper-class white females. When on a binge, bulimics secretly devour large amounts of food until they feel bloated, nauseated, and physically sick. For most bulimic individuals, binge eating is followed by purging of food through vomiting, use of laxatives or enemas, or by other means. Self-induced vomiting after a binge brings a sense of relief, peace, and even euphoria. This often is followed by self-condemnation and shame. A cycle of compulsive binging and purging develops, accompanied by feelings of guilt, shame, anxiety, and hopelessness and by thoughts of suicide. This cycle may be repeated dozens of times a week (Halmi, 1987; Herzog, Keller, Lavori, & Bradburn, 1991; Leitenberg & Rosen, 1988; Muuss, 1986; Weinstein, 1996).

The current multifactorial model of eating disorders cites biological, personality, family, and cultural factors, including a possible hereditary component; pressure on women to be slim; distorted ideas about nutrition, weight, and appearance; interpersonal stressors; low self-esteem; body dissatisfaction; fear of rejection; poor eating habits and inappropriate dieting; childhood trauma such as sexual abuse; and a chaotic or conflictual family history including depression, drug abuse, family preoccupation with food, conflict during meals, and the use of food as a tool for manipulation or punishment (Bailey, 1991; Dacey, Newlson, Clark, & Aikman, 1991; Halmi, 1987; Heatherton, Mahamedi, Striepe, Field, & Keel, 1997; La Porte, 1997; Lask & Bryant-Waugh, 1992; Leitenberg & Rosen, 1988; Lyon, Chatoor, Atkins, Silber, Mosimann, & Gray, 1997; Miller, McCluskey-Fawcett, & Irving, 1993; Smolak, Levine, & Gralen, 1993; Swarr & Richards, 1996; Woodside, 1995).

For anorectics, body dissatisfaction, obsessiveness about one's appearance (including frequent monitoring of appearance in the mirror), low self-esteem, and a precipitating stressful event (such as a putdown from peers) lead a normally weighted though vulnerable young teenager to diet as a way of regulating the personal mood. Excessive dieting provokes compulsive eating and then purging to avoid weight gain (Crowther, Tennenbaum, Hobfoll, & Stephens, 1992). Parents of anorectic children frequently are insecure, frustrated, and overprotective. Many have had painful childhoods themselves, leading to preoccupation with and overinvolvement in their child's problems.

Muuss (1985) views anorexia as a "compensatory attempt to suppress pubertal changes. In addition, the adolescent needs to feel a sense of mastery and control over her body" (p. 526). Many anorectics are "perfectionists" in that they strive to have perfect bodies and perfect grades. Binge eating serves as a way of coping with feelings of loneliness, anger, and depression. "It commonly starts after an unhappy experience, such as academic or vocational failure, or interpersonal problems. Real or imagined rejection by a male frequently triggers the first binge. . . . Binge eating becomes a symbolic escape from the pressures of life" (Muuss, 1986, p. 259). *Thought Question: How might parents, coaches, and physicians inadvertently put pressure on adolescents to maintain unrealistic weight goals?*

Eating disorders, especially anorexia, are not easy to treat (Graber, Brooks-Gunn, Paikoff, & Warren, 1994; Herzog, Schellberg, & Deter, 1997), although the earlier they are identified, the better the prognosis (Brody, 1996a). Relapses are common. Predictors of a poor outcome include alcohol abuse, suicide attempts, and depression. Youngsters with eating disorders usually deny that they have a problem or rationalize their behavior according to their distorted body image. Eventually, family members notice that something is very wrong and pressure the teenager to eat normally. It is more helpful for parents to help their children understand their insecurities about their appearance and help them decide what to do about them.

Irrational beliefs about food and appearance are difficult to change. For those sufferers like Gloria with life-threatening weight loss, hospitalization and intravenous feeding is a first step in treatment. Although initially resistant to therapy, teenagers with eating disorders benefit from individual or family counseling and cognitive-behavioral approaches. Antidepressants, used when depression accompanies the eating disorder, help 25–40% of bulimics stop binge eating. The best results are obtained when antidepressants are used in conjunction with cognitive-behavioral therapy. Important goals of cognitive-behavioral treatment include (1) helping patients establish sensible eating habits and good nutrition, (2) getting them to monitor the emotional cues that trigger binge eating, and (3) modifying distorted attitudes and beliefs about body size and weight (Leitenberg & Rosen, 1988).

With her father and sister, Gloria received three sessions of cognitive psychotherapy a week. Gloria was not always cooperative but managed to regain her weight of 100 pounds. Most sufferers need to learn to see themselves and their problems realistically, accept reasonable weight levels, and learn ways of regulating their weight that are not self-destructive. They also need to learn how to cope with stress and resolve their life problems more effectively (Halmi, 1987; Harper-Giuffre & MacKenzie, 1992; Moreno & Thelen, 1993; Muuss, 1985, 1986). After subsequent relapses and hospitalizations, Gloria eventually graduated from college and held a fairly responsible job.

## ANTISOCIAL BEHAVIOR AND VIOLENCE

*For Aleysha J., the road to crime has been paved with huge gold earrings and name-brand clothes. At Aleysha's high school in the Bronx, popularity comes from looking the part. Aleysha's mother has no money to buy her nice things so the diminutive 15-year-old steals them, an act that she feels makes her equal parts bad girl and liberated woman. "It's like I don't want to do it, but my friends put a lot of pressure on me," says Aleysha, who spoke on condition that her full name not be used. "Then I see something I want so bad I just take it. The worst time, I pulled a knife on this girl, but I never hurt anybody. I just want things."*

*(Lee, 1991, p. 1)*

**Antisocial behavior** during childhood refers to behavior that violates social rules by inflicting physical or mental harm or property loss on others (Tolan & Loeber, 1993). Examples of antisocial behavior include fighting, lying, theft, truancy, and vandalism. These behaviors often occur together. At their extremes, they are referred to as *delinquent behavior* or as a *conduct disorder*. **Juvenile delinquency** is a technical term that the courts apply to criminal behaviors of teenagers between the ages of 10 and 16 years that can lead to incarceration.

**Delinquent behaviors**, on the other hand, are antisocial (often criminal) behaviors that are not brought to the attention of the court. Offenses range from drawing graffiti on public property and violating school rules to more serious acts such as theft and selling drugs, activities that bring young people to the attention of the authorities (Calhoun, Jurgens, & Chen, 1993; Kelly & Hansen, 1987).

Moffitt (1993) describes two qualitatively different patterns of delinquency, each with a unique history and etiology. According to Moffitt, **adolescence-limited antisocial behavior** is motivated mainly by a gap between biological maturity and social maturity that encourages teenagers to copy antisocial behaviors. Teenagers may occasionally shoplift and use drugs but still obey rules at home and in school. By adulthood, more than three-quarters of this group cease all forms of offending.

**Life-course persistent antisocial behavior** reflects an antisocial personality structure based on neuropsychological vulnerability and a lifelong environment that encourages hostile actions. In this pattern of delinquent behavior, we observe a persistent progression of deviant behaviors from early childhood to adulthood: biting and hitting at age 4, shoplifting and truancy at age 10, selling drugs and stealing cars at 16, robbery and rape at 22, child abuse at 30. "The underlying disposition remains the same, but its expression changes form as new social opportunities arise at different points in development" (Moffitt, 1993, p. 679). Loeber (1985) also distinguishes between two types of delinquents: those who engage in only one type of antisocial behavior and those who engage in a variety of such behaviors at fairly high rates.

Acts that are criminal, whether they are committed by juveniles or adults, are called **index offenses**. Less serious acts that are offenses only if committed by juveniles (e.g., running away, underage drinking, truancy) are called **status**

**offenses**. Clinical psychologists and psychiatrists refer to sustained and repetitive antisocial behaviors of young teenagers as conduct disorders. **Conduct disorder** is a psychiatric term indicating a persistent pattern of antisocial behavior that impairs the everyday functioning of adolescents and is considered uncontrollable by related adults (Borduin, Henggeler, & Manley, 1995). The DSM-IV criteria for diagnosis are satisfied by the presence of at least three serious problem behaviors exhibited over at least a 6-month period. Such behaviors include noncompliance, arson, theft, substance abuse, aggressive behaviors, and the inadequate development of social bonds (Dryfoos, 1990).

Conduct-disordered children ordinarily exhibit low self-esteem and an "attitude problem," and most function poorly in school. Many also engage in precocious sexual behaviors. Displaying the multiple problem disorder discussed earlier, such children also lie, steal, run away from home, and resist attending school (Bornstein, Schuldberg, & Bornstein, 1987).

DSM-IV describes a disorder known as **oppositional defiant disorder (ODD)** in adolescents who frequently lose their temper, argue with adults, defy adult authority, intentionally annoy others, blame others for their mistakes, and other spiteful or vindictive behaviors. For a diagnosis of ODD, the pattern must persist over a period of 6 months and include at least four of the cited behaviors (Borduin et al., 1995). ODD is considered less serious than a conduct disorder (Blau, 1996a).

During adolescence, there is a substantial increase in antisocial conduct in both genders (Pakiz et al., 1992). The FBI (*Uniform Crime Report*, 1991) estimated that 30% of all people arrested in 1990 were under the age of 21, and that 43% of all serious crimes were committed by persons in this age group. A total of 1,750,000 juveniles were arrested that year. The number of arrests of juveniles for violent crimes is expected to double by the year 2010, according to the U.S. Justice Department (Butterfield, 1995), although the arrest rate for homicide among youths 10 to 17 years of age fell almost 23% in 1995 from its all-time peak in 1993 (Butterfield, 1996d). Keep in mind that adolescents, especially African-American and Latino youth who live in high-risk neighborhoods, frequently are victims of violent crime, including homicide (Berton & Stabb, 1996; Butterfield, 1994; Esbensen & Huizinga, 1991; Hammond & Yung, 1993; Paschall et al., 1996). The emotional cost to the families of victims and perpetrators is hard to imagine.

Of the 25,000 juveniles currently confined in state institutions, 93% are male, 40% are African-American, and 12% are Hispanic. Most are poorly educated and drug users. One in four grew up living with both parents, and more than half had a relative who had been incarcerated. Sixty percent have previously been in jail. The average age at first arrest was about 12.8 years (Dryfoos, 1990; U.S. Department of Justice, 1987).

During early adolescence many individuals commit relatively minor offenses that, if discovered, lead to probation for 6 months to 2 years. Alcohol and drug abuse usually precedes or accompanies more serious criminal and violent activity that, if prosecuted, leads to detention (Elliott, Huizinga, & Menard, 1989). Frequently, there are warning signs during childhood that something is wrong. Aggressive behavior, poor self-regulatory and social skills, school failure, drug use, early sexual activity, and family abuse or neglect predict a wide range of later delinquent behaviors (Tolan & Thomas, 1995).

The earlier antisocial behaviors appear and the more frequently they occur, the greater the danger of serious offenses in the future (Dryfoos, 1990; Feldman & Weinberger, 1994; Henggeler et al., 1989). Thus it is not surprising that early childhood intervention programs that are designed to reduce school failure also appear to reduce future delinquency and criminality rates (Zigler, Taussig, & Black, 1992). Violence often is learned in the family, in the community, or both (Crespi & Rigazio-DiGilio, 1996; Straus, 1994). Troubled teenagers usually have family histories of harsh discipline, weak parent–child attachment, and inadequate adult supervision (Marcus & Betzer, 1996; Sampson & Laub, 1994; Seydlitz, 1991; Vazsonyi & Flannery, 1997). Many delinquents report that their families are unsupportive and uncommunicative (Bischof, Stith, & Whitney, 1995; Clark & Shields, 1997; Klein et al., 1997). Gang members have difficulty naming adults whom they consider to be role models (Wang, 1994). Partly due to faulty parenting practices, many young people never learn how to handle frustration or get along with peers. Living in poverty and experiencing discrimination and violence almost daily, large numbers of these children "shut down," unable to feel any emotions other than anger or hopelessness.

Deviant behaviors such as truancy, gambling, and shoplifting, committed by delinquents of past generations, seem mild in comparison to the sophisticated gang activities, drug trafficking, and drive-by shootings we hear about today. Boys in particular engage in serious delinquent behaviors such as robbery and assault. Whereas delinquency in girls was once predominantly sex-related (i.e., prostitution), today female delinquency takes the form of status offenses like truancy and running away. Females in gangs are more likely than nongang members to carry guns (Calhoun et al., 1993; Rhodes & Fischer, 1993).

Gangs attract teenagers from all backgrounds and socioeconomic groups. Suburban gangs, both male and female, are proliferating. Police in the affluent community of Westchester, New York, estimate that there are 70 gangs with about 1,500 members. Groups of teenagers, many of whom say that they expect to attend college, give themselves gang names, engage in petty theft and vandalism, and fight with other groups.

> Short-lived alliances are one of the hallmarks of suburban gangs, which unlike city gangs do not always revolve around neighborhood groups protecting their home turf and, often, the drug business that goes with it. . . . Suburban gang members are more likely to meet at school than on the block, and when trouble breaks out it is often at malls and movie theaters. Both the police and gang members said most fights in suburbia were not about territory at all, but start when a member of one group offends, or "disses" a member of another group.
>
> (Henneberger, 1993, p. 25)

Drive-by beatings with baseball bats are more common than drive-by shootings, although the use of dangerous weapons is escalating. According to one 17-year-old gang member in Yonkers, New York, who had 13 stitches removed from his head the previous week from a fight with a rival gang, "It went from punches to razors, bats and bottles, and now to guns" (quoted by

Henneberger, 1993, p. 25). *Thought Question: What, if anything, does the prevalence of antisocial behavior during adolescence tell us about family life?*

Social learning models maintain that teenagers' deviant and antisocial behaviors reflect social skills deficits, poor problem-solving skills, and low resistance to deviant peer pressure. According to Patterson's life-course model (DeBaryshe et al., 1993), undereducated, distressed parents unintentionally elicit and maintain children's antisocial behavior through inconsistent and punitive discipline practices. A coercive parent–child relationship teaches children a negative, aggressive behavior style that leads to academic disruption and peer rejection during the school years. As discussed in Chapter 8, rejected children often join deviant peer groups whose members model bossy and coercive behavior (Dishion et al., 1995; Ma, Shek, Cheung, & Lee, 1996). In such groups we observe fighting, destruction of property, theft, and truancy. Problems become more serious with age. Antisocial behaviors during preadolescence and adolescence predict continuing maladaptive behavior such as substance abuse in adulthood.

Although most troubled adolescents suffer inwardly, some strike out against others—their family members, other teenagers, or strangers. According to recent government reports, youths under 18 years of age account for 10% of all homicide arrests. About 20% of juvenile homicides involve family members. This is not surprising given that most children who assault or kill have witnessed or have been victimized by family violence. Teenagers also are 2.5 times more likely to be victims of violence than are adults. According to the U.S. Justice Department, about a million teenagers a year are raped, robbed, or assaulted, often by their peers (*Newsweek*, August 2, 1993, p. 43). In 1990 alone, 4,200 teenagers were shot to death (National Center for Health, 1991).

The U.S. Justice Department reported in 1995 that 23% of the people arrested on weapons charges in 1993 were juveniles (compared to 16% in 1974). According to the Children's Defense Fund (1996), gunfire is the second leading cause of death among teenagers in the United States (accidents are the leading cause). These deaths include homicides, suicides, and accidents. The death rate from guns for African-American teenagers is about five times higher than for white teenagers. About one-third of high school students report that they have easy access to handguns. Guns are seen as a means of protection or as a source of status. Many of those who are not victims have seen someone shot, robbed, or murdered (DeAngelis, 1993; Freiberg, 1991; *The New York Times*, June 10, 1992).

Violent behavior reflects an ongoing developmental process like that described by Patterson and his colleagues—coercive family behavior and witnessing violent behavior at home or in the community, including various forms of child or spouse abuse. Poverty, unemployment, discrimination, access to drugs and alcohol, and the availability of weapons make it probable that these problems will be passed on from generation to generation. Many aggressive and substance-abusing teenagers have psychological problems like depression or a learning disability that are expressed partly through antisocial or self-destructive behavior (Dawkins, 1997; McLaughlin et al., 1996; Ralph & McMenamy, 1996).

There is no shortage of very angry, very hostile teenage girls. Some join male gangs, and others belong to exclusively female gangs. Increases in female delinquency partly reflect coercive family environments, family neglect, and sexual abuse. Many urban girls join gangs for protection but also to enjoy a sense of belonging that they may not get at home. Beyond the family, there is a profusion of weapons and dead bodies on TV and in the movies that reinforces teenage interest in violence, power, and revenge (Snyder, 1991, 1995).

From their family experiences or from media portrayals of machismo, many teenage males, both urban and suburban, come to view fighting as a way of life. One way or another, most delinquent youth learn that "violence is an appropriate way to solve interpersonal problems, to vent frustration and to get material rewards one feels one deserves but has not attained" (researcher L. Eron, quoted by DeAngelis, 1993, p. 40).

Not only has incarceration lost its ability to frighten teenagers away from a life of crime, to some it has become a rite of passage—a source of respect and status. Jail also is a place where they can receive free living quarters and balanced meals. According to one 25-year-old convict from Chicago, "Some young brothers seem like they don't care if they go to prison. They think it's macho, that it gives them more rank out on the street. I wasn't too worried about going because my uncle came back all built up. I kind of wanted the experience. He told me it was smooth in there, that doing time was a piece of cake" (quoted by Terry, 1992, p. 1).

Those who have a minimal stake in society to begin with have little to lose by going to jail (Hagell & Newburn, 1996). About two-thirds of the 1 million people in prison have not completed high school and had incomes of less than $10,000 a year. The U.S. Justice Department reports that more than half of all juvenile delinquents in state prisons have close relatives who also have been in jail. According to a 22-year-old facing 5 years in prison for selling drugs, "I might have to go to prison, and it don't make me feel good. How's it going to correct me? All it can do is confine me. All you hear around my house is somebody is going to jail and somebody is coming home" (quoted by Terry, 1992, p. 40).

Out of desperation, many U.S. towns and cities use daytime or nighttime curfews and fines for parents as a way of curbing juvenile crime (Butterfield, 1996b). For example, the town of Wapato, Washington, made it illegal for children younger than 18 to be in a public place on school days during school time. Parents of repeat offenders could be fined up to $300. In 1995, Dallas police picked up about 4,000 teenagers, of whom 2,500 were repeat offenders. The latter were given citations ordering them to appear in court. Sixty-five parents were given citations for knowing that their children violated the curfew. New Orleans has a dusk-to-dawn curfew that begins at 8 P.M. in the winter and 9 P.M. in the summer (Butterfield, 1996b).

These measures reflect a growing belief that parents should be responsible for their children. Critics argue that curfews are a simplistic solution to a complex problem. The American Civil Liberties Union maintains that curfews violate teenagers' rights to freedom of speech and assembly. Minority children and parents are most likely to be targeted by law enforcement officials. State and federal laws generally have upheld curfew laws as long as juveniles accompanied by adults and those traveling to and from work are exempted (Butterfield, 1996b; Varner, 1995).

Most formal programs that attempt to reduce delinquent and predelinquent behavior have not been successful, perhaps because they follow a long history of antisocial interaction with parents, teachers, and members of the community (Rice, 1997; Zigler et al., 1992). Since detention seems to reinforce rather than discourage deviant behavior, nontraditional programs currently are being tested, including the use of boot camps, group and foster homes, therapeutic communities, and community-based rehabilitation programs. Such programs emphasize supervision, tutoring, job training, and counseling (Dryfoos, 1990; Edwards, 1995; Mann-Feder, 1996; Preston, 1996). Social skills training programs also have been implemented in the treatment of young offenders (Cunliffe, 1992).

Comprehensive early intervention programs reviewed by Zigler et al., (1992) have been somewhat successful in reducing delinquency. These programs are called *comprehensive* because they address family, school, and community factors in development (Sullivan & Wilson, 1995). Since academic failure and delinquency appear to be linked, such programs may be successful in preventing antisocial behavior by alleviating the risk factors associated with antisocial behavior, especially school failure. A *snowball effect* occurs, meaning that successful social and academic experiences during childhood generate higher aspirations, self-confidence, and positive interactions during adolescence. Adolescent female offenders require programs that take into account their unique developmental needs, including the fact that many have been sexually or physically abused (Miller, Trapani, Fejes-Mendoza, Eggleston et al., 1995).

## SUBSTANCE USE AND ABUSE

> *In the eighth grade, smoking marijuana would be an easy ticket to being cooler. I know there would be a good social result if I started smoking.*
>
> *(17-year-old boy quoted by Wren, 1996, p. A20)*

> *If you want them [drugs], you can get them.*
>
> *(14-year-old high school freshman)*

Adolescence appears to be the critical time in life regarding substance use and abuse. Society sets limits on the availability of substances to teenagers because we strongly believe that drug use both threatens their health and interferes with the necessary developmental tasks of adolescence (Brook, Gordon, Brook, & Brook, 1989; Luthar & Cushing, 1997; National Highway Traffic Safety Administration, 1989; Van Kammen, Loeber, & Stouthamer-Loeber, 1991). The irony is that for those who claim that they want more freedom, dependence on a drug is the ultimate loss of freedom.

During the middle school years, young adolescents, especially those who live in affluent environments, are surprised to learn how easy it is to purchase illegal drugs from peers. High school students become accustomed to the easy availability of drugs in and out of school. Many distinguish between drug dealing (selling and delivering), which is viewed as dangerous, and illicit drug use, which most view negatively or tolerate. The use of mood-altering drugs to relieve boredom, pressure, and stress is so common that many teenagers come to see it as "no big deal." Young people who live in impoverished communities can be seduced by the financial and status rewards of drug selling ("living the high life") despite the dangers (Li, Stanton, Black, & Feigelman, 1996). For some of these youth, drug trafficking appears to be a precursor to drug use (Feigelman, Stanton, & Ricardo, 1993; Li, Stanton, Feigelman, Black, & Romer, 1994).

Although there is no single pathway to substance use and abuse, drugs like alcohol, marijuana, and cocaine temporarily distract teenagers from their current life problems and pressures. Some teenagers use drugs as self-medication for anxiety or depression, especially when such use is supported by their peers (Curran, Spice, & Chassin, 1997; Simons, Whitbeck, Conger, & Melby, 1991). Based on their survey of 823 high school students, Mainous and his colleagues maintain that adolescents whose everyday needs and desires (underlying feeling states) are not being fulfilled use drugs as an indirect way of meeting their needs (Mainous, Martin, Oler, Richardson, & Haney, 1996).

A vicious cycle can result because drug use and drug-related behaviors become part of the problem. It doesn't take long for the psychoactive effects of a drug (stimulation, distraction, and pleasure) to increase users' psychological or physiological dependence. At that point, giving up the drug becomes more difficult (Hartnagel, 1996; Kolata, 1997). DSM-IV criteria for substance use disorder include continued use despite social, psychological, or physical problems; significant impairment and distress; recurrent use that results in a failure to fulfill role obligations; and repeated sustance-related legal problems (Bukstein & Van Hasselt, 1995). Chronic drug abusers ingest a greater variety of drugs, spend more money on them, and purchase them more frequently than occasional users. They also spend considerably more time involved in drug-related activities (Horan & Straus, 1987; Petersen & Hamburg, 1986; Shilts, 1991).

### Experimenting with Drugs

*If you want to find out what it's like, you're going to do it. I've adjusted to friends who call us the freaks of the school. Someone told me we were worthless forms of life, and we just laughed in his face.*
(15-year-old girl quoted by Wren, 1996, p. A20)

Partly out of curiosity, large numbers of adolescents experiment with legal and illegal substances (Petraitis, Flay, & Miller, 1995). Experimentation is so common that many observers outside of the United States consider experimentation with drugs (especially alcohol) to be normative adolescent behavior and abstinence to be deviant (e.g., Lowe, Foxcroft, & Sibley, 1993). Experimentation typically begins with beer and wine, followed by cigarettes and liquor, and then marijuana (Kandel, 1982). The younger the age at initial use, the greater the risk of subsequent drug abuse. Relatively few people use illicit drugs during adulthood if they did not first use them by age 18. During this period of experimentation, no particular substance is preferred or commonly used. A few adolescents move on to harder drugs (Tang, Wong, & Schwarzer, 1996). Whether or not dabblers become users depends on a balance of risk factors and protective factors that we survey below (Beman, 1995; Jessor, 1992; Petraitis et al., 1995; Wills, McNamara, Vaccaro, & Hirky, 1996). (See Table 13-7.)

## Extent of Use

> *I could never use drugs. I would hear my mother's voice in one ear and the voices of the nuns in the other.*
>
> *(15-year-old high school student)*

Relatively few teenagers experimented with illegal substances prior to the 1960s. Nowadays, about two-thirds of adolescents will have used an illegal drug by the time they graduate from high school (Johnston, O'Malley, & Bachman, 1985). A national survey of eighth graders released in 1993 by the University of Michigan at Ann Arbor revealed that 70% of the students reported

**Table 13-7  Psychoactive Drugs and Their Effects**

| Category | Common Name | Method of Administration | Desired Effects |
|---|---|---|---|
| *Stimulants* | | | *Alertness, excitation, energy, euphoria* |
| amphetamines | speed, uppers | oral, injected, inhaled | |
| cocaine | coke, blow, snow | oral, inhaled | |
| caffeine | coffee, tea, soda | oral | |
| nicotine | tobacco | smoked | |
| *Depressants* | | | *Relaxation, euphoria, reduced anxiety and inhibitions, induce sleep* |
| alcohol | beer, wine, liquor | oral | |
| barbiturates | downers, barbs | oral, injected | |
| tranquilizers | valium, librium, xanax | oral | |
| methaqualone | quaaludes, ludes | oral | |
| *Narcotics* | | | *Euphoria, pain relief, relaxation* |
| heroin | smack, horse, junk | oral, injected, smoked | |
| morphine | | | |
| opium | poppy | oral, injected, smoked | |
| | | oral, injected, smoked | |
| *Psychedelics (Hallucinogens)* | | | *Altered perception and awareness, euphoria, hallucinations, time distortion* |
| MDMA | ecstacy | oral | |
| cannabis | marijuana, weed, pot, grass | oral, smoked | |
| LSD | acid | oral | |
| phencyclidine | PCP, angel dust | oral, smoked | |

using alcohol and 27% acknowledged getting drunk. Forty-five percent said that they smoked cigarettes, and 11% admitted using marijuana or hashish. Experimenting with tobacco, alcohol, and marijuana peaked in the late 1970s, and drug use by teenagers gradually diminished until the early 1990s. To some extent, decreased use has led to a sense of complacency among parents and educators. However, recent studies report increases in cigarette and marijuana smoking and LSD use among teenagers (National Institute on Drug Abuse, 1995; Treaster, 1994; *University of Michigan Annual Survey*, 1995). A drug culture flourishes on the internet (Wren, 1997).

Two-thirds of high school seniors drink regularly, and about one-quarter smoke marijuana. Fifteen percent report drinking heavily or using hard drugs. Regular smokers and heavy drinkers are much more likely to use hard drugs than occasional users or nondrinkers. Although experimentation with drugs (other than tobacco) is decreasing among high school students, those who use drugs are doing so more frequently. Drug use does not differ much according to gender, although males are heavier drinkers and are more likely than females to drive when drunk (Dryfoos, 1990).

Not all young people are casual regarding drug use (Adlaf & Smart, 1991). A survey released by the Center on Addiction and Substance Abuse at Columbia University in 1995 revealed that adolescents overwhelmingly view drug use as the greatest problem they face, outranking crime, peer pressure, grades, and sex (Lewin, 1995b). Three-quarters of the respondents reported believing that marijuana use leads to lower grades. Twenty percent said they were afraid of permanent physical or mental damage from drug use.

## Health Risks

We have already acknowledged the role that drugs, especially alcohol, play in unwanted pregnancy, antisocial behavior, and other self-destructive, risk-taking behaviors (Dawkins, 1997). For example, motor vehicle crashes account for 40% of the deaths of young people, making them the top killer of youths aged 15 to 20. (More than half of those killed were not wearing seat belts.) Teenage drivers were involved in 7,993 fatal crashes in 1995, down 23% from 1988 (Centers for Disease Control and Prevention, 1996). Between a quarter and a half of those accidents involved alcohol use. Young drivers also were involved in about 2 million nonfatal crashes in 1995 alone.

Although people differ in their sensitivity to particular drugs, excessive drinking and cigarette smoking are associated with a number of serious health risks. Cigarette smoking is known to cause several deadly diseases, including lung cancer and heart disease. According to a 15-year study of 10,000 youths in Boston, parents are right. Smoking does stunt at least one aspect of a child's growth. The more cigarettes young people smoked, the greater the damage to their lung growth and breathing capacity (Brody, 1996b).

Frequent users of legal or illegal substances can be considered at high risk for many unnecessary life problems (Dryfoos, 1990). To the extent that teenagers view themselves as immortal, they will ignore information that links cigarette smoking to lung cancer and heart disease. "I guess if I really wanted to,

I think I could stop. Maybe when I get older or have kids or something" (15-year-old female quoted by Verhovek, 1995, p. 24). By young adulthood, she may be trapped in a nicotine habit.

## Social Factors

It is difficult to discourage adolescent curiosity about cigarettes, alcohol, and other drugs when family members or other admired adults condone or model the use of these substances (Andrews, Hops, Ary, Tildesley, & Harris, 1993; Stanton, Currie, Oei, & Silva, 1996). Wren (1996) quotes a 16-year-old Massachusetts girl named Nicole: "I smoke weed with my dad. Obviously, he feels fine about it. Since I started smoking weed, we've gotten closer. I smoke every single day" (p. A20). Referring to President Clinton, Nicole observes, "He said that if he tried it again, he'd inhale" (p. A20). Parents are a major influence on the initiation and maintenance of young adolescents' substance use (Andrews et al., 1993; Foxcroft & Lowe, 1995; Stephenson, Henry, & Robinson, 1996). Parents who use drugs, including alcohol and cigarettes, will have more difficulty convincing their children that these substances are potentially dangerous.

Drug taking (and addiction) of parents, siblings, and peers is one of the best predictors of adolescent drug use (Anderson & Henry, 1994; Chassin, Curran, Hussong, & Colder, 1996; Denton & Kampfe, 1994; Duncan, Duncan, & Hops, 1996; Stephenson et al., 1996; Tang et al., 1996; Wills et al., 1996). Conversely, adolescent closeness to parents and peers who do not use drugs appears to "protect" them from experimenting with legal and illegal drugs (Anderson & Henry, 1994; Coombs, Paulson, & Richardson, 1991; Dinges & Oetting, 1993; Halebsky, 1987; McDonald & Towberman, 1993; Shucksmith et al., 1997; Thorne & DeBlassie, 1985; Turner, Irwin, & Millstein, 1991).

## First-Time Use

> [Smoking cigarettes] mellows me out. The first time I tried it, last year, I was like, "This is totally gross." I was coughing, and I turned green, and I thought I was going to throw up. So I had to learn to like it.
> (16-year-old girl, quoted by Verhovek, 1995, p. 24)

Since drugs like alcohol and cigarettes are toxic, first contact frequently is unpleasant, causing feelings of dizziness and nausea. Given the potentially destructive consequences of habitual use of legal and illegal substances, it is remarkable that so many young people overcome their initial aversion and continue to use them into adulthood (Ferguson & McKinlay, 1991; Hartnagel, 1996; Horan & Straus, 1987; Tang et al., 1996). *Thought Question: What factors might lead someone to continue to smoke cigarettes or drink alcohol after an unpleasant first experience?*

Despite increasing knowledge about their adverse effects, first use of alcohol, tobacco, and other drugs is occurring at younger ages. According to the National Institute on Drug Abuse, there is an increase in use of marijuana, cocaine, and LSD among the youngest teenagers. Although the percentage of

13- and 14-year-olds who use drugs still is relatively small, rehabilitation specialists worry that the drug-using behavior of these young people may signal the reversal of previously improving trends. Experimentation sometimes begins as early as elementary school. The fact that drug use can occur at such an early age suggests that drug prevention programs should begin in the earliest grades and continue through the senior year in high school (Treaster, 1993).

First-time users usually obtain illegal substances from peers who already use and implore them to partake (Alberts, Hecht, Miller-Rassulo, & Krizek, 1992). After a first experience, some youth continue to use a drug occasionally and a relatively small number become heavy users or abusers (Petraitis et al., 1995). Members of a drug-using peer group tend to use the same drug (Dinges & Oetting, 1993). Factors that predict substance use are similar across gender and ethnicity (Flannery, Vazsonyi, & Rowe, 1996).

Fortunately, most young people who experiment with drugs during their teenage years do not become regular users or abusers. As one Texas teenager put it, "Man, you have to be some kind of idiot to be putting that crap in your lungs" (quoted by Verhovek, 1995, p. 24). Use of a particular drug does not inevitably lead to use of harder drugs, although multiple-drug abusers usually follow a predictable path, beginning with drugs like nicotine and alcohol and progressing to increasingly dangerous and controlled substances (Kandel, 1975).

### Risk Factors

As we have seen, substance abuse usually is part of a larger cluster of antisocial and self-destructive behaviors that often go back to early childhood (Dobkin et al., 1995). A thorough understanding of any behavior requires an analysis of the social environment and cultural milieu surrounding the behavior, more immediate contextual and social factors, personal dispositions, the behavior itself and its consequences, and the interaction of these factors (Petraitis, Flay, & Miller, 1996). Risk factors for substance abuse include availability of drugs, economic deprivation, early first use, low value placed on achievement, poor school performance (especially in junior high school), dropping out, inadequate parental warmth and guidance, parents and peers who use drugs, family conflict, attention deficit disorder, and stressful family life (Beman, 1995; Brook, Whiteman, Balka, & Cohen, 1995; Doherty & Needle, 1991; Dryfoos, 1990; Hawkins, Catalano, & Miller, 1992; Jenkins, 1996; Segal & Stewart, 1996; Stephenson et al., 1996; Thompson, Riggs, Mikulich, & Crowley, 1996; Thorlindsson & Vilhjalmsson, 1991).

Teenagers offer a variety of reasons for their drug use, including wanting to feel that they belong to a group, reputation enhancement, coping with stress, feeling better about themselves, conviviality, relaxation, pleasure, and increasing creativity. Rather than viewing drug use in moral or social terms, many users believe that their decision is personal (Ennett & Bauman, 1994; Novacek, Raskin, & Hogan, 1991; Nucci, Guerra, & Lee, 1991; Odgers, Houghton, & Douglas, 1996).

## Marijuana

*Some girls in my school say that they smoke pot but really I know that they don't. For some strange reason they think it's cool. Yeah, killing your brain cells is really smart. I don't want you to think I'm a nerd or nothing, I'm in the popular crowd. I just don't do all the things they do—but we still hang out.*

*(16-year-old girl)*

Since the 1960s, marijuana use has been a symbol of adolescent rebellion. Although many teenagers consider marijuana to be relatively harmless compared to crack cocaine or heroin, marijuana today is much more potent (and expensive) than it used to be. "If you're smoking marijuana, you're not using drugs. I don't think that marijuana is the same thing as using cocaine or heroin" (17-year-old high school senior quoted by Wren, 1996, p. A20). Only about 5% of high school students report smoking marijuana daily, but use of the drug is increasing. At some schools, students will tell you that "everybody smokes."

Early marijuana use is associated with later substance use, dropping out of school, deviant behavior, and greater rebelliousness (Fergusson, Lynskey, & Horwood, 1996a). Marijuana use has been attributed to inability to cope with rejection, loss of motivation to conform to social norms, peer use, and especially peer reinforcement of marijuana use (Johnson & Kaplan, 1991). Regular users tend to be male, more socially alienated and lonely, defiant, emotionally distressed, and less interested in achievement than nonusers (Brook et al., 1989; Henneberger, 1994; Page & Cole, 1991).

## Cigarettes

According to the U.S. Food and Drug Administration, 1 million children take up smoking each year. Thus, each day, about 3,000 adolescents begin to smoke (Brody, 1996b; Feder, 1996a). There has been a surge in cigarette smoking among teenagers during this decade (Feder, 1997; Hilts, 1995b). Nineteen percent of adolescent girls and 17% of adolescent boys smoke cigarettes. About 20% of high school seniors smoke every day. Almost all adults who smoke began smoking as teenagers. Cigarette manufacturers spend about 5 billion dollars a year advertising their product. Advertising (often using sports heroes and cartoon characters) and packaging (such as wine coolers in "soft drink" cans) make substance use more attractive to children (Hilts, 1991). Those who succumb can expect to spend $55,000 over their lifetime to support a pack a day habit (Herring, 1997).

Many teenagers deny that they smoke because of advertising. They insist that they smoke because their friends do or because they see their parents smoke (Verhovek, 1995). Exposure to smokers, family permissiveness about smoking, low family cohesion, beliefs about smokers and viewing oneself as a cigarette smoker increase the odds that teenagers will take up the habit (Aloise-Young & Hennigan, 1996; Doherty & Allen, 1994; Lloyd, Lucas, & Fernbach, 1997; Prince, 1995; Thrush, Fife-Schaw, & Breakwell, 1997). Most teenagers who smoke purchase their own cigarettes (Feder, 1996b).

According to a 1993 survey by the Institute for Social Research at the University of Michigan, white teenagers are five times more likely to smoke cigarettes than African-American teenagers. Although the latter are as susceptible to peer influence as white teenagers when it comes to cigarette smoking (Botvin, Epstein, Schinke, & Diaz, 1994), many have come to view smoking cigarettes as "a white thing" (Hilts, 1995a). However, in 1996, a Federal Centers for Disease Control and Prevention survey reported a sharp increase in smoking among young African-American males. The overall percentage of teenagers 17 or younger who reported smoking during the month before the survey was about 35%, up from 30% in 1993 and 27.5% in 1991. In a separate study, Native-Indian adolescents in Canada showed higher rates and more frequent use of cigarettes and marijuana than their white counterparts (Gfellner, 1994).

Cigarette smoking has become quite appealing to young adolescent females (Van Roosmalen & McDaniel, 1992), especially as a way of suppressing appetite (Lawson, 1994). Until the 1960s, most cigarette smokers were male. (Over half of adult men smoked in the 1960s. Now 27% do.) Young female teenagers matched and then surpassed their male counterparts in this habit (Foxcroft & Lowe, 1995). As a result, the incidence of lung cancer among women has increased fivefold over the past 30 years (American Cancer Society, 1993). Although tobacco use continues to decline among adult women, teenage girls seem to be less concerned about the dangers of smoking.

## Alcohol

*My mom thinks I'm going to be an alcoholic like my father. My mom perceives me as a drunk. I try to keep it hidden from her. I'm not open about it at all, although it would make things easier. I just lie. I didn't start drinking until my junior year in high school. My friends influenced me. Now I drink because I like it. I remember when I drank every day for a year and then I stopped. I had the worst shakes and was always depressed.*

*(18-year-old male)*

Alcohol remains the drug of choice among high school and college students, even though the legal drinking age is 21 years in all states (Newcomb & Bentler, 1989). Like the young man quoted above, the drinkers who need the most help are those who started drinking earliest. Those who wait to drink until they are away at college also tend to drink compulsively.

Unlike most adult imbibers, a significant number of teenagers drink alcohol to get drunk. One study revealed that 44% of all college students in the United States had engaged in binge drinking at least once in the 2 weeks before the survey (Honan, 1995a). The survey's principal investigator, Dr. Henry Wechsler, defined a binge drinker as a male who reports consuming five or more drinks in a row, or a female who reports consuming four or more drinks in a row, in the past 2 weeks. Binge drinking is surprisingly common among college students, especially those who live in fraternity houses. A study by the Harvard School of Public Health reported that 86% of fraternity men and 80% of sorority women are binge drinkers (Honan, 1995b). Many colleges are experimenting with policies that prohibit alcohol use in school-based fraternities.

A Columbia University study released in June 1994 reported that 35% of the 58,000 college women polled in 1993 said they drank to get drunk. They claimed that they drank to relieve academic pressure and to fit into campus life. Unfortunately, abusive drinking by women leads to an increased likelihood of rape, violence, accidents, and contracting venereal diseases and AIDS. Just as cigarette smoking gradually is becoming stigmatized, so (we hope) is drinking to the point of getting "wrecked" (Barringer, 1991).

Schulenberg and his colleagues identify being male, having low self-efficacy, and drinking primarily to get drunk as risk factors for increased binge drinking over time (Schulenberg, Wadsworth, O'Malley, Bachman, & Johnston, 1996). There is some evidence that college students are becoming less willing to risk their lives, health, and driver's licenses by drinking to excess (Celis, 1995; Gose, 1995; Honan, 1995b).

Alcohol use varies with ethnicity. Several studies report particularly high rates of alcohol use among Hispanic and white adolescents. Alva and Jones (1994) speculate that heightened alcohol use among Hispanic teenagers reflects their attempt to cope with the stress of acculturation (leaving friends behind in their country of origin, learning a new language, generational conflicts, and sharing a home with too many people). These investigators had 207 Hispanic students in a Los Angeles public junior high school complete a questionnaire including demographic information, personal attributes, and alcohol-related attitudes and behavior. Alcohol users were more likely to report the following stressors: getting into trouble, feeling pressured by friends to get into fights, poor communication with parents, being teased because of their English, and feeling excluded from school because of their cultural background. Hispanic adolescents with positive self-concepts were least likely to use alcohol or have friends who used it.

## Prevention of Drug Abuse

Legal and illegal drugs will be with us as long as their sale is profitable. As with all adjustment problems, prevention is the most sensible strategy for addressing drug use and abuse (Kolata, 1996). Since the 1960s, drug use has been losing some of its glamour among older teenagers. Advertising campaigns and school presentations by recovering addicts apparently have helped students recognize the risk of drugs like cocaine and crack, if not of cigarettes and alcohol. It makes sense for parents and teachers to use positive means to discourage drug use—for example, by providing accurate information about the effects of drugs (St. Pierre, Mark, Kaltreider, & Aikin, 1997). Parents also should listen to their children's points of view and make it safe for their children to tell them the truth about their experimentation. Although some parents claim that they don't want to know about their children's drug use, if we are not aware of what our children are doing, we lose valuable opportunities to let them know why we object to high-risk behaviors (Beck, Scaffa, Swift, & Ko, 1995). *Thought Question: How should parents respond when a child admits to experimenting with a controlled substance like alcohol or marijuana?*

## SELECTED ADJUSTMENT PROBLEMS

### Loneliness

*Study Question: Why might adolescents feel lonelier than elementary school children?*

Most people want and need to feel close to other people. During the teenage years, the desire for intimacy and self-disclosure increases but often is unrequited (Brage, Meredith, & Woodward, 1993). Feeling disconnected from others is heightened by adolescents' attempts to distance themselves from family members. In any case, loneliness is associated with other, more serious adjustment problems, including drug abuse, delinquency, depression, and suicide (Culp, Clyman, & Culp, 1995).

In contrast to solitude (the desire to be alone), loneliness reflects a dissatisfaction with the quality or quantity of one's social contacts. National surveys suggest that 20–50% of adolescents feel moderately lonely at least some of the time. Sixty-six percent of the high school and middle school students in one study identified loneliness as a problem (Culp et al., 1995). A smaller number report feeling very lonely and depressed. Girls usually report feeling lonelier than do boys. Rejection, isolation, conflict with peers, and disappointing romantic experiences contribute to these feelings (Ammaniti, Ercolani, & Tambelli, 1989; Woodward & Kalyan-Masih, 1990).

Like lonely adults, lonely adolescents typically have low self-esteem (especially males) and high social anxiety (especially females) (Brage et al., 1993). Many are deficient in the social skills necessary to form and maintain close personal relationships—for example, the ability to assess the appropriateness of their actions and learn from their mistakes. They see themselves as unattractive and unlikable. Rather than seek out the company of others, they withdraw into solitary activities such as reading, watching television, or listening to music (Brage et al., 1993; Carr & Schellenbach, 1993; Inderbitzen-Pisaruk, Clark, & Solano, 1992).

Unlike lonely teenagers, nonlonely teenagers deliberately seek the company of others. They extend their social contacts, keep busy, and try to think constructively about their social status. Effective interventions help adolescents evaluate their thoughts about loneliness and foster social support and social skills (Brage et al., 1993; Roscoe & Skomski, 1989; Woodward & Kalyan-Masih, 1990).

### Depression

*Study Question: What role does hopelessness play in adolescent depression?*

Most adolescents, although not totally carefree, cope adequately with their everyday life problems. However, about one in three become increasingly discouraged and hopeless with each successive stressor. The alarming rate of teenage suicide attempts (discussed below) has led some observers to conclude that growing up is becoming more difficult and that feelings of hopelessness and alienation are more widespread than we would like to believe (McLaughlin et al., 1996). Others point to the weakening of family bonds, competition in school and in the job market, and less opportunity to find meaning in adolescent life. Also, the "tools" of self-destruction, guns and pills, are more widely available than ever (Clark & Mokros, 1993; Kazdin, 1990).

Biological models of depression cite the possible role of a genetically based vulnerability for the expression of depressive disorders (Pike, McGuire, Hetherington, Reiss, & Plomin, 1996; Riddle & Cho, 1989). Social learning models attribute adolescent depression to low levels of contingent reinforcement, hostile parenting practices, parental depression, or dysfunctional parent–adolescent relationships and communication (e.g., Fergusson, Horwood, & Lynskey, 1995; Ge, Best, Conger, & Simons, 1996; Greenberger & Chen, 1996; Lasko et al., 1996; Slesnick & Waldron, 1997).

Learned helplessness models suggest that depression reflects beliefs that negative outcomes will occur that are beyond the control of the individual. Many adolescents think in ways that make them less tolerant of frustration (Marcotte, 1996). Other cognitive models attribute depression to gender-typed or pessimistic thinking patterns and self-defeating beliefs (Hammond & Romney, 1995; Hart & Thompson, 1996; Lau & Lau, 1996; Marcotte, 1996; Mikulincer, 1994; Reynolds, 1995).

During adolescence, there is a noticeable increase in the occurrence of depressive disorders, including depressed mood, depressive syndromes, and clinical depression. As common as these disorders are (affecting 4–12% of adolescents), they often go undetected and untreated (Reynolds, 1995). It is helpful to distinguish between typical adolescent moodiness and the much more intense pattern of symptoms that characterizes **clinical depression** (Brooks-Gunn & Petersen, 1991; Cantwell & Baker, 1991; Stanley, Dai, & Nolan, 1997).

Like adult depression, adolescent depression refers to a constellation of thoughts, behaviors, and emotions, including feeling sad, tired, lonely, unloved, and unworthy, crying, self-consciousness, and worrying. Depressed adolescents display little interest in and derive minimal pleasure from their daily lives. Changes in eating and sleeping patterns and complaints about physical illness also are typical of this syndrome (Kazdin, 1990; Lewinsohn, Gotlib, & Seeley, 1997; Petti & Larson, 1987; Reynolds, 1995). Clinical depression, the most serious depressive disorder, includes frequent depressed mood and irritability, sleep and eating problems, loss of energy, feelings of worthlessness, and thoughts of suicide (Petersen et al., 1993). Adolescent depression often coexists with conduct disorders, substance abuse, anxiety disorders, and suicidal thoughts (Kearney & Silverman, 1995; Reynolds, 1995; Scafidi, Field, Prodromidis, & Rahdert, 1997). (See Table 13-8.)

Most studies report that adolescent girls are two to three times more likely than adolescent boys to suffer from depression, although most individuals learn to express their emotional distress in gender-related ways (Buntaine & Costenbader, 1997; Hart & Thompson, 1996). Girls develop depressive symptoms in response to stressful life events, beginning at about age 13 (Ge, Lorenz, Conger, Elder, & Simons, 1994).

Teenage depression is persistent and recurrent and is a precursor to adult depression. Although mild depression during the teenage years often goes unrecognized and untreated, its link to suicide and other self-destructive behav-

**Table 13-8 Common Signs of Depression**

Feeling sad, tired, lonely, unloved, and unworthy

Crying, self-consciousness, and worrying

Little interest in and minimal pleasure from daily life

Changes in eating and sleeping patterns

Complaints about physical illness

Decline in school performance

Decline in personal habits and dress

Loss of self-confidence

Self-medicating with alcohol and other drugs

**Clinical Depression**

Frequent depressed mood and irritability

Difficulty with concentration and decision making

Chronic sleep and eating problems

Loss of energy

Feelings of worthlessness

Thoughts of suicide

iors has brought it considerable public attention during the past few years (Connelly, Johnston, Brown, Mackay, & Blackstock, 1993; Ehrenberg, Cox, & Koopman, 1990, 1991; Roberts & Sobhan, 1992). Antisocial behavior in girls also is linked to depressive symptomatology (Pakiz et al., 1992). Although the use of antidepressant medication to treat adolescent depression has not been very successful, several types of psychotherapeutic interventions alleviate depressive symptoms (Marcotte, 1997; Petersen et al., 1993).

Depression typically is precipitated by a series of painful encounters that diminish self-esteem and overwhelm a teenager's coping resources. The greater the number of stressors, the more intense the depressed mood. Having a depressed parent is a major risk factor (Davies & Windle, 1997; Downey & Coyne, 1990; Fergusson et al., 1995). Sources of stress include pressure from parents to achieve in school, perceived parental unavailability and rejection, family discord, parental divorce, low popularity, fear of failure, the onset of puberty and emergence of adult sexuality, negative body image, and the loss of a close family member or friend. Depressed teenagers (especially girls) blame themselves for their life problems and have poor or disrupted social support networks. Use of alcohol or other drugs increases their feeling of helplessness (Adams & Adams, 1991; Davis & Katzman, 1997; Goodyer, Cooper, Vize, & Ashsby, 1993; King, Akiyama, & Elling, 1996; O'Brien et al., 1991; Robertson & Simons, 1989; Rubin et al., 1992; Smart & Walsh, 1993; Youngs et al., 1990).

Although a series of negative events can trigger depression, positive encounters and a positive outlook improve coping ability (Lau & Lau, 1996; Siegel & Brown, 1988). One important buffer against adolescent depression is a well-developed social support system, especially close relationships with family members and friends (Bennett & Bates, 1995). As noted, depressed adolescents (especially girls) often have depressed parents (Gallimore & Kurdek, 1992). It is not known whether parent–child shared depression is biological or psychosocially induced or in which direction it operates (parent to child, child to parent). Perhaps constant bickering and strife in a family depress all family members. Given that the presence of a depressed parent seems to be a key predictor of adolescent depression, prevention efforts should be directed to such families (Petersen et al., 1993).

Based on their study of high school students, Rubin et al. (1992) report that for boys and girls, friendship protects against depression. Adolescents were less likely to report feeling depressed when they were accepted by their peers and when their parents supported their friendships. Family closeness also served as a buffer for girls but not for boys, possibly because high school boys continued to distance themselves from family members.

Feelings of self-efficacy ("I can handle it") help adolescents cope with negative stressors. Depressed individuals usually have pessimistic explanatory styles that undermine any attempts to improve their life circumstances ("I'll never be happy"). Optimistic individuals are much less vulnerable to depressed mood (Seligman, 1990). Ehrenberg, Cox, and Koopman (1991) examined the self-efficacy status of 366 high school students, some depressed and some nondepressed. Students with high self-efficacy were the least likely to be depressed. Self-efficacy was a better predictor of depression for males than for females. For males, academic self-efficacy was the best predictor of depression status during early adolescence, general self-efficacy during middle adolescence, and social self-efficacy during late adolescence. For females, social self-efficacy best predicted depression scores during early adolescence, and physical self-efficacy was the best predictor during middle and late adolescence.

## Suicide

Jody White, age 17 years, shot himself in his bedroom on May 9, 1977.

> *In the year before his death he had been expelled from school for lying about his participation in minor vandalism in the library and transferred to a new school; he regularly used marijuana and told his mother he needed it to concentrate on his studies; he took unreasonable risks with his motorcycle and had gone through a turbulent romance. In fact, he had told his girlfriend that unless they repaired their relationship, he would kill himself. Two and a half years earlier, in November, 1974, his father, John O'Donnell White, also killed himself at home. After several separations, the Whites had been divorced eight months earlier. Mr. White returned for one more attempt at reconciliation. When his wife refused, he kissed her goodbye and shot himself.*
>
> (Brozan, 1986)

Accidental injury, homicide, and suicide are the three leading causes of death among adolescents, together accounting for 75% of the deaths in this age group. Suicide accounts for 14% of all deaths in the 15- to 19-year-old age group (National Center for Health Statistics, 1992). About 2,245 adolescents in this age group take their own lives each year in the United States. According to the Centers for Disease Control and Prevention in Atlanta, the suicide rate for children aged 10 to 14 more than doubled from 1980 to 1992. The rate increased 86% for white boys, 233% for white girls, 300% for African-American boys, and 100% for African-American girls (Leary, 1995).

Estimates of attempted suicides among persons aged 15 to 24 years range from 50,000 to 500,000 a year. Suicide is underreported, partly because many intentional deaths are reported as accidents. Although accidents are considered to be the primary cause of death in this age group, many deaths that are considered accidental really are suicides but are recorded as accidents to avoid family embarrassment (Neiger & Hopkins, 1988; Peck & Warner, 1995). Nevertheless, each year, at least 5,000 "suicide completers" (age 15–24) accomplished their deadly mission—most after previously unsuccessful attempts (Petti & Larson, 1987).

A survey by the U.S. Department of Health and Human Services of 11,419 8th and 10th graders found that 42% of the girls and 25% of the boys reported that they had seriously considered ending their lives (Dismuke, 1988). Eighteen percent of the girls and 11% of the boys claimed that they had attempted suicide. From 16% to 33% of high school and college students report thinking about taking their lives (suicidal ideation). Many of them are depressed, have low self-esteem and poor family relationships, school-related problems, and a drug habit (Culp et al., 1995; Kerr & Milliones, 1995; McLaughlin et al., 1996; Shagle & Barber, 1995). Fortunately, most do not follow through on their self-destructive thoughts (Choquet, Kovess, & Poutignat, 1993; de Man, Leduc, & Labreche-Gauthier, 1993).

The majority of those who think about and attempt suicide are female (Zhang & Jin, 1996), but most of those who succeed (80%) are male, probably because males choose more lethal means (such as guns) to end their lives. Zhang and Jin (1996) found a lower overall rate of suicide ideation for Chinese than for American college students. Rarely does a single problem or stressor precipitate thoughts of suicide. Usually, a sequence of troubling events and a moment of vulnerability are part of the equation. Not realizing the temporary nature of their troubles, some adolescents view suicide as a sure way to end their suffering. Others, in desperation, are crying out for help. Some act impulsively, giving little thought to the consequences of their actions. The all-or-none thinking of some adolescents encourages extreme actions when dealing with difficult but temporary problems (Morano, Cisler, & Lemerond, 1993; Petti & Larson, 1987; Stein, Witztum, Brom, & DeNour, 1992).

Like Jody White, many adolescents who attempt suicide report serious family problems. These include parental divorce, poor parent–adolescent communication (excessive criticism, arguing), unrealistic parental expectations, school pressures, and sexual abuse (Henry, Stephenson, Hanson, & Hargett, 1994; Vannatta, 1996). Many adolescents report feeling unwanted or believing they are a burden to their family. Intense family conflict involving the adolescent appears to generate self-derogatory feelings, which, in turn, encourage suicidal thinking (Campbell, Milling, Laughlin, & Bush, 1993; Neiger & Hopkins, 1988; Shagle & Barber, 1993, 1995; Shaunesey, Cohen, Plummer, &

**Not realizing the temporary nature of their troubles, some adolescents view suicide as a way to end their suffering.**

Berman, 1993; Woznica & Shapiro, 1990). It remains to be demonstrated that these risk factors precede the development of suicidal symptoms (Wagner, 1997).

Parental alcoholism may be a more potent factor than adolescent alcohol use (Allen, 1987). Children of parents who have committed suicide also are considered to be at special risk. Like Jody White, they are prone to adopt this extreme way of coping with temporary problems that seem unresolvable. Loss of a close relative, friend, or confidant often precipitates feelings of despair and hopelessness and suicidal ideation. Peers usually are not well enough informed about suicide to respond sensitively and appropriately to suicidal communications (Allen, 1987; Lester, 1989, 1993; Neiger & Hopkins, 1988; Norton, Durlak, & Richards, 1989).

Adolescents overwhelmed by intense feelings may not fully appreciate the irreversibility of death. "They see this as an easy way out of their troubles, a way to get even with people they have a grudge with, 'I'll die and you'll be sorry'" (Eron, quoted by Barron, 1987).

### Signs of Suicide: "I'd Be Better Off Dead"

Jody White's mother explained that he "was screaming with problems, though he was not talking about them. His appearance was different, he stopped caring about his clothes or his hair, and he was no longer concerned about making plans for the future. He did once ask another boy what it was like to be in therapy, but he didn't want to worry me by asking me" (Brozan, 1986).

Depressed behaviors, such as crying and hopelessness, as well as statements about wanting to die ("I wish I were dead," "No one cares about me"), are considered signs of suicide (Culp et al., 1995; Levy, Jurkovic, & Spirito, 1995). They are signals that 'telegraph' an impending act of self-destruction" (Allen, 1987). Although undecided about death, desperate adolescents view suicide as a way of avoiding further suffering (Blau, 1996b).

Hawton, Cole, O'Grady, and Osborn (1982) asked 50 adolescents who had attempted suicide by overdosing on drugs about their reasons for trying to end their lives. Most reported feeling lonely, angry, and ashamed before their attempts. Three reasons commonly given for suicide attempts were to relieve their suffering, escape from an impossible situation, and make people understand how desperate they felt.

Other signs include previous suicide attempts, social isolation, drug abuse, a recent suicide of a loved one, preoccupation with death, giving away personal belongings, changes in eating and sleeping patterns and school performance, and self-derogation. Families of suicidal adolescents may deny the reality of the problem, block out the threat, dissociate themselves from it, or don't really care (Allen, 1987; Garland & Zigler, 1993; Lester, 1993; Shagle & Barber, 1993; Spirito et al., 1992). Lester (1993) implores parents who observe signs of suicide to believe it, check it out, show that they care, and get help. Given the role that family conflict often plays in teenage and preadolescent suicide, family counseling should be considered (Campbell et al., 1993).

How do you target someone who might commit suicide? It is not possible to predict which adolescents are most vulnerable to self-destructive behavior. Current profiles of children at risk miss a large percentage of actual suicides (Clark & Mokros, 1993). Parents can attempt to prepare children for life's inevitable problems by teaching them problem-solving and coping skills. They also can provide children with the emotional support that we all require during difficult times. Most life problems have several possible solutions, but these do not occur automatically to adolescents or younger children. Schools can offer programs that help teenagers develop skills for coping with life problems. Such programs also should help parents, teachers, and students recognize the warning signals listed below (Blau, 1996b; Brennan, 1993; Garland & Zigler, 1993; Henry, Stephenson, Hanson, & Hargett, 1993). (See Table 13-9.)

Fortunately, the vast majority of adolescents learn to deal effectively with their problems. The signs of suicide are not subtle. Parents would have to exercise extreme denial to avoid noticing them. It happens every day.

## Table 13-9  Signs of Suicide

| | |
|---|---|
| Depressed behaviors, such as crying and hopelessness | Preoccupation with death |
| | Giving away personal belongings |
| Statements about wanting to die | Changes in eating and sleeping patterns and school performance |
| Previous suicide attempts | |
| A recent suicide of a loved one | Self-derogation |
| Social isolation | Unusual personality changes |
| Drug abuse | |

## ABUSE OF ADOLESCENTS

*Study Question: Why might adolescents be more vulnerable to abuse than younger children?*

Although adolescents are twice as likely as preschoolers to be maltreated by family members, their plight has not received the same degree of attention from the media or child protective services. Lacking the dependency of younger children and the independence of adults, teenagers are relatively defenseless in the face of physical, emotional, and sexual abuse. Most come to the attention of authorities, if at all, through disruptive behavior or other "cries" for help, such as running away (Kurtz, Kurtz, & Jarvis, 1991; Rotheram-Borus, Mahler, Koopman, & Langabeer, 1996).

There is no one particular cause of abuse. Maltreatment of children and adolescents is determined by a variety of factors operating over time. Belsky (1993) suggests that child abuse occurs in a family when family stressors outweigh family supports but acknowledges that "there are many pathways to child abuse and neglect" (p. 413).

Reports of sexual abuse have increased since the enactment of the Child Abuse and Neglect Prevention Treatment Act in 1974. Victims and caregivers are reluctant to report acts of abuse because of the social stigma attached to it. Adolescent victims of abuse are vulnerable because they are afraid of getting into trouble for what has happened to them. They are also afraid that they will not be believed or that the perpetrator will retaliate. Most are sexually inex-

Like younger children, teenagers are relatively defenseless in the face of physical, emotional, and sexual abuse.

perienced and do not know how to resist unwanted advances, especially by their own relatives (Rickel & Hendren, 1993).

Sexual abuse and incest are most likely to occur during preadolescence, between ages 9 and 12 years. However, disclosures are most likely in the 12- to 15-year age group. Usually, older males take advantage of younger female relatives. Watkins and Bentovim (1992) estimate that one boy is abused for every two to four girls. Abuse of adolescent girls usually begins during childhood and continues for many years.

The specific effects of abuse depend partly on the relationship between perpetrator and adolescent and partly on the frequency and duration of abuse. Abuse usually is not limited to a single encounter. Incest, in particular, usually persists for years and probably is underreported. Pregnancy and venereal disease sometimes are the first indications of incest. The psychological impact of incest increases with the age of the child, her closeness to the abuser, and the number of abusers (Farrell, 1988).

Older children probably are harmed more than younger children because they understand and are ashamed of the sexual nature of the assault. Male victims often are reluctant to admit being abused because they fear being branded homosexual. They feel stigmatized, humiliated, and outraged. Effects of sexual abuse include running away from home, promiscuity, multiple personality development, and many emotional and behavioral problems (see Spotlight • Running Away and Teenage Prostitution). Abused boys are at increased risk of aggressive actions, substance abuse, confusion about their sexual identity, inappropriate assertion of their masculinity, abusing others, and suicidality (Farrell, 1988; Fisher, 1985; Gordon & Gilgun, 1987; Watkins & Bentovim, 1992).

### SPOTLIGHT • Running Away and Teenage Prostitution

Each year, hundreds of thousands of teenagers in the United States run away from a family life characterized by conflict, rejection, neglect, and inconsistent parenting (Crespi & Sabatelli, 1993). Most teenagers who leave home are escaping from multiproblem families and a range of personal problems that even adults would find overwhelming. Many adolescent prostitutes report that they left home following sexual abuse by their parents or other adults (Seng, 1989). Parents of runaways often are preoccupied with their own needs or so consumed by marital conflict that they overlook their children's needs (Crespi & Sabatelli, 1993).

On the streets, vulnerable teenagers face manipulation and exploitation by adults who entice them into drug use and prostitution (Rotheram-Borus et al., 1996; Ferrell, 1997). Some maltreated youths go to runaway centers for help. They need protection from further exploitation and placement in a safe, stable living environment. They also need to be treated for abuse and family problems (Kurtz et al., 1991; Windle, 1989).

Seng (1989) studied a sample of 14-year-old white, female teenagers who were sexually abused, involved in prostitution, or both. Many were de-

Teenage prostitutes typically have low self-esteem and histories of family violence and/or drug abuse.

pressed and potentially suicidal, had poor self-images, and reported histories of domestic violence and/or drug and alcohol abuse. Sexually abused children came from more troubled families than did the teenagers involved in prostitution. Those who were prostitutes were much more likely to have run away from home and were more likely to abuse drugs and alcohol than were those who were sexually abused. Seng concluded that running away links sexual abuse to prostitution.

## PREVENTION AND
## THE PROBLEM-BEHAVIOR SYNDROME

What can be done to prevent or at least reduce the risk of the cluster of problem behaviors described in this chapter? There is little consensus on this topic (Kolata, 1996), although prevention of problem behavior makes far more sense than treatment, which is much more costly in human and economic terms (Butterfield, 1996c; Hamburg, 1989; Martin, 1996).

Prevention programs differ in their objectives, their focus, the populations they address, and the settings in which they operate. Regarding objectives, we can distinguish different levels of prevention. **Primary prevention** attempts to prevent the occurrence of new cases of a disorder or dysfunction by reducing risk factors or increasing protective factors. **Secondary prevention** (or treatment) attempts to minimize the severity, duration, and manifestation of problem behavior at its earliest stages. **Tertiary prevention** (or rehabilitation) attempts to minimize the effects of the dysfunction once it is established, that is, prevent it from getting worse (Kazdin, 1993).

Programs also differ in their main focus. Some interventions try to cultivate young people's social competence and problem-solving skills (Thompson, Bundy, & Wolfe, 1996); others try to minimize or prevent a specific problem behavior like drug use or unwanted pregnancy (Zavela, Battistich, Dean, Flores, Barton, & Delaney, 1997). Psychotherapy with adolescents appears to be more effective when specific problem behaviors are targeted (Berger & Shechter, 1996; Richards & Sullivan, 1996; Weisz, Weiss, Han, Granger, & Morton, 1995). (See Figure 13-2.) Multidimensional family therapy (MDFT) attempts to improve the personal functioning of parents and adolescents, parent–adolescent

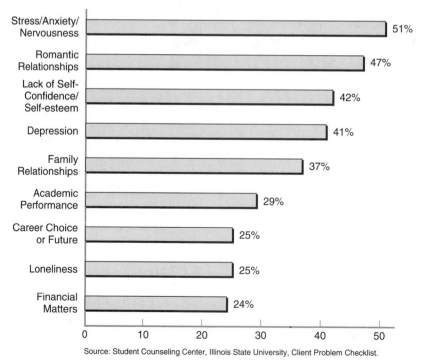

STUDENTS' TOP REASONS FOR SEEKING COUNSELING

These data were compiled from Illinois State University's Client Problem Checklist and reflect national trends in the reasons students seek counseling, according to psychologist Robert Gallagher, PhD, of the University of Pittsburgh's Counseling Center.

Source: Student Counseling Center, Illinois State University, Client Problem Checklist.

**FIGURE 13.2 Students' reasons for seeking counseling. (From Murray, 1996c)**

Box 13-2
Types of
Prevention
Programs

1. **Social skills training.** Enhancing adolescent competence, including self-expression skills, assertiveness and peer pressure resistance strategies, and pregnancy prevention.
2. **Community-based alternatives.** Private and public community agencies that attempt to alleviate the burden on families and schools of addressing adolescent problems. They include youth organizations like Scouts and Boys and Girls Clubs.
3. **Organized youth sports.** The use of organized sports activities as a way of contributing to adolescents' social development and self-confidence.
4. **Youth volunteer service opportunities.** Encouraging young people to help others, perhaps by tutoring or working with the aged.
5. **Peer helping programs.** Training young people to help their peers as mentors or as big brothers and sisters.
6. **Mentor programs.** Increasing contact with adult identification figures who try to help adolescents succeed in school and other adult-type roles.
7. **Work training programs.** Providing adolescents with work experience to ease the transition to adult roles by teaching them the skills they will need as adults.
8. **Substance abuse and pregnancy prevention programs.** Providing relevant information and counseling to high-risk teenagers.

(From Davis & Tolan, 1993)

interactions, and family interactions with nonfamily sources of influence (e.g., school personnel) (Crespi, 1996; Schmidt, Liddle, & Dakof, 1996).

Some programs are aimed at all youth, perhaps through the mass media, whereas others target a particular subgroup that is considered to be at high risk, such as underachievers (e.g., Moote & Wodarski, 1997). Some programs, such as youth hotlines, employ adolescent volunteers (Schondel, Boehm, Rose, & Marlowe, 1996). Finally, some programs are limited to a specific setting such as a school or clinic population (Switzer, Simmons, Dew, Regalski, & Wang, 1995), while others attempt to be multidimensional in scope, employing multiple community resources and addressing the diverse settings in which problem behavior originates and persists (Corvo, 1997; Dryfoos, 1990; Kazdin, 1993; St. Pierre, Mark, Kaltreider, & Aiken, 1997). (See Box 13-2.)

Prevention strategies appear to be most effective when tailored to the different ethnic, sex, and age groups according to what we know about differences among these groups (e.g., Graham, 1996). The impact of a specific intervention (e.g., role playing) on an individual is moderated by that individual's age, stage of development, family, ethnic, and cultural factors (Kazdin, 1993). When possible, programs should be tailored to meet the needs and address the circumstances of the individual adolescent (Andrews et al., 1993; Lloyd, Lucas, & Fernbach, 1997). Protective factors (discussed in an earlier section) such as problem-solving abilities and self-efficacy can be cultivated through educational interventions and through policies that support family stability (Kenny, 1996). Those who work with adolescents, either in groups or individually, certainly should have at least a minimum understanding of adolescent development (Holmbeck & Updegrove, 1995).

To be effective, programs must be very accessible to those who need them the most, especially traditionally underserved youth from poor and fragmented families, who may resist attempts to help them (Fitzgerald, 1994). Even when resources are available, many teenagers do not know where to go or what to do when they are troubled (Boehm, Chessare, Valko, & Sager, 1991; Culp et al., 1995; Windle, Miller-Tutzauer, Barnes, & Welte, 1991).

The most popular antidrug program, Drug Abuse Resistance Education (DARE), taught by specially trained police officers, teaches children how to resist drugs. The program is available in most of the country's schools from kindergarten to 12th grade. But researchers have failed to find long-term behavioral effects of the program (Kolata, 1996). Merely providing information to high-risk youth appears to have little influence. Further, programs aimed at one particular problem behavior, whether drug use, unwanted pregnancy, or staying in school, have not been very effective. To be effective, programs must recognize the interrelatedness of problem behaviors and their common origin in the social institutions children inhabit, especially the school, family, peer group, and community (Mills, 1987; Sullivan & Wilson, 1995; Zigler et al., 1992). Newer prevention models are multidimensional, emphasizing family, school, and community factors (Blau, 1996b; Palmer & Liddle, 1996).

A "war on drugs" will not be effective if it ignores most of the antecedent factors that dispose youth to drug use, especially poverty, discrimination, and family conflict (Dryfoos, 1990). Teenagers might use drugs, for example, for pleasure, because of peer pressure, as a way of rebelling, or simply out of curiosity. If using drugs is a means of coping with stress, trying to eliminate drug use without addressing the source of stress is bound to fail.

Since many of the problems we have surveyed in this chapter are rooted in early childhood experiences, prevention efforts must begin as early as possible and be as comprehensive as possible (O'Donnell, Hawkins, Catalano, Abbott et al., 1995). This means reducing known risk factors and nurturing those protective factors that provide resilience and encourage competence and self-efficacy (Kazdin, 1993). Suicide prevention efforts should emphasize family

**Table 13.10  Characteristics of Successful Intervention Programs**

| | |
|---|---|
| Early identification and intervention | Program located in school |
| Accessible to those who need them the most | Social skills training |
| | Use of peer interventions |
| Intensive individualized attention | Involvement of parents |
| Recognize the interrelatedness of problem behaviors and their common origin in the social institutions children inhabit | Career planning and preparation |
| | Sensitivity to cultural diversity |
| Communitywide multiagency collaboration | Maintained over time |

support and competence-building interventions that address a wide range of adolescent problems. The efficacy of crisis intervention services such as telephone hotlines staffed by trained volunteers remains to be demonstrated (Garland & Zigler, 1993).

As noted previously, early childhood intervention programs show promise in preventing juvenile delinquency. Programs such as Head Start that reach children early in life seem to reduce factors that increase the risk of school failure, drug use, and delinquency (Kazdin, 1993; Zigler et al., 1992). Staff training is crucial so that the prevention program is carried out as planned. Program evaluation is important to determine whether the short- and long-term goals of the intervention are being achieved (Kazdin, 1993).

Based on a review of about 100 programs designed to change the behavior of high-risk adolescents, Dryfoos (1990) suggests that the following components increase the likelihood of success: (1) intensive individualized attention (high-risk children are assigned to a responsible adult, such as a counselor or family worker, who addresses the child's needs); (2) communitywide multiagency collaboration, which assumes primarily that several different programs and services are needed within each community; (3) early identification and intervention; (4) programs located in schools; (5) social skills training, which involves teaching children about their risky behaviors and giving them the skills they need to cope with peer pressure and make good decisions about their futures; (6) use of peers in interventions; (7) involvement of parents; (8) career planning and preparation; (9) sensitivity to cultural diversity; and (10) maintaining prevention efforts over time. (See Table 13-10.)

## SUMMARY

**1.** Although the majority of adolescents are well adjusted, serious psychological disorders occur more frequently during adolescence than during other life stages. Large numbers of adolescents, perhaps 10–20% of all adolescents, are at risk of developing serious adjustment problems, including depression, antisocial behavior, and substance abuse. If ignored or untreated, these problems are likely to persist into adulthood.

**2.** Serious behavior and emotional problems prevent young people from working on normative developmental challenges such as creating an adult identity and developing conventional moral values and behaviors.

**3.** It is sometimes difficult to distinguish normal behavior from problem behavior, partly because most adolescents occasionally engage in behavior that adults disapprove of, such as experimenting with drugs. Thus, the frequency and seriousness of the problem behavior must be taken into account. Concepts like adjustment and mental health imply a sense of personal well-being, as well as the presence of personal and interpersonal strengths that allow optimal functioning.

**4.** Most adolescents experience both normative stressors (e.g., conflict with parents) and atypical stressors (e.g., poverty). Girls report more life problems than boys and may be more vulnerable to stressful life events. Each additional life problem makes it more difficult for young people to cope. Coping ability is determined by a balance of risk and protective factors. Healthy relationships with parents and peers are especially important coping resources.

**5.** Adolescents with disabilities, about 7% of early adolescents, have difficulty meeting developmental challenges such as forming close relationships with peers and separating from their families. Parental overprotectiveness and peer rejection threaten their self-confidence.

**6.** Most theories of deviant behavior attribute such behavior to faulty socialization, including lack of opportunity to develop prosocial behavior and inadequate parenting. A history of antisocial behavior usually begins with inconsistent and lax or punitive parenting practices during early childhood. Through coercive behaviors, parents and children bring out the worst in each other. Aggressive behavior spills over into peer relationships, often leading to peer rejection. Members of deviant peer groups model and reinforce antisocial behavior for each other.

**7.** Multiple problem behavior syndrome consists of a combination of interrelated behaviors and personal qualities including antisocial behavior, school failure and dropping out, susceptibility to deviant peer influence, and substance abuse.

**8.** Teenage girls seem to be especially susceptible to developing anorexia nervosa, a form of self-starvation. Bulimia nervosa, binge eating and then purging oneself through vomiting or other means, usually emerges during the college years. Eating disorders partly reflect the cultural ideal that females with lean bodies are happier and more popular. Up to 10% of anorectics are males, many of whom are involved in sports that require a lean body. Additional risk factors for eating disorders include distorted body image, interpersonal problems, and low self-esteem. Counseling may help, but relapses are not uncommon.

**9.** During adolescence, especially in males, there is a substantial increase in a variety of antisocial behaviors, including vandalism, stealing, and lying. Forty-three percent of all serious crimes are committed by people under the age of 21. Antisocial and delinquent behaviors usually reflect a troubled family environment where parents provide harsh, inconsistent discipline and inadequate supervision.

**10.** Experimenting with legal and illegal drugs has become normative behavior during adolescence. First use of drugs is occurring at increasingly younger ages. Although there are multiple pathways to substance use and abuse, risk factors that stand out include deviant behavior and stimulation seeking, peer use and peer reinforcement, parental drug use, and low family cohesion. Substance use usually is part of a cluster of antisocial and self-destructive behaviors.

**11.** Partly because of stereotypes of adolescent moodiness, mild depression during the teenage years often goes unrecognized and untreated. Its link to suicide and other self-destructive behaviors has led to increased public attention. Depression usually is precipitated by a series of painful life events that overwhelm a teenager's coping resources. Having a depressed parent is a major risk factor. A healthy support system of close relationships protects against depression.

**12.** Over 2,000 adolescents take their lives each year in the United States. Far more, perhaps one out of six teenagers, have thought about suicide without making an attempt. Most of those who think about suicide are female, but most who succeed are male because males usually select more lethal means for taking their lives. Most who attempt suicide feel helpless in the face of family or peer problems or school pressures. Families and friends often miss the warning signs.

**13.** Victims of child abuse are vulnerable because they are afraid of being blamed for what happened or of not being believed. Sexually abused teenagers are at risk of substance abuse, suicide, and other self-destructive behaviors.

**14.** The optimal strategy for all forms of adolescent maladjustment is prevention. Prevention programs differ in their objectives, focus, the populations they treat, and the settings in which they operate. They work best when they are multidimensional (taking into account family, school, and community factors) and tailored to the specific ethnic, gender, and age group and

individual at risk. Multidimensional programs that begin during the elementary school years have proven most effective.

# GLOSSARY

**Deficit model of adolescence** Assumes that maladjustment during the teenage years is inevitable and universal

**Adjustment** Mastery of one's environment and being at peace with oneself; efforts to cope with stressful life events

**Mental health** Optimal functioning or well-being in social and emotional domains

**Optimal psychological functioning** Achieved when individuals feel good about themselves, others feel good about them, and they are able to achieve goals that they and significant others value

**DSM-IV** *Diagnostic and Statistical Manual of Mental Disorders* (4th revision); used by clinicians to diagnose serious psychological problems

**Normative stressors** Stressful life events experienced by most people in a given age group

**Nonnormative stressors** Stressful life events that are not typical for a cohort group

**Problem-solving skills** Skills such as defining a problem and generating possible solutions to help resolve difficulties that pose a threat or keep us from achieving our goals

**Coping skills** A set of learned responses (actions and cognitions) that enable individuals to tolerate, avoid, or minimize stress

**Risk factors** Personal or situational factors that increase the likelihood of developing a problem behavior or a psychological disorder

**Vulnerability** Susceptibility to developing an emotional disorder or adjustment problem

**Resilience** Personal qualities and situational factors that allow individuals to adapt to difficult life circumstances

**Protective factors** Personal qualities or life circumstances that buffer the effects of chronic stressors

**Social-psychological and sociological models of deviant behavior** Emphasize the relationship between an individual and stressful social conditions, such as poverty and discrimination

**Psychoanalytic theory of deviant behavior** Attributes maladjustment to poor early relationships and unresolved emotional conflicts

**Social learning models of deviant behavior** Attribute deviant behavior to faulty learning experiences

**Trait theories of deviant behavior** Hypothesize that the temperamental or noncompliant child induces ineffective parenting, which, in turn, leads to behavioral problems

**Cognitive (attributional) models of deviant behavior** Maintain that faulty thinking styles lead to emotional and behavior problems

**Developmental trajectories** Fairly predictable sequences of behavior beginning during childhood and continuing into adulthood

**Multiple problem behavior syndrome** A combination of behaviors and personal qualities including antisocial conduct, low academic achievement, mood disorders, low self-esteem, truancy and dropping out of school, drug use, and precocious sexual activity

**Anorexia nervosa** An emotional disorder characterized by a strong desire for a thin body and a concurrent fear of gaining weight or being fat

**Bulimia nervosa** An emotional disorder characterized by a preoccupation with food and uncontrolled binge eating

**Antisocial behavior** Behavior that violates social norms

**Delinquent behaviors** A technical term that the courts apply to criminal behaviors of teenagers between the ages of 10 and 16 years that can lead to incarceration

**Adolescence-limited antisocial behavior** Antisocial behavior motivated mainly by a gap between biological maturity and social maturity. Teenagers may occasionally shoplift and use drugs, but they obey rules at home and in school

**Life-course persistent antisocial behavior** Reflects an antisocial personality structure based on neuropsychological vulnerability and a lifelong environment that encourages hostile actions. In this pattern of delinquent behavior, we observe a persistent progression of deviant behaviors from early childhood to adulthood

**Index offenses** Acts that are criminal whether they are committed by juveniles or by adults

**Status offenses** Less serious acts that are offenses only if committed by juveniles (e.g., running away)

**Conduct disorder** A psychiatric term indicating a persistent pattern of antisocial behavior that impairs the everyday functioning of adolescents and is considered uncontrollable by related adults

**Oppositional defiant disorder (ODD)** Diagnosed when adolescents frequently lose their temper, argue with adults, defy adult authority, intentionally annoy others, blame others for their mistakes, and engage in other spiteful or vindictive behaviors

**Clinical depression** Disorder in which a person is overwhelmed by feelings of sadness, hopelessness, and guilt

**Primary prevention** Programs that attempt to prevent the occurrence of new cases of a disorder or dysfunction by reducing risk factors or by increasing protective factors

**Secondary prevention (or treatment)** Programs that attempt to minimize the severity, duration, and manifestation of problem behavior at its earliest signs

**Tertiary prevention (or rehabilitation)** Programs that attempt to minimize the effects of a dysfunction once it is established

## THOUGHT QUESTIONS

**1.** Are adolescents better equipped than younger children to cope with stressful life problems?

**2.** What life circumstances make it harder for adolescents to adjust to normative life transitions?

**3.** What criteria would you use to define optimal adolescent functioning?

**4.** Is antisocial behavior during adolescence normal? Explain.

**5.** How can parents help their children become less vulnerable to stressful life events?

**6.** What kinds of family interactions increase the risk of adolescent maladjustment?

**7.** What might be the cultural origin of a distorted body image?

**8.** Is the use of psychoactive drugs always a sign of maladjustment? Explain.

**9.** Why is so much attention given to the treatment of psychological disorders and so little to prevention?

**10.** Should parents be held responsible for their children's antisocial behavior?

# SELF-TEST

1. A deficit model of adolescence assumes that maladjustment is
   a. rare
   b. inevitable
   c. treatable
   d. unmeasurable

2. Which one of the following is *not* an indicator of optimal psychological functioning?
   a. a sense of well-being
   b. achieving one's goals
   c. social acceptance
   d. financial success

3. An example of a normative stressor during adolescence is
   a. peer conflict
   b. poverty
   c. family violence
   d. serious illness

4. Girls are more likely than boys to _____ their distress.
   a. ignore
   b. internalize
   c. externalize
   d. disclose

5. An example of maladaptive coping is
   a. communicating distress
   b. seeking help
   c. avoiding thinking about a problem
   d. reappraising a problem situation

6. Susceptibility to adjustment problems is called
   a. immunity
   b. resilience
   c. vulnerability
   d. plasticity

**7.** As a group, adolescents with disabilities are

    **a.** depressed

    **b.** dependent

    **c.** frustrated

    **d.** diverse

**8.** Social learning models of deviant behavior emphasize

    **a.** reinforcement and observational learning

    **b.** inept parenting practices

    **c.** faulty thinking styles

    **d.** learning disabilities

**9.** About what percent of the adolescent population is considered at high risk for deviant behavior?

    **a.** 15

    **b.** 20

    **c.** 25

    **d.** 30

**10.** Males who try to lose weight usually are

    **a.** obese

    **b.** involved in sports that require leanness

    **c.** both a and b

    **d.** neither a nor b

**11.** Most bulimics

    **a.** binge and purge

    **b.** are normally weighted

    **c.** feel ashamed of their behavior

    **d.** all of the above

**12.** Acts that are considered criminal, regardless of the offender's age, are called

    **a.** index offenses

    **b.** status offenses

    **c.** conduct disorders

    **d.** delinquent

**13.** Most people in prison
   **a.** are poor
   **b.** are undereducated
   **c.** have relatives who have been in prison
   **d.** all of the above

**14.** Drug experimentation usually begins with
   **a.** cigarettes
   **b.** alcohol
   **c.** marijuana
   **d.** stimulants

**15.** Learned helplessness is associated with what disorder?
   **a.** loneliness
   **b.** depression
   **c.** anorexia
   **d.** bulimia

**16.** Attempting to prevent the occurrence of a disorder is called
   **a.** primary prevention
   **b.** secondary prevention
   **c.** tertiary prevention
   **d.** intervention

# EPILOGUE

Textbooks contain so much information that it is easy to become overwhelmed by details and overlook the big picture. Let's review some of this book's key themes and ideas.

**1.** Over the past several hundred years, childhood and adolescence have come to be recognized as distinct, formative periods of life. Today we view adolescence as a time of exploration and experimentation, an extended life period during which we are expected to "find ourselves" and prepare for adult life.

**2.** Because adolescents are so different from each other, no simple characterization fits all. Stereotypes such as moody and materialistic have a grain of truth, but most adolescents are hard-working, responsible, and well-adjusted.

**3.** Inventionists maintain that each society invents its own version of adolescence, or no version at all. According to this view, in industrialized societies the life stage that we call adolescence was invented as a period of preparation for demanding adult roles. School attendance in particular requires that children remain dependent on their parents financially and emotionally for an extended period. Thus, adolescence becomes a time of deferred adult privileges and deferred adult responsibilities (the moratorium arrangement).

**4.** Even in societies that do not require prolonged dependency on parents, young people still undergo physical, sexual, and cognitive changes. Thus, others claim that adolescence is not an invention at all, but a "natural" stage of development whose specific form depends on the conditions existing in a particular time and culture.

**5.** For practical purposes, we define adolescence as the life period that begins with the onset of puberty or entry into middle school and that ends when one has taken on several adult roles and is relatively self-sufficient.

**6.** Adolescence is a time of biological, emotional, cognitive, and social transitions. Simultaneous transitions are particularly stressful and motivate the learning of new problem solving and coping skills.

**7.** Most adolescents live at home with their parents, attend school, and spend their leisure time with friends, listening to music, or watching television. Many have part-time jobs or extensive household chores. They worry about school, peer acceptance, and having to choose a career. Those who are susceptible to deviant peer pressure or who lack adequate parental supervision are at greatest risk of developing antisocial or self-destructive behaviors.

**8.** Theories of development, by organizing and summarizing existing knowledge, are intended to describe, predict, and explain changes in behavior, thinking, emotions, and experience. Although there is no single, widely accepted theory of adolescent development, by taking multiple levels of influence into account, ecological-interactional models offer the most comprehensive view of adolescent development.

**9.** Most factors that affect development do not operate independently. Rather, individual influences interact with each other to produce outcomes that cannot always be anticipated.

**10.** Puberty is a period of transition from reproductive immaturity to reproductive maturity. Changes in hormone levels, bone structure, fat deposits, and sex organs begin almost simultaneously. Secondary sexual characteristics include growth of body hair, breast development, adult facial features, voice deepening, and increasing fat deposits.

**11.** Children who are prepared for their physical and sexual changes usually are more accepting of them and cope better. Girls who are given little or no information about menstruating may come to view their periods as a burden rather than as a sign of femininity. Most boys enjoy their growth and sexual maturation but those who are not prepared for their first ejaculation may experience embarrassment, guilt, or confusion.

**12.** The timing and duration of physical change have important psychological consequences for how adolescents view and feel about themselves. Although timing effects could have a direct biological origin (early maturers show different changes from late maturers), they usually reflect the interaction between timing of puberty relative to that of one's peers and adolescents' feelings about their own changes.

**13.** Early maturation generally is advantageous to boys and is either disadvantageous or has minimal effect on girls' adjustment. Early-maturing boys usually adjust best and late-maturing boys adjust most poorly. Timing has modest, temporary effects on early- and late-maturing girls. Gender differences in the effects of timing may be culture-specific.

**14.** Adolescent girls often are dissatisfied with their appearance. They tend to be self-conscious about their body shape and weight. For most girls, it is almost impossible to attain the slender, shapely body depicted in fashion magazines, movies, and television.

**15.** Although we can attribute some moodiness to hormonal fluctuations, it is probably the combination of hormonal arousal and stressful or annoying life events that trigger irritable moods and aggressive behaviors during adolescence.

**16.** Adolescents show remarkable advances in thinking and reasoning abilities. Compared to younger children, they can think about themselves and their world more flexibly, abstractly, and hypothetically. They are better able to generate and evaluate hypotheses, to think ahead, and plan for the future. How adolescents think and reason about the world has a considerable impact on their self-concept, behavior, relationships, and emotional life.

**17.** Adolescents are active participants in their own development, creating physical and social environments that shape their experiences and guide their behavior.

**18.** Despite improvements in reasoning, adolescent thinking remains flawed. Adolescents tend to be self-conscious about their appearance and personal qualities and overly concerned about how other people view them (the imaginary audience). Partly reflecting limitations in their reasoning abilities, adolescents may appear argumentative, hypocritical, indecisive, and self-centered. Many create a dramatic storyline (a personal fable) that suggests a unique destiny. They may have difficulty believing that their parents understand what they are going through.

**19.** It is likely that cognitive maturation, socialization, and contextual factors play an important role in the development of prosocial behavior during childhood and adolescence. Parental modeling of altruistic and caring behaviors is especially powerful in teaching moral standards and behaviors. Adolescents should be encouraged to evaluate their moral reasoning when it is challenged by others and to consider other viewpoints.

**20.** Self-concept refers to who we think we are. Identity is the part of self-concept that provides a feeling of coherence of personality and that gives us a sense of continuity or connectedness between past, present, and future. Adolescents construct a sense of identity in the process of making decisions, commitments, and choices in their everyday lives.

**21.** Traditionally, male identity has focused more on achievement and vocation and female identity has been more strongly linked to feelings of connectedness to others. Individuation and separation appear to be more conflictual for females. Most adolescents try to balance independence with caring and connectedness. There is considerable variation **within** each gender regarding gender identity and self-esteem.

**22.** Parent-child relationships provide the main context in which children's socialization occurs. Much of what children know about getting along with people is learned by observing and participating in family relationships. Parents exert optimal influence by staying emotionally in touch with their children, taking their ideas and issues seriously, and setting firm limits on their behavior.

**23.** Parent-adolescent conflict contributes to a realignment of family relationships as adolescents gain a greater voice in family decision making. Family disagreements are normal and healthy. However, teenagers will test their parents resolve to "stay in relationship." Gains in autonomy usually lead to decreased time with parents and temporary decreased closeness.

**24.** Adolescents inhabit a complex, overlapping network of relationships consisting of family members, peers, teachers, coaches, counselors, employers, and many others. Although their parents remain the most important people in their lives, teenagers increasingly turn to their peers for companionship, support, understanding, and fun. Adolescent peer networks include best friends, close friends, acquaintances, cliques, crowds, and eventually, romantic relationships.

**25.** Most parents realize that peer influence is mainly positive and encourage their children to have friendships. Peer groups function as a normative reference group for early and middle adolescents. Peer groups provide a safe haven for acquiring new beliefs and behaviors and experimenting with adult roles and values. Close friendships appear to be crucial to adolescents' social and emotional development. Within close relationships, teenagers learn how to trust, self-disclose, express positive and negative emotions, and become intimate with others.

**26.** The emergence of fertility and sexual desire are important elements of becoming an adult. Reproductive maturity usually emerges before most young people have the judgment and responsibility needed to make good decisions about sexual behavior.

**27.** About half of the teenagers in the United States are sexually experienced by the age of 19 years with age of first intercourse occurring at about age 16. Relatively few teenagers use condoms consistently during intercourse, resulting in about one million unwanted pregnancies each year and increasing the risk of sexually transmitted diseases including AIDS.

**28.** Adolescents say that they engage in sex out of curiosity, for pleasure, to prove their popularity, or as a means of feeling close to a partner. Early sexual experiences usually are unplanned and infrequent, and are not always satisfying. Older adolescents who have intercourse are more likely to be in committed relationships and to use contraception. Casual sex is more acceptable to males than to females.

**29.** Although use of contraceptives has increased over the past decade, many sexually active adolescents report that they rarely if ever use them. Most parents have little to say to their children about sex and romance. Comprehensive sex education programs that take into account personal, social, and cognitive factors have been the most effective in reducing unwanted pregnancies.

**30.** The United States has one of the highest rates of teenage pregnancies in the industrial world. Few pregnant females live with or marry their sexual partner or give the child up for adoption. Most are undereducated, economically disadvantaged, and lead stressful lives, especially those who lack family support. Many claim that they intended to become pregnant, perhaps as a way of gaining love or attention. Although as a group adolescent mothers are emotionally immature and not very competent parents, those with good coping resources and enthusiastic social support usually adjust well and provide adequate caregiving.

**31.** Engaged students seek and enjoy challenging work and persist during learning tasks. Disaffected students have little interest in school and avoid difficult subject matter. Parental interest and involvement, close parent-child relationships, the quality of instruction, and many other contextual factors have a significant impact on adolescents' academic performance. Achievement is self-perpetuating in that children who do well in their early schooling usually continue to succeed during secondary school and college.

**32.** To be plausible, vocational decision models must take into account individual differences in ability and interests, home and family influences, education and training, job opportunities, personal contacts, and luck. Leisure-time activities and socializing also are part of the career exploration process.

**33.** Although the majority of adolescents are well-adjusted, serious psychological disorders occur more frequently during adolescence than during other life stages. Large numbers of adolescents, perhaps 10 to 20 percent of all adolescents, are at risk for developing serious adjustment problems, including depression, antisocial behavior, and substance abuse. If ignored or untreated, these problems are likely to persist into adulthood. Serious behavior and emotional problems prevent young people from addressing normative developmental challenges such as creating an adult identity, forming intimate relationships, and developing moral values and behaviors.

# APPENDIX

# METHODS OF STUDYING ADOLESCENT DEVELOPMENT

## Preview Questions

1. Why do developmental psychologists prefer objective research methods to casual observation of behavior?
2. What is meant by objective observation?
3. What is one advantage and one limitation of each of the following research methods?

   **a.** Naturalistic observation    **d.** Survey
   **b.** Correlational study    **e.** Experiment
   **c.** Case study

4. What is a cohort effect?
5. How does cross-cultural research help us to understand our own culture?
6. What ethical guidelines govern research with children and adolescents?

## Contents

# RESEARCH ON ADOLESCENT DEVELOPMENT

*Study Question: Why should students care where the information in textbooks comes from?*

Years of teaching adolescent development have led me to conclude that students who take this course are more interested in adolescents than in research methodology. However, it behooves students in any discipline to know something about the credibility of the information they are permanently storing in memory. When citing information to prove a point, it is not enough to say "I read it in a textbook." It is surprising how rarely in life we have convincing evidence to back up our opinions and beliefs. And (I'm getting a little defensive now) there really are people who enjoy the logic of research design. You can find them thumbing through the method sections of research journals in your school library. Do not disturb them.

Obviously, not all "facts" are equally credible. Information derived from objective research is more credible than that gained through informal, everyday observation. Information gained from informal observation is more reliable than that offered by tabloid newspapers ("Adolescent gangs from Mars"). However, we cannot automatically assume that the knowledge we derive from empirical research is valid or that what we learn from informal encounters with adolescents is useless. We can have varying degrees of confidence in our observations. I give considerable credence to the findings of research studies cited in the reference section of this text, although I don't always agree with their conclusions and interpretations.

It is the nature of science to measure the events that we are interested in studying, including human behavior. We must supply evidence that our measures are valid. Although the term **validity** has several meanings, the validity of a measure generally refers to its degree of accuracy. "A perfectly valid measure assesses the trait it is supposed to assess, assesses all aspects of the trait, and assesses only that trait" (Whitley, 1996, p. 100). So, when we invoke the trait (or construct) of self-esteem, for example, we need to demonstrate that it plausibly measures how people feel about themselves. The **reliability** of a measure "is its degree of consistency: a perfectly reliable measure gives the same result every time it is applied to the same person or thing" (Ibid., p. 100). If we use the same test several days in a row to measure someone's self-esteem, it had better keep giving us the same score. If a measure is not reliable, it is not likely to be valid; however, high reliability does not guarantee validity.

The study of adolescence is interdisciplinary, with important contributions coming from anthropology, biology, sociology, psychology, psychiatry, and medicine. Every empirical discipline has rules that govern how researchers perform their investigations. These rules, and the logical strategies that are derived from them, are called its **methodology**. Researchers use a variety of observational techniques to obtain evidence (known as *data*) to help them understand developmental change. Most of the material in this text is based on carefully planned research studies that have been conducted during the past few years. In this section, I will describe and illustrate the most common methods of observation in developmental psychology using interesting studies from the adolescent research literature.

The primary source of knowledge in psychology and all other scientific disciplines is **objective observation**. The term *objective* means that we try to recognize our biases and prejudices and do everything that we can to prevent them from influencing our observations and conclusions. We try to adopt a neutral stance toward our research topic, whether it be the psychological effects of having an abortion, why so many adolescents experiment with alcohol, or how gay adolescents react to hostility and rejection. Unlike casual observers, scientists can't afford the luxury of seeing what they want or expect to see. But sometimes it happens. Scientists are human and occasionally draw conclusions that are not warranted by their observations.

There are two important qualifications that need to be made regarding research in adolescent psychology. The first is that the subject matter we are studying, adolescent development, is very complex. Imagine someone trying to account for all facets of your personality, including your thoughts, beliefs, opinions, and attitudes. What would they have to know about your heredity, family history, education, socialization, peer group experiences, and so on? Can anyone, including you, explain why you have turned out the way you have?

The other qualification is that all research methods are limited in their ability to describe the world accurately. Experienced researchers will be the first to admit that their techniques are not perfect and that their interpretations of data are just that—interpretations. You will find researchers' interpretations of their results, along with their description of the limits of their findings, in the discussion section of their research reports. The conclusions we draw from scientific studies are best viewed as tentative.

## PORTRAYING SEXUAL AWAKENING: LITERATURE VERSUS RESEARCH

Objective research methods such as experiments and surveys sacrifice much of the flavor of real-life events. We find flavor and drama in entertainment media such as soap operas and films. But how much light do they shed on real life? What does a television talk show with husbands and wives shouting at each other tell us about family life? Written literature does provide many dramatic and insightful portrayals of adolescent life. It can reveal aspects of development that would be difficult, if not impossible, to derive from more objective methods. Consider the following excerpt from a short story by Philip F. O'Connor called "The Thumping of the Grass" (Gregory, 1978).

*I was playing around the willow tree and my mother was hanging up the wash and Sylvia said over the back fence, "I'll make him lunch," and my mother said do you hear Sylvia and I said yes and she turned to Sylvia and said, "I think it's the best thing for him. He misses his brother." So I went. "She said I'm going to take a bath, do you want to watch, and I said I don't care but I did, I wanted to watch, and she filled the tub and took off her clothes and got in and the suds came up to her breasts and she told me to soap them, easy, and she put her head back on*

> *the rim and closed her eyes and said all over them, all over, and I did it all over until the sweetness came out of me, burst out of me, and flooded the room and the house and the neighborhood and the town. I fell forward into the tub and held her very tight my face between those enormous breasts. When it was over I cried.*

This provocative tale of sexual awakening in a young adolescent boy conveys thoughts and feelings that we might recognize from our own experiences or fantasies. However, such an encounter could not be orchestrated or observed by any ethical investigator. Dramatic portrayals of adolescent life in classic books like *The Catcher in the Rye* and on semi-realistic TV programs like *Friends* and *The Real World* (on MTV) shed light on what it's like to be an adolescent. TV dramatizations and movies, however, cannot provide a deeper understanding or explanation of the events depicted. Objective study and entertainment have quite different goals, although some media can inform and entertain us at the same time.

Compare the above literary passage to an objective study entitled "The Relationship Between Early Development and Psychosexual Behaviors in Adolescent Females," published in the journal *Adolescence* (Phinney, Jensen, Olsen, & Cundick, 1990). Not a very sexy title, I admit. The researchers who performed this *correlational* study wondered whether early menstruation is related to precocious sexual behavior. As discussed in Chapter 3, girls who begin puberty at a very early age (9 or 10 years old) are a bit more likely to have adjustment problems than their later-maturing peers. Early-maturing girls are not as popular as their peers, are less sociable, and may be more likely to engage in self-destructive behaviors. Is early puberty and menstruation associated with relatively early dating and precocious intercourse?

The data used to test this hypothesis were taken from a national survey of a **representative sample** of married and unmarried women in the United States. A representative sample is similar in composition to the larger population. Representative samples increase our confidence when we generalize from smaller to larger groups. Participants were asked to respond to such items as "age at menarche," "age began dating," and "age at first intercourse." An item "ever had intercourse?" allowed two possible answers, yes or no. To detect possible racial differences, the data were analyzed separately for African-American (581) and white and Hispanic (1,253) females, all between the ages of 15 and 19 years.

The study revealed that most girls began menstruating between the ages of 12 and 13 years. White and Hispanic female adolescents began dating, on the average, a year before African-Americans (15 versus 16 years). For African-American girls, first intercourse occurred, on the average, a year earlier than in whites and Hispanics (15 versus 16 years). The hypothesis was supported: "Early-maturing girls are more likely to engage in dating and sexual intercourse at earlier ages than are their later-maturing peers" (p. 328). The article addresses the possible causes of the racial differences and emphasizes the importance of sex education for females, hopefully by the time of first menstruation.

We can see that researchers and those who create literature pursue their common goal—describing and understanding human behavior—in different ways. Writers of literature portray our life experiences personally and dramatically, often capturing the conflict and confusion inherent in real-life events. Researchers attempt to describe and explain behavior, including sexual awakening, by subtracting the drama, simplifying the events being studied, and observing and measuring behavior. Objective observation "protects" our observations from our biases. However, it sacrifices some of the excitement and complexity of real-life events. Science and literature both offer approximations of the truth. Scientists treat objective data as an approximation of the truth, as a best guess about what really happens, but only as an educated guess.

Of course, one also learns about adolescence by living through this life stage, by experiencing personal changes and observing changes in peers. However, most adolescents do not have a vantage point that would allow them to understand and appreciate their own changes as they are occurring. It would be interesting to teach adolescent development to middle school and high school students in order to gauge their reactions.

One can also learn a great deal about adolescents by living with them, although what we learn about the ones we know and love might not apply to others. Daily life provides countless opportunities to observe behavioral and emotional events that are difficult to capture in a textbook. One parent in my adolescent psychology class recorded in her log: "I'm feeling much more comfortable with my daughter's new boyfriend and with her sexual awakening. Although not normal for me when I was her age, I see that her behavior is definitely age appropriate. I'm trying to allow her to grow in this experience. Of course, I hope she doesn't get hurt but I know I can't protect her from heartbreak. I can only be there for her when it happens. She and I have both been doing a lot of growing." How could we capture the flavor of this narrative through objective observation?

## OBJECTIVE METHODS FOR STUDYING ADOLESCENT DEVELOPMENT

### Naturalistic Observation

Occasionally we have the opportunity to watch small groups of adolescents interact with each other on street corners and in school yards, movie theaters, and shopping malls. Because they are not aware (or don't care) that they are being observed, their behavior is spontaneous and natural. It is interesting and informative to study adolescents in their "natural habitats."

**Naturalistic observation** allows us to study adolescent behavior in real-life settings rather than the strict conditions imposed by a laboratory setting. Naturalistic observations usually are **unobtrusive**; the study participants usually are not aware that they are being observed. Sometimes participants in naturalistic studies are informed that they are being studied. This knowledge probably affects their behavior, but it avoids the ethical problem of studying people without their permission. This type of trade-off is typical when we study people's behavior and development. Due to ethical and methodological concerns, naturalistic observation is not frequently used in adolescent research. Further, much interesting adolescent behavior occurs outside of adult surveillance (Hansen et al., 1995).

Darcy Miller (1991) investigated altruistic (helping) behavior in adolescents. Altruistic behavior is associated with healthy self-concept, popularity, and good relationships. In her study entitled "Do Adolescents Help and Share?" published in the journal *Adolescence*, Professor Miller videotaped and interviewed emotionally disturbed and nonhandicapped high school students in their classrooms over 10 consecutive school days. Participants in the study were aware that they were being videotaped. (Do you think this affected their behavior?) The participants also completed the Self Report Altruism Scale.

During semistructured activities, the students interacted freely with each other and with their teachers. The students' prosocial behaviors—sharing, helping, defending, comforting, donating, rescuing, and cooperating—were videotaped and then coded for analysis at a later time. Professor Miller observed that adolescents with behavioral and emotional handicaps acted *more* prosocially than did the students without disabilities. (Why might this be so?) Professor Miller speculates that the teachers of handicapped children emphasize prosocial behavior more than do the teachers of nonhandicapped children. (Can you think of other explanations?)

Although naturalistic observations are interesting, they're subject to the criticism that the observers' biases influence their interpretation of what is happening. In this study, investigators had to interpret actions as helpful or not helpful, not always an easy distinction to make. Casual observers often see what they want or expect to see. To reduce bias, Professor Miller had trained graduate and undergraduate students code the videotapes in a consistent manner. Their agreement about behavioral categories was frequently monitored.

Even careful naturalistic observations reflect the biases of the individuals who are present, the unique circumstances, and the specific setting. If we hear that a particular adolescent threw her math book at her unfaithful boyfriend, it would be ludicrous to conclude that all adolescents are aggressive or even that this girl behaves aggressively under other circumstances. Thus, we should be wary about drawing unwarranted conclusions about an adolescent's behavior or generalizing from the person or group we are observing to other adolescents or groups.

The main disadvantage of naturalistic observation is that it does not allow us to explain the events we observe. The study cited above reports that adolescents with handicaps act more cooperatively than those without handicaps (at least under the circumstances described in the article), but it doesn't tell us why. Because real-life settings usually are complex and varied, they cannot be arranged as carefully as laboratory settings. In natural settings, situational factors cannot be manipulated systematically while other variables are held constant. This is possible only in a laboratory setting. Although naturalistic studies cannot be used to explain behavior, they are very useful for generating ideas and hypotheses for more rigorous studies.

## Correlational Studies

In everyday life, we notice that certain events go together. The occurrence of one event, dark clouds for example, usually predicts another event, that rain may soon be falling. **Correlational studies** measure the degree to which two or more variables are related to each other. Are boys more competitive than girls, do high-achieving parents have high-achieving children, are adolescents more likely to smoke cigarettes if their friends or parents do? A **positive correlation** indicates that two variables change in the same direction. As temperature increases, so does the number of people at the beach. We would expect a positive correlation between students' grade point averages and their SAT scores. Positive correlations vary between 0 and 1.0. The higher the number, the greater the relationship. A perfect positive correlation is represented by a value of 1.0.

A **negative correlation** means that as one variable increases, a second variable decreases. The more people at the beach, the fewer the number of parking spaces available. The more alcohol you drink, the slower your reaction time. Negative correlations vary between 0 and −1.0. Again, the higher the number, the greater the relationship between variables. A perfect negative correlation is indicated by a value of −1.0. The absence of any correlation between two variables is represented by a value of 0. This means that knowing the value of one variable gives you absolutely no ability to predict the other. We've seen, for example, that gender does not predict IQ.

Since correlations rarely are perfect (1.0 or −1.0), we shouldn't be surprised occasionally to meet a high-achieving student who received a low SAT score or to find a convenient parking space in a crowded lot. *Practice Question: Are the following events positively or negatively correlated with each other? (1) Children's height and weight, (2) children's weight and running speed, (3) time spent studying and grade point average, (4) grade point average and time spent watching television.*

One group of investigators (Inderbitzen-Pisaruk et al., 1992) wondered what personal qualities of adolescents are associated (correlated) with reports of loneliness. National surveys reveal that between one-quarter and one-half of all adolescents experience some degree of loneliness. These investigators questioned 186 ninth graders, using seven different paper-and-pencil measures. They found that loneliness in males is associated with low self-esteem and the belief that they have poor social skills. The best predictors of loneliness in females were high social anxiety and the belief that they have poor social skills. *Thought Question: How could a clinical psychologist who works with adolescents use this information?*

Thus, correlational studies establish whether or not one variable is associated with another and, if so, to what degree. When there is a correlation, we can use one factor to predict the occurrence of the other. Is it hot and Sunday? Forget the beach, too much traffic. Like naturalistic observational studies, correlational studies do not allow us to infer that one of the observed variables (e.g., poor social skills) is causing the other (e.g., loneliness). Tightly controlled research is necessary to reveal exactly how these factors are related in the complex fabric of adolescent personality.

## Case Studies

Another way to study adolescence is to follow the progress of one or a few adolescents over an extended period of time. An in-depth study of one particular person or small group is known as a **case study**. Case studies convey the complexity of individual development, usually shedding light on such aspects of development and personality as self-concept, life goals, adjustment, relationships, and achievement. A collection of case studies, consisting of a cross section of male and female adolescents from different socioeconomic, ethnic, and cultural groups, is more likely to illustrate the similarities and differences of adolescents in general than would a single case study (Garrod et al., 1992).

There are several ways of obtaining information about a person in a case study. With her permission, we can observe the individual in a variety of surroundings, such as school and home, and observe her interact with some of the significant people in her life. Of course, the individual is aware of and will be affected by our presence. We can interact with her informally, as well as administer tests or inventories that provide information about her development and personality. We will certainly interview her at length, probably audiotaping or videotaping the interview for later analysis. We will interview her parents, siblings, and friends if she and they consent. Ethical guidelines ensure complete confidentiality and privacy of the responses of all parties.

Realistically, we have to limit our attention to certain aspects of the individual's development and behavior, and ignore others, so that we are not overwhelmed with information. Segal and Fairchild (1996), for example, performed a case study of an individual's history of polysubstance abuse. They included details about the individual's family life, peer relationships, criminal involvement, and transition from alcohol and marijuana use to amphetamine addiction. In composing our case study report, we try to use terminology that is objective. We try not to be judgmental or too interpretive. Casual judgments and interpretations are more likely to reflect our personal biases and assumptions about development than inform us about someone's actual development.

A director of a counseling center performed a case study of a 20-year-old college student she called "Mary" (Hamilton-Obaid, 1989). Although Mary was performing reasonably well in school and on her part-time job, one of her classmates told her teacher that she had become increasingly withdrawn and isolated. When questioned by her friends and family, she would say things like "It just doesn't matter anymore" and "Nobody cares, anyway." One of Mary's friends, concerned about her welfare, consulted with Mary's teacher about her depression and her family problems. The teacher spoke with Mary. Initially, Mary was antagonistic and felt betrayed by her friend but eventually admitted that she was contemplating suicide. The teacher referred her to an academic advisor who helped Mary construct a plan to reduce her suicidal thoughts and feelings. According to the investigator, "As a result of the consistent and persistent support of family, friends, and faculty, Mary's suicidal ideation decreased and she learned to cope with her problems" (p. 62).

In order to achieve a complete picture of Mary's circumstances, Dr. Hamilton-Obaid gathered in depth information from Mary, her teacher, her friend, and her parents. On the basis of this information, Dr. Hamilton-Obaid formulated a five-stage model of identification and intervention for suicidal adolescents.

The case study approach, although informative, has several limitations. One is that there is no such thing as a typical adolescent. Any particular case study tells us about the person being studied but may or may not enlighten us about adolescence as a general stage or process.

Furthermore, Mary and the significant people in her life may or may not answer our questions honestly. Even if they try to be truthful, they may not understand our questions or know the answers. Several case studies of adolescents (similar age, gender, ethnic group) might reveal patterns that are typical of that group. We must be cautious, however, about generalizing about adolescents based on one case study of any particular adolescent or group of adolescents. Like naturalistic observations, case studies are most useful for generating questions and ideas that can be addressed through more vigorous research methods.

## Surveys

Sometimes we seek information about the characteristics or qualities of members of a particular group. We might be interested in the beliefs, values, opinions, attitudes, or behaviors of high school jocks, Girl Scouts, unwed teenage mothers, or fans of rap music. One way to satisfy our curiosity is to survey group members. **Surveys** allow us to ask a lot of questions about one or more topics or issues.

Surveys take the form of spoken interviews or written questionnaires. Interviews usually are more time-consuming, but they allow the researcher greater flexibility in clarifying questions that study participants don't understand. They also allow interviewers to follow up on responses that are ambiguous or interesting. Written questionnaires lack that flexibility but ensure standardization of format. That is, each participant is exposed to the same questions in the same order.

The principal of a high school might want to know whether or not students are interested in taking an SAT preparation course. The principal could informally ask several students who enter his office that day, but students visiting a principal's office might not be typical of other students in the high school. If they are not, the principal might draw the wrong conclusion regarding general interest in taking such a course.

To be useful, surveys should be administered to a *representative* sample of the group we are studying. As in case studies, we can never be sure that participants are responding honestly. Particularly in face-to-face interviews, interviewees may feel pressured to give answers that are socially acceptable. What would you say to a principal who asked you whether or not you were interested in staying after school for additional instruction?

## Self-Report Inventories

Self-report inventories are widely used in the study of adolescents. Such instruments involve asking individual adolescents to evaluate their own behavior or describe their own developmental changes (Hansen et al., 1995). Standardized self-report instruments provide information about almost all facets of adolescents' lives, including close relationships, achievement, physical development, and adjustment. For example, Keefe and Berndt (1996) wondered whether the quality of one's friendships is related to adolescent self-esteem. As discussed in Chapter 8, there is considerable evidence that how adolescents feel about themselves is related to the quality of their close relationships. To measure self-esteem, the investigators used the Harter (1985) Self-Perception Profile for Children. The instrument has six scales, with six items in each scale. All items include statements about two types of children. For example, the scale for scholastic competence contains the item "Some kids do very well at their classwork BUT Other kids don't do well at their classwork." The scale for social acceptance contains the item "Some kids find it hard to make friends BUT Other kids find it pretty easy to make friends." Students completing the instrument decide which one of the two children in each statement is more like them and how true each statement is about themselves. Each student also was asked 26 questions about each of their close friendships (e.g., "How often do you get into arguments with this friend?").

The study revealed that the quality and stability of peer relationships are related to adolescent self-esteem. Although self-report measures allow investigators to obtain a considerable amount of information about adolescent behavior, like surveys self-report measures assess subjective perceptions of behavior rather than behavior itself. In addition, the social desirability effect could motivate adolescents to present themselves in a positive light.

## Experiments

A major goal of behavioral scientists is to understand or *explain* behavior. Of all the research methods, only experiments allow us to infer that one event is actually causing another. Concluding that one event is causing another requires convincing evidence. The main problem in attributing causality to a single factor is eliminating alternative explanations. For example, if you are walking down the street and your best friend passes you by without saying hello, many possible explanations come to mind. Your friend may not have seen you, may be annoyed with you, may be teasing you, may not feel well, or, less plausibly, may have temporary amnesia. Or maybe it wasn't your friend. People often draw conclusions about other people's motives and behavior prematurely, that is, before they have enough information to eliminate alternative explanations.

Experimental design allows us to eliminate alternative explanations so that only one explanation is left (presumably, the correct one). Given the complexity of behavior and development, this is not easily accomplished. In most experiments, several values of a single so-called **independent variable** are presented to participants (formerly called *subjects*) to determine how they affect (if they do) a specific behavior or developmental change, called the **dependent variable**. Typically, an independent variable is some aspect of the environment that can be systematically manipulated—for example, the dose of a drug, the difficulty of a test, or the amount of an incentive. Extraneous variables that could affect the dependent variable are held constant, usually by exposing all participants in the study to the same amounts of the same variables (e.g., room temperature). The concept of **control** refers to all the rules that scientists must follow to ensure that the conclusion drawn is the only one that can reasonably be drawn concerning the effect of the independent variable on the dependent variable. The better controlled the study, the more confident we are in the conclusions we draw.

A group of investigators, for example, wanted to determine whether young adolescents could benefit from assertiveness training (Wise, Bundy, Bundy, & Wise, 1991). *Assertiveness* means standing up for oneself while respecting the rights and opinions of others. The investigators reasoned that assertive self-expression is an important social skill for young adolescents that could enhance self-concept and other measures of positive adjustment.

Participants consisted of 42 sixth graders in two comparable social studies classes. One class received assertiveness training, and the other class served as a control group. Thus, the independent variable had two values, assertiveness training versus no assertiveness training. There was approximately the same number of boys and girls in each class, controlling for possible gender differences. Students were pretested, posttested, and then given a follow-up test 6 months after training. Each test consisted of 26 multiple-choice questions about assertion and aggression. The students' scores on these tests comprised the dependent variable.

When possible, investigators prefer that study participants be *randomly selected* from a larger population so that the results of the study can be generalized to the larger population. If these students were randomly selected from among all sixth graders at the school, the findings could be generalized to that group (but not beyond it). Researchers also prefer to assign people to groups randomly because *random assignment* ensures that the groups will be equivalent on most or all relevant variables. In this study, neither procedure was possible because scheduling and other factors precluded assigning students to their classes randomly. Students might have resisted being told when they had to take a certain class. However, the investigators made sure that the two classes were as comparable as possible (e.g., the same number of males and females in each class).

In most studies, some form of statistical analysis is performed to determine whether group differences in dependent variable scores reflect the influence of the independent variable or are due just to chance fluctuations. Statistical analysis revealed that the two groups did not differ in assertiveness on the pretest. That's good—the two groups were comparable on their knowledge of assertion before training began. The experimental group (one of the two classes) then received six semiweekly 40-minute lessons on assertiveness. Students were taught, through a variety of role-playing activities and written materials, how to assert themselves in appropriate ways while respecting the rights of others. Students in the **control group** (the other class) received no such training. It sometimes is the case that the control (comparison) group receives zero value of the independent variable. What were the results? The experimental group performed better than the control group on both the posttest and the follow-up test 6 months later. The researchers concluded that, like adults, young adolescents benefit from assertiveness training.

Experiments can be performed in a laboratory or a natural setting. Laboratory experiments usually are tightly controlled but are more difficult to organize. **Field experiments** like this one, conducted in natural settings such as school or work locations, may be less well controlled but are more conveniently arranged.

In this study, the investigators had to settle for another trade-off—the two classes preexisted. The pretest results assure us that the two groups were comparable on their knowledge of assertiveness before training. But the absence of random assignment of students to the two classes raises the question of whether they were comparable in other ways that could have affected the outcome of the study. Again, a more rigorous study would randomly assign participants to the two classes to ensure group equivalence.

### Cross-Sectional and Longitudinal Designs

A **cross-sectional design** studies individuals of different ages at the same time. Sherryl Goodman and her colleagues (Goodman et al., 1993) wondered how age and gender are related to children's ability to cope with stress. Life pressures have been shown to be related to anxiety, depression, and other forms of distress in children and adults. The investigators had fifth graders (preadolescents) and seventh graders (early adolescents) from middle-class, intact families complete the Life Events Checklist (LEC). The LEC indicates whether any of 35 listed life events (e.g., serious illness) happened within the past year and how the event made the child feel (from very bad to very good). Two measures are derived: positive stress and negative stress. It is mainly negative stress that is correlated with maladjustment. The investigators had the students' teachers assess each child's current emotional, behavioral, social, and general adjustment to school using the Teacher-Child Rating Scale (TCRS). The TCRS taps a variety of school adjustment problems, including being disruptive in class and displaying poor work habits. Like many other studies, this study revealed that boys are more vulnerable to stress than girls. Specifically, the high-stress boys were rated as more maladjusted (but not less competent) than the high-stress girls. Although the early adolescents did not report more stressors than the younger children, they did appear to be a bit more vulnerable to stress. Gender appears to be a more influential factor than age or developmental level in determining how stress affects adolescents.

Cross-sectional designs have a characteristic that makes them difficult to interpret. Participants in cross-sectional studies differ in age. It is tempting to assume that any changes observed are age related. For example, a study might reveal that 18-year-olds have less conflict with their parents than 13-year-olds. What is responsible for this difference? It is tempting to attribute the difference to the greater maturity of the older group. However, it is possible that the different amount of family conflict between the age groups is due not to aging (or maturing) but to other factors, such as amount of contact between family members (younger children have more) or social conditions (such as peer influence) that affect one group more than the other.

Note that cross-sectional designs, by studying different age groups at the same time, give us immediate feedback concerning our research questions. For those who are more patient, a **longitudinal design** permit them to look for changes in the same group of people over an extended period of time. Regarding the study described above, Goodman and her colleagues could have studied a group of children when they were in the fifth grade and then the same group when they were in the seventh grade. Although there are advantages in studying one group of participants over time, longitudinal studies are time-consuming and require repeated testing at predetermined intervals.

If some individuals become unavailable for testing and are not representative of those who remain, then the findings of the study may not be valid. Naturally, this is frustrating for researchers who have invested several years in a study. Another problem with longitudinal studies is that repeated testing may sensitize participants to the variable being studied. Being asked questions about life stressors could heighten children's awareness of and sensitivity to their life experiences and might influence their subsequent responses on the checklist. Once again, we see that the very act of observing or questioning someone can lead to changes in his or her behavior.

## Cohort Effects

**Cohort effects** reflect the influences associated with being raised at a particular place or time in history. The children living in the Russian city of Chernobyl when the nuclear reactor blew are developing differently from their peers who were not irradiated or forced to leave their homes forever. The lives of people growing up during the Great Depression and World War II were profoundly influenced by these events. It is evident that people who were adolescents in the relatively peaceful 1950s turned out somewhat differently from those whose adolescence occurred during the turbulent 1960s. In other words, cohorts share the events of their time, place, and generation. When we do find differences among individuals of different ages in a cross-sectional design, are they due to maturation, cohort effects, or something else? This is not an easy question to answer. A **cohort-sequential design** (or *cross-sequential design*) combines cross-sectional and longitudinal designs by starting a new longitudinal cohort group each time an assessment is made (Whitley, 1996). See Wigfield and Eccles (1994) for an example.

## Subcultural and Cross-Cultural Research

One of the best ways to understand our own culture is to study other cultures. In Chapter 1, we considered the possibility that adolescence is a cultural invention. If this is true, then each culture presumably invents its own version of this life stage—or no version at all. Contact with people from other societies allows us to test our assumptions about how they may be similar to or different from us. Comparing cultures helps us to lessen the risk of *ethnocentrism*, the tendency to view one's own group more favorably than other groups (Judd et al., 1995). Most developmental researchers are white, middle-class, educated individuals and, at least until recently, they studied mainly white, middle-class families. It is important that we not generalize the results of such studies to other ethnic or socioeconomic groups.

**Subcultural studies** allow us to compare the development of youth in a particular culture who belong to different ethnic, racial, and socioeconomic groups. It is important that we study adolescent development in a variety of cultural contexts. It would be misguided to assume that what is true of white, middle-class adolescents automatically applies to African-American, Hispanic, or Native-American adolescents. By comparing different cultures and different subcultures, we arrive at a better understanding of what is universal about adolescence, what is cultural, and what is personal.

For example, we can see whether Piaget's theory of cognitive development, based largely on the study of privileged Swiss and French children, applies to Chinese, Sudanese, and North American children. Studying similarities and differences among adolescents in various cultures or subcultures is an excellent way to test our developmental theories. It broadens our perspectives and helps us recognize our biases.

Tanioka and Glaser (1991) wondered why reported rates of juvenile delinquency are so much higher in the United States than in Japan. Since students in the United States had already been questioned about their prosocial and antisocial behaviors in previous studies, these investigators decided to administer an equivalent questionnaire to Japanese students. They administered questionnaires to public and private high school students in Osaka and compared these students' responses to those of students questioned previously in Richmond, California, and Seattle, Washington.

They asked Japanese students how many times over a 6-month period they had engaged in different forms of criminal and antisocial behavior, including vandalism and theft. Since respondents' names were not solicited (to increase honest responding), students' reports of criminal or antisocial behavior could not be confirmed by police or school records. The investigators found that Japanese students reported engaging in much more antisocial behavior than was acknowledged by Japanese police officials but much less than that reported by students in the two cities in the United States.

There are several possible national differences that might explain the large disparity in delinquency rates between the two cultures. Japanese students live under more informal social control than do students in the United States. About 97% of the Japanese high schoolers reported having two or more adults living at home compared to 75% of the American students. Japanese neighborhoods are highly cohesive, and neighbors know and watch out for each other's children.

Japanese parents are more likely than parents in the United States to report to each other anything unusual they notice about each other's child. There are also closer ties between police and citizens in Japan and a sense of obligation to maintain one's family honor. The transition to adulthood in Japan also is more predictable and therefore less stressful than for students in the United States. Finally, the link between poverty and antisocial behavior that we observe is not as applicable to Japanese families, who generally have low rates of unemployment and less divorce (Tanioka & Glaser, 1991).

This cross-cultural study not only reveals differences between adolescent behavior in the two cultures, it also suggests possible causes of the differences. If we wonder what we can do about high delinquency rates in the United States, a study like this one points our attention to family life, neighborhood cohesion, and economic inequality. As with most studies, however, the interpretations and conclusions are tentative and merit further investigation.

## ETHICS OF RESEARCH WITH ADOLESCENTS

When we study adolescence, our population includes adolescents and the significant people in their lives. Some studies compare adolescents to members of other age groups, such as preadolescents or adults. Just as the scientific method consists of rules about how we observe people so that we draw valid conclusions, the discipline of psychology has rules regarding the ethical treatment of research participants.

Our main concern is that no harm come to anyone as a result of having participated in psychological research. Researchers must never expose study participants to conditions that could cause them physical harm or serious emotional discomfort without their prior knowledge of and consent to these possible outcomes. The principle of **informed consent** states that individuals must know about any aspect of the research situation that might influence their decision to participate. People can refuse to participate and end their participation at any time. When children and adolescents are involved, the informed consent of their parents or caregivers also is required.

Temporary deception regarding the true purpose of the study and some aspects of its procedure is allowable if the research requires it. However, participants cannot be deceived about conditions of discomfort or possible physical harm. Following the study, participants must be fully debriefed about the real purpose of the study and reassured about their performance if appropriate. People's privacy must be protected; their participation in the study is confidential. If researchers have doubts about the ethical correctness of any aspect of their study, they must seek **peer review**. That is, they consult with knowledgeable colleagues who will provide an objective evaluation of the project's ethical status.

## SUMMARY

**1.** Developmental psychologists follow certain rules and procedures, called methodology, for studying the changes that occur over the life span. We want to know what these changes are. We also are interested in what causes these changes. Understanding human development is not easy. Adolescent development, in particular, is very complex because of simultaneous changes in physical, cognitive, and psychosocial domains.

**2.** We strive to be objective in our observations of adolescents to prevent our biases and expectations from influencing our conclusions. Because our methods of observation always involve a trade-off between accuracy and practicality, our interpretations of data and our conclusions about development are always tentative.

**3.** Naturalistic observation consists of observing behavior in natural settings. For adolescents this includes home, school, shopping malls, street corners, and any other gathering places.

**4.** Correlational studies measure the degree to which variables are related to each other. If we know, for example, that depressed teenagers are at increased risk of committing suicide, we can provide appropriate interventions.

**5.** A case study consists of an in-depth investigation of one person or a small group. It pro-

vides insight about an individual that is not readily obtainable from other research methods.

**6.** Surveys and questionnaires are time-consuming, but they can provide a wealth of information about people's opinions, attitudes, characteristics, and behaviors.

**7.** None of the above methods allows us to conclude that one event is causing another. Only a well-controlled experimental study permits us to infer that one variable—for example, peer pressure—is influencing another—for example, cheating on a test. Although experimental studies are a powerful research technique, what we learn about development in a laboratory cannot automatically be generalized to natural settings. Most research in adolescence involves the use of surveys, questionnaires, and correlational methods.

**8.** Cross-cultural research in adolescence reveals similarities and differences among adolescents in different cultures. Such studies help us understand what is distinctive about our culture and what is universal to all cultures.

**9.** All research in psychology must conform to ethical guidelines that protect participants from harm. Adolescents and their parents must provide informed consent before they can participate in a research study.

## GLOSSARY

**Validity** Degree of accuracy of a measurement; ability of a test or another method of observation to measure what it is designed to measure

**Reliability** Ability of a test or another method of observation to produce consistent and stable scores

**Methodology** Rules that guide the conduct of research and the logical strategies derived from them

**Objective observation** Unbiased, nonjudgmental observation of some aspect of the natural world

**Representative sample** Sample in which the characteristics of the study participants reflect those of a larger population

**Naturalistic observation** Observing behavior in a real-life or natural setting rather than in a laboratory

**Unobtrusive** Observing behavior so that the observer is not noticed

**Correlational study** A study to determine how two or more variables are related to each other

**Positive correlation** Two variables change (increase or decrease) in the same direction (e.g., temperature and number of people at the beach)

**Negative correlation** As the value of one variable increases, the value of the other decreases (e.g., weight and running speed)

**Case studies** In-depth studies of one particular person or small group

**Surveys** Research studies based on verbal interviews or written questionnaires

**Experiments** A powerful research technique involving the manipulation and observation of variables under controlled conditions; allows inferences about cause and effect

**Independent variable** The variable manipulated by the experimenter

**Dependent variable** A specific behavioral or developmental change that reflects the influence of the independent variable

**Control** Rules and strategies that allow researchers to draw valid conclusions about the phenomenon being studied

**Control group** In a controlled experiment, the group that is not subject to the independent variable, to allow comparison with the experimental group

**Field experiments** Studies conducted in natural settings; less well controlled than laboratory experiments

**Cross-sectional design** Observing several age groups at one time

**Longitudinal design** Observing one group of participants over an extended period of time

**Cohort effects** Reflect the shared effects on a group of people of being raised at a particular place or time

**Cohort-sequential designs** Combines cross-sectional and longitudinal designs by starting a new longitudinal cohort group each time an assessment is made

**Subcultural studies** Comparing the development of young people in a particular culture who belong to different ethnic, racial, and socioeconomic groups

**Informed consent** Ethical guideline requiring that study participants be told everything that they need to know in order to decide whether they are willing to participate in a study

**Peer review** Consulting with knowledgeable colleagues who will provide an objective evaluation of a project's ethical status

## THOUGHT QUESTIONS

**1.** How would you test the hypothesis that adolescents are more self-conscious than persons in other age groups?

**2.** What can you learn about adolescents from living with them that you cannot learn from objective research?

**3.** Briefly describe how you would apply each of the following methodologies to shed light on the effects of part-time employment on self-concept during adolescence:

  **a.** Case study
  **b.** Naturalistic observation
  **c.** Correlational study
  **d.** Survey
  **e.** Experiment

**4.** Should researchers have the right to observe adolescents without their permission?

# ANSWERS TO SELF-TESTS

| Question No. | Chapter | | | | | | | | | | | | |
|---|---|---|---|---|---|---|---|---|---|---|---|---|---|
| | 1 | 2 | 3 | 4 | 5 | 6 | 7 | 8 | 9 | 10 | 11 | 12 | 13 |
| 1 | D | B | D | B | D | D | D | A | C | D | A | D | B |
| 2 | D | C | C | D | D | D | B | A | B | D | D | B | D |
| 3 | B | A | D | A | B | A | B | C | B | B | B | B | A |
| 4 | C | D | B | C | B | B | C | D | D | B | C | C | B |
| 5 | A | A | B | C | B | C | D | B | D | D | C | A | C |
| 6 | B | B | B | B | D | A | B | C | D | B | D | C | C |
| 7 | A | D | A | B | A | A | B | A | B | C | A | B | D |
| 8 | B | C | D | D | D | D | D | A | A | C | A | A | A |
| 9 | C | A | A | A | D | C | C | D | C | C | D | D | A |
| 10 | D | D | B | A | C | B | A | C | A | D | A | A | C |
| 11 | A | B | D | D | A | D | B | C | C | A | B | D | D |
| 12 | C | C | D | B | | A | D | B | A | A | D | D | A |
| 13 | D | | A | | | A | A | B | D | | A | | D |
| 14 | | | D | | | | D | D | D | | D | | B |
| 15 | | | | | | | D | | | | B | | B |
| 16 | | | | | | | A | | | | | | A |
| 17 | | | | | | | B | | | | | | |

# REFERENCES

AAUW Report. (1993, March). How schools shortchange girls. *NJEA Review*, pp. 20–25.

AAUW Report. (1997, April). Girls in middle grades. *NJEA Review*, pp. 16–25.

Abell, S. C., & Richards, M. H. (1996). The relationship between body shape satisfaction and self-esteem: An investigation of gender and class differences. *Journal of Youth and Adolescence*, 25(5), 691–703.

Abelsohn, D., & Saayman, G. S. (1991). Adolescent adjustment to parental divorce: An investigation from the perspective of basic dimensions of structural family theory. *Family Process*, 30, 177–191.

Ablard, K. E., & Mills, C. J. (1996). Implicit theories of intelligence and self-perceptions of academically talented adolescents and children. *Journal of Youth and Adolescence*, 25(2), 137–148.

Ackerman, N. (1980). The family with adolescents. In E. Carter & M. McGoldrick (Eds.), *The family life cycle: A framework for family therapy*. New York: Gardner Press.

Adams, G. R. (1996). Reflections: On the past and the future. In G. R. Adams, R. Montemayor, & T. P. Gullotta (Eds.), *Psychosocial development during adolescence: Progress in developmental contextualism*. Thousand Oaks, CA: Sage.

Adams, G. R., Dyk, P., & Bennion, L. D. (1987). Parent–adolescent rela-tionships and identity formation. *Family Perspective*, 21, 249–260.

Adams, G. R., & Jones, R. M. (1982). Adolescent egocentrism: Exploration into possible contributions of parent–child relations. *Journal of Youth and Adolescence*, 11(1), 25–31.

Adams, M., & Adams, J. (1991). Life events, depression, and perceived problem solving alternatives in adolescents. *Journal of Child Psychology & Psychiatry & Allied Disciplines*, 32(5), 811–820.

Adamson, L., & Lyxell, B. (1996). Self-concept and questions of life: Identity development during late adolescence. *Journal of Adolescence*, 19, 569–582.

Adelman, H. S., Taylor, L., & Nelson, P. (1989). Minors' dissatisfaction with their life circumstances. *Child Psychiatry & Human Development*, 20(2), 135–147.

Adelson, J. (1979, February). Adolescence and the generalization gap. *Psychology Today*, 12, 33–37.

Adlaf, E. M., & Smart, R. G. (1991). Drug use among Canadian students: The past, present, and future. *Journal of Drug Issues*, 21, 51–64.

Adwere-Boamah, J., & Curtis, D. A. (1993). A confirmatory factor analysis of a four-factor model of adolescent concerns revisited. *Journal of Youth and Adolescence*, 22(3), 297–312.

Aiken, L. R. (1987). *Assessment of intellectual functioning*. Boston: Allyn & Bacon.

Alan Guttmacher Institute. (1991). *Teenage sexual and reproductive behavior (Facts in brief)*. New York: Author.

Alan Guttmacher Institute. (1992). New York: Author

Alan Guttmacher Institute. (1994a). *Sex and America's teenagers*. New York: Author.

Alan Guttmacher Institute. (1994b). *National teenage pregnancy rate*. New York: Author.

Alan Guttmacher Institute. (1995). New York: Author.

Alberts, J. K., Hecht, M. L., Miller-Rassulo, M., & Krizek, R. L. (1992). The communicative process of drug resistance among high school students. *Adolescence*, 27(105), 203–226.

Alexander, K. L., Entwisle, D. R., & Dauber, S. L. (1993). First-grade classroom behavior: Its short- and long-term consequences for school performance. *Child Development*, 64, 801–814.

Alfieri, T., Ruble, D. N., & Higgins, E. T. (1996). Gender stereotypes during adolescence: Developmental changes and the transition to junior high school. *Developmental Psychology*, 32(6), 1129–1137.

Allen, B. P. (1987). Youth suicide. *Adolescence*, 22(86), 271–290.

Almeida, D. M., & Galambos, N. L. (1991). Examining father involvement and the quality of father–adolescent relations. *Journal of Research on Adolescence*, 1, 155–172.

Aloise-Young, P. A., & Hennigan, K. M. (1996). Self-image, the smoker stereotype and cigarette smoking: Developmental patterns from fifth through eighth grade. *Journal of Adolescence, 19*, 163–177.

Alsaker, F. D. (1992). Pubertal timing, overweight, and psychological adjustment. *Journal of Early Adolescence, 12*(4), 396–419.

Alsaker, F. D. (1995). Is puberty a critical period for socialization? *Journal of Adolescence, 18*, 427–444.

Alsaker, F. D. (1996). Annotation: The impact of puberty. *Journal of Child Psychology & Psychiatry, 37*(3), 249–258.

Alva, S. A. (1993). Differential patterns of achievement among Asian-American adolescents. *Journal of Youth and Adolescence, 22*(4), 407–424.

Alva, S. A., & Jones, M. (1994). Psychosocial adjustment and self-reported patterns of alcohol use among Hispanic adolescents. *Journal of Early Adolescence, 14*(4), 432–448.

Amato, P. R. (1989). Family process and the competence of adolescents and primary school children. *Journal of Youth and Adolescence, 18*(1), 39–53.

American Cancer Society. (1993). Cancer statistics, 1993. *Cancer Journal for Clinicians, 43*, 7–26.

American Institutes for Research (1988). *Report # 1: Summary results from the 1987–1988 national study of intercollegiate athletes.* Palo Alto, CA: Author.

American Psychiatric Association. (1994). *Diagnostic and statistical manual of mental disorders.* (4th ed.)(DSM-IV). Washington, D.C.

Ammaniti, M., Ercolani, A. P., & Tambelli, R. (1989). Loneliness in the female adolescent. *Journal of Youth and Adolescence, 18*(4), 321–329.

Ammerman, R. T., Van Hasselt, V. B., & Hersen, M. (1987). The handicapped adolescent. In V. B. Van Hasselt & M. Hersen (Eds.), *Handbook of adolescent psychology.* New York: Pergamon Press.

Anastasi, A. (1988). *Psychological testing.* New York: Macmillan.

Anderson, A. R., & Henry, C. S. (1994). Family system characteristics and parental behaviors as predictors of adolescent substance abuse. *Adolescence, 29*(114), 405–420.

Anderson, C., & Ford, C. M. (1987). Affect of the game player: Short-term effects of highly and mildly aggressive video games. *Personality and Social Psychology Bulletin, 12*, 390–402.

Anderson, E. M., Clarke, L., & Spain, B. (1982). *Disability in adolescence.* London: Methuen.

Anderson, E. R., Hetherington, E. M., & Clingempeel, W. G. (1989). Transformations in family relations at puberty: Effects of family context. *Journal of Early Adolescence, 9*(3), 310–334.

Anderson, H. L., & Young, V. M. (1992). Holistic attitudes of high school students toward themselves and their school experiences. *Adolescence, 27*(107), 719–730.

Anderson, P. B., Arceneaux, E. R., Carter, D., Miller, A. M., et al. (1995). Changes in the telephone calling patterns of adolescent girls. *Adolescence, 30*(120), 779–784.

Anderssen, E. C., Myburgh, C. P. H., van Zyl, M. A., & Wiid, A. J. B. (1992). A differential analysis of time-use attitudes of high school students. *Adolescence, 27*(105), 63–72.

Andrews, J. A., Hops, H., Ary, D., Tildesley, E., & Harris, J. (1993). Parental influence on early adolescent substance use: Specific and nonspecific effects. *Journal of Early Adolescence, 13*(3), 285–310.

Andrich, D., & Styles, I. (1994). Psychometric evidence of intellectual growth spurts in early adolescence. *Journal of Early Adolescence, 14*(3), 328–344.

Anesko, K. M., & O'Leary, S. O. (1983). The effectiveness of brief parent training for the management of children's homework problems. *Child and Family Behavior, 4*, 113–126.

Angier, N. (1995, June 20). Does testosterone equal aggression? Maybe not. *The New York Times*, pp. A1, C3.

Angier, N. (1997, April 22). Evolutionary necessity or glorious accident? Biologists ponder the self. *The New York Times*, pp. C1, C9.

Applebome, P. (1995a, May 14). Study ties educational gains to more productivity growth. *The New York Times*, p. A22.

Applebome, P. (1995b, December 13). Have schools failed? Revisionists use army of statistics to argue no. *The New York Times*, p. B16.

Applebome, P. (1996a, November 21). Americans straddle the average mark in math and science. *The New York Times*, p. B14.

Applebome, P. (1996b, June 12). Blacks show gains in getting college degrees. *The New York Times*, p. B9.

Applebome, P. (1996c, December 29). After years of gains, minority students start falling behind. *The New York Times*, p. A12.

Applebome, P. (1997a, May 7). Gender gap in testing narrower than believed, study finds. *The New York Times*, p. A16.

Applebome, P. (1997b, May 19). Era of downsizing creates job boom for class of '97. *The New York Times*, pp. A1, B8.

Applebome, P. (1997c, June 26). Children place low in adults' esteem, a study finds. *The New York Times*, p. A25.

Apter, D., & Vihko, R. (1977). Serum pregnenolone, progesterone, 17-hydroxyprogesterone, testosterone, and 5 [alpha]-dihydrotestosterone during human puberty. *Journal of Clinical Endocrinologost and Metabolism, 45*, 1039.

Apter, D., Viinikka, L., & Vihko, R. (1978). Hormonal pattern of adolescent menstrual cycles. *Journal of Clinical Endocrinology and Metabolism, 47*, 944–954.

Aquilino, W. S. (1991). Predicting parents' experiences with coresident adult children. *Journal of Family Issues, 12*(3), 323–342.

Archer, S. L. (1989a). Gender differences in identity development: Issues of process, domain and timing. *Journal of Adolescence, 12*, 117–138.

Archer, S. L. (1989b). The status of identity: Reflections on the need for intervention. *Journal of Adolescence, 12,* 345–359.

Archer, S. L. (1992). A feminist's approach to identity research. In G. R. Adams, T. P. Gullotta, & R. Montemayor (Eds.), *Adolescent identity formation.* Newbury Park, CA: Sage.

Arenson, K. W. (1996a, August 23). Students continue to improve, college board says. *The New York Times,* p. A10.

Arenson, K. W. (1996b, October 2). College board revises test to improve chances for girls. *The New York Times.*

Aries, P. (1962). *Centuries of childhood: A social history of family life.* New York: Vintage.

Arnett, J. (1990). Contraceptive use, sensation seeking, and adolescent egocentrism. *Journal of Youth and Adolescence, 19*(2), 171–180.

Arnett, J. (1991a). Heavy metal music and reckless behavior among adolescents. *Journal of Youth and Adolescence, 20*(6), 573–592.

Arnett, J. (1991b). Adolescents and heavy metal music: From the mouths of metalheads. *Youth & Society, 23*(1), 76–98.

Arnett, J. (1992a). Reckless behavior in adolescence: A developmental perspective. *Developmental Review, 12,* 339–373.

Arnett, J. (1992b). Socialization and adolescent reckless behavior: A reply to Jessor. *Developmental Review, 12,* 391–409.

Arnett, J. J. (1994). Are college students adults? Their conceptions of the transition to adulthood. *Journal of Adult Development, 1,* 213–224.

Arnett, J. J. (1995). Adolescents' use of media for self-socialization. *Journal of Youth and Adolescence, 24*(5), 519–534.

Arnett, J., & Balle-Jensen, L. (1993). Cultural bases of risk behavior: Danish adolescents. *Child Development, 64,* 1842–1855.

Arnett, J. J., Larson, R., & Offer, D. (1995). Beyond effects: Adolescents as active media users. *Journal of Youth and Adolescence, 24*(5), 511–518.

Arnett, J. J., & Taber, S. (1994). Adolescence terminable and interminable: When does adolescence end? *Journal of Youth and Adolescence, 23*(5), 517–537.

Aro, H. M., & Palosaari, U. K. (1992). Parental divorce, adolescence and transition to young adulthood: A follow-up study. *American Journal of Orthopsychiatry, 62*(3), 421–429.

Aronson, P. J., Mortimer, J. T., Zierman, C., & Hacker, M. (1996). Generational differences in early work experiences and evaluations. In J. T. Mortimer & M. D. Finch (Eds.), *Adolescents, work, and family: An intergenerational developmental analysis.* Thousand Oaks, CA: Sage.

Arroyo, C. G., & Zigler, E. (1995). Racial identity, academic achievement, and the psychological well-being of economically disadvantaged adolescents. *Journal of Personality and Social Psychology, 69*(5), 903–914.

Ascher, C. (1991). *School programs for African American male students.* Trends and Issues No. 15, Institute for Urban and Minority Education. New York: Eric Clearinghouse on Urban Education.

Asher, S. R. (1983). Social competence and peer status: Recent advances and future directions. *Child Development, 54,* 1427–1434.

Asher, S. R., & Coie, J. D. (Eds.). (1990). *Peer rejection in childhood.* New York: Cambridge University Press.

Astin, A. (1974). *The American freshman: National norms for fall, 1973.* Washington, DC: American Council of Education.

Astin, A. (1993). *What matters in college? Four critical years revisited.* San Francisco: Jossey-Bass.

Atkinson, R. C., & Shiffrin, R. M. (1971). The control of short-term memory. *Scientific American, 225,* 82–90.

Austin, J. S., & Martin, N. K. (1992). College-bound students: Are we meeting their needs? *Adolescence, 27*(105), 115–121.

Ayalah, D., & Weinstock, I. J. (1979). *Breasts: Women speak about their breasts and their lives.* New York: Summit Books.

Azar, B. (1995, July). Which traits predict job performance? *APA Monitor,* pp. 30–31.

Azar, B. (1996a, June). Schools the source of rough transitions. *APA Monitor,* p. 14.

Azar, B. (1996b, June). People are becoming smarter—why? *APA Monitor,* p. 20.

Azar, B. (1996c, November). Project explores landscape of midlife. *APA Monitor,* p. 26.

Azar, B. (1996d, October). What factors lead to child drug abuse? *APA Monitor,* p. 50.

Bachman, J. G., & Schulenberg, J. (1993). How part-time work intensity relates to drug use, problem behavior, time use, and satisfaction among high school seniors: Are these consequences or merely correlates? *Developmental Psychology, 29*(2), 220–235.

Bacon, C. S. (1993). Student responsibility for learning. *Adolescence, 28*(109), 199–212.

Bagley, C., Bolitho, F., & Bertrand, L. (1997). Sexual assault in school, mental health, and suicidal behaviors in adolescent women in Canada. *Adolescence, 32*(126), 361–366.

Bailey, C. A. (1991). Family structure and eating disorders. *Youth & Society, 23*(2), 251–272.

Bailey, J. M., Bobrow, D., Wolfe, M., & Mikach, S. (1995). Sexual orientation of adult sons of gay fathers. *Developmental Psychology, 31*(1), 124–129.

Bakan, D. (1972). Adolescence in America: From idea to social fact. In J. Kagan & R. Coles (Eds.), *Twelve to sixteen: Early adolescence.* New York: W. W. Norton.

Baker, D. P., & Stevenson, D. L. (1986). Mothers' strategies for children's school achievement: Managing the transition to high school. *Sociology of Education, 59,* 156–166.

Bakken, L., & Romig, C. (1992). Interpersonal needs in middle adolescents: Companionship, leadership, and intimacy. *Journal of Adolescence*, 15, 301–316.

Balassone, M. L. (1991). A social learning model of adolescent contraceptive behavior. *Journal of Youth and Adolescence*, 20(6), 593–616.

Baldwin, S. E., & Baranoski, M. V. (1990). Family interactions and sex education in the home. *Adolescence*, 25(99), 573–582.

Ball, L., & Chandler, M. (1989). Identity formation in suicidal and nonsuicidal youth: The role of self-continuity. *Development and Psychopathology*, 1, 257–275.

Ball, S. J. (1981). *Beachside comprehensive*. Cambridge: Cambridge University Press.

Ballard, M. E., & Coates, S. (1995). The immediate effects of homicidal, suicidal, and nonviolent heavy metal and rap songs on the moods of college students. *Youth & Society*, 27(2), 148–168.

Bancroft, J. (1987). A physiological approach. In J. Geer & W. T. O'Donohue (Eds.), *Theories of human sexuality* (pp. 411–421). New York: Plenum.

Bandura, A. (1964). The stormy decade: Fact or fiction? *Psychology in the Schools*, 1, 224–231.

Bandura, A. (1986). *Social foundations of thought and action: A social cognitive theory*. Englewood Cliffs, NJ: Prentice-Hall.

Bandura, A. (1989). Human agency in social cognitive theory. *American Psychologist*, 44, 1175–1184.

Bandura, A., Barbaranelli, C., Caprara, G. V., & Pastorelli, C. (1996). Multifaceted impact of self-efficacy beliefs on academic functioning. *Child Development*, 67, 1206–1222.

Baranowski, M. D., Schilmoeller, G. L., & Higgins, B. S. (1990). Parenting attitudes of adolescent and older mothers. *Adolescence*, 25(100), 781–790.

Barber, B. L. (1995). Preventive intervention with adolescents and divorced mothers: A conceptual framework for program design and evaluation. *Journal of Applied Developmental Psychology*, 16(4), 481–503.

Barber, B. L., & Eccles, J. S. (1992). Long-term influence of divorce and single parenting on adolescent family- and work-related values, behaviors, and aspirations. *Psychological Bulletin*, 111(1), 108–126.

Barnes, E. J. (1980). The black community as the source of positive self-concept for black children: A theoretical perspective. In R. Jones (Ed.), *Black psychology*. New York: Harper & Row.

Barnes, H. L., & Olson, D. H. (1985). Parent–adolescent communication and the circumplex model. *Child Development*, 56, 437–447.

Barnett, J. K., Papini, D. R., & Gbur, E. (1991). Familial correlates of sexually active pregnant and nonpregnant adolescents. *Adolescence*, 26(102), 457–472.

Baron, J. B., & Sternberg, R. J. (Eds.). (1987). *Teaching thinking skills: Theory and practice*. New York: W. H. Freeman.

Barringer, F. (1991, June 23). With teens and alcohol, it's just say when. *The New York Times*, section 4, p. 1.

Barron, J. (1987, April 15). Suicide rates of teenagers: Are their lives harder to live? *The New York Times*.

Bar-Tal, D., & Nissimn, R. (1984). Helping behavior and moral judgment among adolescents. *British Journal of Developmental Psychology*, 2, 329–336.

Bartling, C. A., & Eisenman, R. (1992). Attitudes of American youth concerning military and civilian jobs. *Adolescence*, 27(106), 407–416.

Baumeister, R. F. (Ed.). (1993). *Self-esteem: The puzzle of low self-regard*. New York: Plenum.

Baumeister, R. F. (1996, Summer). Should schools try to boost self-esteem? *American Educator*, pp. 14–19, 43.

Baumeister, R. F., & Muraven, M. (1996). Identity as adaptation to social, cultural, and historical context. *Journal of Adolescence*, 19, 405–416.

Baumeister, R. F., Smart, L., & Boden, J. M. (1996). Relation of threatened egotism to violence and aggression: The dark side of self-esteem. *Psychological Review*, 103(1), 5–33.

Baumeister, R. F., & Tice, D. (1986). How adolescence became the struggle for self: A historical transformation of psychological development. In J. Suls & A. Greenwald (Eds.), *Psychological perspectives on the self*, Volume 3. Hillsdale, NJ: Erlbaum.

Baumrind, D. (1966). Effects of authoritative parental control on children. *Child Development*, 37, 887–906.

Baumrind, D. (1967). Child care practices anteceding three patterns of preschool behavior. *Genetic Psychology Monographs*, 75, 43–88.

Baumrind, D. (1968). Authoritarian vs. authoritative parental control. *Adolescence*, 3, 255–272.

Baumrind, D. (1971). Current patterns of parental authority. *Developmental Psychology Monographs*, 4(1, Pt. 2), 1–103.

Baumrind, D. (1975). *Early socialization and the discipline controversy*. Morristown, NJ: General Learning Press.

Baumrind, D. (1987). Developmental perspective on adolescent risk taking in contemporary America. *New Directions in Child Development*, 37, 93–125.

Baumrind, D. (1989). Raising competent children. In W. Damon (Ed.), *Child development today and tomorrow*. San Francisco: Jossey Bass.

Baumrind, D. (1991a). Effective parenting during the early adolescent transition. In P. Cowan & M. Hetherington (Eds.), *Family transitions*. Hillsdale, NJ: Erlbaum.

Baumrind, D. (1991b). Parenting styles and adolescent development. In R. M. Lerner, A. C. Petersen, & J. Brooks-Gunn (Eds.), *The encyclopedia of adolescence*. New York: Garland.

Baumrind, D. (1991c). The influence of parenting style on adolescent competence and substance use. *Journal of Early Adolescence*, 11, 56–95.

Baumrind, D., & Moselle, K. A. (1985). A developmental perspective on adolescent drug abuse. *Advances in Alcohol and Substance Abuse*, 4(3/4), 41–67.

Baxter Magolda, M. B. (1992). *Knowing and reasoning in college: Gender-related patterns in students' intellectual development.* San Francisco: Jossey-Bass.

Baydar, N., Brooks-Gunn, J., & Furstenberg, F. F. (1993). Early warning signs of functional illiteracy: Predictors in childhood and adolescence. *Child Development, 64,* 815–829.

Bazar, J. (1990, July). Psychologists can help youths stay out of gangs. *APA Monitor,* p. 39.

Beal, C. R. (1994). *Boys and girls: The development of gender roles.* New York: McGraw–Hill.

Beaty, L. A. (1995). Effects of paternal absence on male adolescents' peer relations and self-image. *Adolescence, 30*(120), 873–880.

Beck, K. H., Scaffa, M., Swift, R., & Ko, M. (1995). A survey of parent attitudes and practices regarding underage drinking. *Journal of Youth and Adolescence, 24*(3), 315–334.

Beech, R., & Schoeppe, A. (1974). Development of value systems in adolescents. *Developmental Psychology, 10,* 644–656.

Beilin, H., & Pufall, P. (Eds.). (1992). *Piaget's theory: Prospects and possibilities.* Hillsdale, NJ: Erlbaum.

Bell, A. P., & Weinberg, M. S. (1978). *Homosexualities: A study of diversity among men and women.* New York: Simon & Schuster.

Bell, N. J., & Bell, R. W. (Eds.). (1993). *Adolescent risk taking.* Newbury Park, CA: Sage.

Beller, M., & Gafni, N. (1996). 1991 International Assessment of Educational Progress in Mathematics and Sciences: The gender differences perspective. *Journal of Educational Psychology, 88*(2), 365–377.

Belsky, J. (1984). The determinants of parenting: A process model. *Child Development, 55,* 83–96.

Belsky, J. (1993). Etiology of child maltreatment: A developmental-ecological analysis. *Psychological Bulletin, 114*(3), 413–434.

Belsky, J., Steinberg, L., & Draper, P. (1991). Childhood experience, inter-

personal development, and reproductive strategy: An evolutionary theory of socialization. *Child Development, 62,* 647–670.

Bem, D. J. (1996). Exotic becomes erotic: A developmental theory of sexual orientation. *Psychological Review, 103*(2), 320–335.

Beman, D. S. (1995). Risk factors leading to adolescent substance abuse. *Adolescence, 30*(117), 201–208.

Benenson, J. F. (1990). Gender differences in social networks. *Journal of Early Adolescence, 10*(4), 472–495.

Bengston, V. L., & Kuypers, J. A. (1971). Generational differences and the developmental stake. *Aging and Human Development, 2,* 240–260.

Bennett, D. S., & Bates, J. E. (1995). Perspective models of depressive symptoms in early adolescence. *Journal of Early Adolescence, 15*(3), 299–315.

Berger, R., & Shechter, Y. (1996). Guidelines for choosing an "intervention package" for working with adolescent girls in distress. *Adolescence, 31*(123), 709–719.

Berk, L. E. (1996). *Infants, children, and adolescents* (2nd ed.). Needham Heights, MA: Allyn & Bacon.

Berman, S. L., Kurtines, W. M., Silverman, W. K., & Serafini, L. T. (1996). The impact of exposure to crime and violence on urban youth. *American Journal of Orthopsychiatry, 66*(3), 329–336.

Berman, W. H., & Sperling, M. B. (1991). Parental attachment and emotional distress in the transition to college. *Journal of Youth and Adolescence, 20*(4), 427–440.

Berndt, T. J. (1979). Developmental changes in conformity to peers and parents. *Developmental Psychology, 15,* 608–616.

Berndt, T. J. (1987, April). *Changes in friendship and school adjustment after the transition to junior high school.* Paper presented at the biennial meeting of the Society for Research in Child Development, Baltimore.

Berndt, T. J., & Keefe, K. (1995). Friends' influence on adolescents' ad-

justment to school. *Child Development, 66,* 1312–1329.

Berndt, T. J., Laychak, A. E., & Park, K. (1990). Friends' influence on adolescents' academic achievement motivation: An experimental study. *Journal of Educational Psychology, 82*(4), 664–670.

Berndt, T. J., Miller, K., & Park, K. (1989). Adolescents' perceptions of friends' and parents' influence on aspects of their school adjustment. *Journal of Early Adolescence, 9,* 419–435.

Berndt, T. J., & Perry, T. B. (1986). Children's perceptions of friendships as supportive relationships. *Developmental Psychology, 22,* 640–648.

Berndt, T. J., & Perry, T. B. (1990). Distinctive features and effects of early adolescent friendships. In R. Montemayor, G. R. Adams, & T. P. Gullotta (Eds.), *From childhood to adolescence: A transitional period?* Newbury Park, CA: Sage.

Berndt, T. J., & Savin-Williams, R. C. (1993). Peer relations and friendships. In P. H. Tolan & B. J. Cohler (Eds.), *Handbook of clinical research and practice with adolescents.* New York: Wiley.

Bernstein, A. (1993, August 16). The young and the jobless. *Business Week,* p. 107.

Bernstein, E. M. (1995, July 15). And then he kissed her. . . . Gross! *The New York Times,* pp. 23, 27.

Berton, M. W., & Stabb, S. D. (1996). Exposure to violence and post-traumatic stress disorder in urban adolescents. *Adolescence, 31*(122), 489–498.

Berzonsky, M. D. (1992). A process perspective on identity and stress management. In G. R. Adams, T. P. Gullotta, & R. Montemayor (Eds.), *Adolescent identity formation.* Newbury Park, CA: Sage.

Beyth-Marom, R., Austin, L., Fischoff, B., Palmgren, C., & Jacobs-Quadrel, M. (1993). Perceived consequences of risky behaviors: Adults and adolescents. *Developmental Psychology, 29,* 549–563.

Bickham, N. L., & Fiese, B. H. (1997). Extension of the children's perceptions of interparental conflict scale for use with late adolescents. *Journal of Family Psychology, 11*(2), 246–250.

Bierman, K. L., Smoot, D. L., & Aumiller, K. (1993). Characteristics of aggressive-rejected, aggressive (nonrejected), and rejected (nonaggressive) boys. *Child Development, 64,* 139–151.

Bills, D. B., Helms, L. B., & Ozcan, M. (1995). The impact of student employment on teachers' attitudes and behaviors toward working students. *Youth & Society, 27*(2), 169–193.

Billy, J. O. G., Brewster, K. L., & Grady, W. R. (1994). Contextual effects on the sexual behavior of adolescent women. *Journal of Marriage and the Family, 56,* 387–404.

Billy, J. O. G, Landale, N. S., Grady, W. R., & Zimmerle, D. M. (1988). Effect of sexual activity on adolescent social and psychological development. *Social Psychology Quarterly, 51,* 190–212.

Billy, J. O. G., & Udry, J. R. (1985). Patterns of adolescent friendship and effects on sexual behavior. *Social Psychology Quarterly, 48,* 27–41.

Binet, A. (1916). *The development of intelligence in children.* Baltimore: Williams & Wilkins.

Bingham, C. R., & Crockett, L. J. (1996). Longitudinal adjustment patterns of boys and girls experiencing early, middle, and late intercourse. *Developmental Psychology, 32*(4), 647–658.

Bird, G. W., & Harris, R. L. (1990). A comparison of role strain and coping strategies by gender and family structure among early adolescents. *Journal of Early Adolescence, 10,* 141–158.

Bischof, G. P., Stith, S. M., & Whitney, M. L. (1995). Family environments of adolescent sex offenders and other juvenile delinquents. *Adolescence, 30*(117), 157–170.

Bishop, J. (1995, Fall). The power of external standards. *American Educator,* pp. 10–18, 42.

Bishop, J. A., & Inderbitzen, H. M. (1995). Peer acceptance and friendship: An investigation of their relation to self-esteem. *Journal of Early Adolescence, 15*(4), 476–489.

Bishop, J. H. (1989). Why the apathy in American high schools? *Educational Researcher, 18,* 6–10.

Bjorklund, D. F. (1997). In search of a metatheory for cognitive development (or, Piaget is dead and I don't feel so good myself). *Child Development, 68,* 144–148.

Bjorklund, D. F., & Green, B. L. (1992). The adaptive nature of cognitive immaturity. *American Psychologist, 47,* 46–54.

Black, C. A., & DeBlassie, R. R. (1993). Sexual abuse in male children and adolescents: Indicators, effects, and treatments. *Adolescence, 28*(109), 123–134.

Blasi, A. (1980). Bridging moral cognition and moral action: A critical review of the literature. *Psychological Bulletin, 88,* 1–45.

Blasi, A., & Hoeffel, E. C. (1974). Adolescence and formal operations. *Human Development, 17,* 344–363.

Blau, G. M. (1996a). Oppositional defiant disorder. In G. M. Blau & T. P. Gullotta (Eds.), *Adolescent dysfunctional behavior: Causes, interventions, and prevention.* Thousand Oaks, CA: Sage.

Blau, G. M. (1996b). Adolescent suicide and depression. In G. M. Blau & T. P. Gullotta (Eds.), *Adolescent dysfunctional behavior: Causes, interventions, and prevention.* Thousand Oaks, CA: Sage.

Blau, G. M., & Gullotta, T. P. (1993). Promoting sexual responsibility in adolescence. In T. P. Gullotta, G. R. Adams, & R. Montemayor (Eds.), *Adolescent sexuality.* Newbury Park, CA: Sage.

Blechman, E. A., & Culhane, S. E. (1993). Aggressive, depressive, and prosocial coping with affective challenges in early adolescence. *Journal of Early Adolescence, 13*(4), 361–382.

Bleeden, E. (1995, February). Should schools offer all-girl math classes? *NEA Today,* p. 55.

Block, J., Block, J. H., & Keyes, S. (1988). Longitudinally foretelling drug usage in adolescence: Early childhood personality and environmental precursors. *Child Development, 59,* 336–355.

Block, J., & Robins, R. W. (1993). A longitudinal study of consistency and change in self-esteem from early adolescence to early adulthood. *Child Development, 64,* 909–923.

Bloom, M. V. (1987). Leaving home: A family transition. In J. Bloom-Feshback & S. Bloom-Feshbach (Eds.), *The psychology of separation and loss.* San Francisco: Jossey-Bass.

Blos, P. (1962). *On adolescence: A psychoanalytic interpretation.* New York: Free Press.

Blos, P. (1979). *The adolescent passage.* New York: International Universities Press.

Blyth, D. A., Hill, J. P., & Thiel, K. P. (1982). Early adolescents' significant others. *Journal of Youth and Adolescence, 11,* 425–450.

Blyth, D. A., Simmons, R. G., & Carlton-Ford, S. (1983). The adjustment of early adolescents to school transitions. *Journal of Early Adolescence, 3,* 105–120.

Blyth, D. A., Simmons, R. G., & Zakin, D. (1985). Satisfaction with body image for early adolescent females: The impact of pubertal timing within different school environments. *Journal of Youth and Adolescence, 14,* 207–225.

Bø, I. (1996). The significant people in the social networks of adolescents. In K. Hurrelmann & S. F. Hamilton (Eds.), *Social problems and social contexts in adolescence.* New York: Aldine De Gruyter.

Bock, R. D., & Moore, E. G. (1986). *Advantage and disadvantage: A profile of American youth.* Hillsdale, NJ: Erlbaum.

Boehm, K., Chessare, J. B., Valko, T. R., & Sager, M. S. (1991). Teen line: A descriptive analysis of a peer telephone listening service. *Adolescence, 26*(103), 643–648.

Boggiano, A. K., & Katz, P. (1991). Maladaptive achievement patterns in students: The role of teachers' controlling strategies. *Journal of Social Issues, 47*(4), 35–51.

Boldero, J., & Fallon, B. (1995). Adolescent help-seeking: What do they get help for and from whom? *Journal of Adolescence, 18,* 193–209.

Bolognini, M., Plancherel, B., Bettschart, W., & Halfon, O. (1996). Self-esteem and mental health in early adolescence: Development and gender differences. *Journal of Adolescence, 19,* 233–245.

Bolton, J. O. G., & MacEachran, A. E. (1988). Adolescent male sexuality: A developmental perspective. *Adolescence, 20,* 21–32.

Bonate, D. L., & Jessell, J. C. (1996). The effects of educational intervention on perceptions of sexual harassment. *Sex Roles, 35*(11/12), 751–764.

Borduin, C. M., Henggeler, S. W., & Manley, C. M. (1995). Conduct and oppositional disorders. In V. B. Van Hasselt & M. Hersen (Eds.), *Handbook of adolescent psychopathology: A guide to diagnosis and treatment.* New York: Lexington.

Bornstein, P. H., Schuldberg, D., & Bornstein, M. T. (1987). Conduct disorders. In V. B. Van Hasselt & M. Hersen (Eds.). *Handbook of adolescent psychology.* New York: Pergamon Press.

Borus, M., Crowley, J., Rumberger, R., Santos, R., & Shapiro, D. (1980). *Findings of the national longitudinal survey of young Americans, 1979.* (Youth Knowledge Development Report 2.7). Washington, DC: U.S. Government Printing Office.

Bosma, H. A. (1992). Identity in adolescence: Managing commitments. In G. R. Adams, T. P. Gullotta, & R. Montemayor (Eds.), *Adolescent identity formation.* Newbury Park, CA: Sage.

Boswell, J. (1980). *Christianity, social tolerance, and homosexuality.* Chicago: University of Chicago Press.

Botvin, G. J., Epstein, J. A., Schinke, S. P., & Diaz, T. (1994). Predictors of cigarette smoking among inner-city minority youth. *Journal of Developmental and Behavioral Pediatrics, 15*(2), 67–73.

Bouffard-Bouchard, T., Parent, S., & Larivee, S. (1991). Influence of self-efficacy on self-regulation and performance among junior and senior high-school age students. *International Journal of Behavioral Development, 14*(2), 153–164.

Boxer, A. M., Cohler, B. J., Herdt, G., & Irvin, F. (1993). Gay and lesbian youth. In P. H. Tolan & B. J. Cohler (Eds.), *Handbook of clinical research and practice with adolescents.* New York: Wiley.

Boyd, M. P., & Yin, Z. (1996). Cognitive-affective sources of sport enjoyment in adolescent sports participants. *Adolescence, 31*(122), 383–395.

Boyer, C. B., Shafer, M., & Taschann, J. M. (1997). Evaluation of a knowledge- and cognitive-behavioral skills-building intervention to prevent STDs and HIV infection in high school students. *Adolescence, 32*(125), 25–42.

Boyes, M. C., & Chandler, M. (1992). Cognitive development, epistemic doubt, and identity formation in adolescence. *Journal of Youth and Adolescence, 21*(3), 277–301.

Brack, C. J., Brack, G., & Orr, D. P. (1994). Dimensions underlying problem behaviors, emotions and related psychosocial factors in early and middle adolescents. *Journal of Early Adolescence, 14*(3), 345–370.

Brage, D., Meredith, W., & Woodward, J. (1993). Correlates of loneliness among midwestern adolescents. *Adolescence, 28*(111), 685–693.

Brake, M. (1985). *Comparative youth culture.* London: Routledge & Kegan Paul.

Bray, J. H., & Harvey, D. M. (1995). Adolescents in stepfamilies: Developmental family interventions. *Psychotherapy, 32,* 122–130.

Breakwell, G. M., & Millward, L. J. (1997). Sexual self-concept and sexual risk-taking. *Journal of Adolescence, 20,* 29–41.

Brennan, C. (1993, April). Helping teens cope. *NJEA Review,* pp. 20–23.

Bretherton, I. (1987). New perspectives on attachment relations: Security, communication and internal working models. In J. Osofsky (Ed.), *Handbook of infant development.* New York: Wiley.

Brier, N. (1995). Predicting antisocial behavior in youngsters displaying poor academic achievement: A review of risk factors. *Journal of Developmental and Behavioral Pediatrics, 16*(4), 271–276.

Brinckerhoff, L. C. (1996). Making the transition to higher education: Opportunities for student empowerment. *Journal of Learning Disabilities, 29*(2), 118–136.

Brochin, H. A., & Horvath, J. A. (1996). Attention-deficit/hyperactivity disorder. In G. M. Blau & T. P. Gullotta (Eds.), *Adolescent dysfunctional behavior: Causes, interventions, and prevention.* Thousand Oaks, CA: Sage.

Brody, G. H., Neubaum, E., & Forehand, R. (1988). Serial marriage: A heuristic analysis of an emerging family form. *Psychological Bulletin, 103*(2), 211–222.

Brody, G. H., Stoneman, Z., & Flor, D. (1996). Parental religiosity, family processes, and youth competence in rural, two-parent African American families. *Developmental Psychology, 32*(4), 696–706.

Brody, G. H., Stoneman, Z., & Gauger, K. (1996). Parent–child relationships, family problem-solving behavior, and sibling relationship quality: The moderating role of sibling temperaments. *Child Development, 67,* 1289–1300.

Brody, J. E. (1986, April 30). Guidelines for parents of teen-agers who are, or are about to be, sexually active. *The New York Times.*

Brody, J. E. (1996a, January 31). Help for youths beset by eating disorders. *The New York Times,* p. C10.

Brody, J. E. (1996b, September 26). Study finds stunted lungs in young smokers. *The New York Times,* p. B10.

Bronfenbrenner, U. (1979). *The ecology of human development: Experiments by nature and design.* Cambridge, MA: Harvard University Press.

Bronfenbrenner, U. (1985). Freedom and discipline across the decades. In G. Becker, H. Becker, & H. Huber

(Eds.), *Ordnung und unordnung* [Order and disorder]. Weinheim, West Germany: Beltz Berlag.

Bronfenbrenner, U. (1986). Ecology of the family as a context for human development: Research perspectives. *Developmental Psychology, 22*(6), 723–742.

Bronfenbrenner, U. (1989). Ecological system theories. *Annals of Child Development, 6,* 187–249.

Bronstein, P., Fitzgerald, M., Briones, M., Pieniadz, J., & D'Ari, A. (1993). Family emotional expressiveness as a predictor of early adolescent social and psychological adjustment. *Journal of Early Adolescence, 13*(4), 448–471.

Brook, J. S., Gordon, A. S., Brook, A., & Brook, D. W. (1989). The consequences of marijuana use on intrapersonal and interpersonal functioning in black and white adolescents. *Genetic, Social and General Psychology Monographs,* pp. 351–369.

Brook, J. S., Whiteman, M., Balka, E. B., & Cohen, P. (1995). Parent drug use, parent personality, and parenting. *Journal of Genetic Psychology, 156*(2), 137–151.

Brooke, J. (1996, October 28). An old law chastises pregnant teenagers. *The New York Times,* p. A10.

Brooks, A. (1995, March 30). Heavy angst when it's "ivy or else." *The New York Times,* p. C1.

Brooks-Gunn, J. (1984). The psychological significance of different pubertal events to young girls. *Journal of Early Adolescence, 4*(4), 315–327.

Brooks-Gunn, J. (1987). Pubertal processes: Their relevance for developmental research. In V. B. Van Hasselt & M. Hersen (Eds.), *Handbook of adolescent psychology.* New York: Pergamon Press.

Brooks-Gunn, J. (1988). Antecedents and consequences of variation in girls' maturational timing. *Journal of Adolescent Health Care, 9,* 365–373.

Brooks-Gunn, J. (1990). Overcoming barriers to adolescent research on pubertal and reproductive development. *Journal of Youth and Adolescence, 19*(5), 425–434.

Brooks-Gunn, J., Attie, I., Burrow, C., Rosso, J. T., & Warren, M. P. (1989). The impact of puberty on body and eating concerns in athletic and nonathletic contexts. *Journal of Early Adolescence, 9*(3), 269–290.

Brooks-Gunn, J., & Furstenberg, F. F., Jr. (1989). Adolescent sexual behavior. *American Psychologist, 44,* 249–257.

Brooks-Gunn, J., Newman, D. L., Holderness, C., & Warren, M. P. (1994). The experience of breast development and girls' stories about the purchase of a bra. *Journal of Youth and Adolescence, 23*(5), 539–564.

Brooks-Gunn, J., & Petersen, A. C. (1984). Problems in studying and defining pubertal events. *Journal of Youth and Adolescence, 13,* 181–196.

Brooks-Gunn, J., & Petersen, A. C. (1991). Studying the emergence of depression and depressive symptoms during adolescence. *Journal of Youth and Adolescence, 20*(2), 115–119.

Brooks-Gunn, J., & Reiter, E. O. (1990). The role of pubertal processes. In S. S. Feldman & G. R. Elliot (Eds.), *At the threshold: The developing adolescent.* Cambridge, MA: Harvard University Press.

Brooks-Gunn, J., & Ruble, D. N. (1982). The development of menstrual-related beliefs and behaviors during early adolescence. *Child Development, 53,* 1567–1577.

Brooks-Gunn, J., & Warren, M. (1988). The psychological significance of secondary sexual characteristics in nine-to-eleven-year-old girls. *Child Development, 59,* 1061–1069.

Brophy, J. (1986). Teacher influences on student achievement. *American Psychologist, 41,* 1069–1077.

Brown, A. L. (1997). Transforming schools into communities of thinking and learning about serious matters. *American Psychologist, 52*(4), 399–413.

Brown, B. B. (1990). Peer groups and peer culture. In S. S. Feldman & G. R. Elliot (Eds.), *At the threshold: The developing adolescent.* Cambridge, MA: Harvard University Press.

Brown, B. B. (1996). Visibility, vulnerability, development, and context: Ingredients for fuller understanding of peer rejection in adolescence. *Journal of Early Adolescence, 16*(1), 27–36.

Brown, B. B., Clasen, D. R., & Eicher, S. A. (1986). Perceptions of peer pressure, peer conformity dispositions, and self-reported behavior among adolescents. *Developmental Psychology, 22,* 521–530.

Brown, B. B., Lohr, M. J., & McClenahan, E. L. (1986). Early adolescents' perceptions of peer pressure. *Journal of Early Adolescence, 6,* 139–154.

Brown, B. B., Mory, M. S., & Kinney, D. (1994). Casting adolescent crowds in a relational perspective: Caricature, channel, and context. In R. Montemayor, G. R. Adams, & T. P. Gullotta (Eds.), *Personal relationships during adolescence.* Thousand Oaks, CA: Sage.

Brown, B. B., Mounts, N., Lamborn, S. D., & Steinberg, L. (1993). Parenting practices and peer group affiliation in adolescence. *Child Development, 64,* 467–482.

Brown, L. M., & Gilligan, C. (1992). *Meeting and the crossroads: Women's psychology and girls' development.* Cambridge, MA: Harvard University Press.

Brown, S. (1988). *Treating adult children of alcoholics: A developmental perspective.* New York: Wiley.

Browne, C. S., & Rife, J. C. (1991). Social, personality, and gender differences in at-risk and not-at-risk sixth-grade students. *Journal of Early Adolescence, 11*(4), 482–495.

Brownell, K. D. (1991). Dieting and the search for the perfect body: Where physiology and culture collide. *Behavior Therapy, 22,* 1–12.

Brownell, K. D., Rodin, J., & Wilmore, J. H. (1992). *Eating, body weight, and performance in athletes: Disorders of modern society.* Philadelphia: Lea & Febiger.

Brozan, N. (1986, January 13). Life after a son's suicide: One family's struggle. *The New York Times.*

Bruchac, J. (1993). Notes of a translator's son. In P. Riley (Ed.), *Growing up Native-American.* New York: Avon.

Bruno, J. E. (1996). Time perceptions and time allocation preferences among adolescent boys and girls. *Adolescence, 31*(121), 109–126.

Brush, S. G. (1991). Women in science and engineering. *American Scientist, 79*, 404–419.

Bryan, T., & Nelson, C. (1994). Doing homework: Perspectives of elementary and junior high school students. *Journal of Learning Disabilities, 27*(8), 488–499.

Bryant-Waugh, R., Hankins, M., Shafran, R., Lask, B. et al. (1996). A prospective follow-up of children with anorexia nervosa. *Journal of Youth and Adolescence, 25*(4), 431–437.

Bryant-Waugh, R., & Lask, B. (1995). Eating disorders in children. *Journal of Child Psychology & Psychiatry & Allied Disciplines, 36*(2), 191–202.

Buchanan, C. M. (1991). Pubertal status in early-adolescent girls: Relations to moods, energy, and restlessness. *Journal of Early Adolescence, 11*(2), 185–200.

Buchanan, C. M., Eccles, J. S., & Becker, J. B. (1992). Are adolescents the victims of raging hormones: Evidence for activational effects of hormones on moods and behavior at adolescence. *Psychological Bulletin, 111*(1), 62–107.

Buchanan, C. M., Maccoby, E. E., & Dornbusch, S. M. (1991). Caught between parents: Adolescents' experience in divorced homes. *Child Development, 62*, 1008–1029.

Buchholz, E. S., & Gol, B. (1986). More than playing house: A developmental perspective on the strengths in teenage motherhood. *American Journal of Orthopsychiatry, 56*(3), 347–359.

Buchholz, E. S., & Korn-Bursztyn, C. (1993). Children of adolescent mothers: Are they at risk for abuse? *Adolescence, 28*(110), 361–382.

Buckley, S., & Wilgoren, D. (1996). Young and experienced: Area's teenagers are having sex earlier with little concern for safety, monogamy. In F. C. Leeming, W. Dwyer, & D. P. Oliver (Eds.), *Issues in adolescent sexuality: Readings from The Washington Post*

*Writers Group.* Needham Heights, MA: Allyn & Bacon.

Buhrmester, D. (1990). Intimacy of friendship, interpersonal competence, and adjustment during preadolescence and adolescence. *Child Development, 61*, 1101–1111.

Buhrmester, D., & Furman, W. (1990). Perceptions of sibling relationships during middle childhood and adolescence. *Child Development, 61*, 1387–1398.

Buhrmester, D., Goldfarb, J., & Cantrell, D. (1992). Self-presentation when sharing with friends and nonfriends. *Journal of Early Adolescence, 12*(1), 61–79.

Buis, J. M., & Thompson, D. N. (1989). Imaginary audience and personal fable: A brief review. *Adolescence, 24*, 773–782.

Bukowski, W. M., Gauze, C., Hoza, B., & Newcomb, A. F. (1993). Differences and consistency between same-sex and other-sex peer relationships during early adolescence. *Developmental Psychology, 29*(2), 255–263.

Bukowski, W. M., & Hoza, B. (1989). Popularity and friendship: Issues in theory, measurement, and outcome. In T. J. Berndt & G. W. Ladd (Eds.), *Peer relationships in child development*. New York: Wiley.

Bukstein, O. G., & Van Hasselt, V. B. (1995). Substance use disorders. In V. B. Van Hasselt & M. Hersen (Eds.), *Handbook of adolescent psychopathology: A guide to diagnosis and treatment*. New York: Lexington.

Bulcroft, R. A. (1991). The value of physical change in adolescence: Consequences for the parent-adolescent exchange relationship. *Journal of Youth and Adolescence, 20*(1), 89–106.

Buntaine, R. L., & Costenbader, V. K. (1997). Self-reported differences in the experience and expression of anger between girls and boys. *Sex Roles, 36*(9/10), 625–638.

Burge, D., Hammen, C., Davila, J., Daley, S. E., Paley, B., Herzberg, D., & Lindberg, N. (1997). Attachment cognitions and college and work functioning two years later in late adolescent

women *Journal of Youth and Adolescence, 26*(3), 285–302.

Burleson, B. R. (1982). The development of comforting strategies in childhood and adolescence. *Child Development, 53*, 1578–1588.

Burnette, E. (1995, June). Black males retrieve a noble heritage. *APA Monitor*, pp. 1, 32.

Burnette, E. (1996, July). Sports lift esteem in young athletes. *APA Monitor*, p. 34.

Burroughs Wellcome Company. (1990). *STD*. Research Triangle Park, NC: Author.

Buss, D. M. (1995). Psychological sex differences: Origins through sexual selection. *American Psychologist, 50*(3), 164–168.

Butterfield, F. (1994, October 14). Teen-age homicide rate has soared. *The New York Times*, p. A22.

Butterfield, F. (1995, September 8). Grim forecast is offered on rising juvenile crime. *The New York Times*.

Butterfield, F. (1996a, May 5). A team's shoplifting spree shocks quiet Boston suburb. *The New York Times*.

Butterfield, F. (1996b, June 3). Successes reported for curfews, but doubts persist. *The New York Times*, pp. A1, B7.

Butterfield, F. (1996c, June 23). Intervening early costs less than "3-strikes" laws, study says. *The New York Times*, p. A24.

Butterfield, F. (1996d, August 9). After a decade, juvenile crime begins to drop. *The New York Times*, p. A1.

Buysse, A. (1996). Adolescents, young adults and AIDS: A study of actual knowledge vs. perceived need for additional information. *Journal of Youth and Adolescence, 25*(2), 259–272.

Buysse, A., & Van Oost, P. (1997). Impact of a school-based prevention programme on traditional and egalitarian adolescents' safer sex intentions. *Journal of Adolescence, 20*, 177–188.

Byrnes, J. P., & Takahira, S. (1993). Explaining gender differences on SAT-Math items. *Developmental Psychology, 29*(5), 805–810.

Cairns, R. B., Neckerman, H. J., & Cairns, B. D. (1989). Social networks and the shadows of synchrony. In G. R. Adams, R. Montemayor, & T. P. Gullotta (Eds.), *Biology of adolescent behavior and development.* Newbury Park, CA: Sage.

Cairns, R. B., Perrin, J. E., & Cairns, B. D. (1985). Social cognitions in early adolescence: Affiliative patterns. *Journal of Early Adolescence, 5,* 339–355.

Calhoun, G., Jurgens, J., & Chen, F. (1993). The neophyte female delinquent: A review of the literature. *Adolescence, 28*(110), 461–471.

Call, K. T. (1996). The implications of helpfulness for possible selves. In J. T. Mortimer & M. D. Finch (Eds.), *Adolescents, work, and family: An intergenerational developmental analysis.* Thousand Oaks, CA: Sage.

Callan, V. J., & Noller, P. (1986). Perceptions of communicative relationships in families with adolescents. *Journal of Marriage and the Family, 48,* 813–820.

Cameron, J. L. (1990). Factors controlling the onset of puberty in primates. In J. Bancroft & J. M. Reinisch (Eds.), *Adolescence and puberty.* New York: Oxford University Press.

Cameron, P., & Cameron, K. (1996). Homosexual parents. *Adolescence, 31*(124), 757–776.

Camp, B. W. (1996). Adolescent mothers and their children: Changes in maternal characteristics and child developmental and behavioral outcomes at school. *Journal of Developmental & Behavioral Pediatrics, 17*(3), 162–169.

Camp, B. W., Holman, S., & Ridgway, E. (1993). The relationship between social support and stress in adolescent mothers. *Journal of Developmental and Behavioral Pediatrics, 14*(6), 369–374.

Campbell, N. B., Milling, L., Laughlin, A., & Bush, E. (1993). The psychosocial climate of families with suicidal preadolescent children. *American Journal of Orthopsychiatry, 63*(1), 142–145.

Campbell, T. L., Byrne, B. B., & Baron, P. (1992). Gender differences in the expression of depressive symptoms in

early adolescents. *Journal of Early Adolescence, 12*(3), 326–338.

Canetti, L., Bachar, E., Galili-Weisstub, E., De-Nour, A. K., & Shalev, A. Y. (1997). Parental bonding and mental health in adolescence. *Adolescence, 32*(126), 381–394.

Cantwell, D. P. (1996). Attention deficit disorder: A review of the past 10 years. *Journal of the American Academy of Child and Adolescent Psychiatry, 35*(8), 978–987.

Cantwell, D. P., & Baker, L. (1991). Manifestations of depressive affect in adolescence. *Journal of Youth and Adolescence, 20*(2), 121–133.

Capaldi, D. M., Crosby, L., & Stoolmiller, M. (1996). Predicting the timing of first sexual intercourse for at-risk adolescent males. *Child Development, 67,* 344–359.

Capaldi, D. M., & Patterson, G. R. (1991). Relation of parental transitions to boys' adjustment problems: I. A linear hypothesis. II. Mothers at risk for transitions and unskilled parenting. *Developmental Psychology, 27,* 489–504.

Carlo, G., Koller, S. H., Eisenberg, N., Da Silva, M. S., & Frohlich, C. B. (1996). A cross-national study on the relations among prosocial moral reasoning, gender role orientations, and prosocial behaviors. *Developmental Psychology, 32*(2), 231–240.

Carlton-Ford, S., & Collins, W. A. (1988, August). *Family conflict: Dimensions, differential reporting, and developmental differences.* Paper presented at the annual meeting of the American Sociological Association, Chicago.

Carmody, D. (1993, January 18). Reaching teen-agers, without using a phone. *The New York Times.*

Carnegie Council on Adolescent Development (1989). *Turning points: Preparing American youth for the 21st century.* New York: Carnegie Corporation.

Carpendale, J. I. M., & Krebs, D. L. (1992). Situational variation in moral judgment: In a stage or on a stage? *Journal of Youth and Adolescence, 21*(2), 203–224.

Carr, M., & Schellenbach, C. (1993). Reflective monitoring in lonely adolescents. *Adolescence, 28*(111), 737–747.

Carruth, B. R., Goldberg, D. L., & Skinner, J. D. (1991). Do parents and peers mediate the influence of television advertising on food-related purchases? *Journal of Adolescent Research, 6*(2), 253–271.

Carter, B., & McGoldrick, M. (Eds.). (1988). *The changing family life cycle: A framework for family therapy* (2nd ed.). New York: Gardner Press.

Case, R. (1985). *Intellectual development: A systematic reinterpretation.* New York: Academic Press.

Case, R. (1992). The role of the frontal lobes in the regulation of cognitive development. *Brain and Cognition, 20,* 51–73.

Casey, M. B., Nuttall, R. L., & Pezaris, E. (1997). Mediators of gender differences in mathematics college entrance test scores: A comparison of spatial skills with internalized beliefs and anxieties. *Developmental Psychology, 33*(4), 669–680.

Caspi, A., Henry, B., McGee, R. O., Moffitt, T. E., & Silva, P. A. (1995). Temperamental origins of child and adolescent behavior problems: From age three to age fifteen. *Child Development, 66,* 55–68.

Cattell, R. B. (1971). *Abilities: Their structure, growth and action.* Boston: Houghton Mifflin.

Cauffman, E., & Steinberg, L. (1996). Interactive effects of menarcheal status and dating on dieting and disordered eating among adolescent girls. *Developmental Psychology, 32*(4), 631–635.

Celis, W. (1993, August 1). The fight over national standards. *The New York Times Education Life,* pp. 14–15.

Celis, W. (1995, February 5). Tradition on the wane: College drinking. *The New York Times,* pp. 1, 20.

Centers for Disease Control and Prevention. (1988). *Sexually transmitted disease statistics: 1987.* Atlanta, GA: Center for Infectious Disease Control.

Centers for Disease Control and Prevention. (1992). *HIV/AIDS surveillance report*. Atlanta, GA: Center for Infectious Disease Control.

Centers for Disease Control and Prevention. (1994). *Preventing tobacco use among young people: A report of the Surgeon General*. Atlanta, GA: U.S. Department of Health and Human Services.

Centers for Disease Control and Prevention. (1995). *HIV/AIDS surveillance report, 7*. Atlanta, GA: U.S. Department of Health and Human Services.

Centers for Disease Control and Prevention. (1996). *AIDS information: Statistical projections/trends*. Atlanta, GA: U.S. Department of Health and Human Services.

Chandler, T. J. L. (1990). The academic All-American as vaunted adolescent role-identity. *Sociology of Sport Journal, 7*, 287–293.

Chao, R. K. (1994). Beyond parental control and authoritarian parenting: Understanding Chinese parenting through the cultural notion of training. *Child Development, 65*, 1111–1119.

Chapman, P., Toma, R. B., Tuveson, R. V., & Jacob, M. (1997). Nutrition knowledge among adolescent high school female athletes. *Adolescence, 32*(126), 437–446.

Chase-Lansdale, P. L., Cherlin, A. J., & Kiernan, K. K. (1995). The long-term effects of parental divorce on the mental health of young adults: A developmental perspective. *Child Development, 66*(6), 1614–1634.

Chassin, L., Curran, P. J., Hussong, A. M., & Colder, C. R. (1996). The relation of parent alcoholism to adolescent substance use: A longitudinal follow-up study. *Journal of Abnormal Psychology, 105*(1), 70–80.

Chen, C., & Stevenson, H. W. (1995). Motivation and mathematics achievement: A comparative study of Asian-American, Caucasian-American, and East Asian high school students. *Child Development, 66*, 1215–1234.

Chess, S., & Thomas, A. (1984). *Origins and evolution of behavior disorders: From infancy to early adult life*. New York: Brunner/Mazel.

Chira, S. (1991, October 23). Educators ask if all-girl schools would make a difference in inner cities. *The New York Times*, p. B5.

Chira, S. (1992a, February 12). Bias against girls is found rife in schools, with lasting damage. *The New York Times*, p. 1.

Chira, S. (1992b, April 8). Renegade researchers offer rebuttal: U.S. schools are better than many say. *The New York Times*, p. A23.

Chira, S. (1992c, May 13). An Ohio college says women learn differently, so it teaches that way. *The New York Times*, p. B7.

Chira, S. (1992d, August 4). Minority students cite bias in higher-education quest. *The New York Times*, p. 1.

Chira, S. (1993, July 14). Is smaller better? Educators now say yes for high school. *The New York Times*, p. 1.

Chira, S. (1994, September 5). Parents take less of a role as pupils age. *The New York Times*.

Chisholm, L., & Bergeret, J. M. (1991). *Youth in the European Community*. Brussels: Commission of the European Community.

Chisholm, L., & Hurrelmann, K. (1995). Adolescence in modern Europe. Pluralized transition patterns and their implications for personal and social risks. *Journal of Adolescence, 18*, 129–158.

Chiu, L. (1990). The relationship of career goal and self-esteem among adolescents. *Adolescence, 25*(99), 593–598.

Choquet, M., Kovess, V., & Poutignat, N. (1993). Suicidal thoughts among adolescents: An intercultural approach. *Adolescence, 28*(111), 649–659.

Christopher, F. S. (1995). Adolescent pregnancy prevention. *Family Relations, 44*, 384–391.

Christopher, J. S., Nangle, D. W., & Hansen, D. J. (1993). Social-skills interventions with adolescents: Current issues and procedures. *Behavior Modification, 17*, 314–338.

Chu, L., & Powers, P. A. (1995). Synchrony in adolescence. *Adolescence, 30*(118), 453–461.

Chubb, N. H., Fertman, C. I., & Ross, J. L. (1997). Adolescent self-esteem and locus of control: A longitudinal study of gender and age differences. *Adolescence, 32*(125), 113–130.

Chung, W. S., & Pardeck, J. T. (1997). Explorations in a proposed national policy for children and families. *Adolescence, 32*(126), 429–436.

Claes, M. E. (1992). Friendship and personal adjustment during adolescence. *Journal of Adolescence, 15*, 39–55.

Clark, D. C., & Mokros, H. B. (1993). Depression and suicidal behavior. In P. H. Tolan & B. J. Cohler (Eds.), *Handbook of clinical research & practice with adolescents*. New York: Wiley.

Clark, M. L. (1989). Friendship and peer relations in black adolescents. In M. L. Clark (Ed.), *Black adolescents*. Berkeley, CA: Cobb and Henry.

Clark, M. L., & Ayers, M. (1993). Friendship expectations and friendship evaluations. *Youth & Society, 24*(3), 299–313.

Clark, R. D., & Shields, G. (1997). Family communication and delinquency. *Adolescence, 32*(125), 81–92.

Clarke, A. E., & Ruble, D. N. (1978). Young adolescents' beliefs concerning menstruation. *Child Development, 49*, 231–234.

Clausen, J. A. (1975). The social meaning of differential physical and sexual maturation. In S. E. Dragastin & G. H. Elder, Jr. (Eds.), *Adolescence in the life cycle: Psychological change and the social context*. New York: Halsted.

Cleverley, J., & Phillips, D. C. (1986). *Visions of childhood: Influential models from Locke to Spock*. New York: Teachers College Press.

Clingempeel, W. G., Colyar, J. J., Brand, E., & Hetherington, E. M. (1992). Children's relationships with maternal grandparents: A longitudinal study of family structure and pubertal status effects. *Child Development, 63*, 1404–1422.

Coates, D. L. (1987). Gender differences in the structure and support characteristics of black adolescents' social networks. *Sex Roles, 17*(11/12), 667–687.

Cochran, M., & Bø, I. (1989). The social networks, family involvement, and pro- and antisocial behavior of adolescent males in Norway. *Journal of Youth and Adolescence, 4,* 377–398.

Cohen, D., & Strayer, J. (1996). Empathy in conduct-disordered and comparison youth. *Developmental Psychology, 32*(6), 988–998.

Cohen, L. H., Burt, C. E., & Bjorck, J. P. (1987). Life stress and adjustment: Effects of life events experienced by young adolescents and their parents. *Developmental Psychology, 23,* 583–592.

Cohen, S. E., Beckwith, L., Parmelee, A. H., Sigman, M., Asarnow, R., & Espinosa, M. P. (1996). Prediction of low and normal school achievement in early adolescents born preterm. *Journal of Early Adolescence, 16*(1), 46–70.

Cohn, L. D. (1991). Sex differences in the course of personality development: A meta-analysis. *Psychological Bulletin, 109*(2), 252–266.

Coie, J. D., & Dodge, K. A. (1983). Continuities and changes in children's social status: A five year long longitudinal study. *Merrill-Palmer Quarterly, 29,* 261–282.

Coie, J. D., Dodge, K. A., & Kupersmidt, J. B. (1990). Peer group behavior and social status. In S. R. Asher & J. D. Coie (Eds.), *Peer rejection in childhood.* Cambridge: Cambridge University Press.

Colangelo, N. (1982). Characteristics of moral problems as formulated by gifted adolescents. *Journal of Moral Education, 11,* 219–232.

Colby, A., & Kohlberg, L. (1987). *The measurement of moral judgment. Volume 1. Theoretical foundations and research validation.* Cambridge: Cambridge University Press.

Coleman, J. C. (1978). Current contradictions in adolescent theory. *Journal of Youth and Adolescence, 7,* 1–11.

Coleman, J. S. (1961). *The adolescent society.* New York: Free Press.

Coleman, M., Ganong, L. H., & Ellis, P. (1985). Family structure and dating behavior of adolescents. *Adolescence, 20*(79), 537–543.

Coles, R., & Stokes, G. (1985). *Sex and the American teenager.* New York: Harper & Row.

Collins, W. A. (1990). Parent–child relationships in the transition to adolescence: Continuity and change in interaction, affect, and cognition. In R. Montemayor, G. R. Adams, & T. P. Gullotta (Eds.), *From childhood to adolescence: A transitional period?* Newbury Park, CA: Sage.

Collins, W. A., & Repinski, D. J. (1994). Relationships during adolescence: Continuity and change in interpersonal perspective. In R. Montemayor, G. R. Adams, & T. P. Gullotta (Eds.), *Personal relationships during adolescence.* Thousand Oaks, CA: Sage.

Collins, W. A., & Russell, G. (1991). Mother–child and father–child relationships in middle childhood and adolescence: A developmental analysis. *Developmental Review, 11,* 99–136.

Collins, W. E., Newman, B. M., & McKenry, P. C. (1995). Intrapsychic and interpersonal factors related to adolescent psychological well-being in stepmother and stepfather families. *Journal of Family Psychology, 9*(4), 433–445.

Compas, B. E. (1987a). Stress and life events during childhood and adolescence. *Clinical Psychology Review, 7,* 275–302.

Compas, B. E. (1987b). Coping with stress during childhood and adolescence. *Psychological Bulletin, 101*(3), 393–403.

Comstock, G. (1991). *Television and the American child.* San Diego, CA: Academic Press.

Conger, J. (1981). Freedom and commitment: Families, youth, and social change. *American Psychologist, 36,* 1475–1484.

Conger, J. C., & Conger, R. D. (1994). Differential parenting and change in sibling differences in delinquency. *Journal of Family Psychology, 8*(3), 287–302.

Conger, R. D., Conger, K. J., Elder, G. H., Lorenz, F. O., Simons, R. L., & Whitbeck, L. B. (1992). A family process model of economic hardship and adjustment of early adolescent boys. *Child Development, 63,* 526–541.

Conger, R. D., Conger, K. J., Elder, G. H., Lorenz, F. O., Simons, R. L., & Whitbeck, L. B. (1993). Family economic stress and adjustment of early adolescent girls. *Developmental Psychology, 29*(2), 206–219.

Conger, R. D., Ge, X., Elder, G. H., Lorenz, F. O., & Simons, R. L. (1994). Economic stress, coercive family process, and developmental problems of adolescents. *Child Development, 65,* 541–561.

Conger, R. D., Lorenz, F. O., Elder, G. H., Jr., Melby, J. N., Simons, R. L., & Conger, K. J. (1991). A process model of family economic pressure and early adolescent alcohol use. *Journal of Early Adolescence, 11*(4), 430–449.

Connelly, B., Johnston, D., Brown, I. D. R., Mackay, S., & Blackstock, E. G. (1993). The prevalence of depression in a high school population. *Adolescence, 28*(109), 149–158.

Connolly, S. D., Paikoff, R. L., & Buchanan, C. M. (1996). Puberty: The interplay of biological and psychosocial processes in adolescence. In G. R. Adams, R. Montemayor, & T. P. Gullotta (Eds.), *Psychosocial development during adolescence: Progress in developmental contextualism.* Thousand Oaks, CA: Sage.

Cook, R., Golombok, S., Bish, A., & Murray, C. (1995). Disclosure of donor insemination: Parental attitudes. *American Journal of Orthopsychiatry, 65*(4), 549–559.

Coombs, R. H., & Landsverk, J. (1988). Parenting styles and substance use during childhood and adolescence. *Journal of Marriage and the Family, 50,* 473–482.

Coombs, R. H., Paulson, M. J., & Richardson, M. A. (1991). Peer vs. parental influence in substance use among Hispanic and Anglo children and adolescents. *Journal of Youth and Adolescence, 20*(1), 73–88.

Cooney, T. M., Hutchinson, M. K., & Leather, D. M. (1995). Surviving the breakup? Predictors of parent–adult child relations after parental divorce. *Family Relations, 44*, 153–161.

Cooper, C. R. (1994). Cultural perspectives on continuity and change in adolescents' relationships. In R. Montemayor, G. R. Adams, & T. P. Gullotta (Eds.), *Personal relationships during adolescence.* Thousand Oaks, CA: Sage.

Cooper, C. R., & Carlson, C. I. (1990). *Shifts in family discourse from early to late adolescence: Age and gender patterns.* Paper presented at the meetings of NIMH Family Research Consortium, Monterey, CA.

Cooper, C. R., Grotevant, H. D., & Condon, S. M. (1983). Individuality and connectedness in the family as a context for adolescent identity formation and role-taking skill. In H. D. Grotevant & C. R. Cooper (Eds.), *Adolescent development in the family.* San Francisco: Jossey-Bass.

Cooper, C. S., Dunst, C. J., & Vance, S. D. (1990). The effect of social support on adolescent mothers' styles of parent–child interaction as measured on three separate occasions. *Adolescence, 25*(97), 49–58.

Cooper, L. (Trans.). (1932). *The Rhetoric of Aristotle.* New York: Appleton-Century-Crofts.

Copeland, E. P., & Hess, R. S. (1995). Differences in young adolescents' coping strategies based on gender and ethnicity. *Journal of Early Adolescence, 15*(2), 203–219.

Cornwell, G. T., Eggebeen, D. J., & Meschke, L. L. (1996). The changing family context of early adolescence. *Journal of Early Adolescence, 16*(2), 141–156.

Corvo, K. N. (1997). Community-based youth violence prevention. *Youth & Society, 28*(3), 291–316.

Côté, J. E. (1996). Identity: A multidimensional analysis. In G. R. Adams, R. Montemayor, & T. P. Gullotta (Eds.), *Psychosocial development during adolescence: Progress in developmental contextualism.* Thousand Oaks, CA: Sage.

Cotterell, J. L. (1992). School size as a factor in adolescents' adjustment to the transition to secondary school. *Journal of Early Adolescence, 12*(1), 28–45.

Cousins, S. D. (1989). Culture and self-perception in Japan and the United States. *Journal of Personality and Social Psychology, 56*(1), 124–131.

Covell, K., Rose-Krasnor, L., & Fletcher, K. (1994). Age differences in understanding peace, war, and conflict resolution. *International Journal of Behavioral Development, 17*(4), 717–737.

Covey, L. A., & Feltz, D. L. (1991). Physical activity and adolescent female psychological development. *Journal of Youth and Adolescence, 20*(4), 463–474.

Crain, W. (1992). *Theories of development: Concepts and applications* (3rd ed.). Englewood Cliffs, NJ: Prentice-Hall.

Crawford, J. D., & Osler, D. C. (1975). Body composition at menarche: The Frisch-Revelle hypothesis revisited. *Pediatrics, 56*, 449–458.

Creasey, G. L., & Koblewski, P. J. (1991). Adolescent grandchildren's relationships with maternal and paternal grandmothers and grandfathers. *Journal of Adolescence, 14*, 373–387.

Crespi, T. D. (1997). Violent children and adolescents: Facing the treatment crisis in child and family interaction. *Family Therapy, 23*(1), 43–50.

Crespi, T. D., & Rigazio-DiGilio, S. A. (1996). Adolescent homicide and family pathology: Implications for research and treatment with adolescents. *Adolescence, 31*(122), 353–367.

Crespi, T. D., & Sabatelli, R. M. (1993). Adolescent runaways and family strife: A conflict-induced differentiation framework. *Adolescence, 28*(112), 867–878.

Crespi, T. D., & Sabatelli, R. M. (1997). Children of alcoholics and adolescence: Individuation, development, and family systems. *Adolescence, 32*(126), 407–418.

Crockett, L. J., Bingham, C. R., Chopak, J. S., & Vicary, J. R. (1996). Timing of first sexual intercourse: The role of social control, social learning, and problem behavior. *Journal of Youth and Adolescence, 25*(1), 89–112.

Crockett, L. J., & Petersen, A. C. (1987). Pubertal status and psychosocial development: Findings from the early adolescence study. In R. M. Lerner & T. T. Bock (Eds.), *Biosocial-psychosocial interactions in early adolescence* (pp. 173–188). Hillsdale, NJ: Erlbaum.

Crockett, L. J., Petersen, A. C., Graber, J. A., Schulenberg, J. E., & Ebata, A. (1989). School transitions and adjustment during early adolescence. *Journal of Early Adolescence, 9*(3), 181–210.

Cross, S., & Markus, H. (1991). Possible selves across the lifespan. *Human Development, 34*, 230–255.

Crouter, A. C., Manke, B. A., & McHale, S. M. (1995). The family context of gender intensification in early adolescence. *Child Development, 66*, 317–329.

Crowther, J. H., Tennenbaum, D. L., Hobfoll, S. E., & Stephens, M. A. P. (Eds.) (1992). *The etiology of bulimia nervosa: The individual and family context.* Washington, DC: Hemisphere.

Crystal, D. S., Kato, K., Olson, S., & Watanabe, H. (1995). Attitudes toward self-change: A comparison of Japanese and American university students. *International Journal of Behavioral Development, 18*(4), 577–593.

Csikszentmihalyi, M., & Larson, R. (1984). *Being adolescent: Conflict and growth in the teenage years.* New York: Basic Books.

Csikszentmihalyi, M., Rathunde, K., & Whalen, S. (1993). *Talented teenagers: The roots of success and failure.* New York: Cambridge University Press.

Culp, A. M., Clyman, M. M., & Culp, R. E. (1995). Adolescent depressed mood, reports of suicide attempts, and asking for help. *Adolescence, 30*(120), 827–837.

Cummings, E. M., & Davies, P. (Eds.). (1994). *Children and marital conflict: The impact of family dispute and resolution.* New York: Guilford Press.

Cunliffe, T. (1992). Arresting youth crime: A review of social skills training with young offenders. *Adolescence, 27*(108), 891–900.

Curran, P. J., Stice, E., & Chassin, L. (1997). The relation between adolescent alcohol use and peer alcohol use: A longitudinal random coefficients model. *Journal of Consulting and Clinical Psychology, 65*(1), 130–140.

Curry, C., Trew, K., Turner, I., & Hunter, J. (1994). The effect of life domains on girls' possible selves. *Adolescence, 29*(113), 133–150.

Custer, G. (1994, November). Psychologists ease school transitions. *APA Monitor*, p. 44.

Custer, M. (1993). Adoption as an option for unmarried pregnant teens. *Adolescence, 28*(112), 891–902.

Dacey, C. M., Nelson, W. M., Clark, V. F., & Aikman, K. G. (1991). Bulimia and body image dissatisfaction in adolescence. *Child Psychiatry and Human Development, 21*(3), 179–184.

Damon, W., & Hart, D. (1988). *Self understanding in childhood and adolescence.* New York: Cambridge University Press.

D'Angelo, L. L., Weinberger, D. A., & Feldman, S. S. (1995). Like father, like son? Predicting male adolescents' adjustment from parents' distress and self-restraint. *Developmental Psychology, 31*(6), 883–896.

Darling, C. A., Davidson, J. K., & Passarello, L. C. (1992). The mystique of first intercourse among college youth: The role of partners, contraceptive practices, and psychological reactions. *Journal of Youth and Adolescence, 21*(1), 97–117.

Darling, N., Hamilton, S. F., & Niego, S. (1994). Adolescents' relations with adults outside the family. In R. Montemayor, G. R. Adams, & T. P. Gullotta (Eds.), *Personal relationships during adolescence.* Thousand Oaks, CA: Sage.

Darling, N., & Steinberg, L. (1993). Parenting style as context: An integrative model. *Psychological Bulletin, 113*(3), 487–496.

Darling-Hammond, L. (September, 1991). Achieving the national education goals. *NJEA Review, 65*(1), 18–24.

Darmody, J. P. (1991). The adolescent personality: Formal reasoning and values. *Adolescence, 26*(103), 731–742.

Da Vanzo, J., & Goldscheider, F. (1990). Coming home again: Returns to the parental home of young adults. *Population Studies, 44,* 241–255.

Davies, P. T., & Windle, M. (1997). Gender-specific pathways between maternal depressive symptoms, family discord, and adolescent adjustment. *Developmental Psychology, 33*(4), 657–668.

Davis, C., & Katzman, M. (1997). Charting new territory: Body esteem, weight satisfaction, depression, and self-esteem among Chinese males and females in Hong Kong. *Sex Roles, 36*(7/8), 449–460.

Davis, L., & Tolan, P. H. (1993). Alternative and preventive interventions. In P. H..Tolan & B. J. Cohler (Eds.), *Handbook of clinical research and practice with adolescents.* New York: Wiley.

Dawkins, M. P. (1997). Drug use and violent crime among adolescents. *Adolescence, 32*(126), 395–406.

DeAngelis, T. (1993, October). Despite rise of violence by youth, solutions exist. *APA Monitor*, p. 40.

DeAngelis, T. (1994, August). Women less likely to pursue technology-related careers. *APA Monitor*, p. 30.

DeAngelis, T. (1996a, October). Minorities' performance is hampered by stereotypes. *APA Monitor*, p. 38.

DeAngelis, T. (1996b, October). Data are emerging on the psychology of bisexuals. *APA Monitor*, p. 58.

DeBaryshe, B. D., Patterson, G. R., & Capaldi, D. M. (1993). A performance model for academic achievement in early adolescent boys. *Developmental Psychology, 29*(5), 795–804.

DeBlassie, A. M., & DeBlassie, R. R. (1996). Education of Hispanic youth: A cultural lag. *Adolescence, 31*(121), 205–216.

De Gaston, J. F., Jensen, L., & Weed, S. (1995). A closer look at adolescent sexual activity. *Journal of Youth and Adolescence, 24*(4), 465–479.

De Gaston, J. F., Weed, S., & Jensen, L. (1996). Understanding gender differences in adolescent sexuality. *Adolescence, 31*(121), 217–231.

deGroot, G. (1994, July). Do single-sex classes foster better learning? *APA Monitor*, pp. 60–61.

Deković, M., & Meeus, W. (1997). Peer relations in adolescence: effects of parenting and adolescents' self-concept. *Journal of Adolescence, 20,* 163–176.

Delaney, C. H. (1995). Rites of passage in adolescence. *Adolescence, 30*(120), 891–897.

Delaney, M. E. (1996). Across the transition to adolescence: Qualities of parent/adolescent relationships and adjustment. *Journal of Early Adolescence, 16*(3), 274–300.

de Luccie, M. F., & Davis, A. J. (1991). Father–child relationships from the preschool years through mid-adolescence. *Journal of Genetic Psychology, 152*(2), 225–238.

de Man, A. F., Leduc, C. P., & Labreche-Gauthier, L. (1993). Correlates of suicidal ideation in French-Canadian adolescents: Personal variables, stress, and social support. *Adolescence, 28*(112), 819–830.

Demos, J., & Demos, V. (1969). Adolescence in historical perspective. *Journal of Marriage and the Family, 31,* 632–638.

Dencker, M. (1996, March 14). Perfect match: Mentorship lifts black achievers program. *The Star-Ledger*, p. CE-8.

Denholm, C. (1995). ''I am neither general nor diplomat'': Reflections on the Persian Gulf War by gifted Canadian adolescents. *Adolescence, 30*(118), 381–401.

Denton, R. E., & Kampfe, C. M. (1994). The relationship between family variables and adolescent substance abuse: A literature review. *Adolescence, 29*(114), 475–495.

DeParle, J. (1992, November 26). Teaching high school students how to work. *The New York Times*, pp. A1, D15.

DeRosier, M. E., Kupersmidt, J. B., & Patterson, C. J. (1994). Children's academic and behavioral adjustment as a function of the chronicity and proximity of peer rejection. *Child Development, 65*(6), 1799–1813.

DeSantis, J. P., Ketterlinus, R. D., & Youniss, J. (1990). Black adolescents' concerns that they are academically able. *Merrill-Palmer Quarterly, 36*(2), 287–299.

Desiderato, L., & Crawford, H. J. (1995). Risky sexual behavior in college students: Relationships between number of sexual partners, disclosure of previous risky behavior, and alcohol use. *Journal of Youth and Adolescence, 24*(1), 55–68.

Dewey, J. (1916). *Democracy and education.* New York: Macmillan.

De Witt, K. (1997, June 23). Girl games on computers, where shoot 'em up simply won't do. *The New York Times,* p. D3.

Deyoung, Y., & Zigler, E. F. (1994). Machismo in two cultures: Relation to punitive child-rearing practices. *American Journal of Orthopsychiatry, 64,* 386–395.

Dickerson, V. C., & Zimmerman, J. (1992). Families with adolescents: Escaping problem lifestyles. *Family Process, 31,* 341–353.

Dinges, M. M., & Oetting, E. R. (1993). Similarity in drug use patterns between adolescents and their friends. *Adolescence, 28*(110), 253–266.

Dishion, T. J., Andrews, D. W., & Crosby, L. (1995). Antisocial boys and their friends in early adolescence: Relationship characteristics, quality, and interactional process. *Child Development, 66,* 139–151.

Dishion, T. J., Patterson, G. R., Stoolmiller, M., & Skinner, M. L. (1991). Family, school, and behavioral antecedents to early adolescent involvement with antisocial peers. *Developmental Psychology, 27*(1), 172–180.

Dismuke, D. (1988, November). Reducing suicides. *NEA Today,* p. 21.

Dobkin, P. L., Tremblay, R. E., Masse, L. C., & Vitaro, F. (1995). Individual and peer characteristics in predicting boys' early onset of substance abuse: A seven-year longitudinal study. *Child Development, 66,* 1198–1214.

Dodge, K. A. (1983). Behavioral antecedents: A peer social status. *Child Development, 54,* 1386–1399.

Doherty, W. J., & Allen, W. (1994). Family functioning and parental smoking as predictors of adolescent cigarette use: A six-year prospective study. *Journal of Family Psychology, 8*(3), 347–353.

Doherty, W. J., & Needle, R. H. (1991). Psychological adjustment and substance use among adolescents before and after a parental divorce. *Child Development, 62,* 328–337.

Donald, M., Lucke, J., Dunne, M., & Raphael, B. (1995). Gender differences associated with young people's emotional reactions to intercourse. *Journal of Youth and Adolescence, 24*(4), 453–464.

Donnerstein, E., Linz, D., & Penrod, S. (1987). *The question of pornography: Research findings and policy implications.* New York: Free Press.

Donovan, J. E., & Jessor, R. (1985). Structure of problem behavior in adolescence and young adulthood. *Journal of Consulting and Clinical Psychology, 53,* 890–904.

Dorn, L. D., Nottelmann, E. D., Inoff-Germain, G., Susman, E. J., & Chrousos, G. P. (1990). Perceptions of puberty: Adolescent, parent, and health care personnel. *Developmental Psychology,* **26**(2) 322–329.

Dornbusch, S. M., Carlsmith, J. M., Bushwall, S. J., Ritter, P. L., Leiderman, H., Hastorf, A. H., & Gross, R. T. (1985). Single parents, extended households, and control of adolescents. *Child Development, 56,* 326–341.

Dornbusch, S. M., Herman, M. R., & Morley, J. A. (1996). Domains of adolescent achievement. In G. R. Adams, R. Montemayor, & T. P. Gullotta (Eds.), *Psychosocial development during adolescence: Progress in developmental contextualism.* Thousand Oaks, CA: Sage.

Downey, G., & Coyne, J. C. (1990). Children of depressed parents: An integrative review. *Psychological Bulletin, 108,* 50–76.

Downs, A. C. (1990). The social biological constructs of social competency. In T. P. Gullotta, G. R. Adams, & R. Montemayor (Eds.), *Developing social competency in adolescence.* Newbury Park, CA: Sage.

Downs, A. C., & Hillje, L. S. (1993). Historical and theoretical perspectives on adolescent sexuality: An overview. In T. P. Gullotta, G. R. Adams, & R. Montemayor (Eds.), *Adolescent sexuality.* Newbury Park, CA: Sage.

Downs, W. R., & Rose, S. R. (1991). The relationship of adolescent peer groups to the incidence of psychosocial problems. *Adolescence, 26*(102), 473–492.

Draper, P., & Harpending, H. (1982). Father absence and reproductive strategy: An evolutionary perspective. *Journal of Anthropological Research, 38,* 255–273.

Drevets, R. K., Benton, S. L., & Bradley, F. O. (1996). Students' perceptions of parents' and teachers' qualities of interpersonal relations. *Journal of Youth and Adolescence, 25*(6), 787–802.

Driscoll, M. P. (1994). *Psychology of learning for instruction.* Needham Heights, MA: Allyn & Bacon.

Dryfoos, J. G. (1990). *Adolescents at risk: Prevalence and prevention.* New York: Oxford University Press.

Dubas, J. S., Graber, J. A., & Petersen, A. C. (1991). A longitudinal investigation of adolescents' changing perceptions of pubertal timing. *Developmental Psychology, 27,* 4, 580–586.

Dubas, J. S., & Petersen, A. C. (1993). Differential cognitive development in adolescent girls. In M. Sugar (Ed.), *Female adolescent development* (2nd ed.). New York: Brunner/Mazel.

DuBois, D. L., & Hirsch, B. J. (1990). School and neighborhood friendship patterns of blacks and whites in early adolescence. *Child Development, 61,* 524–536.

DuBois, D. L., & Hirsh, B. J. (1993). School-nonschool friendship patterns in early adolescence. *Journal of Early Adolescence, 13*(1), 102–122.

du Bois-Reymond, M., & Ravesloot, J. (1996). The roles of parents and peers in the sexual and relational socialization of adolescents. In K. Hurrelmann & S. F. Hamilton (Eds.), *Social problems and social contexts in adolescence: Perspectives across boundaries.* New York: Aldine De Gruyter.

Duckett, E., & Richards, M. H. (1995). Maternal employment and the quality of daily experience for young adolescents of single mothers. *Journal of Family Psychology*, 9(4), 418–432.

Dugger, C. W. (1995, March 9). Guiding hand to college for ghetto youth. *The New York Times*, pp. A1, B12.

Dukes, R. L., & Martinez, R. (1994). The impact of ethgender on self-esteem among adolescents. *Adolescence*, 29(113), 105–115.

Duncan, T. E., Duncan, S. C., & Hops, H. (1996). The role of parents and older siblings in predicting adolescent substance use: Modeling development via structural equation latent growth methodology. *Journal of Family Psychology*, 10(2), 158–172.

Dunn, J., & Plomin, R. (1990). *Separate lives: Why siblings are so different*. New York: Basic Books.

Dunphy, D. (1963). The social structure of urban adolescent peer groups. *Sociometry*, 26, 230–246.

Dunphy, D. (1969). *Cliques, crowds, and gangs: Group life in Sydney adolescents*. Melbourne, Australia: Cheshire.

Dunphy, D. (1972). Peer group socialization. In R. Muuss (Ed.), *Adolescent behavior and society* (3rd. ed.). New York: Random House.

duToit, B. M. (1987). Menarche and sexuality among a sample of black South African schoolgirls. *Social Science and Medicine*, 24, 561–571.

Dweck, C. S., & Leggett, E. L. (1988). A social-cognitive approach to motivation and personality. *Psychological Review*, 95, 256–272.

Dye, J. S. (1989). Parental involvement in curriculum matters: Parents, teachers and children working together. *Educational Research*, 31, 20–35.

Dyk, P. H., & Adams, G. R. (1990). Identity and intimacy: An initial investigation of three theoretical models using cross-lag panel correlations. *Journal of Youth and Adolescence*, 19(2), 91–110.

Eagly, A. H. (1995). The science and politics of comparing men and women. *American Psychologist*, 50(3), 145–158.

East, P. L. (1996). The younger sisters of childbearing adolescents: Their attitudes, expectations, and behaviors. *Child Development*, 67, 267–282.

East, P. L., & Felice, M. E. (1990). Outcomes of parent–child relationships of former adolescent mothers and their 12-year-old children. *Journal of Developmental and Behavioral Pediatrics*, 11(4), 175–183.

East, P. L., & Felice, M. E. (1992). Pregnancy risk among the younger sisters of pregnant and childbearing adolescents. *Journal of Developmental and Behavioral Pediatrics*, 13(2), 128–136.

East, P. L., Lerner, R. M., Lerner, J. V., Soni, R. T., & Jacobson, L. P. (1992). Early adolescent-peer group fit, peer relations, and psychosocial competence: A short-term longitudinal study. *Journal of Early Adolescence*, 12(2), 132–152.

Eaton, Y. M., Mitchell, M. L., & Jolley, J. M. (1991). Gender differences in the development of relationships during late adolescence. *Adolescence*, 26(103), 565–568.

Ebata, A. T., & Moos, R. H. (1991). Coping and adjustment in distressed and healthy adolescents. *Journal of Applied Developmental Psychology*, 12(1), 33–54.

Eberly, M. B., Montemayor, R., & Flannery, D. J. (1993). Variation in adolescent helpfulness toward parents in a family context. *Journal of Early Adolescence*, 13(3), 228–244.

Eccles, J. S., Buchanan, C. M., Flanagan, C., Fuligni, A., Midgley, C., & Yee, D. (1991). Control versus autonomy during early adolescence. *Journal of Social Issues*, 47(4), 53–68.

Eccles, J. S., Flanagan, C., Lord, S., Midgley, C., et al. (1996). Schools, families, and early adolescents: What are we doing wrong and what can we do instead? *Journal of Developmental & Behavioral Pediatrics*, 17(4), 267–276.

Eccles, J. S., & Midgley, C. (1989). Stage/environment fit: Developmentally appropriate classrooms for early adolescents. In R. Ames & C. Ames (Eds.), *Research on motivation in education* (Vol. 3). San Diego, CA: Academic Press.

Eccles, J. S., & Midgley, C. (1990). Changes in academic motivation and self-perception during early adolescence. In R. Montemayor, G. R. Adams, & T. P. Gullotta (Eds.), *From childhood to adolescence: A transitional period?* Newbury Park, CA: Sage.

Eccles, J. S., Midgley, C., & Adler, T. (1984a). Gender-related changes in the school environment: Effects on achievement motivation. In J. G. Nicholls (Ed.), *The development of achievement motivation*. Greenwich, CT: JAI Press.

Eccles, J. S., Midgley, C., & Adler, T. (1984b). Grade-related changes in the school environment: Effects on achievement motivation. In J. G. Nicholls (Ed.), *The development of achievement motivation*. Greenwich, CT: JAI.

Eccles, J. S., Midgley, C., Wigfield, A., Buchanan, C. M., Reuman, D., Flanagan, C., & MacIver, D., (1993). Development during adolescence: The impact of stage-environment fit on young adolescents' experiences in schools and in families. *American Psychologist*, 48(2), 90–101.

Eccles-Parsons, J., Adler, T., & Kaczala, C. (1982). Socialization of achievement attitudes and beliefs: Parental influences. *Child Development*, 53, 310–321.

Eder, D. (1985). The cycle of popularity: Interpersonal relations among female adolescents. *Sociology and Education*, 58, 154–165.

Edwards, R. (1995, December). The search for a proper punishment. *APA Monitor*, p. 30.

Edwards, W. J. (1996a). A sociological analysis of an invisible minority group: Male adolescent homosexuals. *Youth & Society*, 27(3), 334–355.

Edwards, W. J. (1996b). A measurement of delinquency differences between a delinquent and nondelinquent sample: What are the implications? *Adolescence*, 31(124), 973–989.

Ehrenberg, M. F., Cox, D. N., & Koopman, R. F. (1990). The prevalence of depression in high school students. *Adolescence*, 25(100), 905–912.

Ehrenberg, M. F., Cox, D. N., & Koopman, R. F. (1991). The relationship between self-efficacy and depression in adolescents. *Adolescence, 26*(102), 361–374.

Eicher, J. B., Baizerman, S., & Michelman, J. (1991). Adolescent dress, Part II: A qualitative study of suburban high school students. *Adolescence, 26,* 103, 678–686.

Eichorn, D. H. (1975). Asynchronization in adolescent development. In S. E. Dragastin & G. H. Elder, Jr. (Eds.), *Adolescence in the life cycle: Psychological change and social context.* Washington, DC: Hemisphere.

Eisele, J., Hertsgaard, D., & Light, H. K. (1986). Factors related to eating disorders in young adolescent girls. *Adolescence, 21*(82), 283–290.

Eisenberg, N. (1986). *Altruistic emotion, cognition and behavior.* Hillsdale, NJ: Erlbaum.

Eisenberg, N. (1990). Prosocial development in early and mid-adolescence. In R. Montemayor, G. R. Adams, & T. P. Gullotta (Eds.), *From childhood to adolescence: A transitional period?* Newbury Park, CA: Sage.

Eisenberg, N., Carlo, G., Murphy, B., & Van Court, P. (1995). Prosocial development in late adolescence: A longitudinal study. *Child Development, 66,* 1179–1197.

Eisenberg, N., & Lennon, R. (1983). Sex differences in empathy and related capacities. *Psychological Bulletin, 94*(1), 100–131.

Eisenberg, N., & Miller, P. A. (1987). The relation of empathy to prosocial and related behaviors. *Psychological Bulletin, 101,* 91–119.

Eisenberg, N., Miller, P. A., Shell, R., McNalley, S., & Shea, C. (1991). Prosocial development in adolescence: A longitudinal study. *Developmental Psychology, 27*(5), 849–857.

Eisenberg, N., & Mussen, P. H. (1989). *The roots of prosocial behavior in children.* Cambridge: Cambridge University Press.

Elder, G. H., Jr. (1971). *Adolescent socialization and personality development.* Chicago: Rand McNally.

Elder, G. H., Jr. (1975). Adolescence in the life cycle: An introduction. In S. E. Dragastin & G. H. Elder (Eds.), *Adolescence in the life cycle: Psychological change in social context.* New York: Wiley.

Elder, G. H., Jr., Eccles, J. S., Ardelt, M., & Lord, S. (1995). Inner-city parents under economic pressure: Perspectives on the strategies of parenting. *Journal of Marriage and the Family, 57,* 771–784.

Elkind, D. (1967). Egocentrism in adolescence. *Child Development, 38,* 1025–1034.

Elkind, D. (1978). Understanding the young adolescent. *Adolescence, 13,* 127–134.

Elkind, D. (1984). *All grown up and no place to go.* Reading, MA: Addison-Wesley.

Elkind, D. (1988). *Miseducation.* New York: Knopf.

Elkind, D. (1994a). *A sympathetic understanding of the child: Birth to sixteen* (3rd ed.). Needham Heights, MA: Allyn & Bacon.

Elkind, D. (1994b). *Ties that stress: The new family imbalance.* Cambridge, MA: Harvard University.

Elkind, D., & Bowen, R. (1979). Imaginary audience behavior in children and adolescents. *Developmental Psychology, 15,* 33–44.

Elkins, I. J., McGue, M., & Iacono, W. G. (1997). Genetic and environmental influences on parent-son relationships: Evidence for increasing genetic influence during adolescence. *Developmental Psychology, 33*(2), 351–363.

Elliot, D. S., Huizinga, D., & Menard, S. (1989). *Multiple problem youth: Delinquency, substance use, and mental health problems.* New York: Springer-Verlag.

Ellis, L., & Wagemann, B. M. (1993). The religiosity of mothers and their offspring as related to the offspring's sex and sexual orientation. *Adolescence, 28*(109), 227–234.

Ellis, N. B. (1991). An extension of the Steinberg acceleration hypothesis. *Journal of Early Adolescence, 11*(2), 221–235.

Ellis-Schwabe, M., & Thornburg, H. D. (1986). Conflict areas between parents and their adolescents. *Journal of Psychology, 120,* 59–68.

Elmen, J. (1991). Achievement orientation in early adolescence: Developmental patterns and social correlates. *Journal of Early Adolescence, 11*(1), 125–151.

Elmen, J., & Offer, D. (1993). Normality, turmoil, and adolescence. In P. H. Tolan & B. J. Cohler (Eds.), *Handbook of clinical research and practice with adolescents.* New York: Wiley.

Emery, R. (1982). Interparental conflict and the children of discord and divorce. *Psychological Bulletin, 92,* 310–330.

Emmons, L. (1996). The relationship of dieting to weight in adolescents. *Adolescence, 31*(121), 167–178.

Engel, A. (1994). Sex roles and gender stereotyping in young women's participation in sport. *Feminism and Psychology, 4,* 439–448.

Ennett, S. T., & Bauman, K. E. (1994). The contribution of influence and selection to adolescent peer group homogeneity: The case of adolescent cigarette smoking. *Journal of Personality and Social Psychology, 67*(4), 653–663.

Enright, R. D., & Deist, S. H. (1979). Social perspective taking as a component of identity formation. *Adolescence, 14,* 517–522.

Enright, R., & Lapsley, D. K. (1980). Social role-taking: A review of the construct, measures, and measurement prospectives. *Review of Educational Research, 56,* 647–674.

Enright, R., Lapsley, D. K., & Shukla, D. (1979). Adolescent egocentrism in early and late adolescence. *Adolescence, 14,* 687–695.

Enright R., Levy, V., Harris, D., & Lapsley, D. (1987). Do economic conditions influence how theorists view adolescents? *Journal of Youth and Adolescence, 16,* 541–560.

Enright, R. D., Shukla, D. G., & Lapsley, D. K. (1980). Adolescent egocentrism-sociocentrism and self-consciousness. *Journal of Youth and Adolescence, 9,* 101–116.

Ensminger, M. E. (1990). Sexual activity and problem behaviors among black, urban adolescents. *Child Development, 61,* 2032–2046.

Entwisle, D. R. (1990). Schools and the adolescent. In S. S. Feldman & G. R. Elliot (Eds.), *At the threshold: The developing adolescent.* Cambridge, MA: Harvard University Press.

Epstein, J. L. (1983). The influence of friends on achievement and affective outcomes. In J. L. Epstein & N. L. Karweit (Eds.), *Friends in school.* New York: Academic Press.

Epstein, J. L. (1992). School and family partnerships. In M. Alkin (Ed.), *Encyclopedia of educational research* (6th ed.). New York: Macmillan.

Erb, T. O. (1983). Career preferences of early adolescents: Age and sex differences. *Journal of Early Adolescence, 3,* 349–359.

Erikson, E. H. (1950). *Childhood and society.* New York: W. W. Norton.

Erikson, E. H. (1960, March–April). Youth and the life cycle. *Children* (now *Children today*), pp. 43–49.

Erikson, E. H. (1963). *Childhood and society* (2nd ed.). New York: W. W. Norton.

Erikson, E. H. (1964). *Insight and responsibility: Lectures on the ethical implications of psychoanalytic insight.* New York: W. W. Norton.

Erikson, E. H. (1968). *Identity, youth, and crisis.* New York: W. W. Norton.

Erikson, E. H. (1974). Womanhood and the inner space (1968). In J. Strouse, (Ed.), *Women and analysis.* New York: Dell.

Erikson, E. H. (1980). *Identity and the life cycle.* New York: W. W. Norton.

Esbensen, F., & Huizinga, D. (1991). Juvenile victimization and delinquency. *Youth and Society, 23*(2), 202–228.

Esman, A. H. (1991). Mid-adolescence: Foundations for later psychopathology. In S. I. Greenspan & G. H. Pollock (Eds.), *The course of life,* Volume IV: *Adolescence.* Madison, CT: International Universities Press.

Etlin, M. (1988, April). Is there a gifted underachiever? *NEA Today,* pp. 10–11.

Evans, C., & Eder, D. (1993). "No exit": Processes of social isolation in the middle school. *Journal of Contemporary Ethnography, 22,* 139–170.

Evans, E. D., Rutberg, J., Sather, C., & Turner, C. (1991). Content analysis of contemporary teen magazines for adolescent females. *Youth & Society, 23*(1), 99–120.

Evans, S., Vallano, G., & Pelham, W. E. (1995). Attention-deficit hyperactivity disorder. In V. B. Van Hasselt & M. Hersen (Eds.), *Handbook of adolescent psychopathology: A guide to diagnosis and treatment.* New York: Lexington.

Eveleth, P., & Tanner, J. (1976). *Worldwide variation in human growth.* New York: Cambridge University Press.

Fabrega, H., Jr. (1989). Cultural relativism and psychiatric illness. *Journal of Nervous and Mental Disease, 177,* 415–425.

Fabrega, H., Jr. (1992). The role of culture in a theory of psychiatric illness. *Social Science and Medicine, 35,* 91–103.

Fabrega, H., Jr., & Miller, B. (1995). Cultural and historical foundations. In V. B. Van Hasselt & M. Hersen (Eds.), *Handbook of adolescent psychopathology: A guide to diagnosis and treatment.* New York: Lexington.

Fagan, R. W. (1994). Social well-being in university students. *Journal of Youth and Adolescence, 23*(2), 237–249.

Falbo, T., & Polit, D. F. (1986). Quantitative review of the only child literature: Research evidence and theory development. *Psychological Bulletin, 100*(2), 176–189.

Falchikov, N. (1986). Images of adolescence: An investigation into the accuracy of the image of adolescence constructed by British newspapers. *Journal of Adolescence, 9,* 167–180.

Falchikov, N. (1989). Adolescent images of adolescence. *Journal of Adolescence, 12,* 139–154.

Fallon, A. (1990). Culture in the mirror: Sociocultural determinants of body image. In T. F. Cash & T. Pruzinsky (Eds.), *Body image: Development, deviance, and change.* New York: Guilford Press.

Farrell, L. T. (1988). Factors that affect a victim's self-disclosure in father-daughter incest. *Child Welfare, 67*(5), 462–470.

Fasick, F. A. (1988). Patterns of formal education in high school as rites de passage. *Adolescence, 23*(90), 457–468.

Fasick, F. A. (1994). On the "invention of adolescence." *Journal of Early Adolescence, 14*(1), 6–23.

Fassinger, R. E. (1991). The hidden minority: Issues and challenges in working with lesbian women and gay men. *The Counseling Psychologist, 19,* 157–176.

Fauber, R., Forehand, R., Thomas, A. M., & Wierson, M. (1990). A mediational model of the impact of marital conflict on adolescent adjustment in intact and divorced families: The role of disrupted parenting. *Child Development, 61,* 1112–1123.

Faubert, M., Locke, D. C., Sprinthall, N. A., & Howland, W. H. (1996). Promoting cognitive and ego development of African-American rural youth: A program of deliberate psychological education. *Journal of Adolescence, 19,* 533–543.

Faulkenberry, J. R., Vincent, M., James, A., & Johnson, W. (1987). Coital behaviors, attitudes, and knowledge of students who experience early coitus. *Adolescence, 22*(86), 321–332.

Feather, N. (1980). Values in adolescence. In J. Adelson (Ed.), *Handbook of adolescent psychology.* New York: Wiley.

Featherstone, D. R., Cundick, B. P., & Jensen, L. C. (1992). Differences in school behavior and achievement between children from intact, reconstituted, and single-parent families. *Adolescence, 27*(105), 1–12.

Feder, B. J. (1996a, May 24). Increase in teen-age smoking sharpest among black males. *The New York Times,* p. A20.

Feder, B. J. (1996b, February 16). A study finds minors buying more cigarettes. *The New York Times.*

Feder, B. J. (1997, April 20). Surge in teen-age smoking left an industry vulnerable. *The New York Times*, pp. 1, 28.

Federal Bureau of Investigation (FBI). (1991). *Crime in the United States: Uniform Crime Report*. Washington, D.C.: U.S. Department of Justice.

Feigelman, S., Stanton, B. F., & Ricardo, I. (1993). Perceptions of drug selling and drug use among urban youths. *Journal of Early Adolescence, 13*(3), 267–284.

Feiring, C., & Lewis, M. (1993). Do mothers know their teenagers' friends? Implications for individuation in early adolescence. *Journal of Youth and Adolescence, 22*(4), 337–354.

Feldman, S., & Rosenthal, D. (1991). Age expectations for behavioral autonomy in Hong Kong, Australian, and American youth: The influence of family variables and adolescents' values. *International Journal of Psychology, 26*, 1–23.

Feldman, S. S., & Gehring, T. M. (1988). Changing perceptions of family cohesion and power across adolescence. *Child Development, 59*, 1034–1045.

Feldman, S. S., & Weinberger, D. A. (1994). Self-restraint as a mediator of family influences on boys' delinquent behavior: A longitudinal study. *Child Development, 65*, 195–211.

Feldman, S. S., & Wentzel, K. R. (1990). The relationship between parenting styles, sons' self-restraint, and peer relations in early adolescence. *Journal of Early Adolescence, 10*(4), 439–454.

Feldman, S. S., & Wentzel, K. R. (1995). Relations of marital satisfaction to peer outcomes in adolescent boys: A longitudinal study. *Journal of Early Adolescence, 15*(2), 220–237.

Feltey, K. M., Ainslie, J. J., & Geib, A. (1991). Sexual coercion attitudes among high school students: The influence of gender and rape education. *Youth & Society, 23*, 229–250.

Fenzel, L. M. (1989). Role strains and the transition to middle school: Longitudinal trends and sex differences. *Journal of Early Adolescence, 9*(3), 211–226.

Fenzel, L. M. (1992). The effect of relative age on self-esteem, role strain, and anxiety. *Journal of Early Adolescence, 12*(3), 253–266.

Ferguson, A., & McKinlay, I. (1991). Adolescent smoking. *Child: Care, Health and Development, 17*(3), 213–224.

Fergusson, D. M., & Horwood, L. J. (1996). The role of adolescent peer affiliations in the continuity between childhood behavioral adjustment and juvenile offending. *Journal of Abnormal Child Psychology, 24*(2), 205–221.

Fergusson, D. M., Horwood, L. J., & Lynskey, M. (1994). The childhoods of multiple problem adolescents: A 15-year longitudinal study. *Journal of Child Psychology & Psychiatry & Allied Disciplines, 35*(6), 1123–1140.

Fergusson, D. M., Horwood, L. J., & Lynskey, M. (1995). Maternal depressive symptoms and depressive symptoms in adolescents. *Journal of Child Psychology & Psychiatry & Allied Disciplines, 36*(7), 1161–1178.

Fergusson, D. M., Lynskey, M., & Horwood, L. J. (1996a). The short-term consequences of early onset cannabis use. *Journal of Abnormal Child Psychology, 24*(4), 499–512.

Fergusson, D. M., Lynskey, M. T., & Horwood, L. J. (1996b). Factors associated with continuity and changes in disruptive behavior patterns between childhood and adolescence. *Journal of Abnormal Child Psychology, 24*(5), 533–553.

Fichman, L., Koestner, R., & Zuroff, D. C. (1997). Dependency and distress at summer camp. *Journal of Youth and Adolescence, 26*(2), 217–232.

Fiedler, E. D., Lange, R. E., & Winebrenner, S. (1994, January). Ability grouping: Geared for the gifted. *The Educational Digest*, pp. 52–55.

Field, T., Lang, C., Yando, R., & Bendell, D. (1995). Adolescents' intimacy with parents and friends. *Adolescence, 30*(117), 133–140.

Finch, M. D., & Mortimer, J. T. (1996). Future directions for research on adolescents, work, and family. In J. T. Mortimer & M. D. Finch (Eds.), *Adolescents, work, and family: An intergenerational developmental analysis*. Thousand Oaks, CA: Sage.

Fine, G. A., Mortimer, J. T., & Roberts, D. F. (1990). Leisure, work, and the mass media. In S. S. Feldman & G. R. Elliot (Eds.), *At the threshold: The developing adolescent*. Cambridge, MA: Harvard University Press.

Fine, M. A. (1993). Current approaches to understanding family diversity: An overview of the special issue. *Family Relations, 42*, 235–237.

Fischer, C. T. & Alapack, R. J. (1987). A phenomenological approach to adolescence. In V. B. Van Hasselt and M. Hersen (Eds.), *Handbook of adolescent psychology*. New York: Pergamon.

Fischer, J. L., Munsch, J., & Greene, S. M. (1996). Adolescence and intimacy. In G. R. Adams, R. Montemayor, & T. P. Gullotta (Eds.), *Psychosocial development during adolescence: Progress in developmental contextualism*. Thousand Oaks, CA: Sage.

Fischer, K. W. (1980). A theory of cognitive development: The control and construction of hierarchies of skills. *Psychological Review, 87*, 477–531.

Fisher, I. (1992, August 2). The comeback trail. *The New York Times Education Section*, p. 21.

Fisher, K. (1985, November). Parental support vital in coping with abuse. *APA Monitor*, p. 12.

Fisher, L. A., & Baumann, K. E. (1988). Influence and selection in the friend-adolescent relationship: Findings from studies of adolescent smoking and drinking. *Journal of Applied Social Psychology, 18*, 289–314.

Fisher, T. D. (1986). Parent–child communication about sex and young adolescents' sexual knowledge and attitudes. *Adolescence, 21*(83), 517–527.

Fishman, J. (1980). Fatness, puberty and ovulation. *New England Journal of Medicine, 303*, 42.

Fitzgerald, M., Joseph, A. P., Hayes, M., & O'Regan, M. (1995). Leisure activities of adolescent schoolchildren. *Journal of Adolescence, 18*, 349–358.

Fitzgerald, M. D. (1994). Resistant attitudes and behaviors of adolescents in residential care: Considerations and strategies. *Child and Youth Care Forum*, 23(6), 365–375.

Flanagan, C., Schulenberg, J., & Fuligni, A. (1993). Residential setting and parent–adolescent relationships during the college years. *Journal of Youth and Adolescence*, 22(2), 171–187.

Flanagan, C. A., & Eccles, J. (1993). Changes in parents' work status and adolescents' adjustment at school. *Child Development*, 64(1), 246–257.

Flannery, D. J., Rowe, D. C., & Gulley, B. L. (1993). Impact of pubertal status, timing, and age on adolescent sexual experience and delinquency. *Journal of Adolescent Research*, 8, 21–40.

Flannery, D. J., Vazsonyi, A. T., & Rowe, D. C. (1996). Caucasian and Hispanic early adolescent substance use: Parenting, personality, and school adjustment. *Journal of Early Adolescence*, 16(1), 71–89.

Flavell, J. H. (1985). *Cognitive development*. Englewood Cliffs, NJ: Prentice-Hall.

Fletcher, A. C., Darling, N. E., Dornbusch, S. M., & Steinberg, L. (1995). The company they keep: Relation of adolescents' adjustment and behavior to their friends' perceptions of authoritative parenting in the social network. *Developmental Psychology*, 31(2), 300–310.

Fletcher, J., Branen, L. J., & Lawrence, A. (1997). Late adolescents' perceptions of their caregiver's feeding styles and practices and those they will use with their own children. *Adolescence*, 32(126), 287–298.

Flint, L. (1992). Adolescent parental affinity-seeking: Age- and gender-mediated strategy use. *Adolescence*, 27(106), 417–434.

Florsheim, P. (1997). Chinese adolescent immigrants: Factors related to psychosocial adjustment. *Journal of Youth and Adolescence*, 26(2), 143–164.

Flum, H. (1994). The evolutive style of identity formation. *Journal of Youth and Adolescence*, 23(4), 489–498.

Flynn, K., & Fitzgibbon, M. (1996). Body image ideals of low-income African American mothers and their pre-adolescent daughters. *Journal of Youth and Adolescence*, 25(5), 615–630.

Folkenberg, J. (1985, May). Teen pregnancy: Who opts for adoption? *Psychology Today*, p. 16.

Foltz, C., Overton, W. F., & Ricco, R. B. (1995). Proof construction: Adolescent development from inductive to deductive problem-solving strategies. *Journal of Experimental Child Psychology*, 59(2), 179–195.

Fontaine, J. H., & Hammond, N. L. (1996). Counseling issues with gay and lesbian adolescents. *Adolescence*, 31(124), 817–830.

Ford, D. Y. (1992). Self-perceptions of underachievement and support for the achievement ideology among early adolescent African-Americans. *Journal of Early Adolescence*, 12(3), 228–252.

Ford, D. Y., & Harris, J. J., III. (1996). Perceptions and attitudes of black students toward school, achievement, and other educational variables. *Child Development*, 67, 1141–1152.

Ford, M. R., & Lowery, C. R. (1986). Gender differences in moral reasoning: A comparison of the use of justice and care orientations. *Journal of Personality and Social Psychology*, 50, 777–783.

Fordham, S. (1988). Racelessness as a factor in black students' school success: Pragmatic strategy or pyrrhic victory? *Harvard Educational Review*, 58, 326–341.

Fordham, S., & Ogbu, J. U. (1986). Black students' school success: Coping with the "burden of 'acting white.'" *The Urban Review*, 18, 176–205.

Forehand, R. (1992). Parental divorce and adolescent maladjustment: Scientific inquiry vs. public information. *Behavior Research and Therapy*, 30(4), 319–327.

Forehand, R., Middleton, K., & Long, N. (1987). Adolescent functioning as a consequence of recent parental divorce and the parent-adolescent relationship. *Journal of Applied Developmental Psychology*, 8(3), 305–315.

Forehand, R., Neighbors, B., & Wierson, M. (1991). The transition of adolescence: The role of gender and stress in problem behavior and competence. *Journal of Child Psychology & Psychiatry & Allied Disciplines*, 32(6), 929–937.

Forehand, R., & Nousiainen, S. (1993). Maternal and paternal parenting: Critical dimensions in adolescent functioning. *Journal of Family Psychology*, 7(2), 213–221.

Forman, S. G. (1993). *Coping skills interventions for children and adolescents*. San Francisco: Jossey-Bass.

Forrest, J. D. (1990). Cultural influences on adolescents' reproductive behavior. In J. Bancroft and J. M. Reinish (Eds.), *Adolescence and puberty*. New York: Oxford University Press.

Forste, R. T., & Heaton, T. B. (1988). Initiation of sexual activity among female adolescents. *Youth & Society*, 19(3), 250–268.

Foster, V., & Sprinthall, N. A. (1992). Developmental profiles of adolescents and young adults choosing abortion: Stage sequence, decalage, and implications for policy. *Adolescence*, 27(107), 655–673.

Fowler, B. A. (1989). The relationship of body image perception and weight status to recent change in weight status of the adolescent female. *Adolescence*, 24(95), 557–568.

Foxcroft, D. R., & Lowe, G. (1995). Adolescent drinking, smoking and other substance use involvement: links with perceived family life. *Journal of Adolescence*, 18, 159–177.

Frank, A., Avery, C., & Laman, M. (1988). Young adults' perceptions of their relationships with their parents: Individual differences in connectedness, competence, and emotional autonomy. *Developmental Psychology*, 24, 729–737.

Frank, S., Pirsch, L., & Wright, V. (1990). Late adolescents' perceptions of their relationships with their parents: Relationships among deidealization, autonomy, relatedness, and insecurity and implications for adolescent adjustment and ego identity status. *Journal of Youth and Adolescence*, 19, 571–588.

Franklin, C., & Streeter, C. L. (1995). Assessment of middle class youth at-risk to dropout: School, psychological and family correlates. *Child and Youth Services Review, 17,* 433–448.

Franz, W., & Reardon, D. (1992). Differential impact of abortion on adolescents and adults. *Adolescence, 27*(105), 161–172.

Fraser, B. J. (1989). Research synthesis on school and instructional effectiveness. *International Journal of Educational Research, 13,* 707–719.

Freedman-Doan, C. R., Arbreton, A. J. A., Harold, R. D., & Eccles, J. S. (1993). Looking forward to adolescence: Mothers' and fathers' expectations for affective and behavioral change. *Journal of Early Adolescence, 13*(4), 472–502.

Freeman, S. C. (1993). Donald Super: A perspective on career development. *Journal of Career Development, 19*(4), 255–266.

Freiberg, P. (1991a, April). Killing by kids "epidemic" forecast. *APA Monitor,* pp. 1, 31.

Freiberg, P. (1991b, April). Self-esteem gender gap widens in adolescence. *APA Monitor,* p. 29.

Freiberg, P. (1995, June). Psychologists examine attacks on homosexuals. *APA Monitor,* pp. 30–31.

French, D. C., & Waas, G. A. (1985). Behavior problems of peer-neglected and peer-rejected elementary-age children: Parent and teacher perspectives. *Child Development, 56,* 246–252.

Freud, A. (1946). *The ego and the mechanisms of defense.* New York: International Universities Press.

Freud, A. (1958). Adolescence. *Psychoanalytic Study of the Child, 13,* 255–278.

Freud, A. (1966). Instinctual anxiety during puberty. In *The writings of Anna Freud: The ego and the mechanisms of defense.* New York: International Universities Press.

Freud, A. (1969). Adolescence as a developmental disturbance. In G. Caplan & S. Lebovici (Eds.), *Adolescence.* New York: Basic Books.

Freud, S. (1920/1965). *A general introduction to psychoanalysis.* New York: Washington Square Press.

Freud, S. (1925/1961). Some psychical consequences of the anatomical distinction between the sexes. In J. Strachey (Ed.), *The standard edition of the complete psychological works of Sigmund Freud* (Vol. 19). London: Hogarth Press.

Frey, C. U., & Röthlisberger, C. (1996). Social support in healthy adolescents. *Journal of Youth and Adolescence, 25*(1), 17–31.

Friedman, S. (1991, October 13). Teaching young fathers responsibility. *The New York Times* (New Jersey Section), p. 10.

Friedman, W. J., Robinson, A. B., & Friedman, B. L. (1987). Sex differences in moral judgments? A test of Gilligan's theory. *Psychology of Women Quarterly, 11,* 37–46.

Friesen, D. (1968). Academic-athletic-popularity syndrome in the Canadian high school. *Adolescence, 3,* 39–52.

Frisch, R. E. (1983). Fatness, puberty and fertility: The effects of nutrition and physical training on menarche and ovulation. In J. Brooks-Gunn & A. C. Petersen (Eds.), *Girls at puberty: Biological and psychosocial perspectives.* New York: Plenum Press.

Frisch, R. E., & McArthur, J. W. (1974). Menstrual cycles: Fatness as a determinant of minimum weight for height necessary for their maintenance or onset. *Science, 185,* 949–951.

Frisch, R. E., & Revelle, R. (1970). Height and weight at menarche and a hypothesis of critical body weights and adolescent events. *Science, 169,* 397–399.

Fromme, K., & Rivet, K. (1994). Young adults' coping style as a predictor of their alcohol use and response to daily events. *Journal of Youth and Adolescence, 23*(1), 85–97.

Frost, A. K., & Pakiz, B. (1990). The effects of marital disruption on adolescents: Time as a dynamic. *American Journal of Orthopsychiatry, 60*(4), 544–554.

Fryer, D. (1997). International perspectives on youth unemployment and mental health: Some central issues. *Journal of Adolescence, 20,* 333–342.

Fuhrman, W., & Buhrmester, D. (1992). Age and sex differences in perceptions of networks of personal relationships. *Child Development, 63,* 103–115.

Fuligni, A. J. (1997). The academic achievement of adolescents from immigrant families: The roles of family background, attitudes, and behavior. *Child Development, 68*(2), 351–363.

Fuligni, A. J., & Eccles, J. S. (1993). Perceived parent–child relationships and early adolescents' orientation toward peers. *Developmental Psychology, 29*(4), 622–632.

Fuligni, A. J., Eccles, J. S., & Barber, B. L. (1995). The long-term effects of seventh-grade ability grouping in mathematics. *Journal of Early Adolescence, 15*(1), 58–89.

Fulton, A. M., Murphy, K. R., & Anderson, S. L. (1991). Increasing adolescent mothers' knowledge of child development: An intervention program. *Adolescence, 26*(101), 73–81.

Funk, J. (1993). Reevaluating the impact of video games. *Clinical Pediatrics, 32,* 86–90.

Furby, L., & Beyth-Marom, R. (1992). Risk-taking in adolescence: A decision-making perspective. *Developmental Review, 12,* 1–44.

Furman, W., & Wehner, E. A. (1994). Romantic views: Toward a theory of adolescent romantic relationships. In R. Montemayor, G. R. Adams, & T. P. Gullotta (Eds.), *Personal relationships during adolescence.* Thousand Oaks, CA: Sage.

Furstenberg, F. F., Jr. (1990). Coming of age in a changing family system. In S. S. Feldman & G. R. Elliot (Eds.), *At the threshold: The developing adolescent.* Cambridge, MA: Harvard University Press.

Furstenberg, F. F., Jr., Brooks-Gunn, J., & Chase-Lansdale, L. (1989). Teenaged pregnancy and childbearing. *American Psychologist, 44*(2), 313–320.

Furstenberg, F. F., Jr., Brooks-Gunn, J., & Morgan, S. P. (1987). *Adolescent mothers in later life.* New York: Cambridge University Press.

Furstenberg, F. F., Jr., & Cherlin, A. J. (1991). *Divided families: What happens to children when parents part?.* Cambridge, MA: Harvard University Press.

Furstenberg, F. F., Jr., Moore, K. A., & Peterson, J. L. (1986). Sex education and sexual experience among adolescents. *American Journal of Public Health, 75,* 1221–1222.

Furstenberg, F. F., Jr., Morgan, S. P., Moore, K. A., & Peterson, J. L. (1987). Race differences in the timing of first intercourse. *American Sociological Review, 52,* 511–518.

Furstenberg, F. F., Jr., & Nord, C. W. (1985). Parenting apart: Patterns of child-rearing after marital disruption. *Journal of Marriage and the Family, 47,* 893–904.

Gaddis, A., & Brooks-Gunn, J. (1985). The male experience of pubertal change. *Journal of Youth and Adolescence, 14*(1), 61–69.

Gagnon, J. H. (1990). The explicit and implicit use of the scripting perspective in sex research. *Annual Review of Sex Research, 1,* 1–43.

Galambos, N. L., & Maggs, J. L. (1991). Out-of-school care of young adolescents and self-reported behavior. *Developmental Psychology, 27*(4), 644–655.

Galbo, J. J. (1984). Adolescents' perceptions of significant adults: A review of the literature. *Adolescence, 19,* 951–970.

Galbo, J. J. (1986). Adolescents' perceptions of significant adults: Implications for the family, the school, and youth serving agencies. *Children and Youth Services Review, 8,* 37–51.

Galbo, J. J., & Demetrulias, D. M. (1996). Recollections of nonparental significant adults during childhood and adolescence. *Youth & Society, 27*(4), 403–420.

Gallimore, M., & Kurdek, L. A. (1992). Parent depression and parent authoritative discipline as correlates of young adolescents' depression. *Journal of Early Adolescence, 12*(2), 187–196.

Galotti, K. M. (1989). Gender differences in self-reported moral reasoning: A review and new evidence. *Journal of Youth and Adolescence, 18*(5), 475–489.

Galotti, K. M., & Kozberg, S. F. (1996). Adolescents' experience of a life-framing decision. *Journal of Youth and Adolescence, 25*(1), 3–16.

Galotti, K. M., Kozberg, S. F., & Appleman, D. (1990). Younger and older adolescents' thinking about commitments. *Journal of Experimental Child Psychology, 50,* 324–339.

Galotti, K. M., Kozberg, S. F., & Farmer, M. C. (1991). Gender and developmental differences in adolescents' conceptions of moral reasoning. *Journal of Youth and Adolescence, 20*(1), 13–30.

Gamble, W. C. (1994). Perceptions of controllability and other stressor event characteristics as determinants of coping among young adolescents and young adults. *Journal of Youth and Adolescence, 23*(1), 65–84.

Garbarino, J. (1996). Youth in dangerous environments: Coping with the consequences. In K. Hurrelmann & S. F. Hamilton (Eds.), *Social problems and social contexts in adolescence: Perspectives across boundaries.* New York: Aldine De Gruyter.

Garcia-Coll, C. T., Hoffman, J., & Oh, W. (1987). The social ecology and early parenting of Caucasian adolescent mothers. *Child Development, 58,* 955–963.

Gardner, F. E. M. (1987). Positive interaction between mothers and conduct-problem children: Is there training for harmony as well as fighting? *Journal of Abnormal Child Psychology, 15*(2), 283–294.

Gardner, H. (1983). *Frames of mind: Theory of multiple intelligence.* New York: Basic Books.

Gardner, H. (1993). *Multiple intelligence: The theory in practice.* New York: Basic Books.

Gardner, O. S., Keller, J. W., & Piotrowski, C. (1996). Retention issues as perceived by African-American university students. *Psychology: A Journal of Human Behavior, 33*(1), 20–21.

Gargiulo, J., Attie, I., Brooks-Gunn, J., & Warren, M. P. (1985). *Girls dating behavior as a function of social context and maturation.* Paper presented at a symposium on "Love and Sex in Early and Middle Adolescence" at the biennial meeting of the Society for Research in Child Development, Toronto.

Garland, A. F., & Zigler, E. (1993). Adolescent suicide prevention: Current research and social policy implications. *American Psychologist, 48*(2), 169–182.

Garmezy, N., & Masten, A. S. (1986). Stress, competence, and resilience: Common frontiers for therapist and psychopathologist. *Behavior Therapy, 17*(5), 500–521.

Garmon, L. C., Basinger, K. S., Gregg, V. R., & Gibbs, J. C. (1996). Gender differences in stage and expression of moral judgment. *Merrill-Palmer Quarterly, 42*(3), 418–437.

Garnefski, N., & Diekstra, R. F. W. (1997a). Adolescents from one parent, stepparent, and intact families: emotional problems and suicide attempts. *Journal of Adolescence, 20,* 201–208.

Garnefski, N., & Diekstra, R. F. W. (1997b). "Comorbidity" of behavioral, emotional, and cognitive problems in adolescence. *Journal of Youth and Adolescence, 26*(3), 321–338.

Garnefski, N., & Okma, S. (1996). Addiction-risk and aggressive/criminal behaviour in adolescence: influences of family, school and peers. *Journal of Adolescence, 19,* 503–512.

Garrod, A., Smulyan, L., Powers, S. I., & Kilkenny, R. (1992). *Adolescent portraits: Identity, relationships and challenges.* Needham Heights, MA: Allyn & Bacon.

Garton, A. F., & Pratt, C. (1987). Participation and interest in leisure activities by adolescent schoolchildren. *Journal of Adolescence, 10,* 341–351.

Garwood, S. G., & Allen, L. (1979). Self-concept and identified problem differences between pre and postmenarchial adolescents. *Journal of Clinical Psychology, 35,* 528–537.

Garzarelli, P., Everhart, B., & Lester, D. (1993). Self-concept and academic performance in gifted and academically weak students. *Adolescence, 28*(109), 235–238.

Gauze, C., Bukowski, W. M., Aquan-Assee, J., & Sippola, L. K. (1996). Interactions between family environment and friendship and associations with self-perceived well-being during early adolescence. *Child Development, 67*, 2201–2216.

Gavin, L. A., & Furman, W. (1996). Adolescent girls' relationships with mothers and best friends. *Child Development, 67*, 375–386.

Ge, X., Best, K. M., Conger, R. D., & Simons, R. L. (1996). Parenting behaviors and the occurrence and co-occurrence of adolescent depressive symptoms and conduct problems. *Developmental Psychology, 32*(4), 717–731.

Ge, X., Conger, R. D., Cadoret, R. J., Neiderhiser, J. M., et al. (1996). The developmental interface between nature and nurture: A mutual influence model of child antisocial behavior and parent behaviors. *Developmental Psychology, 32*(4), 574–589.

Ge, X., Conger, R. D., Lorenz, F. O., Shanahan, M., et al. (1995). Mutual influences in parent and adolescent psychological distress. *Developmental Psychology, 31*(3), 406–419.

Ge, X., Lorenz, F. O., Conger, R. D., Elder, G. H., Jr., & Simons, R. L. (1994). Trajectories of stressful life events and depressive symptoms during adolescence. *Developmental Psychology, 30*(4), 467–483.

Geary, D. C., Salthouse, T. A., Chen, C., & Fan, L. (1996). Are East Asian versus American differences in arithmetical ability a recent phenomenon? *Developmental Psychology, 32*(2), 254–262.

Gecas, V., & Burke, P. J. (1995). Self and identity. In K. S. Cook, G. A. Fine, & J. S. House (Eds.), *Sociological perspectives on social psychology*. Boston: Allyn & Bacon.

Gelles, R. J., & Straus, M. A. (1987). Is violence toward children increasing? A comparison of 1975 and 1985 national survey rates. *Journal of Interpersonal Violence, 2*, 212–222.

Gelman, R., & Baillargeon, R. (1983). A review of some Piagetian concepts. In J. H. Flavell & E. M. Markman (Eds.), *Manual of child psychology*. Volume 3, *Cognitive Development*. New York: Wiley.

Geohegan, T. (1996, December 1). Child labor in the 1990's. *The New York Times*, News of the Week in Review, p. 9.

George, T. P., & Hartmann, D. P. (1996). Friendship networks of unpopular, average, and popular children. *Child Development, 67*, 2301–2316.

Gerstein, M., Lichtman, M., & Barokas, J. U. (1988). Occupational plans of adolescent women compared to men: A cross-sectional examination. *The Career Development Quarterly, 36*, 222–230.

Gesell, A., & Ilg, F. L. (1943/1949). *Infant and child in the culture of today*. In A. Gesell & F. L. Ilg, (Eds.), *Child development*. New York: Harper & Row.

Gfellner, B. M. (1990). Culture and consistency in ideal and actual child-rearing practices: A study of native and white Canadian parents. *Journal of Comparative Family Studies, 21*, 413–423.

Gfellner, B. M. (1994). A matched-group comparison of drug use and problem behavior among Canadian Indian and white adolescents. *Journal of Early Adolescence, 14*(1), 24–48.

Gibbons, F. X., & Gerrard, M. (1995). Predicting young adults' health risk behavior. *Journal of Personality and Social Psychology, 69*(3), 505–517.

Gibbs, J. C. (1991). Toward an integration of Kohlberg's and Hoffman's moral development theories. *Human Development, 34*, 88–104.

Gibbs, J. T. (1987). Identity and marginality: Issues in the treatment of biracial adolescents. *American Journal of Orthopsychiatry, 57*(2), 265–278.

Gies, F., & Gies, J. (1987). *Marriage and the family in the middle ages*. New York: Harper & Row.

Gifford, V. D., & Dean, M. M. (1990). Differences in extracurricular activity participation, achievement, and attitudes toward school between ninth-grade students attending junior high school and those attending senior high school. *Adolescence, 25*(100), 799–802.

Gilbert, M. C. (1996). Attributional patterns and perceptions of math and science among fifth-grade through seventh-grade girls and boys. *Sex Roles, 35*(7/8), 489–504.

Gilbert, S. (1997, April 9). Early puberty onset seems prevalent. *The New York Times*, p. C10.

Gilchrist, L. D., & Schinke, S. P. (1987). Adolescent pregnancy and marriage. In V. B. Van Hasselt & M. Hersen (Eds.), *Handbook of adolescent psychology*. New York: Pergamon Press.

Giles-Sims, J., Straus, M. A., & Sugarman, D. B. (1995). Child, maternal, and family characteristics associated with spanking. *Family Relations, 44*, 170–176.

Gilligan, C. (1982). New maps of development: New visions of maturity. *American Journal of Orthopsychiatry, 52*, 199–212.

Gilligan, C. (1988). Remapping the moral domain: New images of self in relationship. In C. Gilligan, J. V. Ward, & J. M. Taylor (Eds.), *Mapping the moral domain*. Cambridge, MA: Harvard University Press.

Gilligan, C., & Wiggins, G. (1987). The origins of morality in early childhood relationships. In J. Kagan & S. Lamb (Eds.), *The emergence of morality in young children*. Chicago: University of Chicago Press.

Gillmore, M. R., Hawkins, J. D., Day, L. E., & Catalano, R. F. (1992). Friendship and deviance: New evidence on an old controversy. *Journal of Early Adolescence, 12*(1), 80–95.

Ginsberg, B. G. (1995). Parent–adolescent relationship program (PARD): Relationship enhancement therapy with adolescents and their families (fathers and sons). *Psychotherapy, 32*(1), 108–112.

Ginsburg, G. S., & Bronstein, P. (1993). Family factors related to children's intrinsic/extrinsic motivational orientation and academic performance. *Child Development, 64*, 1461–1474.

Ginzberg, E. (1972). Toward a theory of occupational choice: A restatement. *Vocational Guidance Quarterly, 20,* 169–176.

Ginzberg, E. (1990). Career development. In D. Brown, L. Brooks, & Associates (Eds.), *Career choice and development.* San Francisco: Jossey-Bass.

Giordano, P. C., Cernkovich, S. A., & DeMaris, A. (1993). The family and peer relations of black adolescents. *Journal of Marriage and the Family, 55,* 277–287.

Gjerde, P. F. (1986). The interpersonal structure of family interaction settings: Parent–adolescent relations in dyads and triads. *Developmental Psychology, 22*(3), 297–304.

Glaberson, W. (1992, April 5). A new twist on lost youth: The mall rats. *The New York Times,* pp. 1, 31.

Glasgow, K. L., Dornbusch, S. M., Troyer, L., Steinberg, L., & Ritter, P. L. (1997). Parenting styles, adolescents' attributions, and educational outcomes in nine heterogeneous high schools. *Child Development, 68*(3), 507–529.

Glass, G., Cohen, L., Smith, M., & Filby, N. (1982). *School class size: Research and policy.* Beverly Hills, CA: Sage.

Glasser, W. (1990). *The quality school.* New York: Harper & Row.

Glick, P. C., & Lin, S. (1986). Recent changes in divorce and remarriage. *Journal of Marriage and the Family, 48,* 737–747.

Goddard, N., Subotsky, F., & Fombonne, E. (1996). Ethnicity and adolescent deliberate self-harm. *Journal of Adolescence, 19,* 513–521.

Godenne, G. D. (1978). *Counseling handicapped adolescents.* Keynote address at the 2nd Annual Goucher College Education Conference,

Goff, J. L. (1990). Sexual confusion among certain college males. *Adolescence, 25*(99), 599–614.

Goldberg, A. D., & Chandler, T. J. L. (1989). The role of athletics: The social world of high school adolescents. *Youth & Society, 21*(2), 238–250.

Goldberg, P. A. (1968). Are women prejudiced against women? *Transaction, 5,* 28–30.

Golombok, S., & Tasker, F. (1996). Do parents influence the sexual orientation of their children? Findings from a longitudinal study of lesbian families. *Developmental Psychology, 32*(1), 3–11.

Gonzalez, J., Field, T., Yando, R., Gonzalez, K., Lasko, D., & Bendell, D. (1994). Adolescents' perceptions of their risk-taking behaviors. *Adolescence, 29*(115), 701–710.

Good, T., & Weinstein, R. (1986). Schools make a difference: Evidence, criticisms, new directions. *American Psychologist, 41,* 1090–1097.

Goodenow, C. (1993). Classroom belonging among early adolescent students: Relationships to motivation and achievement. *Journal of Early Adolescence, 13*(1), 21–43.

Goodman, S. H., Brumley, H. E., Schwartz, K. R., & Purcell, D. W. (1993). Gender and age in the relation between stress and children's school adjustment. *Journal of Early Adolescence, 13*(3), 329–345.

Goodyer, I. M., Cooper, P. J., Vize, C. M., & Ashby, L. (1993). Depression in 11–16 year-old girls: The role of past parental psychopathology and exposure to recent life events. *Journal of Child Psychology & Psychiatry & Allied Disciplines, 34*(7), 1103–1115.

Goossens, L. (1984). Imaginary audience behavior as a function of age, sex and formal operational thinking. *International Journal of Behavior Development, 7,* 77–93.

Goossens, L., & Phinney, J. S. (1996). Commentary: Identity, context, and development. *Journal of Adolescence, 19,* 491–496.

Gordon, C. P. (1996). Adolescent decision making: A broadly based theory and its application to the prevention of early pregnancy. *Adolescence, 31*(123), 561–584.

Gordon, D. E. (1990). Formal operational thinking: The role of cognitive-developmental processes in adolescent decision-making about pregnancy and contraception. *American Journal of Orthopsychiatry, 60*(3), 346–356.

Gordon, S., & Gilgun, J. F. (1987). Adolescent sexuality. In V. B. Van Hasselt & M. Hersen (Eds.), *Handbook of adolescent psychology.* New York: Pergamon Press.

Gorman, K. S., & Pollitt, E. (1996). Does schooling buffer the effects of early risk? *Child Development, 67,* 314–326.

Gose, B. (1995, March 17). Partying without alcohol. *Chronicle of Higher Education,* p. A31.

Gottfredson, M. R., & Hirschi, T. (1990). *A general theory of crime.* Stanford, CA: Stanford University Press.

Gottlieb, B. (1993). *The family in the western world.* New York: Oxford University Press.

Gottlieb, B. H., & Sylvestre, J. C. (1996). Social support in the relationships between older adolescents and adults. In K. Hurrelmann & S. F. Hamilton (Eds.), *Social problems and social contexts in adolescence: Perspectives across boundaries.* New York: Aldine De Gruyter.

Gottlieb, D., & Bronstein, P. (1996). Parents' perceptions of children's worries in a changing world. *Journal of Genetic Psychology, 157*(1), 104–118.

Graafsma, T. L. G. (1994a). Psychoanalysis. In H. A. Bosma, T. L. G. Graafsma, H. D. Grotevant, & D. J. de Levita (Eds.), *Identity and development: An interdisciplinary approach* (pp. 21–24). Thousand Oaks, CA: Sage.

Graafsma, T. L. G. (1994b). A psychoanalytic perspective on the concept of identity. In H. A. Bosma, T. L. G. Graafsma, H. D. Grotevant, & D. J. de Levita (Eds.), *Identity and development: An interdisciplinary approach.* Thousand Oaks, CA: Sage.

Graber, J. A., & Brooks-Gunn, J. (1995). Biological and maturational factors in development. In V. B. Van Hasselt & M. Hersen (Eds.), *Handbook of adolescent psychopathology: A guide to diagnosis and treatment.* New York: Lexington.

Graber, J. A., & Brooks-Gunn, J. (1996). Transitions and turning points: Navigating the passage from childhood through adolescence. *Developmental Psychology, 32*(4), 768–776.

Graber, J. A., Brooks-Gunn, J., Paikoff, R. L., & Warren, M. P. (1994). Prediction of eating problems: An 8-year study of adolescent girls. *Developmental Psychology, 30*(6), 823–834.

Graber, J. A., Brooks-Gunn, J., & Warren, M. P. (1995). The antecedents of menarcheal age: Heredity, family environment, and stressful life events. *Child Development, 66*, 346–359.

Grace, N. C., Kelley, M. L., & McCain, A. P. (1993). Attribution processes in mother–adolescent conflict. *Journal of Abnormal Child Psychology, 21*(2), 199–211.

Graham, N. (1996). The influence of predictors on adolescent drug use: An examination of individual effects. *Youth & Society, 28*(2), 215–235.

Graham, S., Hudley, C., & Williams, E. (1992). Attributional and emotional determinants of aggression among African-American and Latino young adolescents. *Developmental Psychology, 28*(4), 731–740.

Granleese, J., & Joseph, S. (1993). Self-perception profile of adolescent girls at a single-sex and a mixed-sex school. *Journal of Genetic Psychology, 154*(4), 525–530.

Grannis, J. C. (1992). Students' stress, distress, and achievement in an urban intermediate school. *Journal of Early Adolescence, 12*(1), 4–27.

Grauerholz, E. (1987). Balancing the power in dating relationships. *Sex Roles, 17*(9/10), 563–571.

Gray, R. L. (1979). Toward observing that which is not directly observable. In J. Lochhead & J. Clement (Eds.), *Cognitive process instruction.* Philadelphia: Franklin Institute.

Gray, W. M., & Hudson, L. M. (1984). Formal operations and the imaginary audience. *Developmental Psychology, 20*, 619–627.

Green, D. L. (1990). High school student employment in social context: Adolescents' perceptions of the role of part-time work. *Adolescence, 25*(98), 425–435.

Green, V., Johnson, S., & Kaplan, D. (1992). Predictors of adolescent female decision making regarding contraceptive use. *Adolescence, 27*(107), 613–631.

Greenberg, M., Siegel, J., & Leitch, C. (1984). The nature and importance of attachment relationships to parents and peers during adolescence. *Journal of Youth and Adolescence, 12*, 373–386.

Greenberger, E. (1984). Defining psychosocial maturity in adolescence. In P. Karoly & J. Steffen (Eds.), *Adolescent behavior disorders: Foundations and contemporary concerns.* Lexington, MA: D. C. Heath.

Greenberger, E., & Chen, C. (1996). Perceived family relationships and depressed mood in early and late adolescence: A comparison of European and Asian Americans. *Developmental Psychology, 32*(4), 707–716.

Greenberger, E., & Steinberg, L. D. (1986). *When teenagers work: The psychological and social costs of adolescent employment.* New York: Basic Books.

Greene, A. L. (1990). Patterns of affectivity in the transition to adolescence. *Journal of Experimental Child Psychology, 50*, 340–356.

Greene, A. L., & Grimsley, M. D. (1990). Age and gender differences in adolescents' preferences for parental advice: Mum's the word. *Journal of Adolescent Research, 5*, 396–413.

Greening, L. (1997). Adolescent stealers' and nonstealers' social problem-solving skills. *Adolescence, 32*(125), 51–56.

Gregory, T. W. (1978). *Adolescence in literature.* New York: Longman.

Grief, E. B., & Ulman, K. J. (1982). The psychological impact of menarche on early adolescent females: A review of the literature. *Child Development, 53*, 1413–1430.

Griffin-Carlson, M. S., & Mackin, K. J. (1993). Parental consent: Factors influencing adolescent disclosure regarding abortion. *Adolescence, 28*(109), 1–12.

Grolnick, W. S., & Slowiaczek, M. L. (1994). Parents' involvement in children's schooling: A multidimensional conceptualization and motivational model. *Child Development, 65*, 237–252.

Grolnick, W. S., Weiss, L., McKenzie, L., & Wrightman, J. (1996). Contextual, cognitive, and adolescent factors associated with parenting in adolescence. *Journal of Youth and Adolescence, 25*(1), 33–54.

Gross, J. (1993, March 29). Where "boys will be boys" and adults are befuddled. *The New York Times*, p. A1.

Grossman, F. K., Beinashowitz, J., Anderson, L., Sakurai, M., Finnin, L., & Flaherty, M. (1992). Risk and resilience in young adolescents. *Journal of Youth and Adolescence, 21*(5), 529–550.

Grotevant, H. D. (1987). Toward a process model of identity formation. *Journal of Adolescent Research, 2*, 203–222.

Grotevant, H. D. (1992). Assigned and chosen identity components: A process perspective on their integration. In G. R. Adams, T. P. Gullotta, & R. Montemayor (Eds.), *Adolescent identity formation.* Newbury Park, CA: Sage.

Grotevant, H. D. (1994). Psychology. In H. A. Bosma, T. L. G. Graafsma, H. D. Grotevant, & D. J. de Levita (Eds.), *Identity and development: An interdisciplinary approach* (pp. 63–65). Thousand Oaks, CA: Sage.

Grotevant, H. D., Bosma, H. A., De Levita, D. J., & Graafsma, T. L. G. (1994). Introduction. In H. A. Bosma, T. L. G. Graafsma, H. D. Grotevant, & D. J. de Levita (Eds.). *Identity and development: An interdisciplinary approach.* Thousand Oaks, CA: Sage.

Grotevant, H. D., & Cooper, C. (1986). Individuation in family relationships: A perspective on individual differences in the development of identity and role-taking skill in adolescence. *Human Development, 29*, 82–100.

Grotevant, H. D., & Thornbecke, W. (1982). Sex differences in styles of occupational identity formation in late adolescence. *Developmental Psychology, 18*, 396–405.

Grove, K. J. (1991). Identity development in interracial Asian/white late adolescents: Must it be so problematic? *Journal of Youth and Adolescence, 20*(6), 617–628.

Grusec, J. E., Goodnow, J. J., & Cohen, L. (1996). Household work and the development of concern for others. *Developmental Psychology, 32*(6), 999–1007.

Guerin, D. W., Gottfried, A. W., Oliver, P. H., & Thomas, C. W. (1994). Temperament and school functioning during early adolescence. *Journal of Early Adolescence, 14*(2), 200–225.

Guerra, N. G. (1993). Cognitive development. In P. H. Tolan & B. J. Cohler (Eds.), *Handbook of clinical research and practice with adolescents.* New York: Wiley.

Guggino, J. M., & Ponzetti, Jr. J. J. (1997). Gender differences in affective reactions to first coitus. *Journal of Adolescence, 20,* 189–200.

Gurney, R. (1993, March). Looking for a safe haven. *NEA Today,* p. 27.

Gysbers, N., & Henderson, P. (1988). *Developing and managing your school guidance program.* Alexandria, VA: American Association for Counseling and Development.

Hacker, D. J. (1994). An existential view of adolescence. *Journal of Early Adolescence, 14*(3), 300–327.

Hagbork, W. J. (1995). High school student television viewing time: A study of school performance and adjustment. *Child Study Journal, 25*(3), 155–167.

Hagell, A., & Newburn, T. (1996). Family and social contexts of adolescent re-offenders. *Journal of Adolescence, 19,* 5–18.

Hajcak, F., & Garwood, P. (1988). Quick-fix sex: Pseudosexuality in adolescents. *Adolescence, 23,* 755–760.

Hale, S. (1990). A global developmental trend in cognitive processing speed. *Child Development, 61,* 653–663.

Halebsky, M. A. (1987). Adolescent alcohol and substance abuse: Parent and peer effects. *Adolescence, 22*(88), 961–968.

Hall, G. S. (1904). *Adolescence: Its psychology and its relations to physiology, anthropology, sociology, sex, crime, religion and education* (Vols. 1 and 2). New York: Appleton.

Hall, G. S. (1923). *Life and confessions of a psychologist.* New York: Appleton.

Hall, J. A. (1987). Parent–adolescent conflict: An empirical review. *Adolescence, 22*(88), 767–789.

Haller, A. O. (1982). Social psychological aspects of schooling and achievement. In R. M. Haller, D. Mechanic, A. O. Haller, & T. S. Hauser (Eds.), *Social structure and behavior.* New York: Academic Press.

Hallinan, M. T., & Smith, S. S. (1985). The effects of classroom racial composition on students' interracial friendliness. *Social Psychology Quarterly, 48*(1), 3–16.

Halmi, K. A. (1987). Anorexia nervosa and bulimia. In V. B. Van Hasselt & M. Hersen (Eds.), *Handbook of adolescent psychology.* New York: Pergamon Press.

Halpern, C. T., & Udry, J. R. (1992). Variation in adolescent hormone measures and implications for behavioral research. *Journal of Research on Adolescence, 2,* 103–122.

Halpern, D. F. (1992). *Sex differences in cognitive abilities* (2nd ed.). Hillsdale, NJ: Erlbaum.

Hamburg, D. A. (1992). *Today's children: Creating a future for a generation in crisis.* New York: Times Books (Random House).

Hamburg, D. A., & Takanishi, R. (1989). Preparing for life: The critical transition of adolescence. *American Psychologist, 44*(5), 825–827.

Hamburg, G. (1989). *Life skills training: Preventive interventions for early adolescents.* Washington, DC: Carnegie Council on Adolescent Development.

Hamilton, J. A. (1984). Psychobiology in context: Reproductive-related events in men's and women's lives. *Contemporary Psychiatry, 3,* 325–328.

Hamilton, S. F. (1990). *Apprenticeship for adulthood: Preparing youth for the future.* New York: Free Press.

Hamilton, S. F., & Darling, N. (1996). Mentors in adolescents' lives. In K. Hurrelmann & S. F. Hamilton (Eds.), *Social problems and social contexts in adolescence: Perspectives across boundaries.* New York: Aldine De Gruyter.

Hamilton, S. F., & Hamilton, M. A. (1992). Mentoring programs: Promise and paradox. *Phi Delta Kappan, 73*(7), 546–550.

Hamilton-Obaid, B. (1989). Helping adolescents in crisis: A case study. *Adolescence, 24*(93), 59–63.

Hamlett, K. W., & Curry, J. F. (1990). Anorexia nervosa in adolescent males: A review and case study. *Child Psychiatry and Human Development, 21*(2), 79–94.

Hammond, W. A., & Romney, D. M. (1995). Cognitive factors contributing to adolescent depression. *Journal of Youth and Adolescence, 24*(6), 667–683.

Hammond, W. R., & Yung, B. (1993). Psychology's role in the public health response to assaultive violence among young African-American men. *American Psychologist, 48*(2), 142–154.

Handler, A. (1990). The correlates of the initiation of sexual intercourse among young urban black females. *Journal of Youth and Adolescence, 19*(2), 159–170.

Hanley, R. (1996, March 13). Backpack: An inalienable right? *The New York Times,* pp. B1, B4.

Hanna, N. A., & Berndt, T. J. (1995). Relations between friendship, group acceptance, and evaluations of summer camp. *Journal of Early Adolescence, 15*(4), 456–475.

Hannon, R., Kuntz, T., Van Laar, S., Williams, J., & Hall, D. S. (1996). College students' judgments regarding sexual aggression during a date. *Sex Roles, 35*(11/12), 765–780.

Hansen, D. J., Giacoletti, A. M., & Nangle, D. W. (1995). Social interactions and adjustment. In V. B. Van Hasselt & M. Hersen (Eds.), *Handbook of ado-*

*lescent psychopathology: A guide to diagnosis and treatment.* New York: Lexington Books.

Hansen, L. S. (1993). Career development: Trends and issues in the United States. *Journal of Career Development, 20*(1), 7–24.

Harding, C. G., & Snyder, K. (1991). Tom, Huck, and Oliver Stone as advocates in Kohlberg's just community. *Adolescence, 26*(102), 319–329.

Hardy, D. F., Power, T. G., & Jaedicke, S. (1993). Examining the relation of parenting to children's coping with everyday stress. *Child Development, 64,* 1829–1841.

Harlan, W. R., Harlan, E. A., & Grillo, P. (1980). Secondary sex characteristics of girls 12 to 17 years of age: The U.S. Health Examination Survey. *Journal of Pediatrics, 96,* 1074–1078.

Harold, G. T., & Conger, R. D. (1997). Marital conflict and adolescent distress: The role of adolescent awareness. *Child Development, 68*(2), 333–350.

Harold, G. T., Fincham, F. D., Osborne, L. N., & Conger, R. D. (1997). Mom and dad are at it again: Adolescent perceptions of marital conflict and adolescent psychological distress. *Developmental Psychology, 33*(2), 333–350.

Harper, J. F., & Marshall, E. (1991). Adolescents' problems and their relationship to self-esteem. *Adolescence, 26*(104), 799–808.

Harper-Giuffre, H., & MacKenzie, K. R. (Eds.). (1992). *Group psychotherapy for eating disorders.* Washington, DC: American Psychiatric Press.

Harris, E. S. (1991). Adolescent bereavement following the death of a parent: An exploratory study. *Child Psychiatry and Human Development, 21*(4), 267–281.

Harris, K. M., & Marmer, J. K. (1996). Poverty, paternal involvement, and adolescent well-being. *Journal of Family Issues, 17*(5), 614–640.

Harris, K. M., & Morgan, S. P. (1991). Fathers, sons, and daughters: Differential paternal involvement in parenting. *Journal of Marriage and the Family, 53,* 531–544.

Harris, L. (1996, September 22). The hidden world of dating violence. *Parade Magazine,* pp. 4–6.

Harris, L., & Associates, Inc. (1986). *American teens speak: Sex, myths, TV, and birth control* (Planned Parenthood poll). New York: Author.

Harris, L., & Associates, Inc. (1988). *Sexual material on American network television during the 1987–1988 season.* New York: Planned Parenthood Federation of America.

Harris, P. L. (1983). Infant cognition. In P. H. Mussen (Ed.), *Handbook of child psychology: infancy and developmental psychobiology,* Volume II. New York: Wiley.

Harrison, A. O., Wilson, M. N., Pine, C. J., Chan, S. Q., & Buriel, R. (1990). Family ecologies of ethnic minority children. *Child Development, 61,* 347–362.

Harrison, P. L., & Turner, T. E. (1995). Intellectual development and retardation. In V. B. Van Hasselt & M. Hersen (Eds.), *Handbook of adolescent psychopathology: A guide to diagnosis and treatment.* New York: Lexington Books.

Hart, B. I., & Thompson, J. M. (1996). Gender role characteristics and depressive symptomatology among adolescents. *Journal of Early Adolescence, 16*(4), 407–426.

Hart, D., & Fegley, S. (1995). Prosocial behavior and caring in adolescence: Relations to self-understanding and social judgment. *Child Development, 66,* 1346–1359.

Harter, S. (1985). *Manual for the self-perception profile for children.* Denver: University of Denver, Press.

Harter, S. (1986). Processes underlying the construction, maintenance and enhancement of the self-concept in children. In J. Suls & A. Greenwald (Eds.), *Psychological perspectives on the self* (Vol. 3). Hillsdale, NJ: Erlbaum.

Harter, S. (1987). The determinants and mediational role of global self-worth in children. In N. Eisenberg (Ed.), *Contemporary issues in developmental psychology.* New York: Wiley.

Harter, S. (1988). Developmental and dynamic changes in the nature of the self concept: Implications for child psychotherapy. In S. Shirk (Ed.), *Cognitive development and child psychotherapy.* New York: Plenum.

Harter, S. (1989). Causes, correlates and the functional role of global self-worth: A life-span perspective. In J. Kolligian & R. A. Sternberg (Eds.), *Perceptions of competence and incompetence across the life-span.* New Haven, CT: Yale University Press.

Harter, S. (1990a). Self and identity development. In S. S. Feldman & G. R. Elliot (Eds.), *At the threshold: The developing adolescent.* Cambridge, MA: Harvard University Press.

Harter, S. (1990b). Processes underlying adolescent self-concept formation. In R. Montemayor, G. R. Adams, & T. P. Gullotta (Eds.), *From childhood to adolescence: A transitional period?* Newbury Park, CA: Sage.

Harter, S., & Jackson, B. K. (1993). Young adolescents' perceptions of the link between low self-worth and depressed affect. *Journal of Early Adolescence, 13*(4), 383–407.

Harter, S., & Lee, L. (1989). *Manifestations of true and false selves in early adolescence.* Presented at the meeting of the Society for Research in Child Development, Kansas City, MO.

Harter, S., Marold, D. B., Whitesell, N. R., & Cobbs, G. (1996). A model of the effects of perceived parent and peer support on adolescent false self behavior. *Child Development, 67,* 360–374.

Hartnagel, T. F. (1996). Cannabis use and the transition to young adulthood. *Journal of Youth and Adolescence, 25*(2), 241–258.

Hartup, W. W. (1989). Behavioral manifestations of children's friendships. In T. J. Berndt & G. W. Ladd (Eds.), *Peer relationships in child development.* New York: Wiley.

Hartup, W. W. (1996). The company they keep: Friendships and their developmental significance. *Child Development, 67*, 1–13.

Harvey, S. M., & Spigner, C. (1995). Factors associated with sexual behavior among adolescents: A multivariate analysis. *Adolescence, 30*(118), 253–264.

Hauser, S. T., & Bowlds, M. K. (1990). Stress, coping, and adaptation. In S. S. Feldman & G. R. Elliot (Eds.), *At the threshold: The developing adolescent.* Cambridge, MA: Harvard University Press.

Havens, B., & Swenson, I. (1988). Imagery associated with menstruation in advertising targeted to adolescent women. *Adolescence, 23*(89), 89–97.

Havighurst, R. J. (1972). *Developmental tasks and education* (3rd ed.). New York: McKay.

Havighurst, R. J. (1987). Adolescent culture and subcultures. In V. B. Van Hasselt & M. Hersen (Eds.), *Handbook of adolescent psychology.* New York: Pergamon Press.

Hawkins, J., Catalano, R., & Miller, J. (1992). Risk and protective factors for alcohol and other drug problems in adolescence and early adulthood: Implications for substance abuse prevention. *Psychological Bulletin, 112*, 64–105.

Hawton, K., Cole, D., O'Grady, J., & Osborn, M. (1982). Adolescents who take overdoses: Their characteristics, problems, and contacts with helping agencies. *British Journal of Psychiatry, 140*, 118–123.

Hayes, D. (Ed.). (1987). *Risking the future: Adolescent sexuality, pregnancy, and childbearing* (Vol. 1). Washington, DC: National Academy Press.

Heath, S. B. (1983). *Ways with words.* New York: Cambridge University Press.

Heatherton, T. F., Mahamedi, F., Striepe, M., Field, A. E., & Keel, P. (1997). A 10-year longitudinal study of body weight, dieting, and eating disorder symptoms. *Journal of Abnormal Psychology, 106*(1), 117–125.

Henderson, V. L., & Dweck, C. S. (1990). Motivation and achievement.

In S. S. Feldman & G. R. Elliot (Eds.), *At the threshold: The developing adolescent.* Cambridge, MA: Harvard University Press.

Hendry, L. B., Roberts, W., Glendinning, A., & Coleman, J. C. (1992). Adolescents' perceptions of significant individuals in their lives. *Journal of Adolescence, 15*, 255–270.

Henggeler, S. W., Edwards, J., & Borduin, C. M. (1987). The family relations of female juvenile delinquents. *Journal of Abnormal Child Psychology, 15*, 199–209.

Henggeler, S. W., McKee, E., & Borduin, C. M. (1989). Is there a link between maternal neglect and adolescent delinquency? *Journal of Clinical Child Psychology, 18*(3), 242–246.

Henker, B., Whalen, C. K., & O'Neil, R. (1995). Worldly and workaday worries: Contemporary concerns of children and young adolescents. *Journal of Abnormal Child Psychology, 23*(6), 685–702.

Henneberger, M. (1993, July 24). Gang membership grows in middle-class suburbs. *The New York Times,* pp. 1, 25.

Henneberger, M. (1994, February 6). "Pot" surges back, but it's, like, a whole new world. *The New York Times.*

Henry, B., Caspi, A., Moffitt, T. E., & Silva, P. A. (1996). Temperamental and familial predictors of violent and nonviolent criminal convictions: Age 3 to age 18. *Developmental Psychology, 32*(4), 614–623.

Henry, C. S., & Lovelace, S. G. (1995). Family resources and adolescent family life satisfaction in remarried family households. *Journal of Family Issues, 16*(6), 765–786.

Henry, C. S., & Peterson, G. W. (1995). Adolescent social competence, parental qualities, and parental satisfaction. *American Journal of Orthopsychiatry, 65*(2), 249–262.

Henry, C. S., Stephenson, A. L., Hanson, M. F., & Hargett, W. (1993). Adolescent suicide and families: An ecological approach. *Adolescence, 28*(110), 291–308.

Henry, C. S., Stephenson, A. L., Hanson, M. F., & Hargett, W. (1994). Adolescent suicide and families: An ecological approach. *Family Therapy, 21*(1), 63–80.

Hensley, W. E. (1994). Height as a basis for interpersonal attraction. *Adolescence, 29*(114), 469–474.

Hergenhahn, B. R. (1992). *An introduction to the history of Psychology* (2nd ed.). Belmont, CA: Wadsworth.

Herold, E. S., & Marshall, S. K. (1996). Adolescent sexual development. In G. R. Adams, R. Montemayor, & T. P. Gullotta (Eds.). *Psychosocial development during adolescence: Progress in developmental contextualism.* Thousand Oaks, CA: Sage.

Herr, E. L. (1991, January). Advancing the agenda. *Vocational Education Journal,* 31–32.

Herr, K. M. (1989). Adoption vs. parenting decisions among pregnant adolescents. *Adolescence, 24*(96), 795–799.

Herring, H. B. (1997, April 27). Where there's smoke, there's outlay. *The New York Times Business Section,* p. 9.

Hershberger, S. L., & D'Augelli, A. R. (1995). The impact of victimization on the mental health and suicidality of lesbian, gay and bisexual youths. *Developmental Psychology, 31*(1), 65–74.

Herzog, D. B., Keller, M. B., Lavori, P. W., & Bradburn, I. S. (1991). Bulimia nervosa in adolescence. *Journal of Developmental and Behavioral Pediatrics, 12*(3), 191–195.

Herzog, W., Schellberg, D., & Deter, H. (1997). First recovery in anorexia nervosa patients in the long-term course: A discrete-time survival analysis. *Journal of Consulting and Clinical Psychology, 65*(1), 169–177.

Hess, R. D., & Holloway, S. D. (1984). Family and school as educational institutions. In R. D. Parke (Ed.), *Review of child development research* (Vol. 7). Chicago: University of Chicago Press.

Hetherington, E. M. (1987). Family relations six years after divorce. In K. Pasley & M. Ihinger-Tallman (Eds.), *Remarriage and stepparenting: Current research and theory*. New York: Guilford.

Hetherington, E. M. (1989). Coping with family transition: Winners, losers, and survivors. *Child Development, 60*, 1–14.

Hetherington, E. M., & Clingempeel, W. G. (1992). Coping with marital transitions: A family systems perspective. *Monographs of the Society for Research in Child Development, 57*(2–3), 1–242.

Hetherington, E. M., Stanley-Hagan, M., & Anderson, E. R. (1989). Marital transitions: A child's perspective. *American Psychologist, 44*, 303–312.

Hetrick, E. S., & Martin, A. D. (1987). Developmental issues and the resolution for gay and lesbian adolescents. *Journal of Homosexuality, 2*(1/2), 25–43.

Hieshima, J. A., & Schneider, B. (1994). Intergenerational effects on the cultural and cognitive socialization of third- and fourth-generation Japanese Americans. *Journal of Applied Developmental Psychology, 15*(3), 319–327.

Higgins, R. L., Snyder, C. R., & Berglas, S. (1990). *Self-handicapping: The paradox that isn't*. New York: Plenum.

Higher Education Research Institute, UCLA. (1995, January 9).

Hill, J. P. (1985). Family relations in adolescence: Myths, realities, and new directions. *Genetic, Social and General Psychology Monographs, 111*(2), 233–248.

Hill, J. P. (1987). Research on adolescents and their families: Past and prospect. In W. Damon (Ed.), *New directions in child psychology*. San Francisco: Jossey-Bass.

Hill, J. P., & Holmbeck, G. (1986). Attachment and autonomy during adolescence. In G. Whitehurst (Ed.), *Annals of child development*. Greenwich, CT: JAI Press.

Hill, J. P., & Holmbeck, G. (1987). Disagreements about rules in families with seventh-grade girls and boys. *Journal of Youth and Adolescence, 16*(3), 221–246.

Hill, J. P., & Lynch, M. E. (1983). The intensification of gender-related role

expectations during early adolescence. In J. Brooks-Gunn & A. C. Petersen (Eds.), *Girls at puberty*. New York: Plenum.

Hill, P. (1993). Recent advances in selected aspects of adolescent development. *Journal of Child Psychology & Psychiatry & Allied Disciplines, 34*(1), 69–99.

Hilton, J. L., & von Hippel, W. (1996). Stereotypes. *Annual Review of Psychology, 47*, 237–271.

Hilts, P. J. (1991, November 5). Beverage ads appealing to youth are criticized. *The New York Times*.

Hilts, P. J. (1995a, April 19). Black teenagers are turning away from smoking, but whites puff on. *The New York Times*.

Hilts, P. J. (1995b, July 20). Survey finds surge in smoking by young. *The New York Times*.

Hines, S., & Groves, D. L. (1989). Sports competition and its influence on self-esteem development. *Adolescence, 24*(96), 861–869.

Hinshaw, S. P. (1992). Externalizing behavior problems and academic underachievement in childhood and adolescence: Causal relationships and underlying mechanisms. *Psychological Bulletin, 111*(1), 127–155.

Hinton-Nelson, M. D., Roberts, M. C., & Snyder, C. R. (1996). Early adolescents exposed to violence: Hope and vulnerability to victimization. *American Journal of Orthopsychiatry, 66*(3), 346–353.

Hirsh, B. J., & DuBois, D. L. (1991). Self-esteem in early adolescence: The identification and prediction of contrasting longitudinal trajectories. *Journal of Youth and Adolescence, 20*(1), 53–72.

Hockenberry-Eaton, M., Richman, M. J., DiIorio, C., Rivero, T., & Maibach, E. (1996). Mother and adolescent knowledge of sexual development: The effects of gender, age, and sexual experience. *Adolescence, 31*(121), 35–47.

Hofferth, S. L. (1990). Trends in adolescent sexual activity, contraception,

and pregnancy in the United States. In J. Bancroft & J. M. Reinisch (Eds.), *Adolescence and puberty*. New York: Oxford University Press.

Hoffman, L. W. (1996). Progress and problems in the study of adolescence. *Developmental Psychology, 32*(4), 777–780.

Hoffman, M. A., Levy-Schiff, R., Sohlberg, S. C., & Zarizki, J. (1992). The impact of stress and coping: Developmental changes in the transition to adolescence. *Journal of Youth and Adolescence, 21*(4), 451–469.

Hoffman, M. L. (1983). Affective and cognitive processes in moral internalization. In E. T. Higgins, D. N. Ruble, & W. W. Hartup (Eds.), *Social cognitions and social development: A sociocultural perspective*. New York: Cambridge University Press.

Hoge, D. R., Smit, E. K., & Hanson, S. L. (1990). School experiences predicting change in self-esteem of sixth- and seventh-grade students. *Journal of Educational Psychology, 82*(1), 117–127.

Hoge, R. D., Andrews, D. A., & Leschied, A. W. (1996). An investigation of risk and protective factors in a sample of youthful offenders. *Journal of Child Psychology & Psychiatry & Allied Disciplines, 37*(4), 419–424.

Hogue, A., & Steinberg, L. (1995). Homophily of internalized distress in adolescent peer groups. *Developmental Psychology, 31*(6), 897–906.

Holahan, C. J., Valentiner, D. P., & Moos, R. H. (1994). Parent support and psychological adjustment during the transition to young adulthood in a college sample. *Journal of Family Psychology, 8*(2), 215–223.

Holahan, C. J., Valentiner, D. P., & Moos, R. H. (1995). Parental support, coping strategies, and psychological adjustment: An integrative model with late adolescents. *Journal of Youth and Adolescence, 24*(6), 633–648.

Holden, G. W., Nelson, P. B., Velasquez, J., & Ritchie, K. L. (1993). Cognitive, psychosocial, and reported sexual behavior differences between pregnant and nonpregnant adolescents. *Adolescence, 28*(111), 557–572.

Holland, A., & Andre, T. (1994). The relationship of self-esteem to selected personal and environmental resources of adolescents. *Adolescence, 29*(114), 345–360.

Holland, B. (1995, September 17). No praise for pop? It's a bum rap. *The New York Times*, Arts and Entertainment Section, p. 27.

Holland, J. (1985). *Making vocational choices: A theory of vocational personalities and work environments.* (2nd ed.). Englewood Cliffs, NJ: Prentice-Hall.

Holland, J. (1996). Exploring careers with a typology: What we have learned and some new directions. *American Psychologist, 51*(4), 397–406.

Hollingshead, A. B. (1949). *Elmtown's youth: The impact of social class on adolescents.* New York: Wiley.

Holmbeck, G. N. (1987). *The role of familial conflict in adaptation to menarche: Sequential analysis of family interaction.* Unpublished doctoral dissertation, Virginia Commonwealth University, Richmond, VA.

Holmbeck, G. N., & Hill, J. P. (1988). Storm and stress beliefs about adolescence: Prevalence, self-reported antecedents, and effects of an undergraduate course. *Journal of Youth and Adolescence, 17,* 285–306.

Holmbeck, G. N., & Hill, J. P. (1991a). Rules, rule behaviors, and biological maturation in families with seventh-grade boys and girls. *Journal of Early Adolescence, 11*(2), 236–257.

Holmbeck, G. N., & Hill, J. P. (1991b). Conflictive engagement, positive affect, and menarche in families with seventh-grade girls. *Child Development, 62,* 1030–1048.

Holmbeck, G. N., & O'Donnell, K. (1991). Discrepancies between perceptions of decision-making and behavioral autonomy. In R. Paikoff (Ed.), *Shared views of the family during adolescence: New directions for child development.* San Francisco: Jossey-Bass.

Holmbeck, G. N., & Updegrove, A. L. (1995). Clinical-developmental inter-

face: Implications of developmental research for adolescent psychotherapy. *Psychotherapy, 32*(1), 16–33.

Holmes, S. A. (1997, July 6). It's awful! It's terrible! It's . . . never mind. *The New York Times News of The Week in Review*, p. 3.

Honan, W. H. (1995a, November 3). Lowest level of binge drinking is found at western colleges. *The New York Times*, p. A16.

Honan, W. H. (1995b, December 6). Study ties binge drinking to fraternity house life. *The New York Times.*

Honan, W. H. (1996, June 17). Income found to predict education level better than race. *The New York Times*, p. A11.

Hong, E., Milgram, R. M., & Whiston, S. C. (1993). Leisure activities in adolescents as a predictor of occupational choice in young adults: A longitudinal study. *Journal of Career Development, 19*(3), 221–229.

Hooker, K., Fiese, B. H., Jenkins, L., Morfei, M. Z., & Schwagler, J. (1996). Possible selves among parents of infants and preschoolers. *Developmental Psychology, 32*(3), 542–550.

Hopwood, N. J., Kelch, R. P., Hale, P. M., Mendes, T. M., Foster, C. M., & Beitins, I. Z. (1990). The onset of human puberty: Biological and Environmental Factors. In J. Bancroft & J. M. Reinisch (Eds.), *Adolescence and puberty.* New York: Oxford University Press.

Horan, J. J., & Straus, L. K. (1987). Substance abuse in adolescence. In V. B. Van Hasselt & M. Hersen (Eds.), *Handbook of adolescent psychology.* New York: Pergamon Press.

Hornton, C. B., & Oakland, T. (1997). Temperament-based learning styles as moderators of academic achievement. *Adolescence, 32*(125), 131–142.

Hortaçsu, N. (1989). Targets of communication during adolescence. *Journal of Adolescence, 12,* 253–263.

Hotvedt, M. E. (1990). Emerging and submerging adolescent sexuality: Culture and sexual orientation. In J. Bancroft & J. M. Reinisch (Eds.), *Adoles-*

*cence and puberty.* New York: Oxford University Press.

Houchins, S. C. (1991). *Parent scaffolding of early adolescents' interpersonal negotiation skills.* Dissertation, University of Texas at Austin.

Hoyle, R. H., & Leff, S. S. (1997). The role of parental involvement in youth sport participation and performance. *Adolescence, 32*(125), 233–243.

Hubbs-Tait, L., & Garmon, L. C. (1995). The relationship of moral reasoning and AIDS knowledge to risky sexual behavior. *Adolescence, 30*(119), 549–564.

Hudley, C. A. (1995). Assessing the impact of separate schooling for African American male adolescents. *Journal of Early Adolescence, 15*(1), 38–57.

Huerta-Franco, R., Diáz de León, J., & Malacara, J. M. (1996). Knowledge and attitudes toward sexuality in adolescents and their association with the family and other factors. *Adolescence, 31*(121), 179–192.

Hultsman, W. Z. (1992). Constraints to activity participation in early adolescence. *Journal of Early Adolescence, 12*(3), 280–299.

Hunter, C. St. J., & Harman, D. (1979). *Adult illiteracy in the United States.* New York: McGraw-Hill.

Hunter, F. T. (1985). Adolescents' perception of discussions with parents and friends. *Developmental Psychology, 21*(3), 433–440.

Hurlock, E. B. (1973). *Adolescent development* (4th ed.). New York: McGraw-Hill.

Hurrelmann, K. (Ed.). (1994). *International handbook of adolescence.* Westport, CT: Greenwood Press.

Hurrelmann, K. (1996). The social world of adolescents: A sociological perspective. In K. Hurrelmann & S. F. Hamilton (Eds.), *Social problems and social contexts in adolescence: Perspectives across boundaries.* New York: Aldine De Gruyter.

Hutnik, N. (1991). *Ethnic minority identity: A social psychological perspective.* Oxford: Clarendon Press.

Hyde, J. S. (1994). Can meta-analysis make feminist transformations in psychology? *Psychology of Women Quarterly, 18*, 451–462.

Hyde, J. S., Fennema, E., & Lamon, S. J. (1990). Gender differences in mathematics performance: A meta-analysis. *Psychological Bulletin, 107*, 139–155.

Imbimbo, P. V. (1995). Sex differences in the identity formation of college students from divorced families. *Journal of Youth and Adolescence, 24*(6), 745–761.

Inazu, J. K., & Fox, G. L. (1980). Maternal influence on the sexual behavior of teenage daughters. *Journal of Family Issues, 1*, 81–102.

Inderbitzen-Pisaruk, H., Clark, M. L., & Solano, C. H. (1992). Correlates of loneliness in midadolescence. *Journal of Youth and Adolescence, 21*(2), 151–167.

Ingersoll, G. M., & Orr, D. P. (1989). Behavioral and emotional risk in early adolescents. *Journal of Early Adolescence, 9*, 396–408.

Inhelder, B., & Piaget, J. (1958). *The growth of logical thinking from childhood to adolescence.* New York: Basic Books.

Inoff-Germain, G., Arnold, G. S., Nottelmann, E. D., Susman, E. J., Cutler, G. B., Jr., & Chrousos, G. P. (1988). Relations between hormone levels and observational measures of aggressive behavior of young adolescents in family interactions. *Developmental Psychology, 24*(1), 129–139.

Isay, R. A. (1989). *Being homosexual: Gay men and their development.* New York: Farrar-Straus-Giroux.

Isberg, R. S., Hauser, S. T., Jacobson, A. M., Powers, S. I., Noam, G., Weiss-Perry, B., & Follansbee, D. (1989). Parental contexts of adolescent self-esteem: A developmental perspective. *Journal of Youth and Adolescence, 18*(1), 1–23.

Jackson, A. W., & Hornbeck, D. W. (1989). Educating young adolescents: Why we must restructure middle grade schools. *American Psychologist, 44*(5), 831–836.

Jacobs, J. E., Bennett, M. A., & Flanagan, C. (1993). Decision making in one-parent and two-parent families: Influence and information selection. *Journal of Early Adolescence, 13*(3), 245–266.

Jacobvitz, D. B., & Bush, N. F. (1996). Reconstructions of family relationships: Parent–child alliances, personal distress, and self-esteem. *Developmental Psychology, 32*(4), 732–743.

Jadack, R. A., Hyde, J. S., Moore, C. F., & Keller, M. L. (1995). Moral reasoning about sexually transmitted diseases. *Child Development, 66*(1), 167–177.

Jaffe, M. L. (1997). *Understanding parenting* (2nd ed.). Needham Heights, MA: Allyn & Bacon.

Jagers, R. J. (1996). Culture and problem behaviors among inner-city African-American youth: Further explorations. *Journal of Adolescence, 19*, 371–381.

Jahnke, H. C., & Blanchard-Fields, F. (1993). A test of two models of adolescent egocentrism. *Journal of Youth and Adolescence, 22*, 313–326.

Jakobsen, R., Rise, J., Aas, H., & Anderssen, N. (1997). Noncoital sexual interactions and problem behaviour among young adolescents: The Norwegian Longitudinal Health Behaviour Study. *Journal of Adolescence, 20*, 71–83.

Jankowiak, W. R., & Fischer, E. F. (1992). A cross-cultural perspective on romantic love. *Ethos, 31*, 149–156.

Jaquish, G. A., & Savin-Williams, R. C. (1981). Biological and ecological factors in the expression of adolescent self-esteem. *Journal of Youth and Adolescence, 10*, 473–485.

Jarvinen, D. W., & Nicholls, J. G. (1996). Adolescents' social goals, beliefs about the causes of social success, and satisfaction in peer relations. *Developmental Psychology, 32*(3), 435–441.

Jenkins, J. E. (1996). The influence of peer affiliation and student activities on adolescent drug involvement. *Adolescence, 31*(122), 297–306.

Jessor, R. (1982). Problem behavior and developmental transition in adolescence. *Journal of School Health, 52*, 295–300.

Jessor, R. (1987). Problem-behavior theory, psychosocial development, and adolescent problem drinking. *British Journal of Addiction, 82*, 331–342.

Jessor, R. (1992). Risk behavior in adolescence: A psychosocial framework for understanding and action. *Developmental Review, 12*(4), 374–390.

Jessor, R. (1993). Successful adolescent development among youth in high-risk settings. *American Psychologist, 48*(2), 117–126.

Jessor, R., Donovan, J. E., & Costa, F. M. (1991). *Beyond adolescence: Problem behavior and young adult development.* Cambridge: Cambridge University Press.

Jessor, R., & Jessor, S. L. (1977). *Problem behavior and psychosocial development.* New York: Academic Press.

Jessor, R., Van Den Bos, J., Vanderryn, J., Costa, F. M., & Turbin, M. S. (1995). Protective factors in adolescent problem behavior: Moderator effects and developmental change. *Developmental Psychology, 31*(6), 923–933.

Johnson, B. E., Kuck, D. L., & Schander, P. R. (1997). Rape myth acceptance and sociodemographic characteristics. A multidimensional analysis. *Sex Roles, 36*(11/12), 693–708.

Johnson, B. M., & Collins, W. A. (1988). *Developmental differences in perceptions and expectations: Implications for family relationships and psychosocial functioning in the second decade of life.* Unpublished manuscript, University of Minnesota.

Johnson, K. (1996, March 7). For Bucknell's class of '96, pressure to focus, and fast. *The New York Times*, p. A22.

Johnson, R. J., & Kaplan, H. B. (1991). Developmental processes leading to marijuana use: Comparing civilians and the military. *Youth & Society, 23*(1), 3–30.

Johnson, S. A., & Green, V. (1993). Female adolescent contraceptive decision making and risk taking. *Adolescence, 28*(109), 81–96.

Johnston, D. K. (1985). *Two moral orientations—two problem-solving strategies: Adolescent's solutions to dilemmas in fables.* Unpublished doctoral dissertation, Harvard University, School of Education.

Johnston, D. K., Brown, L. M., & Christopherson, S. B. (1990). Adolescents' moral dilemmas: The context. *Journal of Youth and Adolescence, 19*(6), 615–622.

Johnston, J. S., Jr. (1992). Liberal education: Preparation for life. *Private Colleges.*

Johnston, L. D., O'Malley, P. M., & Bachman, J. G. (1985). *Use of licit and illicit drugs by America's high school students 1975–1984* (DHHS Publication No. ADM 85-1394). Washington, DC: National Institute on Drug Abuse.

Jonah, B. A. (1986). Accident risk and risk-taking behavior among young drivers. *Accident analysis and prevention, 16*, 255–271.

Jones, D. C., & Costin, S. E. (1995). Friendship quality during preadolescence and adolescence: The contributions of relationship orientations, instrumentality, and expressivity. *Merrill-Palmer Quarterly, 41*(4), 517–535.

Jones, E. F., Forrest, J. D., Goldman, N., Henshaw, S. K., Lincoln, R., Rosoff, J. I., Westoff, C. F., & Wulf, D. (1985). Teenage pregnancy in developed countries: Determinants and policy implications. *Family Planning Perspectives, 17*(2), 53–63.

Jordan, W. J., Lara, J., & McPartland, J. M. (1996). Exploring the causes of early dropout among race-ethnic and gender groups. *Youth & Society, 28*(1), 62–94.

Jorgensen, S. R. (1993). Adolescent pregnancy and parenting. In T. P. Gullotta, G. R. Adams, & R. Montemayor (Eds.), *Adolescent sexuality.* Newbury Park, CA: Sage.

Jory, B., Rainbolt, E., Karns, J. T., Freeborn, A., & Greer, C. V. (1996). Communication patterns and alliances between parents and adolescents during a structured problem-solving task. *Journal of Adolescence, 19*, 339–346.

Josephs, R. A., Markus, H. R., & Tafarodi, R. W. (1992). Gender and self-esteem. *Journal of Personality & Social Psychology, 63*(3), 391–402.

Josselson, R. (1987). *Finding herself: Pathways to identity development in women.* San Francisco: Jossey-Bass.

Josselson, R. (1988). The embedded self: I and thou revisited. In D. K. Lapsley & F. C. Power (Eds.), *Self, ego, and identity: Integrative approaches.* New York: Springer-Verlag.

Josselson, R. (1994). Identity and relatedness in the life cycle. In H. A. Bosma, T. L. G. Graafsma, H. D. Grotevant, & D. J. de Levita (Eds.), *Identity and development: An interdisciplinary approach.* Thousand Oaks, CA: Sage.

Judd, C. M., Park, B., Ryan, C. S., Brauer, M., & Kraus, S. (1995). Stereotypes and ethnocentrism: Diverging interethnic perceptions of African-American and white American youth. *Journal of Personality and Social Psychology, 69*(3), 460–481.

Judson, G. (1992, August 2). Lost in the middle. *The New York Times Education Section,* p. 19.

Judson, G. (1993, September 14). Zen of first impressions about being in college. *The New York Times,* p. B8.

Juhasz, A. M. (1989). Significant others and self-esteem: Methods for determining who and why. *Adolescence, 24*(95), 581–594.

Julian, W., McHenry, P. S., & McKelvey, M. W. (1994). Cultural variation in parenting: Perceptions of Caucasian, African-American, Hispanic, and Asian Americans. *Family Relations, 43*, 30–37.

Jurich, A. P., & Collins, O. P. (1996). 4-H night at the movies: A program for adolescents and their families. *Adolescence, 31*(124), 863–874.

Kaczmarek, M. G., & Backlund, B. A. (1991). Disenfranchised grief: The loss of an adolescent romantic relationship. *Adolescence, 26*(102), 253–259.

Kagan, J. (1972). A conception of early adolescence. In J. Kagan & R. Coles (Eds.), *Twelve to sixteen: Early adolescence.* New York: W. W. Norton.

Kagan, J. (1987). Introduction. In J. Kagan & S. Lamb (Eds.), *The emergence of morality in young children.* Chicago: University of Chicago Press.

Kalof, L. (1995). Sex, power, and dependency: The politics of adolescent sexuality. *Journal of Youth and Adolescence, 24*(2), 229–249.

Kamptner, N. L. (1995). Treasured possessions and their meanings in adolescent males and females. *Adolescence, 30*(118), 301–318.

Kandel, D. B. (1975). Stages in adolescent involvement in drug use. *Science, 190*, 912–914.

Kandel, D. B. (1978). Homophily, selection, and socialization in adolescent friendships. *American Journal of Sociology, 84*, 427–436.

Kandel, D. B. (1982). Epidemiological and psychosocial perspectives on adolescent drug use. *Journal of the American Academy of Clinical Psychology, 21*, 328–347.

Kandel, D. B. (1985, July). Effects of drug use from adolescence to young adulthood on participation in family and work roles. In R. Jessor (Chair), *Longitudinal resarch on substance use in adolescence.* Symposium conducted at the meeting of the International Society for the Study of Behavioral Development, Tours, France.

Kaplan, H. B., Johnson, R. J., & Bailey, C. A. (1987). Deviant peers and deviant behaviors: Further elaboration of a model. *Social Psychology Quarterly, 50*, 277–284.

Kaplan, S. L., Grumbach, M. M., & Aubert, M. L. (1976). The ontogenesis of pituitary hormones and hypothalamic factors in the human fetus: Maturation of the central nervous system regulation of anterior pituitary function. *Recent Progress in Hormone Research, 32*, 161–243.

Karraker, K. H., & Evans, S. L. (1996). Adolescent mothers' knowledge of child development and expectations for their own infants. *Journal of Youth and Adolescence, 25*(5), 651–666.

Karweit, N., & Hansell, S. (1983). Sex differences in adolescent relationships: Friendship and status. In J. Epstein & N. Karweit (Eds.), *Friends in school*. New York: Academic Press.

Kasser, T., Ryan, R. M., Zax, M., & Sameroff, A. J. (1995). The relations of maternal and social environments to late adolescents' materialistic and prosocial values. *Developmental Psychology*, *31*(6), 907–914.

Katchadourian, H. (1990). Sexuality. In S. S. Feldman & G. R. Elliot (Eds.), *At the threshold: The developing adolescent*. Cambridge, MA: Harvard University Press.

Kaywell, J. F. (1993). *Adolescents at risk: A guide to fiction and nonfiction for young adults, parents, and professionals*. Westport, CT: Greenwood Press.

Kazdin, A. E. (1987). *Child psychotherapy: Developing and identifying effective treatments*. Elmsford, NY: Pergamon Press.

Kazdin, A. E. (1990). Childhood depression. *Journal of Child Psychology and Psychiatry*, *31*, 121–160.

Kazdin, A. E. (1993). Adolescent mental health: Prevention and treatment programs. *American Psychologist*, *48*(2), 127–141.

Kean, T. H. (1989). The life you save may be your own. *American Psychologist*, *44*(5), 828–830.

Kearney, C. A., & Silverman, W. K. (1995). Anxiety disorders. In V. B. Van Hasselt & M. Hersen (Eds.), *Handbook of adolescent psychopathology: A guide to diagnosis and treatment*. New York: Lexington.

Keating, D. P. (1990). Adolescent thinking. In S. S. Feldman & G. R. Elliot (Eds.), *At the threshold: The developing adolescent*. Cambridge, MA: Harvard University Press.

Keating, D. P. (in press). Understanding human intelligence: Toward a developmental synthesis. In C. Benbow & D. Lubinski (Eds.), *From psychometrics to giftedness: Essays in honor of Julian Stanley*. Baltimore: Johns Hopkins University Press.

Keating, D. P., & Clark, L. V. (1980). Development of physical and social reasoning in adolescence. *Developmental Psychology*, *16*, 23–30.

Keating, D. P., & Sasse, D. K. (1996). Cognitive socialization in adolescence: Critical period for a critical habit of mind. In G. R. Adams, R. Montemayor, & T. P. Gullotta (Eds.), *Psychosocial development during adolescence: Progress in developmental contextualism*. Thousand Oaks, CA: Sage.

Keefe, K., & Berndt, T. J. (1996). Relations of friendship quality to self-esteem in early adolescence. *Journal of Early Adolescence*, *16*(1), 110–129.

Keel, P. K., Fulkerson, J. A., & Leon, G. R. (1997). Disordered eating precursors in pre- and early adolescent girls and boys. *Journal of Youth and Adolescence*, *26*(2), 203–216.

Keelan, J. P. R., Dion, K. K., & Dion, K. L. (1992). Correlates of appearance anxiety in late adolescence and early adulthood among young women. *Journal of Adolescence*, *15*, 193–205.

Keith, J. B., McCreary, C., Collins, K., Smith, C. P., & Bernstein, I. (1991). Sexual activity and contraceptive use among low-income urban black adolescent females. *Adolescence*, *26*(104), 769–785.

Keith, V. M., & Finlay, B. (1988). The impact of parental divorce on children's educational attainment, marital timing, and likelihood of divorce. *Journal of Marriage and the Family*, *50*, 797–809.

Kelly, J. A., & Hansen, D. J. (1987). Social interactions and adjustment. In V. B. Van Hasselt & M. Hersen (Eds.), *Handbook of adolescent psychology*. New York: Pergamon Press.

Kenny, M. E. (1987). The extent and function of parental attachment among first-year college students. *Journal of Youth and Adolescence*, *16*, 17–29.

Kenny, M. E. (1996). Promoting optimal development from a developmental and contextual framework. *The Counseling Psychologist*, *24*(3), 475–481.

Kenrick, D. T., Gabrielidis, C., Keefe, R. C., & Cornelius, J. S. (1996). Adolescents' age preferences for dating partners: Support for an evolutionary model of life-history strategies. *Child Development*, *67*(4), 1499–1511.

Kernis, M. H., Cornell, D. P., Sun, C., Berry, A., & Harlow, T. (1993). There's more to self-esteem than whether it is high or low: The importance of stability of self-esteem. *Journal of Personality and Social Psychology*, *65*(6), 1190–1204.

Kerr, M. M., & Milliones, J. (1995). Suicide and suicidal behavior. In V. B. Van Hasselt & M. Hersen (Eds.), *Handbook of adolescent psychopathology: A guide to diagnosis and treatment*. New York: Lexington.

Kershner, R. (1996). Adolescent attitudes about rape. *Adolescence*, *31*(121), 29–34.

Kett, J. F. (1977). *Rites of passage: Adolescence in America 1790 to the present*. New York: Basic Books.

Kidwell, J. S., Dunham, R. M., Bacho, R. A., Pastorino, E., & Portes, P. R. (1995). Adolescent identity exploration: A test of Erikson's theory of transitional crisis. *Adolescence*, *30*(120), 785–794.

Kilborn, P. T. (1994, May 30). For high school graduates, a job market of dead ends. *The New York Times*, pp. 1, 23.

Kim, U., & Chun, M. B. J. (1994). Educational "success" of Asian Americans: An indigenous perspective. *Journal of Applied Developmental Psychology*, *15*(3), 329–339.

Kimbrough, V. D., & Salomone, P. R. (1993). African Americans: Diverse people, diverse career needs. *Journal of Career Development*, *19*(4), 265–272.

Kindermann, T. A. (1993). Natural peer groups as contexts for individual development: The case of children's motivation in school. *Developmental Psychology*, *29*(6), 970–977.

King, A., Beazley, R., Warren, W., Hankins, C., Robertson, A., & Radford, J. (1988). *Canada youth and AIDS study*. Kingston, Ontario: Queen's University.

King, C. A., Akiyama, M., & Elling, K. A. (1996). Self-perceived competencies and depression among middle school students in Japan and the United States. *Journal of Early Adolescence*, 16(2), 192–210.

King, N. J., Ollier, K., Iacuone, R., & Schuster, S. (1989). Fears of children and adolescents: A cross-sectional Australian study using the Revised-Fear Survey Schedule for Children. *Journal of Child Psychology & Psychiatry & Allied Disciplines*, 30(5), 775–784.

Kinney, D. A. (1993). From "nerds" to "normals": The recovery of identity among adolescents from middle school to high school. *Sociology of Education*, 66, 21–40.

Kirby, D. (1994). Sexuality education: It can reduce unprotected intercourse. *Siecus Report*, 22, 19–20.

Kirshnit, C. E., Ham, M., & Richards, M. H. (1989). The sporting life: Athletic activities during early adolescence. *Journal of Youth and Adolescence*, 18(6), 601–615.

Kiselica, M. S., & Sturmer, P. (1993). Is society giving teenage fathers a mixed message? *Youth & Society*, 24(4), 487–501.

Klaczynski, P. A. (1990). Cultural-developmental tasks and adolescent development: Theoretical and methodological considerations. *Adolescence*, 25(100), 811–823.

Klaczynski, P. A. (1997). Bias in adolescents' everyday reasoning and its relationship with intellectual ability, personal theories, and self-serving motivation. *Developmental Psychology*, 33(2), 273–283.

Klaczynski, P. A., Laipple, J. S., & Jurden, F. H. (1992). Educational context differences in practical problem solving during adolescence. *Merrill-Palmer Quarterly*, 38(3), 417–438.

Klein, H. (1990). Adolescence, youth, and young adulthood: Rethinking current conceptualizations of life stage. *Youth & Society*, 21(4), 446–471.

Klein, H. A. (1992). Temperament and self-esteem in late adolescence. *Adolescence*, 27(107), 689–695.

Klein, H. A., O'Bryant, K., & Hopkins, H. R. (1996). Recalled parental authority style and self-perception in college

men and women. *Journal of Genetic Psychology*, 157(1), 5–17.

Klein, J. D., Brown, J. D., Childers, K. W., Oliveri, J., Porter, C., & Dykers, C. (1993). Adolescents' risky behavior and mass media use. *Pediatrics*, 92, 24–31.

Klein, K., Forehand, R., Armistead, L, & Long, P. (1997). Delinquency during the transition to early adulthood: Family and parenting predictors from early adolescence. *Adolescence*, 32(125), 61–80.

Knight, G. P., Virdin, L. M., & Roosa, M. (1994). Socialization and family correlates of mental health outcomes among Hispanic and Anglo American children: Consideration of cross-ethnic scalar equivalence. *Child Development*, 65, 212–224.

Koff, E., & Rierdan, J. (1995). Preparing girls for menstruation: Recommendations from adolescent girls. *Adolescence*, 30(120), 795–811.

Koff, E., Rierdan, J., & Sheingold, K. (1982). Memories of menarche: Age, preparation, and prior knowledge as determinants of initial menstrual experience. *Journal of Youth and Adolescence*, 11, 1–19.

Kohlberg, L. (1958). *Global rating guide with new materials*. Cambridge, MA: School of Education, Harvard University.

Kohlberg, L. (1975). The cognitive-developmental approach to moral education. *Phi Delta Kappan*, 56, 670–677.

Kohlberg, L. (1985). Resolving moral conflicts within the just community. In C. G. Harding (Ed.), *Moral dilemmas: Philosophical and psychological issues in the development of moral reasoning*. Chicago: Precendent.

Kohlberg, L., & Gilligan, C. (1971). The adolescent as philosopher: The discovery of the self in a post-conventional world. *Daedalus*, 100, 1051–1086.

Kohlberg, L., & Kramer, R. (1969). Continuities and discontinuities in childhood and adult moral development. *Human Development*, 12, 93–120.

Kohn, P. M., & Milrose, J. A. (1993). The inventory of high-school students'

recent life experiences: A decontaminated measure of adolescents' hassles. *Journal of Youth and Adolescence*, 22(1), 43–54.

Koizumi, R. (1995). Feelings of optimism and pessimism in Japanese students' transition to junior high school. *Journal of Early Adolescence*, 15(4), 412–428.

Kolaric, G. C., & Galambos, N. L. (1995). Face-to-face interactions in unacquainted female–male adolescent dyads: How do girls and boys behave? *Journal of Early Adolescence*, 15(3), 363–382.

Kolata, G. (1996, September 18). Experts are at odds on how best to tackle rise in teen-agers' drug use. *The New York Times*, p. B7.

Kolata, G. (1997, July 29). Hard-core smokers, last-ditch remedies. *The New York Times*, pp. C1, C8.

Kornhaber, A. (1996). *Contemporary grandparenting*. Thousand Oaks, CA: Sage.

Kornhaber, A., & Woodward, K. L. (1981). *Grandparents/grandchild: The vital connection*. New York: Anchor Press.

Koyle, P. F., Jensen, L. C., Olsen, J., & Cundick, B. (1989). Comparison of sexual behaviors among adolescents. *Youth & Society*, 20(4), 461–476.

Kramer, L. R. (1986). Career awareness and personal development: A naturalistic study of gifted adolescent girls' concerns. *Adolescence*, 21(81), 123–131.

Kramer, L. R. (1991). The social construction of ability perceptions: An ethnographic study of gifted adolescent girls. *Journal of Early Adolescence*, 11(3), 340–362.

Kroger, J. (1997). Gender and identity: The intersection of structure, content, and context. *Sex Roles*, 36(11/12), 747–770.

Kroger, J., & Green, K. E. (1996). Events associated with identity status change. *Journal of Adolescence*, 19, 477–490.

Krueger, J. (1996). Personal beliefs and cultural stereotypes about racial characteristics. *Journal of Personality & Social Psychology*, 71(3), 536–548.

Kruger, A. C. (1992). The effect of peer and adult-child transactive discussions on moral reasoning. *Merrill-Palmer Quarterly, 38*(2), 191–211.

Kulin, H. E., Buibo, N., Mutie, D., & Sorter, S. (1982). The effect of chronic childhood malnutrition on pubertal growth and development. *American Journal of Clinical Nutrition, 36*, 527–536.

Kunen, S., Tang, W., & Ducey, S. J. (1991). Sex and age differences in adolescents' value judgments of historically important events: Theory, stereotypes and data. *Adolescence, 26*(101), 159–182.

Kupersmidt, J. B., & Coie, J. D. (1990). Preadolescent peer status, aggression, and school adjustment as predictors of externalizing problems in adolescence. *Child Development, 61*, 1350–1362.

Kurdek, L. A., & Fine, M. A. (1993). Parent and nonparent residential family members as providers of warmth and supervision to young adolescents. *Journal of Family Psychology, 7*(2), 245–249.

Kurdek, L. A., & Fine, M. A. (1994). Family acceptance and family control as predictors of adjustment in young adolescents: Linear, curvilinear, or interactive effects? *Child Development, 65*, 1137–1146.

Kurdek, L. A., Fine, M. A., & Sinclair, R. J. (1994). The relation between parenting transitions and adjustment in young adolescents: A multisample investigation. *Journal of Early Adolescence, 14*(4), 412–431.

Kurdek, L. A., Fine, M. A., & Sinclair, R. J. (1995). School adjustment in sixth graders: Parenting transitions, family climate, and peer norm effects. *Child Development, 66*(2), 430–445.

Kurtz, P. D., Kurtz, G. L., & Jarvis, S. V. (1991). Problems of maltreated runaway youth. *Adolescence, 26*(103), 543–555.

Kutner, L. (1991a, February 21). When you don't like your teen-ager's date. *The New York Times*, p. C8.

Kutner, L. (1991b, November 14). A teen-age risk: The abusive relationship. *The New York Times*.

Kutner, L. (1991c, November 28). What's worse than an argumentative teen-ager? *The New York Times*.

Kutner, L. (1992a, April 16). When to start dating? It depends on the child. *The New York Times*, p. C9.

Kutner, L. (1992b, October 8). Sometimes a date is just a meeting of eyes. *The New York Times*.

Kutner, L. (1993a, January 21). Children's self-esteem colors their whole world. *The New York Times*, p. C12.

Kutner, L. (1993b, February 11). A good summer job offers a chance to group up a little. *The New York Times*, p. C12.

Kutner, L. (1993c, June 17). Troubleshooting unrealistic career goals. *The New York Times*, p. C10.

Kutner, L. (1994, February 24). Harmless teasing, or sexual harassment? *The New York Times*.

Kvernmo, S., & Heyerdahl, S. (1996). Ethnic identity in aboriginal Sami adolescents: The impact of the family and the ethnic community context. *Journal of Adolescence, 19*, 453–463.

LaBreche, L. (1995, March). Switching schools can hurt self-esteem. *APA Monitor*, pp. 40–41.

Lackovic-Grgin, K., & Deković, M. (1990). The contribution of significant others to adolescents' self-esteem. *Adolescence, 25*(100), 839–846

Lackovic-Grgin, K., Deković, M., & Opacic, G. (1994). Pubertal status, interaction with significant others, and self-esteem of adolescent girls. *Adolescence, 29*(115), 691–700.

Ladd, G. W., & Cairns, E. (1996). Children: Ethnic and political violence. *Child Development, 67*, 14–18.

LaFromboise, T., Coleman, H. L. K., & Gerton, J. (1993). Psychological impact of biculturalism: Evidence and theory. *Psychological Bulletin, 114*(3), 395–412.

Lagana, L., & Hayes, D. M. (1993). Contraceptive health programs for adolescents: A critical review. *Adolescence, 28*(110), 347–359.

Lakey, J. F. (1994). The profile and treatment of male adolescent sex offenders. *Adolescence, 29*(116), 755–761.

Lambert, B. G., & Mounce, N. B. (1987). Career planning. In V. B. Van Hasselt & M. Hersen (Eds.), *Handbook of adolescent psychology*. New York: Pergamon Press.

Lamborn, S. D., Dornbusch, S. M., & Steinberg, L. (1996). Ethnicity and community context as moderators of the relations between family decision making and adolescent adjustment. *Child Development, 67*, 283–301.

Lamborn, S. D., Mounts, N. S., Steinberg, L., & Dornbusch, S. M. (1991). Patterns of competence and adjustment among adolescents from authoritative, authoritarian, indulgent, and neglectful families. *Child Development, 62*, 1049–1065.

Landers, S. (1988, July). Sex, drugs 'n' rock: Relation not causal. *APA Monitor*, p. 40.

Lansdown, R., & Walker, M. (1991). *Your child's development from birth through adolescence*. New York: Knopf.

LaPorte, D. J. (1997). Gender differences in perceptions and consequences of an eating binge. *Sex Roles, 36*(7/8), 479–490.

Lapsley, D. K. (1990). Continuity and discontinuity in adolescent social cognitive development. In R. Montemayor, G. R. Adams, & T. P. Gullotta (Eds.), *From childhood to adolescence: A transitional period?* Newbury Park, CA: Sage.

Lapsley, D. K., Enright, R. D., & Serlin, R. C. (1985). Toward a theoretical perspective on the legislation of adolescence. *Journal of Early Adolescence, 5*, 441–466.

Lapsley, D. K., & Murphy, M. N. (1985). Another look at the theoretical assumptions of adolescent egocentrism. *Developmental Review, 5*, 227–236.

Lapsley, D. K., & Rice, K. (1988). History, puberty, and the textbook consensus on adolescent development (book review). *Contemporary Psychology, 33*, 210–213.

Larson, R. (1995). Secrets in the bedroom: Adolescents' private use of media. *Journal of Youth and Adolescence, 24*(5), 535–550.

Larson, R., & Ham, M. (1993). Stress and "storm and stress" in early adolescence: The relationship of negative events with dysphoric affect. *Developmental Psychology, 29*(1), 130–140.

Larson, R., Kubey, R., & Colletti, J. (1989). Changing channels: Early adolescent media choices and shifting investments in family and friends. *Journal of Youth and Adolescence, 18*(6), 583–599.

Larson, R., & Richards, M. H. (1989). The changing life space of early adolescence. *Journal of Youth and Adolescence, 18*, 501–509.

Larson, R., & Richards, M. H. (1991). Daily companionship in late childhood and early adolescence: Changing developmental contexts. *Child Development, 62*, 284–300.

Larson, R., & Richards, M. H. (1994). *Divergent realities: The emotional lives of mothers, fathers, and adolescents.* New York: Basic Books.

Larson, R., Richards, M. H., Moneta, G., Holmbeck, G., & Duckett, E. (1996). Changes in adolescents' daily interactions with their families from ages 10 to 18: Disengagement and transformation. *Developmental Psychology, 32*(4), 744–754.

Larson, R. W. (1997). The emergence of solitude as a constructive domain of experience in early adolescence. *Child Development, 68*(1), 80–93.

Lask, B., & Bryant-Waugh, R. (1992). Early-onset anorexia nervosa and related eating disorders. *Journal of Child Psychology & Psychiatry & Allied Disciplines, 33*(1), 281–300.

Lasko, D. S., Field, T. M., Gonzalez, K. P., Harding, J., Yando, R., & Bendell, D. (1996). Adolescent depressed mood and parental unhappiness. *Adolescence, 31*(121), 49–57.

Lau, S., & Lau, W. (1996). Outlook on life: How adolescents and children view the life-style of parents, adults and self. *Journal of Adolescence, 19*, 293–296.

Laursen, B., & Collins, W. A. (1994). Interpersonal conflict during adolescence. *Psychological Bulletin, 115*(2), 197–209.

Laursen, B., Hartup, W. W., & Koplas, A. L. (1996). Towards understanding peer conflict. *Merrill-Palmer Quarterly, 42*(1), 76–102.

Laursen, B., & Koplas, A. L. (1995). What's important about important conflicts? Adolescents' perceptions of daily disagreements. *Merrill-Palmer Quarterly, 41*(4), 536–553.

Lavery, B., Siegel, A. W., Cousins, J. H., & Rubovits, D. S. (1993). Adolescent risk-taking: An analysis of problem behaviors in problem children. *Journal of Experimental Child Psychology, 55*, 277–294.

Lawrence, C. M., & Thelen, M. H. (1995). Body image, dieting, and self-concept: Their relation in African-American and Caucasian children. *Journal of Clinical Child Psychology, 24*(1), 41–48.

Lawson, C. (1990, May 3). 4th-grade lament: "Everyone's dating." *The New York Times.*

Lawson, C. (1991, April 4). A bedtime story that's different. *The New York Times.*

Lawson, C. (1992, January 9). The freshman is home. Bi-zarre! *The New York Times*, pp. C1, C5.

Lawson, E. J. (1994). The role of smoking in the lives of low-income pregnant adolescents: A field study. *Adolescence, 29*(113), 61–79.

Lazarus, R. S., & Folkman, S. (1984). *Stress, appraisal, and coping.* New York: Springer.

Leadbeater, B. J., Bishop, S. J., & Raver, C. C. (1996). Quality of mother–toddler interactions, maternal depressive symptoms, and behavior problems in preschoolers of adolescent mothers. *Developmental Psychology, 32*(2), 280–288.

Leary, W. E. (1995, April 21). Young people who try suicide may be succeeding more often. *The New York Times*, p. A15.

LeCroy, C. W. (1988). Parent–adolescent intimacy: Impact on adolescent functioning. *Adolescence, 23*(89), 137–147.

Ledlow, S. (1992). Is cultural discontinuity an adequate explanation for dropping out? *Journal of American Indian Education, 31*, 21–36.

Lee, F. R. (1990, March 20). "Model minority" label taxes Asian youths. *The New York Times*, p. B1.

Lee, F. R. (1991, November 25). For gold earrings and protection, more girls take road to violence. *The New York Times*, pp. A1, B7.

Lee, F. R. (1992, November 19). Growing up under the eyes of a probation officer. *The New York Times*, pp. B1, B8.

Lee, M., & Larson, R. (1996). Effectiveness of coping in adolescence: The case of Korean examination stress. *International Journal of Behavioral Development, 19*(4), 851–869.

Lefkowitz, E. S., Kahlbaugh, P. E., & Sigman, M. D. (1996). Turn-taking in mother-adolescent conversations about sexuality and conflict. *Journal of Youth and Adolescence, 25*(3), 307–322.

Leftwich, K. (1992, February). Outlook: Where the jobs are. *Vocational Education Journal*, 18–21.

Leigh, B. C., & Aramburu, B. (1996). The role of alcohol and gender in choices and judgments about hypothetical sexual encounters. *Journal of Applied Social Psychology, 26*(1), 20–30.

Leitenberg, H., & Rosen, J. C. (1988). Cognitive-behavioral treatment of bulimia nervosa. In M. Hersen, R. M. Eisler, & P. M. Miller (Eds.), *Progress in behavior modification* (Vol. 23). Newbury Park, CA: Sage.

Lempers, J. D., & Clark-Lempers, D. S. (1997). Economic hardship, family relationships, and adolescent distress: An evaluation of a stress–distress mediation model in mother–daughter and mother–son dyads. *Adolescence, 32*(126), 339–356.

Leonardson, G. R. (1986). The relationship between self-concept and selected academic and personal factors. *Adolescence, 21*, 467–474.

Leone, C. M., & Richards, M. H. (1989). Classwork and homework in early adolescence: The ecology of achievement. *Journal of Youth and Adolescence, 18*(6), 531–548.

Lerner, R. M. (1986). *Concepts and theories of human development* (2nd ed.). New York: Random House.

Lerner, R. M. (1992). Dialectics, developmental contextualism, and the further enhancement of theory about puberty and psychosocial development. *Journal of Early Adolescence, 12*(4), 366–388.

Lerner, R. M. (1996). Relative plasticity, integration, temporality, and diversity in human development: A developmental contextual perspective about theory, process, and method. *Developmental Psychology, 32*(4), 781–786.

Lerner, R. M., Lerner, J. V., Hess, L. E., Schwab, J., Jovanovic, J., Talwar, R., & Kucher, J. S. (1991). Physical attractiveness and psychosocial functioning among early adolescents. *Journal of Early Adolescence, 11*(3), 300–320.

Lerner, R. M., Lerner, J. V., & Tubman, J. (1989). Organismic and contextual bases of development in adolescence: A developmental contextual view. In G. R. Adams, R. Montemayor, & T. P. Gullotta (Eds.), *Biology of adolescent behavior and development.* Newbury Park, CA: Sage.

le Roux, J. (1996). The worldwide phenomenon of street children: Conceptual analysis. *Adolescence, 31*(124), 965–972.

Lesko, N. (1996). Denaturalizing adolescence: The politics of contemporary representations. *Youth & Society, 28*(2), 139–161.

Lester, D. (1993). *The cruelist death: The enigma of adolescent suicide.* Philadelphia: Charles Press.

Leukefeld, C. G., & Haverkos, H. W. (1993). Sexually transmitted diseases. In T. P. Gullotta, G. R. Adams, & R. Montemayor (Eds.), *Adolescent sexuality.* Newbury Park, CA: Sage.

Leung, J., & Leung, K. (1992). Life satisfaction, self-concept, and relationship with parents in adolescence. *Journal of Youth and Adolescence, 21*(6), 653–665.

Leung, J. J., Wright, B., & Foster, S. F. (1987). Perceived parental influence and adolescent post-secondary career plans. *High-School Journal, 70*, 173–179.

Levine, J. A., & Gislason, I. A. (1985). The college student in conflict with parents over career choice. *Medical Aspects of Human Sexuality, 19*, 17–23.

Levine, M. P., Smolak, L., & Hayden, H. (1994). The relation of sociocultural factors to eating attitudes and behaviors among middle school girls. *Journal of Early Adolescence, 14*(4), 471–490.

Levinson, R. A. (1995). Reproductive and contraceptive knowledge, contraceptive self-efficacy, and contraceptive behavior among teenage women. *Adolescence, 30*(117), 65–86.

Levitt, M. J., Guacci-Franco, N., & Levitt, J. L. (1993). Convoys of social support in childhood and early adolescence: Structure and function. *Developmental Psychology, 29*(5), 811–818.

Levy, S. R., Jurkovic, G. L., & Spirito, A. (1995). A multisystems analysis of adolescent suicide attempters. *Journal of Abnormal Child Psychology, 23*(2), 221–234.

Lewin, K. (1980). Field theory and experiment in social psychology. In R. E. Muuss (Ed.), *Adolescent behavior and society: A book of readings* (3rd ed., pp. 4–13). New York: Random House. (Originally published in 1939).

Lewin, T. (1995a, May 30). Family decay global, study says. *The New York Times*, p. A5.

Lewin, T. (1995b, July 18). Adolescents say drugs are biggest worry. *The New York Times*.

Lewin, T. (1995c, November 29). In home schooling, a new type of student. *The New York Times*, p. D20.

Lewin, T. (1996, October 6). Kissing cases highlight schools' fears of liability for sexual harassment. *The New York Times*, p. A22.

Lewin, T. (1997, April 5). Teen-agers alter sexual practices, thinking risks will be avoided. *The New York Times*, p. 8.

Lewinsohn, P., Gotlib, I. H., & Seeley, J. R. (1997). Depression-related psychosocial variables: Are they specific to depression in adolescents? *Journal of Abnormal Psychology, 106*(3), 365–375.

Lewis, C. C. (1981). The effects of parental firm control: A reinterpretation of findings. *Psychological Bulletin, 90*(3), 547–563.

Li, X., Stanton, B., Black, M. M., & Feigelman, S. (1996). Persistence of drug trafficking behaviors and intentions among urban African American early adolescents. *Journal of Early Adolescence, 16*(4), 469–487.

Li, X., Stanton, B., Feigelman, S., Black, M. M., & Romer, D. (1994). Drug trafficking and drug use among African-American early adolescents. *Journal of Early Adolescence, 14*(4), 491–508.

Liebert, R. M., & Sprafkin, J. (1988). *The early window—Effects of television on children and youth* (3rd ed.). New York: Pergamon.

Liestol, K. (1982). Social conditions and menarcheal age: The importance of the early years of life. *Annals of Human Biology, 9*, 521–536.

Lindemann, J. E. (1981). General considerations for evaluating and counseling the physically handicapped. In J. E. Lindemann (Ed.), *Psychological and behavioral aspects of physical disability: A manual for health practitioners.* New York: Plenum.

Lindsay, P., & Knox, W. E. (1984). Continuity and change in work values among young adults: A longitudinal study. *American Journal of Sociology, 89*, 918–931.

Linn, M. C. (1980). Teaching children to control variables: Some investigations using free choice experiences. In S. Modgil & C. Modgil (Eds.), *Toward a theory of psychological development with the Piagetian framework.* London: National Foundation for Educational Research.

Linn, M. C. (1983). Content, context, and process in reasoning during adolescence. *Journal of Early Adolescence, 3*, 63–82.

Linn, M. C., & Hyde, J. S. (1991). Trends in cognitive and psychosocial gender differences. In R. M. Lerner, A. C. Petersen, & J. Brooks-Gunn (Eds.),

*Encyclopedia of adolescence.* New York: Garland.

Linn, R. (1991). Sexual and moral development of Israeli female adolescents from city and kibbutz: Perspectives of Kohlberg and Gilligan. *Adolescence, 26*(101), 58–71.

Linney, J. A., & Seidman, E. (1989). The future of schooling. *American Psychologist, 44,* 336–340.

Linney, J. A., & Vernberg, E. (1983). Changing patterns of parental employment and the family–school relationship. In C. D. Hayes & S. G. Kamerman (Eds.), *Children of working parents: Experiences and outcomes.* Washington, DC: National Academy Press.

Linver, M. R., & Silverberg, S. B. (1997). Maternal predictors of early adolescent achievement-related outcomes: Adolescent gender as moderator. *Journal of Early Adolescence, 17*(3), 294–318.

Liu, X., Kaplan, H. B., & Risser, W. (1992). Decomposing the reciprocal relationships between academic achievement and general self-esteem. *Youth & Society, 24*(2), 123–148.

Lloyd, B., Lucas, K., & Fernbach, M. (1997). Adolescent girls' constructions of smoking identities: implications for health promotion. *Journal of Adolescence, 20,* 43–56.

Locke, J. (1690/1961). *Essay concerning human understanding.* London: J. M. Dent and Sons, Ltd.

Locke, J. (1693/1964). *Some thoughts concerning education.* In P. Gay (Ed.), *John Locke on Education.* New York: Bureau of Publications, Teacher's College, Columbia University.

Lockheed, M., & Hall, K. (1976). Conceptualizing sex as a status characteristic: Applications to leadership training strategies. *Journal of Social Issues, 32*(3), 111–124.

Locust, C. (1988). Wounding the spirit: Discrimination and traditional American Indian belief systems. *Harvard Educational Review, 58,* 315–340.

Loewenstein, G., & Furstenberg, F., Jr. (1991). Is teenage sexual behavior rational? *Journal of Applied Social Psychology, 21*(12), 957–986.

Lohr, S. (1987, Summer). Swedes instill a sense of responsibility. *The New York Times,* Education Supplement, p. 19.

Lomsky-Feder, E. (1996). Youth in the shadow of war, war in the light of youth: Life stories of Israeli veterans. In K. Hurrelmann & S. F. Hamilton (Eds.), *Social problems and social contexts in adolescence: Perspectives across boundaries.* New York: Aldine De Gruyter.

Long, B. H. (1989). Heterosexual involvement of unmarried undergraduate females in relation to self-evaluations. *Journal of Youth and Adolescence, 18*(5), 489–500.

Long, N., & Forehand, R. (1987). The effects of parental divorce and parental conflict on children: An overview. *Journal of Developmental and Behavioral Pediatrics, 8*(5), 292–296.

Lord, S. E., Eccles, J. S., & McCarthy, K. A. (1994). Surviving the junior high school transition: Family processes and self-perceptions as protective and risk factors. *Journal of Early Adolescence, 14*(2), 162–199.

Losel, F., & Bliesener, T. (1994). Some high-risk adolescents do not develop conduct problems: A study of protective factors. *International Journal of Behavioral Development, 17*(4), 753–777.

Lourenço, O., & Machado, A. (1996). In defense of Piaget's theory: A reply to 10 common criticisms. *Psychological Review, 103*(1), 143–164.

Lowe, G., Foxcroft, D. R., & Sibley, D. (1993). *Adolescent drinking and family life.* Langhorne, PA: Harwood Academic/Gordon and Breach Science.

Lu, S. (1990). The development of self-conceptions from childhood to adolescence in China. *Child Study Journal, 20*(2), 129–137.

Lueck, T. J. (1996, June 2). A few bright spots for young people seeking summer jobs. *The New York Times,* p. A38.

Luster, T., & Mittelstaedt, M. (1993). Adolescent mothers. In T. Luster & L. Okagaki (Eds.), *Parenting: An ecological perspective.* Hillsdale, NJ: Erlbaum.

Luster, T., & Small, S. A. (1994). Factors associated with sexual risk-taking behaviors among adolescents. *Journal of Marriage and the Family, 56,* 622–632.

Luthar, S. S. (1991). Vulnerability and resilience: A study of high-risk adolescents. *Child Development, 62,* 600–616.

Luthar, S. S. (1995). Social competence in the school setting: Prospective cross-domain associations among inner-city teens. *Child Development, 66,* 416–429.

Luthar, S. S., & Cushing, G. (1997). Substance use and personal adjustment among disadvantaged teenagers: A six-month prospective study. *Journal of Youth and Adolescence, 26*(3), 353–371.

Luthar, S. S., Zigler, E., & Goldstein, D. (1992). Psychosocial adjustment among intellectually gifted adolescents: The role of cognitive-developmental and experiential factors. *Journal of Child Psychology and Psychiatry, 33*(2), 361–373.

Lyon, M., Chatoor, I., Atkins, D., Silber, T., Mosimann, J., & Gray, J. (1997). Testing the hypothesis of the multidimensional model of anorexia nervosa in adolescents. *Adolescence, 32*(125), 101–112.

Ma, H. K., Shek, D. T. L., Cheung, P. C., & Lee, R. Y. P. (1996). The relation of prosocial and antisocial behavior to personality and peer relations of Hong Kong Chinese adolescents. *Journal of Genetic Psychology, 157*(3), 255–266.

Maccoby, E. E. (1988). Gender as a social category. *Developmental Psychology, 24,* 755–765.

Maccoby, E. (1991). Different reproductive strategies in males and females. *Child Development, 62,* 676–681.

Maccoby, E. E., Buchanan, C. M., Mnookin, R. H., & Dornbusch, S. M. (1993). Postdivorce roles of mothers and fathers in the lives of their children. *Journal of Family Psychology, 7*(1), 24–38.

Maccoby, E. E., & Jacklin, C. N. (1974). *The psychology of sex differences.* Stanford, CA: Stanford University Press.

Maccoby, E. E., & Martin, J. A. (1983). Socialization in the context of the family: Parent–child interaction. In E. M. Hetherington (Ed.), *Handbook of child psychology, Volume 4: Socialization, personality, and social development* (4th ed.). New York: Wiley.

Maggs, J. L., Almeida, D. M., & Galambos, N. L. (1995). Risky business: The paradoxical meaning of problem behavior for young adolescents. *Journal of Early Adolescence, 15*(3), 344–362.

Maggs, J. L., Frome, P. M., Eccles, J. S., & Barber, B. L. (1997). Psychosocial resources, adolescent risk behavior and young adult adjustment: is risk taking more dangerous for some than others? *Journal of Adolescence, 20*, 103–119.

Magnusson, D., Stattin, H., & Allen, V. L. (1986). Differential maturation among girls and its relation to social adjustment in a longitudinal perspective. In D. L. Featherman & R. M. Lerner (Eds.), *Life span development* (Vol. 7). New York: Academic Press.

Mahoney, J. L., & Cairns, R. B. (1997). Do extracurricular activities protect against early school dropout? *Developmental Psychology, 33*(2), 241–253.

Mahoney, M. J. (1991). *Human change processes: The scientific foundations of psychotherapy*. New York: Basic Books.

Maier, E., & Herman, A. (1974). The relationship of vocational indecisiveness and satisfaction with dogmatism and self-esteem. *Journal of Vocational Behavior, 5*, 95–102.

Mainous, A. G., III., Martin, C. A., Oler, M. J., Richardson, E. T., & Haney, A. S. (1996). Substance use among adolescents: Fulfilling a need state. *Adolescence, 31*(124), 807–816.

Malina, R. M. (1985). Growth and physical performance of Latin American children and youth: Socio-economic and nutritional contrasts. *Collegian Antropologicum, 9*, 9–31.

Malina, R. M., & Bouchard, C. (1991). *Growth, maturation, and physical activity*. Champaign, IL: Human Kinetics.

Mallik, N. B., Ghosh, K. K., & Chattopadhyay, P. K. (1986). Hormonal and psychological changes in adolescent boys. *Journal of Psychological Researches, 30*, 165–169.

Manegold, C. S. (1994, August 18). Students gain but fall short of goals. *The New York Times*, p. B11.

Mann, L., Harmoni, R., & Power, C. (1989). Adolescent decision making: The development of competence. *Journal of Adolescence, 12*, 265–278.

Mann-Feder, V. R. (1996). Adolescents in therapeutic communities. *Adolescence, 31*(121), 17–28.

Manning, M. L. (1992). Developmentally appropriate middle schools. *Child Education, 68*(5), 305–307.

Manning, W. D. (1990). Parenting employed teenagers. *Youth & Society, 22*, 184–200.

Mansnerus, L. (1992a, August 2). Mediocrity in the classroom. *The New York Times Education Section*, pp. 22–23.

Mansnerus, L. (1992b, November 1). Should tracking be derailed? *The New York Times*, pp. 1, 4.

Mansnerus, L. (1994, August 7). New pressures on vocational education. *The New York Times* (Education Life Section), pp. 14–16.

Marano, H. E. (1997a, July 1). Puberty may start at 6 as hormones surge. *The New York Times*, pp. C1, 6.

Marano, H. E. (1997b, July 2). Sexual issues fan parents' fears. *The New York Times*, p. C9.

Marcia, J. E. (1966). Development and validation of ego-identity status. *Journal of Personality and Social Psychology, 3*, 551–558.

Marcia, J. E. (1967). Ego identity status: Relationship to change in self-esteem, "general maladjustment," and authoritarianism. *Journal of Personality, 35*, 119–133.

Marcia, J. E. (1980). Identity in adolescence. In J. Adelson (Ed.), *Handbook of adolescent psychology*. New York: Wiley

Marcia, J. E. (1994). The empirical study of ego identity. In H. A. Bosma, T. L. G. Graafsma, H. D. Grotevant, & D. J. de Levita (Eds.), *Identity and development: An interdisciplinary approach*. Thousand Oaks, CA: Sage.

Marcotte, D. (1996). Irrational beliefs and depression in adolescence. *Adolescence, 31*(124), 935–954.

Marcotte, D. (1997). Treating depression in adolescence: A review of the effectiveness of cognitive-behavioral treatments. *Journal of Youth and Adolescence, 26*(3), 273–284.

Marcus, I. M. (1991). The influence of development in career achievement. In S. I. Greenspan & G. H. Pollock (Eds.), *The course of life*, Volume IV, *Adolescence*. Madison, CT: International Universities Press.

Marcus, R. F. (1996). The friendships of delinquents. *Adolescence, 31*(121), 145–158.

Marcus, R. F., & Betzer, P. D. S. (1996). Attachment and antisocial behavior in early adolescence. *Journal of Early Adolescence, 16*(2), 229–248.

Marjoribanks, K. (1986). A longitudinal study of adolescents' aspirations as assessed by Seginer's model. *Merrill-Palmer Quarterly, 32*(3), 211–230.

Marjoribanks, K. (1996). Ethnicity, proximal family environment, and young adolescents' cognitive performance. *Journal of Early Adolescence, 16*(3), 340–359.

Markel, G., & Greenbaum, J. (1996). *Performance breakthroughs for adolescents with learning disabilities or ADD*. Champaign, IL: Research Press.

Marks, N. F. (1995). Midlife marital status differences in social support relationships with adult children and psychological well-being. *Journal of Family Issues, 16*(1), 5–28.

Markstrom-Adams, C. (1992). A consideration of intervening factors in adolescent identity formation. In G. R. Adams, T. P. Gullotta, & R. Montemayor (Eds.), *Adolescent identity formation*. Newbury Park, CA: Sage.

Markstrom-Adams, C., & Adams, G. R. (1995). Gender, ethnic group, and grade differences in psychosocial functioning during middle adolescence. *Journal of Youth and Adolescence, 24*(4), 397–417.

Markus, H., & Nurius, P. (1986). Possible selves. *American Psychologist, 41,* 954–969.

Marsh, H. W. (1989). Age and sex effects in multiple dimensions of self-concept: Preadolescence to early adulthood. *Journal of Educational Psychology, 81*(3), 417–430.

Marsh, H. W. (1991). Employment during high school: Character building or a subversion of academic goals? *Sociology of Education, 64,* 172–189.

Marshall, W. A., & Tanner, J. M. (1969). Variations in the pattern of pubertal changes in girls. *Archives of Diseases in Childhood, 44,* 291–303.

Marshall, W. A., & Tanner, J. M. (1970). Variations in the pattern of pubertal changes in boys. *Archives of Diseases in Childhood, 45,* 13–23.

Marshall, W. A. & Tanner, J. M. (1986). Puberty. In F. Falkner & J. M. Tanner (Eds.), *Human growth*, Volume 2, *Postnatal growth neurobiology*. New York: Plenum.

Marsiglio, W., & Menaghan, E. G. (1990). Pregnancy resolution and family formation. *Journal of Family Issues, 11*(3), 313–333.

Martin, B. (1990). The transmission of relationship difficulties from one generation to the next. *Journal of Youth and Adolescence, 19*(3), 181–199.

Martin, E. P., & Martin, J. M. (1978). *The black extended family.* Chicago: University of Chicago Press.

Martin, S. (1996; October). Programs should nurture, not punish, black youth. *APA Monitor,* p. 25.

Martin, S., & Murray, B. (1996, October). Social toxicity undermines youngsters in inner cities. *APA Monitor,* p. 27.

Maslow, A. (1971). *The farther reaches of human nature.* New York: Viking.

Mason, C. A., Cauce, A. M., Gonzales, N., & Hiraga, Y. (1996). Neither too sweet nor too sour: Problem peers, maternal control, and problem behavior in African American adolescents. *Child Development, 67*(5), 2115–2130.

Mason, N. K. (1992, February). Career guidance: The teacher's role. *Vocational Education Journal,* 22–23.

Massalam, V. S., Marcus, R. F., & Stunkard, C. L. (1990). Parent–adolescent communication, family functioning, and school performance. *Adolescence, 25*(99), 725–737.

Masten, A. S., Coatsworth, J. D., Neemann, J., Gest, S. D., et al. (1995). The structure and coherence of competence from childhood through adolescence. *Child Development, 66*(6), 1635–1659.

Matarazzo, J. D. (1992). Psychological testing and assessment in the 21st century. *American Psychologist, 47*(8), 1007–1018.

Mates, D., & Allison, K. R. (1992). Sources of stress and coping responses of high school students. *Adolescence, 27*(106), 461–474.

Mathews, D. J., & Keating, D. P. (1995). Domain specificity and habits of mind: An investigation of patterns of high-level development. *Journal of Early Adolescence, 15*(3), 319–343.

Maticka-Tyndale, E. (1991). Modification of sexual activities in the era of AIDS: A trend analysis of adolescent sexual activities. *Youth & Society, 23*(1), 31–49.

Mau, R. Y. (1992). The validity and devolution of a concept: Student alienation. *Adolescence, 27*(107), 731–741.

Mazor, A., Shamir, R., & Ben-Moshe, J. (1990). The individuation process from a social-cognitive perspective in kibbutz adolescents. *Journal of Youth and Adolescence, 19*(2), 73–90.

Mboya, M. M. (1995). Variations in parenting practices: Gender- and age-related differences in African adolescents. *Adolescence, 30*(120), 955–962.

McAdams, D. P. (1987). A life-story model of identity. In R. Hogan & W. H. Jones (Eds.), *Perspectives in personality: A research annual* (Vol. 2). Greenwich, CT: JAI Press.

McAdams D. P. (1989). The development of a narrative identity. In D. M. Buss & N. Cantor (Eds.), *Personality psychology: Recent trends and emerging directions.* New York: Springer-Verlag.

McBride, S., & Belsky, J. (1988). Characteristics, determinants, and consequences of maternal separation anxiety. *Developmental Psychology, 24*(3), 407–414.

McCabe, M. P., & Collins, J. K. (1984). Measurement of depth of desired and experienced sexual involvement at different stages of dating. *Journal of Sex Research, 20,* 377–390.

McCall, R. B., Evahn, C., & Kratzer, L. (1992). *High school underachievers: What do they achieve as adults?* Newbury Park, CA: Sage.

McCarn, S. R., & Fassinger, R. E. (1996). Revisioning sexual minority identity formation: A new model of lesbian identity and its implication for counseling and research. *The Counseling Psychologist, 24*(3), 508–534.

McCarron, B. (1996, May 9). An alternative prom: Feeling shunned, gay teens dance on to own galas. *The Star Ledger,* pp. 1, 18.

McCarthy, J. B. (1995). *Adolescence and character disturbance.* Lanham, MD: University Press of America.

McClean, A. L., & Flanigan, B. J. (1993). Transition-marking behaviors of adolescent males at first intercourse. *Adolescence, 28*(111), 579–595.

McClelland, D. C. (1973). Testing for competence rather than for "intelligence." *American Psychologist, 28,* 1–14.

McCombs, A., & Forehand, R. (1989). Adolescent school performance following parental divorce: Are there family factors that can enhance success? *Adolescence, 24*(96), 871–880.

McConaghy, N. (1995). Adolescent sexuality. In V. B. Van Hasselt & M. Hersen (Eds.), *Handbook of adolescent psychopathology: A guide to diagnosis and treatment.* New York: Lexington Books.

McCord, J. (1990). Problem behaviors. In S. S. Feldman & G. R. Elliot (Eds.), *At the threshold: The developing adolescent.* Cambridge, MA: Harvard University Press.

McCormick, N., Izzo, A., & Folcik, J. (1985). Adolescents' values, sexuality, and contraception in a rural New York county. *Adolescence, 20*(78), 385–395.

McCullum, C., & Achterberg, C. L. (1997). Food shopping and label use behavior among high school-aged adolescents. *Adolescence*, *32*(125), 181–198.

McCurdy, S. J., & Scherman, A. (1996). Effects of family structure on the adolescent separation-individuation process. *Adolescence*, *31*(122), 307–319.

McDermott, P. A. (1996). A nationwide study of developmental and gender prevalence for psychopathology in childhood and adolescence. *Journal of Abnormal Child Psychology*, *24*(1), 53–65.

McDonald, J. L., & Jessell, J. C. (1992). Influence of selected variables on occupational attitudes and perceived occupational abilities of young adolescents. *Journal of Career Development*, *18*(4), 239–250.

McDonald, R. M., & Towberman, D. B. (1993). Psychological correlates of adolescent drug involvement. *Adolescence*, *28*(112), 925–936.

McFarlane, A. H., Bellissimo, A., & Norman, G. R. (1995). Family structure, family functioning, and adolescent well-being: The transcendent influence of parental style. *Journal of Child Psychology & Psychiatry & Allied Disciplines*, *36*(5), 847–864.

McGrory, A. (1990). Menarche: Responses of early adolescent females. *Adolescence*, *25*(98), 265–270.

McHolland, J. D. (1985). Strategies for dealing with resistant adolescents. *Adolescence*, *20*(78), 349–368.

McIntosh, H. (1996, June). Adolescent friends not always a bad influence. *APA Monitor*, p. 16.

McKechnie, J., Lindsay, S., Hobbs, S., & Lavalette, M. (1996). Adolescents' perceptions of the role of part-time work. *Adolescence*, *31*(121), 193–204.

McKinney, J. P., & Vogel, J. (1987). Developmental theories. In V. B. Van Hasselt & M. Hersen (Eds.), *Handbook of adolescent psychology*. New York: Pergamon Press.

McLaughlin, J., Miller, P., & Warwick, H. (1996). Deliberate self-harm in adolescents: hopelessness, depression, problems and problem-solving. *Journal of Adolescence*, *19*, 523–532.

McLean, A. L., & Flanigan, B. J. (1993). Transition-marking behaviors of adolescent males at first intercourse. *Adolescence*, *28*(111), 579–595.

McLoyd, V. C. (1990). The impact of economic hardship on black families and children: Psychological distress, parenting, and socioemotional development. *Child Development*, *61*, 311–346.

McLoyd, V. C., Jayaratne, T. E., Ceballo, R., & Borquez, J. (1994). Unemployment and work interruption among African American single mothers: Effects on parenting and adolescent socioemotional functioning. *Child Development*, *65*(2), 562–589.

McNair, D., & Brown, D. (1983). Predicting the occupational aspirations, occupational expectations, and career maturity of black and white male and female 10th graders. *Vocational Guidance Quarterly*, *32*, 29–36.

McNally, S., Eisenberg, N., & Harris, J. D. (1991). Consistency and change in maternal child-rearing practices and values: A longitudinal study. *Child Development*, *62*, 190–198.

Meece, J. L., Parsons, J. E., Kaczala, C. M., Goff, S. B., & Futterman, R. (1982). Sex differences in math achievement: Toward a model of academic choice. *Psychological Bulletin*, *91*, 324–348.

Meeus, W. (1989). Parental and peer support in adolescence. In K. Hurrelmann & U. Engel (Eds.), *The social world of adolescents: International perspectives*. Berlin: de Gruyter.

Meier, B. (1992, September 5). Credit cards on the rise in high schools. *The New York Times*.

Mellor, S. (1989). Gender differences in identity formation as a function of self-other relationships. *Journal of Youth and Adolescence*, *18*(4), 361–375.

Mendelberg, H. E. (1986). Identity conflict in Mexican-American adolescents. *Adolescence*, *21*, 215–222.

Mendelson, B. K., White, D. R., & Mendelson, M. J. (1996). Self-esteem and body esteem: Effects of gender, age, and weight. *Journal of Applied Developmental Psychology*, *17*(3), 321–346.

Merten, D. E. (1996a). Visibility and vulnerability: Responses to rejection by nonaggressive junior high school boys. *Journal of Early Adolescence*, *16*(1), 5–26.

Merten, D. E. (1996b). Information versus meaning: Toward a further understanding of early adolescent rejection. *Journal of Early Adolescence*, *16*(1), 37–45.

Mesco, R. H., Rao, K., Amaya-Jackson, L., & Cantwell, D. M. (1995). Diagnostic classification of adolescents. In V. B. Van Hasselt & M. Hersen (Eds.), *Handbook of adolescent psychopathology: A guide to diagnosis and treatment*. New York: Lexington Books.

Meyer, V. F. (1991). A critique of adolescent pregnancy prevention research: The invisible white male. *Adolescence*, *26*(101), 217–222.

Meyer-Bahlburg, H. F. L., Ehrhardt, A. A., Rosen, L. R., Gruen, R. S., Veridiano, N. P., Vann, F. H., & Neuwalder, H. F. (1995). Prenatal estrogens and the development of homosexual orientation. *Developmental Psychology*, *31*(1), 12–21.

Mezzich, A., Bukstein, O. G., & Grim, M. R. (1995). Epidemiology and adolescent diagnosis. In V. B. Van Hasselt & M. Hersen (Eds.), *Handbook of adolescent psychopathology: A guide to diagnosis and treatment*. New York: Lexington.

Michel, C., Thomas, R. M., & Maimbolwa-Sinyangwe, I. (1989). Adolescents' conceptions of "moral": Haiti, the United States, and Zambia. *Youth & Society*, *21*(2), 196–206.

Mickelson, R. (1990). The attitude-achievement paradox among black adolescents. *Sociology of Education*, *63*, 44–61.

Middleton, E. B., & Loughead, T. A. (1993). Parental influence on career development: An integrative framework for adolescent career counseling. *Journal of Career Development*, *19*(3), 161–174.

Midgley, C., Anderman, E., & Hicks, L. (1995). Differences between elementary and middle school teachers and students: A goal theory approach.

*Journal of Early Adolescence, 15*(1), 90–113.

Midgley, C., Feldlaufer, H., & Eccles, J. (1988). The transition to junior high school: Beliefs of pre- and post-transition teachers. *Journal of Youth and Adolescence, 17,* 543–562.

Midgley, C., Feldlaufer, H., & Eccles, J. (1989). Student/teacher relations and attitudes toward mathematics before and after the transition to junior high school. *Child Development, 60,* 981–992.

Midgley, C., & Urdan, T. (1995). Predictors of middle school students' use of self-handicapping strategies. *Journal of Early Adolescence, 15*(4), 389–411.

Mifflin, L. (1996, December 3). TV aims few shows at a teen-age audience. *The New York Times,* pp. C13, C18.

Mifflin, L. (1997, March 27). TV rating system may actually lure youths to violent shows, study finds. *The New York Times,* p. A22.

Mikulincer, M. (1994). *Human learned helplessness: A coping perspective.* New York: Plenum.

Miller, B. C. (1992). Adolescent parenthood, economic issues, and social policies. *Journal of Family and Economic Issues, 13*(4), 467–475.

Miller, B. C. (1993). Families, science, and values: Alternative views of parenting effects and adolescent pregnancy. *Journal of Marriage and the Family, 55,* 7–21.

Miller, B. C., Christopherson, C. R., & King, P. K. (1993). Sexual behavior in adolescence. In T. P. Gullotta, G. R. Adams, & R. Montemayor (Eds.), *Adolescent sexuality.* Newbury Park, CA: Sage.

Miller, B. C., & Dyk, P. A. H. (1993). Sexuality. In P. H. Tolan & B. J. Cohler (Eds.), *Handbook of clinical research and practice with adolescents.* New York: Wiley.

Miller, B. C., & Fox, G. L. (1987). Theories of heterosexual behavior. *Journal of Adolescent Research, 2,* 269–282.

Miller, B. C., McCoy, J., Olson, T., & Wallace, C. (1986). Parental discipline and control attempts in relation to adolescent sexual attitudes and behavior. *Journal of Marriage and the Family, 48*(3), 503–512.

Miller, C. L., Miceli, P. J., Whitman, T. L., & Borkowski, J. G. (1996). Cognitive readiness to parent and intellectual-emotional development in children of adolescent mothers. *Developmental Psychology, 32*(3), 533–541.

Miller, D. (1991). Do adolescents help and share? *Adolescence, 26*(102), 449–456.

Miller, D., Trapani, C., Fejes-Mendoza, K., Eggleston, C., et al. (1995). Adolescent female offenders: Unique considerations. *Adolescence, 30*(118), 429–435.

Miller, D. A. F., McCluskey-Fawcett, K., & Irving, L. M. (1993). Correlates of bulimia nervosa: Early family mealtime experiences. *Adolescence, 28*(111), 621–635.

Miller, J. B., & Lane, M. (1991). Relations between young adults and their parents. *Journal of Adolescence, 14,* 179–194.

Mills, C. S., & Granoff, B. J. (1992, November). Date and acquaintance rape among a sample of college students. *Social Work,* 504–509.

Mills, M. C. (1987). An intervention program for adolescents with behavior problems. *Adolescence, 22*(85), 91–96.

Millstein, S. G., & Litt, I. F. (1990). Adolescent health. In S. S. Feldman & G. R. Elliot (Eds.), *At the threshold: The developing adolescent.* Cambridge, MA: Harvard University Press.

Miner, M. H. (1991). The self-concept of homeless adolescents. *Journal of Youth and Adolescence, 20*(5), 545–560.

Minton, L. (1994, February 20). Have you ever been sexually harassed? *Parade Magazine,* p. 30.

Minton, L. (1995a, April 16). Is it cool to be friends with a "nerd"? *Parade Magazine,* p. 22.

Minton, L. (1995b, November 5). Sexism in high school: Readers say girls go along and teachers allow it. *Parade Magazine,* p. 6.

Minton, L. (1996, May 19). Sexism is not cool. *Parade Magazine,* p. 15.

Mitchell, C. E. (1988). Preparing for vocational choice. *Adolescence, 23*(90), 331–334.

Modell, J., & Goodman, M. (1990). Historical perspectives. In S. S. Feldman & G. R. Elliot (Eds.), *At the threshold: The developing adolescent.* Cambridge, MA: Harvard University Press.

Moffitt, T. E. (1993). Adolescence-limited and life-course-persistent antisocial behavior: A developmental taxonomy. *Psychological Review, 100*(4), 674–701.

Moffitt, T. E., Caspi, A., Belsky, J., & Silva, P. A. (1992). Childhood experience and the onset of menarche: A test of a sociobiological model. *Child Development, 63,* 47–58.

Molina, B. S. G., & Chassin, L. (1996). The parent–adolescent relationship at puberty: Hispanic ethnicity and parental alcoholism as moderators. *Developmental Psychology, 32*(4), 675–686.

Monaco, N. M., & Gaier, E. L. (1992). Single-sex versus coeducational environment and achievement in adolescent females. *Adolescence, 27*(107), 579–594.

Monck, E. (1991). Patterns of confiding relationships among adolescent girls. *Journal of Child Psychology and Psychiatry, 32*(2), 333–345.

Montemayor, R. (1982). The relationship between parent–adolescent conflict and the amount of time adolescents spend alone and with parents and peers. *Child Development, 53,* 1512–1519.

Montemayor, R. (1983). Parents and adolescents in conflict: All families some of the time and some families most of the time. *Journal of Early Adolescence, 3,* 83–103.

Montemayor, R. (1986). Family variation in parent–adolescent storm and stress. *Journal of Adolescent Research, 1,* 15–31.

Montemayor, R., Eberly, M., & Flannery, D. J. (1993). Effects of pubertal status and conversation topic on parent and adolescent affective expression. *Journal of Early Adolescence, 13*(4), 431–447.

Montemayor, R., & Flannery, D. J. (1990). Making the transition from childhood to early adolescence. In R. Montemayor, G. R. Adams, & T. P. Gullotta (Eds.), *From childhood to adolescence: A transitional period?* Newbury Park, CA: Sage.

Montemayor, R., & Hanson, E. (1985). A naturalistic view of conflict between adolescents and their parents and siblings. *Journal of Early Adolescence, 5,* 23–30.

Moore, D. (1987). Parent–adolescent separation: The construction of adulthood by late adolescents. *Developmental Psychology, 23*(2), 298–307.

Moore, D., & Schultz, N. R., Jr. (1983). Loneliness at adolescence: Correlates, attributions, and coping. *Journal of Youth and Adolescence, 21*(2), 95–100.

Moore, K. A., Peterson, J. L., & Furstenburg, F. F., Jr. (1986). Parental attitudes and the occurrence of early sexual activity. *Journal of Marriage and the Family, 48,* 777–782.

Moore, S., & Gullone, E. (1996). Predicting adolescent risk behavior using a personalized cost-benefit analysis. *Journal of Youth and Adolescence, 25*(3), 343–359.

Moore, S., & Rosenthal, D. (1991). Adolescent invulnerability and perceptions of AIDS risk. *Journal of Adolescent Research, 6*(2), 164–180.

Moote, G. T., Jr., & Wodarski, J. S. (1997). The acquisition of life skills through adventure-based activities and programs: A review of the literature. *Adolescence, 32*(125), 143–168.

Morano, C. D., Cisler, R. A., & Lemerond, J. (1993). Risk factors for adolescent suicidal behavior: Loss, insufficient familial support, and hopelessness. *Adolescence, 28*(112), 851–865.

Moreno, A. B., & Thelen, M. H. (1993). A preliminary prevention program for eating disorders in a junior high school population. *Journal of Youth and Adolescence, 22*(2), 109–124.

Moreno, A. B., & Thelen, M. H. (1995). Eating behavior in junior high school females. *Adolescence, 30*(117), 171–174.

Morgan, C. S. (1992). College students' perceptions of barriers to women in science and engineering. *Youth & Society, 24*(2), 228–236.

Morin, S. M., & Welsh, L. A. (1996). Adolescents' perceptions and experiences of death and grieving. *Adolescence, 31*(123), 585–595.

Morris, G. B. (1992). Adolescent leaders: Rational thinking, future beliefs, temporal perspective, and other correlates. *Adolescence, 27*(105), 173–181.

Morris, H. (Ed.). (1961). *Freedom and responsibility.* Stanford, CA: Stanford University Press.

Morrison, D. (1985). Adolescent contraceptive behavior: A review. *Psychological Bulletin, 98*(3), 538–568.

Mortimer, J. T., & Finch, M. D. (1996). Work, family, and adolescent development. In J. T. Mortimer & M. D. Finch (Eds.), *Adolescents, work, and family: An intergenerational developmental analysis.* Thousand Oaks, CA: Sage.

Mortimer, J. T., Finch, M. D., Ryu, S., Shanahan, M. J., & Call, K. T. (1996). The effects of work intensity on adolescent mental health, achievement, and behavioral adjustment: New evidence from a prospective study. *Child Development, 67,* 1243–1261.

Mortimer, J. T., Finch, M. D., Seongryeol, R., Shanahan, M. J., & Call, K. T. (1996). The effects of work intensity and adolescent mental health, achievement, and behavioral adjustment: New evidence from a prospective study. *Child Development, 67,* 1243–1261.

Moser, M. R., Paternite, C. E., & Dixon, Jr., W. E. (1996). Late adolescents' feelings toward parents and siblings. *Merrill-Palmer Quarterly, 42*(4), 537–553.

Moses, S. (1992, July). All the lonely children: How can they be helped? *APA Monitor,* p. 39.

Mosle, S. (1996, September 8). Scores count. *The New York Times Magazine,* pp. 41–45.

Mounts, N. S., & Steinberg, L. (1995). An ecological analysis of peer influence on adolescent grade point average and drug use. *Developmental Psychology, 31*(6), 915–922.

Muehlenhard, C. L. (1988). Misinterpreting dating behaviors and the risk of date rape. *Journal of Social and Clinical Psychology, 6,* 20–37.

Mueller, C., Field, T., Yando, R., Harding, J., et al. (1995). Under-eating and over-eating concerns among adolescents. *Journal of Child Psychology & Psychiatry & Allied Disciplines, 36*(6), 1019–1025.

Mullis, A. K., Mullis, R. L., & Normandin, D. (1992). Cross-sectional and longitudinal comparisons of adolescent self-esteem. *Adolescence, 27*(105), 51–62.

Mulsow, M. H., & Murry, V. M. (1996). Parenting on edge: Economically stressed, single, African American adolescent mothers. *Journal of Family Issues, 17*(5), 704–721.

Munsch, J., & Kinchen, K. M. (1995). Adolescent sociometric status and social support. *Journey of Early Adolescence, 15*(2), 181–202.

Munsch, J., & Wampler, R. S. (1993). Ethnic differences in early adolescents' coping with school stress. *American Journal of Orthopsychiatry, 63*(4), 633–646.

Munson, H. L., & Rubenstein, B. J. (1992). School IS work: Work task learning in the classroom. *Journal of Career Development, 18*(4), 289–296.

Murphey, J. (1987). Education influences. In V. B. Van Hasselt & M. Hersen (Eds.), *Handbook of adolescent psychology.* New York: Pergamon Press.

Murphy, M. C., & Archer, J., Jr. (1996). Stressors on the college campus: A comparison of 1985 and 1993. *Journal of College Student Development, 37*(1), 20–28.

Murray, B. (1995a, September). Kids learn keys to healthy relationships. *APA Monitor,* p. 48.

Murray, B. (1995b, September). Key skill for teen parents: having realistic expectations. *APA Monitor,* p. 51.

Murray, B. (1995c, September). Good mentoring keeps at-risk youth in school. *APA Monitor*, p. 49.

Murray, B. (1995d, November). Gender gap in math scores is closing. *APA Monitor*, p. 43.

Murray, B. (1996a, January). Program helps kids map realistic goals. *APA Monitor*, p. 40.

Murray, B. (1996b, April). Students stretch beyong the "three R's." *APA Monitor*, p. 46.

Murray, B. (1996c, April). College youth haunted by increased pressures. *APA Monitor*, p. 47.

Murray, B. (1996d, November). Judges, courts get tough on spanking. *APA Monitor*, p. 10.

Murray, B. (1996e, November). Self-esteem varies among ethnic-minority girls. *APA Monitor*, p. 42.

Murray, B. (1996f, November). Greek system sparks scrutiny, debate. *APA Monitor*, p. 48.

Murray, B. (1997a, March). Teaching today's pupils to think more critically. *APA Monitor*, p. 51.

Murray, B. (1997b, April). Is the internet feeding junk to students? *APA Monitor*, p. 50.

Murstein, B. I., & Mercy, T. (1994). Sex, drugs, relationships, contraception, and fears of disease: On a college campus over 17 years. *Adolescence*, 29(114), 303–322.

Murtaugh, M., & Zetlin, A. G. (1990). The development of autonomy among learning handicapped and nonhandicapped adolescents: A longitudinal perspective. *Journal of Youth and Adolescence*, 19(3), 245–255.

Muuss, R. E. (1985). Adolescent eating disorder: Anorexia nervosa. *Adolescence*, 20(79), 525–536.

Muuss, R. E. (1986). Adolescent eating disorder: Bulimia. *Adolescence*, 21(82), 257–267.

Muuss, R. E. (1988a). *Theories of adolescence* (5th ed.). New York: Random House.

Muuss, R. E. (1988b). Carol Gilligan's theory of sex differences in the development of moral reasoning during adolescence. *Adolescence*, 23(89), 229–243.

Mwamwenda, T. S. (1993). Formal operations and academic achievement. *The Journal of Psychology*, 127(1), 99–103.

Nasar, S. (1992, August 7). More college graduates taking low-wage jobs. *The New York Times*, p. D5.

Nasserbakht, A., Araujo, K., & Steiner, H. (1996). A comparison of adolescent and adult defense styles. *Child Psychiatry & Human Development*, 27(1), 3–14.

National Center for Health Statistics. (1993). Advance report of final natality statistics, 1991. *Monthly vital statistics report: Vol. 42*. Washington, DC: Public Health Service.

National Institute on Drug Abuse. (1995). Washington, DC: Government Printing Office.

Navarro, M. (1992, May 6). Left behind by AIDS: A parent dies and a teenager aches. *The New York Times*, pp. B1, B10.

Navarro, M. (1996, May 19). Teen-age mothers viewed as abused prey of older men. *The New York Times*, pp. 1, 18.

Necessary, J. R., & Parish, T. S. (1996). Relationships between college students' perceptions of their family members and how they interact with one another. *Adolescence*, 31(123), 747–750.

Neiger, B. L., & Hopkins, R. W. (1988). Adolescent suicide: Character traits of high-risk teenagers. *Adolescence*, 23(90), 469–475.

Neighbors, B., Forehand, R., & Armistead, L. (1992). Is parental divorce a critical stressor for young adolescents? Grade point average as a case in point. *Adolescence*, 27(107), 639–646.

Neighbors, B., Forehand, R., & McVicar, D. (1993). Resilient adolescents and interparental conflict. *American Journal of Orthopsychiatry*, 63(3), 462–471.

Neisser, U. (1976). General, academic, and artificial intelligence. In L. Resnick (Ed.), *Human intelligence: Perspectives on its theory and measurement*. Norwood, NJ: Ablex.

Neisser, U., Boodoo, G., Bouchard, T. J., Jr., Boykin, A. W., Brody, N., Ceci, S. J., Halpern, D. F., Loehlin, J. C., Perloff, R., Sternberg, R. J., & Urbina, S. (1996). Intelligence: Knowns and unknowns. *American Psychologist*, 51(2), 77–101.

Neisser, U., & Fivush, R. (Eds.). (1994). *The remembering self: Construction and accuracy in self-narrative*. New York: Cambridge University Press.

Nelson, W. L., Hughes, H. M., Handal, P., Katz, B., & Searight, H. R. (1993). The relationship of family structure and family conflict to adjustment in young adult college students. *Adolescence*, 28(109), 29–40.

Netting, N. S. (1992). Sexuality in youth culture: Identity and change. *Adolescence*, 27(108), 961–976.

Neubauer, G., & Melzer, W. (1989). Sexual development of the adolescent. In K. Hurrelmann & U. Engel (Eds.), *The social world of adolescents: International perspectives*. Berlin: de Gruyter.

Neugarten, B. L. (1969). Continuities and discontinuities of psychological issues into adult life. *Human Development*, 12, 121–130.

Neugarten, B. L. (1979). Time, age and life cycle. *American Journal of Psychiatry*, 136, 887–894.

Newcomb, M. D. (1996). Adolescence: Pathologizing a normal process. *The Counseling Psychologist*, 24(3), 482–490.

Newcomb, M. D., & Bentler, P. M. (1989). Substance use and abuse among children and teenagers. *American Psychologist*, 44(2), 242–248.

Newcombe, N. S., & Baenninger, M. (1989). Biological change and cognitive ability in adolescence. In G. R. Adams, R. Montemayor, & T. P. Gullotta (Eds.), *Biology of adolescent behavior and development*. Newbury Park, CA: Sage.

Newcombe, N., & Dubas, J. S. (1987). Individual differences in cognitive ability: Are they related to the timing of puberty? In R. M. Lerner & T. T. Foch (Eds.), *Biological–psychosocial in-*

teractions in early adolescence. Hillsdale, NJ: Erlbaum.

Newcomer, S. F., & Udry, J. R. (1985). Oral sex in an adolescent population. *Archives of Sexual Behavior, 14,* 41–56.

Newman, B. M. (1989). The changing nature of the parent–adolescent relationship from early to late adolescence. *Adolescence, 24*(96), 915–924.

Newman, B. S., & Muzzonigro, P. G. (1993). The effects of traditional family values on the coming out process of gay male adolescents. *Adolescence, 28*(109), 213–226.

Newman, J. (1985). Adolescents: Why they can be so obnoxious. *Adolescence, 20*(79), 635–646.

Newman, J. (1991). College students' relationships with siblings. *Journal of Youth and Adolescence, 20*(6), 629–644.

Newman, P. R., & Newman, B. M. (1997). *Childhood and adolescence.* Pacific Grove, CA: Brooks/Cole.

Newstead, S. E., Franklyn-Stokes, A., & Armstead, P. (1996). Individual differences in student cheating. *Journal of Educational Psychology, 88*(2), 229–241.

Nicholls, J. G. (1984). Achievement motivation: Conceptions of ability, subjective experience, task choice, and performance. *Psychological Bulletin, 91,* 328–346.

Nickerson, R. S. (1987). Why teach thinking? In J. B. Baron & R. J. Sternberg, (Eds.), *Teaching thinking skills: Theory and practice.* New York: W. H. Freeman.

Nielsen Media Research. (1993). 1992–1993 report on television. New York: Author.

Nielson, D. M., & Metha, A. (1994). Parental behavior and adolescent self-esteem in clinical and nonclinical samples. *Adolescence, 29*(115), 525–542.

Noam, G. (1996). High-risk youth: Transforming our understanding of human development. *Human Development, 39*(1), 1–17.

Noller, P. (1994). Relationships with parents in adolescence: Process and outcome. In R. Montemayor, G. R. Adams, & T. P. Gullotta (Eds.), *Personal relationships during adolescence.* Thousand Oaks, CA: Sage.

Noller, P., & Bagi, S. (1985). Parent–adolescent communication. *Journal of Adolescence, 8,* 125–144.

Noller, P., & Callan, V. J. (1986). Adolescent and parent perceptions of family cohesion and adaptability. *Journal of Adolescence, 9,* 97–106.

Noller, P., & Callan, V. J. (1988). Understanding parent–adolescent interactions: Perceptions of family members and outsiders. *Developmental Psychology, 24*(5), 707–714.

Noller, P., & Callan, V. J. (1990). Adolescents' perceptions of the nature of their communication with parents. *Journal of Youth and Adolescence, 19,* 349–362.

Nordheimer, J. (1996, June 23). Blue-collar training gets the black-tie touch. *The New York Times,* Business Section, pp. 1, 11.

Norton, E. M., Durlak, J. A., & Richards, M. H. (1989). Peer knowledge of and reactions to adolescent suicide. *Journal of Youth and Adolescence, 18*(5), 427–437.

Nottelmann, E. D. (1987). Competence and self-esteem during transition from childhood to adolescence. *Developmental Psychology, 23,* 441–450.

Nottelmann, E. D., Inoff-Germain, G., Susman, E. J., & Chrousos, G. P. (1990). Hormones and behavior at puberty. In J. Bancroft & J. M. Reinisch (Eds.), *Adolescence and puberty.* New York: Oxford University Press.

Nottelmann, E. D., Susman, E. J., Blue, J. H., Inoff-Germain, G., Dorn, L. D., Loriaux, D. L., Cutler, G. B., & Chrousos, G. P. (1987). Gonadal and adrenal hormonal correlates of adjustment in early adolescence. In R. M. Lerner & T. T. Foch (Eds.), *Biological–psychological interactions in early adolescence: A life-span perspective.* Hillsdale, NJ: Erlbaum.

Nottelmann, E. D., & Welsh, C. J. (1986). The long and the short of physical stature in early adolescence. *Journal of Early Adolescence, 6,* 15–27.

Novacek, J., Raskin, R., & Hogan, R. (1991). Why do adolescents use drugs? Age, sex, and user differences. *Journal of Youth and Adolescence, 20*(5), 475–492.

Nucci, L., Guerra, N., & Lee, J. (1991). Adolescent judgments of the personal, prudential, and normative aspects of drug usage. *Developmental Psychology, 27*(5), 841–848.

Nunn, G. D., & Parish, T. S. (1992). The psychosocial characteristics of at-risk high school students. *Adolescence, 27*(106), 435–440.

Nurius, P. S., Norris, J., Dimeff, L. A., & Graham, T. L. (1996). Expectations regarding acquaintance sexual aggression among sorority and fraternity members. *Sex Roles, 37*(7/8), 427–444.

Nurmi, J. E., Poole, M. E., & Kalakoski, V. (1996). Age differences in adolescent identity exploration and commitment in urban and rural environments. *Journal of Adolescence, 19,* 443–452.

Nurmi, J. E., Poole, M. E., & Virpi, K. (1996). Age differences in adolescent identity exploration and commitment in urban and rural environments. *Journal of Adolescence, 19,* 443–452.

Nwadiora, E., & McAdoo, H. (1996). Acculturative stress among Amerasian refugees: Gender and racial differences. *Adolescence, 31*(122), 477–487.

Nydegger, C. (1974). Timing of fatherhood role perception and socialization. *Dissertation Abstracts International, 34,* 9629.

Oakes, J. (1985). *Keeping track: How schools structure inequality.* New Haven, CT: Yale University Press.

Oakes, J. (1987). Curriculum inequality and school reform. *Equity and excellence, 23,* 8–14.

O'Brien, J. M., Goodenow, C., & Espin, O. (1991). Adolescents' reactions to the death of a peer. *Adolescence, 26*(102), 431–440.

O'Connell, L. (1996). Not at home alone. . . and lots of parents know it. In F. C. Leeming, W. Dwyer, & D. P. Oliver (Eds.), *Issues in adolescent sexu-*

*ality: Readings from The Washington Post Writers Group*. Needham Heights, MA: Allyn & Bacon.

O'Connor, B. P., & Nikolic, J. (1990). Identity development and formal operations as sources of adolescent egocentrism. *Journal of Youth and Adolescence, 19*(2), 149–158.

O'Connor, T. G., & Rutter, M. (1996). Risk mechanisms in development: Some conceptual and methodological considerations. *Developmental Psychology, 32*(4), 787–795.

Odgers, P., Houghton, S., & Douglas, G. (1996). Reputation enhancement theory and adolescent substance abuse. *Journal of Child Psychology & Psychiatry & Allied Disciplines, 37*(8), 1015–1022.

O'Donnell, J., Hawkins, J. D., Catalano, R. F., Abbott, R. D., et al. (1995). Preventing school failure, drug use, and delinquency among low-income children: Long-term intervention in elementary schools. *American Journal of Orthopsychiatry, 65*(1), 87–100.

Offer, D. (1984). *The adolescent: A psychological self-portrait*. New York: Basic Books.

Offer, D. (1985, Summer). A portrait of normal adolescence. *American Educator*, pp. 34–37.

Offer, D., Ostrov, E., & Howard, K. K. (1989). Adolescence: What is normal? *American Journal of Diseases of Children, 143*, 731–736.

Offer, D., & Schonert-Reichl, K. A. (1992). Debunking the myths of adolescence: Findings from recent research. *Journal of the American Academy of Child and Adolescent Psychiatry, 31*, 1003–1014.

Ogbu, J. U. (1982). Cultural discontinuities and schooling. *Anthropology and Education Quarterly, 13*, 280–307.

Ohannessian, C. M., Lerner, R. M., Lerner, J. V., & von Eye, A. (1994). A longitudinal study of perceived family adjustment and emotional adjustment in early adolescence. *Journal of Early Adolescence, 14*(3), 371–390.

Ohannessian, C. M., Lerner, R. M., Lerner, J. V., & von Eye, A. (1995). Discrepancies in adolescents' and par-

ents' perceptions of family functioning and adolecent emotional adjustment. *Journal of Early Adolescence, 15*(4), 490–516.

O'Koon, J. (1997). Attachment to parents and peers in late adolescence and their relationship with self-image. *Adolescence, 32*(126), 471–482.

Oláh, A. (1995). Coping strategies among adolescents: A cross-cultural study. *Journal of Adolescence, 18*, 491–512.

Olderburg, C. M., & Kerns, K. A. (1997). Associations between peer relationships and depressive symptoms: Testing moderator effects of gender and age. *Journal of Early Adolescence, 17*(3), 319–337.

Oliver, M. B., & Hyde, J. S. (1993). Gender differences in sexuality: A meta-analysis. *Psychological Bulletin, 114*(1), 29–51.

Olsen, J. A., Jensen, L. C., & Greaves, P. M. (1991). Adolescent sexuality and public policy. *Adolescence, 26*(102), 419–430.

Olsen, J. A., Weed, S., Nielsen, A., & Jensen, L. (1992). Student evaluation of sex education programs advocating abstinence. *Adolescence, 27*(106), 369–380.

Olsen, J. A., Weed, S. E., Ritz, G. M., & Jensen, L. C. (1991). The effects of three abstinence sex education programs on student attitudes toward sexual activity. *Adolescence, 26*(103), 631–641.

Olweus, D., Mattsson, A., Schalling, D., & Low, H. (1980). Testosterone, aggression, physical, and personality dimensions in normal adolescent males. *Psychosomatic Medicine, 42*, 253–269.

Olweus, D., Mattsson, A., Schalling, D., & Low, H. (1988). Circulating testosterone levels and aggression in adolescent males: A causal analysis. *Psychosomatic Medicine, 50*, 261–272.

O'Malley, P., & Bachman, J. (1983). Self-esteem: Change and stability between ages 13 and 23. *Developmental Psychology, 19*, 257–268.

Orenstein, P. (1994). *School girls: Young women, self-esteem, and the confidence gap*. New York: Doubleday.

Orwoll, L., & Achenbaum, W. A. (1993). Gender and the development of wisdom. *Human Development, 36*(5), 274–296.

Osborne, L. N., & Fincham, F. D. (1996). Marital conflict, parent–child relationships, and child adjustment: Does gender matter? *Merrill-Palmer Quarterly, 42*(1), 48–75.

Overmier, K. (1990). Biracial adolescents: Areas of conflict in identity formation. *The Journal of Applied Social Sciences, 14*(2), 157–176.

Overton, W. F., Steidl, J. H., Rosenstein, D., & Horowitz, H. A. (1992). Formal operations as regulatory context in adolescence. In S. C. Feinstein (Ed.), *Adolescent psychiatry: Developmental and clinical studies* (Vol. 18). Chicago: University of Chicago Press.

Owens, T. J. (1992). Where do we go from here? Post–high school choices of American men. *Youth & Society, 23*(4), 452–477.

Oyserman, D., Gant, L., & Ager, J. (1995). A socially contextualized model of African American identity: Possible selves and school persistence. *Journal of Personality and Social Psychology, 69*(6), 1216–1232.

Oyserman, D., Radin, N., & Benn, R. (1993). Dynamics in a three-generational family: Teens, grandparents, and babies. *Developmental Psychology, 29*(3), 564–572.

Oz, S., Tari, A., & Fine, M. (1992). A comparison of the psychological profiles of teenage mothers and their nonmother peers: I. Ego development. *Adolescence, 27*(105), 193–202.

Page, R. M., & Cole, G. E. (1991). Loneliness and alcoholism risk in late adolescence: A comparative study of adults and adolescents. *Adolescence, 26*(104), 925–930.

Paige, K. E. (1983). A bargaining theory of menarcheal responses in preindustrial cultures. In J. Brooks-Gunn & A. C. Petersen (Eds.), *Girls at puberty: Biological and psychosocial perspectives*. New York: Plenum Press.

Paikoff, R. L. (1995). Early heterosexual debut: Situations of sexual possibility during the transition to adolescence. *American Journal of Orthopsychiatry, 65*(3), 389–401.

Paikoff, R. L., & Brooks-Gunn, J. (1990). Physiological processes: What role do they play during the transition to adolescence? In R. Montemayor, G. R. Adams, & T. P. Gullotta (Eds.), *From childhood to adolescence: A transitional period?* Newbury Park, CA: Sage.

Paikoff, R. L., & Brooks-Gunn, J. (1991). Do parent–child relationships change during puberty? *Psychological Bulletin, 110*(1), 47–66.

Paikoff, R. L., Brooks-Gunn, J., & Carlton-Ford, S. (1991). Effect of reproductive status changes on family functioning and well-being of mothers and daughters. *Journal of Early Adolescence, 11*(2), 201–220.

Paikoff, R. L., Brooks-Gunn, J., & Warren, M. P. (1991). Effects of girls' hormonal status on depressive and aggressive symptoms over the course of one year. *Journal of Youth and Adolescence, 20*(2), 191–215.

Pakiz, B., Reinherz, H. Z., & Frost, A. K. (1992). Antisocial behavior in adolescence: A community study. *Journal of Early Adolescence, 12*(3), 300–313.

Palladino, G. (1996). *Teenagers: An American history.* New York: Basic Books.

Palmer, R. B., & Liddle, H. A. (1996). Adolescent drug abuse: Contemporary perspectives on etiology and treatment. In G. M. Blau & T. P. Gullotta (Eds.), *Adolescent dysfunctional behavior: Causes, interventions, and prevention.* Thousand Oaks, CA: Sage.

Palmer, S., & Cochran, L. (1988). Parents as agents of career development. *Journal of Counseling Psychology, 35,* 71–76.

Papalia, D. E., & Olds, S. W. (1996). *A child's world: Infancy through adolescence* (6th ed.). New York: McGraw-Hill.

Papini, D. R., Clark, S., Barnett, J. K., & Savage, C. L. (1989). Grade, pubertal status, and gender-related variations in conflictual issues among adolescents. *Adolescence,* **24**(96), 977–987.

Papini, D. R., Farmer, F. F., Clark, S. M., Micka, J. C., & Barnett, J. K.

(1990). Early adolescent age and gender differences in patterns of emotional self-disclosure to parents and friends. *Adolescence, 25*(100), 959–976.

Papini, D. R., Roggman, L. A., & Anderson, J. (1991). Early-adolescent perceptions of attachment to mother and father: A test of the emotional-distancing and buffering hypotheses. *Journal of Early Adolescence, 11*(2), 258–275.

Pardeck, J. A., & Pardeck, J. T. (1990). Family factors related to adolescent autonomy. *Adolescence, 25*(98), 311–319.

Parish, T. S. (1993). Perceived parental actions and evaluations of the family and its members. *Adolescence, 28*(111), 749–752.

Parish, T. S., & McCluskey, J. J. (1992). The relationship between parenting styles and young adults' self-concepts and evaluations of parents. *Adolescence, 27*(108), 915–918.

Parish, T. S., & Necessary, J. R. (1994). Parents' actions: Are they related to children's self-concepts, evaluations of parents, and to each other? *Adolescence, 29*(116), 943–948.

Parish, T. S., & Parish, J. G. (1991). The effects of family configuration and support system failures during childhood and adolescence on college students' self-concepts and social skills. *Adolescence, 26*(102), 441–447.

Parke, R. D., & Ladd, G. W. (Eds.). (1992). *Family–peer relationships: Modes of linkage.* Hillsdale, NJ: Erlbaum.

Parker, J. G., & Asher, S. R. (1987). Peer relations and later personal adjustment: Are low-accepted children "at risk?" *Psychological Bulletin, 102,* 357–389.

Parker, J. G., & Gottman, J. M. (1989). Social and emotional development in a relational context: Friendship interaction from early childhood to adolescence. In T. J. Berndt & G. W. Ladd (Eds.), *Peer relationships in child development.* New York: Wiley.

Parkhurst, J. T., & Asher, S. R. (1992). Peer rejection in middle school: Subgroup differences in behavior, loneliness, and interpersonal concerns. *Developmental Psychology, 28,* 231–241.

Parmer, T. (1993). The athletic dream—But what are the career dreams of other African American urban high school students? *Journal of Career Development, 20*(2), 131–146.

Paschall, M. J., Ennett, S. T., & Flewelling, R. L. (1996). Relationships among family characteristics and violent behavior by Black and white male adolescents. *Journal of Youth and Adolescence, 25*(2), 177–198.

Passino, A. W., Whitman, T. L., Borkowski, J. G., Schellenbach, C. J., Maxwell, S. E., Keogh, D., & Rellinger, E. (1993). Personal adjustment during pregnancy and adolescent parenting. *Adolescence, 28*(109), 97–122.

Patel, N., Power, T. G., & Bhavnagri, N. P. (1996). Socialization values and practices of Indian immigrant parents: Correlates of modernity and acculturation. *Child Development, 67*(2), 302–313.

Patrick, H., Hicks, L., & Ryan, A. M. (1997). Relations of perceived social efficacy and social goal pursuit to self-efficacy for academic work. *Journal of Early Adolescence, 17*(2), 109–128.

Patterson, G. R. (1982). *Coercive family processes.* Eugene, OR: Castalia Press.

Patterson, G. R. (1986). Performance models for antisocial boys. *American Psychologist, 41,* 432–444.

Patterson, G. R., DeBaryshe, B. D., & Ramsey, E. (1989). A developmental perspective on antisocial behavior. *American Psychologist, 44,* 329–335.

Patterson, G. R., & Dishion, T. J. (1985). Contributions of families and peers to delinquency. *Criminology, 23,* 63–79.

Patterson, J. M., & McCubbin, H. I. (1987). Adolescent coping style and behaviors: Conceptualization and treatment. *Journal of Adolescence, 10,* 163–186.

Patterson, L. J. M. (1997). Long-term unemployment amongst adolescents: A longitudinal study. *Journal of Adolescence, 20,* 261–280.

Patterson, S. J., Sochting, I., & Marcia, J. E. (1992). The inner space and beyond: Women and identity. In G. R. Adams, T. P. Gullotta, & R. Montemayor (Eds.), *Adolescent identity formation*. Newbury Park, CA: Sage.

Paulson, S. E. (1994). Relations of parenting style and parental involvement with ninth-grade students' achievement. *Journal of Early Adolescence, 14*(2), 250–267.

Paulson, S. E., Hill, J. P., & Holmbeck, G. N. (1991). Distinguishing between perceived closeness and parental warmth in families with seventh-grade boys and girls. *Journal of Early Adolescence, 11*(2), 276–293.

Paulson, S. E., & Sputa, C. L. (1996). Patterns of parenting during adolescence: Perceptions of adolescents and parents. *Adolescence, 31*(122), 369–381.

Pawliuk, N., Grizenko, N., Chan-Yip, A., Gantous, P., et al. (1996). Acculturation style and psychological functioning in children of immigrants. *American Journal of Orthopsychiatry, 66*(1), 111–121.

Paxton, S. J., Wertheim, E. H., Gibbons, K., Szmukler, G. K., Hillier, L., & Petrovich, J. (1991). Body image satisfaction, dieting beliefs, and weight loss behaviors in adolescent girls and boys. *Journal of Youth and Adolescence, 20*(3), 361–379.

Pearce, K., & Jones, J. P. (1992, December). Debate: Is vocational education tracking in disguise? *NEA Today*, p. 35.

Peck, D. L., & Warner, K. (1995). Accident or suicide? Single-vehicle car accidents and the intent hypothesis. *Adolescence, 30*(118), 463–472.

Peiser, N. C., & Heaven, P. C. L. (1996). Family influences on self-reported delinquency among high school students. *Journal of Adolescence, 19*, 557–568.

Pendley, J. S., & Bates, J. E. (1996). Mother/daughter agreement on the eating attitudes test and the eating disorder inventory. *Journal of Early Adolescence, 16*(2), 179–191.

Perkins, D. F., & Lerner, R. M. (1995). Single and multiple indicators of physical attractiveness and psychosocial behaviors among young adolescents. *Journal of Early Adolescence, 15*(3), 269–298.

Perlmutter, R., & Shapiro, E. R. (1987). Morals and values in adolescence. In V. B. Van Hasselt & M. Hersen (Eds.), *Handbook of adolescent psychology*. New York: Pergamon Press.

Perosa, L. M., Perosa, S. L., & Tam, H. P. (1996). The contribution of family structure and differentiation to identity development in females. *Journal of Youth and Adolescence, 25*(6), 817–837.

Perry, C. M., & McIntire, W. G. (1995). Modes of moral judgment among early adolescents. *Adolescence, 30*(119), 707–715.

Perry, T. B. (1987). *The relation of adolescents' self-perceptions to their social relationships*. Unpublished doctoral dissertation, University of Oklahoma, Norman, OK.

Perry, W. G. (1970). *Forms of intellectual and ethical development in the college years*. New York: Holt, Rinehart & Winston.

Peskin, H. (1972). Pubertal onset and ego functioning. In J. Kestenberg (Ed.), *The adolescent: Physical development, sexuality and pregnancy*. New York: MSS Information Co.

Peskin, H. (1973). Influence of the developmental schedule of puberty on learning and ego functioning. *Journal of Youth and Adolescence, 2*, 273–290.

Pestrak, V. A., & Martin, D. (1985). Cognitive development and aspects of adolescent sexuality. *Adolescence, 20*(80), 981–987.

Pete, J. M., & DeSantis, L. (1990). Sexual decision making in young black adolescent females. *Adolescence, 25*(97), 145–154.

Peters, J. F. (1994). Gender socialization of adolescents in the home: Research and discussion. *Adolescence, 29*(116), 913–934.

Petersen, A. C. (1983). Menarche: Meaning of measure and measuring meaning. In A. Golub (Ed.), *Menarche*. New York: Heath.

Petersen, A. C. (1988). Adolescent development. In L. W. Porter and M. Rosenzweig (Eds.), *Annual Review of Psychology, 39*, 583–607.

Petersen, A. C., Compas, B. E., Brooks-Gunn, J., Stemmler, S. E., & Grant, K. E. (1993). Depression in adolescence. *American Psychologist, 48*(2), 155–168.

Petersen, A. C., & Crockett, L. (1985). Pubertal timing and grade effects on adjustment. *Journal of Youth and Adolescence, 14*, 191–206.

Petersen, A. C., Crockett, L., Richards, M., & Boxer, A. (1988). A self-report measure of pubertal status: Reliability, validity, and initial norms. *Journal of Youth and Adolescence, 17*, 117–133.

Petersen, A. C., & Hamburg, B. A. (1986). Adolescence: A developmental approach to problems and psychopathology. *Behavior Therapy, 17*(5), 480–499.

Petersen, A. C., Sarigiani, P. A., & Kennedy, R. E. (1991). Adolescent depression: Why more girls? *Journal of Youth and Adolescence, 20*(2), 247–271.

Petersen, A., Silbereisen, R. K., & Sörenson, S. (1996). Adolescent development: A global perspective. In K. Hurrelmann & S. F. Hamilton (Eds.), *Social problems and social contexts in adolescence: Perspectives across boundaries*. New York: Aldine De Gruyter.

Petersen, A. C., Tobin-Richards, M., & Boxer, A. (1983). Puberty: Its measurement and its meaning. *Journal of Early Adolescence, 3*, 47–62.

Petersen, M. (1997, July 27). Teaching abstinence: The price of federal money for sex education. *The New York Times New Jersey Section*, p. 7.

Peterson, C. (1982). The imaginary audience and age, cognition, and dating. *Journal of Genetic Psychology, 140*, 317–318.

Peterson, G. I., Kiesler, S. B., & Goldberg, P. A. (1971). Evaluation of the performance of women as a function of their sex, achievement, and personal history. *Journal of Personality and Social Psychology, 19*, 114–118.

Peterson, K. L., & Roscoe, B. (1991). Imaginary audience behavior in older adolescent females. *Adolescence, 26*, 195–200.

Peterson, L., & Gelfand, D. M. (1984). Causal attributions of helping as a function of age and incentives. *Child Development, 55,* 504–511.

Petraitis, J., Flay, B. R., & Miller, T. Q. (1995). Reviewing theories of adolescent substance use: Organizing pieces in the puzzle. *Psychological Bulletin, 117*(1), 67–86.

Petri, E. (1934). Untersuchungen zur Erbedingtheir der Menarche. *Z. Morph. Anthr. 33,* 43–48.

Petti, T. A., & Larson, C. N. (1987). Depression and suicide. In V. B. Van Hasselt & M. Hersen (Eds.), *Handbook of adolescent psychology.* New York: Pergamon Press.

Phares, V., & Compas, B. E. (1992). The role of fathers in child and adolescent psychopathology: Make room for daddy. *Psychological Bulletin, 111*(3), 387–412.

Phares, V., & Danforth, J. S. (1994). Adolescents' parents', and teachers' distress over adolescents' behavior. *Journal of Abnormal Child Psychology, 22*(6), 721–732.

Philip, K., & Hendry, L. B. (1996). Young people and mentoring—towards a typology? *Journal of Adolescence, 19,* 189–201.

Phinney, J. S. (1989). Stages of ethnic identity development in minority group adolescents. *Journal of Early Adolescence, 9,* 34–49.

Phinney, J. S. (1990). Ethnic identity in adolescents and adults: Review of research. *Psychological Bulletin, 108*(3), 499–514.

Phinney, J. S., & Alipuria, L. L. (1990). Ethnic identity in college students from four ethnic groups. *Journal of Adolescence, 13,* 171–183.

Phinney, J. S., Cantu, C. L., & Kurtz, D. A. (1997). Ethnic and American identity as predictors of self-esteem among African American, Latino, and white adolescents. *Journal of Youth and Adolescence, 26*(2), 165–186.

Phinney, J. S., & Chavira, V. (1992). Ethnic identity and self-esteem: An exporatory longitudinal study. *Journal of Adolescence, 15,* 271–281.

Phinney, J. S., & Goossens, L. (1996). Introduction: Identity development

in context. *Journal of Adolescence, 19,* 401–403.

Phinney, J. S., & Rosenthal, D. A. (1992). Ethnic identity in adolescence: Process, context, and outcome. In G. R. Adams, T. P. Gullotta, & R. Montemayor (Eds.), *Adolescent identity formation.* Newbury Park, CA: Sage.

Phinney, V. G., Jensen, L. C., Olsen, J. A., & Cundick, B. (1990). The relationship between early development and psychosexual behaviors in adolescent females. *Adolescence, 25*(98), 321–332.

Piaget, J. (1926). *The language and thought of the child.* New York: Harcourt, Brace, & World. (Originally published in 1923).

Piaget, J. (1932/1965). *The moral judgment of the child* (M. Gabain, trans.). New York: Free Press.

Piaget, J. (1950). *The psychology of intelligence.* New York: International Universities Press.

Piaget, J. (1952). *The origins of intelligence in children.* New York: International Universities Press.

Piaget, J. (1951/1965). *Play, dreams and imitation.* New York: W. W. Norton.

Piaget, J. (1972). Intellectual evolution from adolescence to adulthood. *Human Relations, 15,* 1–12.

Pick, S., & Palos, P. A. (1995). Impact of the family on the sex lives of adolescents. *Adolescence, 30*(119), 667–675.

Pike, A., McGuire, S., Hetherington, E. M., Reiss, D., & Plomin, R. (1996). Family environment and adolescent depressive symptoms and antisocial behavior: A multivariate genetic analysis. *Developmental Psychology, 32*(4), 590–603.

Pimentel, E. F. (1996). Effects of adolescent achievement and family goals on the early adult transition. In J. T. Mortimer & M. D. Finch (Eds.), *Adolescents, work, and family: An intergenerational developmental analysis.* Thousand Oaks, CA: Sage.

Pintrich, P. R., & De Groot, E. V. (1990). Motivational and self-regulated learning components of class-

room academic performance. *Journal of Educational Psychology, 82*(1), 33–40.

Pintrich, P. R., Roeser, R. W., & De Groot, A. M. (1994). Classroom and individual differences in early adolescents' motivation and self-regulated learning. *Journal of Early Adolescence, 14*(2), 139–161.

Pipes, R. B., & LeBov-Keeler, K. (1997). Psychological abuse among college women in exclusive heterosexual dating relationships. *Sex Roles, 36*(9/10), 585–604.

Plancherel, B., & Bolognini, M. (1995). Coping and mental health in early adolescence. *Journal of Adolescence, 18,* 459–474.

Pleck, J. H., Sonenstein, F. L., & Ku, L. C. (1990). Contraceptive attitudes and intention to use condoms in sexually experienced and inexperienced adolescent males. *Journal of Family Issues, 11*(3), 294–312.

Pledger, L. M. (1992). Development of self-monitoring behavior from early to late adolescence. *Adolescence, 27*(106), 329–339.

Plomin, R. (1994). *Genetics and experience: The interplay between nature and nurture.* Thousand Oaks, CA: Sage.

Plopper, B. L., & Ness, M. E. (1993). Death as portrayed to adolescents through top 40 rock and roll music. *Adolescence, 28*(112), 793–807.

Pogrebin, R. (1996a, May 9). Hard-core threat to health: Moshing at rock concerts. *The New York Times,* pp. B1, B9.

Pogrebin, R. (1996b, November 4). Magazines learning to take not-so-clueless (and monied) teenagers more seriously. *The New York Times,* p. D8.

Pollack, L. A. (1983). *Forgotten children.* Cambridge: Cambridge University Press.

Pombeni, M. L., Kirchler, E., & Palmonari, A. (1990). Identification with peers as a strategy to muddle through the troubles of the adolescent years. *Journal of Adolescence, 13,* 351–369.

Poole, M. E., Cooney, G. H., & Cheong, A. C. S. (1986). Adolescent perceptions of family cohesiveness, autonomy, and independence in Australia and

Singapore. *Journal of Comparative Family Studies, 17*, 311–332.

Poole, M. E., & Gelder, A. J. (1985). Family cohesiveness and adolescent autonomy in decision making. *Australian Journal of Sex, Marriage and Family, 5*, 65–75.

Poppen, P. J. (1994). Adolescent contraceptive use and communication: Changes over a decade. *Adolescence, 29*(115), 503–514.

Poston, W. S. C. (1990). The biracial identity development model: A needed addition. *Journal of Counseling and Development, 69*, 152–155.

Powers, S. I., Hauser, S. T., & Kilner, L. A. (1989). Adolescent mental health. *American Psychologist, 44*, 200–208.

Pratt, W. F., & Eglash, S. (1990). *Premarital sexual behavior, multiple partners, and marital experience.* Paper presented at the annual meeting of the Population Association of America, Toronto.

Preston, J. (1996, September 3). After youth boot camp comes a harder discipline. *The New York Times*, pp. B1, B5.

Prince, F. (1995). The relative effectiveness of a peer-led and adult-led smoking intervention program. *Adolescence, 30*(117), 187–194.

Pritchard, M. E., Myers, B. K., & Cassidy, D. J. (1989). Factors associated with adolescent saving and spending patterns. *Adolescence, 24*(95), 711–723.

Prouse, J., & Dooley, D. (1997). Effect of underemployment on school-leavers' self-esteem. *Journal of Adolescence, 20*, 243–260.

Pungello, E. P., Kupersmidt, J. B., Burchinal, M. R., & Patterson, C. J. (1996). Environmental risk factors and children's achievement from middle childhood to early adolescence. *Developmental Psychology, 32*(4), 755–767.

Purkey, S. C., & Smith, M. S. (1983). Effective schools: A review. *The Elementary School Journal, 83*(4), 427–452.

Quadrel, M. J., Fischoff, B., & Davis, W. (1993). Adolescent (in)vulnerability. *American Psychologist, 48*(2), 102–116.

Queen, K. W. (1994). Meeting affective needs of at-risk adolescents. *Psychological Reports, 74*, 753–754.

Quigley, E. V. (1987, October 30). ABC, CBS, and NBC refuse to air "pill" commercials. *The Los Angeles Times.*

Rabow, J., Radcliffe-Vasile, S., Newcomb, M. D., & Hernandez, A. C. R. (1992). Teachers', students', and others' contributions to educational outcomes. *Youth & Society, 24*(1), 71–91.

Raeff, C. (1994). Viewing adolescent mothers on their own terms: Linking self-conceptualization and adolescent motherhood. *Developmental Review, 14*(3), 215–244.

Ralph, N., & McMenamy, C. (1996). Treatment outcomes in an adolescent chemical dependency program. *Adolescence, 31*(121), 91–107.

Ramasamy, R. (1996). Post-high school employment: A follow-up of Apache Native American youth. *Journal of Learning Disabilities, 29*(2), 174–179.

Rathus, S. A., & Nevid, J. S. (1991). *Abnormal psychology.* Englewood Cliffs, NJ: Prentice-Hall.

Rauch-Elnekave, H. (1994). Teenage motherhood: Its relationship to undetected learning problems. *Adolescence, 29*(113), 91–103.

Rauste–von Wright, M. (1989). Body image satisfaction in adolescent girls and boys: A longitudinal study. *Journal of Youth and Adolescence, 18*(1), 71–83.

Ravert, A. A., & Martin, J. (1997). Family stress, perception of pregnancy, and age of first menarche among pregnant adolescents. *Adolescence, 32*(126), 261–270.

Ravitch, D. (1996, August 28). Defining literacy downward. *The New York Times*, p. A19.

Raviv, A., Bar-Tal, D., Raviv, A., & Ben-Horin, A. (1996). Adolescent idolization of pop singers: Causes, expressions, and reliance. *Journal of Youth and Adolescence, 25*(5), 631–650.

Ravo, N. (1996, October 14). 25-year low in a measure of well-being. *The New York Times.*

Readdick, C. A., & Mullis, R. L. (1997). Adolescents and adults at the mall. *Adolescence, 32*(126), 313–322.

Rees, J. M., & Trahms, C. M. (1989). Nutritional influences on physical growth and behavior in adolescence. In G. R. Adams, R. Montemayor, & T. P. Gullotta (Eds.), *Biology of adolescent behavior and development.* Newbury Park, CA: Sage.

Reese, F. L., & Roosa, M. W. (1991). Early adolescents' self-reports of major life stresses and mental health risk status. *Journal of Early Adolescence, 11*(3), 363–378.

Regan, P. C. (1996). Sexual acts: Doing what comes (un)naturally. Review of L. Tiefer (1995). Sex is not a natural act and other essays. Boulder, CO: Westview Press. In *Contemporary Psychology, 41*(4), pp. 367–368.

Rehman, S. N., & Reilly, S. S. (1985). Music videos: A new dimension of televised violence. *The Pennsylvania Speech Communication Annual, 41*, 61–64.

Reimer, M. S. (1996). "Sinking into the ground": The development and consequences of shame in adolescence. *Developmental Review, 16*(4), 321–363.

Reis, J., & Herz, E. (1989). An examination of young adolescents' knowledge of and attitude toward sexuality according to perceived contraceptive responsibility. *Journal of Applied Social Psychology, 19*(3), 231–250.

Reischl, T. M., & Hirsch, B. J. (1989). Identity commitments and coping with a difficult developmental transition. *Journal of Youth and Adolescence, 18*(1), 55–69.

Reisman, J. M. (1985). Friendship and its implications for mental health or social competence. *Journal of Early Adolescence, 5*, 383–391.

Reisman, J. M., & Shorr, S. I. (1978). Friendship claims and expectations among children and adults. *Child Development, 49*, 913–916.

Reitman, D., Gross, A. M., & Messer, S. C. (1995). Role of family and home environment. In V. B. Van Hasselt & M. Hersen (Eds.), *Handbook of adolescent psychopathology: A guide to diagnosis and treatment.* New York: Lexington.

Remafedi, G. (1987). Male homosexuality: The adolescent perspective. *Pediatrics, 79*, 326–330.

Remafedi, G., Resnick, M., Blum, R., & Harris, L. (1992). Demography of sexual orientation in adolescents. *Pediatrics, 89*, 714–721.

Repucci, N. D. (1987). Prevention and ecology: Teenage pregnancy, child sexual abuse, and organized youth sports. *American Journal of Community Psychology, 15*(1), 1–22.

Resnick, M. D., Blum, R. W., Bose, J., Smith, M., & Toogood, R. (1990). Characteristics of unmarried adolescent mothers: Determinants of child rearing versus adoption. *American Journal of Orthopsychiatry, 60*(4), 577–584.

Reuters News Service. (1991, October 5). 1.5 million people have AIDS, U. N. world health group says. *Houston Chronicle,* p. 27A.

Reyes, O., & Jason, L. A. (1993). Pilot study examining factors associated with academic success for Hispanic high school students. *Journal of Youth and Adolescence, 22*(1), 57–71.

Reynolds, A. J. (1991). The middle schooling process: Influences on science and mathematics achievement from the longitudinal study of American youth. *Adolescence, 26*(101), 133–158.

Reynolds, W. M. (1995). Depression. In V. B. Van Hasselt & M. Hersen (Eds.), *Handbook of adolescent psychopathology: A guide to diagnosis and treatment.* New York: Lexington Books.

Rhodes, J. E. (1994). Older and wiser: Mentoring relationships in childhood and adolescence. *Journal of Primary Prevention, 14*, 75–86.

Rhodes, J. E., & Fischer, K. (1993). Spanning the gender gap: Gender differences in delinquency among inner-city adolescents. *Adolescence, 28*(112), 879–889.

Rice, M. E. (1997). Violent offender research and implications for the criminal justice system. *American Psychologist, 52*(4), 414–423.

Rich, Y., & Golan, R. (1992). Career plans for male-dominated occupations among female seniors in religious and secular high schools. *Adolescence, 27*(105), 73–86.

Richards, I., & Sullivan, A. (1996). Psy-chotherapy for delinquents? *Journal of Adolescence, 19*, 63–73.

Richards, M. H., Abell, S. N., & Petersen, A. C. (1993). Biological development. In P. H. Tolan & B. J. Cohler (Eds.), *Handbook of clinical research and practice with adolescents.* New York: Wiley.

Richards, M., & Petersen, A. C. (1987). Biological theoretical models of adolescent development. In V. B. Van Hasselt & M. Hersen (Eds.), *Handbook of adolescent psychology.* New York: Pergamon Press.

Rickel, A. U., & Hendren, M. C. (1993). Aberrant sexual experiences in adolescence. In T. P. Gullotta, G. R. Adams, & R. Montemayor (Eds.), *Adolescent sexuality.* Newbury Park, CA: Sage.

Riddle, M. A., & Cho, S. C. (1989). Biological aspects of adolescent depression. In G. R. Adams, R. Montemayor, & T. P. Gullotta (Eds.), *Biology of adolescent behavior and development.* Newbury Park, CA: Sage.

Rierdan, J., Koff, E., & Stubbs, M. L. (1989). Timing of menarche, preparation, and initial menstrual experience: Replication and further analyses in a prospective study. *Journal of Youth and Adolescence, 18*(5), 413–425.

Riggan, D. (1991, December 1). Dated practices (letter to the editor). *The New York Times.*

Riley, P. (Ed.). (1993). *Growing up Native-American.* New York: Avon.

Rindfuss, R. R. (1991). The young adult years: Diversity, structural change, and fertility. *Demography, 28*(4), 493–512.

Risman, B. J. (1989). Can men "mother"? Life as a single father. In B. J. Risman & P. Schwartz (Eds.), *Gender in intimate relationships: A microstructural approach.* Belmont, CA: Wadsworth.

Roberts, A., & Cotton, L. (1994). Note on assessing a mentor program. *Psychological Reports, 75*, 1369–1370.

Roberts, L. R., & Petersen, A. C. (1992). The relationship between academic achievement and social self-image during early adolescence. *Journal of Early Adolescence, 12*(2), 197–219.

Roberts, R. E., & Sobhan, M. (1992). Symptoms of depression in adolescence: A comparison of Anglo, African, and Hispanic Americans. *Journal of Youth and Adolescence, 21*(6), 639–651.

Robertson, E. B., Skinner, M. L., Love, M. M., Elder, G. H., Jr., Conger, R. D., Dubas, J. S., & Petersen, A. C. (1992). The pubertal development scale: A rural and suburban comparison. *Journal of Early Adolescence, 12*(2), 174–186.

Robertson, J. F., & Simons, R. D. (1989). Family factors, self-esteem, and adolescent depression. *Journal of Marriage and the Family, 51*, 125–138.

Robins, R. W., John, O. P., Caspi, A., Moffitt, T. E., Stouthamer-Loeber, M. (1996). Resilient, overcontrolled, and undercontrolled boys: Three replicable personality types. *Journal of Personality and Social Psychology, 70*(1), 157–171.

Robinson, B. E., & Barret, R. L. (1985, December). Teenage fathers. *Psychology Today,* pp. 66–70.

Roche, J. P., & Ramsbey, T. W. (1993). Premarital sexuality: A five-year follow-up study of attitudes and behavior by dating stage. *Adolescence, 28*(109), 67–80.

Rodgers, J. L., & Rowe, D. (1988). Influence of siblings on adolescent sexual behavior. *Developmental Psychology, 24*(5), 722–728.

Rodgers, J. L., & Rowe, D. C. (1990). Adolescent sexual activity and mildly deviant behavior. *Journal of Family Issues, 11*(3), 274–293.

Rodman, H. (1990). Legal and social dilemmas of adolescent sexuality. In J. Bancroft & J. M. Reinisch (Eds.), *Adolescence and puberty.* New York: Oxford University Press.

Rodriguez, C., & Moore, N. B. (1995). Perceptions of pregnant/parenting teens: Reframing issues for an integrated approach to pregnancy problems. *Adolescence, 30*(119), 685–706.

Rodriguez, R. A. (1988). *Significant events in gay identity development: Gay men in Utah.* Paper presented at the 96th Annual Convention of the American Psychological Association, Atlanta.

Roe, K. (1995). Adolescents' use of socially disvalued media: Towards a theory of media delinquency. *Journal of Youth and Adolescence, 24*(5), 617–631.

Rogers, C. (1961). *On becoming a person.* Boston: Houghton Mifflin.

Rogers, M. J., & Holmbeck, G. N. (1997). Effects of interpersonal aggression on children's adjustment: The moderating role of cognitive appraisal and coping. *Journal of Family Psychology, 11*(1), 125–130.

Rogoff, B., & Chavajay, P. (1995). What's become of research on the cultural basis of cognitive development? *American Psychologist, 50*(10), 859–877.

Rojewski, J. W. (1996). Educational and occupational aspirations of high school seniors with learning disabilities. *Exceptional Children, 62*(5), 463–476.

Romeo, F. (1994). Adolescent boys and anorexia nervosa. *Adolescence, 29*(115), 643–648.

Romig, C., & Bakken, L. (1992). Intimacy development in middle adolescence: Its relationship to gender and family cohesion and adaptability. *Journal of Youth and Adolescence, 21*(3), 325–338.

Roscoe, B., & Kruger, T. L. (1990). AIDS: Late adolescents' knowledge and its influence on sexual behavior. *Adolescence, 25*(97), 39–47.

Roscoe, B., & Skomski, G. G. (1989). Loneliness among late adolescents. *Adolescence, 24*(96), 947–955.

Roscoe, B., Strouse, J. S., & Goodwin, M. P. (1994). Sexual harassment: Early adolescents' self-reports of experiences and acceptance. *Adolescence, 29*(115), 515–524.

Rosenbaum, M. (1979). The changing body image of the adolescent girl. In M. Sugar (Ed.), *Female adolescent development.* New York: Brunner/Mazel.

Rosenbaum, M. (1993). The changing body image of the adolescent girl. In M. Sugar (Ed.), *Female adolescent development* (2nd ed.). New York: Brunner/Mazel.

Rosenberg, M. (1979). *Concerning the self.* New York: Basic Books.

Rosenberg, M. (1985). Self-concept and psychological well-being in adolescence. In R. L. Leahy (Ed.), *The development of self.* Orlando, FL: Academic Press.

Rosenberg, M. (1986). Self-concept from middle childhood through adolescence. In J. Suls & A. G. Greenwald (Eds.), *Psychological perspective on the self.* Hillsdale, NJ: Erlbaum.

Rosenthal, D., & Peart, R. (1996). The rules of the game: Teenagers communicating about sex. *Journal of Adolescence, 19*, 321–332.

Rosenthal, S. L., Cohen, S. S., & Biro, F. M. (1996). Developmental sophistication among adolescents of negotiation strategies for condom use. *Journal of Developmental and Behavioral Pediatrics, 17*(2), 94–97.

Rosenthal, S. L., Lewis, L. M., & Cohen, S. S. (1996). Issues related to the sexual decision-making of inner-city adolescent girls. *Adolescence, 31*(123), 731–739.

Rosenthal, S. L., & Simeonsson, R. J. (1989). Emotional disturbance and the development of self-consciousness in adolescence. *Adolescence, 24*(95), 689–698.

Rosseel, E. (1989). The impact of attitudes toward the personal future on study motivation and work orientations of nonworking adolescents. *Adolescence, 24*(93), 75–93.

Roth, R., & Constantine, L. M. (1995, January). Conference aims to create safe schools. *APA Monitor,* 42–43.

Rothenberg, M. B. (1975). Effect of television violence on children and youth. *Journal of the American Medical Association, 234*, 1043–1046.

Rotheram-Borus, M. J., Mahler, K. A., Koopman, C., & Langabeer, K. (1996). Sexual abuse history and associated multiple risk behavior in adolescent runaways. *American Journal of Orthopsychiatry, 66*(3), 390–400.

Rotheram-Borus, M. J., Rosario, M., Van Rossem, R., Reid, H., & Gillis, R. (1995). Prevalence, course, and predictors of multiple problem behaviors among gay and bisexual male adolescents. *Developmental Psychology, 31*(1), 75–85.

Rousseau, J. J. (1762/1948). *Emile* (B. Foxley, trans). London: J. M. Dent & Sons, Ltd.

Rowen, B., Bossert, S. T., & Dwyer, D. C. (1983). Research on effective schools: A cautionary note. *Educational Researcher, 12*, 24–31.

Rubin, C., Rubenstein, J. L., Stechler, G., Heeren, T., Halton, A., Housman, D., & Kasten, L. (1992). Depressive affect in "normal" adolescents: Relationship to life stress, family, and friends. *American Journal of Orthopsychiatry, 62*(3), 430–441.

Rubin, L. (1979). *Women of a certain age.* New York: Harper & Row.

Rubin, R. (1990). Mood changes during adolescence. In J. Bancroft & J. M. Reinisch (Eds.), *Adolescence and puberty.* New York: Oxford University Press.

Rubin, S. (1988). College freshmen: Turmoil or maturity? *Adolescence, 23*(91), 585–591.

Ruble, D. N., & Brooks-Gunn, J. (1982). The experience of menarche. *Child Development, 53*, 1557–1566.

Rudd, N. M., McKenry, P. C., & Nah, M. (1990). Welfare receipt among black and white adolescent mothers: A longitudinal perspective. *Journal of Family Issues, 11*(3), 334–352.

Rumberger, R. W. (1983). Dropping out of high school: The influence of race, sex, and family background. *American Educational Research Journal, 20*, 199–220.

Ruscoe, G., Morgan, J. C., & Peebles, C. (1996). Students who work. *Adolescence, 31*(123), 625–632.

Russell, A., Brewer, N., & Hogben, N. (1997). Psychological variables associated with the household work of girls and boys in early adolescence. *Journal of Early Adolescence, 17*(2), 197–215.

Rutter, M. (1983). School effects on pupil progress: Research findings and policy implications. *Child Development, 54*, 1–29.

Rutter, M. (1985). Family and school influences in behavioral development.

*Journal of Child Psychology and Psychiatry, 26*, 349–368.

Rutter, M. (1986). The developmental psychopathology of depression: Issues and perspectives. In C. E. Izard, P. B. Read, & M. Rutter (Eds.), *Depression in young people*. New York: Guilford Press.

Rutter, M. (1990). Changing patterns of psychiatric disorders during adolescence. In J. Bancroft & J. M. Reinisch (Eds.), *Adolescence and puberty*. New York: Oxford University Press.

Rutter, M. L. (1997). Nature-nurture integration: The example of antisocial behavior. *American Psychologist, 52*(4), 390–398.

Ryan, A. M., Hicks, L., & Midgley, C. (1997). Social goals, academic goals, and avoiding seeking help in the classroom. *Journal of Early Adolescence, 17*(2), 152–171.

Ryan, C. M. (1990). Age-related improvement in short-term memory efficiency during adolescence. *Developmental Neuropsychology, 6*, 193–205.

Ryan, R. M., & Lynch, J. H. (1989). Emotional autonomy versus detachment: Revisiting the vicissitudes of adolescence and young adulthood. *Child Development, 60*, 340–356.

Ryan, R. M., Stiller, J. D., & Lynch, J. H. (1994). Representations of relationships to teachers, parents, and friends as predictors of academic motivation and self-esteem. *Journal of Early Adolescence, 14*(2), 226–249.

Ryu, S., & Mortimer, J. T. (1996). The "occupational linkage hypothesis" applied to occupational value formation in adolescence. In J. T. Mortimer & M. D. Finch (Eds.), *Adolescents, work, and family: An intergenerational developmental analysis*. Thousand Oaks, CA: Sage.

St. Pierre, T. L., Mark, M. M., Kaltreider, D. L., & Aikin, K. J. (1997). Involving parents of high-risk youth in drug prevention: A three-year longitudinal study in boys and girls clubs. *Journal of Early Adolescence, 17*(1), 21–50.

Salomone, P. R. (1996). Tracing Super's theory of vocational development: A 40-year retrospective. *Journal of Career Development, 22*(3), 167–184.

Salt, R. E. (1991). Affectionate touch between fathers and preadolescent sons. *Journal of Marriage and the Family, 53*, 545–554.

Saltiel, J. (1985). A note on models and definers as sources of influence in the status attainment process: Male–female differences. *Social Forces, 63*, 129–143.

Salts, C. J., Seismore, M. D., Lindholm, B. W., & Smith, T. A. (1994). Attitudes toward marriage and premarital sexual activity of college freshmen. *Adolescence, 29*(116), 775–780.

Sam, D. L. (1995). Acculturation attitudes among young immigrants as a function of perceived parental attitudes toward cultural change. *Journal of Early Adolescence, 15*(2), 238–258.

Sampson, R. J., & Laub, J. H. (1994). Urban poverty and the family context of delinquency: A new look at structure and process in a classic study. *Child Development, 65*, 523–540.

Sanders, D. (1987). Cultural conflicts: An important factor in the academic failures of American Indian students. *Journal of Multicultural Counseling and Development, 15*.

Sanders, G., & Mullis, R. (1988). Family influences on sexual attitudes and knowledge as reported by college students. *Adolescence, 23*(92), 837–845.

Sanders, S. A., & Reinisch, J. M. (1990). Biological and social influences on the endocrinology of puberty: Some additional considerations. In J. Bancroft & J. M. Reinisch (Eds.), *Adolescence and puberty*. New York: Oxford University Press.

Sanderson, C. A., & Cantor, N. (1995). Social dating goals in late adolescence: Implications for safer sexual practices. *Journal of Personality & Social Psychology, 68*(6), 1121–1134.

Sandler, J. (1992). Comments on the self and its objects. In S. C. Feinstein (Ed.), *Adolescent psychiatry: Developmental and clinical studies* (Vol. 18). Chicago: University of Chicago Press.

Sandven, K., & Resnick, M. D. (1990). Informal adoption among black adolescent mothers. *American Journal of Orthopsychiatry, 60*(2), 210–224.

Sanger, D. E. (1993, February 1). Shedding teens (and jeans), they're now of age. *The New York Times*, p. A5.

Sansbury, L. L., & Wahler, R. G. (1992). Pathways to maladaptive parenting with mothers and their conduct disordered children. *Behavior Modification, 16*(4), 574–592.

Santilli, N. R., & Hudson, L. M. (1992). Enhancing moral growth: Is communication the key? *Adolescence, 27*(105), 145–161.

Sapolsky, R. (1997, March). Testosterone rules. *Discover*, pp. 45–50.

Sarason, I. G., & Sarason, B. R. (1993). *Abnormal psychology: The problem of maladaptive behavior* (7th ed.). Englewood Cliffs, NJ: Prentice-Hall.

Sarigiani, P. A., Camarena, P. M., & Petersen, A. C. (1993). Cultural factors in adolescent girls' development: the role of ethnic minority group status. In M. Sugar (Ed.), *Female adolescent development*. New York: Brunner/Mazel.

Savickas, M. L. (1995). Donald E. Super (1910–1994) (obituary). *American Psychologist, 50*(9), 794–795.

Savin-Williams, R. C. (1979). Dominance hierarchies in groups of early adolescents. *Child Development, 50*, 923–935.

Savin-Williams, R. C. (1990). *Gay and lesbian youth: Expressions of identity*. Washington, DC: Hemisphere.

Savin-Williams, R. C. (1994). Dating those you can't love and loving those you can't date. In R. Montemayor, G. R. Adams, & T. P. Gullotta (Eds.), *Personal relationships during adolescence*. Thousand Oaks, CA: Sage.

Savin-Williams, R. C. (1995). An exploratory study of pubertal maturation timing and self-esteem among gay and bisexual youths. *Developmental Psychology, 31*(1), 56–64.

Savin-Williams, R. C., & Berndt, T. J. (1990). Friendship and peer relations. In S. S. Feldman & G. R. Elliot (Eds.), *At the threshold: The developing adolescent*. Cambridge, MA: Harvard University Press.

Savin-Williams, R. C., & Rodriguez, R. G. (1993). A developmental, clinical perspective on lesbian, gay male, and bisexual youths. In T. P. Gullotta, G. R. Adams, & R. Montemayor (Eds.), *Adolescent sexuality*. Newbury Park, CA: Sage.

Savin-Williams, R. C., & Weisfeld, G. E. (1989). An ethological perspective on adolescence. In G. R. Adams, R. Montemayor, & T. P. Gullotta (Eds.), *Biology of adolescent behavior and development*. Newbury Park, CA: Sage.

Scafidi, F. A., Field, T., Prodromidis, M., & Rahdert, E. (1997). Psychosocial stressors of drug-abusing disadvantaged adolescent mothers. *Adolescence*, 32(125), 93–100.

Scales, P. C., & Gibbons, J. L. (1996). Extended family members and unrelated adults in the lives of young adolescents: A research agenda. *Journal of Early Adolescence*, 16(4), 365–389.

Scarr, S. (1992). Developmental theories for the 1990s: Development and individual differences. *Child Development*, 63, 1–19.

Schab, F. (1991). Schooling without learning: Thirty years of cheating in high school. *Adolescence*, 26(104), 839–847.

Schamess, S. (1993). The search for love: Unmarried adolescent mothers' views of, and relationships with, men. *Adolescence*, 28(110), 425–438.

Schechternman, A. L., & Hutchinson, R. L. (1991). Causal attributions, self-monitoring, and gender differences among four virginity status groups. *Adolescence*, 26(103), 659–678.

Scheer, S. D., Unger, D. G., & Brown, M. B. (1996). Adolescents becoming adults: Attributes for adulthood. *Adolescence*, 31(121), 127–131.

Schellenbach, C. J., Whitman, T. L., & Borkowski, J. G. (1992). Toward an integrative model of adolescent parenting. *Human Development*, 35(2), 100–106.

Schilmoeller, G. L., & Baranowski, M. D. (1985). Childrearing of firstborns by adolescent and older mothers. *Adolescence*, 20(80), 805–822.

Schlegel, A., & Barry, H. (1991). *Adolescence: An anthropological inquiry*. New York: Free Press.

Schmidt, F. L. (1992). What do data really mean? Research findings, meta-analysis, and cumulative knowledge in psychology. *American Psychologist*, 47(10), 1173–1181.

Schmidt, S. E., Liddle, H. A., & Dakof, G. A. (1996). Changes in parenting practices and adolescent drug abuse during multidimensional family therapy. *Journal of Family Psychology*, 10(1), 12–27.

Schmitt, D. P., & Buss, D. M. (1996). Strategic self-promotion and competitor derogation: Sex and context effects on the perceived effectiveness of mate attraction tactics. *Journal of Personality & Social Psychology*, 70(6), 1185–1204.

Schneider, B. H., & Younger, A. J. (1996). Adolescent–parent attachment and adolescents' relations with their peers: A closer look. *Youth & Society*, 28(1), 95–108.

Schneider, S. (1992). Separation and individuation issues in psychosocial rehabilitation. *Adolescence*, 27(105), 137–144.

Schoenberger, C. (1995, November 5). Am I really ready for this? *New York Times Education Life*, pp. 17–18.

Schondel, C., Boehm, K., Rose, J., & Marlowe, A. (1996). Adolescent volunteers: An untapped resource in the delivery of adolescent preventive health care. *Youth & Society*, 27(2), 123–135.

Schonert-Reichl, K. A., & Muller, J. R. (1996). Correlates of help-seeking in adolescence. *Journal of Youth and Adolescence*, 25(6), 705–732.

Schulenberg, J., & Ebata, A. T. (1994). The United States. In K. Hurrelmann (Ed.), *International handbook of adolescence*. Westport, CT: Greenwood Press.

Schulenberg, J., Goldstein, A. E., & Vondracek, F. W. (1991). Gender differences in adolescents' career interests: Beyond main effects. *Journal of Research on Adolescence*, 1(1), 37–61.

Schulenberg, J., Vondracek, F. W., & Crouter, A. C. (1984). The influence of the family on vocational development. *Journal of Marriage and the Family*, 46(1), 129–143.

Schulenberg, J., Wadsworth, K. N., O'Malley, P. M., Bachman, J. G., & Johnston, L. D. (1996). Adolescent risk factors for binge drinking during the transition to young adulthood: Variable- and pattern-centered approaches to change. *Developmental Psychology*, 32(4), 659–674.

Schulman, S., & Collins, W. A. (Eds.). (1993). *Father–adolescent relationships*. San Francisco: Jossey-Bass.

Schwalb, D. W., Schwalb, B. J., & Nakazawa, J. (1995). Competitive and cooperative attitudes: A longitudinal survey of Japanese adolescents. *Journal of Early Adolescence*, 15(1), 145–168.

Schwartz, D. B., & Darabi, K. F. (1986). Motivations for adolescents' first visit to a family planning clinic. *Adolescence*, 21(83), 535–545.

Schweder, R. A., Mahapatra, M., & Miller, J. G. (1987). Culture and moral development. In J. Kagan & S. Lamb (Eds.), *The emergence of morality in young children*. Chicago: University of Chicago Press.

Schweitzer, R. D., Seth-Smith, M., & Callan, V. (1992). The relationship between self-esteem and psychological adjustment in young adolescents. *Journal of Adolescence*, 15, 83–97.

Sebald, H. (1992). *Adolescence: A social psychological analysis* (4th ed.). Englewood Cliffs, NJ: Prentice-Hall.

Secord, P., & Peevers, B. (1974). The development of person concepts. In T. Mischel (Ed.), *Understanding other persons*. Oxford: Blackwell.

Seelow, D. (1996). Listening to youth: Woodstock, music, America, and Kurt Cobain's suicide. *Child & Youth Care Forum*, 25(1), 49–60.

Seelye, K. Q. (1997a, March 14). Groups seeks to alter S. A. T. to raise girls' scores. *The New York Times*.

Seelye, K. Q. (1997b, June 15). Concealing a pregnancy to avoid telling mom. *The New York Times News of the Week in Review*, p. 5.

Segal, B. M., & Stewart, J. C. (1996). Substance use and abuse in adolescence: A review. *Child Psychiatry and Human Development*, 26(4), 193–210.

Segal, S. D., & Fairchild, H. H. (1996). Polysubstance abuse—A case study. *Adolescence, 31*(124), 797–806.

Seginer, R. (1983). Parents' educational expectations and children's academic achievements: A literature review. *Merrill-Palmer Quarterly, 29*, 1–23.

Seidman, E., Allen, L., Aber, J. L., Mitchell, C., & Feinman, J. (1994). The impact of school transitions in early adolescence on the self-esteem and perceived social context of poor urban youth. *Child Development, 65*, 507–522.

Seiffge-Krenke, I. (1997). Imaginary companions in adolescence: sign of a deficient or positive development? *Journal of Adolescence, 20*, 137–154.

Seiffge-Krenke, I., & Shulman, S. (1990). Coping style in adolescence: A cross-cultural study. *Journal of Cross-Cultural Psychology, 21*(3), 351–377.

Seligman, M. E. P. (1990). *Helplessness: On depression, development and death.* San Francisco: Freeman.

Selman, R. L. (1976). Social-cognitive understanding. In T. Lickona (Ed.), *Moral development and behavior.* New York: Holt, Rinehart, & Winston.

Selman, R. L. (1980). *The growth of interpersonal understanding*: Developmental and clinical analyses. New York: Academic Press.

Selman, R., & Demorest, A. (1984). Observing troubled children's interpersonal negotiation strategies: Implications of and for a developmental model. *Child Development, 55*, 288–304.

Seltzer, V. C. (1989). *The psychosocial worlds of the adolescent: Public and private.* New York: Wiley.

Seng, M. J. (1989). Child sexual abuse and adolescent prostitution: A comparative analysis. *Adolescence, 24*(95), 665–675.

Seppa, N. (1996a, July). Keeping young athletic fires burning. *APA Monitor*, p. 32.

Seppa, N. (1996b, August). Moving appears hardest on adolescents. *APA Monitor*, p. 10.

Seppa, N. (1997, March). What is society teaching to boys? *APA Monitor*, p. 11.

Sessa, F. M., & Steinberg, L. (1991). Family structure and the development of autonomy during adolescence. *Journal of Early Adolescence, 11*(1), 38–55.

Seydlitz, R. (1991). The effects of age and gender on parental control and delinquency. *Youth & Society, 23*(2), 175–201.

Shagle, S. C., & Barber, B. K. (1993). Effects of family, marital, and parent–child conflict on adolescent self-derogation and suicidal ideation. *Journal of Marriage and the Family, 55*, 964–974.

Shagle, S. C., & Barber, B. K. (1995). A social-ecological analysis of adolescent suicide ideation. *American Journal of Orthopsychiatry, 65*(1), 114–124.

Shaheen, J. (1994, January 30). Early-grade sex course is debated. *The New York Times* (Section 13, p. 1).

Shanahan, M. J., Elder, G. H., Jr., Burchinal, M., & Conger, R. D. (1996a). Adolescent earnings and relationships with parents: The work-family nexus in urban and rural ecologies. In J. T. Mortimer & M. D. Finch (Eds.), *Adolescents, work, and family: An intergenerational developmental analysis.* Thousand Oaks, CA: Sage.

Shanahan, M. J., Elder, G. H., Jr., Burchinal, M., & Conger, R. D. (1996b). Adolescent paid labor and relationships with parents: Early work-family linkages. *Child Development, 67*, 2183–2200.

Shapiro, J. R., & Mangelsdorf, S. C. (1994). The determinants of parenting competence in adolescent mothers. *Journal of Youth and Adolescence, 23*(6), 621–641.

Shaughnessy, M. F., & Shakesby, P. (1992). Adolescent sexual and emotional intimacy. *Adolescence, 27*(106), 475–480.

Shaunesey, K., Cohen, J. L., Plummer, B., & Berman, A. (1993). Suicidality in hospitalized adolescents: Relationship to prior abuse. *American Journal of Orthopsychiatry, 63*(1), 113–119.

Shavelson, R. J., Hubner, J. J., & Stanton, G. C. (1976). Validation of construct interpretations. *Review of Educational Research, 46*, 407–441.

Sheppard, M. A., Wright, D., & Goodstadt, M. S. (1985). Peer pressure and drug use—Exploding the myth. *Adolescence, 20*, 949–958.

Sherman, B. R., & Donovan, B. R. (1991). Relationship of perceived maternal acceptance-rejection in childhood and social support networks of pregnant adolescents. *American Journal of Orthopsychiatry, 61*(1), 103–113.

Shilts, L. (1991). The relationship of early adolescent substance use to extracurricular activities, peer influence, and personal attitudes. *Adolescence, 26*(103), 613–617.

Shobris, J. G. (1996). The anatomy of intelligence. *Genetic, Social & General Psychology Monographs, 122*(2), 135–158.

Shorter-Gooden, K., & Washington, N. C. (1996). Young, black, and female: The challenge of weaving an identity. *Journal of Adolescence*, 465–475.

Shucksmith, J., Glendinning, A., & Hendry, L. (1997). Adolescent drinking behaviour and the role of family life: a Scottish perspective. *Journal of Adolescence, 20*, 85–101.

Shucksmith, J., Hendry, L. B., & Glendinning, A. (1995). Models of parenting: Implications for adolescent well-being within different types of family contexts. *Journal of Adolescence, 18*, 253–270.

Siegel, J., & Schaughnessy, M. F. (1995). There's a first time for everything: Understanding adolescence. *Adolescence, 30*(117), 217–222.

Siegel, J. M., & Brown, J. D. (1988). A prospective study of stressful circumstances, illness symptoms, and depressed mood among adolescents. *Developmental Psychology, 24*(5), 715–721.

Siegler, R. S. (1991). *Children's thinking.* Englewood Cliffs, NJ: Prentice-Hall.

Sigurdsson, J. F., & Gudjonsson, G. H. (1996). Psychological characteristics of juvenile alcohol and drug users. *Journal of Adolescence, 19*, 41–46.

Silbereisen, R. K., Petersen, A. C., Albrecht, H. T., & Kracke, B. (1989). Maturational timing and the development of problem behavior: Longitudinal studies in adolescence. *Journal of Early Adolescence, 9*(3), 247–268.

Silberman, H. F. (1991, January). Improvements coming, but problems remain. *Vocational Education Journal*, 30–31.

Silverberg, S. B., & Gondoli, D. M. (1996). Autonomy in adolescence: A contextualized perspective. In G. R. Adams, R. Montemayor, & T. P. Gullotta (Eds.), *Psychosocial development during adolescence: Progress in developmental contextualism*. Thousand Oaks, CA: Sage.

Silverberg, S. B., & Steinberg, L. (1990). Psychological well-being of parents with early adolescent children. *Developmental Psychology*, 26(4), 658–666.

Sim, H., & Vuchinich, S. (1996). The declining effects of family stressors on antisocial behavior from childhood to adolescence and early adulthood. *Journal of Family Issues*, 17(3), 408–427.

Simmons, R. G., & Blyth, D. A. (1987). *Moving into adolescence: The impact of pubertal change and school context*. New York: Aldine de Gruyter.

Simmons, R. G., Blyth, D. A., Van Cleave, E. F., & Bush, D. M. (1979). Entry into early adolescence: The impact of school structure, puberty, and early dating on self-esteem. *American Sociological Review*, 44, 948–967.

Simmons, R. G., Burgeson, R., Carlton-Ford, S., & Blyth, D. (1987). The impact of cumulative change in early adolescence. *Child Development*, 58(5), 1220–1234.

Simmons, R. G., & Rosenberg, F. (1975). Sex, sex-roles, and self image. *Journal of Youth and Adolescence*, 4(3), 229–258.

Simons, M. (1993, April 9). The sex market: Scourge on the world's children. *The New York Times*.

Simons, R. L., Johnson, C., & Conger, R. D. (1994). Harsh corporal punishment versus quality of parental involvement as an explanation of adolescent maladjustment. *Journal of Marriage and the Family*, 56, 591–607.

Simons, R. L., Robertson, J. F., & Downs, W. R. (1989). The nature of the association between parental rejection and delinquent behavior. *Journal of Youth and Adolescence*, 18(3), 297–310.

Simons, R. L., Whitbeck, L. B., Beaman, J., & Conger, R. D. (1994). The impact of mothers' parenting, involvement by nonresidential fathers, and parental conflict on the adjustment of adolescent children. *Journal of Marriage and the Family*, 56, 356–371.

Simons, R. L., Whitbeck, L. B., Conger, R. D., & Chyi-In, W. (1991). Intergenerational transmission of harsh parenting. *Developmental Psychology*, 27(1), 159–171.

Simons, R. L., Whitbeck, L. B., Conger, R. D., & Conger, K. J. (1991). Parenting factors, social skills, and value commitments as precursors to school failure, involvement with deviant peers, and delinquent behavior. *Journal of Youth and Adolescence*, 20(6), 645–664.

Simons, R. L., Whitbeck, L. B., Conger, R. D., & Melby, J. N. (1991). The effect of social skills, values, peers, and depression on adolescent substance use. *Journal of Early Adolescence*, 11(4), 466–481.

Singh, K., & Hernández-Gantes, V. M. (1996). The relation of English language proficiency to educational aspirations of Mexican American eighth graders. *Journal of Early Adolescence*, 16(3), 253–273.

Skaalvik, E. M., & Rankin, R. J. (1992). Math and verbal achievement and self-concepts: Testing the internal/external frame of reference model. *Journal of Early Adolescence*, 12(3), 267–279.

Skandhan, K. P., Pandya, A. K., Skandhan, S., & Mehta, Y. (1988). Menarche: Prior knowledge and experience. *Adolescence*, 23(89), 149–154.

Skinner, B. F. (1974). *About behaviorism*. New York: Knopf.

Skinner, E. A., Wellborn, J. G., & Connell, J. P. (1990). What it takes to do well in school and whether I've got it: A process model of perceived control and children's engagement and achievement in school. *Journal of Educational Psychology*, 82(1), 22–32.

Skoe, E. E., & Gooden, A. (1993). Ethic of care and real-life moral dilemma content in male and female early adolescents. *Journal of Early Adolescence*, 13(2), 154–167.

Slaughter-Defoe, D. T., Nakagawa, K., Takanishi, R., & Johnson, D. J. (1990). Toward cultural/ecological perspectives on schooling and achievement in African- and Asian-American children. *Child Development*, 61, 363–383.

Sleek, S. (1996, October). Research identifies causes of internal homophobia. *APA Monitor*, p. 57.

Sleek, S., & Burnette, E. (1996, July). Coaches may be ill-prepared for the job. *APA Monitor*, pp. 42–43.

Slesnick, N., & Waldron, H. B. (1997). Interpersonal problem-solving interactions of depressed adolescents and their parents. *Journal of Family Psychology*, 11(2), 234–245.

Small, S., Eastman, G., & Cornelius, S. (1988). Adolescent autonomy and parental stress. *Journal of Youth and Adolescence*, 17, 377–392.

Small, S. A., & Kerns, D. (1993). Unwanted sexual activity among peers during early and middle adolescence: Incidence and risk factors. *Journal of Marriage and the Family*, 55, 941–952.

Small, S. A., Silverberg, S. B., & Kerns, D. (1993). Adolescents' perceptions of the costs and benefits of engaging in health-compromising behaviors. *Journal of Youth and Adolescence*, 22(1), 73–87.

Smart, R. G., & Walsh, G. W. (1993). Predictors of depression in street youth. *Adolescence*, 28(109), 41–53.

Smetana, J. G. (1988a). Adolescents' and parents' conceptions of parental authority. *Child Development*, 59, 321–335.

Smetana, J. G. (1988b). Concepts of self and social convention. Adolescents' and parents' reasoning about hypothetical and actual family conflicts. In M. Gunnar (Ed.), *Minnesota symposium on child psychology*. Hillsdale, NJ: Erlbaum.

Smetana, J. G. (1989). Adolescents' and parents' reasoning about actual family conflict. *Child Development*, 60, 1052–1067.

Smetana, J. G. (1995). Parenting styles and conceptions of parental authority during adolescence. *Child Development*, 66, 299–316.

Smetana, J. G., & Asquith, P. (1994). Adolescents' and parents' conceptions of parental authority and personal autonomy. *Child Development*, *65*, 1147–1162.

Smetana, J. G., & Bitz, B. (1996). Adolescents' conceptions of teachers' authority and their relations to rule violations in school. *Child Development*, *67*, 1153–1172.

Smetana, J. G., Killen, M., & Turiel, E. (1991). Children's reasoning about interpersonal and moral conflicts. *Child Development*, *62*, 629–644.

Smetana, J. G., Yau, J., Restrepo, A., & Braeges, J. L. (1991). Adolescent-parent conflict in married and divorced families. *Developmental Psychology*, *27*(6), 1000–1010.

Smith, A. M. A., & Rosenthal, D. A. (1995). Adolescents' perceptions of their risk environment. *Journal of Adolescence*, *18*, 229–245.

Smith, C., & Krohn, M. D. (1995). Delinquency and family life among male adolescents: The role of ethnicity. *Journal of Youth and Adolescence*, *24*(1), 69–93.

Smith, D. J., & Rutter, M. (1995). Introduction. In M. Rutter & D. J. Smith (Eds.), *Psychosocial disorders in young people: Time trends and their causes*. New York: Wiley.

Smith, E. A., & Udry, J. R. (1985). Coital and non-coital sexual behaviors of white and black adolescents. *American Journal of Public Health*, *75*, 1200–1203.

Smith, K. A., & Forehand, R. (1986). Parent-adolescent conflict: Comparison and prediction of the perceptions, of mothers, fathers, and daughters. *Journal of Early Adolescence*, *6*, 353–367.

Smith, S. L. (1975). Mood and the menstrual cycle. In E. J. Sachar (Ed.), *Topics in psychoendocrinology* (pp. 19–58). New York: Grune & Stratton.

Smith, S. P. (1996). Dating-partner preferences among a group of inner-city African-American high school students. *Adolescence*, *31*(121), 79–90.

Smith, T. E. (1990). Time and academic achievement. *Journal of Youth and Adolescence*, *19*(6), 539–558.

Smith, T. E. (1991). Agreement of adolescent educational expectations with perceived maternal and paternal educational goals. *Youth & Society*, *23*(2), 155–174.

Smith, T. E. (1992). Time use and change in academic achievement: A longitudinal follow-up. *Journal of Youth and Adolescence*, *21*(6), 725–747.

Smith, T. E. (1997). Adolescent gender differences in time alone and time devoted to conversation. *Adolescence*, *32*(126), 483–496.

Smolak, L., Levine, M. P., & Gralen, S. (1993). The impact of puberty and dating on eating problems among middle school girls. *Journal of Youth and Adolescence*, *22*(4), 355–368.

Smollar, J., & Youniss, J. (1989). Transformations in adolescents' perceptions of parents. *International Journal of Behavioural Development*, *12*, 71–84.

Snodgrass, D. M. (1991). The parent connection. *Adolescence*, *26*(101), 83–87.

Snyder, S. (1991). Movies and juvenile delinquency: An overview. *Adolescence*, *26*(101), 121–132.

Snyder, S. (1995). Movie portrayals of juvenile delinquency: I. Epidemiology and criminology. *Adolescence*, *30*(117), 53–64.

Sobol, M. P., & Daly, K. J. (1992). The adoption alternative for pregnant adolescents: Decision making, consequences, and policy implications. *Journal of Social Issues*, *48*(3), 143–161.

Sokol-Katz, J., Dunham, R., & Zimmerman, R. (1997). Family structure versus parental attachment in controlling adolescent deviant behavior: A social control model. *Adolescence*, *32*(125), 199–215.

Sommer, B., & Nagel, S. (1991). Ecological and typological characteristics in early adolescent truancy. *Journal of Early Adolescence*, *11*(3), 379–392.

Sommer, K., Whitman, T. L., Borkowski, J. G., Schellenbach, C., Maxwell, S., & Keogh, D. (1993). Cognitive readiness and adolescent parenting. *Developmental Psychology*, *29*(2), 389–398.

Sonenstein, F. L. (1986). Risking paternity: Sex and contraception among adolescent males. In A. B. Elser & M. E. Lamb (Eds.), *Adolescent fatherhood*. Hillsdale, NJ: Erlbaum.

Sorell, G. T., & Nowak, C. A. (1981). The role of physical attractiveness as a contributor to individual development. In R. M. Lerner & N. A. Busch-Rossnagel (Eds.), *Individual as producers of their own development: A life-span perspective*. New York: Academic Press.

Spencer, M. B., & Dornbusch, S. M. (1990). Challenges in studying minority youth. In S. S. Feldman & G. R. Elliot (Eds.), *At the threshold: The developing adolescent*. Cambridge, MA: Harvard University Press.

Spencer, M. B., Kim, S., & Marshall, S. (1987). Double stratification and psychological risk: Adaptational processes and school achievement of black children. *Journal of Negro Education*, *56*, 77–87.

Spencer, M. B., & Markstrom-Adams, C. (1990). Identity processes among racial and ethnic minority children in America. *Child Development*, *61*, 290–310.

Spirito, A., Francis, G., Overholser, J., & Natalie, F. (1996). Coping, depression, and adolescent suicide attempts. *Journal of Clinical Child Psychology*, *25*(2), 147–155.

Spirito, A., Plummer, B., Gispert, M., Levy, S., Kurkjian, J., Lewander, W., Hagberg, S., & Devost, L. (1992). Adolescent suicide attempts: Outcomes at follow-up. *American Journal of Orthopsychiatry*, *62*(3), 464–468.

Spirito, A., Stark, L. J., Grace, N., & Stamoulis, D. (1991). Common problems and coping strategies reported in childhood and early adolescence. *Journal of Youth and Adolescence*, *20*(5), 531–544.

Stanley, P. D., Dai, Y., & Nolan, R. F. (1997). Differences in depression and self-esteem reported by learning disabled and behavior disordered middle school students. *Journal of Adolescence*, *20*, 219–222.

Stanton, B. F., Black, M., Kaljee, L., & Ricardo, I. (1993). Perceptions of sexual behavior among urban early adolescents: Translating theory through focus groups. *Journal of Early Adolescence, 13*(1), 44–66.

Stanton, W. R., Currie, G. D., Oei, T. P. S., & Silva, P. A. (1996). A developmental approach to influences on adolescents' smoking and quitting. *Journal of Applied Developmental Psychology, 17*(3), 307–319.

Stark, E. (1986, October). Young, innocent and pregnant. *Psychology Today,* pp. 28–35.

Stattin, H. (1995). Introduction: The adolescent is a whole person. *Journal of Adolescence, 18,* 381–386.

Steele, C. M. (1992, April). Race and the schooling of black Americans. *Atlantic Monthly,* 68–78.

Steele, C. M. (1997). A threat in the air: How stereotypes shape intellectual identity and performance. *American Psychologist, 52*(6), 613–629.

Steele, J. R., & Brown, J. D. (1995). Adolescent room culture: Studying media in the context of everyday life. *Journal of Youth and Adolescence, 24*(5), 551–576.

Steenland, S. (1988). *Growing up in prime time: An analysis of adolescent girls on television.* Washington, DC: National Commission on Working Women of Wide Opportunities for Women.

Stefanko, M. (1987). Adolescents and adults: Ratings and expected ratings of themselves and each other. *Adolescence, 22*(85), 208–221.

Stein, D., Witztum, E., Brom, D., & DeNour, A. K. (1992). The association between adolescents' attitudes toward suicide and their psychosocial background and suicidal tendencies. *Adolescence, 27*(108), 949–959.

Stein, J. H., & Reiser, L. W. (1994). A study of white middle-class adolescent boys' responses to ''semenarche'' (the first ejaculation). *Journal of Youth and Adolescence, 23*(3), 373–384.

Steinberg, J. (1996, August 19). Where the boys aren't, schoolgirls both eager and not so. *The New York Times,* pp. B1, B6.

Steinberg, L. (1981). Transformations in family relations at puberty. *Developmental Psychology, 17,* 833–840.

Steinberg, L. (1986). Latchkey children and susceptibility to peer pressure: An ecological analysis. *Developmental Psychology, 22,* 435–439.

Steinberg, L. (1987a, September). Bound to bicker. *Psychology Today,* 36–39.

Steinberg, L. (1987b). Family processes at adolescence: A developmental perspective. *Family Therapy, 14*(2), 77–86.

Steinberg, L. (1987c). Impact of timing on family relations: Effects of pubertal status and pubertal timing. *Developmental Psychology, 23,* 451–460.

Steinberg, L. (1987d). Single parents, stepparents, and the susceptibility of adolescents to antisocial peer pressure. *Child Development, 58,* 269–275.

Steinberg, L. (1988). Reciprocal relation between parent–child distance and pubertal maturation. *Developmental Psychology, 24*(1), 122–128.

Steinberg, L. (1989). Pubertal maturation and parent–adolescent distance: An evolutionary perspective. In G. R. Adams, R. Montemayor, & T. P. Gullotta (Eds.), *Biology of adolescent behavior and development.* Newbury Park, CA: Sage.

Steinberg, L. (1990). Autonomy, conflict, and harmony in the family relationship. In S. S. Feldman & G. R. Elliot (Eds.), *At the threshold: The developing adolescent.* Cambridge, MA: Harvard University Press.

Steinberg, L. (1996a, Summer). Ethnicity and adolescent achievement. *American Educator,* pp. 28–35, 44–48.

Steinberg, L. (1996b). *Beyond the classroom.* New York: Simon & Schuster.

Steinberg, L., Blinn, P., & Chan, K. (1984). Dropping out among language minority youth. *Review of Educational Research, 54,* 113–132.

Steinberg, L., & Dornbusch, S. M. (1991). Negative correlates of part-time employment during adolescence: Replication and elaboration. *Developmental Psychology, 27*(2), 304–313.

Steinberg, L., Dornbusch, S. M., & Brown, B. B. (1992). Ethnic differences in adolescent achievement. *American Psychologist, 47*(6), 723–729.

Steinberg, L., Elmen, J. D., & Mounts, N. S. (1989). Authoritative parenting, psychosocial maturity, and academic success among adolescents. *Child Development, 60,* 1424–1436.

Steinberg, L., Fegley, S., & Dornbusch, S. M. (1993). Negative impact of part-time work on adolescent adjustment: Evidence from a longitudinal study. *Developmental Psychology, 29*(2), 171–180.

Steinberg, L., Lamborn, S. D., Darling, N., Mounts, N. S., & Dornbusch, S. M. (1994). Over-time changes in adjustment and competence among adolescents from authoritative, authoritarian, indulgent, and neglectful families. *Child Development, 65*(3), 754–770.

Steinberg, L., Lamborn, S. D., Dornbusch, S. M., & Darling, N. (1992). Impact of parenting practices on adolescent achievement: Authoritative parenting, school involvement, and encouragement to succeed. *Child Development, 63,* 1266–1281.

Steinberg, L., & Silverberg, S. (1986). The vicissitudes of autonomy in early adolescence. *Child Development, 57,* 841–851.

Steinberg, L., & Silverberg, S. (1987). Influences on marital satisfaction during the middle stages of the family life cycle. *Journal of Marriage and the Family, 49,* 751–760.

Steinberg, L., & Steinberg, W. (1994). *Crossing paths: How your child's adolescence triggers your own crisis.* New York: Simon & Schuster.

Steinhauer, J. (1995, May 23). Most men avoid birth control responsibility, poll finds. *The New York Times.*

Steitz, J. A., & Owen, T. P. (1992). School activities and work: Effects on adolescent self-esteem. *Adolescence, 27*(105), 37–49.

Stephenson, A. L., Henry, C. S., & Robinson, L. C. (1996). Family characteristics and adolescent substance use. *Adolescence, 31*(121), 59–77.

Stern, D., McMillion, M., Hopkins, C., & Stone, J. (1990). Work experience for students in high school and college. *Youth & Society, 21*(3), 355–389.

Sternberg, R. J. (1984). Mechanisms of cognitive development: A componential approach. In R. J. Sternberg (Ed.), *Mechanisms of cognitive development.* New York: Freeman.

Sternberg, R. J. (1985). *Beyond I. Q.: A triarchic theory of human intelligence.* New York: Cambridge University Press.

Sternberg, R. J. (1988). Intellectual development: Psychometric and information-processing approaches. In M. H. Bornstein & M. E. Lamb (Eds.), *Developmental psychology: An advanced textbook.* Hillsdale, NJ: Erlbaum.

Sternberg, R. J. (1990, April). *Academic and practical cognition as different aspects of intelligence.* Paper presented at the Twelfth West Virginia Conference on Life-Span Developmental Psychology, Morgantown, WV.

Sternberg, R. J., & Powell, J. S. (1983). The development of intelligence. In J. H. Flavell & E. M. Markman (Eds.), *Handbook of child psychology*, Volume III, Cognitive development. New York: Wiley.

Sternberg, R. J., Wagner, R. K., Williams, W. M., & Horvath, J. A. (1995). Testing common sense. *American Psychologist, 50*(11), 912–927.

Stevenson, D. L., & Baker, D. P. (1987). The family–school relation and the child's school performance. *Child Development, 58*, 1348–1357.

Stevenson, H. W., Chen, C., & Lee, S. (1993). Mathematics achievement of Chinese, Japanese, and American children: Ten years later. *Science, 259*, 53–58.

Stevenson, H. W., & Stigler, J. W. (1992). *The learning gap: Why our schools are failing and what we can learn from Japanese and Chinese education.* New York: Summit Books.

Stevenson, H. W., Stigler, J. W., Lees, S. Y., Lucker, G., Kitamura, S., & Hsu, C. C. (1985). Cognitive performance and academic achievement of Japa-nese, Chinese, and American children. *Child Development, 56*, 718–734.

Stewart, B. (1996, March 24). Girl's life. *The New York Times.* New Jersey Section, pp. 1, 10.

Stice, E., & Barrera, M., Jr. (1995). A longitudinal examination of the reciprocal relations between perceived parenting and adolescents' substance use and externalizing behaviors. *Developmental Psychology, 31*(2), 322–334.

Stiffman, A. R., Dore, P., & Cunningham, R. M. (1994). Inner-city youths and condom use: Health beliefs, clinic care, welfare, and the HIV epidemic. *Adolescence, 29*(116), 805–820.

Stiles, D. A., Gibbons, J. L., Hardardottir, S., & Schnellmann, J. (1987). The ideal man or woman as described by young adolescents in Iceland and the United States. *Sex Roles, 17*(5/6), 313–320.

Stiles, D. A., Gibbons, J. L., & Peters, E. (1993). Adolescents' views of work and leisure in the Netherlands and the United States. *Adolescence, 28*(110), 473–489.

Stipek, D. J., & Tannatt, L. M. (1984). Children's judgments of their own and their peers' academic competence. *Journal of Educational Psychology, 76*, 75–84.

Stoutjesdyk, D., & Jevne, R. (1993). Eating disorders among high performance athletes. *Journal of Youth and Adolescence, 22*(3), 271–282.

Strachen, A., & Jones, D. (1982). Changes in identification during adolescence: A personal construct theory approach. *Journal of Personality Assessment, 46*, 139–148.

Strage, A. (1997). Agency, communion, and achievement motivation. *Adolescence, 32*(126), 299–312.

Strasburger, V. C. (1988, July 31). Children need national TV network. *Hartford Courant.*

Strasburger, V. C. (1992). Children, adolescents, and television. *Pediatrics in Review, 13*, 144–151.

Strasburger, V. C. (1995). *Adolescents and the media: Medical and psychological impact.* Thousand Oaks, CA: Sage.

Straus, M. A., & Donnelly, D. A. (1993). Corporal punishment of adolescents by American parents. *Youth & Society, 24*(4), 419–442.

Straus, M. A., & Kantor, G. K. (1994). Corporal punishment of adolescents by parents: A risk factor in the epidemiology of depression, suicide, alcohol abuse, child abuse, and wife beating. *Adolescence, 29*(115), 543–562.

Straus, M. B. (1994). *Violence in the lives of adolescents.* New York: W. W. Norton.

Strauss, N. (1994, October 2). A guitar god finds redemption. *The New York Times*, pp. 1, 32.

Streitmatter, J. (1993). Gender differences in identity development: An examination of longitudinal data. *Adolescence, 28*(109), 55–66.

Strouse, J. S., Buerkel-Rothfuss, N., & Long, E. C. J. (1995). Gender and family as moderators of the relationship between music video exposure and adolescent sexual permissiveness. *Adolescence, 30*(119), 505–522.

Strouse, J. S., Goodwin, M. P., & Roscoe, B. (1994). Correlates of attitudes toward sexual harassment among early adolescents. *Sex Roles, 31*(9/10), 559–578.

Stubbs, M. L. (1982). Period piece. *Adolescence, 17*, 45–55.

Stubbs, M. L., Rierdan, J., & Koff, E. (1989). Developmental differences in menstrual attitudes. *Journal of Early Adolescence, 9*, 480–498.

Stumpf, H., & Stanley, J. C. (1996). Gender-related differences on the College Board's Advanced Placement and Achievement tests, 1982–1992. *Journal of Educational Psychology, 88*(2), 353–364.

Sue, S., & Okazaki, S. (1990). Asian-American educational achievements: A phenomenon in search of an explanation. *American Psychologist, 45*, 913–920.

Suitor, J. J., & Reavis, R. (1995). Football, fast cars, and cheerleading: Adolescent gender norms, 1978–1989. *Adolescence, 30*(118), 265–272.

Sullivan, H. S. (1953). *The interpersonal theory of psychiatry.* New York: Norton.

Sullivan, J. F. (1987, October 29). Pregnancy task force hears from teenagers. *The New York Times.*

Sullivan, R., & Wilson, M. F. (1995). New directions for research in prevention and treatment of delinquency: A review and proposal. *Adolescence, 30*(117), 1–17.

Super, D. E. (1953). A theory of vocational development. *American Psychologist, 8,* 185–190.

Super, D. E. (1963). Vocational development in adolescence and early adulthood: Tasks and behaviors. In D. E. Super, R. Starishe, & J. P. Jordan (Eds.), *Career development: Self-concept.* New York: College Entrance Examination Board.

Super, D. E. (1967). *The psychology of careers.* New York: Harper & Row.

Super, D. E. (1984). Career and life development. In D. Brown, L. Brooks, & Associates (Eds.), *Career choice and development.* San Francisco: Jossey-Bass.

Super, D. E. (1985). Coming of age in Middletown: Careers in the making. *American Psychologist, 40*(4), 405–414.

Super, D. E., Crites, J. O., Hummel, R. C., Moser, H. P., Overstreet, P. L., & Warnath, C. F. (1957). *Vocational development: A framework for research.* New York: Teachers College Press.

Susman, E. J., Dorn, L. D., & Chrousos, G. P. (1991). Negative affect and hormone levels in young adolescents: Concurrent and predictive perspectives. *Journal of Youth and Adolescence, 20*(2), 167–190.

Swarr, A. E., & Richards, M. H. (1996). Longitudinal effects of adolescent girls' pubertal development, perceptions of pubertal timing, and parental relations on eating problems. *Developmental Psychology, 32*(4), 636–646.

Swisher, K., & Hoisch, M. (1992). Dropping-out among American Indians and Alaskan natives: A review of studies. *Journal of American Indian Education, 31,* 3–15.

Switzer, G. E., Simmons, R. G., Dew, M. A., Regalski, J. M., & Wang, C. (1995). The effect of a school-based helper program on adolescent self-image, attitudes, and behavior. *Journal of Early Adolescence, 15*(4), 429–455.

Tabor, M. B. W. (1992a, June 14). For gay high-school seniors, nightmare is almost over. *The New York Times.*

Tabor, M. B. W. (1992b, August 2). Living on the edge. *The New York Times Education Section,* pp. 16–18.

Tabor, M. B. W. (1996, August 7). Comprehensive study finds parents and peers are most crucial influences on students. *The New York Times,* p. A15.

Tajfel, H. (1978). *The social psychology of minorities.* New York: Minority Rights Group.

Takanishi, R. (1993a). The opportunities of adolescence—Research, interventions, and policy. *American Psychologist, 48*(2), 85–87.

Takanishi, R. (1993b). *Adolescence in the 1990s: Risk and opportunity.* New York: Teachers College Press.

Talwar, R., Nitz, K., & Lerner, R. M. (1990). Relations among early adolescent temperament, parent and peer demands, and adjustment: A test of the goodness of fit model. *Journal of Adolescence, 13,* 279–298.

Talwar, R., Schwab, J., & Lerner, R. M. (1989). Early adolescent temperament and academic competence: Tests of "direct effects" and developmental contextual models. *Journal of Early Adolescence, 9*(3), 291–309.

Tang, C. S. K., Wong, C. S. Y., & Schwarzer, R. (1996). Psychosocial differences between occasional and regular adolescent users of marijuana and heroin. *Journal of Youth and Adolescence, 25*(2), 219–240.

Tanioka, I., & Glaser, D. (1991). School uniforms, routine activities, and the social control of delinquency in Japan. *Youth & Society,* **23**(1) 50–75.

Tannenbaum, L., Neighbors, B., & Forehand, R. (1992). The unique contribution of four maternal stressors to adolescent functioning. *Journal of Early Adolescence, 12*(3), 314–325.

Tanner, J. M. (1962). *Growth at adolescence.* Oxford: Basil Blackwell.

Tanner, J. M. (1970). Physical growth. In P. H. Mussen (Ed.), *Carmichael's manual of child psychology* (Vol. 1). New York: Wiley.

Tanner, J. M. (1990). *Foetus into man* (2nd ed.). Cambridge, MA: Harvard University Press.

Taub, D. E., & Blinde, E. M. (1992). Eating disorders among adolescent female athletes: Influence of athletic participation and sport team membership. *Adolescence, 27*(108), 833–848.

Taylor, R. D. (1996). Adolescents' perceptions of kinship support and family management practices: Association with adolescent adjustment in African American families. *Developmental Psychology, 32*(4), 867–695.

Taylor, R. D., Casten, R., & Flickinger, S. M. (1993). Influence of kinship social support on the parenting experiences and psychological adjustment of African-American adolescents. *Developmental Psychology, 29*(2), 382–388.

Taylor, R. D., & Roberts, D. (1995). Kinship support and maternal and adolescent well-being in economically disadvantaged African-American families. *Child Development, 66*(6), 1585–1597.

Teare, J. F., Garrett, C. R., Coughlin, D. G., Shanahan, D. L., et al. (1995). America's children in crisis: Adolescents' requests for support from a national telephone hotline. *Journal of Applied Developmental Psychology, 16*(1), 21–33.

Teeter, R. (1988). The travails of 19th-century urban youth as a precondition to the invention of modern adolescence. *Adolescence, 23*(89), 15–18.

TerLouw, J. (1994, January). Understanding Asian students. *NJEA Review,* pp. 16–19.

Terrell, F., Terrell, S. L., & Miller, F. (1993). Level of cultural mistrust as a function of educational and occupational expectations among black students. *Adolescence, 28*(111), 573–578.

Terrell, N. E. (1997). Street life: Aggravated and sexual assaults among homeless and runaway adolescents. *Youth & Society, 28*(3), 267–290.

Terry, D. (1992, September 13). More familiar, life in a cell seems less terrible. *The New York Times,* pp. 1, 40.

Tevendale, H. D., DuBois, D. L., Lopez, C., & Prindiville, S. L. (1997). Self-esteem and early adolescent adjustment. An exploratory study. *Journal of Early Adolescence, 17*(2), 216–237.

Thatcher, R. W., Walker, R. A., & Giudice, S. (1987). Human cerebral hemispheres develop at different rates and ages. *Science, 236,* 1110–1113.

Theriot, J. G., Pecoraro, A. G., & Ross-Reynolds, J. (1991). Revelations of adolescent mothers: An intensive case-study approach. *Adolescence, 26*(102), 349–360.

Thomas, A. M., & Forehand, R. (1993). The role of paternal variables in divorced and married families: Predictability of adolescent adjustment. *American Journal of Orthopsychiatry, 63*(1), 126–135.

Thomas, R. M. (1996). *Comparing theories of child development* (4th ed.). Pacific Grove, CA: Brooks/Cole.

Thomas, V. G., & Shields, L. C. (1987). Gender influences on work values of Black adolescents. *Adolescence, 22*(85), 37–43.

Thompson, K. L., Bundy, K. A., & Wolfe, W. R. (1996). Social skills training in young adolescents:Cognitive and performance components. *Adolescence, 31*(123), 505–521.

Thompson, L. L., Riggs, P. D., Mikulich, S. K., & Crowley, T. J. (1996). Contribution of ADHD symptoms to substance problems and delinquency in conduct-disorder adolescents. *Journal of Abnormal Child Psychology, 24*(3), 325–347.

Thompson, R. L., & Larson, R. (1995). Social context and the subjective experience of different types of rock music. *Journal of Youth and Adolescence, 24*(6), 731–744.

Thompson, S. C., Anderson, K., Freedman, D., & Swan, J. (1996). Illusions of safety in a risky world: A study of college students' condom use. *Journal of Applied Social Psychology, 26,* 189–210.

Thorbecke, W., & Grotevant, H. D. (1982). Gender differences in interpersonal identity formation. *Journal of Youth and Adolescence, 11,* 479–492.

Thorlindsson, T., & Vilhjalmsson, R. (1991). Factors related to cigarette smoking and alcohol use among adolescents. *Adolescence, 26*(102), 399–418.

Thorne, C. R., & DeBlassie, R. R. (1985). Adolescent substance abuse. *Adolescence, 20*(78), 335–347.

Thornton, A. (1990). The courtship process and adolescent sexuality. *Journal of Family Issues, 11,* 239–273.

Thornton, A., & Camburn, D. (1987). The influence of the family on premarital sexual attitudes and behavior. *Demography, 24,* 323–340.

Thornton, A., & Camburn, D. (1989). Religious participation and adolescent sexual behavior and attitudes. *Journal of Marriage and the Family, 51,* 641–652.

Thornton, A., Orbuch, T. L., & Axinn, W. G. (1995). Parent–child relationships during the transition to adulthood. *Journal of Family Issues, 16*(5), 538–564.

Thornton, A., Young-DeMarco, L., & Goldscheider, F. (1993). Leaving the parental nest: The experience of a young white cohort in the 1980s. *Journal of Marriage and the Family, 55,* 216–229.

Thrush, D., Fife-Schaw, C., & Breakwell, G. M. (1997). Young people's representations of others' view of smoking: is there a link with smoking behavior? *Journal of Adolescence, 20,* 57–70.

Tidwell, R. (1988). Dropouts speak out: Qualitative data on early school departures. *Adolescence, 23*(92), 939–941.

Tiefer, L. (1995). *Sex is not a natural act and other essays.* Boulder, CO: Westview Press.

Tierno, M. J. (1991). Responding to the socially motivated behaviors of early adolescents: Recommendations for classroom management. *Adolescence, 26*(103), 569–577.

Tiger, L., & Fox, R. (1989). *The imperial animal.* New York: Holt.

Timimi, S. B. (1995). Adolescence in immigrant Arab families. *Psychotherapy, 32*(1), 141–149.

Tisak, M. S., & Tisak, J. (1996). My sibling's but not my friend's keeper: Reasoning about responses to aggressive acts. *Journal of Early Adolescence, 16*(3), 324–339.

Tizard, B., & Phoenix, A. (1995). The identity of mixed parentage adolescents. *Journal of Child Psychology and Psychiatry, 36*(8), 1399–1410.

Tobin-Richards, M. H., Petersen, A. C., & Boxer, A. M. (1983, April). *The significance of weight to feelings of attractiveness in pubertal girls.* Paper presented at the meeting of the Society for Research in Child Development, Detroit.

Tolan, P. H. (1988). Delinquent behaviors and male adolescent development: A preliminary study. *Journal of Youth and Adolescence, 17,* 413–427.

Tolan, P. H., & Loeber, R. (1993). Antisocial behavior. In P. H. Tolan & B. J. Cohler (Eds.), *Handbook of clinical research and practice with adolescents.* New York: Wiley.

Tolan, P. H., & Thomas, P. (1995). The implications of age of onset for delinquency risk II: Longitudinal data. *Journal of Abnormal Child Psychology, 23*(2), 157–181.

Took, K. J., & Weiss, D. S. (1994). The relationship between heavy metal and rap music and adolescent turmoil: Real or abstract? *Adolescence, 29*(115), 613–623.

Traub, S. H., & Dodder, R. A. (1988). Intergenerational conflict of values and norms: A theoretical model. *Adolescence, 23*(92), 975–989.

Treaster, J. B. (1993, April 14). Drug use by younger teen-agers appears to rise, counter to trend. *The New York Times,* p. 1.

Treaster, J. B. (1994, February 1). Survey finds marijuana use is up in high schools. *The New York Times,* p. 1.

Trickett, E. J., & Schmid, K. D. (1993). The school as a social context. In P. H. Tolan & B. J. Cohler (Eds.), *Handbook of clinical research and practice with adolescents*. New York: Wiley.

Trigg, M., Davis, R., Kirschner, D., Marolis, M., & Wittenstrom, K. (1995, March). Sexual harassment in schools. *NJEA Review*, pp. 22–31.

Trost, J. E. (1985). Contraception for teenagers: Swedish solutions. *Transaction/Society, 23,* 44–48.

Trost, J. E. (1990). Social support and pressure and their impact on sexual behavior. In J. Bancroft & J. M. Reinisch (Eds.), *Adolescence and puberty*. New York: Oxford University Press.

Trotter, R. J. (1986). Three heads are better than one. *Psychology Today, 20,* 56–62.

Trzcinski, J. (1992). Heavy metal kids: Are they dancing with the devil? *Child and Youth Care Forum, 21*(1), 7–22.

Tubman, J. G., Windle, M., & Windle, R. C. (1996). The onset and cross-temporal patterning of sexual intercourse in middle adolescence: Prospective relations with behavioral and emotional problems. *Child Development, 67,* 327–343.

Turiel, E., & Smetana, J. G. (1984). Social knowledge and action: The coordination of domains. In W. M. Kurtines & J. L. Gewirtz (Eds.), *Morality and moral development*. New York: Wiley.

Turner, R. A., Irwin, C. E., Jr., & Millstein, S. G. (1991). Family structure, family processes, and experimenting with substances during adolescence. *Journal of Research on Adolescence, 1*(1), 93–106.

Ubell, E. (1995, February 12). Sex-education programs that work—and some that don't. *Parade Magazine*, pp. 18–20.

Udry, J. R. (1988). Biological predispositions and social control in adolescent sexual behavior. *American Sociological Review, 53,* 709–722.

Udry, J. R., & Billy, J. O. G. (1987). Initiation of coitus in early adolescence. *American Sociological Review, 52,* 841–855.

Udry, J. R., Halpern, C., & Campbell, B. (1991). *Hormones, pubertal development, and sexual behavior in adolescent females. Reproduction as social development in adolescent females*. Symposium presented at the biennial meeting of the Society for Research in Child Development, Seattle, WA.

Udry, J. R., & Talbert, L. M. (1988). Sex hormone effects on personality in puberty. *Journal of Personality and Social Psychology, 54,* 291–295.

Udry, J. R., Talbert, L. M., & Morris, N. (1986). Biosocial foundations for adolescent female sexuality. *Demography, 23,* 217–227.

Unger, D. G., & Wandersman, L. P. (1988). The relation of family and partner support to the adjustment of adolescent mothers. *Child Development, 59,* 1056–1060.

Unger, R., & Crawford, M. (1992). *Women and gender: A feminist psychology*. New York: McGraw-Hill.

University of Michigan Annual Survey (1995). Monitoring the Future Survey. University of Michigan.

University of Michigan Annual Survey. (1997). Monitoring the Future Survey. University of Michigan.

Updergraff, K. A., McHale, S. M., & Crouter, A. C. (1996). Gender roles in marriage: What do they mean for girls' and boys' school achievement? *Journal of Youth and Adolescence, 25*(1), 73–88.

Urberg, K. A., Degirmencioglu, S. M., Tolson, J. M., & Halliday-Scher, K. (1995). The structure of adolescent peer networks. *Developmental Psychology, 31*(4), 540–547.

Urdan, T., Midgley, C., & Wood, S. (1995). Special issues in reforming middle level schools. *Journal of Early Adolescence, 15*(1), 9–37.

Useem, E. L. (1992). Middle schools and math groups: Parents' involvement in children's placement. *Sociology of Education, 5,* 263–279.

U.S. Bureau of the Census. (1995). *Educational attainment in the United States*. Washington, DC: U.S. Government Printing Office.

U.S. Bureau of the Census. Department of Commerce. (1996). *Statistical Abstract of the United States*, 1996. Washington, DC: U.S. Government Printing Office.

U.S. Department of Education. (1991). *Youth indicators 1991: Trends in well-being of American youth*. Washington, DC: Office of Educational Research and Improvement.

U.S. Department of Justice, *Survey of Youth in Custody* (1987). Washington, DC: U.S. Government Printing Office.

U.S. Department of Labor, Bureau of Labor Statistics. (1992). *Employment and earnings*. Washington, DC: U.S. Department of Labor.

U.S. Office of Technology Assessment (1991). *Adolescent health: Volume 3. Crosscutting issues in the delivery of health and related services* (Publication No. OTA-H-467). Washington, DC: U.S. Congress.

Valde, G. A. (1996). Identity closure: A fifth identity status. *Journal of Genetic Psychology, 157*(3), 245–254.

Valery, J. H., O'Connor, P., & Jennings, S. (1997). The nature and amount of support college-age adolescents request and receive from parents. *Adolescence, 32*(126), 323–338.

Van Boxtel, H. W., & Monks, F. J. (1992). General, social, and academic self-concepts of gifted adolescents. *Journal of Youth and Adolescence, 21*(2), 169–186.

Van Buskirk, A. M., & Duke, M. P. (1991). The relationship between coping style and loneliness in adolescents: Can "sad passivity" be adaptive? *Journal of Genetic Psychology, 152*(2), 145–157.

Van de Ven, P. (1995). Talking with juvenile offenders about gay males and lesbians: Implications for combating homophobia. *Adolescence, 30*(117), 19–42.

Van Kammen, W. B., Loeber, R., & Stouthamer-Loeber, M. (1991). Substance use and its relationship to conduct problems and delinquency in young boys. *Journal of Youth and Adolescence, 20*(4), 399–413.

Vannatta, R. A. (1996). Risk factors related to suicidal behavior among male and female adolescents. *Journal of Youth and Adolescence, 25*(2), 149–160.

Van Roosmalen, E. H., & Krahn, H. (1996). Boundaries of youth. *Youth & Society, 28*(1), 3–39.

Van Roosmalen, E. H., & McDaniel, S. A. (1992). Adolescent smoking intentions: Gender differences in peer context. *Adolescence, 27*(105), 87–105.

Varner, L. K. (1995, September 17). Towns try daytime curfews, fine for parents in juvenile crime fight. *The Star Ledger.*

Vartanian, L. R. (1997). Separation-individuation, social support, and adolescent egocentrism: An exploratory study. *Journal of Early Adolescence, 17*(3), 245–270.

Vartanian, L. R., & Powlishta, K. K. (1996). A longitudinal examination of the social-cognitive foundations of adolescent egocentrism. *Journal of Early Adolescence, 16*(2), 157–178.

Vazsonyi, A. T., & Flannery, D. J. (1997). Early adolescent delinquent behaviors: Associations with family and school domains. *Journal of Early Adolescence, 17*(3), 271–293.

Vernberg, E. M. (1990a). Psychological adjustment and experiences with peers during early adolescence: Reciprocal, incidental, or unidirectional relationships? *Journal of Abnormal Child Psychology, 18*(2), 187–198.

Vernberg, E. M. (1990b). Experiences with peers following relocation during early adolescence. *American Journal of Orthopsychiatry, 60*(3), 466–472.

Verhovek, S. H. (1995, July 30). Young, carefree and in love with cigarettes. *The New York Times,* pp. 1, 24.

Vest, J. (1996). The school that's put sex to the test: At Antioch, a passionate reaction to consent code. In F. C. Leeming, W. Dwyer, & D. P. Oliver (Eds.), *Issues in adolescent sexuality: Readings from The Washington Post Writers Group.* Needham Heights, MA: Allyn & Bacon.

Violato, C., & Wiley, A. J. (1990). Images of adolescence in English literature: The middle ages to the modern period. *Adolescence, 25*(98), 253–264.

Vitaro, F., Ladouceur, R., & Bujold, A. (1996). Predictive and concurrent correlates of gambling in early adolescent boys. *Journal of Early Adolescence, 16*(2), 211–228.

Vizard, E., Monck, E., & Misch, P. (1995). Child and adolescent sexual abuse perpetrators: A review of the research literature. *Journal of Child Psychology & Psychiatry & Allied Disciplines, 36*(5), 731–756.

Volkmar, F. R., & Schwab-Stone, M. (1996). Childhood disorders in DSM-IV. *Journal of Child Psychology & Psychiatry & Allied Disciplines, 37*(7), 779–784.

Vuchinich, S., Bank, L., & Patterson, G. R. (1992). Parenting, peers, and the stability of antisocial behavior in preadolescent boys. *Developmental Psychology, 28*(3), 510–521.

Vuchinich, S., Hetherington, E. M., Vuchinich, R. A., & Clingempeel, W. G. (1991). Parent–child interaction and gender differences in early adolescents' adaptation to stepfamilies. *Developmental Psychology, 27*(4), 618–626.

Vygotsky, L. S. (1978). *Mind in society.* Cambridge, MA: Harvard University Press. (Originally published in 1930, 1935, and 1960).

Waber, D. P. (1977). Sex differences in mental abilities, hemispheric lateralization, and rate of physical growth at adolescence. *Developmental Psychology, 13,* 29–38.

Wachs, T. D. (1992). *The nature of nurture.* Newbury Park, CA: Sage.

Wachs, T. D. (1996). Known and potential processes underlying developmental trajectories in childhood and adolescence. *Developmental Psychology, 32*(4), 796–801.

Wagner, B. M. (1997). Family risk factors for child and adolescent suicidal behavior. *Psychological Bulletin, 121*(2), 246–298.

Wagner, W. G. (1996). Optimal development in adolescence. *The Counseling Psychologist, 24*(3), 360–399.

Waldner-Haugrud, L. K., & Magruder, B. (1996). Homosexual identity expression among lesbian and gay adolescents: An analysis of perceived structural associations. *Youth & Society, 27*(3), 313–333.

Walker, L. J. (1984). Sex differences in the development of moral reasoning: A critical review. *Child Development, 55*(3), 183–201.

Walker, L. J., & Taylor, J. H. (1991). Family interactions and the development of moral reasoning. *Child Development, 62,* 264–283.

Wallerstein, J. S., & Blakeslee, S. (1989). *Second chances.* New York: Ticknor and Fields.

Wallerstein, J. S., & Corbin, S. B. (1989). Daughters of divorce: Report from a ten-year follow-up. *American Journal of Orthopsychiatry, 59*(4), 593–604.

Walsh, F., & Scheinkman, M. (1993). The family context of adolescence. In P. H. Tolan & B. J. Cohler (Eds.), *Handbook of clinical research and practice with adolescents.* New York: Wiley.

Wang, A. Y. (1994). Pride and prejudice in high school gang members. *Adolescence, 29*(114), 279–291.

Ward, L. M. (1995). Talking about sex: Common themes about sexuality in the prime-time television programs children and adolescents view most. *Journal of Youth and Adolescence, 24*(5), 595–616.

Ward, R. A., & Spitze, G. (1992). Consequences of parent–adult child coresidence. *Journal of Family Issues, 13*(4), 553–572.

Ward, R. A., & Spitze, G. (1996a). Gender differences in parent–child coresidence experiences. *Journal of Marriage and the Family, 58,* 718–725.

Ward, R. A., & Spitze, G. (1996b). Will the children ever leave? Parent–child coresidence history and plans. *Journal of Family Issues, 17*(4), 514–539.

Wark, G. R., & Krebs, D. L. (1996). Gender and dilemma differences in real-life moral judgment. *Developmental Psychology, 32*(2), 220–230.

Warner, B. S., & Weist, M. D. (1996). Urban youth as witnesses to violence: Beginning assessment and treatment efforts. *Journal of Youth and Adolescence, 25*(3), 361–377.

Warren, M. P. (1983). Physical and biological aspects of puberty. In J. Brooks-Gunn & A. C. Petersen (Eds.), *Girls at puberty: Biological and psychosocial perspectives.* New York: Plenum Press.

Warren, M. P., & Brooks-Gunn, J. (1989). Mood and behavior at adolescence: Evidence for hormonal factors. *Journal of Clinical Endocrinology and Metabolism, 69*(1), 77–83.

Warzak, W. J., Grow, C. R., Poler, M. M., & Walburn, J. N. (1995). Enhancing refusal skills: Identifying contexts that place adolescents at risk for unwanted sexual activity. *Journal of Developmental and Behavioral Pediatrics, 16*(2), 98–100.

Wassef, A., Ingham, D., Collins, M. L., & Mason, G. (1995). In search of effective programs to address students' emotional distress and behavioral problems. Part I: Defining the problem. *Adolescence, 30*(119), 523–538.

Waterman, A. S. (1985). Identity in the context of adolescent psychology. In A. S. Waterman (Ed.), *New directions for child development: No. 30. Identity in adolescence: Processes and contents.* San Francisco: Jossey-Bass.

Waterman, A. S. (1992). Identity as an aspect of optimal psychological functioning. In G. R. Adams, T. P. Gullotta, & R. Montemayor (Eds.), *Adolescent identity formation.* Newbury Park, CA: Sage.

Watkins, B., & Bentovim, A. (1992). The sexual abuse of male children and adolescents: A review of current research. *Journal of Child Psychology and Psychiatry, 33*(1), 197–248.

Watts, R., Machabanski, H., & Karrer, B. M. (1993). Adolescence and diversity. In P. H. Tolan & B. J. Cohler (Eds.), *Handbook of clinical research and practice with adolescents.* New York: Wiley.

Weinberg, R. A. (1989). Intelligence and IQ: Landmark issues and great debates. *American Psychologist, 44,* 98–104.

Weiner, B. (1985). An attributional theory of achievement motivation and emotion. *Psychological Review, 92,* 548–573.

Weinmann, L. L., & Newcombe, N. (1990). Relational aspects of identity: Late adolescents' perceptions of their relationships with parents. *Journal of Experimental Child Psychology, 50*(3), 357–369.

Weinstein, E., & Rosen, E. (1991). The development of adolescent sexual intimacy: Implications for counseling. *Adolescence, 26*(102), 331–339.

Weinstein, E., & Rosen, E. (1994). Decreasing sex bias through education for parenthood or prevention of adolescent pregnancy: A developmental model with integrative strategies. *Adolescence, 29*(115), 723–732.

Weinstein, R. J. (1996). Eating disorders. In G. M. Blau & T. P. Gullotta (Eds.), *Adolescent dysfunctional behavior: Causes, interventions, and prevention.* Thousand Oaks, CA: Sage.

Weiss, L. H., & Schwarz, J. C. (1996). The relationship between parenting types and older adolescents' personality, academic achievement, adjustment, and substance use. *Child Development, 67,* 2101–2114.

Weiss, S. (1996, May). From school to work. *NEA Today,* p. 17.

Weisz, J. R., Weiss, B., Han, S. S., Granger, D. A., & Morton, T. (1995). Effects of psychotherapy with children and adolescents revisited: A meta-analysis of treatment outcome studies. *Psychological Bulletin, 117*(3), 450–468.

Welsh, P. (1992, Spring). It takes two to tango. *American Educator, 16*(1), pp. 18–46.

Wentzel, K. R. (1991). Relations between social competence and academic achievement in early adolescence. *Child Development, 62,* 1066–1078.

Wentzel, K. R. (1993a). Motivation and achievement in early adolescence: The role of multiple classroom goals. *Journal of Early Adolescence, 13*(1), 4–20.

Wentzel, K. R. (1993b). Does being good make the grade? Social behavior and academic competence in middle school. *Journal of Educational Psychology, 85*(2), 357–364.

Wentzel, K. R. (1994). Family functioning and academic achievement in middle school: A social-emotional perspective. *Journal of Early Adolescence, 14*(2), 268–291.

Wentzel, K. R. (1996). Social and academic motivation in middle school: Concurrent and long-term relations to academic effort. *Journal of Early Adolescence, 16*(4), 390–406.

Wentzel, K. R., & Erdley, C. A. (1993). Strategies for making friends: Relations to social behavior and peer acceptance in early adolescence. *Developmental Psychology, 29*(5), 819–826.

Wentzel, K. R., & Feldman, S. S. (1993). Parental predictors of boys' self-restraint and motivation to achieve at school: A longitudinal study. *Journal of Early Adolescence, 13*(2), 183–203.

Wentzel, K. R., Feldman, S. S., & Weinberger, D. A. (1991). Parental child rearing and academic achievement in boys: The mediational role of social-emotional adjustment. *Journal of Early Adolescence, 11*(3), 321–339.

Wenz-Gross, M., Siperstein, G. N., Untch, A. S., & Widaman, K. F. (1997). Stress, social support, and adjustment of adolescents in middle school. *Journal of Early Adolescence, 17*(2), 129–151.

Werner, E. E., & Smith, R. S. (1992). *Overcoming the odds: High-risk children from birth to adulthood.* Ithaca, NY: Cornell University Press.

Westerman, M. A., & La Luz, E. J. (1995). Marital adjustment and children's academic achievement. *Merrill-Palmer Quarterly, 41*(4), 453–470.

White, J. L. (1989). *The troubled adolescent.* Elmsford, NY: Pergamon Press.

White, K. D., Pearson, J. C., & Flint, L. (1989). Adolescents' compliance-resistance: Effects of parents' compliance strategy and gender. *Adolescence, 24*(95), 595–621.

White, L. (1992). The effect of parental divorce and remarriage on parental support for adult children. *Journal of Family Issues, 13*(2), 234–250.

White, S. D., & DeBlassie, R. R. (1992). Adolescent sexual behavior. *Adolescence, 27*(105), 183–191.

White, S. H. (1992). G. Stanley Hall: From philosophy to developmental psychology. *Developmental Psychology, 28*(1), 25–34.

Whitehead, B. D. (1994–1995, Winter). The failure of sex education. *American Educator,* 22–29.

Whitley, B. E., Jr. (1996). *Principles of research in behavioral science.* Mountain View, CA: Mayfield.

Widmer, M. A., Ellis, G. D., & Trunnell, E. P. (1996). Measurement of ethical behavior in leisure among high- and low-risk adolescents. *Adolescence, 31*(122), 397–408.

Wierson, M., Armistead, L., Forehand, R., Thomas, A. M., & Fauber, R. (1990). Parent–adolescent conflict and stress as a parent: Are there differences between being a mother and father? *Journal of Family Violence, 5,* 187–197.

Wierson, M., & Forehand, R. (1992). Family stressors and adolescent functioning: A consideration of models for early and middle adolescents. *Behavior Therapy, 23,* 671–688.

Wierson, M., Long, P. J., & Forehand, R. L. (1993). Toward a new understanding of early menarche: The role of environmental stress in pubertal timing. *Adolescence, 28*(112), 913–924.

Wigfield, A., & Eccles, J. S. (1992). The development of achievement task values: A theoretical analysis. *Developmental Review, 12,* 265–310.

Wigfield, A., & Eccles, J. S. (1994). Children's competence beliefs, achievement values, and general self-esteem: Changes across elementary school and middle school. *Journal of Early Adolescence, 14*(2), 107–138.

Wigfield, A., Eccles, J. S., MacIver, D. A. R., & Midgley, C. (1991). Transitions during early adolescence: Changes in children's domain-specific self-perceptions and general self-esteem across the transition to junior

high school. *Developmental Psychology, 27*(4), 552–565.

Wilks, J. (1986). The relative importance of parents and friends in adolescent decision making. *Journal of Youth and Adolescence, 15*(4), 323–335.

Williams, E., & Radin, N. (1993). Paternal involvement, maternal employment, and adolescents' academic achievement: An 11-year follow-up. *American Journal of Orthopsychiatry, 63*(2), 306–312.

Williams, L. (1993, December 2). Pregnant teen-agers are outcasts no longer. *The New York Times,* p. C1.

Williams, M. C., & Sackley, G. (1990, October). Debate: Should all high school graduates go to college? *NEA Today,* p. 35.

Williams, S., & McGee, R. (1991). Adolescents' self-perceptions of their strengths. *Journal of Youth and Adolescence, 20*(3), 325–337.

Williams, S. S., Kimble, D. L., Covell, N. H., Weiss, L. H., Newton, K. J., Fisher, J. D., & Fisher, W. A. (1992). College students use implicit personality theory instead of safer sex. *Journal of Applied Social Psychology, 22,* 921–933.

Willits, F. K., & Crider, D. M. (1988). Transition to adulthood and attitudes toward traditional morality. *Youth & Society, 20*(1), 88–105.

Wills, T. A., McNamara, G., Vaccaro, D., & Hirky, A. E. (1996). Escalated substance use: A longitudinal grouping analysis from early to middle adolescence. *Journal of Abnormal Psychology, 105*(2), 166–180.

Wilson, S. M., & Medora, N. P. (1990). Gender comparisons of college students' attitudes toward sexual behavior. *Adolescence, 25*(99), 615–627.

Windle, M. (1989). Substance use and abuse among adolescent runaways: A four-year follow-up study. *Journal of Youth and Adolescence, 18*(4), 331–344.

Windle, M. (1992). A longitudinal study of stress buffering for adolescent problem behaviors. *Developmental Psychology, 28*(3), 522–530.

Windle, M. (1994). A study of friendship characteristics and problem behaviors among middle adolescents. *Child Development, 65*(6), 1764–1777.

Windle, M., Miller-Tutzauer, C., Barnes, G. M., & Welte, J. (1991). Adolescent perceptions of help-seeking resources for substance abuse. *Child Development, 62,* 179–189.

Winn, N. N., & Priest, R. (1993). Counseling biracial children: A forgotten component of multicultural counseling. *Family Therapy, 20*(1), 29–36.

Wise, K. L., Bundy, K. A., Bundy, E. A., & Wise, L. A. (1991). Social skills training for young adolescents. *Adolescence, 26*(101), 233–242.

Witt, S. D. (1997). Parental influence on children's socialization to gender roles. *Adolescence, 32*(126), 253–260.

Wood, J., Chapin, K., & Hannah, M. E. (1988). Family environment and its relationship to underachievement. *Adolescence, 23*(90), 283–290.

Wood, K. C., Becker, J. A., & Thompson, J. K. (1996). Body image dissatisfaction in preadolescent children. *Journal of Applied Developmental Psychology, 17*(1), 85–100.

Wood, P., & Clay, W. C. (1996). Perceived structural barriers and academic performance among American Indian high school students. *Youth & Society, 28*(1), 40–61.

Woodside, D. B. (1995). Anorexia nervosa and bulimia nervosa. In V. B. Van Hasselt & M. Hersen (Eds.), *Handbook of adolescent psychopathology: A guide to diagnosis and treatment.* New York: Lexington.

Woodward, J. C., & Kalyan-Masih, V. (1990). Loneliness, coping strategies, and cognitive styles of the gifted rural adolescent. *Adolescence, 25*(100), 977–988.

Worden, M. (1991). *Adolescents and their families: An introduction to assessment and intervention.* New York: Haworth Press.

Woznica, J. G., & Shapiro, J. R. (1990). An analysis of adolescent suicide attempts: The expendable child. *Journal of Pediatric Psychology, 15*(6), 789–796.

Wren, C. S. (1996, October 10). Teenagers find drugs easy to obtain and warnings easy to ignore. *The New York Times*, p. A20.

Wren, C. S. (1997, June 20). A seductive drug culture flourishes on the internet. *The New York Times*, pp. A1, A22.

Wren, D. J. (1997). Adolescent females' "voice" changes can signal difficulties for teachers and administrators. *Adolescence*, 32(126), 463–470.

Wright, P. H., & Keple, T. W. (1981). Friends and parents of a sample of high school juniors: An exploratory study of relationship intensity and interpersonal rewards. *Journal of Marriage and the Family*, 43, 559–570.

WuDunn, S. (1996, March 13). Stigma curtails single motherhood in Japan. *The New York Times*, pp. A1, A11.

Wulff, M. B., & Steitz, J. A. (1997). Curricular track, career choice, and androgyny among adolescent females. *Adolescence*, 32(125), 43–50.

Wyatt, G. E. (1990). Changing influences on adolescent sexuality over the past forty years. In J. Bancroft & J. M. Reinisch (Eds.), *Adolescence and puberty*. New York: Oxford University Press.

Wylie, R. C. (1979). *The self-concept* (Vol. 2). Lincoln: University of Nebraska Press.

Yamamoto, K., Davis, O. L., Jr., Dylak, S., Whittaker, J., et al. (1996). Across six nations: Stressful events in the lives of children. *Child Psychiatry and Human Development*, 26(3), 139–150.

Yau, J., & Smetana, J. G. (1996). Adolescent–parent conflict among Chinese adolescents in Hong Kong. *Child Development*, 67, 1262–1275.

Yee, D. K., & Flanagan, C. (1985). Family environments and self-consciousness in early adolescence. *Journal of Early Adolescence*, 5, 59–68.

Yeh, C. J., & Huang, K. (1996). The collectivistic nature of ethnic identity development among Asian-American college students. *Adolescence*, 31(123), 645–661.

Yeoman, T., & Griffiths, M. (1996). Adolescent machine gambling and crime. *Journal of Adolescence*, 19, 99–104.

Yesmont, G. A. (1992). The relationship of assertiveness to college students' safer sex behaviors. *Adolescence*, 27(106), 253–272.

Yildirim, A. (1997). Gender role influences on Turkish adolescents' self-identity. *Adolescence*, 32(125), 217–232.

Yogev, A., & Roditi, H. (1987). School counselors as gatekeepers: Guidance in poor versus affluent neighborhoods. *Adolescence*, 22(87), 625–639.

Young, E. W., Jensen, L. C., Olsen, J. A., & Cundick, B. P. (1991). The effects of family structure on the sexual behavior of adolescents. *Adolescence*, 26(104), 977–986.

Young, I. L., Anderson, C., & Steinbrecher, A. (1995). Unmasking the phantom: Creative assessment of the adolescent. *Psychotherapy*, 32(1), 134–138.

Youngs, G. A., Rathge, R., Mullis, R., & Mullis, A. (1990). Adolescent stress and self-esteem. *Adolescence*, 25(98), 333–341.

Youngstrom, N. (1991, October). Warning: Teens at risk for AIDS. *APA Monitor*, pp. 38–39.

Youniss, J., & Haynie, M. A. (1992). Friendship in adolescence. *Development and Behavioral Pediatrics*, 13(1), 59–66.

Youniss, J., & Ketterlinus, R. D. (1987). Communication and connectedness in mother– and father–adolescent relationships. *Journal of Youth and Adolescence*, 16, 265–280.

Youniss, J., McLellan, J. A., & Strouse, D. (1994). "We're popular, but we're not snobs": Adolescents describe their crowds. In R. Montemayor, G. R. Adams, & T. P. Gullotta (Eds.), *Personal relationships during adolescence*. Thousand Oaks, CA: Sage.

Youniss, J., & Smollar, J. (1985). *Adolescent relations with mothers, fathers, and friends*. Chicago: University of Illinois Press.

Yowell, C. M. (1997). Risks of communication: Early adolescent girls' conversations with mothers and friends about sexuality. *Journal of Early Adolescence*, 17(2), 172–196.

Yussen, S. (1977). Characteristics of moral dilemmas written by adolescents. *Developmental Psychology*, 13, 162–163.

Zabin, L. S., & Hayward, S. C. (1993). *Adolescent sexual behavior and childbearing*. Newbury Park, CA: Sage.

Zahn-Waxler, C. (1996). Environment, biology, and culture. Implications for adolescent development. *Developmental Psychology*, 32(4), 571–573.

Zani, B. (1991). Male and female patterns in the discovery of sexuality during adolescence. *Journal of Adolescence*, 14, 163–178.

Zarbatany, L., Ghesquiere, K., & Mohr, K. (1992). A context perspective on early adolescents' friendship expectations. *Journal of Early Adolescence*, 12(1), 111–126.

Zavela, K. J., Battistich, V., Dean, B. J., Flores, R., Barton, R., & Delaney, R. J. (1997). Say yes first: A longitudinal, school-based alcohol and drug prevention project for rural youth and families. *Journal of Early Adolescence*, 17(1), 67–96.

Zelizer, V. (1985). *Pricing the priceless child:The changing social value of children*. New York: Basic Books.

Zera, D. (1992). Coming of age in a heterosexist world: The development of gay and lesbian adolescents. *Adolescence*, 27(108), 849–854.

Zern, D. S. (1991). Stability and change in adolescents' positive attitudes toward guidance in moral development. *Adolescence*, 26(102), 261–272.

Zhang, J., & Jin, S. (1996). Determinants of suicide ideation: A comparison of Chinese and American college students. *Adolescence*, 31(122), 451–467.

Zick, C. D., & Allen, C. R. (1996). The impact of parents' marital status on the time adolescents spend in productive activities. *Family Relations*, 45, 65–71.

Zigler, E., Taussig, C., & Black, K. (1992). Early childhood intervention: A promising preventative for juvenile delinquency. *American Psychologist*, 47(8), 997–1006.

Zimbardo, P., & Radl, S. (1981). *Shyness*. New York: McGraw-Hill.

Zimiles, H., & Lee, V. E. (1991). Adolescent family structure and educational progress. *Developmental Psychology*, 27(2), 314–320.

Zimmerman, M. A., Copeland, L. A., Shope, J. T., & Dielman, T. E. (1997). A longitudinal study of self-esteem: Implications for adolescent development. *Journal of Youth and Adolescence*, 26(2), 117–142.

Zimmerman, M. A., Salem, D. A., & Maton, K. (1995). Family structure and psychosocial correlates among urban African-American adolescent males. *Child Development*, 66(6), 1598–1613.

Zoccolillo, M., Meyers, J., & Assiter, S. (1997). Conduct disorder, substance dependence, and adolescent motherhood. *American Journal of Orthopsychiatry*, 67(1), 152–157.

# PHOTO CREDITS

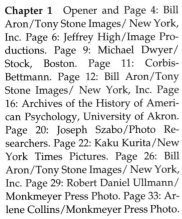

**Chapter 10** Opener: Harry Cutting Photography. Page 363: Tony Anderson/FPG International. Page 364: Harry Cutting Photography. Page 365: Jonathan Elderfield/Gamma Liaison. Page 367: Paul Conklin/Monkmeyer Press Photo. Page 369: Harry Cutting Photography. Page 371: Arlene Collins/Monkmeyer Press Photo. Page 373: David De Lossy/The Image Bank. Page 382: Erica Lansner/Black Star.

**Chapter 11** Opener, Page 393, and Page 400: Ansell Horn/Impact Visuals. Page 403: Spencer Grant/The Picture Cube. Page 405: Daily News L.P. Photo. Page 405 (background): Ansell Horn/Impact Visuals. Page 417: Barbara Rios/Photo Researchers. Page 418: Paul Perez/From The Hip/The Image Works. Page 420: Jeffrey High/Image Productions. Page 423: Spencer Grant/Monkmeyer Press Photo. Page 428: Barbara Rios/Photo Researchers. Page 429: Ansell Horn/Impact Visuals.

**Chapter 12** Opener and Page 449: Stephanie Rausser/FPG International. Page 452: Lewis Hine/Corbis-Bettmann. Page 461: Stephanie Rausser/FPG International. Page 462: Stacy Rosenstock/Impact Visuals. Page 466: Drawing by P. Steiner; ©1993 The New Yorker Magazine, Inc. Page 468: Hazel Hankin/Stock, Boston. Page 470: Harvey Finkle/Impact Visuals. Page 478: Rafael Macia/Photo Researchers.

**Chapter 13** Opener, Page 491, and Page 493: Tom Trierweiler/Zephyr Pictures. Page 501: Bill Burke/Impact Visuals. Page 509: George S. Zimbel/Monkmeyer Press Photo. Page 531: Steve Goldberg/Monkmeyer Press Photo. Page 533: Mimi Forsyth/Monkmeyer Press Photo. Page 535: Michael Goldman/FPG International. Page 537: Tom Trierweiler/Zephyr Pictures.

# AUTHOR INDEX

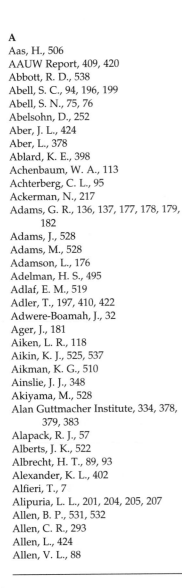